NATIONAL SOCIALISM

BASIC PRINCIPLES, THEIR APPLICATION BY THE NAZI PARTY'S FOREIGN ORGANIZATION, AND THE USE OF GERMANS ABROAD FOR NAZI AIMS

✦

PREPARED IN THE SPECIAL UNIT
OF THE DIVISION OF EUROPEAN AFFAIRS
BY
RAYMOND E. MURPHY
FRANCIS B. STEVENS
HOWARD TRIVERS
JOSEPH M. ROLAND

UNITED STATES
GOVERNMENT PRINTING OFFICE
WASHINGTON : 1943

DEPARTMENT OF STATE

PUBLICATION 1864

For sale by the
Superintendent of Documents
Government Printing Office
Washington, D. C.
Price, $1.00

FOREWORD

This treatise has been prepared by competent officials of the Department of State from studies of German literature and philosophy; German statutes, decrees, and other official records; authoritative writings and statements of German leaders under the National Socialist (Nazi) regime; and confidential reports and information obtained over a period of years by representatives of the Department of State.

Source material has been carefully analyzed, and only that known to be reliable and accurate has been used. Except in those instances where its confidential nature precludes this being done, the source material is identified and reflects its authoritative nature. In general, translations are those of officers of the Department of State who are experts in the German language and who are also cognizant of German National Socialist ideology and understand the connotation of its terminology. The only other translations used are taken from well-known publications previously established to be reliable.

The National Socialist Government of Germany has clearly defined its doctrines and has not concealed its attempt to extend their applicability to persons of German extraction abroad. This treatise provides a study of Nazi ideology and the general precepts of National Socialism, particularly the Nazi viewpoint toward citizenship, loyalty, individual rights, and their relation to the state. The structure and methods of the major Nazi organizations which have their headquarters in Germany and which work among Germans abroad are given in detail and likewise the use of organized German minorities in furtherance of Nazi interests.

It is the Department's opinion that, from evidence available, it is clear that Nazi efforts to indoctrinate our loyal American citizens of German descent met with little response and that only a small fraction of our immigrants from Germany were receptive to Nazi ideas.

A study of the Nazi movement and its ramifications abroad entails the use of the terminology which is characteristic of the movement. In many cases, the use of German words for ideas and concepts through which the Nazi ideology finds expression appears preferable, since satisfactory English equivalents which convey the full significance of these German expressions are not available. Although the significance of many of these expressions is explained in the text, a glossary of such terms is included at the end of the study for the convenience of the reader.

December 1, 1942.

CONTENTS

PART I

THE NAZI PARTY: IDEOLOGY, PROGRAM, METHODS

PART II

GERMAN CITIZENSHIP LAWS AND NAZI POLICY REGARDING DUAL NATIONALITY, EXPATRIATION, AND NATURALIZATION OF GERMANS IN OTHER COUNTRIES

PART III

NAZI ORGANIZATIONS WORKING AMONG GERMANS IN FOREIGN COUNTRIES AND USE OF ORGANIZED GERMAN MINORITIES IN FURTHERANCE OF GERMAN INTERESTS

PART I

THE NAZI PARTY
Ideology, Program, Methods

INTRODUCTION

The political and economic principles of National Socialism are diametrically opposed to those of American democracy. Each of the basic tenets of National Socialist ideology is the antithesis of its counterpart in American political organization. The Nazis consider dictatorship the ideal and natural form of government in human society, and their spokesmen express nothing but contempt for democracy and democratic institutions. The internal political aim of the Nazis, which has been realized almost in its entirety, is the establishment of a totalitarian state which exercises complete control over all phases of individual activity. The guaranty of individual liberty and the exercise of free economic initiative are foreign to the concepts of the totalitarian state. Such political activity as is permitted under such a system is limited to a single political party, which, in the case of Germany, is the Nazi Party. The extermination of opposing political parties results in the elimination of free elections, and the legislative branch of the Government, composed entirely of members of the only existing party, becomes merely a rubber stamp for the decisions reached by the party leadership. All powers are concentrated in the chief of state, who has not been chosen by the freely expressed will of his countrymen but has attained power as head of the single political party. Nazi ideology, furthermore, rejects the doctrine of individual political equality, which is expressed in the Declaration of Independence and the Bill of Rights, and proclaims the racial supremacy of the Germans. Proceeding on this premise, the Nazis have adopted and pursued with great energy a foreign policy aimed at the establishment of complete German hegemony in Europe and eventual world domination.

After the Nazis had gained power in Germany, their spokesmen stated clearly that their program was not composed of temporary measures, as some German circles had been led to believe. In a lecture on *The Nature and Form of National Socialism*, delivered in 1934, Propaganda Minister Dr. Paul Joseph Goebbels frankly stated that National Socialism had used the privileges of democracy in order to crush the democratic system and to establish a regime based on principles directly opposed to democracy:

> "National Socalism is now engaged in gradually stabilizing in Germany the new legal situation which has been brought about by the revolution. This is basically different from the old legality and dispenses with the possibility of criticism which it made use of itself under the old system. If democracy permitted us to

3

use democratic methods in the time of our opposition, it was because this was necessary under a democratic system. We National Socialists have never maintained that we were representatives of a democratic viewpoint, but we have openly declared that we only made use of democratic means in order to gain power, and that after the seizure of power we would ruthlessly deny to our opponents all those means which they had granted to us during the time of our opposition." [1]

The irreconcilable conflict between National Socialism and democracy was affirmed by Hitler in his most important speech to the workers of the Rheinmetall-Borsig plant on December 10, 1940, when he declared war to the death against the democracies:

"We are involved in a conflict in which more than the victory of any one country or the other is at stake; it is rather a war of two opposing worlds . . ." [2]

". . . In this Anglo-French world, there exists, as it were, democracy, which means the rule of the people by the people. Now, the people must possess some means for giving expression to their thoughts or their wishes. Examining this problem more closely, we see that the people themselves have originally no convictions of their own. Their convictions are formed, of course, just as everywhere else. The decisive question is, who enlightens the people, who educates them? In those countries it is actually capital that rules; that is, nothing more than a clique of a few hundred men who possess untold wealth and, as a consequence of the peculiar structure of their national life, are more or less independent and free." [3]

"I could continue to cite examples indefinitely. The fact remains that two worlds are face to face with one another. Our opponents are quite right when they say: 'Nothing can reconcile us to the National Socialist World'. How can narrow-minded capitalists ever agree to my principles? It would be easier for the devil to go to church and cross himself with holy water than for these people to comprehend the ideas which are accepted facts to us today. But we have solved our problems." [4]

"These are the two worlds. *I grant that one of the two must succumb.* Yes, one or the other . . .
"If in this war everything points to the fact that gold is fighting against work, capitalism against peoples, and reaction against the progress of humanity, then work, the peoples and progress will be victorious." [5]

The ideological concepts on which the Nazi movement and the Third Reich are based have well-defined antecedents in certain as-

---

[1] Goebbels, *Wesen und Gestalt des Nationalsozialismus* (Berlin, 1935), pp. 12–13.

[2] *My New Order* (extracts from Hitler's speeches, ed. by Raoul de Roussy de Sales: New York, Reynal and Hitchcock, 1941), p. 874.

[3] *Ibid.*, p. 879.

[4] *Ibid.*, p. 882.

[5] *Ibid.*, p. 889.

pects of German political thought of the eighteenth and nineteenth centuries. The theses of these nineteenth-century doctrinaires were amalgamated and expanded by the Nazis for their own purposes. Opposed to these doctrines was that great element of German liberals, many of whom, led by Karl Schurz, came to the United States in the nineteenth century.

In these certain aspects of German political thought of the past century and a half are to be found the origin and development of all the basic ideological concepts of the Nazi movement: *Volk*, racial supremacy, the leadership principle, rule by an elite class or a single party, the totalitarian state, *Lebensraum*, and the use of military force as an instrument of policy. The contribution of the Nazis has not been to create a new political ideology but rather to crystallize the political aspirations of these doctrinaires and to achieve them by unscrupulous and ruthless methods.

The Volk

The underlying concept of the Nazi state is the *Volk* or the German people. The nature and function of the *Volk* have long been a subject of great interest to German political writers.

It was the father of the German school of historical thought, Johann Gottfried Herder (1744–1803), who first developed the idea of the organic folk-nation in contrast to the hitherto prevalent concept of the politico-juridical state. "There is a living organic force", he wrote, "I know not whence its origin nor what its essence; but that it exists, that it is a living force, that it fashions organic units from the chaos of homogeneous matter, that I see, that is indisputable." [6] Herder sought to point out the conformity of the organization of human life to the laws of nature; he spoke of nationality as "a plant of nature" [7] and the development of national cultures as "a phase of a perpetual system of nature".[8] The various nations were marked for him by distinctive characteristics; he wrote of "those peculiar national characters which are so deeply imprinted in the older peoples and which appear so unmistakably in all their manifestations upon the earth".[9] "Every nationality", he said, "bears within itself the standard of its perfection totally independent of its comparison with that of others." [10] Behind the national character, moreover,

---

[6] Herder, "*Sämmtliche Werke* (Suphan ed.: Berlin, 1877–1913), vol. III, p. 269.

[7] *Ibid.*, vol. XII, p. 451.

[8] *Ibid.*, vol. XV, p. 3.

[9] *Herders Philosophie* (selections ed. by Horst Stephan: Leipzig, 1909), p. 149.

[10] Herder, *Sämmtliche Werke* (Suphan ed.), vol. XIV, p. 227.

there stood a national soul, which he described as "the mother of all culture upon the earth".[11]

Herder believed that the place of the individual was derived from his connection with the folk-heritage and the folk-community, "for none of us became a man by himself. The whole pattern of humanity within him is bound up through the spiritual genesis of education with his parents, teachers, and friends and with all circumstances attending the course of his life; that is, with his folk and his fore-fathers."[12]

Patriotism, therefore, became a basic character value. Herder wrote, "Devotion to the fatherland is a great human virtue"[13] and "He that has lost his patriotic spirit has lost himself and the whole world about himself."[14] He felt that the Germans had failed to develop their own folk-character sufficiently, and many of his works deplored the foreign influences which then dominated German culture. Among his posthumous writings appeared a treatise entitled "Plan for the First Patriotic Institute To Foster a Common Spirit in Germany".[15]

The Romantic philosopher, Karl Friedrich Schlegel (1772–1829), seized upon Herder's idea of the *Volk*, which he made the basis of the nation; for him the highest type of state was the state embracing all descendants of one tribe or the members of one *Volk*. He wrote, "The older and purer and more unmixed the racial stock, the more national customs it will have, and the more national customs and stead-fastness and attachment to these, the more it will be a nation."[16] "Every state is an individual existing independently for itself [*ein selbstständig für sich bestehendes Individuum*]; it is unconditionally its own master; it has its peculiar character and governs itself accord-ing to its peculiar laws, customs, and usages."[17]

During the period of fervent German nationalism which resulted from the Napoleonic wars, the patriotic writer and professor of history at the University of Munich, Joseph Görres (1776–1848), introduced the idea of the ties of blood which bind the *Volk* together, which sub-sequently became one of the basic tenets of Nazi ideology. In his treatise, "The Growth of History", he developed a mystical concept of the *Volk*, which he made the basis of all history; he said of the *Volk* that "all history is nothing but the growth of this plant of heaven;

---

[11] *Ibid.*, vol. III, p. 29.

[12] *Herders Philosophie*, p. 136.

[13] Herder, *Sämmtliche Werke* (Suphan ed.), vol. XIII, p. 149.

[14] *Ibid.*, vol. XVIII, p. 337.

[15] *Ibid.*, vol. XVI, pp. 600ff.

[16] Schlegel, *Philosophische Vorlesungen aus den Jahren 1804 bis 1806*, vol. II, p. 357 (quoted by Friedrich Meinecke in *Weltbürgertum und Nationalstaat*: Munich and Berlin, 1928, p. 85).

[17] *Ibid.*, vol. II, p. 382 (quoted by Meinecke, *op. cit.*, p. 89).

it goes creeping through all species; it has struck its roots in the matter of the primeval world".[18] In another place he wrote, "It is the most fatal of all delusions for a folk to abandon its native characteristics . . ."[19] "No human power can hold back a folk which matures from within itself to great historical character . . . What is above all necessary is that in the center of the nation a firm and definite public opinion should form itself which expresses decisively and unmistakably the peculiarities of the racial strain."[20]

Friedrich Wilhelm Joseph Schelling (1775–1854), the last of the great Romantic philosophers, espoused the metaphysical totality of the folk-nation. "Metaphysics", according to Schelling, "is that which creates states organically and allows a mass of human beings to become of one heart and one mind, i.e. a folk."[21] With Schelling also appears the tendency, which has reached its zenith under the Nazis, to sacrifice the individual for the totality of the *Volk*.

This concept of the submergence of the individual in the *Volk* was also advocated by the economist, Adam Heinrich Müller (1779–1829), who believed that the individual derived his significance from his membership in the eternal *Volk*, which is "the exalted community of a long succession of species—those who have departed, who are now living, and who are still to come—who are all associated for life and death in one great intimate union".[22]

The great German philosopher, Georg Wilhelm Friedrich Hegel (1770–1831), for many years a professor at the University of Berlin, whose teachings have had so deep an influence in Germany, likewise subscribed to the idea of the *Volk* as the basis of the nation. He taught that the state was grounded in the *Volk* and that "the *Volk* as state is the spirit in its substantial rationality and direct reality, hence the absolute power upon earth".[23] For him, too, the individual *per se* had slight value, while the organically conceived "folk-spirit", or the state, was accorded both value and actual power. In his *Philosophy of History* Hegel wrote, "The individuals vanish for the universal substantial [the folk-spirit or the state], and this forms for itself the individuals which it requires for its own purpose."[24]

---

[18] Görres, *Gesammelte Schriften* (Schellberg ed.: Cologne, 1926), vol. III, p. 413.

[19] Görres, *"Über den Fall Teutschlands und die Bedingungen seiner Wiedergeburt", Politische Schriften* (ed. by Marie Görres: Munich, 1854), vol. I, p. 125.

[20] *Ibid.*, p. 127.

[21] Schelling, *Sämmtliche Werke* (K.F.A. Schelling ed.: Stuttgart and Augsburg, 1861), vol. VIII, p. 9.

[22] Müller, *Elemente der Staatskunst* (Baxa ed.: 1922), vol. I, p. 204 (quoted by Meinecke, *op. cit.*, p. 141).

[23] Hegel, *Grundlinien der Philosophie des Rechtes* (Glockner ed.: Stuttgart, 1938), p. 441.

[24] Hegel, *Die Vernunft in der Geschichte* (Lasson ed.: Leipzig, 1930), p. 37.

Like Schelling and Müller, the famous German philologist and founder of the University of Berlin, Wilhelm von Humboldt (1767–1835), looked forward to a time "in which for us the individuals lose themselves in the mass of folk".[25]   He wrote, "The individual human being is always associated with a whole, with that of his nation, of the stock to which this belongs, and of the whole species." [26]   "The individualities which are to be found inside the same nation are embraced by the national uniformity, which in its turn separates every single disposition from its like in another folk." [27]

From the concept of the *Volk* as the basic element in the state and the submergence of the individual in the totality of the *Volk* derives the Nazi principle of *Gemeinnutz vor Eigennutz* or the precedence of community interests over the interests of the individual.   This idea, too, has long been current in Germany.   One of the first glorifiers of the state, King Frederick William I of Prussia, is alleged to have said: "In affairs of state, the good of the whole always takes precedence over the good of the individual."   Likewise Leopold von Ranke (1795–1886), an outstanding German historian who was associated with the University of Berlin for several decades, taught that the individual should sacrifice his time and, if need be, himself for the good of the state.   "Nobody is exempted from the fulfilment of military service; purely private life, indeed, no longer exists.   Our activity belongs above all, in and for itself, to the community . . .   The development even of personal characteristics depends upon the reality of one's participation, I do not say in the forms of the constitution, but in the progress of the general welfare, in the common being." [28]

RACIAL SUPREMACY

Another corollary from the concept of the *Volk* is the idea of the racial supremacy of the Germans, which has been enthusiastically proclaimed by the Nazis, and the effect of which, as this study will show, has been so great in determining the relation of Germans abroad to the Third Reich.   The fact that the Germans had first appreciated the significance of the folk concept lent support to their feeling of difference from all other peoples and superiority to all other peoples.   At the beginning of the nineteenth century, Schelling warned the Germans that in order to recapture their true spirit they must cast out all decadent foreign elements and influences which had

---

[25] Humboldt, *Über die Verschiedenheit des menschlichen Sprachbaus* (Pott ed.: Berlin, 1880), vol. II, p. 22.

[26] *Ibid.*, vol. II, p. 44.

[27] *Ibid.*, vol. II, p. 209.

[28] Ranke, *"Politisches Gespräch"*, *Sämmtliche Werke* (Dove ed.: Leipzig, 1887), vol. 49–50, pp. 333–334.

been introduced by their forefathers. Müller, who foresaw a European community of states dominated by Germany, believed that Germanity would become a supernational ideal through the high genius and wisdom of the German folk. "The great federation of European peoples", he wrote, "which will come some day as sure as we live, will also bear German hues, for everything great, fundamental, and eternal in all European institutions is certainly German . . . The seed of German life has indeed, in these recent folk-tumults, only been extended ever further and further over the ground of our continent; it will proceed in its rampant growth and from quite unpretentious beginnings will gradually advance to mighty effects; let its growth be left to eternal nature." [29]

Friedrich List (1789–1846), a prominent German economist, who in the first half of the nineteenth century advocated a customs and political union embracing the German states, Netherlands, and Belgium, believed that the Germanic peoples were eminently qualified and designated by Providence not only to form the leading industrial nation but also to colonize and civilize wild or uninhabited countries and to lead world affairs in general. The ideas of Aryan supremacy which were clearly formulated by the French racial theorist, Arthur de Gobineau (1816–1882), in his *Essai sur l'inégalité des races humaines* (*Essay on the Inequality of the Human Races*), were seized upon and developed by German racial fanatics of the Wagner - Stewart Chamberlain - Rosenberg school. Gobineau had proclaimed the superiority of the white race over the colored races and the supremacy of the "Aryan" among white men. The composer, Richard Wagner (1813–1883), incorporated Gobineau's ideas into his own writings and made them the basis of his anti-Semitism. For Wagner, racial purity was the touchstone for the value of a people, and he attributed the decay of the Germans, i.e. their falling away from the tradition of the romantic hero, to Jewish penetration.

Friedrich Wilhelm Nietzsche (1844–1900), whose writings were so profoundly stimulating to German imperialism, glorified the blond Teuton beast and advocated the use of utter ruthlessness by the Germans in achieving their goals. "The Germans are a dangerous people", he wrote, "they are experts at inventing intoxicants. Gothic, rococo . . . the historical sense and exoticism, Hegel, Richard Wagner." [30]

The racial ideas of Wagner were elaborated by his son-in-law, the expatriate Englishman, Houston Stewart Chamberlain (1855–1927). Chamberlain rejected the scientific study of races, contending that

---

[29] Müller, *Über König Friedrich II* (1810), p. 58 (quoted by Meinecke, *op. cit.*, pp. 155–156).

[30] Nietzsche, *Peoples and Countries* (translated by J. M. Kennedy in *Nietzsche's Philosophy*: The Modern Library, New York, 1937), pp. 182–183.

the differences between them were self-evident. "The races of man-kind", he wrote, "are markedly different in the nature and also in the extent of their gifts, and the Germanic races belong to the most highly gifted group, the group usually termed Aryan." [31] He held the Germans to be the supreme people within the Germanic race and he considered the German language to be the supreme vehicle of intellectual and cultural achievement. In 1901 he wrote in a letter to Kaiser Wilhelm II, "Science, Philosophy and Religion can today take no onward step save in the German tongue . . . And because the German soul is indissolubly linked with the German tongue, the higher development of mankind is bound up with Germany, a mighty Germany spreading far across the earth the sacred heritage of her language, affirming herself everywhere and imposing herself on others . . . God builds today upon the Germans alone. This is the knowledge, the certain truth, that has filled my soul for years; to the service of this truth I have sacrificed my repose; for it I will live and die." [32]

This view of the German language as a symbol of German racial superiority is of particular interest in view of the persistent efforts which have been made by various official and semi-official Nazi organizations to foster the use of the German language in foreign countries and particularly to insure that children of German blood in foreign countries shall wherever possible receive their education in German.

The racial theories of Wagner and Chamberlain soon found ex-pression in a violent campaign of anti-Semitism. Toward the end of the nineteenth century Eugen Dühring (1833–1921), another pro-fessor at the University of Berlin, denounced Jewish penetration in Germany and in vehement terms deplored the influence of the Jews in education, the press, and the learned professions. Racially mixed marriages, he said, upset the natural cohesion of the whole Gentile community, destroyed the unity and harmony of family life, and could under all circumstances result only in degeneration. In his most significant treatise, *Die Judenfrage*, he wrote, "When the Jews are in the foreground, there is the most corruption." [33] "A political rise of the Jews signifies a corresponding decline and deterioration of peoples and societies." [34] He regarded anti-Semitic agitation as a primary means of promoting that social solidarity which was the necessary basis for a national socialist community.

---

[31] Chamberlain, *The Foundations of the Nineteenth Century* (translated by John Lees: London, 1911), vol. I, p. 541.

[32] Quoted by Wickham Steed in *International Affairs* (London, Sept.–Oct. 1938), vol. XVII, pp. 667–668.

[33] Dühring, *Die Judenfrage* (Leipzig, 1930), p. 7.

[34] *Ibid.*, p. 113.

Particularly outspoken in his conviction of the superiority and the manifest destiny of the German race was the anthropologist, Ludwig Woltmann (1871–1907), who asserted, "It is susceptible of anthropological proof that all European civilization, even in the Slavonic and Latin lands, is a product of the German race." [35] And farther along in the same work: "The Germanic race is called to fetter the earth in its domination, to exploit the treasures of nature and the physical forces of man." [36]

The philosophical writer, Count Hermann Keyserling (born 1880), another disciple of Chamberlain, likewise proclaimed the racial supremacy of the German. "The Germanic people", he wrote, "who destroyed the old world, were rough and cruel, but they were also courageous, loyal and ready to sacrifice; this enabled them, given their talents, to become continuously better in the course of centuries, whereas Greeks and Romans, who were refined and false, perished through degeneration." [37]

The Führer Principle

According to Nazi ideology, the first pillar of the state is the *Volk*. The second is the Führer or leader. In Nazi ideology, the leader is supposed in some mysterious manner to embody and give expression to the aspirations and wishes of the *Volk*. His authority is supreme, his decisions are final and always right, and his followers owe him the duty of unquestioning obedience. Like the concept of the *Volk*, the Führer principle has deep roots in German political thought.

It is interesting to note that the ardently nationalistic philosopher, Johann Gottlieb Fichte (1762–1814), who at the beginning of the nineteenth century advocated the establishment of a self-contained autarchic state, later, under the influence of Napoleon's example, opposed absolutism in the state and accurately foretold the character which a future Führer would have to possess and the conditions under which he might attain power. He declared that only if a ruler succeeded in nullifying in his people all those virtues of an ordered society which had been built up in Europe throughout the centuries and in delivering them over to barbarism could he fill them with the spirit necessary to build up a universal monarchy. "Besides barbaric brutality", Fichte wrote, "the world conqueror of our time would have to educate his people to cool and deliberate piracy; he would not have to punish extortion but to encourage it. Moreover, the shame

---

[35] Woltmann, *Politische Anthropologie* (Eisenach and Leipzig, 1903), p. 293.

[36] *Ibid.*, p. 298.

[37] Keyserling, *The Travel Diary of a Philosopher* (translated by J. Holroyd Reece: London, 1925), vol. I, p. 302.

which is naturally identified with such matters would have to fall away and robbery would have to be made the honorable token of a fine reason; it would have to be regarded as a great deed, leading the way to all honor and dignity. Where is the nation in modern Europe so dishonorable that it could be brought into this condition? Or granted that a ruler succeeded in thus transforming his people, the achievement of his aims would be thwarted by these very means. Such a people would see in the conquered men, lands, and cultural products nothing more than a means for making money quickly in order to go farther and make more money . . . With such a people one can plunder the earth, lay waste to it, and grind it into a dismal chaos, but one can never form it into a universal monarchy." [38]

On this subject, however, Fichte's ideas, although prescient, were without influence on subsequent German thought. Fichte's contemporary, Görres, wrote of the Germans' innate longing for a leader, which would impel the German princes "to choose a chief, after their ancient custom, to remain faithful to him in life and death, and to bind their own independence with the liberty of their peoples".[39] Of particularly far-reaching influence upon subsequent historical thought was Hegel's concept of the great heroic personalities which shape the course of history; accepting the necessary ruthlessness of such a "hero", he wrote, "A great figure, marching along his historic course, tramples upon many innocent flowers, and must destroy many things on his way." [40]

Even the Socialist leader and agitator, Ferdinand Lassalle (1825–1864), believed that the nation must be led by a single forceful personality. "We must forge our wills together into a single hammer", he wrote, "and must lay this hammer in the hands of a man in whose intelligence, character, and good-will we have the necessary confidence, in order that he may be able to strike with this hammer!" [41] In a letter to Bismarck, dated June 8, 1863, Lassalle wrote, "The working class instinctively feels attracted to dictatorship, if they can first be convinced that it will be practiced in their interests." [42]

Even liberal political thought in Germany subscribed to the Führer principle. Walter Rathenau (1867–1922), for example, the Foreign Minister in the Ebert government, who is stigmatized by the Nazis as a traitor to Germany and who paid with his life for his policy of fulfilment of the terms of the Treaty of Versailles, subscribed to the idea that democracy is only justified as a foundation

---

[38] Fichte, *Reden an die deutsche Nation* (Berlin, Deutsche Bibliothek Verlags Gesellschaft, undated), p. 254.

[39] Görres, *Gesammelte Schriften* (Schellberg ed.: Cologne, 1926), vol. IV, p. 449.

[40] Hegel, *Die Vernunft in der Geschichte* (Lasson ed.: Leipzig, 1930), p. 83.

[41] Lassalle, *Gesamtwerke* (Blum ed.: Leipzig, 1899), vol. II, p. 334.

[42] Gustav Mayer, *Bismarck und Lassalle* (Berlin, 1928), p. 60.

for autocratic rule. "Government should everywhere be autocratic", he wrote, "all governments except autocratic ones are powerless and incompetent. Autocracy and democracy are not opposites which exclude one another; on the contrary they become effective only when they are united. An autocratic government can only exist on a democratic basis; democracy is only justified when it has an autocratic superstructure. At all times it is persons who have ruled, not corporate bodies and masses." [43] He pictured an elite ruling class and a supreme leader enjoying a sort of mystical prestige who enforced absolute subordination and identified the state with himself.

Oswald Spengler (1880–1936), the post-war German philosopher, was one of the most convinced advocates of dictatorship. The very nature of the German character, "our unbounded necessity to serve, to follow, to venerate no matter whom or no matter what, faithful as a dog, to believe blindly despite all reproaches",[44] lent itself to the establishment of a strong Prussianized state, which could be accomplished only through a return to "Caesarism". "I call Caesarism", Spengler wrote, "the way of government which despite all constitutional formulation is once more wholly formless in its inner being . . . There is significance only in the purely personal power which is wielded by the Caesar or by someone else in his place through his capabilities. It is the return from a world of completed form into the primitive . . . The powers of the blood, the primeval, growing, germinating force of life, unbroken corporeal strength enter once again into their ancient mastery. Race breaks forth pure and irresistible: the success of the strongest and the rest as prey. It seizes the governance of the world, and the realm of books and problems becomes torpid or sinks into oblivion. From now on heroic destinies in the style of antiquity become possible again." [45]

Artur Moeller van den Bruck (1876–1925) was a post-war patriot who proclaimed the regeneration of Germany. In his book *Das dritte Reich* (*The Third Reich*), published in 1923, he sketched the outlines of the Nazi state, holding that all great Germans had been anti-liberal and that German youth of the post-war period was rising up against liberalism. He sought the basis for a constructive political order for modern Germany in the Dark Ages, when free men chose a "Duke" to lead them: "The people in their confederations established the law; and the leader . . . put the law into effect as the executor of the people's will." [46] Moeller believed that in the same

[43] Rathenau, *An Deutschlands Jugend* (Berlin, 1918), p. 102.

[44] Spengler, *"Vom deutschen Volkscharakter"*, *Reden und Aufsätze* (Munich, 1937), p. 133.

[45] Spengler, *Der Untergang des Abendlandes* (Munich, 1922), vol. II, pp. 541–542.

[46] Moeller van den Bruck, *Germany's Third Empire* (translated by E. O. Lorimer: London, 1934), p. 123.

way the Germans could retrieve the failure of 1918. The nation should seek "a form far more truly German than Western parliamentary government and party systems—leadership".[47] "Leadership", he wrote, "is not a matter of ballot boxes but of choice based on confidence." [48] The leaders of the new empire should not be "concerned that a party should always be right but that one person's will should prevail".[49] "Youth demands a leader who will march in the van: a leader who will make decisions, not the typical westerner who only sums up." [50] "If once the people feel that they have found a real leader in the country, they will joyfully accept his leadership and send to the devil all the democratic and socialist party leaders." [51] "A leader of today will need to persuade the masses to permit him to act for the whole nation, to preserve or win the values that are essential . . . He must rejoice at being called to lead the proletarian masses, to direct their will into national channels." [52] In this way true German democracy would find itself again anchored in a national solidarity which would render class war a thing of the past.

THE ELITE CLASS

Intermediate between the *Volk* and the Führer is the elite ruling class, which owes unconditional allegiance to the leader and represents not only a link between him and the *Volk* but also the instrument through which his plans are realized and his orders executed. The need for an elite class was powerfully championed by Keyserling, who argued that the republican form of government can result only in enslavement of the people and that government by the will of the people manifests itself in general as a rule of incompetence. Within the nation, as within the individual, Keyserling believed, "the emphasis should be laid on what is of highest value, and the inferior values should play a subordinate role".[53] "In all her great periods", he wrote, "the German structure has, in one way or another been aristocratic . . . the tone must be given, for this caste-people, by a real caste which has, as it were, taken an official oath to have a noble point of view; nothing else will do with a people which has the German turn of mind . . . no rule of the masses, or even of the majority, can ever be worth anything to Germany if she wishes to 'keep fit'." [54]

[47] *Ibid.*, p. 228.
[48] *Ibid.*
[49] *Ibid.*
[50] *Ibid.*, p. 74.
[51] *Ibid.*, p. 117.
[52] *Ibid.*, p. 142.
[53] Keyserling, *Europe* (translated by Maurice Samuel: New York, 1928), p. 116.
[54] *Ibid.*, p. 118.

He continued, "I certainly do not believe in a restoration of the rule of the princes in Germany; our development has carried us beyond that point. Nevertheless its *equivalent* will have to emerge once more if Germany's again to become 'fit'. The ruling class will have to be recruited not from the ranks of the scholars . . . but from the ranks of a special and different breed of men, quite alien to the masses of the people." [55]

Keyserling was an accurate prophet. A ruling caste and the equivalent of the princes has indeed emerged in the hierarchy of the Nazi Party.

The Totalitarian State

Another conception which has always appealed strongly to the German mind and has been realized in practice by the Nazis is that of the totalitarian state. The readiness to sacrifice the individual for the community and to accord dictatorial powers to the head of the state led naturally to the conclusion that the state should be all-powerful and should have complete control over the lives of its subjects.

Fichte in 1800 in his treatise entitled "The Closed Commercial State" accurately forecast the outlines of the totalitarian state. He maintained that "it is the state alone which unites an indeterminate mass of human beings into an enclosed whole, into a totality", [56] and advocated that the state should virtually eliminate private enterprise, setting up a rigidly planned corporate economy. The main features of the system which he outlined bear striking resemblance to the system instituted by the Nazis. Aiming at national self-sufficiency, he advocated strict government control of labor and production, concealed inflation and blocked currency, international barter agreements, development of domestic substitutes for imported materials wherever feasible, and intensive armament as a prelude to territorial expansion. Even the methods which he prescribes for the occupation and economic coordination of foreign territory correspond surprisingly with those actually put into practice by the Nazis.

The metaphysical conception of the absoluteness and all-encompassing reality of the state was further developed and propounded by the great German philosophers, who succeeded Fichte. Schelling wrote, "Neither true science nor true religion nor true art has any objectivity other than in the state." [57] For Hegel, whose views in this matter exerted such wide influence, the state was supreme,

---

[55] *Ibid.*, p. 120.

[56] *Fichte für heute* (selections ed. by Ludwig Roselius : Berlin, 1938), p. 133.

[57] Schelling, *Sämmtliche Werke* (K.F.A. Schelling ed.: Stuttgart and Augsburg, 1861), vol. VI, p. 575.

something "earthly-divine" (*ein Irdisch-Göttliches*),[58] and to be revered as such: "Everything that man is, he owes to the state; he only has his true being therein. All value which man has, all spiritual reality, he only has through the state." [59]

Lassalle, the Socialist, likewise believed that great power should be centered in the state. His socialism was state-controlled and his whole political system was based upon the might of the state. "The state", he said, "is a unity of individuals in a moral whole, a unity which increases a millionfold the powers of all the particular persons who are included in this union; this unity multiplies a millionfold the powers which would be at the disposal of them all as individuals . . . the last and most significant purpose of the state, therefore, is to wrest forth and to shape human destiny; that is, all culture of which the human race is capable." [60]

Heinrich von Treitschke (1834–1896), a member of the Reichstag and professor of history at the University of Berlin, who was one of the most outspoken advocates of German imperialism during the Empire, urged the greatest concentration of power in the hands of the state. He expressed admiration for Machiavelli's "conviction that even the most oppressive despotism must be welcome if it insures might and unity for the mother country . . ." [61] He believed that the state should bring about religious and cultural unity within the nation at all costs. Individual feelings were of no consequence; obedience must be the rule. "The state is power", he wrote. "The consequences of this thought are far-reaching. It is the truth and those who dare not face it had better leave politics alone." [62]

Friedrich Naumann (1860–1919), another proponent of pan-Germanism, who in 1896 had founded an abortive national socialist party known as the *Nationalsozialer Verein,* foresaw the development of Germany into a totalitarian state. In his significant book *Mitteleuropa (Central Europe)* composed during the World War of 1914–18, he wrote, "What 40 years ago seemed to be an unearthly ideology of socialistic and state-socialistic dreamers now appears with fabulous assurance as a concrete form which has in the meantime been made ready. Germany is on the way toward becoming not only an industrial state but an organizational state altogether." [63] "On all sides state socialism or national socialism grows up; 'regulated economy' grows up. Fichte and Hegel nod approval from the walls; after the war for the first time the German becomes an economic state-citizen

---

[58] Hegel, *Die Philosophie des Rechtes* (Glockner ed.: Stuttgart, 1928), p. 370.

[59] Hegel, *Die Vernunft in der Geschichte* (Lasson ed.: Leipzig, 1930), p. 90.

[60] Lassalle, *op. cit.,* vol. III, pp. 269ff.

[61] Treitschke's *Briefe* (ed. by Max Cornelius: Leipzig, 1914), vol. 1, p. 352.

[62] Treitschke, *Politics* (translated by Blanche Dugdale and Torben de Bille: New York, 1916), vol. I, p. 85.

[63] Naumann, *Mitteleuropa* (Berlin, 1915), p. 100.

body and soul; his ideal is and remains the organism, not free will . . . That is our freedom, our self-development. Therewith shall we experience our day in history . . . Germany foremost in the world." [64]

The last prophet of national socialism, Moeller van den Bruck, gave expression to the German admiration for autocracy in a description of the German socialism of the future, which he hoped would be realized in a corporative state characterized by totalitarian unity. "Every people has its own socialism",[65] he wrote.

> "Instead of government by party we offer the ideal of the *Third Empire*. It is an old German conception and a great one . . . The *Third Empire* will be an empire of organization in the midst of European chaos." [66]

> "In no country have . . . values tended so definitely toward a unity—a unity which we have never enjoyed since our First Empire, a unity which in our Second Empire we failed to achieve—a unity which it must be the task of our Third Empire to establish. The antitheses of our history will remain, but it is reserved for our Third Empire to bring our values to their fulfilment." [67]

IMPERIALISM

The glorification of the *Volk*, the adulation of the strong leader, and the tendency to concentrate power in an autocratic totalitarian state led naturally to the imperialistic foreign policy which was vigorously pursued after the establishment of the Empire. German imperialism has expressed itself primarily in terms of pan-Germanism and *Lebensraum* (living-space). Pan-Germanism, a direct corollary of the *Volk* concept, aimed at the gathering of all persons of German blood into a greater German Reich. The complementary concept of *Lebensraum* sought to provide ample territory for the development of this greater German state into a nation whose material possessions, economic resources, and standard of living would be adequate for the racially superior German. Again it is possible to adduce abundant evidence of the prevalence of these ideas in German political thought.

Following the Napoleonic wars the poets, Theodor Körner (1791–1813) and Ernst Moritz Arndt (1769–1860), glorified battle and looked forward to the day when a greater Germany would be established by the sword. One of Arndt's political tracts was entitled "The Rhine, Germany's Stream but Not Germany's Frontier". He proclaimed that the Germans were the heirs to the Netherlands, Denmark, Sweden, and Norway—and even to England and Scotland.

---

[64] *Ibid.*, p. 106.

[65] Moeller van den Bruck, *op. cit.*, p. 71.

[66] Moeller van der Bruck, prefatory letter to Heinrich von Gleichen, *op. cit.*, pp. 13–15.

[67] *Ibid.*, p. 249.

List, the economist, likewise believed that Germany needed supple-mentary territories. He was convinced that the superior Germanic race would be able to solve the problem of securing vital living-space, but he sought expansion to the east rather than to the west; for him Hungary represented the gateway to a great new empire: "But why turn one's eyes to lands overseas," he wrote, "when on our southeastern frontier we find immense stretches of country toward which we could easily direct our surplus population . . . What a prodigious flood of power Germany of the southwest allows to flow down to the ocean! How much that flood could produce if it were directed toward the channel of the Danube! Nothing less than the foundation of a powerful eastern German-Magyar empire, bathed on the one hand by the Black Sea, on the other by the Adriatic Sea." [68]

Pan-Germanism was actively fostered by the Universal German League, founded in 1891 and renamed the Pan-German League in 1894. Not only did the League lend active support to colonial and naval expansion but it sought particularly to foster a nationalistic spirit among all citizens of Germany.

One of the most ardent German militarists of the years preceding the World War of 1914–18 was General Friedrich von Bernhardi. In his book *Vom heutigen Kriege* (*Of Present-day War*), published in 1912, he gave clear expression to the arrogant claims of pan-German-ism:

> "We have recognized in ourselves a factor as powerful as it is necessary for the development of all humanity. Our knowledge of this fact imposes on us the obligation to assert our intellectual and moral influence as far as possible, and to open out all over the world a free road to German labor and German idealism.
> "But we can fulfil these higher cultural tasks only if our cul-tural work is carried on and sustained by increasing *political* power, a power which must find its expression in an enlargement of our colonial domain, the extension of foreign commerce, the increased influence of Germanism in all regions of the earth, and, above all, in the complete consolidation of our power in Eu-rope." [69]

Naumann, another exponent of pan-Germanism, believed that the task of the Empire was to unite all the Germanic lands of central Europe in a firm nucleus to which further acquisitions might subse-quently be added. The Europe which he envisaged was to be con-trolled entirely by power politics. Small or weak states would not be able to maintain themselves in the new system. Economy was to be rigidly regulated under an "organizational state" to serve the inter-ests of a militant nationalism. He, too, expressed imperialistic am-

---

[68] List, *"Die Ackerverfassung and die Auswanderung"*, *Werke* (Berlin, 1928), vol. V, p. 299.

[69] Bernhardi, *Vom heutigen Kriege* (Berlin, 1912), vol. I, pp. 8–9.

bitions in terms of Germany's world destiny: "A growing people on a confined territory, with comparatively little natural wealth, must not think otherwise than: *We want to work for the whole world, so that the whole world should have to work for us!* That is our way to become a master nation, that is our national destiny, that is the way to alleviate our social problems." [70]

Even Germany's defeat in the World War did not eradicate German imperialist ambitions or faith in Germany's destiny. Keyserling, for example, proclaimed that "Germany must naturally continue to assert herself as a people and as a nation . . . it would be a crime for Germany to relinquish without a struggle one jot or tittle of her rights." [71] Spengler predicted "a final struggle between democracy and Caesarism, between the leading powers of a dictatorial cash economy and the purely political will to order of the Caesars".[72] Moeller van den Bruck formulated the Nazi approach to the problem of *Lebensraum.* "The population problem is *the* problem of Germany . . . Since access to the outer world is forbidden us, we must look for its solution within our own borders; and since it cannot there be solved, a day must come when we shall burst our frontiers and seek and find it outside." [73] "The population problem unites all conquered peoples in a common cause; and wherever it remains unsolved the nation is in effect a conquered people." [74]

WAR AS AN INSTRUMENT OF POLICY

German writers have never been under any illusion as to how German imperialist aims were to be realized. They have prided themselves on their realistic approach to political problems and have accepted without hesitation the conclusion which to them appears inescapable that German aims can only be realized in the long run by the use of force. It is natural, therefore, to find a martial spirit and militaristic attitude among German writers and it is striking that many of the most influential of them advocate and justify war as an instrument of national policy. In his *Philosophy of Right* Hegel asserted, "In what has been said lies the *ethical moment of war*, which is not to be considered as an absolute evil and as a merely external matter of chance." [75] By means of war "the moral health of nations

[70] Naumann, *Das blaue Buch von Vaterland und Freiheit* (Leipzig, 1913), p. 127.

[71] Keyserling, *Europe* (translated by Maurice Samuel: New York, 1928), p. 132.

[72] Spengler, *Der Untergang des Abendlandes* (Munich, 1922), vol. II, p. 583.

[73] Moeller van den Bruck, *op. cit.*, pp. 64–65.

[74] *Ibid.*, p. 67.

[75] Hegel, *Grundlinien der Philosophie des Rechtes* (Glockner ed.: Stuttgart, 1928), p. 433.

is maintained in opposition to the permanence of finite determinations, just as the passage of a wind saves the sea from putrid stagnation".[76] "The peoples not only come out of wars strengthened but nations which are internally disunited gain an inner peace by foreign wars." [77]

Leopold von Ranke, the Berlin professor, did not believe that Germany could attain her rightful place among the nations simply through cultural superiority. "The esteem in which this country is held in Europe", he wrote, "depends upon its military power . . . This military power demands its needs, undiminished, without interruption; it demands unity and stern subordination." [78] And later he said, "In order to be something, one must raise oneself by one's own strength; we must develop free independence and we must fight to obtain the right which is not conceded to us." [79]

The foremost exponent of war as an instrument of policy was General Carl von Clausewitz (1780–1831), who in his famous *Vom Kriege (Of War)* stated, "War is an act of force in order to compel the opponent to fulfil our will",[80] and again, "War is an act of force and there are no limits to the use of the same." [81] He believed that the whole people must become infused with a warlike spirit which would overcome all sentiments of humanity: "He who uses this force ruthlessly, without sparing blood, will win preponderance over an opponent who does not do likewise." [82] For Clausewitz war and politics were necessary complements of one another. "War is not merely a political act", he wrote, "but a true political instrument, a continuation of political intercourse, an execution of the same with other means." [83] "War knows only one method: force. There is no other; it is destruction, wounds, death, and this employment of brute force is an absolute rule. As to international law, which all lawyers are so full of, it imposes on the object and the law of war only insignificant restrictions; in effect, none whatever." [84]

Treitschke, who was an enthusiastic follower of Clausewitz, likewise considered war to be "the forceful continuation of politics" and he designated the conduct of war as an "essential function of the State." [85] "War is politics par excellence", he wrote, "Again and

---

[76] *Ibid.*, p. 434.

[77] *Ibid.*, p. 436.

[78] Ranke, *"Ueber die Trennung und Einheit von Deutschland"*, *Sämmtliche Werke* (Dove ed.: Leipzig, 1887), vol 49–50, p. 150.

[79] Ranke, *"Politisches Gespräch"*, *ibid.*, p. 327.

[80] Clausewitz, *Vom Kriege* (Berlin, 1832), vol. I, p. 4.

[81] *Ibid.*, p. 6.

[82] *Ibid.*, p. 4.

[83] *Ibid.*, p. 28.

[84] *"Paroles allemandes"*, *Pages d'histoire* (Nancy and Paris, Librairie Berger-Levrault, 1914–18), no. 40, p. 94.

[85] Treitschke, *Politics*, vol. I, p. 64.

again it has been proved that it is war which turns a people into a nation, and that only great deeds, wrought in common, can forge the indissoluble links which bind them together." [86] He was a firm believer in Prussian hegemony in Europe and advocated the formation of a well-organized army in order to obtain the imperialist aims which he envisaged. Militarism alone, he held, could bring out the highest virtues of a people: "Our liberalism must return to the old German conviction that martial force is the basis of all political virtues; in the rich treasure of Germany's glories the Prussian military glory is a jewel as precious and as loyally acquired as the masterpieces of our poets and our thinkers. The sacred character of the allegiance to the flag is a witness to the moral force of our people." [87] "Our military organization remains a glorious manifestation of German political idealism." [88] He believed that there was no place for pacifism in the Germanic nature: "To Aryan races, who are before all things courageous, the foolish preaching of everlasting peace has always been in vain. They have always been men enough to maintain with the sword what they have attained through the spirit." [89]

One of the most rabid German militarists, General Friedrich von Bernhardi, sought to show in his book *Deutschland und der nächste Krieg (Germany and the Next War)*, published in 1911, that "war is in the first place a biological necessity, a regulator of the life of mankind which is quite indispensable".[90] Moreover, "it is not only a biological necessity but also a moral demand, and as such, an indispensable factor of culture".[91] "To increase its might", he wrote, "is the first task of the state, determining all other tasks".[92] "All efforts which have the elimination of war as their goal must be characterized not only as foolish but as absolutely immoral and branded as unworthy of humanity." [93] "Our folk must come to understand that the preservation of peace can and must never be the aim of politics." [94] These teachings fell upon receptive soil; by 1913 the book had run into six editions.

The concept of might in German thought likewise survived the World War. Spengler, for example, wrote, "We do not need any

---

[86] *Ibid.*, p. 51.

[87] Treitschke, *"Das constitutionelle Königtum in Deutschland"*, *Historische und politische Aufsätze* (Berlin, 1886), vol. III, p. 476.

[88] *Ibid.*, p. 481.

[89] Treitschke, *Politics*, vol. I, p. 67.

[90] Bernhardi, *Deutschland und der nächste Krieg* (Stuttgart and Berlin, 1912), p. 11.

[91] *Ibid.*, p. 18.

[92] *Ibid.*, p. 46.

[93] *Ibid.*, p. 30.

[94] *Ibid.*, p. 34.

more ideologists, or any talk about the culture and cosmopolitanism and spiritual mission of the Germans. We need hardness, we need brave skepticism, we need a class of socialist master-natures. Once more: socialism means might, might, might, again and again. Plans and ideas are nothing without might."[95]

This emphasis on the importance of war as a political instrument led to its glorification by German writers as a *Volk* activity. Germans were admonished to cultivate heroic virtues and were told that the greatest glory was to sacrifice their lives on the field of battle. A quotation from Treitschke is typical: "Just where, to the superficial observer, war appears as something brutal and inhuman, we have learned to discern its moral force. That, for the sake of the fatherland, men should stifle their natural human feelings, that they should murder one another, men who have done each other no wrong, who perhaps even respect one another as gallant enemies—at first sight this seems the revolting side of war; and yet herein consists its grandeur. A man must sacrifice not only his life, but also the profoundly just and natural impulses of the human soul. He must renounce his whole ego for the sake of the great patriotic idea. Therein lies the moral sublimity of war." [96]

PROPAGANDA

In view of the deliberate policy of Nazi propaganda to employ falsehood and duplicity as a political weapon, it is interesting to find pre-Nazi German writers who also pay tribute to lying. Nietzsche's superman, for instance, would "rather lie than tell the truth because lying requires more spirit and will . . ." [97] And Spengler, who accurately forecast the age of demagogy, wrote, "What is truth? For the multitude it is that which they constantly read and hear . . . What it [the press] wants, is true. Its commanding officers engender, transform, and exchange truths. Three weeks' work by the press, and all the world has perceived the truth." [98]

---

[95] Spengler, *Preussentum and Sozialismus* (Munich, 1934), pp. 102–103 (1st ed. 1919).

[96] Treitschke, *Politik* (Leipzig, 1899–1900), vol. II, p. 362 (translated by H. W. C. Davis in *The Political Thought of Heinrich von Treitschke* (New York, 1915), p. 155).

[97] "The Will to Power", *The Complete Works of Friedrich Nietzsche* (ed. by Oscar Levy: Edinburgh and London, 1910), vol. XV, p. 367.

[98] Spengler, *Der Untergang des Abendlandes* (Munich, 1922), vol. II, p. 579.

ELEMENTS OF NAZI IDEOLOGY

The line of thought which we have traced from Herder to the immediate forerunners of the Nazi movement embodies an anti-democratic tradition which National Socialism has utilized, reduced to simple but relentless terms, and exploited in what is known as the National Socialist *Weltanschauung* for the greater aggrandizement of Nazi Germany. The complete agreement between the Nazi ideology and the previously described political concepts of the past is revealed in the forthcoming exposition of the main tenets of Naziism.

THE VOLK

Ernst Rudolf Huber, in his basic work *Verfassungsrecht des grossdeutschen Reiches* (*Constitutional Law of the Greater German Reich*) (document 1, *post* p. 155), published in 1939, states:

"The new constitution of the German Reich . . . is not a constitution in the formal sense such as was typical of the nineteenth century. The new Reich has no written constitutional declaration, but its constitution exists in the unwritten basic political order of the Reich. One recognizes it in the spiritual powers which fill our people, in the real authority in which our political life is grounded, and in the basic laws regarding the structure of the state which have been proclaimed so far. The advantage of such an unwritten constitution over the formal constitution is that the basic principles do not become rigid but remain in a constant, living movement. Not dead institutions but living principles determine the nature of the new constitutional order."[1]

In developing his thesis Huber points out that the National Socialist state rests on three basic concepts, the *Volk* or people, the Führer, and the movement or party. With reference to the first element, the *Volk*, he argues that the democracies develop their concept of the people from the wrong approach: They start with the concept of the state and its functions and consider the people as being made up of all the elements which fall within the borders or under the jurisdiction of the state. National Socialism, on the other hand, starts with the concept of the people, which forms a political unity, and builds the state upon this foundation.

"There is no people without an objective unity, but there is also none without a common consciousness of unity. A people is determined by a number of different factors: by racial deri-

---

[1] Huber, *Verfassungsrecht des grossdeutschen Reiches* (Hamburg, 1939), pp. 54–55.

vation and by the character of its land, by language and other forms of life, by religion and history, but also by the common consciousness of its solidarity and by its common will to unity. For the concrete concept of a people, as represented by the various peoples of the earth, it is of decisive significance which of these various factors they regard as determinants for the nature of the people. The new German Reich proceeds from the concept of the political people, determined by the natural characteristics and by the historical idea of a closed community. The political people is formed through the uniformity of its natural characteristics. Race is the natural basis of the people . . . As a political people the natural community becomes conscious of its solidarity and strives to form itself, to develop itself, to defend itself, to realize itself. 'Nationalism' is essentially this striving of a people which has become conscious of itself toward self-direction and self-realization, toward a deepening and renewing of its natural qualities.

"This consciousness of self, springing from the consciousness of a historical idea, awakens in a people its will to historical formation: the will to action. The political people is no passive, sluggish mass, no mere object for the efforts of the state at government or protective welfare work . . . The great misconception of the democracies is that they can see the active participation of the people only in the form of plebiscites according to the principle of majority. In a democracy the people does not act as a unit but as a complex of unrelated individuals who form themselves into parties . . . The new Reich is based on the principle that real action of a self-determining people is only possible according to the principle of leadership and following." [2]

According to Huber, geographical considerations play a large part in the shaping of a people:

"The people stands in a double relation, to its lands; it settles and develops the land, but the land also stamps and determines the people . . . That a certain territory belongs to a certain people is not justified by state authority alone but it is also determined objectively by its historical, political position. Territory is not merely a field for the exercise of state control but it determines the nature of a people and thereby the historical purpose of the state's activity. England's island position, Italy's Mediterranean position, and Germany's central position between east and west are such historical conditions, which unchangeably form the character of the people." [3]

But the new Germany is based upon a "unity and entirety of the people" [4] which does not stop at geographical boundaries:

"The German people forms a closed community which recognizes no national borders. It is evident that a people has not

---

[2] *Ibid.*, pp. 153–155.
[3] *Ibid.*, pp. 156–157.
[4] *Ibid.*, p. 157.

exhausted its possibilities simply in the formation of a national state but that it represents an independent community which reaches beyond such limits." [5]

The state justifies itself only so far as it helps the people to develop itself more fully. In the words of Hitler, quoted by Huber from *Mein Kampf*, " 'It is a basic principle, therefore, that the state represents not an end but a means. It is a condition for advanced human culture, but not the cause of it . . . Its purpose is in the maintenance and advancement of a community of human beings with common physical and spiritual characteristics.' " [6]

Huber continues:

"In the theory of the folk-Reich [*völkisches Reich*], people and state are conceived as an inseparable unity. The people is the prerequisite for the entire political order; the state does not form the people but the people moulds the state out of itself as the form in which it achieves historical permanence . . ." [7]

"The state is a function of the people, but it is not therefore a subordinate, secondary machine which can be used or laid aside at will. It is the form in which the people attains to historical reality. It is the bearer of the historical continuity of the people, which remains the same in the center of its being in spite of all changes, revolutions, and transformations." [8]

A similar interpretation of the role of the *Volk* is expounded by Gottfried Neesse in his *Die Nationalsozialistische Deutsche Arbeiterpartei—Versuch einer Rechtsdeutung (The National Socialist German Workers Party—An Attempt at Legal Interpretation)*, published in 1935. From the National Socialist viewpoint, according to Neesse, the state is regarded not as an organism superior to the people but as an organization of the people: "In contrast to an organism, an organization has no inherent legality; it is dependent upon human will and has no definite mission of its own. It is a form in which a living mass shapes itself into unity, but it has no life of its own." [9] The people is the living organism which uses the organization of the state as the form in which it can best fulfil its mission. The law which is inherent in the people must be realized through the state.

But the central and basic concept of National Socialist political theory is the concept of the people:

"In contrast to the state, the people form a true organism—a being which leads its own life and follows its own laws, which possesses powers peculiar to itself, and which develops its own

---

[5] *Ibid.*, p. 158.

[6] *Ibid.*, p. 163.

[7] *Ibid.*, p. 164.

[8] *Ibid.*, pp. 165–166.

[9] Neesse, *Die Nationalsozialistische Deutsche Arbeiterpartei—Versuch einer Rechtsdeutung* (Stuttgart, 1935), p. 44.

nature independent of all state forms. . . . This living unity of the people has its cells in its individual members, and just as in every body there are certain cells to perform certain tasks, this is likewise the case in the body of the people. The individual is bound to his people not only physically but mentally and spiritually and he is influenced by these ties in all his manifestations." [10]

The elements which go to make up a people are beyond human comprehension, but the most important of them is a uniformity of blood, resulting in "a similarity of nature which manifests itself in a common language and a feeling of community and is further moulded by land and by history". [11] The unity of the people is increased by its common destiny and its consciousness of a common mission". [12]

Liberalism gave rise to the concept of a "society-people" (*Gesellschaftsvolk*) which consisted of a sum of individuals, each of whom was supposed to have an inherent significance and to play his own independent part in the political life of the nation. National Socialism, on the other hand, has developed the concept of the "community-people" (*Gemeinschaftsvolk*) which functions as a uniform whole. [13]

"The people, however, is never politically active as a whole, but only through those who embody its will. The true will of a people can never be determined by a majority vote. It can only display itself in men and in movements, and history will decide whether these men or movements could rightly claim to be the representatives of the people's will." [14]

"Every identification of the state with the people is false from a legal and untenable from a political standpoint . . . The state is the law-forming organization and the law serves the inner order of the community; the people is the politically active organism and politics serve the outward maintenance of the community . . . But law receives its character from the people and politics must reckon with the state as the first and most important factor." [15]

The "nation" is the product of this interplay and balance between the state and the people. The original and vital force of the people, through the organization of the state, realizes itself fully in the unified communal life of the nation:

"The nation is the complete agreement between organism and organization, the perfect formation of a naturally grown being.

---

[10] *Ibid.*, p. 51.

[11] *Ibid.*, p. 54.

[12] *Ibid.*, p. 58.

[13] *Ibid.*, pp. 54–56.

[14] *Ibid.*, p. 59.

[15] *Ibid.*, pp. 60–61.

... *Nationalism* is nothing more than the outwardly directed striving to maintain this inner unity of people and state, and *socialism* is the inwardly directed striving for the same end." [16]

Dr. Herbert Scurla, Government Councilor and Reich's Minister for Science, Education, and Folk Culture, in a pamphlet entitled *Die Grundgedanken des Nationalsozialismus und das Ausland* (*Basic Principles of National Socialism With Special Reference to Foreign Countries*), also emphasizes the importance of the *Volk* in the National Socialist state. Dr. Scurla points out that National Socialism does not view the nation in the democratic sense of a community to which the individual may voluntarily adhere.

"The central field of force of the National Socialist consciousness is rather the folk, and this folk is in no case mere individual aggregation, i.e. collectivity as sum of the individuals, but as a unity with a peculiar two-sidedness, at the same time 'essential totality' (M. H. Boehm). The folk is both a living creature and a spiritual configuration, in which the individuals are included through common racial conditioning, in blood and spirit. It is that force which works on the individual directly 'from within or from the side like a common degree of temperature' (Kjellén) and which collects into the folk whatever according to blood and spirit belongs to it. This folk, point of departure and goal at the same time, is, in the National Socialist world-view, not only the field of force for political occurrences and bearer of each and every political order, but as well the central factor of the entire world-picture. Neither individuals, as the epoch of enlightenment envisaged, nor states, as in the system of the dynastic and national state absolutism, nor classes, as conceived by Marxism, are the ultimate realities of the political order, but the peoples, who stand over against one another with the unqualifiable right to a separate existence as natural entities, each with its own essential nature and form." [17]

Dr. Scurla claims that National Socialism and Fascism are the strivings of the German and Italian people for final national unification along essentially different national lines natural to each of them. "What took place in Germany", he asserts, "was a political revolution of a total nature." [18] "Under revolution", he states, "we understand rather the penetration of the collective folk-mind [*gesamtvölkischen Bewusstseins*] into all regions of German life." [19] And, he concludes:

"National Socialism is no invented system of rules for the political game, but the world-view of the German people, which

---

[16] *Ibid.*, pp. 65–66.

[17] Scurla, *Die Grundgedanken des Nationalsozialismus und das Ausland* (Berlin, 1938), pp. 10–11.

[18] *Ibid.*, p. 9.

[19] *Ibid.*

experiences itself as a national and social community, and con-
cedes neither to the state nor the class nor the individual any
privileges which endanger the security of the community's right
to live." [20]

Some of the most striking expressions of the race concept are found
in *Die Erziehung im dritten Reich* (*Education in the Third Reich*),
by Friedrich Alfred Beck, which was published in 1936. It is worthy
of note that the tendency which may be observed in Huber (document
1, *post* p. 155) and Neesse to associate the ideas of *Volk* and race
is very marked with Beck. "All life, whether natural or spiritual, all
historical progress, all state forms, and all cultivation by education are
in the last analysis based upon the racial make-up of the people in
question." [21]   *Race* finds its expression in human life through the phenomenon of the *people*:

> "*Race* and *people* belong together. National Socialism has re-
> stored the concept of the people from its modern shallowness and
> sees in the people something different from and appreciably greater
> than a chance social community of men, a grouping of men who
> have the same external interests. By *people* we understand an
> entire living body which is racially uniform and which is held to-
> gether by common history, common fate, a common mission, and
> common tasks. Through such an interpretation the people takes
> on a significance which is only attributed to it in times of great
> historical importance and which makes it the center, the content,
> and the goal of all human work. Only that race still possesses
> vital energy which can still bring its unity to expression in the
> totality of the people. The people is the space in which race can
> develop its strength. Race is the vital law of arrangement which
> gives the people its distinctive form. In the course of time the
> people undergoes historical transformations, but race prevents
> the loss of the people's own nature in the course of these trans-
> formations. Without the people the race has no life; without
> race the people has no permanence . . . Education, from the
> standpoint of race and people, is the creation of a form of life in
> which the racial unity will be preserved through the totality of the
> people." [22]

Beck describes the politically spiritual National Socialist personality
which National Socialist education seeks to develop, in the following
terms:

> "Socialism is the direction of personal life through dependence
> on the community, consciousness of the community, feeling for
> the community, and action in the community; nationalism is the
> elevation of individual life to a unique (microcosmic) expression
> of the community in the unity of the personality." [23]

---

[20] *Ibid.*, p. 13.
[21] Beck, *Die Erziehung im dritten Reich* (Dortmund and Breslau, 1936), p. 20.
[22] *Ibid.*, pp. 20–21.
[23] *Ibid.*, p. 35.

National Socialist education must stress the heroic life and teach German youth the importance of fulfilling their duty to the *Volk*.

"Heroism is that force and that conviction which consecrates its whole life to the service of an idea, a faith, a task, or a duty even when it knows that the destruction of its own life is certain . . . German life, according to the laws of its ideology, is heroic life . . . All German life, every person belonging to the community of Germans must bear heroic character within himself. Heroic life fulfils itself in the daily work of the miner, the farmer, the clerk, the statesman, and the serving self-sacrifice of the mother. Wherever a life is devoted with an all-embracing faith and with its full powers to the service of some value, there is true heroism . . . Education to the heroic life is education to the fulfilment of duty . . . One must have experienced it repeatedly that the inner fruition of a work in one's own life has nothing to do with material or economic considerations, that man keeps all of his faculties alive through his obligation to his work and his devotion to his duty, and that he uses them in the service of an idea without any regard for practical considerations, before one recognizes the difference between this world of heroic self-sacrifice and the liberalistic world of barter. Because the younger generation has been brought up in this heroic spirit it is no longer understood by the representatives of the former era who judge the values of life according to material advantage . . . German life is heroic life. Germany is not a mere community of existence and of interests whose only function is to insure the material and cultural needs of its members, but it also represents an elemental obligation on the part of the members. The eternal Germany cannot be drawn in on the map; it does not consist of the constitution or the laws of the state. This Germany is the community of those who are solemnly bound together and who experience and realize these eternal national values. This Germany is our eternal mission, our most sacred law . . . The developing personality must be submerged in the living reality of the people and the nation from earliest youth on, must take an active and a suffering part in it. Furthermore the heroic life demands a recognition and experiencing of the highest value of life which man must serve with all his powers. This value can perhaps be recognized and presented theoretically in the schools but it can only be directly comprehended and personally experienced in the community of the people. Therefore all education must preserve this *direct connection with the community of the people* and school education must derive from it the form and substance of its instruction." [24]

"This nationalism, which is based upon the laws of life, has nothing in common with the weak and presumptuous patriotism of the liberalistic world; it is not a gift or a favor, not a possession or a privilege, but it is the form of national life which we have won in hard battle and which suits our Nordic-German racial and spiritual heritage. In the nationalistic personality the powers and values which have been established in the socialistic personality

[24] *Ibid.*, pp. 52–55.

will be purposefully exerted for the perfection of the temporal and eternal idea of life." [25]

The National Socialist idea of totality, therefore, and its manifestation in the life of the national community form the principal substance of education in the Third Reich:

"This idea of totality must be radically distinguished from the liberalistic conception of the mass. According to the liberalistic interpretation the whole consists of a summation of its parts. According to the National Socialist organic conception the whole comes before the parts; it does not arise from the parts but it is already contained in the parts themselves; all parts are microcosmic forms of the whole. This organic conception of the whole is the deepest natural justification of the basic political character of all organic life." [26]

Education, Beck continues, must present this total unity as it is manifested in the racial character of the people. Race is the most essential factor in the natural and spiritual unity of a people, and it is also the main factor which separates one people from another. The racial character of the people must determine the substance of education; this substance must be derived primarily from the life of the people.

Even in the specialized field of political science, Nazi education is concerned not with the structure of the state but with the role of the individual in the life of the people:

"National Socialist political science concerns itself not with education to citizenship but with preparation for membership in the German people. . . . Not the structure of the state but the strength of a people determines the value and the strength of an individual life. The state must be an organization which corresponds to the laws of the people's life and assists in their realization." [27]

Such indeed is the supreme goal of all National Socialist education: to make each individual an expression of "the eternal German":

"Whoever wishes fully to realize himself, whoever wishes to experience and embody the eternal German ideal within himself must lift his eyes from everyday life and must listen to the beat of his blood and his conscience . . . He must be capable of that superhuman greatness which is ready to cast aside all temporal bonds in the battle for German eternity . . . National Socialist education raises the eternal German character into the light of our consciousness . . . National Socialism is the eternal law of our German life; the development of the

[25] *Ibid.*, p. 46.
[26] *Ibid.*, p. 57.
[27] *Ibid.*, p. 118.

eternal German is the transcendental task of National Socialist education." [28]

RACIAL SUPREMACY

The theory of the racial supremacy of the Nordic, i.e. the German, which was developed by Wagner and Stewart Chamberlain reaches its culmination in the writings of Alfred Rosenberg, the high priest of Nazi racial theory and herald of the *Herrenvolk* (master race). Rosenberg developed his ideas in the obscure phraseology of *Der Mythus des 20. Jahrhunderts* (*The Myth of the Twentieth Century*) (document 3, *post* p. 174). "The 'meaning of world history'", he wrote, "has radiated out from the north over the whole world, borne by a blue-eyed blond race which in several great waves determined the spiritual face of the world . . . These wander-periods were the legendary migration of the Atlantides across north Africa, the migration of the Aryans into India and Persia; the migration of the Dorians, Macedonians, Latins; the migration of the Germanic tribes; the colonization of the world by the Germanic occident." [29] He discusses at length Indian, Persian, Greek, Roman, and European cultures; in each case, he concludes, the culture is created by the ruling Nordic element and declines through the racial decay of the Nordics resulting from their intermixture with inferior races.

It has long been accepted, Rosenberg claims, that all the states of the west and their creative values have been generated by Germans; and it follows that if the Germanic blood were to vanish away completely in Europe all western culture would also fall to ruin.

Rosenberg acclaims the new faith of the blood which is to replace the non-German religion of Christianity. "A *new* faith is arising today: the myth of the blood, the faith to defend with the blood the divine essence of man. The faith, embodied in clearest knowledge, that the Nordic blood represents that *mysterium* which has replaced and overcome the old sacraments." [30]

Rosenberg accepts the classic German view of the *Volk*, which he relates closely to the concept of race. "The state is nowadays no longer an independent idol, before which everything must bow down; the state is not even an end but is only a means for the preservation of the folk . . . Forms of the state change, and laws of the state pass away; the folk remains. From this alone follows that the nation is the first and *last*, that to which everything else has

---

[28] *Ibid.*, p. 140.

[29] Rosenberg, *Der Mythus des 20. Jahrhunderts* (Munich, 1935), p. 28 (1st ed. 1930).

[30] *Ibid.*, p. 114.

to be subordinated." [31]   "The new thought puts folk and race higher than the state and its forms.   It declares protection of the folk more important than protection of a religious denomination, a class, the monarchy, or the republic; it sees in treason against the folk a greater crime than high treason against the state." [32]

The essence of Rosenberg's racial ideas was incorporated in point 4 of the program of the Nazi Party, which reads as follows: "None but members of the nation [*Volk*] may be citizens of the State. None but those of German blood, whatever their creed, may be members of the nation.   No Jew, therefore, may be a member of the nation." [33]   After the Nazis came to power, this concept was made the basis of the German citizenship law of September 15, 1935.

Commenting upon point 4 of the Nazi program in his pamphlet, *Nature, Principles, and Aims of the NSDAP*, Rosenberg wrote:

> "An indispensable differentiation must be made sometime in the German *Volk* consciousness: The right of nationality should not represent something which is received in the cradle as a gift, but should be regarded as a good which must be earned.   Although every German is a subject of the state, the rights of nationality should only be received when at the age of twenty or twenty-two he has completed his education or his military service or has finished the labor service which he owes to the state and after having given evidence of honorable conduct. The right to nationality, which must be earned, must become an opportunity for every German to strive for complete humanity and achievement in the service of the *Volk*.   This consciousness, which must always be kept alive, will cause him to regard this earned good quite differently from the way it was regarded in the past and today more than ever.
>
> "The prevailing concept of state nationality completely ignores the idea of race.   According to it whoever has a German passport is a German, whoever has Czech documents is a Czech, although he may have not a single drop of Czech blood in his veins . . .
>
> "National Socialism also sees in the nature of the structure and leadership of the state an outflowing of a definite character in the *Volk*.   If one permits a wholly foreign race—subject to other impulses—to participate therein, the purity of the organic expression is falsified and the existence of the *Volk* is crippled. . . .
>
> "This whole concept of the state [parliamentary democracy] is replaced by National Socialism with a basically different concept.   National Socialism recognizes that, although the individual racial strains in German-speaking territory differ, they nevertheless belong to closely related races, and that many mixtures

[31] *Ibid.*, p. 479.
[32] *Ibid.*, p. 542.
[33] Gottfried Feder, *The Programme of the Party of Hitler* (translated by E. T. S. Dugdale: Munich, 1932), p. 18.

among the members of these different branches have produced new and vital strains, among them the complex but still *German* man, but that a mixture with the Jewish enemy race, which in its whole spiritual and physical structure is basically different and antagonistic and has strong resemblances to the peoples of the Near East, can only result in bastardization." [34]

True to the tradition of German imperialism, Rosenberg does not confine his ideas of racial supremacy to the Germans in the Reich alone. He even extends them to the United States, where he envisages the day when the awakening German element will realize its destiny in this country. In *Der Mythus des 20. Jahrhunderts*, for example, he writes, "After throwing off the worn-out idea upon which it was founded . . . i.e. after the destruction of the idea represented by New York, the United States of North America has the great task . . . of setting out with youthful energy to put into force the new racial-state idea which a few awakened Americans have already foreseen." [35]

This idea was developed at length by the German geopolitician, Colin Ross. In his book *Unser Amerika* (*Our America*) (document 4, *post* p. 178), published in 1936, Ross develops the thesis that the German element in the United States has contributed all that is best in American life and civilization and urges it to become conscious of its racial heritage and to prepare for the day when it may take over complete control of the country.

Reference was made in the preceding section to Beck's *Education in the Third Reich*. On the subject of racial supremacy Beck points out that certain new branches of learning have been introduced into the National Socialist schools and certain old ones have been given a new emphasis. The most important of these are the science of race and the cultivation of race (*Rassenkunde und Rassenpflege*), which teach the pupil to recognize and develop those racial powers which alone make possible the fullest self-realization in the national community. An awakening of a true racial consciousness in the people should lead to a "qualitative and quantitative" racial refinement of the German people by inducing a procreative process of selection which would reduce the strains of foreign blood in the national body. "German racial consciousness must have pride in the Nordic race as its first condition. It must be a feeling of the highest personal pride to belong to the Nordic race and to have the possibility and the obligation to work within the German community for the advancement of the Nordic race." [36] Beck points out that pupils must be

---

[34] Rosenberg, *Wesen, Grundsätze und Ziele der NSDAP* (Munich, 1933), pp. 16–18 (1st ed. 1922).

[35] Rosenberg, *Der Mythus des 20. Jahrhunderts*, p. 673.

[36] Beck, *op. cit.*, p. 110.

made to realize "that the downfall of the Nordic race would mean
the collapse of the national tradition, the disintegration of the living
community and the destruction of the individual".[37]

Under the influence of war developments, which have given the
Nazis a chance to apply their racial theories in occupied territories,
their spokesmen have become increasingly open with regard to the
political implications of the folk concept. In an article on "The
Structure and Order of the Reich", published late in 1941, Ernst
Rudolf Huber wrote, "this folk principle has found its full confirmation for the first time in the events of this war, in which the
unity of the folk has been realized to an extent undreamed of through
the return to the homeland of territories which had been torn from
it and the resettlement of German folk-groups. Thus the awakening
of Germandom to become a political folk has had a twofold result:
the unity of the folk-community has risen superior to differences of
birth or wealth, of class, rank, or denomination; and the unity of Germandom above all state boundaries has been consciously experienced
in the European living-space [*Siedlungsraum*]." [38]

THE FÜHRER PRINCIPLE

The second pillar of the Nazi state is the Führer, the infallible
leader, to whom his followers owe absolute obedience. The Führer
principle envisages government of the state by a hierarchy of leaders,
each of whom owes unconditional allegiance to his immediate superior
and at the same time is the absolute leader in his own particular
sphere of jurisdiction.

One of the best expositions of the Nazi concept of the Führer
principle is given by Huber in his *Constitutional Law of the Greater
German Reich* (document 1, *post* p. 155):

> "The Führer-Reich of the [German] people is founded on the
> recognition that the true will of the people cannot be disclosed
> through parliamentary votes and plebiscites but that the will of
> the people in its pure and uncorrupted form can only be expressed
> through the Führer. Thus a distinction must be drawn between
> the supposed will of the people in a parliamentary democracy,
> which merely reflects the conflict of the various social interests,
> and the true will of the people in the Führer-state, in which the
> collective will of the real political unit is manifested . . .
>
> "The Führer is the bearer of the people's will; he is independent
> of all groups, associations, and interests, but he is bound by laws
> which are inherent in the nature of his people. In this twofold

[37] *Ibid.*, p. 110.

[38] Huber, "*Aufbau und Gefüge des Reiches*", published in the book *Idee und
Ordnung des Reiches* (ed. by Huber: Hamburg, Hanseatische Verlagsanstalt,
1941), p. 12.

condition: independence of all factional interests but unconditional dependence on the people, is reflected the true nature of the Führer principle.   Thus the Führer has nothing in common with the functionary, the agent, or the exponent who exercises a mandate delegated to him and who is bound to the will of those who appoint him.   The Führer is no 'representative' of a particular group whose wishes he must carry out. He is no 'organ' of the state in the sense of a mere executive agent. He is rather himself the bearer of the collective will of the people. In his will the will of the people is realized. He transforms the mere feelings of the people into a conscious will . . .   Thus it is possible for him, in the name of the true will of the people which he serves, to go against the subjective opinions and convictions of single individuals within the people if these are not in accord with the objective destiny of the people . . .   He shapes the collective will of the people within himself and he embodies the political unity and entirety of the people in opposition to individual interests . . .

"But the Führer, even as the bearer of the people's will, is not arbitrary and free of all responsibility. His will is not the subjective, individual will of a single man, but the collective national will is embodied within him in all its objective, historical greatness . . .   Such a collective will is not a fiction, as is the collective will of the democracies, but it is a political reality which finds its expression in the Führer. The people's collective will has its foundation in the political idea which is given to a people. It is present in the people, but the Führer raises it to consciousness and discloses it . . .

"In the Führer are manifested also the natural laws inherent in the people: It is he who makes them into a code governing all national activity. In disclosing these natural laws he sets up the great ends which are to be attained and draws up the plans for the utilization of all national powers in the achievement of the common goals. Through his planning and directing he gives the national life its true purpose and value. This directing and planning activity is especially manifested in the lawgiving power which lies in the Führer's hand. The great change in significance which the law has undergone is characterized therein that it no longer sets up the limits of social life, as in liberalistic times, but that it drafts the plans and the aims of the nation's actions . . .

"The Führer principle rests upon unlimited authority but not upon mere outward force. It has often been said, but it must constantly be repeated, that the Führer principle has nothing in common with arbitrary bureaucracy and represents no system of brutal force, but that it can only be maintained by mutual loyalty which must find its expression in a free relation. The Führer-order depends upon the responsibility of the following, just as it counts on the responsibility and loyalty of the Führer to his mission and to his following . . .   There is no greater responsibility than that upon which the Führer principle is grounded." [39]

---

[39] Huber, *Verfassungsrecht des grossdeutschen Reiches* (Hamburg, 1939), pp. 194–198.

The nature of the plebiscites which are held from time to time in a National Socialist state, Huber points out, cannot be understood from a democratic standpoint. Their purpose is not to give the people an opportunity to decide some issue but rather to express their unity behind a decision which the Führer, in his capacity as the bearer of the people's will, has already made:

"That the will of the people is embodied in the Führer does not exclude the possibility that the Führer can summon all members of the people to a plebiscite on a certain question. In this 'asking of the people' the Führer does not, of course, surrender his decisive power to the voters. The purpose of the plebiscite is not to let the people act in the Führer's place or to replace the Führer's decision with the result of the plebiscite. Its purpose is rather to give the whole people an opportunity to demonstrate and proclaim its support of an aim announced by the Führer. It is intended to solidify the unity and agreement between the objective people's will embodied in the Führer and the living, subjective conviction of the people as it exists in the individual members . . . This approval of the Führer's decision is even more clear and effective if the plebiscite is concerned with an aim which has already been realized rather than with a mere intention." [40]

Huber states that the Reichstag elections in the Third Reich have the same character as the plebiscites. The list of delegates is made up by the Führer and its approval by the people represents an expression of renewed and continued faith in him. The Reichstag no longer has any governing or lawgiving powers but acts merely as a sounding board for the Führer:

"It would be impossible for a law to be introduced and acted upon in the Reichstag which had not originated with the Führer or, at least, received his approval. The procedure is similar to that of the plebiscite: The lawgiving power does not rest in the Reichstag; it merely proclaims through its decision its agreement with the will of the Führer, who is the lawgiver of the German people." [41]

Huber also shows how the position of the Führer developed from the Nazi Party movement:

"The office of the Führer developed out of the National Socialist movement. It was originally not a state office; this fact can never be disregarded if one is to understand the present legal and political position of the Führer. The office of the Führer first took root in the structure of the Reich when the Führer took over the powers of the Chancelor, and then when he assumed the position of the Chief of State. But his primary significance is always as leader of the movement; he has absorbed within himself the two highest offices of the political leadership of the Reich and has

[40] *Ibid.*, pp. 199–200.
[41] *Ibid.*, pp. 207–208.

created thereby the new office of 'Führer of the people and the Reich'. That is not a superficial grouping together of various offices, functions, and powers . . . It is not a union of offices but a unity of office. The Führer does not unite the old offices of Chancelor and President side by side within himself, but he fills a new, unified office." [42]

"The Führer unites in himself all the sovereign authority of the Reich; all public authority in the state as well as in the movement is derived from the authority of the Führer. We must speak not of the state's authority but of the Führer's authority if we wish to designate the character of the political authority within the Reich correctly. The state does not hold political authority as an impersonal unit but receives it from the Führer as the executor of the national will. The authority of the Führer is complete and all-embracing; it unites in itself all the means of political direction; it extends into all fields of national life; it embraces the entire people, which is bound to the Führer in loyalty and obedience. The authority of the Führer is not limited by checks and controls, by special autonomous bodies or individual rights, but it is free and independent, all-inclusive and unlimited. It is not, however, self-seeking or arbitrary and its ties are within itself. It is derived from the people; that is, it is entrusted to the Führer by the people. It exists for the people and has its justification in the people; it is free of all outward ties because it is in its innermost nature firmly bound up with the fate, the welfare, the mission, and the honor of the people." [43]

Neesse, in his *The National Socialist German Workers Party— An Attempt at Legal Interpretation*, emphasizes the importance of complete control by the party leadership over all branches of the government. He says there must be no division of power in the Nazi state to interfere with the leader's freedom of action. Thus the Führer becomes the administrative head, the lawgiver, and the highest authority of justice in one person. This does not mean that he stands above the law. "The Führer may be outwardly independent, but inwardly he obeys the same laws as those he leads." [44]

The *leadership* (*Führung*) in the Nazi state is not to be compared with the *government* or *administration* in a democracy:

"*Führung* is not, like government, the highest organ of the state, which has grown out of the order of the state, but it receives its legitimation, its call, and its mission from the people . . ." [45]

"The people cannot as a rule announce its will by means of majority votes but only through its embodiment in one man, or in a few men. The principle of the *identity* of the ruler and those who are ruled, of the government and those who are gov-

[42] *Ibid.*, pp. 213–214.
[43] *Ibid.*, p. 230.
[44] Neesse, *op. cit.*, p. 146.
[45] *Ibid.*, p. 143.

erned has been very forcibly represented as the principle of democracy. But this identity . . . becomes mechanistic and superficial if one seeks to establish it in the theory that the people are at once the governors and the governed . . . A true organic identity is only possible when the great mass of the people recognizes its embodiment in one man and feels itself to be one nature with him . . . Most of the people will never exercise their governing powers but only wish to be governed justly and well . . . National Socialist *Führung* sees no value in trying to please a majority of the people, but its every action is dictated by service to the welfare of the people, even though a majority would not approve it. The mission of the *Führung* is received from the people, but the fulfilment of this mission and the exercise of power are free and must be free, for however surely and forcefully a healthy people may be able to make decisions in the larger issues of its destiny, its decisions in all smaller matters are confused and uncertain. For this reason, *Führung* must be free in the performance of its task . . . The Führer does not stand for himself alone and can be understood not of himself, but only from the idea of a work to be accomplished . . . Both the Führer and his following are subject to the idea which they serve; both are of the same substance, the same spirit, and the same blood. The despot knows only subjects whom he uses or, at best, for whom he cares. But the first consideration of the Führer is not his own advantage nor even, at bottom, the welfare of the people, but only service to the mission, the idea, and the purpose to which Führer and following alike are consecrated." [46]

The supreme position of Adolf Hitler as Führer of the Reich, which Huber and Neesse emphasize in the preceding quotations, is also stressed in the statements of high Nazi officials. For example, Dr. Frick, the German Minister of the Interior, in an article entitled "Germany as a Unitary State", which is included in a book called *Germany Speaks*, published in London in 1938, states:

> "The unity of the party and the state finds its highest realization in the person of the Leader and Chancelor who . . . combines the offices of President and Chancelor. He is the leader of the National Socialist Party, the political head of the state and the supreme commander of the defense forces." [47]

It is interesting to note that, notwithstanding the generally recognized view as expressed in the preceding citations that the authority of the Führer is supreme, Hitler found it necessary in April 1942 to ask the Reichstag to confirm his power to be able at any time, if necessary, to urge any German to fulfil his obligations by all means which appear to the Führer appropriate in the interests of the suc-

---

[46] *Ibid.*, pp. 144–147.

[47] *Germany Speaks* (containing articles by twenty-one leading members of the Nazi Party and the German Government: London, 1938), p. 31.

cessful prosecution of the war.[48]   (The text of the resolution adopted by the Reichstag is included as document 5, *post* p. 183.)

Great emphasis is placed by the Nazi leaders on the infallibility of the Führer and the duty of obedience of the German people. In a speech on June 12, 1935, for instance, Robert Ley, director of the party organization, said, "Germany must obey like a well-trained soldier: the Führer, Adolf Hitler, is always right." Developing the same idea, Ley wrote in an article in the *Angriff* on April 9, 1942 (document 6, *post*, p. 184) : "Right is what serves my people; wrong is what damages it. I am born a German and have, therefore, only one holy mission: work for my people and take care of it." And with reference to the position of Hitler, Ley wrote:

> "The National Socialist Party is Hitler, and Hitler is the party. The National Socialists believe in Hitler, who embodies their will. Therefore our conscience is clearly and exactly defined. Only what Adolf Hitler, our Führer, commands, allows, or does not allow is our conscience. *We have no understanding for him who hides behind an anonymous conscience, behind God, whom everybody conceives according to his own wishes.*"

These ideas of the Führer's infallibility and the duty of obedience are so fundamental in fact that they are incorporated as the first two commandments for party members. These are set forth in the *Organisationsbuch der NSDAP* (*Nazi Party Organization Book*) for 1940, page 7 (document 7, *post* p. 186). The first commandment is "The Führer is always right!" and the second is "Never go against discipline!"

In view of the importance attached to the Führer principle by the Nazis, it is only natural that youth should be intensively indoctrinated with this idea. Neesse points out that one of the most important tasks of the party is the formation of a "select group" or elite which will form the leaders of the future:

> "A party such as the NSDAP, which is responsible to history for the future of the German Reich, cannot content itself with the hope for future leaders but must create a strain of strong and true personalities which should offer the constantly renewed possibility of replacing leaders whenever it is necessary."[49]

Beck, in his work *Education in the Third Reich*, also insists that a respect for the Führer principle be inculcated in youth:

> "The educational value of the Hitler Youth is to be found in this community spirit which cannot be taught but can only be experienced . . . But this cultivation of the community spirit through the experience of the community must, in order to avoid

---

[48] *Reichsgesetzblatt* (1942), p. 247.   (All citations to the *Reichsgesetzblatt* refer to part I thereof.)

[49] Neesse, *op. cit.*, p. 150.

any conception of individual equality which is inconsistent with the German view of life, be based upon inward and outward recognition of the Führer principle . . . In the Hitler Youth, the young German should learn by experience that there are no theoretical equal rights of the individual but only a natural and unconditional subordination to leadership." [50]

German writers often pretend that the Führer principle does not necessarily result in the establishment of a dictatorship but that it permits the embodiment of the will of the people in its leaders and the realization of the popular will much more efficiently than is possible in democratic states. Such an argument, for example, is presented by Dr. Paul Ritterbusch in *Demokratie und Diktatur* (*Democracy and Dictatorship*), published in 1939. Professor Ritterbusch claims that Communism leads to a dictatorial system but that the Nazi movement is much closer to the ideals of true democracy. The real nature of National Socialism, however, cannot be understood from the standpoint of the "pluralistic-party state". It does not represent a dictatorship of one party and a suppression of all others but rather an expression of the will and the character of the whole national community in and through one great party which has resolved all internal discords and oppositions within itself. The Führer of this great movement is at once the leader and the expression of the national will. Freed from the enervating effects of internal strife, the movement under the guiding hand of the Führer can bring the whole of the national community to its fullest expression and highest development.

The highest authority, however, Hitler himself, has left no doubt as to the nature of Nazi Party leaders. In a speech delivered at the Sportpalast in Berlin on April 8, 1933, he said:

"When our opponents say: 'It is easy for you: you are a dictator'—We answer them, 'No, gentlemen, you are wrong; there is no single dictator, but ten thousand, each in his own place.' And even the highest authority in the hierarchy has itself only one wish, never to transgress against the supreme authority to which it, too, is responsible. We have in our movement developed this loyalty in following the leader, this blind obedience of which all the others know nothing and which gave to us the power to surmount everything." [51]

As has been indicated above, the Führer principle applies not only to the Führer of the Reich, Adolf Hitler, but to all the subordinate leaders of the party and the government apparatus. With respect to this aspect of the Führer principle, Huber (document 1, *post* p. 155) says:

---

[50] Beck, *op. cit.*, p. 131.
[51] *My New Order*, p. 159.

"The ranks of the public services are regarded as forces organized on the living principle of leadership and following: The authority of command exercised in the labor service, the military service, and the civil service is Führer-authority . . . It has been said of the military and civil services that true leadership is not represented in their organization on the principles of command and obedience. In reality there can be no political leadership which does not have recourse to command and force as the means for the accomplishment of its ends. Command and force do not, of course, constitute the true nature of leadership, but as a means they are indispensable elements of every fully developed Führer-order." [52]

The Führer principle is officially recognized by the party, and the party interpretation thereof is set forth in the *Party Organization Book* (document 7 and charts 1 and 1–A, *post* pp. 186, 488, 489).

There are also included herein, as charts 2 and 2–A and 3 and 3–A (*post* pp. 490, 491, 492, 493), photostatic copies and translations of two charts from *Der nationalsozialistische Staat* (*The National Socialist State*) by Dr. Walther Gehl, published in 1935. These charts clearly show the concentration of authority in the Führer and the subordinate relation of the minor leaders in both the state and the party.

The Party: Leadership by an Elite Class

1. FUNCTIONS OF THE PARTY

The third pillar of the Nazi state, the link between *Volk* and Führer, is the Nazi Party. According to Nazi ideology, all authority within the nation is derived ultimately from the people, but it is the party through which the people expresses itself. In *Rechtseinrichtungen und Rechtsaufgaben der Bewegung* (*Legal Organization and Legal Functions of the Movement*) (document 8, *post* p. 204), published in 1939, Otto Gauweiler states:

"The will of the German people finds its expression in the party as the political organization of the people. It represents the political conception, the political conscience, and the political will. It is the expression and the organ of the people's creative will to life. It comprises a select part of the German people for 'only the best Germans should be party members' . . . The inner organization of the party must therefore bring the national life which is concentrated within itself to manifestation and development in all the fields of national endeavor in which the party is represented." [53]

---

[52] Huber, *Verfassungsrecht des grossdeutschen Reiches* (Hamburg, 1939), p. 410.

[53] Gauweiler, *Rechtseinrichtungen und Rechtsaufgaben der Bewegung* (Munich, 1939), p. 2.

Gauweiler defines the relationship of the party to the state in the following terms:

> "The party stands above and beside the state as the wielder of an authority derived from the people with its own sovereign powers and its own sphere of sovereignty . . . The legal position of the party is therefore that of a completely sovereign authority whose legal supremacy and self-sufficiency rest upon the original independent political authority which the Führer and the movement have attained as a result of their historical achievements." [54]

Neesse states that "It will be the task of National Socialism to lead back the German people to an organic structure which proceeds from a recognition of the differences in the characters and possibilities of human beings without permitting this recognition to lead to a cleavage of the people into two camps." [55] This task is the responsibility of the party. Although it has become the only political party in Germany, the party does not desire to identify itself with the state. It does not wish to dominate the state or to serve it. It works beside it and cooperates with it. In this respect, Nazi Germany is distinguished from the other one-party states of Europe: "In the one-party state of Russia, the party rules over the state; in the one-party state of Italy, the party serves the state; but in the one-party state of Germany, the party neither serves the state nor rules over it directly but works and struggles together with it for the community of the people." [56] Neesse contends that the party derives its legal basis from the law inherent in the living organism of the German *Volk*:

> "The inner law of the NSDAP is none other than the inner law of the German people. The party arises from the people; it has formed an organization which crystallizes about itself the feelings of the people, which seemed buried, and the strength of the people, which seemed lost." [57]

Neesse states that the party has two great tasks—to insure the continuity of national leadership and to preserve the unity of the *Volk*:

> "The first main task of the party, which is in keeping with its organic nature, is to protect the National Socialist idea and to constantly renew it by drawing from the depths of the German soul, to keep it pure and clear, and to pass it on thus to coming generations: this is predominantly a matter of education of the people.

---

[54] *Ibid.*, p. 9.

[55] Neesse, *op. cit.*, p. 71.

[56] *Ibid.*, p. 119.

[57] *Ibid.*, p. 126.

"The second great task, which is in keeping with its organizational nature, is to form the people and the state into the unity of the nation and to create for the German national community forms which are ever new and suited to its vital development: this is predominantly a matter of state formation. These two tasks, one of which deals with substance and the other with function, belong together. It is as impossible to separate them as it is to split up the party into organism and organization, form and content." [58]

Huber (document 1, *post* p. 155) describes the tasks of the party in similar terms. He states that the party is charged with the "education of the people to a political people" through the awakening of the political consciousness of each individual; the inculcation of a "uniform political philosophy", that is, the teaching of Nazi principles; "the selection of leaders", including the choice and training of especially promising boys to be the Führers of the future; and the shaping of the "political will of the people" in accordance with the Führer's aims. [59]

The educational tasks of the party are stressed by Beck, who develops the idea that the *Volk* can be divided into three main groups, "a supporting, a leading, and a creative class". [60] It is the duty of the leading class, that is, the party, from which the creative class of leaders is drawn, to provide for the education of the supporting class.

"Every member of the body of the people must belong to the politically supporting class, that is, each one who bears within himself the basic racial, spiritual, and mental values of the people . . . Here no sort of leading or creative activity is demanded but only a recognition of the leading and creative will . . . Only those are called to leadership in political life who have recognized the community-bound law of all human life in purest clarity and in the all-embracing extent of its validity and who will place all the powers of their personal lives with the help of a politically moral character in the service of the formation of community life . . . From the politically leading class arise the politically creative personalities. These are the mysterious elemental forces which are beyond all explanation by human reason and which through their action and by means of the living idea within them give to the community of the people an expression which is fresh, young, and eternal. Here is the fulfilment of the highest and purest political humanity . . . The education of the socialistic personality is essentially the forming of the politically supporting class within the German people and the encouragement of those political tendencies which make a man a political leader.

---

[58] *Ibid.*, pp. 139–140.

[59] Huber, *Verfassungsrecht des grossdeutschen Reiches* (Hamburg, 1939), pp. 293–296.

[60] Beck, *op. cit.*, p. 37.

To educate to political creativeness is just as impossible as to educate to genius. Education can only furnish the spiritual atmosphere, can only prepare the spiritual living-space for the politically creative personality by forming a uniform political consciousness in the socialistic personality, and in the development of politically creative personalities it can at the most give special attention to those values of character and spirit which are of decisive importance for the development of this personality." [61]

Goebbels in *The Nature and Form of National Socialism* (document 2, *post* p. 170) emphasizes the responsibility of the party for the leadership of the state:

"The party must always continue to represent the hierarchy of National Socialist leadership. This minority must always insist upon its prerogative to control the state. It must keep the way open for the German youth which wishes to take its place in this hierarchy. In reality the hierarchy has fewer rights than duties! It is responsible for the leadership of the state and it solemnly relieves the people of this responsibility. It has the duty to control the state in the best interests and to the general welfare of the nation." [62]

Dr. Frick, German Minister of the Interior, in his chapter in *Germany Speaks* indicates the exclusive position of the party in the Third Reich:

"National Socialist Germany, however, is not merely a unitary state: it is also a unitary nation and its governance is based on the principle of leadership . . .

"In National Socialist Germany, leadership is in the hands of an organised community, the National Socialist Party; and as the latter represents the will of the nation, the policy adopted by it in harmony with the vital interests of the nation is at the same time the policy adopted by the country . . . The National Socialist Party is the only political party in Germany and therefore the true representative of the people . . ." [63]

To Dr. Ley, the party is identical with the Führer. As he wrote in the *Angriff* on April 9, 1942 (document 6, *post* p. 184), "The National Socialist Party is Hitler, and Hitler is the party."

The role of the party in legislation, in political matters, and in the appointment of Government officials is indicated by the Führer's decree of May 29, 1941, [64] as amplified by the order of January 16, 1942, concerning its execution. [65] (Document 9, *post* p. 212). This order provides that all legislative proposals and proposed laws and decrees, as well as any proposed changes therein, must pass through and receive the approval of the Party Chancelry.

[61] *Ibid.*, pp. 37–38.
[62] Goebbels, *op. cit.*, p. 19.
[63] *Germany Speaks*, pp. 30–31.
[64] *Reichsgesetzblatt* (1941), p. 295.
[65] *Ibid.* (1942), p. 35.

2. PARTY MEMBERSHIP

Details concerning the qualifications and duties of party members are contained in the *Party Organization Book* for 1940 (document 7, *post* p. 186).

> "Membership is finally confirmed by the issuance of a membership card or a membership book.   Anyone who becomes a party member does not merely join an organization but he becomes a soldier in the German freedom movement and that means much more than just paying his dues and attending the members' meetings.   He obligates himself to subordinate his own ego and to place everything he has in the service of the people's cause.   Only he who is capable of doing this should become a party member. A selection must be made in accordance with this idea.
>
> "Readiness to fight, readiness to sacrifice, and strength of character are the requirements for a good National Socialist. Small blemishes, such as a false step which someone has made in his youth, should be overlooked; the contribution in the struggle for Germany should alone be decisive.   The healthy will naturally prevail over the bad if the will to health finds sufficient support in leadership and achievement.   Admission to the party should not be controlled by the old bourgeois point of view.   The party must always represent the elite of the people." [66]

German blood is one of the prerequisites for party membership. The *Party Organization Book* for 1940 (document 7, *post* p. 186) also states, "Only those racial comrades who possess German citizenship are eligible for admission." [67]

Party members shall not exceed ten percent of the German population of the region. "The ideal proportion of the number of party members to the number of racial comrades is set at ten percent.   This proportion is to apply also to the individual Province [Gau]." [68]

3. PLEDGES AND SYMBOLS OF ALLEGIANCE

Party members take an oath of loyalty to the Führer in the following terms: "I pledge allegiance to my Führer, Adolf Hitler.   I promise at all times to respect and obey him and the leaders whom he appoints over me." [69]

(a) The Hitler Salute

A pledge of allegiance to the Führer is also implied in the Nazi salute, which is usually accompanied by the greeting, "Heil Hitler". The phrase *mit deutschem Gruss*, which is commonly used as a closing salutation in letters, is another form of the Hitler greeting. *Knaurs*

---

[66] *Organisationsbuch der NSDAP* (ed. by the National Organizational Director of the NSDAP: Munich, 1940), p. 5.

[67] *Ibid.*, p. 6b.

[68] *Ibid.*, p. 6d.

[69] *Ibid.*

Konversations-Lexikon (*Knaur's Conversational Dictionary*), published in Berlin in 1934, contains the following definition:

> "*German greeting*, Hitler greeting: by raising the right arm; used by the old Germans with the spear as a greeting of arms [*Waffengruss*]. Communal greeting of the National Socialists; introduced into general use in 1933."

That this greeting was used by the Nazis as early as 1923 is demonstrated by a photograph which appeared in *Das Buch der NSDAP, Werden, Kampf and Ziel der NSDAP* (*The Book of the NSDAP, Growth, Struggle, and Goal of the NSDAP*) by Walter M. Espe (Berlin, 1934), illustration 34 (document 10, *post* p. 214).

In the same book (page 23 in the supplement entitled *"Die NSDAP"*) the following distinction is made between the usual Nazi greeting and the Storm Troopers' salute:

> "While the German greeting consists merely in raising the right hand in any desired manner and represents rather a general comradely greeting, the SA salute is executed, in accordance with the specifications of the SA service regulations, by placing the left hand on the belt and raising the extended right arm.
>
> "The SA salute is to be given to all higher ranking leaders of the SA and the SS and of the veterans' organization which has been incorporated into the SA, as well as to the Army and the national and security police forces.
>
> "The comradely German greeting is to be exchanged between all equally ranking members of the SA and the SS and members of a corresponding rank in the Army, the police, the veterans' organization, the German air-sport league, the Hitler Youth, the railway guards, and the whole membership of the party so far as they are distinguishable by regulation uniforms."

(b) The Swastika

Early in its history the Nazi Party adopted the swastika banner as its official emblem.[70] It was designed by Hitler himself, who wrote in *Mein Kampf*:

> "I myself after countless attempts had laid down a final form: a flag with a background of red cloth, having a white circle, and, in its center, a black swastika . . .
>
> "As National Socialists we see our program in our flag. In the *red* we see the social idea of the movement, in the *white* the nationalistic idea, and in the *swastika* the fight for the victory of Aryan man and at the same time for the victory of the idea of creative work, which in itself always was and always will be anti-Semitic."[71]

---

[70] The German pocket reference book for current events (*Taschen-Brockhaus zum Zeitgeschehen*: Leipzig, 1942) states that the swastika banner was designed by Hitler for the NSDAP in 1919.

[71] Adolf Hitler, *Mein Kampf* (Munich, Verlag Franz Eher, G.m.b.H., 1933 [copyright 1925]), pp. 556–557.

The swastika banner came into general use after January 30, 1933 as a symbol of allegiance to the Hitler regime, but not until two years later was it made the German national flag by the Reich flag law of September 15, 1935.[72]   Another law, decreed on April 7, 1937,[73] specified that:

> "The insignia which the NSDAP, its formations, and associated organizations use for their officers, their structure, their organization, and their symbols may not be used by other associations either alone or with embellishments."

It is interesting to note that party regulations forbid members to use passport photographs in which they appear in party uniform or wearing party insignia and that party members are forbidden to discuss foreign policy with foreigners unless they are officially designated by the Führer to do so.   The pertinent regulations read:

"Pass Photos on Identification Cards

> "Members of the NSDAP must not use pass photos which show the holder of any identification card in a uniform of the party or of any of its formations.   It is also forbidden to use as pass photos pictures which show the person wearing a party button.

"Conversations With Foreigners

> "It is forbidden to all party members to engage in discussions of foreign policy with foreigners.   Only such persons as have been designated by the Führer are entitled to do so."[74]

THE TOTALITARIAN STATE

The Weimar Constitution, although never formally abrogated by the Nazis, was rendered totally ineffectual by two basic laws, promulgated within two months after the seizure of power by the party. The first of these was the "Decree of the Reich's President for the Protection of the People and State" (document 11–I, *post* p. 215), issued February 28, 1933, the day after the Reichstag was burned down. It suspended "until further notice"[75] articles of the Weimar Constitution guaranteeing essential democratic rights of the individual. Thus, according to article 1 of this decree, "restrictions on personal liberty, on the right of free expression of opinion, including freedom of the press, on the right of assembly and the right of association, and violations of the privacy of postal, telegraphic, and telephonic communications, and warrants for house-searches, orders for confiscations

---

[72] *Reichsgesetzblatt* (1935), p. 1145.
[73] *Ibid.* (1937), p. 442.
[74] *Organisationsbuch der NSDAP* (Munich, 1940), p. 8.
[75] *Reichsgesetzblatt* (1933), p. 83.

as well as restrictions on property, are also permissible beyond the legal limits otherwise prescribed".[76] The abrogation by the Nazis of these fundamental rights of democracy has never been repealed or amended. In fact, this decree represents the presupposition and confirmation of the police sway established throughout Germany by the Nazis.[77]

The second basic law, known as the "Enabling Act", the "Law To Remove the Distress of People and State", of March 24, 1933 (document 11–II, *post* p. 217), swept away parliamentary government entirely. By abrogating the pertinent articles of the Weimar Constitution, it enabled the Nazi Cabinet under Hitler's chancelorship to appropriate money and legislate without any responsibility to the Reichstag or any obligation to respect the Constitution.

The dissolution of democracy in Germany was sealed by the unification of the authoritarian Nazi Party with the German state. Soon after the party came to power in 1933, steps were taken to effect and secure this unity. The process is described by Huber (document 1, *post* p. 155) as follows:

> "On July 14, 1933 was issued the law against the formation of new parties which raised the **NSDAP** to the only political party in Germany [document 11–III] . . . The overthrow of the old party-state was accompanied by the construction of the new movement-state [*Bewegungsstaat*]. Out of a political fighting organization the NSDAP grew to a community capable of carrying the state and the nation. This process was accomplished step by step in the first months after the National Socialist seizure of power. The assumption of the office of Chancelor by the Führer of the movement formed the basis for this development. Various party leaders were appointed as *Reichsminister;* the governors of the provinces were national leaders or *Gauleiter* of the party, such as General von Epp; the Prussian government officials are as a rule *Gauleiter* of the party; the Prussian police chiefs are mostly high-ranking SA leaders. By this system of a union of the personnel of the party and state offices the unity of party and state was achieved."[78]

The culmination of this development was reached in the "Law To Safeguard the Unity of Party and State", of December 1, 1933

---

[76] *Ibid.*

[77] In his book *Die deutsche Polizei* (*The German Police*) (Darmstadt, L.C. Wittich Verlag, 1941), p. 24, the prominent Nazi police official, Dr. Werner Best, wrote that this law "is to be regarded not as a 'police law'—that is, as the regulation of police functions and activities—but as the expression of the new conception of the state as it has been transformed by the National Socialist revolution, from which the new 'police' concept is derived". Also, this law was for the police "the confirmation that the work already begun was in agreement with the law giving will of the Supreme Leadership of the Reich".

[78] Huber, *Verfassungsrecht des grossdeutschen Reiches* (Hamburg, 1939), p. 288.

(document 11–IV, *post* p. 221), which proclaimed the NSDAP "the bearer of the German state-idea and indissolubly joined to the state". In order to guarantee the complete cooperation of the party and SA with the public officials, the Führer's Deputy and the Chief of Staff of the SA were made members of the Cabinet.

With regard to the relation between the party and the state, Neesse writes:

> "The NSDAP is not a structure which stands under direct state control, to which single tasks of public administration are entrusted by the state, but it holds and maintains its claim to totality as the 'bearer of the German state-idea' in all fields relating to the community—regardless of how various single functions are divided between the organization of the party and the organization of the state." [79]

To maintain cooperation between the party and state organizations, the highest state offices are given to the men holding the corresponding party offices. Gauweiler (documents 8, *post* p. 204) attributes to the party supreme leadership in all phases of national life. Thus the state becomes merely an administrative machine which the party has set up in accordance with and for the accomplishment of its aims:

> "As the responsible bearer and shaper of the destiny of the whole German nation the party has created an entirely new state, for that which sought to foist itself upon her as a state was simply the product of a deep human confusion. The state of the past and its political ideal had never satisfied the longing of the German people. The National Socialist movement already carried its state within itself at the time of its early struggles. It was able to place the completely formed body of its own state at the disposal of the state which it had taken over." [80]

The official party interpretation of the relation between party and state, as set forth in the *Party Organization Book* for 1940, appears in the Appendix as document 7 (*post* p. 186).

Goebbels in his lecture on *The Nature and Form of National Socialism* (document 2, *post* p. 170) stressed the importance of *Gleichschaltung* or the penetration of Nazi ideology into all fields of national life. This to his mind must be the result of the National Socialist revolution. The same aims, ideals, and standards must be applied to economics and to politics, to cultural and social development, to education and religion, and to foreign and domestic relations.

The result of this concept of the totalitarian state has been the compulsory regimentation of all phases of German life to conform to the pattern established by the party. The totalitarian state does not recognize personal liberties for the individual. The legal position

---

[79] Neesse, *op. cit.*, p. 131.
[80] Gauweiler, *op. cit.*, p. 3.

of the individual citizen in the Third Reich is clearly set forth by
Huber (document 1, *post* p. 155) :

> "Not until the nationalistic political philosophy had become
> dominant could the liberalistic idea of basic rights be really over-
> come. The concept of personal liberties of the individual as
> opposed to the authority of the state had to disappear; it is not
> to be reconciled with the principle of the nationalistic Reich.
> There are no personal liberties of the individual which fall out-
> side of the realm of the state and which must be respected by the
> state. The member of the people, organically connected with
> the whole community, has replaced the isolated individual; he is
> included in the totality of the political people and is drawn into
> the collective action. There can no longer be any question of
> a private sphere, free of state influence, which is sacred and
> untouchable before the political unity. The constitution of the
> nationalistic Reich is therefore not based upon a system of inborn
> and inalienable rights of the individual." [81]

In place of these rights the constitution of the Third Reich guarantees to the individual his place in the community of the people:

> "The legal position of the individual member of the people
> forms an entirely new concept which is indispensable for the
> construction of a nationalistic order. The legal position of the
> individual is always related to the community and conditioned
> by duty. It is developed not for the sake of the individual but
> for the community, which can only be filled with life, power, and
> purpose when a suitable field of action is insured for the indi-
> vidual member. Without a concrete determination of the indi-
> vidual's legal position there can be no real community.
>
> "This legal position represents the organic fixation of the indi-
> vidual in the living order. Rights and obligations arise from
> the application of this legal position to specific individual rela-
> tionships . . . But all rights must be regarded as duty-bound
> rights. Their exercise is always dependent upon the fulfilment
> by the individual of those duties to which all rights are subordi-
> nate . . ." [82]

The concept of private property in the totalitarian state is also at
variance with the democratic concept of private property. In the
Third Reich the holder of property is considered merely as a manager
responsible to the *Volk* for the use of the property in the common
interest. Huber sets forth the Nazi view in the following words:

> " 'Private property' as conceived under the liberalistic economic
> order was a reversal of the true concept of property. This
> 'private property' represented the right of the individual to
> manage and to speculate with inherited or acquired property as
> he pleased, without regard for the general interests . . . Ger-
> man socialism had to overcome this 'private', that is, unrestrained

---

[81] Huber, *Verfassungsrecht des grossdeutschen Reiches* (Hamburg, 1939),
p. 361.

[82] *Ibid.*, pp. 365–366.

and irresponsible view of property. All property is common property. The owner is bound by the people and the Reich to the responsible management of his goods. His legal position is only justified when he satisfies this responsibility to the community." [83]

Pursuant to this view of the nature of ownership, property may be confiscated whenever the state decides that public management would be in the interests of the community, or if the owner is found guilty of irresponsible management, in which case no compensation is paid him.

Reference has been made to the appointment of party members to important state offices. Gauweiler (document 8, *post* p. 204) points out that the party insured the infusion of the entire structure of the state with its ideology through the civil-service law (*Beamtengesetz*) of January 26, 1937,[84] which provides that a person appointed to a civil-service position must be "filled with National Socialist views, since only thus can he be an executor of the will of the state which is carried by the NSDAP. It demands of him that he be ready at all times to exert himself unreservedly in behalf of the National Socialist state and that he be aware of the fact that the NSDAP, as the mouthpiece of the people's will, is the vital force behind the concept of the German state." [85]

The infiltration of party members into the civil service has now proceeded to such a point that early in 1942 Pfundtner, the Secretary of State in the German Ministry of the Interior, could write in the periodical *Akademie für deutsches Recht:*

"The German civil servant must furthermore be a National Socialist to the marrow of his bones and must be a member of the party or of one of its formations. The state will primarily see to it that the Young Guard of the movement is directed toward a civil-service career and also that the civil servant takes an active part in the party so that the political idea and service of the state become closely welded." [86]

---

[83] *Ibid.*, pp. 372–373.
[84] *Reichsgesetzblatt* (1937), pp. 39–70.
[85] Gauweiler, *op. cit.*, p. 156.
[86] Reported in a bulletin of the official German news agency, DNB, Apr. 14, 1942.

NAZI AIMS AND METHODS

POLITICAL AIMS

The political aims of National Socialism have been written so clearly in history in the past 10 years that it does not appear necessary to discuss them at length here.

The detailed program of the Nazi Party consists of the 25 points which were adopted on February 24, 1920 at a party mass meeting in Munich. (The 25-point program appears in the Appendix as document 12, *post* p. 222.) The points of particular interest in this study are the first four, which are set forth below:

> "1. We demand the union of all Germans to form a Great Germany on the basis of the right of the self-determination enjoyed by nations.
> "2. We demand equality of rights for the German People in its dealings with other nations, and abolition of the Peace Treaties of Versailles and St. Germain.
> "3. We demand land and territory (colonies) for the nourishment of our people and for settling our superfluous population.
> "4. None but members of the nation may be citizens of the State. None but those of German blood, whatever their creed, may be members of the nation. No Jew, therefore, may be a member of the nation." [1]

1. INTERNAL OBJECTIVES

A statement of the internal objectives of National Socialism is made by Gauweiler in his *Legal Organization and Legal Functions of the Movement* (document 8, *post* p. 204). The laws of the Reich must seek to establish and promote the five basic values recognized by Nazi ideology:

> "1. Race: The legal protection of the race, which has created a new concept of nationality [*Volkszugehörigkeit*], is consciously put in first place, for the most significant historical principle which has been established by the victory of National Socialism is that of the necessity for keeping race and blood pure. All human mistakes and errors can be corrected except one: 'the error regarding the importance of maintaining the basic values of a nation'.
> "The purpose of this legal protection of the basic value of *race* must be the prevention for all time of a further mixture of German blood with foreign blood, as well as the pre-

[1] Feder, *op. cit.*, p. 18.

vention of continued procreation of racially unworthy and undesirable members of the people.

"2. Soil [*Boden*]: The living-space and the basis for the food supply of the German people are its territory and soil. The farmer is the first and deepest representative of the people since he nourishes the people from the fertility of the earth and he maintains the nation through the fertility of his own family. Here National Socialism had to accomplish two great legal ends: the reestablishment and the protection of the farmer class and the securing of its land for the farmer family.

"3. Work: The nation's work as a basic national value is grounded on the leading concept of 'work of the hands and of the head' within and for the community of the people and the elevation of work to the only criterion for the value of an individual within the community. In place of the idea of class warfare, National Socialism had to establish the national community legally; in place of the defamation of work and its degradation to an object of barter, National Socialism had to raise it to an ethical duty and the right to work had to become the most clearly defined personal right of the individual. The concept of the honor of work had to be established as the basic concept of the national honor.

"4. The Reich: With the securing of the three basic values of race, soil, and work arises the National Socialist Reich.

"The infusion of foreign cultural and legal influences in Germany was a consequence of the weakening of the central authority of the German Reich since the Middle Ages. The creation and insuring of a strong central authority in contrast to the disorganized, federalistic system of the Weimar Republic became one of the principal lines of National Socialist legal policy. In consequence of the National Socialist revolution, the Reich took on the legal form of a totalitarian state and received a supreme and completely authoritative lawgiver in the person of the Führer. The principle of a division of power could no longer maintain itself: The formulation, the interpretation, and the execution of the law are all performed by the Führer himself or under his authority.

"5. Honor: The fifth great value of the nation is its honor. The honor of the people, the Reich, the party, the Führer, and the individual citizen are all regarded as goods to be protected by law. The basis of national honor is loyalty. National Socialist criminal law is therefore essentially organized as a system of punishment for breaches of faith. Every crime and offense against the community is a breach of faith which must result in loss of honor." [2]

2. FOREIGN POLICY

The close connection between the internal political program of the National Socialist movement, as expressed in the foregoing para-

[2] Gauweiler, *op. cit.*, pp. 149–151.

graphs, and its foreign policy was indicated by Hitler when he wrote in *Mein Kampf* (document 13–I, *post* p. 226):

> "As National Socialists we can further set forth the following principle with regard to the nature of the foreign policy of a folk-state:
> *"It is the task of the foreign policy of a folk-state to secure the existence on this planet of the race which is encompassed by the state and at the same time to establish a healthy, viable, natural relation between the number and growth of the folk on the one hand and the size and quality of its soil and territory on the other hand."* [3]

And in the same work he states:

> "Yes, we can only learn from the past that we must undertake the setting of aims for our political activity in two directions: *Soil and territory as the goal of our foreign policy, and a new, philosophically firm and uniform foundation as the goal of our domestic political activity."* [4]

The political objectives of National Socialism, then, by definition of Hitler himself, are the internal unification of the German people and external expansion.

While the Nazis have never concealed the first of these objectives, the second was the subject for a great deal of dissimulation up to the outbreak of the present war. Typical of the false front which the Nazis presented to the outside world with reference to their foreign-policy objectives are the statements made by Dr. Scurla in *Basic Principles of National Socialism With Special Reference to Foreign Countries*. Dr. Scurla quotes Hitler's speech of May 17, 1933 in which he said, " 'We see the European nations around us as given facts. French, Poles, etc., are our neighbor peoples, and we know that no conceivable historic occurrence could change this reality' ",[5] and comments:

> "This folk principle, which has grown out of the National Socialist ideology, implies the recognition of the independence and the equal rights of each people. We do not see how anyone can discern in this a 'pan-Germanic' and imperialistic threat against our neighbors. This principle does not admit the difference between 'great powers' and 'minor states', between majority peoples and minorities. It means at the same time a clear rejection of any imperialism which aims at the subjugation of foreign peoples or the denationalization of alien populations. It demands the unqualified acknowledgment of the right to live of every folk, and of every folk-group, which is forced to live as a foreign group in another state. The western European national state together with its parliamentary democracy was not

---

[3] *Mein Kampf*, pp. 727–728.
[4] *Ibid.*, pp. 735–736.
[5] Scurla, *op. cit.*, p. 21.

able to do justice to the natural and living entities, the peoples, in their struggle for existence." [6]

Farther on in the same work Scurla states:

"Out of its fundamental ideologic view, however, Germany rejects every form of imperialism, even that of peaceful penetration. It is unable to concede to any people the authority to develop ideas and ways of living, to which then another people has to subordinate itself, even if some other order is suited to its essential nature . . . It does not at all, however, consider the German order obligatory for other peoples. National Socialism, as has been said a hundred times, is exclusively the sum total of the German world-view." [7]

Similar assurances by Nazi leaders were frequently made in order to induce a sense of security in neighboring countries. Hitler, for example, in a proclamation opening the party congress at Nuremberg on September 11, 1935 said:

"National Socialism has no aggressive intentions against any European nation. On the contrary, we are convinced that the nations of Europe must continue their characteristic national existence, as created by tradition, history and economy; if not, Europe as a whole will be destroyed." [8]

But such assurances, which were intended exclusively for foreign consumption, were refuted by the basic policy laid down in *Mein Kampf*, which has been persistently pursued throughout the 10 years of the Nazi regime and has been realized to the extent that Germany now dominates and is in control of most of the European continent. In *Mein Kampf* (document 13–I, *post* p. 226) Hitler wrote:

"Our task, the mission of the National Socialist movement, however, is to lead our folk to such political insight that it will see its future goal fulfilled not in the intoxicating impression of a new Alexandrian campaign but rather in the industrious work of the German plow, which waits only to be given land by the sword." [9]

Hitler suggests a future foreign policy for Germany which would assure *Lebensraum* and domination of the European continent. In *Mein Kampf* he states:

"But the political testament of the German nation for its outwardly directed activity should and must always have the following import:

Never tolerate the establishment of two continental powers in Europe. See an attack against Germany in every attempt to

---

[6] *Ibid.*, pp. 21–22.

[7] *Ibid.*, p. 23.

[8] *Der Parteitag der Freiheit* (official record of the 1935 party congress at Nuremberg: Munich, 1935), p. 27.

[9] *Mein Kampf*, p. 743.

organize a second military power on the German borders, even if it is only in the form of the establishment of a state which is a potential military power, and see therein not only the right but also the duty to prevent the formation of such a state with all means, even to the use of force, or if it has already been established, to destroy it again. See to it that the strength of our folk has its foundations not in colonies but in the soil of the European homeland. Never regard the foundations of the Reich as secure, if it is not able to give every off-shoot of our folk its own bit of soil and territory for centuries to come. Never forget that the most sacred right in the world is the right to the soil which a man wishes to till himself, and the most sacred sacrifice is the blood which he spills for this soil." [10]

It is impossible to adduce from the writings of Hitler or other Nazi leaders direct statements indicating that they aspire to the domination of the entire world. Such expressions, however, may be inferred not only from the direction of German foreign policy and the effusions of the geopoliticians but also from the following statement made by Hitler in *Mein Kampf* (document 13–I, *post* p. 226):

". . . If the German folk, in its historical development, had possessed that herdlike unity which other peoples have enjoyed, the German Reich would today be mistress of the globe. World history would have taken another course, and no one can tell whether in this way that might not have been attained which so many deluded pacifists are hoping today to wheedle by moaning and whining: a peace supported not by the palm branches of tearful pacifistic female mourners but founded by the victorious sword of a master race [*Herrenvolk*] which places the world in the service of a higher culture." [11]

Like Hitler, Rosenberg envisaged the extension of Nazi power far beyond the borders of Germany. In his *Nature, Principles, and Aims of the NSDAP* he stated, "But National Socialism also believes that, far beyond Germany's borders, its principles and its ideology . . . will lead the way in the unavoidable struggles for power in the other countries of Europe and America." [12]

Propaganda

1. PROFESSED PEACEFUL INTENTIONS AS A CLOAK FOR IMPERIALISTIC DESIGNS

The falsity of Nazi propaganda has been demonstrated repeatedly during the past decade. That its keynote was set by Hitler himself becomes evident upon an examination of his statements on foreign

---

[10] *Ibid.*, pp. 754–755.

[11] *Ibid.*, pp. 437–438.

[12] Rosenberg, *Wesen, Grundsätze und Ziele der NSDAP*, p. 48.

policy over a period of years. Not only has his policy been marked by a series of shifts and turns, so that the policy of one year was frequently canceled by the policy of the next, but a comparison of his words with his subsequent deeds makes it evident that he deliberately sought to lull other countries into a feeling of security until he was ready to move against them. On May 17, 1933 he asserted:

> "*No fresh European war is capable of putting something better in the place of unsatisfactory conditions which exist to-day* . . . The outbreak of such madness without end would lead to the collapse of existing social order in Europe . . . The German Government are convinced that to-day there can be only one great task, and that is to assure the peace of the world . . . *The German Government wish to settle all difficult questions with other Governments by peaceful methods.* They know that any military action in Europe, even if completely successful, would, in view of the sacrifice, bear no relation to the profit to be obtained . . .
>
> "Germany will tread no other path than that laid down by the Treaties. The German Government will discuss all political and economic questions only within the framework of, and through, the Treaties.
>
> "*The German people have no thought of invading any country.*" [13]
>
> (Document 14, *post* pp. 232–233.)

And on March 7, 1936 he stated:

> "After three years I believe that I can regard the struggle for German equality as concluded to-day. I believe, moreover, that thereby the first and foremost reason for our withdrawal from European collective collaboration has ceased to exist. *We have no territorial demands to make in Europe.*" [14]   (Document 14, *post* p. 237.)

Moreover, he did not shrink from giving specific assurances of Germany's peaceful intentions toward his subsequent victims:

> "There are Germans and Poles in Europe, and they ought to live together in agreement. The Poles cannot think of Europe without the Germans and the Germans cannot think of Europe without the Poles." (Oct. 24, 1933)
>
> "*Germans and Poles must reconcile themselves as to the fact of each others' existence.* It has seemed to me necessary to demonstrate by an example that it is possible for two nations to talk over their differences without giving the task to a third or a fourth. . . .

---

[13] *London Times*, Sept. 26, 1939, p. 9.
[14] *Ibid.*

"*The assertion that the German Reich plans to coerce the Austrian State is absurd and cannot be substantiated or proved* . . . The assertion of the Austrian Government that from the side of the Reich an attack would be undertaken or planned I must emphatically reject . . . The German Reich is always ready to hold out a hand for a real understanding, with full respect for the free will of Austrian Germans . . ."
(Jan. 13, 1934)

"*The lie goes forth again that Germany to-morrow or the day after will fall upon Austria or Czecho-Slovakia.* I ask myself always: Who can these elements be who will have no peace, who incite continually, who must so distrust, and want no understanding? Who are they? I know they are not the millions who, if these inciters had their way, would have to take up arms." (May 1, 1936)

"Germany and Poland are two nations, and these nations will live, and neither of them will be able to do away with the other. I recognized all of this, and we all must recognize that a people of 33,000,000 will always strive for an outlet to the sea . . . "*We have assured all our immediate neighbors of the integrity of their territory as far as Germany is concerned. That is no hollow phrase; it is our sacred will* . . ."
(Sept. 26, 1938) [15]
(Document 14, *post* pp. 233, 234, 238, 240–241.)

"Yugoslavia is a State that has increasingly attracted the attention of our people since the war. The high regard that the German soldiers then felt for this brave people has since been deepened and has developed into genuine friendship. Our economic relations with this country are undergoing constant development and expansion, just as is the case with the friendly countries of Bulgaria, Greece, Rumania, Turkey, Switzerland, Belgium, Holland, Denmark, Norway, Sweden, Finland, and the Baltic States." (Jan. 30, 1939) [16]

In Hitler's Reichstag speech of April 28, 1939, in which he replied to President Roosevelt's telegraphic message inviting him and Mussolini to pledge themselves not to attack 31 countries mentioned by name, he stated:

". . . *All states bordering on Germany have received much more binding assurances, and above all suggestions, than Mr. Roosevelt asked from me in his curious telegram* . . .
"The German Government is nevertheless prepared to give each of the States named an assurance of the kind desired by Mr. Roosevelt on the condition of absolute reciprocity, provided that the State wishes it and itself addresses to Germany a request for such an assurance together with appropriate proposals." [17]

---

[15] *Ibid.*
[16] *My New Order*, p. 592.
[17] *Ibid.*, pp. 669–671.

And on September 1, 1939, with reference to the recently concluded pact between Germany and Russia, he said:

> "You know that Russia and Germany are governed by two different doctrines. There was only one question that had to be cleared up. Germany has no intention of exporting its doctrine. Given the fact that Soviet Russia has no intention of exporting its doctrine to Germany, I no longer see any reason why we should still oppose one another. On both sides we are clear on that. Any struggle between our people would only be of advantage to others. We have, therefore, resolved to conclude a pact which rules out forever any use of violence between us." [18]

Additional assurances of this nature are quoted in a series of extracts from Hitler's speeches, dating from February 10, 1933 to September 1, 1939, which was printed in the *London Times* of September 26, 1939 (document 14, *post* p. 232).

2. INTERNAL PROPAGANDA

Within Germany the notorious propaganda machine of Dr. Goebbels, together with a systematic terrorization of oppositionist elements, has been the principle support of the rise and triumph of the Nazi movement. In his *Legal Organization and Legal Functions of the Movement* (document 8, *post* p. 204), Gauweiler gives an idea of the permeation of all phases of national life with a propaganda designed to make Nazi "legal principles" acceptable to the masses. He makes it clear that all of the Nazi propaganda machinery is in the service of this program; political lecturers, the press, the radio, and the films all play a part in helping the people to understand and appreciate the new legal code. The schools and Hitler Youth groups provide instruction for all young people in the fundamentals of National Socialist law, and pupils in those schools which train the carefully selected future leaders are given an especially strong dose of Nazi legal theory and practice.

In order to appeal to the broadest audience, Nazi propaganda has always sought to present all questions in the simplest possible terms. Goebbels himself, in his *Nature and Form of National Socialism* (document 2, *post* p. 170), wrote as follows:

> "National Socialism has simplified the thinking of the German people and led it back to its original primitive formulas. It has presented the complicated processes of political and economic life in their simplest terms. This was done with the well-considered intention of leading the broad masses of the people once again to take part in political life. In order to find understanding among the masses, we consciously practiced a popular [*volksgebundene*] propaganda. We have taken complexes of facts which

---

[18] *Ibid.*, p. 687.

were formerly accessible only to a few specialists and experts, carried them to the streets, and hammered them into the brain of the little man. All things were presented so simply that even the most primitive mind could grasp them. We refused to work with unclear or insubstantial concepts but we gave all things a clearly defined sense. Here lay the secret of our success." [19]

The character and quality of Nazi propaganda was fully presaged in *Mein Kampf*. Here Hitler paid a striking tribute to the power of lies, commenting on—

"the very correct principle that the size of the lie always involves a certain factor of credibility, since the great mass of a people will be more spoiled in the innermost depths of its heart, rather than consciously and deliberately bad. Consequently, in view of the primitive simplicity of its mind it is more readily captivated by a big lie than by a small one, since it itself often uses small lies but would be, nevertheless, too ashamed to make use of big lies. Such an untruth will not even occur to it, and it will not even believe that others are capable of the enormous insolence of the most vile distortions. Why, even when enlightened, it will still vacillate and be in doubt about the matter and will nevertheless accept as true at least some cause or other. Consequently, even from the most impudent lie something will always stick . . ." [20]

A number of other passages display Hitler's low opinion of the intellectual capacities and critical faculties of the masses:

"All propaganda has to appeal to the people and its intellectual level has to be set in accordance with the receptive capacities of the most-limited persons among those to whom it intends to address itself. The larger the mass of men to be reached, the lower its purely intellectual level will have to be set." [21]

"The receptive capacity of the great masses is very restricted, its understanding small. On the other hand, however, its forgetfulness is great. On account of these facts all effective propaganda must restrict itself to very few points and impress these by slogans, until even the last person is able to bring to mind what is meant by such a word." [22]

"The task of propaganda is, for instance, not to evaluate diverse rights but to emphasize exclusively the single right of that which it is representing. It does not have to investigate objectively the truth, so far as this is favorable to the others, in order then to present it to the masses in strict honesty, but rather to serve its own side ceaselessly." [33]

"If one's own propaganda even once accords just the shimmer of right to the other side, then the basis is therewith laid for doubt regarding one's own cause. The masses are not able to

---

[19] Goebbels, *op. cit.*, p. 6.
[20] *Mein Kampf*, p. 252.
[21] *Ibid.*, p. 197.
[22] *Ibid.*, p. 198.
[23] *Ibid.*, p. 200.

distinguish where the error of the other side ends and the error of one's own side begins." [24]

"But all talent in presentation of propaganda will lead to no success if a fundamental principle is not always strictly followed. Propaganda has to restrict itself to a few matters and to repeat these eternally. Persistence is here, as with so many other things in the world, the first and most important presupposition for success." [25]

"In view of their slowness of mind, they [the masses] require always, however, a certain period before they are ready even to take cognizance of a matter, and only after a thousandfold repetition of the most simple concept will they finally retain it." [26]

"In all cases in which there is a question of the fulfilment of apparently impossible demands or tasks, the entire attention of a people must be concentrated only on this one question, in such a way as if being or non-being actually depends on its solution . . ."

". . . The great mass of the people can never see the entire way before them, without tiring and doubting the task." [27]

"In general the art of all truly great popular leaders at all times consists primarily in not scattering the attention of a people but rather in concentrating it always on one single opponent. The more unified this use of the fighting will of a people, the greater will be the magnetic attractive force of a movement and the more powerful the force of its push. It is a part of the genius of a great leader to make even quite different opponents appear as if they belonged only to one category, because the recognition of different enemies leads weak and unsure persons only too readily to begin doubting their own cause.

"When the vacillating masses see themselves fighting against too many enemies, objectivity at once sets in and raises the question whether really all the others are wrong and only one's own people or one's own movement is right." [28]

(Document 13–II, *post* pp. 229–231.)

It has been the aim of Nazi propaganda, then, to unite the masses of the people in hatred of certain enemies, designated by such conveniently broad and simple terms as "Jews", "democrats", "plutocrats", "bolshevists", or "Anglo-Saxons", which so far as possible were to be identified with one another in the public mind. The Germans were represented to themselves, on the other hand, as a racial folk of industrious workers. It then became possible to plunge the people into a war on a wave of emotional hatred against those nations which were pictured as combining to keep Germany from attaining her rightful place in the sun.

[24] *Ibid.*, pp. 200–201.
[25] *Ibid.*, p. 202.
[26] *Ibid.*, p. 203.
[27] *Ibid.*, p. 273.
[28] *Ibid.*, p. 129.

The important role which propaganda would have to play in the coming war was fully recognized by Ewald Banse, an ardent Nazi military theorist of the geopolitical school and professor of military science at Brunswick Military College. In his book *Raum und Volk im Weltkrieg* (*Space and People in the World War*) which appeared in 1932 (an English translation by Alan Harris was published under the title *Germany Prepares for War* (New York, Harcourt, Brace and Co., 1934)), he stated:

"Preparation for future wars must not stop at the creation, equipment and training of an efficient army, but must go on to train the minds of the whole people for the war and must employ all the resources of science to master the conditions governing the war itself and the possibility of endurance. In 1914 we had a first-class army, but our scientific mobilization was bad, and the mobilization of men's minds a thing undreamed of. The unveiling of war memorials, parades of war veterans, flag-waggings, fiery speeches and guard-mounting are not of themselves enough to prepare a nation's mind for the dangers that threaten. Conviction is always more lasting than enthusiasm.

". . . Such teaching is necessary at a time and in a world in which countries are no longer represented by monarchs or a small aristocracy or by a specialist army, but in which the whole nation, from the commander-in-chief to the man in the ranks, from the loftiest thought to the simplest wish, from corn to coal, from the treasury vaults to the last trouser-button, must be permeated through and through with the idea of national defense, if it is to preserve its national identity and political independence. The science of national defense is not the same as military science; it does not teach generals how to win battles or company commanders how to train recruits. Its lessons are addressed first and foremost to the whole people. It seeks to train the popular mind to heroism and war and to implant in it an understanding of the nature and prerequisite conditions of modern warfare. It teaches us about countries and peoples, especially our own country and its neighbors, their territories and economic capacity, their communications and their mentality—all for the purpose of creating the best possible conditions for waging future wars in defense of the national existence." [29]

INFILTRATION TACTICS

The Nazis, while entirely without scruple in the pursuit of their objectives, endeavor whenever possible to give their actions the cloak of legality. This procedure was followed in Germany to enable them to gain control of the Government of the Reich and in their foreign policy up to September 1, 1939. It has been a cardinal principle of the Nazis to avoid the use of force whenever their objectives may be

---

[29] Banse, *Germany Prepares for War* (New York, 1934), pp. 348–349.

attained in another manner and they have assiduously studied their enemies in an effort to discover the weak points in their structure which will enable the Nazis to accomplish their downfall. The preceding pages have demonstrated that the Nazis have contributed practically nothing that is original to German political thought. By the use of unscrupulous, deceitful, and uninhibited tactics, however, they have been able to realize many of the objectives which had previously existed only in theory.

The Weimar Constitution provided the Nazis with a convenient basis for the establishment of the totalitarian state. They made no effort to conceal their intention of taking advantage of the weaknesses of the Weimar Republic in order to attain power. On April 30, 1928 Dr. Goebbels wrote in his paper *Der Angriff:*

> "We enter Parliament in order to supply ourselves, in the arsenal of democracy, with its own weapons. We become members of the Reichstag in order to paralyze the Weimar sentiment with its own assistance. If democracy is so stupid as to give us free tickets and salaries for this bear's work, that is its affair . . ." [30]

And later in the same article:

> "We do not come as friends, nor even as neutrals. We come as enemies. As the wolf bursts into the flock, so we come." [31]

Hitler expressed the same idea on September 1, 1933, when, looking back upon the struggle for political power in Germany, he wrote:

> "This watchword of democratic freedom led only to insecurity, indiscipline, and at length to the downfall and destruction of all authority. *Our opponents' objection that we, too, once made use of these rights, will not hold water; for we made use of an unreasonable right, which was part and parcel of an unreasonable system, in order to overthrow the unreason of this system.*" [32]

Discussing the rise to power of the Nazis, Huber (document 1, *post* p. 155) wrote in 1939:

> "The parliamentary battle of the NSDAP had the single purpose of destroying the parliamentary system from within through its own methods. It was necessary above all to make formal use of the possibilities of the party-state system but to refuse real cooperation and thereby to render the parliamentary system, which is by nature dependent upon the responsible cooperation of the opposition, incapable of action." [33]

---

[30] Goebbels, *Der Angriff: Aufsätze aus der Kampfzeit* (Munich, 1936), p. 71.
[31] *Ibid.*, p. 73.
[32] *My New Order*, pp. 195–196.
[33] Huber, *Verfassungsrecht des grossdeutschen Reiches* (Hamburg, 1939), p. 31.

As its parliamentary strength increased, the party was able to achieve these aims:

> "It was in a position to make the formation of any positive majority in the Reichstag impossible . . . Thus the NSDAP was able through its strong position to make the Reichstag powerless as a lawgiving and government-forming body." [34]

The same principle was followed by Germany in weakening and undermining the governments of countries which it had chosen for its victims. While it was Hitler's policy to concentrate on only one objective at a time, German agents were busy throughout the world in ferreting out the natural political, social, and economic cleavages in various countries and in broadening them in order to create internal confusion and uncertainty. Foreign political leaders of Fascist or authoritarian persuasion were encouraged and often liberally subsidized from Nazi funds. Control was covertly obtained over influential newspapers and periodicals and their editorial policies shaped in such a way as to further Nazi ends. In the countries Germany sought to overpower, all the highly developed organs of Nazi propaganda were utilized to confuse and divide public opinion, to discredit national leaders and institutions, and to induce an unjustified feeling of confidence in the false assertions of Nazi leaders disclaiming any aggressive intentions.

One of the most important features introduced by the Nazis into German foreign policy was the appreciation of the value of Germans living abroad and their organization as implements of the Reich for the attainment of objectives in the field of foreign policy. This idea was applied by the Nazis to all the large colonies of Germans which are scattered throughout the world. The potential usefulness of these colonies was early recognized by the men in Hitler's immediate entourage, several of whom were so-called *Auslandsdeutsche* who had spent many years of their life abroad and were familiar with foreign conditions and with the position and influence of German groups in foreign countries. Of particular importance in this group were Rudolf Hess, the Führer's Deputy, who was primarily responsible for elaborating the policy which utilized the services of Germans abroad, and Ernst Wilhelm Bohle, the leader of the Foreign Organization, who was responsible for winning over these Germans to Naziism and for their organization in groups which would serve the purposes of the Third Reich.

Part III of this treatise discusses in detail the agencies employed by the Nazi regime for the organization of *Volksgenossen* abroad and the systematic use of the German racial element in foreign countries for the promotion of German interests.

---

[34] *Ibid.*, p. 32.

PART II

GERMAN CITIZENSHIP LAWS AND NAZI POLICY REGARDING DUAL NATIONALITY, EXPATRIATION, AND NATURALIZATION OF GERMANS IN OTHER COUNTRIES

SUPREMACY OF GERMAN BLOOD OVER ANY FOREIGN CITIZENSHIP

The significance of the concept of *Volk*, both for German political thinking during the past century and a half in general, and for the Nazi ideology in particular, has been shown in the preceding discussion in part I, as has also its correlation with the concept of German racial supremacy, German imperialism, and other aspects of Nazi thought. The *Volk*, as has been shown, is an obscure, compelling, natural entity, bound together by blood and common culture. It is entirely different from our notion of "people", the social community of citizens having an open, conscious, and optional allegiance to a political union of their own making. The *Volk* is rather conceived, on the one hand, as a natural organism and as such exerting a compulsory hold on the individual through blood relationship and, on the other hand, as a supernatural being, imposing an absolute claim for loyalty and allegiance.

The conception of citizenship based on the notion of the *Volk* must, of course, be entirely at variance with American views, especially with regard to the adoption of foreign citizenship by persons of German extraction. Indeed, it would appear, from the Nazi viewpoint, that the adoption of foreign citizenship in a genuine way by a German is really inconceivable, unless the person in question acts as a renegade betraying his own nature and origin. The Nazis have not failed to put the adoption of foreign citizenship in such a light. For instance, when the German film actress, Marlene Dietrich, was naturalized in 1937 as an American citizen, *Der Stürmer*, the weekly published by Julius Streicher, Nazi Gauleiter of Franconia, Germany, presented in an October 1937 issue a picture purporting to show the oath scene, in which Marlene Dietrich was taking the oath "that she betray her fatherland" (document 15, *post* p. 244).

An equally strong Nazi tendency has been to belittle the essential significance of any foreign citizenship, thus enabling the German to adopt foreign citizenship readily and in a casual way. Momentary questions of personal convenience are allowed to be determining factors, while the intrinsic import and implications of naturalization are deliberately ignored. It is known, too, that Nazi Germans have acquired citizenship in other countries on orders from Germany, for reasons of expediency.

The first factor in the depreciation of foreign citizenship lies in the general theoretic subordination of the state to the *Volk*, which was pointed out in part I.   Hitler, himself, in his *Mein Kampf*, declares the state is only a means serving the *Volk* and terms it also "the living organism of a nationality [*Volkstum*]".[1]   In another place he terms the state a "folk organism" and construes its aim as the furtherance of a certain species of human being.[2]   In this connection Hitler makes the foreboding remark that "the state, as such, does not even need to have a territorial limitation as a prerequisite".[3]   And with the usual perfidy, ascribing to the Jews what is later shown herein to be true of the Nazi aims, he declares, "The Jewish state was never in itself territorially restricted; rather it was universally unlimited in space but restricted to the solidarity of one race.   Consequently, this people always formed a state within the other states."[4]

It will be recalled that the first article in the the official program of the NSDAP, the text of which was written in 1927 by Gottfried Feder on Hitler's orders and reviewed by Hitler himself, reads as follows:

> "We demand the union of all Germans to form a Great Germany on the basis of the right of the self-determination enjoyed by nations."[5]

In his subsequent remarks concerning the program, Feder made the following comment:

> "All those of German blood, even if they live at present under Danish, Polish, Czech, Italian, or French sovereignty, are to be united in one German Reich.   We demand, neither more nor less than was demanded on behalf of our enemies, the right of *self-determination of Germans* with regard to their allegiance to the mother-country, the German homeland.
>
> "We will not relinquish our claim to any German in Sudeten Germany, Alsace-Lorraine, Poland, the League of Nations Colony Austria, and the successor states of the old Austria."[6]

These claims, however, are not merely restricted to the European countries adjacent to Germany, for Feder continues with regard to the German emigrants abroad:

> "The best, most capable, Vikinglike Germans are often those who went out into the wide world as bearers of culture, as engineers, explorers, scholars, businessmen, doctors.   They belong to the great German racial family [*Volksfamilie*], which ought not to and dares not let them be lost.   These Germans ought no longer

---

[1] *Mein Kampf*, pp. 433ff.

[2] *Ibid.*, pp. 164ff.

[3] *Ibid.*, p. 165.

[4] *Ibid.*, p. 165.

[5] Gottfried Feder, *Das Programm der NSDAP* (Munich, Franz Eher Verlag, Central Publishing House of the NSDAP, 1933), p. 19 (1st ed. 1927).

[6] *Ibid.*, p. 42.

to be cultural *fertilizers* but rather conscious outposts, champions of Germandom in the world; they ought not to be 'apostles of humanity' but rather bearers of the Nordic idea." [7]

In *Mein Kampf* Hitler mentions the loss to Germany owing to emigration, in a passage which also contains a clear claim of German racial supremacy:

> ". . . also in the future we would remain merely cultural fertilizer, not only in the sense of the limited conception of our present bourgeois viewpoint, which only sees a lost citizen in the individual lost racial comrade, but also in the sense of the most painful recognition that then, despite all our knowledge and ability, our blood nevertheless is destined to decline. Mating again and again with other races, we raise these from their previous cultural level to a higher one, but we sink down forever from our own high level." [8]

Bound together with the general subordination of the state to the *Volk* and with the claim of German racial superiority come open expressions of the supremacy of German blood over any foreign citizenship. In a pamphlet entitled *Citizenship and the Reich's Burgher Law*, which was published in 1939 in an official collection of pamphlets (edited by the Chief of the Reich's Chancelry), Dr. Bernhard Lösener, Ministerial Adviser in the German Ministry of the Interior, declared:

> "The concepts 'citizen' and 'racial member' do not coincide . . . If both concepts are to be considered in the proper relation with regard to their value, the race, or its single member the racial comrade, must stand in first place. To make this, the only healthy view, again common knowledge is one of the aims of National Socialism." [9]

Furthermore, in the same article Dr. Lösener expresses the view that foreign citizenship should not be permitted to make any essential difference nor disrupt the unity of the race:

> "The highest goal, which, however, can only remain always an ideal, would be that the original and more healthy condition of the unity of race and citizenship be again achieved. No imperialistic goals are to be set here, but it must be achieved that the conception of citizenship, independent of the race and carrying on a juridical separate existence in empty space, gradually dies. Not only in the law, but above all in the sentiments of every racial comrade, both the German citizens and the Germans in foreign countries, it must be displaced from the position of a factor which designates a difference in essential nature.

---

[7] *Ibid.*, p. 42.

[8] *Mein Kampf*, p. 476.

[9] Dr. Bernhard Lösener, *Staatsangehörigkeit und Reichsbürgerrecht* (published in *Grundlagen, Aufbau und Wirtschaftsordnung des nationalsozialistischen Staates:* Berlin, 1936), vol. I, group 2, no. 13, p. 3.

Here we are right in hoping for the fruition of the seed which our Führer and his movement have scattered abroad." [10]

In an address at the 1933 meeting of the German Foreign Institute at Stuttgart, Professor Mergenthaler, the Minister-President of Württemberg, declared:

"Previously only a formal concept of citizenship has been current. The German revolution has dispensed with this formal concept of citizenship. Racial relationship based on blood ties is the foundation on which the German Foreign Institute and the entire task of protecting Germanism abroad is erected." [11]

The "formal concept" of citizenship was rejected because according to Nazi ideas it did not and could not include all Germans. As Dr. Lösener asserts with regard to this issue:

"The German citizenship law of 1913 begins with the statement: 'Whoever possesses citizenship in a state of the Federation or possesses direct citizenship in the Reich is a German.' Aside from the fact that, since the law of January 30, 1934 on the reconstruction of the Reich, this article I is invalid and has been replaced, we, as National Socialists, reject also the fact that a basic law of the German Reich pronounces that only he is a German who formally possesses German citizenship. For us the German people is not the sum of German citizens, but there belong to it also all those bound by a common racial extraction. These are, moreover, many more than all those who are able to exhibit a German citizenship certificate. We must again accustom ourselves so to select juridical terms that they do not carry on a special existence 'in the sense of the law', but rather coincide with the deeper-rooted productive conception, whose appropriateness every person of common sense grasps." [12]

The same idea is repeated again and again in propagandistic literature. A prominent pan-Germanist, Friedrich Lange, declares in the *Volksdeutsche Kartenskizzen* (Berlin, 1937):

". . . blood is stronger than a passport! . . . We will never call German people who are citizens of foreign countries aliens but racial comrades! German people will always remain our racial comrades even if foreign citizenship is forced upon them, just as members of an alien race can never become German racial comrades by means of conversion. We will always remember that we, Germans, are not only citizens of the largest German state, of the German Reich, but that we are also racial comrades of more than 30 million Germans outside our borders." [13]

---

[10] *Ibid.*, p. 29.

[11] *N. S. Kurier* (Stuttgart newspaper), Sept. 21, 1933, morning edition.

[12] Lösener, *op. cit.*, p. 16.

[13] Cited in *The German Reich and Americans of German Origin* (New York, Oxford University Press, 1938), p. 20.

In the authoritative pan-Germanist work *The Book of German Volkstum*, Dr. Hans Steinacher, the Director of the League for Germandom Abroad, declared with assurance:

> "We feel and we also know that the bonds of *Volkstum* have an infinitely deeper effect than the alienable possession of citizenship papers." [14]

Pan-Germanist ideas had always stressed the great extent and the importance of the German racial element in non-German countries. The Nazis added further emphasis to these ideas by their use of the notion of the racial or folk community (*Volksgemeinschaft*), which by its very nature demands explicit and total allegiance. In pamphlet 8 of group 1, in the above-mentioned collection (edited by the Chief of the Reich's Chancelry, Dr. Lammers), Fritz Reinhardt, a State-Secretary in the Reich's Treasury Department, wrote under the title *Vom Wesen der Volksgemeinschaft* (*Concerning the Nature of the Folk-Community*):

> "Adolf Hitler has set his stamp on the word folk-community [*Volksgemeinschaft*]. This word is to make completely clear to the members of our people that the individual is *nothing*, when not a member of a community, and that the *natural* community is only the community of men of the same *origin*, same *language*, and same *culture*, i. e. the *folk-community*.

> . . . .

> "The *folk-community* is the *natural presupposition* for the existence of the whole people and indirectly, in the end, for the existence of each individual. Whoever wants to *live* and *thrive* in this world is obligated in the nature of things to orient *his* struggle for existence mainly *toward the struggle for the vital rights of the folk-community and thus of the nation.*
> "The folk-community is *not spatially bounded;* it includes *all* members of the people, without regard to residence or temporary place of abode; thus it includes also those who live outside of the borders of the German state.

> . . . .

> "The German folk-community includes not only all those who are members of the NSDAP, it includes *all* who by *origin*, *language*, and *culture* belong to the German folk-community and in accordance with the rigid law of nature acknowledge their allegiance to the German folk-community. The German folk-community includes therefore not only the members of the folk *within* the German borders but those everywhere in the world, without regard to residence or temporary place of abode, without regard to class and profession, and also without regard to

---

[14] *The Book of German Volkstum* (*Das Buch vom deutschen Volkstum*) (Leipzig, 1935), p. 416.

what former political direction or party the individual may
have formerly adhered to, and without regard to how the individual *formerly* considered *National Socialism* and *Adolf Hitler*,
formerly at a time when he was *not yet enlightened* about the
essence of National Socialism and the NSDAP, about Adolf Hitler and his intentions. The one and only presupposition is that
the folk-member *today pledges allegiance to the German folk-
community* and lets all his thinking, feeling, and acting be directed toward that which *the flag of the German folk-community,
the flag of the National Socialist German Reich, the Adolf Hitler
flag* commands him." [15]

Expressions of solidarity with the whole body of racial comrades
living outside of the borders of Germany were among the common-
places of Nazi thought and propaganda.   At the 1933 meeting of the
Pan-German League for Germandom Abroad, Franz Ritter von Epp,
Governor of Bavaria and a *Reichsleiter* in the Nazi Party, stated
as follows:

"We will not allow ourselves at any future time to be separated
nationally and racially from our racial brethren beyond the borders.   A realistic policy of the part of the German race united in
a state is imaginable only on the basis of the psychological
growth of the race.   The conviction must be established out there
that the German race within the state frontiers is also concerned
about the most remote parts of the race.   The salvation of a
race lies only in the solidarity of the racial whole." [16]

To this solidarity, Nazi Germany also added protection as a right
and duty of the Reich.   In his foreword to *Wir Deutsche in der Welt
(We Germans in the World)*, the official yearbook for 1936 of the
Alliance of German Societies Abroad, the Nazi number-two man,
Hermann Göring, Field Marshal and Minister-President of Prussia,
asserted:

"'We Germans throughout the world', this is the text of our
credo which expresses the unity of Germandom in its full mag-
nitude.   We, that is the racial comrades in the homeland, the
nearly one million German citizens living abroad, and the many
millions of persons of German blood living in Europe and overseas who must not be lost to German culture.   The Third Reich
is not required to prove the truth of this credo to anybody, for
nationality is the cornerstone of the work and the power of the

[15] Fritz Reinhardt, *Vom Wesen der Volksgemeinschaft* (published in *Grundlagen, Aufbau und Wirtschaftsordnung des nationalsozialistischen Staates:* Berlin, 1936), vol. I, group 1, no. 8, pp. 1, 2, 12.

[16] *Der nationalsozialistische Staat* (ed. by Dr. Walther Gehl, Breslau, 1933),
p. 226.

Reich.   But I proclaim it here so that it may be heard and understood by the people beyond our borders, not only by our German brethren abroad but by the whole world.   Protection of German culture and German nationality is the foremost duty of the Reich." [17]

In return for such solidarity and protection Nazi Germany naturally demanded complete loyalty and allegiance to the German *Volk*. In fact, as Professor Walz stated in the November 25, 1934 issue of *Deutsches Recht*, the central organ of the National Socialist Academy for German Law, "The guiding principle of the National Socialist conception of international law is boundless and unalterable loyalty toward one's own race and people [*Volkstum*]." From an article concerning the collection by the German Foreign Institute of the addresses of all the emigrants from the Gau Weser-Ems, which appeared in the Bremen daily newspaper *Bremer Nachrichten* of April 16, 1941, the following is noteworthy:

> "The *Volksdeutscher* living in foreign states must know—besides the natural obligations of the German toward his host state—that he must remain loyal to his nationality [*Volkstum*]; *it is to this he owes the highest values!*"

In his article, "Structure and Order of the Reich," which appeared late in 1941, Ernst Rudolf Huber wrote that the circle of *Volksgenossen*, who are bound by a "duty of loyalty" (*Treupflicht*) to the Reich, "includes all those who as conscious members of the German folk-community live under the sovereignty of a foreign state.   This applies above all to the members of the German folk-groups in foreign countries who hold foreign citizenship without thereby relinquishing their bond of loyalty to the German folk-community. They are not subject to the German state's authority of command and yet they are coordinated with the German folk-community [*der deutschen Volksgemeinschaft zugeordnet*] through bonds of loyalty. But the German folk-community is bound to protect and care for them, as it does all its members." [18]

The comprehensive and unlimited world-wide scope of these German conceptions and the activities for their fulfilment are indicated again in the following statement by Otto Schäfer, a prominent official

[17] *Wir Deutsche in der Welt* (published by the Verband Deutscher Vereine im Ausland: Stuttgart, 1936), p. 6.

[18] Huber, *"Aufbau und Gefüge des Reiches"*, published in the book *Idee und Ordnung des Reiches* (ed. by Huber: Hamburg, Hanseatische Verlagsanstalt, 1941), p. 27.

in the Pan-German League for Germandom Abroad, affiliated with
the Nazi Party:

> "For not in the formation of an entirely autarchic state for
> a part of the great German people, but rather in the assumption
> of the leadership of Europe and of the world in the struggle for
> the triumph of the legal principle, which will determine the
> immediate future of the peoples, lies the natural and God-given
> mission of the united German race, and not in Germany or
> Europe, but rather in the realm of the German race lies the
> German *Lebensraum*, which entails, today more than ever, the
> world." [19]

---

[19] *Sinn und Wesen des VDA*, by Otto Schäfer, VDA District Leader (2d ed.:
Frankfurt-am-Main, 1933), p. 16.

DUAL CITIZENSHIP

The old German law of nationality of June 1, 1870 specified in section 21 [1] that a German citizen living in a foreign country automatically lost his citizenship after a 10-year absence, if he had not enrolled on the register of the local German Consulate. This general provision was quite in accord with the German policy of that time, as manifested in the Bancroft treaties of 1868, in accordance with which in the North German Confederacy and several other German states naturalization in the United States entailed a loss of German citizenship.

Between 1870 and 1914 a change took place in the German attitude, doubtless brought about by the growing insistence on pan-Germanist ideas and the power ambitions of imperial Germany. This change appeared in the German "Imperial and State Citizenship Law", proclaimed on July 22, 1913, with force of law as of January 1, 1914.[2] The most important features of this law are the abandonment of the provision of the prior law regarding the loss of German nationality through 10 years of residence abroad, and the introduction of an entirely novel provision, according to which Germans residing in foreign countries may retain their nationality, after obtaining naturalization as citizens of other countries, provided they have secured consent of the German authorities to such naturalization. This was a part of the German policy to retain or recover the German nationality of all persons of German ancestry regardless of their residence outside of Germany—as was pointed out in an article in the July 1914 issue of the *American Journal of International Law* by Richard W. Flournoy, Jr., Chief of the Bureau of Citizenship of the Department of State. In this way the principle of dual nationality was openly accepted and carried farther than ever before. Aside from certain amendments, made after 1933, none of which have altered the provisions regarding dual nationality, this law of 1913 has remained unchanged to this date as the basic German law regarding citizenship.

The abrogation of section 21 of the old law of 1870 is supplemented by section 13 ot the 1913 law, according to which persons who have already lost their German nationality by residence abroad of

---

[1] *Bundes-Gesetzblatt des norddeutschen Bundes* (Berlin, 1870), pp. 358–359.
[2] *Reichsgesetzblatt* (1913), pp. 583ff.

75

ten years may, without returning to Germany, resume their original German nationality:

> "§ 13. A former German who has not taken up his residence in Germany may on application be naturalized by the State of which he was formerly a citizen, provided his case fulfills the requirements of Nos. 1 and 2 of paragraph 1 of §8 [requirements of "legal competence" and "blameless life"]; the same applies to one who is descended from a former German or has been adopted as a child of such. Prior to naturalization a report must be made to the Imperial Chancellor; if he raises objections, naturalization does not take place." [3]

Delius, a German commentator, expressed the principle underlying these changes as follows:

> "Section 13 aims to facilitate as far as possible the reinstatement of lost members of our population as citizens again. The federal state may (not must), accordingly, renaturalize its former citizens, their descendants, etc., who have not resumed their residence in Germany. In contrast to the citizens of other countries Germans are not in the habit, after they have established themselves abroad, of returning permanently to their homes. Reference is made especially to representatives of commerce, to members of the German communities in Palestine, to missionaries, and in general to persons who by being especially active in the fostering of Germandom abroad, for example in German societies, and particularly by maintaining German schools and churches, do a worthy service.
>
> "The possibility of reinstatement as citizens extends not only to persons who have no citizenship but also to such former Germans and their descendants as have acquired a foreign citizenship." [4]

It is to be especially noted that this provision extends not only to former Germans but to their descendants as well, and that special reference is made to persons who are very active in promoting Germandom abroad. Flournoy furthermore remarks with regard to several other of its provisions that the German law has departed from the principle that residence in the country is a prerequisite to naturalization. Thus, "the performance of services to the state rather than domicil within its territory appears to be made the basis of German nationality". [5]

Section 25 of the 1913 law introduces an express provision for dual nationality. The first paragraph of this section asserts as a

---

[3] *Ibid.*, p. 586 (translated in 8 A.J.I.L. Supp. (1914), p. 220).

[4] *Reichs- und Staatsangehörigkeitsgesetz* (Leipzig, 1913) (cited by R. W. Flournoy, Jr., in 8 A.J.I.L. (1914), p. 478).

[5] 8 A.J.I.L. (1914), p. 479.

general rule that German nationality is lost by naturalization abroad:

> "A German who has neither his residence nor permanent abode in Germany loses his citizenship on acquiring foreign citizenship, provided the foreign citizenship is acquired as a result of his own application therefor . . ."

The next two paragraphs, however, state:

> "Citizenship is not lost by one who before acquiring foreign citizenship has secured on application the written consent of the competent authorities of his home State to retain his citizenship. Before this consent is given the German consul is to be heard.
>
> "The Imperial Chancellor may order, with the consent of the Federal Council, that persons who desire to acquire citizenship in a specified foreign country, may not be granted the consent provided for in paragraph 2." [6]

According to this provision the German Government permits a German to acquire citizenship in a foreign country without giving up his German citizenship if he has secured the prior consent of the German authorities. The 1913 German law also makes it possible for persons who as minors were citizens of one country under the *jus soli* and citizens of another under the *jus sanguinis* to assume of their own volition a dual nationality on reaching their majority.

The principle of dual nationality for the furtherance of political interests, introduced by Imperial Germany, not only was never renounced by the German Republic but has been further enlarged, intensified, and utilized by the Nazi regime. It is true that one can find Nazi professions which indicate the undesirability of dual citizenship. For instance, Dr. Lösener of the German Ministry of the Interior remarks about dual citizenship in the article previously cited:

> "It is just as little desired, as a matter of principle, that one person possess several citizenships (*sujet mixte*). It can occur through the fact that one state does not, according to its laws, cancel its citizenship, if its holder acquires a foreign citizenship. Or it can occur through the fact that one state for special reasons in individual cases expressly allows the acquirer of a foreign citizenship to maintain its own citizenship. (Permissible in the German Reich according to article 25 of the law of 1913.)
>
> "The phenomenon of dual citizenship could only be really avoided by binding agreements between the individual states; legislation of the single states can only diminish its disadvantages. How little desired the possession of dual citizenship

---

[6] *Reichsgesetzblatt* (1913), p. 589 (translated in 8 A.J.I.L. Supp. (1914), p. 223).

is, anyone will understand who values an allegiance to a state more than allegiance to some club or other. If one considers as its real essence the external side of the deep solidarity with the homeland and holds in mind the concept of the obligations deriving therefrom, then dual citizenship brings about an insoluble conflict of the highest duties, especially when both states stand hostile to one another." [7]

Such academic thinking, however, does not at all correspond with the dominant Nazi ideas and Nazi practices. Dual nationality has rather been accepted and promoted, since according to Nazi views the foreign citizenship acquired is merely a convenience, not affecting the primary allegiance to the German mother-country.

A leaflet entitled "When Will Germany Receive a German-blooded Ambassador From America?", which was written in Hamburg by a German-American named Paul Strasser, Jr., and was widely distributed among German-Americans, propounded the need for a wider application of the principles of dual nationality in the following terms:

> "It is Germany's task in the struggle for the recognition of the German-American in American political life to give the German who has emigrated to America a definite position in constitutional law which will strengthen his prestige in America. He should no longer be regarded by Germany as the cast-off scum of the nation, but he who has been born in Germany should remain a German citizen his whole life long regardless of the acquisition of foreign citizenship, as is the case with the citizen of Switzerland, who occupies a position of high esteem in America precisely because he retains his Swiss citizenship along with his newly won American citizenship.
>
> "It would be necessary, therefore, to modify the provisions of the German citizenship law in this sense . . . Such a law would immeasurably strengthen the political backbone of the German element in the United States, and a new victory would be won in the long struggle for political equality of the German-American . . ."
> (Document 16–A, *post* p. 248.)

The Nazi policy with regard to the organization of corporate German minorities throughout the states of eastern and southeastern Europe, which is discussed in detail in part III, illustrates best the wide-spread, calculated use of the principles of dual nationality. For these organized German *Volksgruppen* (folk-groups) in Rumania, Hungary, Slovakia, Croatia, and elsewhere are ostensibly bound by a dual fealty, primarily on the one hand to the Great German Reich and

---

[7] Lösener, *op. cit.*, p. 11.

its leader Adolf Hitler, and incidentally to the local state. The dominant allegiance for all practical purposes is quite clearly to Nazi Germany. The same principle has also been applied in the countries of conquered Europe, where non-German Nazi sympathizers have been recruited to fight with the German Army in special national battalions. SS Volunteers in Norway and Belgium have pledged allegiance both to Adolf Hitler as the leader of all Germanic peoples and at the same time to their respective countries.[8] (Document 17, *post* p. 249.)

Although the Nazi policy concerning dual nationality, for political reasons, has not resulted in the promulgation of a new basic nationality law, nevertheless it has become apparent in various open legal enactments, three of which will be mentioned.

Before doing this it may be well to recall the general legal situation with regard to matters of nationality involving Germany and the United States. The Bancroft conventions of 1868, which specified the loss of German citizenship in the event of naturalization in the United States, were terminated as a result of the World War of 1914–18.[9] Article 278 of the Treaty of Versailles, however, provided as follows:

> "Germany undertakes to recognize any new nationality which has been or may be acquired by her nationals under the laws of the Allied and Associated Powers and in accordance with the decisions of the competent authorities of these Powers pursuant to naturalization laws or under treaty stipulations, and to regard such persons as having, in consequence of the acquisition of such new nationality, in all respects severed their allegiance to their country of origin."

The treaty made between the United States and Germany in 1921 for restoring friendly relations provides that all rights, privileges, indemnities, reparations, or advantages shall be reserved to the United States which in the Treaty of Versailles were reserved for the benefit of the United States or the nationals of the United States.

---

[8] *Zeitschrift für Geopolitik* (monthly magazine published by Professor Karl Haushofer: Heidelberg), Sept. 1941, p. 534.

[9] Article 289 of the Treaty of Versailles, the rights and advantages of which were accorded to the United States by its treaty restoring friendly relations with Germany, concluded Aug. 25, 1921, provides that all bilateral treaties between Germany and each of the Allied or Associated Powers are and shall remain abrogated unless notice of revival is given by the particular Allied or Associated Power concerned. The United States did not give notice of the revival of these conventions within the prescribed period.

Since article 278 of the Treaty of Versailles obligated Germany to recognize any new nationality acquired by her nationals under the laws of the Allied and Associated Powers and explicitly eliminated all questions of dual nationality, the United States Government regarded article 278 as "a substitute for a naturalization treaty".[10]

The Treaty of Versailles, however, was repudiated in general after January 30, 1933 by repeated Nazi pronouncements, and the separate articles were step by step nullified by the German Government before the opening of hostilities in 1939. Article 278 received corresponding treatment. In answer to an American note, regarding a test case, the Nazi Government, on April 11, 1938, declared that article 278 referred to changes of nationality acquired collectively by transfers of territory under the Versailles Treaty. It flatly denied the general application of article 278 to individual cases. By this improvised interpretation the Nazis nullified article 278 and the understanding based thereupon.

Furthermore, no treaty or other agreement has ever been concluded between Germany and the United States regarding persons who were dual nationals through a conflict of *jus sanguinis* and *jus soli*. Under the law governing German citizenship, German citizenship by birth is derived on the doctrine of *jus sanguinis* and therefore persons born abroad of German parents are citizens of Germany *jure sanguinis*. Thus persons born in the United States of German parents are by birth citizens of Germany, *jure sanguinis*, and citizens of the United States, *jure soli*, and may therefore owe dual allegiance. In the absence of any agreement between Germany and the United States, Germany unquestionably has the right to claim the allegiance of such persons, when such persons are within the jurisdiction of Germany.

A clear stand with regard to the status of dual nationals was taken by Nazi Germany at the time of the reinstitution of the German national army in May 1935. Paragraph 2 of article 1 of the German military-service law (*Wehrgesetz*) of May 21, 1935 [11] provides that every German man is subject to military service (*"Jeder deutsche Mann ist wehrpflichtig"*). Paragraph 1 of article 18 then states:

> "A German in the sense of this law is every citizen of Germany, even though he may also be a citizen of another country (*Deutscher im Sinne dieses Gesetzes ist jeder Reichsangehoerige, auch wenn er ausserdem im Besitze einer auslaendischen Staatsangehoerigkeit ist*)."

Paragraph 2 of the same article further specifies that Germans who have already served in the army of another state are not exempt

---

[10] *Digest of International Law*, by G. H. Hackworth, Legal Adviser of the Department of State (Washington, 1942), vol. III, p. 402.

[11] *Reichsgesetzblatt* (1935), pp. 609ff.

from their liability to German military service. During peacetime, however, they will only be allowed to enter active military service upon special request to be decided upon by the German Minister of War. These provisions of the German military-service law bear witness to the Nazi concept of the priority of German citizenship over any foreign citizenship whether acquired by naturalization or by the basic citizenship laws of another country.

In the matter of military service the oath should be mentioned which the soldiers are required to take under the German law of August 20, 1934.[12]   Section 1 states:

> "Government employees and soldiers of the armed forces have to take an oath on entry in service." [13]

The oath for a soldier, given in paragraph 2 of section 2, reads as follows:

> "I swear before God this holy oath, that I shall render absolute obedience to the leader of the German Reich and people, Adolf Hitler, commander in chief of the armed forces, and that as a brave soldier I shall be ready at all times to give my life under this oath." [14]

This oath is an oath of allegiance to Germany and, if taken voluntarily by an American citizen over 21 years of age, would bring about loss of American citizenship under section 2 of the act of March 2, 1907 and section 401(b) of the Nationality Act of 1940.

A further reaffirmation of the Nazi conception of dual nationality has also been indicated in official German decrees issued since the outbreak of the war in 1939. In the decree of September 4, 1939 concerning the naturalization of volunteers, section 3 states that the requirement can be disregarded according to which the applicant in case of the acquisition of German citizenship has to give up his previous citizenship.[15]   (Document 18, *post* p. 251.)

In a recent decree containing very important amendments to the German citizenship law, "The Decree of January 24, 1942, Regulating Matters of Citizenship", section 2 states as follows:

> "The Reich's Minister of the Interior can designate the countries for which citizenship can be acquired on petition, or on petition of the husband or of the legal guardian, without the loss of German citizenship therewith being involved." [16]   (Document 19–A, *post* p. 253.)

Dual nationality could hardly be given a more hearty validation and greater scope for political usefulness.

---

[12] *Ibid.* (1934), p. 785.

[13] *Ibid.*

[14] *Ibid.*

[15] *Ibid.* (1939), p. 1741.

[16] *Ibid.* (1942), p. 40.

EXPATRIATION

Manner of Achieving Expatriation

According to the basic German citizenship law of 1913, the legal grounds which lead to loss of German citizenship are divided into two groups: the loss takes place either necessarily as the consequence of some other action, without the state's making any particular decision in the individual case of loss, or it is brought about by an express sovereign act of the state. The detailed provisions are contained in sections 17 to 32.[1]

The sufficient grounds for the loss of citizenship in the first group are:

(1) The acquisition of a foreign citizenship,
(2) The legitimation of a German child by a foreigner,
(3) The marriage of a German woman with a foreigner,
(4) The non-fulfilment of military obligations.

Sovereign acts of the state, which bring about the loss of citizenship, are:

(1) Denaturalization (*Entlassung*),
(2) An express ruling to this effect, initiated by the authorities themselves.

The loss of German citizenship through the acquisition of a foreign citizenship, it will be recalled, takes place only if the German citizen permanently resides in the foreign country and if the acquisition of foreign citizenship results from his own petition therefor. According to article 25 of the same law, he can avert the loss, if beforehand he obtains from the government of his federal state, in writing, the permission that he may keep his German citizenship as well.

With regard to the loss of citizenship by denaturalization, a petition is always required of a German citizen who wants to be denaturalized. Only the husband can make the petition for a married woman, and the wife of a German citizen can furthermore only be denaturalized together with her husband, the wife's consent, however, always being required. In accordance with the terms of the law, such denaturalization may not be refused, except in the case of active soldiers or public officials—an aspect of the law which has not been followed by Nazi practice and to which we will return later.

---

[1] *Reichsgesetzblatt* (1913), pp. 587ff.

In section 40 a formal legal means of appeal was provided against any refusal of a petition for denaturalization. The denaturalization, however, was canceled, if the denaturalized person one year after the issuance of the certificate of denaturalization still had, or again had, his permanent residence in Germany. The extension of the denaturalization to the members of the family of the denaturalized person did not automatically take place. On the contrary, separate petitions of the family head were necessary for his wife and also for his minor children.

Other cases of state acts effecting the loss of citizenship are distinguished from denaturalization by the fact that they do not take place on the petition of the party concerned but rather on the initiative of the authorities. In the citizenship law of 1913 two cases are mentioned in which a German citizen loses his citizenship "through the decision of his home state", i.e. the government of the federal state, not of the German Empire. These cases were:

(1) If a German citizen failed to obey the order to return in the event of a war, and

(2) If a German citizen has entered the service of a foreign state, either civil or military, without his government's having given its express permission thereto.

In these cases the loss of citizenship included also the wife and the minor children.

To the above-mentioned withdrawals of citizenship by the state authorities have been added, by the Nazi law of July 14, 1933,[2] two further cases of measures effecting the loss of citizenship by the decision of the authorities, namely, the revocation of naturalization and the deprivation (*Aberkennung*) of citizenship.

This law concerned two separate subject-matters. The first section made it possible to revoke undesired naturalizations, which had taken place during the period of the Weimar Republic, namely, between November 9, 1918 and January 30, 1933. This measure, dictated by reason of Nazi racial policy, was primarily designed to revoke the naturalization of Jews from eastern Europe, which had taken place during this period. The measure was limited to one term of two years, later extended a half year, and all such denaturalization proceedings were terminated on December 31, 1935.

The measure provided for in section 2 of this law, the deprivation of German citizenship, however, is general and unlimited in nature. It can be decreed against German citizens who reside in a foreign country, "so far as they have injured German interests by conduct which conflicts with their duty of allegiance to the Reich and the German people. The same applies to German citizens who do not

[2] *Ibid*, p. 480.

obey a summons to return, which the German Minister of the Interior has sent them with regard to this ruling." [3] To make its effect even stronger a confiscation of property is also provided for here. A separate decision is made in each case as to whether the loss of German citizenship includes also the wife and children of the person concerned. The deprivation of citizenship is pronounced by the German Minister of the Interior, under whose Ministry functions the Gestapo, in agreement with the Foreign Office. In order to have legal efficacy, the decision must be published in the *Reichsanzeiger*, the official journal for administrative enactments.

The implications of this measure for Germans living abroad are pointed out thus by Dr. Otto Gauweiler in his authoritative work *Legal Organization and Legal Functions of the Movement*:

> "*The present legal position of foreign Germans and of the foreign groups of the NSDAP* has been decidedly influenced by the historical fact of the seizure of power by the party. It stands in close relation to political developments within the Reich, just as the development of German communities abroad has always been strongly influenced by the political development in the homeland. The basic change in the legal position of foreign Germans has found expression in a series of laws which give a new definition of their legal position, for example, the law regarding the annulment of naturalization and the revocation of German citizenship of July 14, 1933 . . . The loyalty which German citizens residing in foreign countries owe to the Reich finds its expression here in the exclusion of faithless Germans." [4]   (Document 20, *post* p. 256.)

LIMITATIONS PLACED ON EXPATRIATION

According to section 22 of the German citizenship law of 1913, expatriation is not granted:

> "1. To persons liable to military duty, as to whose liability to service a decision has not been made, except in cases where they present a certificate from the recruiting commission that in the opinion of the commission expatriation is not sought with a view to escaping the fulfillment of active service;
>
> "2. To members of the active army, of the active navy or of the active colonial troops;
>
> "3. To members of the reserve of the class defined in Nos. 2 to 4 of Article 56 of the Imperial military law, except in cases where they have obtained the consent of the military authorities;
>
> "4. To other members of the reserve after they have been called to active service;

---

[3] *Ibid.*
[4] Gauweiler, *op. cit.*, p. 73.

> "5. To officials and officers, including those of the reserve, before they have been discharged from duty." [5]

The German military-service law of May 21, 1935 also contains the following provision with regard to expatriation in paragraph 3 of section 18:

> "The release of persons liable to military service from citizenship in the Reich and therewith from their military-service liability requires the approval of the Reich's Minister of War or of a recruiting office designated by him." [6]

At the outbreak of the present war, the German Government prohibited the expatriation of its citizens in the following terms by a decree dated September 1, 1939: "Persons liable to military service will not be released from German citizenship until further notice." [7]

To these bare legal restrictions on expatriation, the Nazis have doubtless added others in their actual administrative practices which accord more adequately with their general theories regarding race and citizenship. In this connection it must be recalled that matters of citizenship in Nazi Germany are not regulated by judicial processes as in the United States. The German Government rules by decree and by administrative orders, only some of which are openly published. In general, too, administrative practices, in conformity with the general Nazi ideology, are often introduced and carried on before official explicit proclamation of a decree or order covering the same. Hence it is necessary to consider the statements of authoritative Nazi spokesmen in order to ascertain the real practices.

National Socialist writers commonly testify to the need for a complete alteration of existing German citizenship laws, especially in matters of expatriation. In a pamphlet entitled *Nationalsozialismus und Staatsrecht (National Socialism and Constitutional Law)*, published in the previously mentioned collection edited by Dr. Lammers, the Chief of the Reich's Chancelry, State-Secretary Wilhelm Stuckart of the Ministry of the Interior declares:

> "In the course of reorganization, a new ruling will have to be made regarding the acquisition and loss of citizenship, and indeed in the development of the idea, which already found expression in the law of May 15, 1935,[8] namely, that citizenship

---

[5] *Reichsgesetzblatt* (1913), p. 588 (translated in 8 A.J.I.L. Supp. (1914), p. 222).

[6] *Reichsgesetzblatt* (1935), p. 611.

[7] *Ibid.* (1939), p. 1656.

[8] The law of May 15, 1935 canceled the provisions of the 1913 citizenship law which *obliged* the state to grant naturalization under various stipulated conditions.

can no longer be acquired, lost, and changed at will like membership in a club." [9]

In his previously cited pamphlet from the same collection, Dr. Lösener of the German Ministry of the Interior states, as one National Socialist demand on a new citizenship law:

"Likewise it is to be considered if the *denaturalization of minors* ought not to be made more difficult. The principle of family unity, which has its justification, must withdraw, if it comes into conflict with the higher principle of racial allegiance." [10]

In his authoritative work *Verfassungsrecht des grossdeutschen Reiches* (*Constitutional Law of the Greater German Reich*), Ernst Rudolf Huber, professor of law at the University of Leipzig, has expressed clearly the Nazi views and administrative practices in matters of expatriation:

"According to the wording of the citizenship law of 1913, denaturalization must be granted, if the stated grounds for objection, membership in the Army or the public service, are not at hand. This regulation of paragraph 2, section 22, corresponds to the extreme individualism, which regards citizenship as a right over which the individual can freely dispose. This view is impossible today; citizenship is a bond, from which one cannot withdraw according to one's own free will. Consequently the competent authorities decide about expatriation in accordance with their own judgment. The conflicting regulation of paragraph 2, section 22, is no longer applicable." [11]

USE OF EXPATRIATION TO CONTROL RACIAL COMRADES ABROAD

The threat of expatriation, initiated and executed by the state authorities, was one of the strongest threats wielded by the Nazis in order to keep Germans abroad obedient to their will. Unsought expatriation could, of course, cause great difficulties for the individual concerned. It made him at once a man without a country, if he had not hitherto possessed another citizenship as well, and could entail serious economic disabilities, as well as hamper his movements and in certain countries prejudice his reputation. Although the Nazis had many lesser means of exerting pressure on Germans abroad, this threat in the background was a powerful factor not only in keeping the activities of Germans abroad from deviating away from the prescribed line but also in forcing them to perform positive services.

---

[9] Dr. Wilhelm Stuckart, *Nationalsozialismus und Staatsrecht* (published in *Grundlagen, Aufbau und Wirtschaftsordnung des nationalsozialistischen Staates*: Berlin, 1936), vol. I, group 2, no. 15, p. 24.

[10] Lösener, *op. cit.*, pp. 28–29.

[11] Huber, *Verfassungsrecht des grossdeutschen Reiches* (Hamburg, 1939), p. 174.

As early as July 1933 the Nazi Government, as we have seen, gave itself the power to deprive Germans residing abroad of their citizenship, if their conduct did not conform to the will of the Nazis. [12] This decree is further strengthened by the law of February 3, 1938, concerning the obligatory registration of German citizens abroad. [13] According to this law every German citizen who resides longer than three months in the district of the same German Consulate is obliged to register with this Consulate. Section 5 of this law states: "Whoever persistently violates the registration obligation incumbent on him and does so in a way which represents an offense against his duty of loyalty toward the German Reich and the German people, can in accordance with existing legal prescriptions be deprived of his German citizenship." By this means the Nazis were able to maintain continuously a direct contact with, and hold over, all Germans abroad. This power, too, was wielded directly by the Nazi Party since, as is discussed at length in the next part, the Nazi Party's Foreign Organization, dealing with Germans abroad, obtained direct control over German consular representatives abroad, after its head, Gauleiter Bohle, entered the Foreign Office on January 30, 1937.

It is known from a reliable source that the German police sent regularly to the German consular offices throughout the world lists of persons whose whereabouts were to be determined. The German Consulates kept these lists current, reporting at once any information ascertained about such persons. In this way constant surveillance was maintained of Germans abroad whose activities might have incurred the displeasure of Nazi authorities. The decree of May 6, 1940 furthermore, among its many legal provisions, made Germans abroad liable under German law for any acts committed abroad, even though, under ordinary concepts of legal jurisdiction, the German Government had no jurisdiction over the person concerned when the act in question was committed. [14] (Document 21, *post* p. 259.)

The power of the Nazi Party's Foreign Organization with regard to Germans abroad is indicated by the work of its Department for Returning Germans (Rückwandereramt). This department is described as follows in an official pamphlet, *The Foreign Organization of the National Socialist Party*, by Dr. Emil Ehrich, personal adviser to the Gauleiter of the Foreign Organization:

"Through the examination of personal details concerning conationals who, as a result of economic pressure or for other reasons, have returned to take up residence in the Reich, and through

[12] *Reichsgesetzblatt* (1933), p. 480.
[13] *Ibid.* (1938), p. 113.
[14] *Ibid.* (1940), p. 754.

the issuance of a passport, this department insures the systematic and purposeful insertion [*Einreihung*] of these co-nationals in the domestic economy. At the same time it prevents the re-insertion [*Wiedereinreihung*] of doubtful and undesirable returning Germans and the unjustified demands of such persons upon welfare institutions." [15]

The role of this department of the Foreign Organization with regard to the issuance of passports should be especially noted.

The way in which the Nazis wielded this threat is revealed by the following remarks from a confidential account by a reliable person in a position to know the facts:

"The German in Holland who was not amenable to the dictation of Butting [the Nazi Party leader in Holland] and his friends had no chance whatever to stay in business. He was threatened first of all with the loss of his passport. Here is a threat so serious that Americans, citizens of a really free republic, can hardly grasp its import. It puts a man before these alternatives: either go back to Germany, or declare yourself a refugee and cut yourself off from your country and your family at home. Had this particular German a job with a German firm in Holland? He was fired automatically. With a Dutch firm? A word in the proper ear and the man was out of work. Was he the agent of a German principal? Butting had only to write to Bohle, in Berlin, that one X, Rotterdam agent of the German firm Y, was *nicht zuverlaessig*, not trustworthy. A peremptory note from Bohle (Party headquarters) to the German firm in question, and X's agency contract was immediately rescinded. Was the man proprietor of his own business? As he was a German, his business was sure to have a German basis or connection, and he was promptly ruined. His source of supply was blocked, his credit line was withdrawn by the banks, his market was closed to him. In one way or another the German in Holland was faced with this grim choice: Come in with us or blow your brains out!"

REPATRIATION

While using the threat of expatriation to control the activities of their nationals abroad, the Nazis have always been ready to repatriate loyal Nazi-minded German racial comrades who were in possession of some foreign citizenship. Easy repatriation was a natural consequence of the Nazi theory of the supremacy of German blood over any foreign citizenship and the casual attitude toward the acquisition of foreign citizenship.

---

[15] Ehrich, *Die Auslands-Organisation der NSDAP* (Berlin, 1937), p. 21.

Adolf Hitler himself, in the Bible of Naziism, *Mein Kampf*, devoted an extensive passage to a general ridicule of naturalization. In a chapter entitled "Subjects and Citizens of the State", Hitler wrote thus of naturalization:

"Aside from acquiring citizenship by birth there is also the possibility later of naturalization. It is contingent upon various prerequisites; for example, that the prospective candidate should not be a burglar or a procurer; furthermore, that he should be politically unobjectionable, i.e. that he should be a harmless political idiot; finally, that he should not become a burden to his new homeland. This refers, of course, in this realistic age, only to a financial burden. Yes, it is even regarded as a favorable recommendation to present a prospectively good future taxpayer in order to facilitate the acquisition of citizenship nowadays.

"Racial considerations play no part in it whatsoever.

"The whole process of the acquisition of citizenship is carried out in a manner not very different, for example, from admission to an automobile club. The man makes his declarations, these are examined and approved, and one day he is notified on a handbill that he has become a citizen, this being clothed even in a comical form." [16]

Viewing the process of naturalization and the acquisition of citizenship in this light, Germans in America who were under the influence of Nazi ideas found it very easy to assume American citizenship for reasons of personal and practical convenience. Moreover, they were assured that their adoption of American citizenship would not impede the reassumption of German citizenship at any future time.

Documentary evidence of the Nazi policy toward Germans who had acquired American citizenship has confirmed this assurance. In the January 1941 *Information Sheet* of the Kameradschaft USA, the organization in Germany of Germans returned from America who had been active in the Nazi movement in the United States, the comrades are advised "in all questions concerning naturalization" to "communicate with: Comrade *Georg Nebbe*, Volksdeutsche Mittelstelle, [17] Berlin W 62, Keithstr. 27" (document 22–A, *post* p. 279).

---

[16] *Mein Kampf*, pp. 488–489.

[17] The Volksdeutsche Mittelstelle (Office for Dealing With Those of German Race) is an official bureau, dealing with problems concerning German racial comrades who are not German citizens. This bureau, working under SS and Police Leader Himmler, played an important role in the resettlement, on territory annexed from conquered Poland, of German racial comrades from Bessarabia, Volhynia, and the Baltic states.

Furthermore, an account of the meeting of the Berlin group of the Kameradschaft USA reported a discussion which was "of interest to most of the comrades", as follows:

> "For example, naturalization affairs were discussed by a representative of the Volksdeutsche Mittelstelle—Berlin, with the result that the re-naturalization of most of the comrades has so far occurred without friction." (Document 22–A, *post* p. 280.)

PART III

NAZI ORGANIZATIONS WORKING AMONG GERMANS IN FOREIGN
COUNTRIES AND USE OF ORGANIZED GERMAN MINORITIES
IN FURTHERANCE OF GERMAN INTERESTS

ORGANIZATIONS EMPLOYED BY THE NAZIS TO REGULATE THE LIFE AND ACTIVITIES OF GERMANS ABROAD

The Foreign Organization

1. HISTORY AND GROWTH OF POWER

The first National Socialist organizations among Germans abroad were for the most part founded independently, without direct stimulus or encouragement from German sources. However, in 1930, a small group of Nazi Party men in Hamburg, having become conscious of the possibilities for organized party activity among Germans abroad, undertook the preparatory work for a Party Office to deal with problems concerning party members and Germans abroad. This Office was formally established by an order of the Reich's Nazi Organization Directorate of May 1, 1931, being designated then as the "Foreign Section of the Reich's Directorate of the NSDAP".[1] (Document 23, *post* p. 285). With headquarters in Hamburg, the Office was placed under the direction of Dr. Hans Nieland. According to this order every party member abroad, or residing permanently in a foreign country, was under the supervision of the Foreign Section of the Nazi Party. The first phase of the work, up to 1933, was devoted to a consolidation of the Nazi groups abroad already in existence and the establishment of numerous new branches and local groups, so that the first unification of these into groups covering an entire foreign country was soon necessary. In fact, the first country-wide Nazi Party organization abroad was founded in Paraguay in 1931.

At that time, however, the Nazi Party was too much concerned with German affairs to place much stress on foreign activities. In the first months after the party's accession to power in January 1933, it was even questioned whether the existence of a Foreign Section was justified. Since then, however, it has apparently consistently proved its usefulness, having grown steadily in power and importance. On May 8, 1933 it was put in charge of its present leader, Ernst Wilhelm Bohle, a protégé of Rudolf Hess, who was Hitler's Deputy at that time, and on October 3, 1933 it was placed directly under Hess, Bohle becoming a member of the staff of the Führer's Deputy with the rank of Gauleiter. The present designa-

[1] Ehrich, *op. cit.*, p. 9.

tion, "Foreign Organization of the NSDAP", [2] was ordered by Hess on February 17, 1934.[3] In view of the growth of the organization under Bohle's energetic leadership and to further an increased development the central office of the Foreign Organization was transferred to Berlin in the middle of March 1936. The Maritime Division, which dealt with German seamen, remained in Hamburg.

Since there had been considerable friction between the agents of the Foreign Organization and the officials of the German Government's foreign services, the German Foreign Service (diplomatic and consular officials) was inducted in October 1935 as a professional group into the Foreign Organization, thus insuring the collaboration of the Foreign Service men abroad with the Nazi Party agents. With regard to this, Dr. Ehrich, one of Gauleiter Bohle's chief aides, is quoted by the Deutsches Nachrichtenbüro, the official German news agency, as saying, "a decisive step has been taken in strengthening National Socialist leadership among Germans abroad; it is to be hoped that this new arrangement will contribute to a close cooperation between party and state in all fields of foreign effort. Every German abroad knew that only through the Foreign Organization and its numerous cells could he maintain a real connection with what was happening in the Reich. The official of the Foreign Service must feel himself to be a true fellow German and the trusted helper and National Socialist friend of his countrymen."

The Foreign Organization received its definitive sanction when on January 30, 1937 Bohle was transferred to the Ministry for Foreign Affairs, assuming the title "Head of the Foreign Organization in the Ministry for Foreign Affairs". Whereas formerly the jurisdiction of his organization had nominally merely extended to Nazi Party members abroad, at this time it was explicitly enlarged to include *all* German citizens abroad. The preamble to this decree gives as the purpose of Bohle's installation in the Foreign Office "the unified care and control [*Betreuung*] of the German citizens in foreign countries".[4] The vast extent of Bohle's powers is clear, the preamble stating further that "the direction and handling of all matters concerning German citizens abroad are transferred to him". Although according to the provision of the decree Bohle was placed personally and directly under the German Foreign Ministry, the Foreign Ministry appears to have exercised only a very general control over his work, and it is known that he possessed the privilege of addressing instructions, through the German diplomatic pouches, to the party's agents abroad.

---

[2] The Foreign Organization of the NSDAP is known in German as "Die Auslands-Organisation der NSDAP", or more familiarly as the "AO".

[3] Ehrich, *op. cit.*, p. 9.

[4] *Ibid.*, p. 31.

To further reinforce the party's grip upon the Foreign Office, which was progressively and effectively tightened during 1937, the officials of the Foreign Office and all members of the Foreign Service throughout the world were organized into a party group, an *"Orts-gruppe"*, under the authority of Bohle.   While the group rested under the supreme authority of Bohle in his capacity as representative of the party sovereignty in the Foreign Office, Dr. Resenberg and a Herr Kruger were named *Ortsgruppenleiter* and deputy leader, respectively, both being Bohle men brought into the Foreign Office from the party's Foreign Organization.   On December 22, 1937 it was announced in the *Völkischer Beobachter*, the official party newspaper, that Bohle had been given the rank of Secretary of State in the Foreign Office and that decisions taken by him and issued in the form of orders with his signature would have the force of "ministerial decisions" or instructions of the Ministry for Foreign Affairs.   It was understood that this established an even greater independence for Bohle and that it would enable Bohle to compel members of the regular Foreign Service to promote the work of his Foreign Organization.

In the official party program of the NSDAP, published first in 1927, Gottfried Feder wrote, "Not to 'assimilate themselves' to foreign ways but to maintain their own superior German ways, that must be the task of Germans abroad and of our official representatives.   An iron broom must go through the dusty Foreign Office for this purpose also." [5]   In fulfilling this demand, as the Nazis have done with such logical consequence in so many other spheres of activity, Bohle and the party's Foreign Organization served as the "iron broom".

2. STRUCTURE AND ACTIVITIES

The Foreign Organization of the Nazi Party has a curious double position and status in the complicated arrangement of the Nazi party-state.   As we have seen, the director of the party's Foreign Organization, Bohle, was appointed Chief of the Foreign Organization in the Foreign Office, and as such he is directly and personally responsible to the Foreign Minister.   However, his field of activity as leader of the party's Foreign Organization and his responsibility as such to the Führer's Deputy [6] remain unchanged.   Although Bohle himself moved to the Foreign Office, taking with him many members of his former staff, the Foreign Organization of the party as such remained in its quarters at 4A Tiergarten Strasse, Berlin, continuing to operate

[5] Feder, *Das Programm der NSDAP* (Munich, Franz Eher Verlag, Central Publishing House of the NSDAP, 1933), p. 42 (1st ed. 1927).

[6] After Hess' flight to England, the Office of the Führer's Deputy was redesignated by a decree of May 29, 1941 the "Party Chancelry" and placed under the direction of Reichsleiter Martin Bormann, formerly Hess' staff leader. *Reichsgesetzblatt* (1941), p. 295.

under Bohle's leadership, although its field of activity apparently became more restricted with the enlargement of Herr Bohle's powers.

The Foreign Organization likewise has a dual status with respect to its position in the party structure. On the one hand, the officials of the Foreign Organization form a part of the staff of the Führer's Deputy, now the Director of the Party Chancelry, and thus are directly responsible to him. On the other hand, the Foreign Organization is also a Gau of the NSDAP and as such is ordered hierarchically like any other party Gau, so far as is permitted by the special conditions abroad and at sea. Like the NSDAP itself, the Foreign Organization is divided into country groups (*Landesgruppen*), regional sections (*Landeskreise*), local groups (*Ortsgruppen*), and branches (*Stützpunkte*). The hierarchic arrangement of the local groups is built up in each country in accordance with the Führer principle, which confers supreme authority upon the party leader in each country in exactly the same manner as the party organization in Germany is built up to the final authority of the Führer. It is to be noted, too, that the party leaders abroad are entitled "Bearers of Sovereignty" (*Hoheitsträger*), just as are analogous leaders in Germany.

A detailed account of the internal structure of the Foreign Organization's home offices in Berlin and Hamburg is to be found in the official pamphlet previously cited, *The Foreign Organization of the NSDAP*, by Dr. Emil Ehrich, personal adviser to Bohle. As Dr. Ehrich states:

> "The diversity of conditions abroad requires that the Central Office of the Foreign Organization have offices which on the one hand are continuously and precisely informed concerning all events abroad which are in any way connected with and exert influence upon the existence of foreign Germandom, and which, on the other hand, must be in a position politically to determine and carry out the work of the party divisions and organizations associated in the AO and the activities of the departments which are charged with functions not limited to specific geographic regions." [7]

For this task the world is divided into eight geographic divisions, with a regional department for each. These *Länderämter* are as follows:

1. Regional Department I, Northeastern Europe.
2. Regional Department II, Western Europe (excluding Great Britain and Ireland).
3. Regional Department III, Southeastern Europe, Austria, and the Near East.
4. Regional Department IV, Italy, Switzerland, and Hungary.
5. Regional Department V, Africa.

---

[7] Ehrich, *op. cit.*, p. 17.

6. Regional Department VI, North America.
7. Regional Department VII, Latin America.
8. Regional Department VIII, the Far East, Australia, Great Britain, and Ireland.

"These constitute the actual political foundation of the Foreign Organization and are responsible to the Gauleiter for the entire development" of the various party groups within their sphere of jurisdiction.[8]

The Director of each *Länderamt* is acquainted through personal experience with the characteristics of the regions under his jurisdiction and the conditions which prevail in them.   All correspondence relating to the activities of the AO in these regions passes through his office, and it is thus possible for him to gain a correlated picture of, and to exert a coordinating influence upon, the policies and the activities of the AO in that part of the world.   It is also possible in this way to keep a close watch on the individual party members and officials abroad, and the Director of the *Länderamt* plays an important part in the selection and appointment of party officials and leaders in the countries over which his control extends.   He also acts as a co-worker and adviser to the Gauleiter of the AO on all matters of general policy.

The general extent of the Foreign Organization's activities may be seen from the following statement in the official party manual:

> "The Foreign Organization has the task of winning German citizens who live abroad or are engaged in navigation for the National Socialist view of the world and of keeping alive in every single German abroad the principle of the racial community which transcends all classes and religious denominations."[9] (Document 7, *post* p. 201.)

In brief, the purpose is to propagate Nazi doctrines among the Germans abroad and to control their economic, political, and cultural activities.

A cursory glance at the list of departments in the Foreign Organization's central office, as given by Ehrich,[10] demonstrates the comprehensive scope of these activities.   The German Labor Front of the Foreign Organization, including all members of the German Labor Front abroad, conducts the social and occupational work of the Foreign Organization.   The Department for Government Employees does the same for all employees in the Foreign Service of the Reich who reside abroad.   The Department for Teachers deals with all German teachers on leave from schools in Germany and serving in German

---

[8] *Ibid.*

[9] *Organisationsbuch der NSDAP* (ed. by the National Organizational Director of the NSDAP: Munich, 1940), p. 143.

[10] Ehrich, *op. cit.*, pp. 18ff.

schools abroad. There are also organizations for German lawyers, professors, and students abroad. Organizations for women and for the youth are maintained in close association with the Reich's Women's Organization and the Hitler Youth. The head of the Youth Department in the Foreign Organization is at the same time the Director of the Foreign Department of the Youth Office in the German Reich.

Aside from these organizations there are the so-called "functional offices", among them the following: The Office for Foreign Trade, subdivided on a regional and functional basis, deals with all questions of foreign trade. The Inspection Department prepares statistics concerning foreign Germandom, attends to registration, expedites mail, and is responsible for transportation and for the control and reporting service. The Department for Culture supervises German cultural institutions abroad, selects the personnel suitable to accomplish National Socialist cultural work abroad, and from the cultural side uses foreign Germandom to further good relations between Germany and the other nations. The Press Office watches the German and foreign press with regard to all developments in foreign Germandom and services the Reich's press and the foreign German press. The Legal Department deals with matters of legal administration, legal policy, and legal protection. The Speakers' Department supervises the organization of festivals in German colonies abroad, sending suitable speakers. It also handles film and radio work. The Department for Returning Germans arranges for the fitting employment in domestic industry of Germans returning to take up residence in the Reich. It also prevents the reinclusion in German society of those who are undesirable. The Instruction Department maintains in Altona, a suburb of Hamburg, a Reich's school for Germans from abroad and for seamen. Finally, the Department for Public Welfare deals with the needy and also directs the Winter Relief [11] work abroad.

Chart 4,[12] taken from the official 1940 Nazi Party manual, shows in graphic form the structure of the Foreign Organization. The Foreign Organization's supervisory authority over the activities abroad of all other Nazi Party offices, including the German Labor Front, is further documented by chart 5 [13] from the same source. The extent of this supervision is indicated by the following regulation:

> "All business communication between all party offices and the organizations of the NSDAP in foreign countries and on board ships is to be forwarded without exception via the Managing

---

[11] *Winterhilfswerk*, a Nazi-organized institution which during the winter collects large sums for distribution among the needy and for the support of welfare agencies.

[12] *Post*, p. 494.

[13] *Post*, p. 496.

Office of the Foreign Organization. Associations affiliated with the party, which intend to include German citizens abroad in their activity, may only do this within the framework of the Foreign Organization." [14]   (Document 7, *post* p. 203.)

3. POLICY AS INDICATED BY OFFICIAL PRONOUNCEMENTS

(a) Regimentation of Germans and German Institutions Abroad

The first task of the Foreign Organization was to unite the German colonies abroad on a National Socialist basis. As Gauleiter Bohle stated in the 1934 *Almanach der nationalsozialistischen Revolution*, an official Nazi publication edited by Wilhelm Kube, then President of Brandenburg:

"Today our fighters abroad are standing at posts which are often desperate. They know, however, that just as at home, so also abroad, only National Socialism can prepare the way for a solid Germandom. Only National Socialists who are ideologically well grounded can unite the German colonies, which outside of the homeland are often still divided, and create a unity in which alone the guaranty for support of the homeland by foreign Germandom can be given. . . .

"Therefore we need party members abroad who have mastered our ideology and who are able to communicate it to other Germans. We know that Germans abroad are still in part cool to the movement because they do not know what they want. The education of racial comrades who still stand apart has, therefore, been made a special task of the group leaders abroad, and it is pointed out to them that there are still many Germans abroad who are not friendly toward us because they have not understood the will of our Führer, although otherwise they are often valuable German comrades." [15]

(Document 24, *post* p. 312.)

In the same article Bohle indicates the importance attached to the absorption of all German institutions abroad, and the methods employed:

"In many countries the skill and vision of our group leaders have already succeeded in persuading German societies and bunds of the most valuable character, which were still standing apart, of the necessity for a positive position toward the National Socialist state. The word '*Gleichschaltung*' [conformity] cannot, because of the absence of the instruments of force of the state, find the same application abroad as in Germany. It is only thanks to the conscientious work of enlightenment carried on by our party members abroad, often under great personal sacrifices, that in many

---

[14] *Organisationsbuch der NSDAP*, p. 144.

[15] *Almanach der nationalsozialistichen Revolution* (ed. by Senior President Wilhelm Kube: Berlin, 1934), p. 95.

places the solidarity of Germandom in our sense of the word has already been established." [16]   (Document 24, *post* p. 313.)

At the Nazi Party congress in September 1936 at Nuremberg, Germany, Bohle was already able to announce:

> "Today, barely four years after the seizure of power, we can proudly and joyfully declare that our party comrades abroad have conquered foreign Germanism—conquered it for the National Socialist idea—conquered it without any external pressure—conquered it *through the strength of persuasion—conquered it through the deeds of the Führer in the Reich!*" [17]   (Document 25, *post* p. 315.)

At the Foreign Organization's assembly at Stuttgart in August 1937 and thereafter, this boast was again repeated.

At the meeting in 1937 Bohle stated:

> "Through its Foreign Organization the party has been able to bring innumerable Germans abroad to the homeland and to show these Germans that they belong to this homeland, are bound and obligated to it.
>
> "*When national holidays are celebrated in the Reich today, then we know that the Germans in foreign countries are celebrating these days in the same spirit, and that all Germans are taking part therein.*" [18]
>
> (Document 26–A, *post* p. 348.)

With regard to the control of the German societies abroad, Bohle declared at that time: *180679*

> "The work of the many groups and societies has taken on a *new significance* through the all-encompassing activity of the party's groups abroad, and this work has been shaped in a more fruitful way for the community."

> "With this presupposition, our societies in foreign countries, which in part have existed for decades and, as one ought to acknowledge, have in many cases performed excellent work for Germandom, constitute an extremely valuable support of the entire work in Germandom abroad." [19]
>
> (Document 26–A, *post* p. 348.)

It will be noted that Bohle set an especially high value on the use of German societies of long standing and good reputation in their respective countries.

---

[16] *Ibid.*, p. 96.

[17] *Der Parteitag der Ehre* (Munich, Central Publishing House of the NSDAP, 1936), p. 125.

[18] Deutsches Nachrichtenbüro (official German news agency, Berlin), 1st morning bulletin of Aug. 30, 1937.

[19] *Ibid.*

In a talk at Vienna on October 24, 1936 Bohle went so far as to say:

"For the Foreign Organization of the NSDAP and for me, as its responsible leader, it is a particular pleasure to be able to say after only a few years that the unconditional will to cooperation with the new state has overcome and swept along every single German national regardless of all boundaries and unto the farthest corners of the earth." [20]   (Document 27, *post* p. 358.)

(b) National Socialist Racial Community as the Basis for Unification

Whatever success the Foreign Organization has had in the unification of all Germandom abroad, from the ideologic side, doubtless comes from the principle of the German "racial community". As Bohle himself stated at the Foreign Organization's meeting in 1937:

"Without the Führer and his conception, which takes hold of and encompasses all Germans, it would be senseless to attempt unification of Germandom abroad. The German racial community, preached by Adolf Hitler, was the only basis on which a unification of Germandom abroad could have taken place. It is necessary to keep this fact in mind, when on looking back we confirm how differently it looks today out there in comparison with the previous period." [21]   (Document 26–A, *post* pp. 347–348.)

No meeting of the Foreign Organization, no address or article of any of its directors, fails to stress the significance of the "racial community" for Germans abroad. At the party congress in 1936 Bohle declared:

". . . our Germanism abroad is composed of individual Germans who can only live as Germans if they form among themselves an *indestructible community* and if this community is incorporated in the community which Adolf Hitler has given the racial comrades in the Reich. *We believe in the eternal value of the race and the blood* and we feel ourselves the appointed *protectors of these values in foreign Germanism.* A state which is built on the iron laws of blood and race, like the National Socialist Reich, cannot do other than accept its own blood always and everywhere even in the remotest corner of the earth." [22] (Document 25, *post* pp. 314–315.)

At the Foreign Organization's annual assembly of Germans living abroad, in 1937 at Stuttgart, Rudolf Hess, at that time the Führer's Deputy, addressed the audience as follows:

"My German racial comrades, men and women! German seamen!

---

[20] *Wir Deutsche in der Welt* (published by the Verband Deutscher Vereine im Ausland: Berlin, 1937), p. 21.

[21] Deutsches Nachrichtenbüro, 1st morning bulletin of Aug. 30, 1937.

[22] *Der Parteitag der Ehre* (Munich, 1936), pp. 124–125.

"You stand before me as a slice of the great German racial community, the racial community which extends beyond the borders of our Reich, for National Socialism has not only at home created a national community transcending all classes and groups in a way previously unknown, but it has also included German racial comrades in foreign countries. It has made them conscious and proud members of this racial community!" [23]
(Document 26-A, *post* pp. 351–352.)

In an account of the Führer's talk to Germans from abroad at the 1935 party congress it is recorded that—

"The Führer then expressed the idea that the German people is today not merely a state, but that it has become a racial corpus [*Volkskörper*] which is pulsing with a vital and inner life. This is the great thing which National Socialism has given to the German people: that the German who goes to a foreign country nowadays is not a lost member but remains a living member of the people's community. The individual knows then that his life for the community is not in any sense a lost life but that he can be somehow useful and helpful for the totality of the people even though he may remain abroad. That is the miracle of the National Socialist organization and leadership of the people." [24]
(Document 28, *post* p. 363.)

Although the "racial community" is the foremost idea propounded as the basis for unifying all Germans abroad, other typically Nazi ideas are often set forth as binding notions for all Germans. For instance, Hess, at the 1937 assembly of Germans living abroad, invited the participants to attend the Reich's party congress in the following terms:

"You will see the man who created the idea of the Führer, and who himself as the first Führer has put with this idea the strongest clamp around Germany and all the Germans of the world." [25]
(Document 26-A, *post* p. 353.)

(c) Systematic Opposition to Assimilation of Germans

The idea of "racial community", of course, entails the repudiation of any assimilation by the populations of foreign countries. Most striking expressions of this are found in Bohle's address at the party congress in 1936:

"The Führer had to come in order to hammer into all of us the fact that the German cannot choose and may not choose whether or not he will be German but that he was sent into this world by God as a German and that God thereby had laid upon him as a German duties of which he cannot divest himself without committing treason to Providence. *Therefore, we believe and we*

[23] Deutsches Nachrichtenbüro, 3d morning bulletin of Aug. 30, 1937.
[24] *Der Parteitag der Freiheit* (Munich, 1935), p. 120.
[25] Deutsches Nachrichtenbüro, 1st forenoon bulletin of Aug. 30, 1937.

know that the German everywhere is a German—whether he lives in the Reich or in Japan, in France or in China, or anywhere else in the world. *Not countries or continents, not climate or environment but blood and race determine the world of ideas of the German.*" [26]   (Document 25, *post* p. 315.)

Accordingly:

"The Foreign Organization wishes to preserve for the Reich every German wherever he may be in the world, be he rich or poor, young or old, in the knowledge that no sin is greater than that of *voluntarily* abandoning German blood." [27]   (Document 25, *post* p. 315.)

Furthermore:

"It is not necessary for the new Reich to permit its racial comrades abroad inactively to fall prey to foreign and un-German ideas so that they may then become estranged from the Reich itself." [28]   (Document 25, *post* p. 316.)

In the 1937 meeting he expressed the same idea thus:

"We foreign German National Socialists reject the conception of the universal German, whose prime endeavor is to adapt himself everywhere, because this universal German not only makes himself ridiculous among the foreigners but also consciously or unconsciously repudiates his Germanism with this self-abandonment." [29]   (Document 26–A, *post* p. 349.)

At the same meeting Rudolf Hess stated clearly and bluntly:

"Under the leadership of the Foreign Organization, Germandom abroad is also becoming more and more *filled with the National Socialist spirit*. The Foreign Organization of the NSDAP has brought together the Germans out there, who even long after the seizure of power were disunited and split by class differences, and joined them with Adolf Hitler's Reich. The National Socialist care for Germandom abroad is maintaining an enormous number of Germans for the nation, who otherwise would be absorbed as cultural fertilizer for other nations." [30]   Document 26–A, *post* p. 352.)

(d) Obligation To Remain Loyal to Nazi Germany

The summons is accordingly issued to all Germans abroad to remain German, and this with its Nazi implications is their prime obligation. At the 1937 meeting Baron von Neurath, then the German Foreign Minister, related this in an old-fashioned way to the notion of protection, saying:

[26] *Der Parteitag der Ehre* (Munich, 1937), p. 125.
[27] *Ibid.*, p. 125.
[28] *Ibid.*, p. 126.
[29] Deutsches Nachrichtenbüro, 2d morning bulletin of Aug. 30, 1937.
[30] Deutsches Nachrichtenbüro, 3d morning bulletin of Aug. 30, 1937.

"Every German living abroad now knows that even in a foreign country he remains a living member of the German national community. He knows that he can count on the sure protection of his home state for himself and his interests. He will in return also feel within himself the obligation to remain a part of his people and to serve it according to his powers." [31]   (Document 26–A, *post* p. 350.)

In a talk at Vienna in 1936, Bohle furnished a more Nazi statement of the matter when he declared:

"In this, the Foreign Organization has followed wholly new paths; it has deliberately turned aside from the old unsuitable idea of the pure protection of foreign Germandom, a protection which is of no use to the Reich and in one way or another must give Germans abroad the feeling of not belonging to the people of the Reich in the same measure as a racial comrade in the Reich itself.

"For a master race, however, a protection of this kind would be humiliating. The Foreign Organization has, therefore, deliberately begun its work by placing upon foreign Germandom obligations to the new Reich, and it is a cause of pride for our German nationals beyond the borders that almost all of them have joyfully accepted these obligations." [32]

(Document 27, *post* p. 358.)

Subsequent sections, especially those which depict the role that German minorities have played in the Nazi conquest of Europe, indicate the nature of the obligations.

(e) Instructions Regarding Behavior Abroad

Germans living abroad are repeatedly ordered and exhorted in these official pronouncements to observe the laws of the country where they are residing and to refrain from any activity connected with its internal affairs. Of the Ten Commandments stamped on the foreign certificate of every party member residing abroad, the first two are as follows:

"1. Observe the laws of the country whose guest you are.
"2. Leave the politics of the country where you reside to its inhabitants. You are not concerned with the internal politics of a foreign country. Take no part in them, even in conversation." [33]

(Document 24, *post* p. 311.)

As Baron von Neurath affirmed at the Foreign Organization's meeting in 1937:

"We know, of course, and we are the last to seek to put any false interpretation on it, that the hospitality which is granted foreign citizens in a country obligates them to abstain strictly from any meddling in the internal affairs of the foreign country and obligates them to observe the general laws prevailing there." [34]

(Document 26–A, *post* p. 351.)

---

[21] *Ibid.*

[32] *Wir Deutsche in der Welt* (Berlin, 1937), pp. 21–22.

[33] *Almanach der nationalsozialistischen Revolution* (Berlin, 1934), p. 94.

[34] Deutsches Nachrichtenbüro, 3d morning bulletin of Aug. 30, 1937.

And he attempts to interpret the installation of Bohle as Chief of the Foreign Organization in the Foreign Office as a guaranty for the observation of these principles, a statement repeated by Bohle some months later at Budapest.[35]

At the 1935 meeting of Germans living abroad, Hess, in giving the oath of allegiance to the Führer, did not hesitate to assure the Germans from abroad that the Führer—

> "will never give you any command which cannot be reconciled with the laws of the country where you are living".[36]   (Document 28, *post* p. 365.)

At the 1937 meeting, Hess' assurances went even further, when he declared:

> "The National Socialist Germans are loyal to the country where they reside just as they are loyal citizens *of their own homeland*." [37] (Document 26–A, *post* p. 353.)

Bohle even had the temerity to state, in a talk before the German colony at Vienna on October 24, 1936:

> "Just as I have repeatedly announced this basic principle of my organization, so I will declare unambiguously here today in Vienna that every German national abroad, regardless of whether he is a member of the party or not, has the primary duty of keeping out of things which do not concern the Reich.   I never permit our German nationals abroad to become involved in the internal political affairs of other countries." [38]   (Document 27, *post* p. 357.)

The events in Austria a year and a half later revealed the value of such assertions.

(f) Professed Harmlessness

Following the usual Nazi practice of bold lying, the Nazi leaders have made repeated professions of the pacific purposes of the Foreign Organization since 1937, when the Foreign Organization was beginning to unfold its fifth-column activities.   At the Foreign Organization's assembly in 1937, Bohle declared:

> "The attempts to make it appear as if National Socialists abroad were exclusively spies or political agents—principally as the last attempt at a discrimination—one sees recently even in newspapers which want to be taken seriously.   It is amusing to read that Germany is training all housemaids abroad as spies and that the Nazi men themselves have as their chief task to transform the foreign countries concerned into Hitler-colonies.

---

[35] *Jahrbuch für auswärtige Politik* (Berlin, 1938), p. 16.

[36] *Der Parteitag der Freiheit* (Munich, 1935), p. 122.

[37] Deutsches Nachrichtenbüro, 1st forenoon bulletin of Aug. 30, 1937.

[38] *Wir Deutsche in der Welt* (Berlin, 1937), pp. 19–20.

"Because there are still people in foreign countries who believe
such things, I should like here especially to assure them that we
are not training the housemaids as spies and that we have not
ordered the Nazis living abroad to conquer foreign countries." [39]
(Document 26-A, *post* p. 349.)

Attempting to pour further ridicule on the same notion, Hess included the following remarks in his address at that meeting:

"From time to time the Foreign Organization of the NSDAP
enjoys the especially loving attention of foreign politicians. . . . Our youngest party Gau is made to appear a
sinister secret organization.

"You, my party comrades abroad, become spiders in the enormous network of espionage. It is really frightening to hear how
you bear the poison of fatal doctrines to foreign peoples and how
great world empires are threatened by you, and it is terrifying
to hear how you poor fellows must constantly report at the central offices of the NSDAP morning, afternoon, and evening, in
order to report, I would almost like to say, whether you have had
a good or bad dream about National Socialism." [40]
(Document 26-A, *post* p. 352.)

And continued, by attributing the Nazis' own activities to others:

"Naturally the wirepullers want nothing else than to divert
attention from those who really threaten the peace of the nations.
For it is not *we* who use our commercial offices as agencies for
the disintegration of the nations who are our hosts. *We* do not
smuggle inflammatory articles in foreign languages into other
countries. *We* are not organizing the underworld of other states
as the storm troops of civil war." [41]   (Document 26-A, *post*
p. 352.)

With cunning blandness Hess then introduced a theme later used
by Bohle in the same way:

"Does one really believe that we are so dumb, that if we wanted
to set up an organization for espionage, we would then use for this
purpose our so visible branches, local groups, and country groups
abroad?" [42]   (Document 26-A, *post* p. 353.)

In his talk at Budapest early in 1938 Bohle stated:

"Not only the structure of our organization but likewise its
entire work is carried on so clearly and openly before the whole
world that it would be simply childish stupidity on our part to
engage in, for example, espionage through such channels. One

---

[39] Deutsches Nachrichtenbüro, 2d morning bulletin of Aug. 30, 1937.
[40] *Ibid.*, 3d morning bulletin of Aug. 30, 1937.
[41] *Ibid.*, 1st forenoon bulletin of Aug. 30, 1937.
[42] *Ibid.*

does not place spies and similar agents in the light of publicity." [43]
(Document 29, *post* p. 370.)

In this connection the Nazi leaders were wont to profess that National Socialism was not an article for export.   In 1937 Hess used these strong words:

> *"We can declare with a pure conscience: We do not want National Socialism to trickle into other peoples as poison! We likewise do not wish to force it on other peoples. We do not even want to give it away to other peoples. On the contrary: We are jealously concerned to keep National Socialism for ourselves."* [44]
> (Document 26–A, *post* p. 352.)

Again at Budapest in 1938 Bohle repeated this:

> "Anyone who has concerned himself even superficially with the doctrines of National Socialism in Germany must know that this philosophy is a purely internal point of view which we jealously protect and never expect to export." [45]   (Document 29, *post* pp. 374–375.)

In 1938 Hess told the assembled Germans from abroad:

> "You have joined up in the Foreign Organization of the NSDAP in order to cultivate your Germanism and in order to be good National Socialists. Your Germanism and your National Socialism are your own private concern. You are not engaged in any '*pénétration pacifique*', you do not at all seek 'in a peaceful way to permeate' the host peoples with National Socialism. No, your Germanism and your National Socialism are your own private concern and remain also your most private concern." [46]
> (Document 30–A, *post* p. 385.)

In October 1937 in London Bohle expressed in classic terms what the National Socialists abroad claimed to be doing:

> "The National Socialists do not disseminate hatred and discord, but are anxious to deliver the messages of goodwill emanating from a country whose Leader loves peace because he loves his people and wants to make them happy." [47]   (Document 31, *post* p. 396.)

(g) German Citizens?   Or All Those of German Origin?

With regard to the question whether the activities of the Foreign Organization extended beyond German citizens to include German racial comrades of foreign citizenship, it will be noted that the activi-

---

[43] *Jahrbuch für auswärtige Politik* (Berlin, 1938), p. 19.
[44] Deutsches Nachrichtenbüro, 1st forenoon bulletin of Aug. 30, 1937.
[45] *Jahrbuch für auswärtige Politik* (Berlin, 1938), p. 25.
[46] *Der Montag* (daily newspaper of Berlin, Germany), 2d ed., Aug. 29, 1938.
[47] *Germany Speaks*, pp. 341–342.

ties of the Foreign Organization are usually discussed in terms of German racial comrades in general.   No distinction is made, especially in the earlier speeches, between German citizens and those of German origin who had adopted citizenship in another country.   From 1937 on, however, in view of the growing opposition to the Foreign Organization's activities from neighboring European countries and countries abroad, the leaders of the Foreign Organization found it expedient to state explicitly that their work was only concerned with German citizens.

At the Foreign Organization's meeting in Stuttgart in 1937 Bohle affirmed:

> "We concern ourselves with our citizens in foreign countries and only with our citizens, and we care for their connection with the Reich and for the maintenance of their Germanism." [48] (Document 26–A, *post* p. 349.)

A month later in London Bohle repeated the same profession:

> "Within the scope of the Foreign Office I am responsible for all questions that concern citizens of the Reich living abroad. The fact that I have nothing whatever to do with non-German nationals—either in my capacity as a member of the National Socialist Party or owing to my connection with the Foreign Office—has been emphasised so often as to require no further reference.   All statements to the effect, for instance, that I make it my business to organise the German minorities in foreign countries are pure inventions; and nobody knows this better than the governments of the countries concerned.   I am here referring, of course, to those of German origin abroad who are citizens of the countries in which they live." [49]   (Document 31, *post* p. 391.)

Again at Budapest in 1938 Bohle explicitly repeated this declaration made in London, adding:

> "The German Reich has never expected or wished that the Germans of Hungarian nationality should be anything but a true and loyal part of the Hungarian state.   If attempts are made by individuals or irresponsible organizations to arouse Germans of Hungarian nationality against the Hungarian state, I can give the emphatic assurance that such plots will be most sharply condemned on the part of Germany." [50]   (Document 29, *post* p. 374.)

As Bohle put the issue:

> "The interest of the German Reich in Germans of Hungarian nationality is not political but purely cultural." [51]   (Document 29, *post* p. 374).

---

[48] Deutsches Nachrichtenbüro, 2d morning bulletin of Aug. 30, 1937.

[49] *Germany Speaks*, p. 334.

[50] *Jahrbuch für auswärtige Politik* (Berlin, 1938), p. 24.

[51] *Ibid*.

In terms of Nazi ideology itself, as may be clearly seen from the discussions in previous sections, such a distinction, however, is entirely specious.   Even in the same address the inevitable connection between the two is implied by Bohle's remark:

> "Since the Nazi Party in the new Reich possesses the exclusive right to determine the philosophical and political views of the entire people, the Foreign Organization has logically been established for the leadership of all German citizens abroad." [52] (Document 29, *post* p. 367.)

In the same passage he stated:

> "Through my appointment as Chief of the Foreign Organization in the Foreign Office on January 30, 1937 this union of party and state received clear expression also in the supervision of foreign Germandom." [53]   (Document 29, *post* p. 368.)

Farther on he admitted:

> "When we speak in general of foreign Germandom we understand thereby not only German nationals abroad but also persons of German origin." [54]   (Document 29, *post* 368.)

Although Bohle immediately professed to make the proper distinction in practice, the evidence indicates that no such distinction in practice ever existed.   There was a convenient ambiguity in modes of expression, there were dummy organizations and diverse subterfuges, but no essential obligatory distinction between German racial comrades of German and foreign citizenship.   Just as the Nazi ideology encompassed all German racial comrades regardless of their citizenship, likewise the Foreign Organization sought to encompass all those of German extraction who could be reached, by whatever means possible.   While Nazi policy contemplated the furtherance of German interests through the establishment of compact German racial minorities wherever Germans resided throughout the world, the Foreign Organization represented the official party organ for the fulfilment of all German aims beyond the borders of the Reich.

The story of Austria and of Czechoslovakia is well known, but in the following account of Hess' address at the Foreign Organization's assembly in August 1938—in the period between the absorption of Austria and the destruction of Czechoslovakia—there is testimony both as to the role of the racial comrades (*Volksdeutsche*) and the facility with which the "outward sign" of foreign citizenship was sloughed off. At the close of this talk Rudolf Hess recalled—

> "the day last year in Stuttgart when German men and women, German boys and girls, in their native costumes . . . appeared

---

[52] *Ibid.*, p. 16.
[53] *Ibid.*
[54] *Ibid.*, p. 17.

here in Stuttgart, completely animated by the great German idea, passionately moved by National Socialism but nevertheless outwardly *Volksdeutsche*, Germans of foreign citizenship [namely, Austrian].

" 'Today', Rudolf Hess continued, 'they also stand openly in our ranks. They will be proud and happy to march in the formations of the National Socialist movement past their Führer in Nuremberg—this time as German citizens! . . .'

"Rudolf Hess then recalls the similar struggle of another German folk-group for its national right to live: The German people looks at the German racial comrades in Czechoslovakia with the profoundest sympathy for their suffering. No one in the world, who loves his own people and is proud of his own people, will find fault with us, if from this place here we also turn our thoughts to the Sudeten Germans, if we say to them that we see with complete admiration how they are maintaining an iron discipline, despite the worst chicanery, despite terror and murder. If it had in general required a proof, that the best German virtues are embodied in Sudeten Germandom, then it is proved by this iron discipline and this steadfast calm, which comes from the feeling of one's own right. You in Sudetenland know: We stand by you, with passionate hearts. (The masses emphasize this greeting of the Führer's Deputy to the Sudeten Germans with jubilant enthusiasm.) *The right of three and one-half million German men lies with you, the right of millions of members of a great people to conduct their life and so to shape it as adherence to this people of culture demands."* [55]

(Document 30–A, *post* 386.)

Presaging future events in a backhanded way, Bohle stated in his speech at Budapest in 1938:

"I think I may also say that the Germans of Hungarian nationality are the last who would wish to serve as a pretext for the assertion that the German Reich has designs on the integrity of the Hungarian state." [56]   (Document 29, *post* p. 374.)

The Germans of Polish nationality, well prepared by Nazi agitation, were ready, however, to serve as the desired pretext against Poland.

4. CENTRAL CONTROLLING AGENCY OVER ALL OTHER ORGANIZATIONS PROMOTING GERMANISM

A large number of quasi-independent German agencies have engaged in diverse activities among those of German extraction living in foreign countries. We shall consider in some detail only those two major institutions which were most active in the United States, the Deutsches Ausland-Institut (DAI, German Foreign Institute), Stuttgart, and the Volksbund für das Deutschtum im Ausland (VDA, League for Germandom in Foreign Countries), Berlin. Before doing

---

[55] *Der Montag* (Berlin daily newspaper), Aug. 29, 1938.
[56] *Jahrbuch für auswärtige Politik* (Berlin, 1938), p. 25.

so, it must be reiterated, however, that the Foreign Organization of the NSDAP functioned as a central agency controlling the activities of all the organizations promoting Germanism abroad. In his monograph entitled *Die Auslands-Organisation der NSDAP*, Dr. Emil Ehrich, personal adviser to the Gauleiter of the Foreign Organization, closes his description of the Foreign Organization's Department for Culture with the following words: "In the last analysis it is the central office for all the numerous organizations and bureaus which are aiming at a spiritual and cultural exchange with Germandom abroad." [57] (Document 23, *post* p. 298.)

The VDA
(Volksbund für das Deutschtum im Ausland)

Both the VDA and the DAI were pre-Nazi institutions, striving to maintain the German language, customs, and culture among those of German extraction outside of German borders. When the Nazis assumed power in 1933, both the VDA and the DAI were quickly reorganized and used by the Nazis, although ostensibly retaining their independence as private institutions. Since these agencies maintained open connections between Germany and German racial comrades of foreign citizenship, in the United States as well as elsewhere, it is important to demonstrate the clear tie-up between both these agencies and the Nazi Party. This appears in common ideas and aims, public professions of adherence, official representation at meetings, and appointments in personnel. It may well be maintained that in the totalitarian state there can be no "independent agencies", in the sense of that term used in reference to a democratic country. However, the subsequent discussion presents direct evidence to refute any argument that the VDA and DAI, after 1933, were acting as private non-official agencies.

1. NATURE AND ACTIVITIES

The VDA was founded as the German School League in 1880 in Austria to support endangered German schools in areas of mixed nationality. A similar organization was founded in Germany at the same time. In 1908 the German association assumed the name "League for Germandom in Foreign Countries" (Verein für das Deutschtum im Ausland). The Austrian association became the Austrian branch of the VDA in 1921, later absorbing other Austrian societies doing similar work. One of these societies, the Südmark, absorbed in 1925, had been founded in 1889 with the aim of providing economic support to Germans residing or settling in the mixed-language areas of Styria, Carinthia, Carniola, and Tyrol.

As a result of the ethnic problems arising after the war, the VDA expanded considerably and reorganized its many groups throughout

---

[57] Ehrich, *op. cit.*, p. 20.

Germany and Austria. As the pamphlet *Nature and Significance of the VDA* by VDA District Leader Otto Schäfer states: "The sphere of activity became extended to the entire realm of life of the German race."[58] (Document 32–A, *post* p. 424.) The extent of the VDA's activities may be seen from the following list of its departments, taken from the same source: Business Management, Publicity and Organizations, Press and Periodicals, Youth Work, Academic Work, Scholarships, Vacation Trips and Hiking, Physical Training, School Department, Libraries Abroad, Library and Archives, Business Department.[59]

The VDA was particularly active in German public schools, spreading its propaganda among the children and arranging exchanges of correspondence between school children at home and those in foreign countries. Remaining true to its original purpose, the VDA functioned as a sort of liaison between the German school system and German schools in foreign countries, sending Nazi schoolbooks and maintaining special agents to supervise German-language schools abroad. Describing this school work, Schäfer writes:

> "Its major feature lies in the establishment and maintenance of German kindergartens and schools, for the first fourteen years are usually decisive with regard to national allegiance, if an especially strong national will is not at hand. Usually the number of children and the particular conditions of the neighborhood are ascertained and then the solution of the matter is begun. If the German children live in a region of very mixed nationality, then the establishment of a German kindergarten is necessary. In unilingual areas, the establishment of German schools suffices. In most cases attempts are made to induce the authorities to fulfil their obligations; if this does not succeed, the VDA acts and arranges for the building of a schoolhouse, in that it either furnishes a subsidy or itself builds the school . . . In other localities it pays for the teachers, or gives subsidies so that able teachers and pastors may be kept in the endangered areas. If the establishment of a school is impossible, then it attempts to arrange for good private instruction and grants subsidies for this also."[60] (Document 32–A, *post* p. 427.)

An important phase of the VDA's work was the collection of money, put at the disposal of all groups propagating the idea of Germandom abroad. The VDA also engaged actively in pan-German propagandistic work both within Germany and abroad. Aside from pamphlets and manifestoes, the chief vehicles for this were the periodicals published by the VDA, "*Volksdeutsche*", "*Deutsche Welt*", and "*Deutsche Arbeit*". The magazine "*Volksdeutsche*" was sent by the VDA to all parts of the world, including the United States. A calendar entitled

---

[58] Otto Schäfer, *op. cit.*, p. 28.
[59] *Ibid.*
[60] *Ibid.*, p. 34.

"Germans All Over the World" was also sent, often as a donation by German firms (document 33, *post* p. 431), and propagandistic literature was forwarded to German women's organizations abroad and to address lists furnished by representatives abroad or other interested parties.

2. GOALS

A standard German encyclopedia of 1925 gives the following brief account of the aims of the VDA, which in 1924 with its 1,914 local groups and 1,172 school groups was "the largest organization working for Germandom":

> "The VDA has borne its present name since 1909 and has since then had as its aim not only the maintenance of German schools but also of other cultural institutions of Germandom abroad. Its protective work extends first to the Alp and Sudeten lands, then also to eastern Europe and overseas. It concerns itself with German kindergartens, schools, libraries, and newspapers abroad, with the support of Germans abroad, and especially of Germans from abroad studying in the Reich, and with propagandistic work through the press, through lectures, and its own publications." [61]

In the pamphlet entitled *Nature and Significance of the VDA*, Otto Schäfer, a VDA district leader, wrote in 1932:

> "The *aim* of the VDA's *work, in its broadest sense,* is the fulfilment of the meaning of German racial unity, the permeation of all Germans with the racial idea; *the aim in the more restricted sense* is the successful work of maintaining and protecting Germandom in all countries of the earth, and especially by the cultivation of German cultural forms of activity and expression." [62] (Document 32–A, *post* pp. 425–426.)

Similarly, in an address at the meeting of the VDA in Passau, Whitsuntide 1933, Dr. Hans Steinacher, the Reich's leader of the VDA, stated:

> "The aim of our work is the maintenance of the race outside of our borders. This work cannot be isolated from the life of the Germans within our borders. Borders can separate the life of states but not the life of a people. No matter if the state be forced here and there to give up its claims and to endure borders, which lie on this side of our ethnic borders, the race does not admit any such resignation of race!" [63] (Document 34, *post* p. 434.)

Closing his review of the history of the VDA in the above-mentioned work, Otto Schäfer declared:

[62] Schäfer, *op. cit.,* p. 30.

[63] *Der nationalsozialistische Staat* (ed. by Dr. Walther Gehl: Breslau, 1933), pp. 222–223.

"Brilliant as this development of the VDA, which encompasses today over 2,000,000 members, and of the whole Germandom movement appears, it is not yet at an end, and ought not to come to an end, until it has reached the entire German race, led the last lost son back into his father's house, has secured the last field fertilized by German sweat and blood." [64]   (Document 32-A, *post* p. 425.)

The general background for the VDA's work is indicated by the explanatory note at the beginning of the chapter in *Der nationalsozialistische Staat* containing extracts of Steinacher's address at Passau:

"There has been a Germandom in foreign countries since the 13th century, when German settlers migrated to the European east and southeast, and since the 17th century, when these isolated German settlements were increased and strengthened, and when Germans as farmers and as artisans migrated to North America.   The small German Reich of Bismarck left millions of Germans outside of its borders, and the Treaty of Versailles separated from the Reich still further territory inhabited by Germans.

"To the pure state-thinking of the 19th century, Germans in foreign countries, who were not citizens of the Reich, were counted as foreigners. . . .   One spoke of German-Russians, instead of Russian-Germans, of German-Bohemians, instead of Sudeten-Germans, etc.   The Reich did not concern itself about them, in order to avoid political complications.   Merely the VDA, the 'Volksbund (formerly Verein) für das Deutschtum im Ausland', maintained the connection between Germandom in the Reich and Germandom in foreign countries.   Its slogan was 'Germans of all countries, unite!' [65]

(Document 34, *post* p. 433.)

The world-wide scope of the VDA's work is also clearly stated by Schäfer:

"We see that the sphere of the VDA's work has become very great, it encompasses the entire planet, and it is by far not able to satisfy the demands made upon it.   Also for this reason its aim must remain: the unification of all Germans to one great community of destiny, to a nation." [66]   (Document 32-A, *post* p. 426.)

Pamphlets and manifestoes of the VDA leave no doubt that among the "lost sons" are millions of citizens of the United States. The United States is included in the long list of countries containing German racial comrades, in an advertisement appearing February 22, 1934 in the *Berliner Börsen Zeitung*, an authoritative Berlin newspaper, which further states:

"The Germans are a people of 100 millions!"

---

[61] *Meyer's Lexikon* (Leipzig, 1925), vol. 3, p. 703.

[64] Schäfer, *op. cit.*, p. 29.

[65] *Der nationalsozialistische Staat*, pp. 215–216.   Verein was changed to Volksbund in 1933.

[66] Schäfer, *op cit.*, p. 32.

"The great German racial community is fighting all over the whole planet."

"The VDA is the trustee of the 30 million Germans in foreign countries!"
(Document 35–A, *post* p. 436.)

Concerning the German emigrants to North America, Dr. Schäfer wrote in his 1933 VDA pamphlet:

"Doubtless the Germans would have possessed greater powers of resistance against America's Anglo-Saxonism, if a strong German Government had stood behind them and supported them in their first measures toward the maintenance and cultivation of Germanism, as did the English Government for its emigrants."

"As long as the German Government or a great part of the German people did not stand behind them [the German emigrants], they were powerless. In these years the German nationality lost 20 million persons in the United States, to the great detriment of Germany later." [67]
(Document 32–A, *post* p. 422.)

In a VDA handbill of the same period, seeking new contributing members, under the title "Every Third German Lives in a Foreign Country" 10 to 12 million Germans are listed as residing in the United States. From this handbill are also taken the following statements:

"There are Germans on the whole planet. How many? That's hard to say. As a result of the indifference of the old homeland countless numbers of these have long since forgotten their German language and German ways. Millions have drowned in the melting pot of the United States alone. The number of Germans in the world, however, certainly still amounts to nearly ONE HUNDRED MILLION!

"Think of these animated by a unified will. They would be an enormous energy, a firm foundation for our future, for the German economy, industry, and prestige in the world, *Lebensraum* for our growing generation, basis for our export trade, and therewith *source of employment opportunity for us all*. We want to create this will! Help us!

.   .   .   .

"Germans are stretched over the planet like a net. There is no city on earth where Germans have not gotten a foothold as businessmen, scarcely a country in which they do not dwell as settlers. The German name rings out throughout the whole world. We lack only one thing: the will to stand together everywhere, as the others do. If this will is once at hand, the German language will never die out, German characteristics will never slip away, and the German economy will always flourish.

"Germans are still migrating out into the world. Thus it was for centuries, so it still is today. The past has cast away German blood, donated it to foreign peoples. This is all over! We also want finally to be a people like all the peoples of the earth. Lend

---

[67] *Ibid.*, pp. 7, 8.

your aid, so that the Germans out there remain German and
shape the German future together with us!"
(Document 36–A, *post* pp. 441–443.)

In his introduction to the VDA calendar "Germans All Over the
World" for 1938, which was widely distributed among Germans
abroad, Dr. Hans Steinacher emphasized the superiority of the
German folk principle to citizenship:

"The individual is nothing without his folk. Every German
folk-comrade is responsible for his work and his whole existence
to the German folk. But the German folk-community extends
far beyond our state borders. We must not think of state
boundaries when we speak of the German folk. To be sure, our
folk-community is divided and cut to pieces by state boundaries,
but it is not destroyed. In all the branches of our hundred
million folk there is the same outpouring of the powers of
growth. . . .
"Thus our calendar wishes to build bridges of community
between Germans and Germans so that they will come to be
acquainted with each other and to know that they are of one
folkdom, regardless of what citizenship they possess and in
what part of the world they live. . . ."

The common aims of the VDA and the Nazi movement, as well as
the role of the VDA with respect to the movement, are revealed in
the following remarks made by Dr. Steinacher in Passau in 1933:

"The movement arises from the depths of the German race.
Because it does so, it is no purely state movement and is therefore not limited by the borders of the state. It affects the entire
extent of our racial corpus. The present moment is decisive, since
the revolution has terminated within the Reich and the entire life
is in a state of transformation. . . .
"And over there beyond our borders: from the Baltic down to
the mouth of the Danube, from Upper Silesia to Egerland, from
Burgenland to Tyrol and to Eupen-Malmedy, we see everywhere
how the young generation is being seized by this movement. We
observe it also beyond the seas in North America, in Brazil, and
in South Africa, where with unique ardor precisely the simple
classes have gained in self-consciousness and are proceeding along
their way everywhere more full of faith and stronger. The entire
German racial corpus has become actually fluid. Whatever belongs to it is being newly formed. A new aspect of German life
has begun. . . .

.   .   .   .

"We are the intermediaries of this exchange between the fight
out there and the renewal here within. To be sure, there is still
a long and difficult path to be traversed, in order really to
arrive at this great goal, the truly entire German nation. . . .
It is necessary to see all important vital occurrences and results of our being in the whole extent of our racial corpus
[*überstaatlichen Volkskörpers*], a racial corpus which extends

beyond and is superior to the state. We do not want German culture, German sentiments, German obligations to be any longer restricted by the sphere of state borders."[68] (Document 34, *post* pp. 433–434.)

In his report of the Passau meeting, Schäfer states the identity of aims with complete clarity:

"The ultimate goals of the VDA and the NSDAP consequently agree. It is a matter of the conquest of the last German person, the guaranteeing of an indestructible German racial unity, which deeply conscious and deeply anchored in the breast of every single German represents his highest and ultimate goal; it is a matter of the abandonment of self. From this goal the VDA is drawing the consequences at present. It is bursting the framework of the League, which for a long time has been too narrow, and it is carrying its old idea in a new form and a new organization out into the world. It is extending its sphere of work over the entire German race. No longer merely sustainer and helper, defender and champion, in the future it will be a mediator, a mediator between Germandom at home and Germandom abroad, a mediator between the government and the people. It will be the leader in a racial policy which extends far beyond the policy of an official government, it will be the leader in the organization of all German states and German men, in the common united great German racial front.

"Thus it stands behind, thus it stands ahead of the government, in complete freedom, but in deepest solidarity. If, in the future, government policy and racial policy may and must necessarily take different courses, nevertheless they will go hand in hand and have only the one goal: 'German *Volk*'."[69]

(Document 32–A, *post* p. 429.)

3. TIE-UP WITH THE NAZI PARTY

A direct tie-up between the VDA and the party ensued immediately after the party's assumption of power. In a circular dated February 24, 1933 the new Nazi Minister of the Interior, Frick, instructed the separate governments of the German federal states to accord preferred treatment to the VDA and to promote its work by official government support. This circular stated in part:

"My Ministry in its attention to national tasks has to a special degree exercised protection over and furtherance of Germandom in the border countries and Germandom in foreign countries. A large number of institutions concerned with special tasks in this sphere are being supported as far as possible by means at my disposal. Among all these the *League for Germandom in Foreign Countries*, German School League, Inc., Berlin, enjoys an *especially favored position*. To its work carried on for half

---

[68] *Der nationalsozialistische Staat*, pp. 218ff.

[69] Schäfer, *op. cit.*, p. 42.

a century is due the maintenance of so many German schools, churches, newspapers, or other institutions in the German settlements in foreign countries. Without such maintenance of these institutions large German folk-groups, especially under the pressure of the post-war period, would have perished as cultural fertilizer for foreign peoples. Unfortunately in past years a certain reserve among wide circles of the population was noticeable with regard to the propaganda work of the above-named national League, and also administrative restrictions on its activities have not been left undone. It appears to me, therefore, as an urgent duty of the Reich and of the federal states not only to set aside such hindrances but also to enable the League for Germandom in Foreign Countries to unfold the increased propaganda work in all spheres which it desires. Also, regard for the needs and misery of the time, and for the lack of work and bread within Germany, ought not to divert attention from the fact that the around 30 million Germans in foreign countries [*Auslanddeutschen*] outside of the present contracted borders of the Reich are an integral part of the entire German people. They are an integral part, which the Reich's Government is not able to help economically, but whose cultural support through the league primarily concerned with this, the League for Germandom in Foreign Countries, it considers it is obligated to make possible.

"I should like accordingly to direct the special attention of the governments of the federal states to the activity of the League for Germandom in Foreign Countries with the idea that it *be accorded privileged treatment*. It is primarily the school groups which carry on the propaganda work of the League, in which at the same time the education of the youth to patriotic thinking takes place, an education which is above denominational and party differences. I will, therefore, attach the greatest value to the fact that its school meetings be accorded the greatest freedom of action and that the pupils be allowed to wear the insignia of the League in the schools. I would expect an effective enlivenment of this work, *if the supervisors of all the schools, in their annual reports to their superior authorities concerning the school activities, will be urged to report the furtherance of the League by the school groups of each school.*"

(Document 37–A, *post* pp. 446–447.)

In May 1933 an agreement was signed between the VDA and the Hitler Youth Organization, arranging for a complete collaboration between the Hitler Youth and the VDA. According to this agreement the Hitler Youth recommends that its members join the VDA, the VDA school groups assist the Hitler Youth in their work, and, "as a visible sign of his solidarity with the Hitler Youth, the VDA member wears a VDA armband with the swastika". Mutual participation of the groups of one organization in the events of the other is arranged, as is a close contact between the VDA group chiefs and the Hitler Youth leaders. According to article 6 of this agreement:

"(6) Solicitor Nabersberg of the NSDAP's National Youth Office becomes a member of the VDA's Council of Leaders. Dr. H. Schoeneich of the VDA becomes a member of the Council of Leaders in the Reich's Board of German Youth Societies. The same reciprocal representation also is to be established in the provincial boards." (Document 38–A, *post* p. 450.)

It is further noteworthy that immediately after the Nazis became the ruling power of Germany, the VDA, under the guidance of its new Reich's leader, Hans Steinacher, was completely reorganized on the basis of the Führer principle.[70] (Document 32–A, *post* p. 421.) It also appears from Schäfer's account that Rudolf Hess, then the deputy leader of the NSDAP, dispatched a letter to the VDA meeting at Passau in 1933, in which he confirmed the service of the VDA as the "bearer of a true National Socialist policy in the racial sense". [71] Also, Schäfer's pamphlet on the VDA, which has been so extensively cited herein, received official confirmation and commendation. Quoted among the letters of approval is the following:

". . . The Führer thanks . . . you. He took very much pleasure in it.

"Signed X.—Adjutant of the Reich's Chancelor." [72]
(Document 32–A, *post* p. 430.)

4. USEFULNESS AS A PSEUDO-INDEPENDENT AGENCY

In his work *Legal Organization and Legal Functions of the Movement*, published by the official Nazi publishing house, Otto Gauweiler remarks:

"A basic principle of the activity of the Foreign Organization is respect for the laws of those countries where Germans are living as guests; the struggles of German minority groups beyond the borders of the Reich are carried on in other organizational forms." [73] (Document 20, *post* p. 255.)

The VDA was one of the most important "organizational forms" for carrying on this struggle. For reasons of political expediency it was necessary for the German Government and the official party embodied in the Government to disassociate itself outwardly from the activities of German minority groups in foreign countries. Con-

---

[70] Schäfer, *op. cit.*, p. 29.
[71] *Ibid.*, pp. 41–42.
[72] *Ibid.*, p. 48.
[73] Gauweiler, *op cit.*, p. 71.

sequently, the pretense of independence had to be maintained for those institutions performing the open liaison work between German minorities abroad and the German mother-country. The following citations from an authorized official of the VDA show the general realization that the VDA had enhanced usefulness for the Nazis as a pseudo-independent agency.

Concerning the recognition which the VDA received from Hitler after he came into power, the VDA District Leader Schäfer writes:

> "At the same time the high political talent of our Führer was exhibited in the fact that he had recognized at once what an important instrument for a successful racial-German [*Volksdeutsche*] policy stands at the German people's disposal in the form of an independent VDA." [74]   (Document 32–A, *post* p. 428.)

Answering the question "Why a Strong VDA?" Schäfer states:

> "(1) Because our racial brothers in foreign countries acknowledge their adherence to us and to the Reich and we ours to them, and therefore a National Socialist Reich ought never to neglect VDA tasks, if it does not want to abandon itself.
>
> "(2) Because we need a racial league, which not being an official government nor official party organization is able to work for its racial fellows, where the government and the party are not able and may not do this on account of political reasons, i. e. because racial policy and government policy are two different things, which it is true have the same point of departure and the same goal but must necessarily proceed along entirely different paths.
>
> .   .   .   .
>
> "(5) Because otherwise the party and the Hitler Youth must form special groups in their own organizations for the solution of VDA's tasks.
>
> "(6) Because the foreign countries most readily reject racial work in this form, but the National Socialist, however, must support and push through precisely racial work in every form.
>
> "(7) Because under present conditions the racial idea can be carried to *all* sections of our German race only through the VDA." [75]
>
> (Document 32–A, *post* pp. 429–430.)

His further points reaffirm the essential identity between the VDA and the Nazi Party:

> "(8) Because the VDA rests unconditionally on the foundation of German racial thinking, i. e. on the National Socialist foundation.
>
> "(9) Because the leaders of the VDA are without exception National Socialists of the spirit and not just the party.
>
> "(10) Because the true VDA member is the true National Socialist, i. e. the VDA leads surely to National Socialism.

---

[74] Schäfer, *op. cit.*, p. 42.

[75] *Ibid.*, p. 45.

"(11) Because our Führer and Chancelor, Adolf Hitler, wants a strong VDA:

> "(a) to permeate the entire people and the party with the racial ideas, the central ideas of National Socialism;
>
> "(b) for the purpose of a strong and successful racial policy." [76]

(Document 32–A, *post* p. 430.)

5. CONNECTION BETWEEN THE VDA, DAI, AND OTHER SIMILAR ORGANIZATIONS

Before proceeding to discuss the DAI in some detail, it may be well to point out that the relation between the VDA and Naziism, as adduced in the evidence presented above, applies in general to the DAI and to all the other minor German institutions and associations devoted to Germandom abroad. The VDA, it is known, worked in close collaboration with the DAI, with the German Protective Association (Deutscher Schutzbund), and with others. Schäfer asserts:

> "The majority of Germandom's associations, over 90 percent, finally united into a large 'Alliance of Free Germandom Associations', whose management is attended to by the VDA. It aims on the one hand to bring about extensive collaboration and mutual supplementation, and on the other hand to help avoid friction and unnecessary double work. Its most important members are the 'Deutscher Schutzbund', the Deutsches Auslandsinstitut, the 'Bund der Auslandsdeutschen', the 'Deutsche Kolonialgesellschaft', the 'Vereinigung für Siedlung und Wanderung', the 'Reichsverband für die katholischen Auslandsdeutschen', and the 'Vereinigung Deutsch Evangelisch im Auslande'. In recent months the Deutscher Schutzbund was absorbed by the VDA; the Alliance of Associations of German Teachers Abroad, which has acquired more and more significance through its Darmstadt meetings under the leadership of State Councilor Block, joined the VDA; and the Deutsches Auslandsinstitut, under the leadership of the Transylvanian Saxon, Dr. Richard Csaki, has entered into a closer connection with the VDA." [77]   (Document 32–A, *post* p. 425.)

In the subsequent section on the DAI it is, in fact, shown that Steinacher, as Reich's leader of the VDA, was appointed by the Württemberg government as chairman of a committee of three to select a new president of the DAI in the spring of 1933. It cannot be too often repeated that all German institutions and associations propagating Germanism abroad worked together after the advent of the Nazis, and under Nazi guidance.

---

[76] *Ibid.*

[77] *Ibid.*, p. 29.

The DAI
(Deutsches Ausland-Institut)
1. NATURE AND SIGNIFICANCE

The Deutsches Ausland-Institut was founded in 1917 with the express purpose of furthering German interests abroad by maintaining contact with all those of German extraction who had migrated or were migrating to foreign countries. Established in Stuttgart because of the heavy emigration originating from southwestern Germany, its scope was not restricted to this section. In fact, the DAI possesses the most comprehensive collection of material concerning all Germandom abroad. Even in pre-Nazi days, however, it was not merely a research institute. Its diverse collections of material were always available in the interest of Germandom abroad, and the DAI, furthermore, not only engaged in propagandistic work through its magazines, press releases, and publication of books but also had departments for advice to emigrants, for employment, legal matters, and information. In the words of a standard German encyclopedia:

> "The DAI represents, especially since the completion in 1925 of its new Home of Germandom [*Haus des Deutschtums*], the appointed central organ for the connection between the homeland and Germandom abroad." [78]

A reliable confidential source, reporting in 1937 on the work of the DAI, furnished the following details concerning the separate branches of the DAI's activities:

"Research and Information Service

> "The Institute keeps itself posted concerning the cultural and business activities of Germans in foreign parts and maintains lists of German clubs and firms which are available to reliable persons wishing to enter into correspondence with these groups. In a certain sense it thus helps to further German trade, as it handles inquiries of a business nature and facilitates the making of initial contacts. The Institute, moreover, keeps a card index file of the family history of Germans who have left the Fatherland, bearing in particular upon their 'racial integrity'. Through its correspondents abroad who report directly to it the Institute is informed of the status and progress of 'Germanism' in particular countries. The reaction of the resident population is also recorded in special reports and clippings from the local press. The Institute is thus in a sense the seismograph which registers everything relating to the cause of 'Germanism'.

"Propaganda Work

> "The Institute is one, but probably the most important, of the agencies which prepare and disseminate propaganda abroad in

---

[78] *Meyer's Lexikon* (Leipzig, 1925), vol. 3, p. 703.

the form of books, pamphlets, periodicals and communiqués. Such material is extensively supplied to public libraries, societies, educational institutions, church organizations, and so forth, provided they are frequented by, or connected in some way with Germans, or persons of German extraction. The Institute can furthermore be relied upon to assist in the preparation and documentation of Congresses held by Germans abroad.

"The Institute also has a hand in organizing the frequent and periodical broadcasts transmitted to foreign Germans by the powerful short-wave stations of the Reich radio system. The Stuttgart broadcasting station is housed in the building of the Institute which furnishes with appropriate material this station as well as others belonging to the German chain. The main object of the programs thus supplied is to keep Germans living in other countries in constant touch with developments in the Reich, to stimulate their interest in the Reich, to develop social, political and economic relationships favorable to Germany, and to convince them of the success of National Socialism. Certain of these broadcasts are also of a cultural nature and include music, theatrical programs, lectures on artistic and historical subjects, as well as also religious discourses.

"Activity in Emigration Matters

"The Institute would appear to exercise a certain function in controlling and directing the source of the small amount of emigration (excepting Jews) that is taking place from the Reich. It is understood to possess a department which acts as a sort of labor exchange able to furnish German workmen for firms doing business abroad. This section also apparently advises persons wishing to proceed to foreign countries as settlers, handling their applications and passing upon their requests for foreign exchange. The Institute's activity in this field is apparently based on the theory that while a large wave of emigration is neither possible nor desirable, nevertheless the establishment of the right kind of German settler is advantageous in certain localities, particularly if they can be encouraged to maintain their ties with the Reich and be bound to National Socialism."

2. TIE-UP WITH NAZIS

Evidence demonstrating the close tie-up between the DAI and the Nazi Party is as conclusive as in the case of the VDA. Here, likewise, immediately after the Nazis came into power, an established institution whose general ideals and aims were in conformity with those of the Nazis was promptly *gleichgeschaltet*, i.e. put under direct Nazi control through reorganization. An account of the procedure appeared in the official National Socialist newspaper organ of Württemberg, the Stuttgart *N. S. Kurier* of September 21, 1933:

"In the course of the revolutionary turn of events, an emergency has ensued, which required the chief supervisory authorities of the Württemberg government to install for the

500386—43——9

maintenance of the work a Committee of Reorganization, to which were transferred all powers. This condition was subsequently recognized as proper by the Assembly. The committee had the task of appointing the new chairman of the Institute, who then himself was to appoint the new Board of Directors, and in agreement with the Government offices work out the new statutes.

"The head of the Committee of Three, Dr. Steinacher, Reich's Führer of the VDA, declared that they have found the right man in Chief Mayor Dr. Strölin, who in view of the situation and his personality appeared most suited to assume this responsible post. The task of the committee had concluded with this."

(Document 39–A, *post* p. 463.)

Dr. Strölin was the Nazi Chief Mayor of Stuttgart, installed by fiat after the advent of the Nazis, although he had been badly beaten in the previous election.

It will be noted in the above citation that after his appointment Dr. Strölin, acting in accordance with the Führer principle, then proceeded to appoint the new Board of Directors. Dr. Eisenmann, director of the provincial parliament, was appointed vice chairman. Also appointed to the Board of Directors were: Senior Government Councilor Dr. Drück from the Ministry of the Interior; Dr. Robert Ernst, leader of the Schutzbund; University Professor Dr. Göring; Senior Director of Education Dr. Krehl; and Dr. Hans Steinacher, Reich's leader of the VDA, among others. The direction of the Institute was entrusted to Professor Csaki,[79] a Transylvanian Saxon who had experience in Germanism activities beyond the borders of Germany.

The first paragraph of a report on the 1933 annual meeting of the DAI, appearing in the authoritative Stuttgart newspaper, *Stuttgarter Neues Tagblatt*, of September 21, 1933, shows the status of the DAI in the new Nazi state:

"This year's annual meeting of the Deutsches Ausland-Institut stood entirely under the sign of the new National Socialist Germany. Only the National Socialist world-view is able to give to the idea of the work for Germandom abroad the great significance which is due it. The racial-German idea has today finally won through. Hence it was to be taken for granted that this year's annual meeting of the Deutsches Ausland-Institut would be participated in by the authoritative Government offices.

---

[79] Dr. Csaki is still mentioned as the Manager of the Institute in a report dated Nov. 30, 1940. However, the March–April 1942 issue of the DAI periodical *Deutschtum im Ausland* names Dr. Hermann Rüdiger as the Institute's Manager, Dr. Csaki having become in the meantime a member of the Board of Directors. The same issue discloses that the notorious Walter Kappe, well known in the United States, is managing editor of the periodical but on leave for military duty.

Representatives of the authorities and of pan-German organizations were present in great numbers at the annual meeting and the demonstration." (Document 39–A, *post* p. 460.)

Another article in the same issue of the above newspaper names the following official representatives:

"The Chairman of the Deutsches Ausland-Institut, Chief Mayor Dr. Strölin, opened the celebration. He greeted among those present, in particular, Minister-President and Minister of Religion in Württemberg Mergenthaler as the representative of the supervisory authorities; General Haushofer of Munich as the representative of Rudolf Hess, who has been entrusted by the Führer with the supreme direction of all matters concerning Germans in foreign countries; the Deputy Gauleiter Schmidt as the Württemberg representative of Reich's Propaganda Minister Dr. Goebbels; Herr Ruberg as the representative of the NSDAP's Foreign Policy Office and its Director Alfred Rosenberg. The President of the Danzig Senate, Dr. Rauschning, was greeted with great applause as the representative of the purely German population of Danzig which has been separated from the mother-country against its will. Chief Mayor Dr. Strölin further greeted Privy Councilor Dr. Rödiger as the representative of the Reich's Ministry of Foreign Affairs and the Reich's Ministry of the Interior, whose presence must be taken as the sign of the Reich's special interest in the work of the Institute. He also greeted Senator Dr. Muth, the tried Führer of the Banat Germandom, and Privy Councilor Professor Dr. von Müller, the President of the German Academy." (Document 39–A, *post* pp. 461–462.)

Privy Councilor Dr. Rödiger, as representative of the Ministry of Foreign Affairs and Ministry of the Interior at the session, brought greetings from Foreign Minister von Neurath and stated that "both Ministries had always followed with great interest the work of the DAI".[80] (Document 39–A, *post* p. 462.)

Deputy Gauleiter Schmidt, representing Dr. Goebbels, stated, "The local party leadership [*Gauleitung*] is prepared to cooperate through thick and thin with the new officers of the DAI."[81] (Document 39–A, *post* p. 462.)

In the course of the 1933 annual meeting, Dr. Strölin read a telegram which had been sent to Reich's Chancelor Hitler:

"The assembled participants of the annual meeting of the Deutsches Ausland-Institut and the newly formed Board of Directors of the Institute greet *the Führer of the German people*. The entire Germandom abroad, accustomed to struggle in the defense of its cultural goods, reveres in you *the renovator of Germandom* and sees in your leadership *the guaranty for the*

---

[80] *Stuttgarter Neues Tagblatt*, Sept. 21, 1933.
[81] *Ibid.*

inseparable unity of Germandom abroad with the mother-country and for the expansion of all racial-German work." [82] (Document 39-A, *post* p. 461.)

Subsequently, Dr. Strölin read the following telegram from Hitler in reply:

"I sincerely thank the assembled participants of the DAI's annual meeting for the pledge of allegiance transmitted to me, and send my most cordial greeting. Signed, Adolf Hitler." [83] (Document 39-A, *post* p. 461.)

The public addresses delivered at that meeting illustrate the complete correspondence between the aims of the DAI and those of the Nazi Party, and contain further the explicit dedication of the DAI to the service of National Socialism. Minister-President Mergenthaler in an address, recorded by the *Stuttgarter Neues Tagblatt*, September 21, 1933, stated:

"The National Socialist movement has had a fructifying effect in all spheres of life. It has also given an entirely new impulse to the work for Germandom. The work for Germandom in foreign countries has thereby received the proper consecration and depth. In the past years of struggle it has often filled us with concern that the work for Germandom in foreign countries could not be carried on in close connection with the Brown fighters of National Socialism. The liberalistic ideology which has been overcome dealt with the formal concept of the citizen. We have gotten rid of that. Today the blood-united German racial-comrade stands in the center. That is the new foundation upon which we must build.

"The work for foreign Germandom must in the future proceed on a racial basis; otherwise it has lost the ground under its feet . . . New paths will be opened up for the work of Germandom by the new conception. The new conception will be a protective wall against the cultural and racial absorption of our comrades in other peoples. National Socialism will give energy to the German racial comrades. We are giving the Germans abroad therewith something enormously great. We also ought not to forget that the Germans abroad in a certain sense stand as guardians around us. Hence I want to impress on the Deutsches Ausland-Institut: Join us therefore in taking care that the spirit of National Socialism also become alive among the German racial-comrades in foreign countries, so that streams of energy may emanate from it!"
(Document 39-A, *post* pp. 462-463.)

The end of Dr. Csaki's annual report, as given in the *N. S. Kurier* of September 21, 1933, included the following:

"After sixteen years of its existence the DAI is concluding the first great span of its development. *The second stage*, upon

---

[82] *N. S. Kurier*, Sept. 21, 1933.
[83] *Stuttgarter Neues Tagblatt*, Sept. 21, 1933.

which we are entering, stands under the influence of the *great happenings in the German fatherland and the great psychic fulfilment of the entire German racial community*. It must and will be borne by the great ideas of the *education and mission of our Nation in foreign countries*. With every part of his [Dr. Csaki's] being he pledges himself to service for Germandom and to the work of the Institute, and *he vows* that it will be *accomplished in the spirit of the new state and in the sense of the National Socialist ideology*." (Document 39–A, *post* p. 464.)

After 1933 the DAI, although remaining nominally a private group, according to reliable sources became independent financially of the industrial and trade concerns engaged in foreign commerce which had previously supported it. Money was lavishly granted it by the German Government and by the city of Stuttgart, and other public funds were also put at its disposal. In this way, its operation could be directly controlled by the Nazi state.

Furthermore, there is direct evidence to show that the DAI worked directly with Nazi Party organizations, especially the Foreign Organization. It was doubtless a tribute to the work of the DAI and a further sanctification of it, when Hitler, on August 27, 1936, designated Stuttgart as the "City of Foreign Germans". At that time, too, Gauleiter Bohle, the head of the party's Foreign Organization, assumed protective sway (*Schirmherrschaft*) over Stuttgart. Furthermore, Dr. Ehrich, in his authoritative pamphlet entitled *The Foreign Organization of the NSDAP*, states explicitly that the DAI "works in hearty cooperation with the Foreign Organization".[84] (Document 23, *post* p. 305.) Also it is known that Dr. Karl Klingenfuss, the Director of the Foreign Organization's Department of Culture in 1937, was a prominent member of the DAI.

The Institute's role as an important adjunct of the party's Foreign Organization appeared especially in the work of indoctrination. The Institute not only gave schooling courses for Germans from abroad but also assisted in the training of the leaders and agents who carried on the party's work abroad. A confidential report on this special schooling work conducted by the DAI for the Foreign Organization states:

"All persons who in the future aspire to hold an office in the Foreign Organization abroad, such as that of *Landesgruppenleiter, Ortsgruppenleiter*, or some other Party function carrying with it the title of *Amtswalter* (office-holder), must now submit to a training course given in one of a number of so-called *Schulungslager* (indoctrination camps) where the candidates take up communal residence for brief periods, usually lasting a fortnight. Many of the present office-holders are indeed being brought

[84] Ehrich, *op cit.*, p. 30.

back to Germany to be lodged in one of these *Schulungslager*, or houses or camps, where they are given the necessary intensive grounding in the principles of National Socialism. It appears, moreover, that the younger men most recently admitted to the official foreign services, as well as those below a certain grade who are called back to serve in the Foreign Office, must also attend one of these camps in summer. (Their wives are schooled in special courses given locally in Berlin.) Not only are Party and Government officials serving abroad forced to submit to this training, but it appears that persons capable of exercising a cultural and professional influence abroad, such as ministers, doctors, lawyers, business leaders, and so forth, are encouraged and sometimes required to attend one of these camps, where Nazi doctrine is mixed with rigid military discipline.

"The Ausland-Institut plays a part in determining the curriculum of the *Schulungslager* as well as serving as an intermediary between the Party authorities who run these camps and Germans from abroad who are to attend them. Its facilities of various kinds are also put at the free disposal of persons of German extraction who visit the Reich and who may be counted upon to promote the National Socialist cause in foreign countries."

Most striking evidence of the relation between the DAI and the Nazi Party is furnished by the following passages from the previously mentioned January 1941 circular letter of the Kameradschaft U.S.A.:

"Collection of Documents Concerning the Movement:

"The collection of pictures, photos, handbills, pamphlets, newspaper clippings, and posters of the German national movement in the United States, which was begun by me in the spring of 1939, will be *continued*.

"The material already at hand is to be built up to a complete collection, which later is to be incorporated into the German Foreign Institute, as well as the Central Archives of the NSDAP in Munich, as an eternal record of our struggle in the United States."

(Document 22–A, *post* p. 278.)

3. VIEWS ON ASSIMILATION EXPRESSED AT DAI MEETING 1937

In accordance with its general nature, the DAI represented one of the foremost German agencies aiming to prevent the assimilation of Germans abroad into the populations of the foreign countries. At the twentieth annual meeting of the DAI held at Stuttgart on August 11–15, 1937, the subject of assimilation was one of the main topics discussed. This meeting was likewise attended by very prominent officials of the German Government, including Foreign Minister Baron von Neurath, Minister of the Interior Frick, and the Governor of Württemberg and his entire Cabinet; officials of the German party; representatives of Alfred Rosenberg's Party Office; and many other prominent persons. Hence the views expressed represented both German party-state officialdom and the DAI.

According to an entirely reliable confidential report, dated August 21, 1937, the German Minister of the Interior, Frick, in his address at the culminating reception of the meeting—

"declared that the new Germany has recognized that its attention and devotion to the welfare of the millions of Germans, who have not the fortune to owe political allegiance to Germany, but who are condemned to live abroad, are not merely a matter of natural sympathy and solidarity, but are in a higher degree dictated by the strong political and economic interests of the Reich. He protested strongly against attempts of foreign nations to assimilate German blood and argued that those nations, which realize that they will gain nothing by such endeavors, but which will recognize the aspirations of Germans living in their midst, will gain the friendship of the mighty German Reich, which will then be prepared to make economic concessions to them . . . Herr Frick also said that the principles of National Socialism, which are directing the cultural and political life of the German nation, will constitute in the future a source of strength and of confidence for millions of *Volksdeutsche* (persons of German blood) living in foreign countries."

Komrad Henlein, at that time leader of the German minority element in Czechoslovakia, was a prominent visitor at the assembly, speaking twice, once in public and once in private. Among his principal statements reported at that time were the following:

"Every person of German extraction regards the Third Reich as a source of strength in his struggle to retain his *Volkstum* [meaning in this sense: the community of all persons of German extraction throughout the world]; . . . the happiness and future of the Sudeten Germans, as well as all Germans in the world, are closely linked with those of the Third Reich; . . . solidarity with and loyalty towards Germany is not incompatible with citizenship in another country; . . . and we have the inalienable right to unite ourselves on the basis of blood with our German brethren and to form one great national family . . ."

In view of the later events in Czechoslovakia, and Henlein's activities in particular, one should note especially his bland assurance of the compatibility between loyalty toward Germany and citizenship in another country.

At an earlier gathering of this DAI meeting, the problem of the German element in the United States was the subject of a special discussion, led by Dr. Kroh, a professor at Tübingen University. According to the same report:

"His entreaty that every possible effort should be made by Germans living in the United States, regardless of allegiance, to preserve their mother tongue met with hearty approval by the whole assembly. He even argued that these efforts should be extended to the reestablishment of the German character which had been submerged in the great melting pot and that every endeavor should be made to guard against the dangers of bilingualism, which has a strong tendency ultimately to end in the triumph of the language of the country of residence."

During the period of the DAI's meeting, an article appeared on August 12, 1937 in the *N.S. Kurier*, the official National Socialist organ of Württemberg, under the title "German Youth in the United States". It appeared as a leader on the front page and was signed with the letter "K". According to reliable information, its author is Dr. Karl Klingenfuss, previously mentioned as Director of the Foreign Organization's Department of Culture and one of the leading members of the DAI. Among the passages of this article are the following:

> "And these German-Americans, who for centuries have made nothing but sacrifices for America, who have made valuable contributions to the culture of the country, and who were too good-natured and honest to interfere with politics and to secure rights for themselves and their nationality, are now prepared for a final struggle. While preserving their national characteristics and their German world-outlook they are prepared to incorporate themselves in the political life of America in order to be able to exercise a decisive influence on the formation of a new America.
>
> "Therefore, the program of this young body of German-Americans, regardless of what unions or organizations it may belong to, is:
>
> "We want to lead the Germans in the United States, who have become partly alienated from their German home country and from German nationality, back to the great community of blood and fate of all Germans. For this purpose a spiritual revival of Germans along the pattern of the old home country will be necessary.
>
> "After attaining this aim we want to organize the Germans in the United States, in order that their spiritual revival may be succeeded by economic recovery and political training."

USE OF ORGANIZED GERMAN MINORITIES

The more open organizational and ideologic features of the Nazi Party's Foreign Organization and its affiliates have hitherto been considered. Although somewhat beyond our general theme, it may not be amiss to set down here certain well-authenticated information concerning the subterranean activities abroad of these Nazi agencies. Since the express purpose of the NSDAP's Foreign Organization and its affiliates was to make every German abroad an active exponent of Naziism, adherence to and service for the Nazi goal of political domination were naturally implied. Notwithstanding all the specious protestations of the party's leaders, subsequent events have revealed the organized German minorities under Nazi control "boring within" foreign countries, undermining established governmental authority, weakening public morale, forwarding vital information to the German military authorities, and in general preparing the way for German military conquest and Gestapo rule.

It may be recalled here that the German minorities formed a considerable part of the German pretext for the destruction of Czechoslovakia and for the opening of hostilities against Poland, and later against Yugoslavia as well. In the course of events in central and eastern Europe during the past years, claims and acts of the organized German minorities have in every case synchronized with claims and acts of the German Reich.

This was especially true in the case of Czechoslovakia, as is well known. In an article in *Böhmen und Mähren*,[1] by SS Group Leader and State-Secretary K.H. Frank, dealing with the activities of the Nazi SS on March 15, 1939, it was even made clear that the Voluntary Protection Squad of the Sudeten German Party (*Freiwilliger Selbstschutz*) functioned as an auxiliary of the Nazi SS, performing various tasks essential to obtaining quick control of political authority in the country. On the day the German armed forces entered Czechoslovakia, and in the following days, many of the Sudeten German Party troopers were at once inducted into the Nazi SS, which had entered Czechoslovakia with the German Army. (Document 40, *post* p. 465.)

---

[1] *Böhmen und Mähren* (official periodical of the Reich's Protector of Bohemia and Moravia, published by State-Secretary and SS Group Leader K. H. Frank: Prague, May 1941), p. 179.

During the German campaign in Poland, according to all reports, the organized German minority functioned as a "fifth column" with great effectiveness, gathering military information, planting signals for the German air force, and undermining the morale of the Polish Army by diversionist activities.

An account published in July 1941 in *Deutsches Wollen*,[2] the magazine of the party's Foreign Organization, relates the activities of the Nazi Party group in Greece before and after the German Army entered Athens. After the entrance of the Germans, in the words of this group's leader, all the party members performed "auxiliary service with the Army". (Document 41, *post* p. 467.)

The following excerpts are taken from a confidential, reliable account, verified by other sources, of the many-sided German fifth-column activity in the Netherlands before the German invasion. Since these excerpts give a sketch of a whole situation, they are set down in proper sequence without interruption. Valuable details concerning the activities of Bohle's Foreign Organization are given, as well as illuminating remarks on Nazi propaganda and tactics. Of special interest, too, is the exposé of the Nazi Party's methods for maintaining its powerful hold on all Germans, in which are mentioned both the threats and inducements given by the Nazis to Germans living abroad in order to secure their loyalty and service. The tie-up with Netherlands Nazis and the clever use of disaffected Netherlanders, especially from among the unemployed, is also worthy of note.

"Few countries were more important in the pre-war Nazi strategy than Holland—and for very good reasons . . . For all these reasons it was imperative that the Nazi party members in the Netherlands be rigorously organized, and their knowledge and influence employed for the destruction of the Dutch morale. This was Dr. Butting's job.

"It was not a job at which any man could work openly. The Dutch government was democratic, wherefore it permitted the existence of a Dutch National-Socialist Party, and that party even had a handful of representatives in the Dutch Parliament. But Germans resident in Holland were forbidden by Dutch law to organize politically. This being so, both their organization and their leader had to work under cover. The cover for the Nazi party organization was an outwardly social and cultural body that went by the innocent name of *Reichsdeutsche Gemeinschaft*, the German Citizens' Association. Every member of this association was a member of the Nazi Party of Germany. The president of the association was Dr. Butting,—and the cover furnished Dr. Butting was an appointment as attaché of the German legation at The Hague.

---

[2] *Deutsches Wollen* (magazine of the Foreign Organization of the NSDAP: Berlin, July 1941), pp. 1ff.

". . . He [Butting] had first become a Nazi, then an ardent Nazi, and in the course of time an agitator in Austria. Among the unfortunate Austrians he had acquired such skill in the art of national disintegration (which is to say, fifth columnism), that, rising in the Party ranks, he was eventually rewarded with the high and lucrative post of *Landesgruppenleiter*, or National Group Leader, for Holland. . . . As Party leader for Holland he was in absolute fact the uncrowned king of every German national resident in that country. He reported solely and directly to Bohle, who was at one and the same time head of the Party's foreign organization and Assistant Secretary for Foreign Affairs.

.   .   .   .

"In 1938 the German legation owned two houses in The Hague. Both were of course the subject of diplomatic immunity and therefore inviolable as concerned search and seizure by the Dutch police. I shall call the house in which Dr. Butting had his office House No. 2.

"What went on in House No. 2? It had been remodelled and was divided like a two-family house—vertically, not horizontally; but between the two halves there was a communicating door. One side of the house was Dr. Butting's. The other half housed the Nazi military intelligence agent for Holland . . .

"S.B. [the military intelligence agent] may have had as many as a dozen subordinates working in Holland, all sub-agents of the Canaris bureau. These were professional spies who knew their trade. But they could not possibly know Holland as intimately as was required by the strategy of the German High Command, as it was revealed following the invasion of May 1940. For this, not a dozen but perhaps several hundred sources of information were necessary. And it is at this point that Butting and the military intelligence agent come together. Through his German Citizens' Association, Butting had a pair of Nazi eyes, a pair of Nazi ears, in every town and hamlet of the Netherlands. They were the eyes and ears of his minor party officials. Whenever the military intelligence agent needed information concerning a corner of Holland which his people had not yet explored, or was anxious to check information relayed to him by one of his own people, he would go to Butting.

"'Have you anybody along such-and-such a canal?' he would ask, 'or in such-and-such a town.'

"Butting always had.

"'Let me see the fellow's card,' S.B. would say. And having driven out to scrutinize the fellow (most often a party member, but sometimes a Hollander), having interviewed him and been satisfied with him, S.B. would mark him down as a *Vertrauensmann*, a man to be trusted. Through such a man he would learn, among other things, which of the Hollanders in the locality might be considered 'reliable.' The *Vertrauensmann* would not, however, become a Canaris sub-agent. If he were a Hollander, he would continue his work for the Dutch National-Socialist Party run by Mussert and Rost van Tonningen. If, as was more likely, he were a German, he would go on working

intermittently for S.B. but would continue his direct and normal
Party service as fifth columnist, that is, as a man who, standing
well in the Dutch community in which he lived, was able to
spread Nazi doctrine and win sympathy for the Nazis of
Germany and their way of life.

What S.B. learnt from one of his own people he checked with
a Butting man; and what the Butting men reported was unfail-
ingly checked with a military intelligence man, or by S.B. himself.

"'I know every stone in Holland,' S.B. once boasted. By
'stone' he meant canal, lock, bridge, viaduct, culvert, highway, by-road, airport, emergency landing field, and the name
and location of Dutch Nazi sympathizers who would help the
invading army when the time came. Had Dr. Butting's Party
organization not existed under the innocent cover of his Citizens' Association, S.B.'s knowledge of Holland would have
been as nothing compared with what it was. Thus the Citizens'
Association served a double purpose: it was invaluable for
espionage at the same time as it fulfilled its primary function
as a fifth column agency. Or, to put it more truly, there is no
such thing as fifth columnism divorced from espionage. Fused
and intertwined, they come to the same thing; and when you
permit fifth columnism, 'mere propaganda', you are at the same
time intensifying the espionage carried out against your country.

.   .   .   .

"There are a scattering of German schools in Holland—a high
school in The Hague and primary schools in other cities.
German children, but also the children of Hollanders and of
some members of the diplomatic corps, attended these schools.
The schools were subsidized by the Nazi Government. Their
teachers were sent out from Germany and were all Party members.
The curriculum was prescribed by Berlin and was exactly that
taught in Nazi Germany.

"Now the great danger of these schools—apart from the poison-
ing of young minds with ludicrous notions of race and history,
and Nazi doctrine generally—comes from the fact that, more than
any other category of German living abroad, these school teachers
are completely under the thumb of the Buttings. They are not
merely Germans and Nazis, they are civil servants participating
in a hierarchy and a pension system in which they cannot afford
to lose their rank and all the benefits accruing from their past
service . . .

"In Holland these teachers had still another function. Dr.
Butting maintained at House No. 2 an enormous *Kartothek*, a
card file, in which he registered everything that his agents knew
about the German population of Holland, as well as about non-
Germans. Having no wish to draw attention upon himself by
the presence of a large clerical staff in House No. 2, he obliged
the teachers to do his clerical work for him after hours . . .

"One of the most pitiful and skilful aspects of Dr. Butting's
domination in Holland was the control he possessed over the

German working population, even those who were indifferent to politics or secretly anti-Nazi.

"We had in Holland, you will recall, at least 100,000 Germans who had not surrendered, and by and large did not intend to surrender, their German nationality. As workers, whether clerks, craftsmen, common laborers, or even housemaids, they were all required by Nazi law to be members of the Labor Front. The Labor Front, you may have forgotten, is that Nazi government department which has replaced the outlawed labor unions of Germany, and administers the workers' insurance, benefit, and pension system first instituted . . . by Bismarck in the 1880's. In and out of Germany, every German worker must carry a Labor Front card and must have entered on that card the monthly contributions he makes to the Fund out of which the benefit payments are disbursed.

"Consider what a boon this represented to Dr. Butting. Who in Holland shall collect these social contributions? Who but the Party members? From whom collect? From every single German in Holland below the status of an executive or proprietor of his own business. Thus, leaving aside the refugees, who had lost their nationality, every German man and woman in Holland was known to Butting's Party men; every one was identified and his personal history summarized in that vast card file upon which the teachers spent their evenings.

"Now to be a German citizen and to be known to the Nazis is to be in the power of the Nazis. So long as you do not surrender your nationality, the Buttings are able to coerce or blackmail or bribe you into doing their bidding. They can break you, or they can induct you into the Party—exactly as these vest-pocket Robespierres choose. That you happen to reside outside instead of inside Germany makes no difference. You are their man; and this is of course especially true of the poor, for the poor by definition live in uncertainty, have no influential friends, and stand in constant dread of authority—whether it be the rent collector or the police.

"In the winter of 1938–39 Butting had received orders to repatriate to Germany, because of the war-economy labor shortage, literally thousands of German housemaids who had been working in Holland. The great card file was consulted, and Butting himself decided which women were to go and which were to be allowed to remain. Those who were most 'useful' to the Party stayed.

.   .   .   .

"It was not far different with the men of German nationality. Somehow, if you didn't toe the line you lost your job. And what then? Holland, like all countries without a war economy, had her share of unemployed. Jobs were scarce, and the foreign unemployed were instantly deported by the Dutch, who had no wish to extend the dole to them. So you found yourself back in Germany. What sort of work could you get in Germany if you were in Butting's black books? Labor camp work and no other.

"But there were other reasons than terrorism why you should submit to Dr. Butting. There were those little everyday reasons which play so large a part in our lives that we never think of them as decisive, never accord them the importance they possess. For example, you—and the women too—enjoy certain advantages by being a 'good' German, that is, at least outwardly a Nazi sympathizer. The 'Social Department' of the Citizens' Association through which your Labor Front dues were collected, also furnished you sports, recreation, and entertainment through its local branches. If you had to send money home to your family in Germany, 'the boys' knew where you could get a favorable exchange rate for your guilders. Suppose you were in funds, and went home to Germany for Christmas. You could get out of Holland all right; but the only way to be reasonably sure that you would be allowed back was to impress 'the boys' with the idea that you could make yourself useful to them. So you spied on your employer; you answered questions about what went on in your shop; you told 'the boys' that the regiment of the Dutch colonel in whose house you worked was being transferred to such-and-such a place next month; you let them know what Mynheer A., the shipping agent, had said about Hitler to Mynheer B., the oil man, at the club where you were a waiter. It didn't occur to you that by this system German morality as a whole was being sapped, that the German people were being turned into stool-pigeons and boot-lickers—merely that you stood in a little better with 'the boys' and had made a friendly gleam come for a moment into a Party official's eye that ordinarily was cold and suspicious. If, two months later at the club, you chanced to overhear that the shipping man was no longer agent for the German line his family had long represented, it meant nothing to you,—unless you were a very clever lad, in which case you were on the way to being one of 'the boys' yourself.

. . . .

". . . It was with the aid of this van Hoeven, and with the advice of certain members of the Dutch national-socialist party, that the Dutch unemployment records were carefully combed for men to be put to work in Germany. A selection was made of those young men who were at once the best workers and most disaffected spirits among the Dutch unemployed.

"The young men were shipped off to Germany and given work at fair wages. The foreign exchange regulations were relaxed in their favor, and they were permitted to send home to their families, in Dutch guilders, up to two-thirds of their pay. They were decently housed, quite well fed, and generously entertained with free beer, movies, and dances, sometimes three evenings a week, by the officials of the 'Strength Through Joy' movement or one of the other Nazi agencies for keeping up the spirits of the Nazi slaves at home. With their habitual cunning, the Nazis rotated these Dutch unemployed. They would keep a man in Germany, in these favorable conditions, not above six months, send him back, and replace him by another. The total turnover was about 80,000 men.

"When one of these men returned to Holland, and found himself again out of a job, he was more than ever dissatisfied with the government and employers of his own country, and more than ever an admirer of Nazi ways.   Often he became a member of the Dutch National-Socialist Party; and even if he did not, he became at least a non-resister of the German invasion . . .

"The result of this manoeuvre was something so extraordinary that it could have been foreseen only in the perverted imagination of its Nazi inventors.   In September 1939, after the Nazis had provoked war against England and France, actually hundreds of Dutchmen appeared at [the German] . . . legation in The Hague to offer their services to Nazi Germany in any capacity—many of them suggesting espionage.   Such was the intensity of the delusion implanted in thousands of Hollanders by the months they had spent in Germany.   Not until Holland was invaded in May 1940, many months later, did it become clear what S.B. had been able to do with these fellows.   Certainly they were among the Hollanders of every social stratum, high and low, who helped to welcome, shelter, and guide the German parachutist troops in whom they saw the saviors of their country.

.   .   .   .

"It was Nazi fifth columnism which saw the weaknesses in the Dutch democratic and capitalistic structure and exploited them. Because you are democratic and capitalistic, they preached, you have unemployment.   Because of this your rich foreign trade has dwindled.   Because of this you have governors who are weak and cowardly and not leaders of men.   Thus Nazi fifth columnism influenced the non-Nazi Hollander by making him skeptical of the value of his traditional Dutch institutions.   Without being actually disloyal to those institutions, the non-Nazi Hollander was not entirely sure that they were worth defending.   He was not absolutely certain that they would not, in reality, be swept away by a 'wave of the future' as the Nazis were constantly telling him they would be.   So he became not a Nazi, of course, but a passive non-resister, a man unsure of himself and of his world. This you may take to be gospel—it is not the converts but the doubters, the non-resisters, who explain the collapse of their nations.   And, the truly decisive product of fifth columnism is not the convert, it is the non-resister.

.   .   .   .

"Whereas in Germany itself the Nazi Party has been closed since 1934 or 1935, and virtually no new members admitted, it is still possible for a 'deserving' German living abroad to attain to the honor and achieve the material advantage of *Parteigenosse*, or Party member.   Out of 80,000,000 inhabitants there are only some 3,500,000 Party members in Greater Germany.   It goes without saying that, each on his own social level, they constitute the prosperous and the preferred class of present-day Germany . . .   Therefore, those Germans who cling to their nationality while they live abroad cannot but yearn to become Party members and enjoy the solid dollars-and-cents advantages of Party membership in the mother country. Any one of them who possesses the least tendency to unscrupulousness can be led round by the nose, if only the promise of Party membership is dangled before him as an eventual reward for his services to the Butting of the country in which he resides.

"The Party organization in Holland followed that at home as closely as its smaller numbers would permit. Under Dr. Butting served a corps of district leaders. Each district leader had his cluster of precinct captains, so to say. And each precinct captain was in command of his troops. In solemn imitation of the Party bureaucracy at home, the Party in Holland was administered by a large staff which included an almost comical variety of specialists (some of them high ranking Party dignitaries) . . .

"There was in Amsterdam a prime fifth column center called The German Chamber of Commerce for the Netherlands. Its officers were exclusively German and Nazi, and its president was a certain Dr. Flesche. Flesche was one of the High Fifteen of the Citizens' Association, a key man who served as a gushing fountain of information for the spy, S.B., even more than for Dr. Butting. It was he, as well as one Sperling, head of the German railway bureau, who were the chief consultants and sources of data for the special war-economy attaché in 1939 to the German Consulate in Amsterdam assigned to make a complete census of Dutch business properties. The same sort of census was taken by the same sort of specialist in other European countries; and it was thanks to the information they gathered that the High Command was able, after the invasion, to see that German supplies of raw materials and manufactures were promptly supplemented by the stocks present in the invaded countries. The same data, also, told the Nazi profiteers what foreign properties to 'buy up' with the paper currencies they issued in the invaded countries and forced upon the stockholders of the properties they coveted.

.   .   .   .

". . . Not as a committee, but individually, each ignorant of the fact that others were also working for the High Command, one German business man was appointed by S.B. agent for the quiet purchase of oil supplies on Nazi behalf; another was employed to engage cargo space in advance for the import of war materials to go to Germany; a third was sent into the market to pick up gold coin; and so on. All this was arranged in May and June 1939 when, having taken Czechoslovakia, the Nazis had made up their minds to risk war that summer and were hastening their final preparations.

.   .   .   .

"The simplest fashion in which the Nazi fifth column worked upon the Dutch business world was to eliminate executives unfriendly to the Nazi regime and replace them by their own tools. In the beginning the process was more or less haphazard, the Nazis being still uncertain how far they might go. As an actual plan, it matured only in 1938. In that year, for the first time, it was determined to get rid of Jews wherever possible *outside* Germany. After the Jews came other undesirables, from the Nazi point of view. And the interesting thing is that it was not the propaganda men but the military intelligence men who first saw the advantage of removing undesirables and replacing them by 'safe' people in foreign businesses.

.   .   .   .   .   .

"Nazi fifth columnism is a three-ring circus, built one ring inside the next. The innermost ring is represented by the normal espionage and intelligence service of the military establishment common to all governments. The middle ring is the Nazi Party organization with its affiliated agencies operating on foreign soil. And the outermost ring is the socio-economic situation of the workers and businessmen in the non-German country where the Nazi spies and fifth columnists are at work."

NAZI POLICY OF FORMING CORPORATE GERMAN MINORITIES IN CONQUERED EUROPE

Any consideration of the purpose of Nazi organs working among Germans in foreign countries must include an examination of the demonstrated Nazi policy in conquered Europe. Especially in eastern and southeastern Europe Nazi racial and political theories are now taking shape in clear policy, and the German minority organizations which had hitherto veiled their ultimate aims are now coming out into the open. There are many aspects to this policy and many far-reaching goals, as yet merely suggested. Two features, however, have definitely emerged, namely, that the German minorities under Nazi influence are gathering themselves together to form in each country compact Nazi-minded German racial entities, leading a separate corporate existence; and that these corporate minorities, professing a dual allegiance while in reality imbued with a single loyalty to Nazi Germany, are coming to function in each case as "a state within a state". The end of such a process must be the disruption of the national and political integrity of the countries involved, leading thereby to a complete German domination of each such country through the reciprocal interplay of the concentrated German minority and the Great German Reich.

German minorities, or *Volksgruppen* (folk-groups), have been organized in Slovakia, Hungary, Rumania, Croatia, and Serbia. All these *Volksgruppen* have been organized in an authoritarian Nazi way in accordance with the Führer principle, and with the usual affiliated Nazi formations and institutions. In each case, the general relation to the country involved is the same, although there are variations in accordance with the extent of the power which the Nazi Reich can exert. All negotiated arrangements are similar in one respect and differ therein from previous treaties concerning minorities, namely, in the fact that whereas previous agreements, such as those made in 1919, were concerned with the protection of the separate individuals, now the *Volksgruppe* as a whole, that is the organized corporate minority, is given the central position. In this regard, the German treaties for the protection of the folk-group (*Volksgruppenschutzverträge*) are believed to represent an entirely novel legal and constitutional arrangement.

On the basis of a brief protocol issued by the German and Rumanian Governments, an agreement was negotiated between the German minority in Rumania and the Rumanian state, the articles of which were announced October 23, 1940, as follows:

"1. The German folk-group in Rumania is declared to be a *legal person* according to public law. It bears the name 'German Folk-group in Rumania'.

"2. All Rumanian citizens belonging to the German people, who acknowledge their allegiance to the German people and are recognized by the leaders of the folk-group and enrolled in the national register of the German folk-group in Rumania, belong to the German folk-group in Rumania.

"3. The *'National Socialist Workers Party (NSDAP) of the German folk-group in Rumania'* expresses the will and constitutes the executive organ of the German folk-group.

"4. The German folk-group in Rumania, in agreement with the Government of the National Legionary State, decrees the laws concerning its own particular life and aiming at the preservation and strengthening of the German folk-group.

"5. The symbol of the allegiance of the German folk-group in Rumania to the German people is the flag of the German people. The symbol of the allegiance to the Rumanian state is the flag of the National Legionary State.

"6. The separate personality, here proclaimed, of the German folk-group in Rumania is anchored in the Constitution of the National Rumanian Legionary State.

"7. The leader of the German folk-group in Rumania and the Minister of Justice are entrusted with the execution of this decree." [1]

(Document 42, *post* p. 471.)

Interpreting this agreement, Dr. Otto Liess wrote in the official Nazi Party organ, *Nationalsozialistische Monatshefte*, of December 1940:

"The Legionary Rumania will respect as a new community the *separate personality of a folk-group* . . .

"The German folk-group can likewise in its *inner* problems look to a tradition of many centuries, and in its realm of action can aim at the ordering of the entire group. Consequently, it is no longer necessary to let the denominations administer the schools and education of the youth. The churches within the German folk-group of Rumania will have the opportunity to lay the emphasis of their work on their own particular realm, namely, care of souls. As a legal community, the folk-group *itself* will be able to look after political, economic, and social matters, without endangering the existence of the group as was the case in the Versailles interval. The meaninglessness of a strife within the common state is definitively set aside through the attainment of the new legal status of the folk-group." [2]

(Document 42, *post* p. 472.)

----

[1] *Nationalsozialistische Monatshefte* (foremost Nazi monthly, ed. by Alfred Rosenberg: Munich, Central Publishing House of the NSDAP, Dec. 1940), pp. 803–804.

[2] *Ibid.*, p. 804.

Extreme professions of allegiance to Nazi Germany, made by Andreas Schmidt, the leader of the German folk-group in Rumania, in a speech on February 9, 1941 at Hermannstadt are recorded as follows in a pan-Germanist publication:

"there is *no personal freedom* in a struggle in which the Great German Reich is being established! *In this struggle there is only the freedom of our own people.* Any personal freedom must be subordinated. Every thought and every action, which does not spring from the consciousness that the person is participating in the present work, is alien to us. And I believe that every breast is animated by the desire to participate in some way or other and to be able to say after the victory has been attained: 'I have also given something for this cause, even if it was only my personal freedom!' "

"My comrades, strengthen the relations between Germany and Rumania, not just by your convictions but by your deeds! Everyone must stand the test, when it is a matter of duty. Lay everything aside, my folk-comrades, which separates you from one another. *What unites us is greater, and that is the struggle of the German people for Great Germany!*" [3]
(Document 43, *post* p. 474.)

The German-Hungarian agreement is much more detailed than the German-Rumanian. Baron von Freytagh-Loringhoven, a member of the German Reichstag, sketches the German-Hungarian protocol as follows in the *Europäische Revue* of January 1941:

"The German folk-group is in it guaranteed the right to organize itself and form associations for special purposes, such as sport, care of the youth, etc. Likewise its authority is acknowledged in matters of economic self-help and the development of cooperatives. Its members may practice their vocations under the same presuppositions as the other Hungarian citizens. They have a claim on as many positions in the magistracy and the administrative bodies, as corresponds to their share in the total population. German officials are to be used preferably in the official posts in regions settled by Germans, and in the central offices superior to these. The children shall be assured the possibility of attending German schools, and care will be taken to train a sufficient number of good teachers. The free use of the German language will also be guaranteed. The German language will also be accepted in official matters in those administrative districts in which the members of the folk-group constitute one third of the entire population. The German press will not be subject to any restrictions which do not have general application. No measures will be taken which aim at Magyarization, and the members of the folk-group are to have the right to a free cultural intercourse with the motherland. On the other hand, the Government of the Reich recognizes that the members

---

[3] *Weltwacht der Deutschen* (pan-Germanist biweekly: Dresden-Hellerau, Mar. 1941).

of the folk-group are obligated to be loyal to the Hungarian state." [4]   (Document 44, *post* pp. 477–478.)

In this agreement, also, the knotty question concerning the determination of membership in the folk-group is settled by the criteria of individual declaration, combined with the consent of the folk-group organization.

In Slovakia the German folk-group is organized into the "German Party", with its "Voluntary SS" and other organs. The leader of the "German Party" and the German folk-group, Franz Karmasin, directs the German Department of State (*Staatssekretariat*), set up in October 1938.   (Document 45, *post* p. 480.)

In the new state of Croatia, the autonomy of the German folk-group and the powers of its leaders have perhaps been extended even further than elsewhere. According to a report in the official Nazi newspaper of Cracow, the *Krakauer Zeitung*, of June 25, 1941—

> "The Croatian state-leader Dr. Pavelitch has issued a law concerning the temporary *legal status of the German folk-group in Croatia*. The law proclaims the 'German Folk-group in the Independent State Croatia' a juristic person for public law. On the basis of equal rights with the members of the Croatian people, the Germans of Croatia are guaranteed the unrestricted preservation of their Germanism and the unimpeded belief in the National Socialist world-view, as well as the unhindered initiation and maintenance of national and cultural relations with the German motherland. The German folk-group can, according to need, set up organizations, units, and arrangements for free unhindered work in the political, economic, and social realm. The Croatian state-leader emphasized in an address that the law represents an expression of the friendly and brotherly relations between Croatia and the Great German Reich. At the occasion of the signing of the law, the Croatian state-leader and the German folk-group leader, Altgayer, sent a common message to the Führer. Further, the Foreign Minister Lorkovitch and the folk-group leader Altgayer sent a telegram to the Reich's Foreign Minister von Ribbentrop."

The final legal status of the German folk-group in Croatia and further details concerning its autonomy were reported in the Riga Nazi organ, *Deutsche Zeitung im Ostland*, of October 31, 1941, as follows:

> "In a solemn act of state on Thursday the Croatian state-leader signed laws concerning the legal status of the leader of the German folk-group, the use of the German language, and the employment in the Croatian public service of officials belonging to the German folk-group. This law represents the necessary supplement of the basic law concerning the legal status of the German folk-group, as well as the law concerning the German school system. The broad

---

[4] *Europäische Revue* (authoritative German monthly political review: Stuttgart, Jan. 1941), pp. 7–8.

law gives to the leader of the folk-group the powers of a director of the state, who within the framework of existing laws possesses the right of issuing decrees and is subordinate only to the Poglavnik [the Croatian leader].

"In all administrative units of the state in which the German population represents more than twenty percent of the total population, both German and Croatian are official languages. Official announcements and place and street names are to be in both languages. Where the German population exceeds ten percent, it has the right to use German in any official business. All Germans have the right to speak the German language, hoist the German flag, and sing the songs of the German nation, without hindrance. The honor of the German people, of the German language, and of German symbols, enjoys legal protection.

"Indigenous German officials are, as far as possible, to be appointed in the regions containing German settlements; indigenous German mayors are to be appointed in communities with a German majority."

The Nazi policy of forming organized German minorities has not at all been restricted to the countries of eastern Europe. In Denmark as well, under the German occupation, the same type of organization has been introduced among the Germans of North Schleswig. Here, too, we find a "German Party", under its leader, and with all the Nazi organizational paraphernalia. The ideologic orientation of these Danish citizens of German extraction was clearly expressed on January 19, 1941 in an address by Dr. Möller, the leader of the "German Party":

"By and large we may say at the end of the year 1940 that we have made a *big step forward.* We have completely reorganized the folk-group; . . . we have carried the National Socialist movement right into the whole folk-group.

.   .   .   .

"Our task must be to take care that the national lines in North Schleswig are not effaced. We serve singly and alone the Führer and the German swastika flag. . . . With regard to the future of our homeland and of our movement, we may be the greatest optimists. Adolf Hitler will shape the future of the new Europe, and in this future we also have our place, not as Europeans, but as Germans." [5]

(Document 46, *post* p. 481.)

The general Nazi claim of the right of the mother-state to protect its folk-groups in other countries and the diverse methods for its fulfilment—annexation, resettlement, folk-group agreements, diplomatic intervention, and retorsion—are set forth as follows in the closing passages of Freytagh-Loringhoven's article previously quoted:

"As important as the two Vienna protocols [agreements with Rumania and Hungary] are in themselves, their full meaning

---

[5] *Weltwacht der Deutschen* (Dresden-Hellerau, Feb. 1941).

is to be recognized, only when one considers them as an effect of the protective right [*Schutzrecht*] of the mother-state over its folk-groups. This protective right, that became formally a necessity after the breakdown of the inadequate Geneva protection of minorities caused by Poland, was proclaimed by the Führer in his speech before the Reichstag on February 20, 1938. It received the practical acknowledgment of the other great powers in the course of the Czech crisis and was the basis of the Munich Agreement of September 20, 1938. It was validated again in the Polish crisis and, along with the disputability of the Treaty of Versailles, formed the legal basis for the reannexation of West Prussia, Posen, and East Upper Silesia. Likewise it is to be considered as the legal basis for the treaties concerning resettlement, which Germany first concluded, and now, following its example, Bulgaria and Rumania have also concluded. Alongside of reannexation and resettlement, the treaty for the protection of the folk-group appears then as a third form for the realization of the protective right.

"In the cases, however, in which the presuppositions for one of these three forms are lacking, still a fourth possibility arises for the exercise of the protective right. This is diplomatic intervention, which if necessary can be supported by the means of pressure which are recognized in international law, especially by retorsion and reprisals. Of course, this possibility also existed formerly, before the recognition .of the protective right. But the essential difference lies therein that now such an intervention can be viewed not as inadmissible intrusion in the internal affairs of a foreign state but as representing the consequence of a right acknowledged by international law.

"Thus there are an abundance of practical ways in which the protective right of the mother-state has already been realized and can be realized in the future. From the standpoint of the German people that in the course of centuries has sent millions of its sons out in the world and unfortunately has lost a great part of them, whose suppression it has had to endure in silence, it may already be welcomed as one of the most valuable results of this war, that the Reich has now not only attained the possibility, but also the right, to stretch out its protective hand over its sons." [6]

(Document 44, *post* pp. 478–479.)

One phase of this Nazi *Volksgruppen* policy merits special attention, namely the systematic endeavor to retrieve for Germandom persons of remote German extraction, who have been completely assimilated in the populations of the countries where they reside. This has been practiced with particular energy in Poland and Rumania. Albert Forster, Governor and Gauleiter of Danzig - West Prussia, the new Nazi Province created largely out of annexed

---

[6] *Europäische Revue* (Stuttgart, Jan. 1941), pp. 8–9.

Polish territory, has stated in an article discussed in the *Krakauer Zeitung* of May 25–26, 1941, that the essential purpose—

> "is to take care that no drop of German blood be lost to the German people. It is certain, District Leader Forster emphasizes, that much German blood and therewith German *Volkstum* is present in the east. Unfortunately, it has been Polonized through the political events of the past and other influences. The conduct of the Polish clergy has been of decisive influence. When inscribing names in the church register, they have deliberately given a Polish form to the pure German family names of their parish children, so that today one can recognize often only with difficulty the former German core. To discover these Germans lost and made unrecognizable by Polish names and to remove this foreign disfigurement will now, corresponding to the general directions of the Reich's Minister of the Interior, be the most important future problem in the Province. Every family must be exactly examined, if one knows that it has a German parent or grandparent or that it has German relations in the old Reich, or if other evidence of German origin is at hand.
>
> "From such an examination has resulted, e.g. in the District Kulm, that of around eleven hundred families some six hundred were entirely or half of German origin. Of course, it is also decisive whether a family wants to become German, and whether in view of its racial appearance there is also some guaranty that it can become German. When one realizes that all the creative deeds among the different peoples of the European east go back to men with Nordic blood or at least to blood which has undergone strong Nordic influences, then it becomes clear how important it is not to let any man of our race and our blood be lost."

This same policy has also been employed with great energy in the part of Poland not directly annexed into Germany, known as the "Government General". The discovery of Polonized Germans around Zamosc in the Lublin District elicited prompt measures to re-Germanize them. The German settlements there date back to the end of the eighteenth century. As Lothar von Seltmann states in the official magazine of the VDA, *Deutsche Arbeit*, for September 1941:

> "it is a question here of men of German extraction, but the Polonization with respect to language and spirit is so far advanced that an almost complete slipping away into the foreign nationality has taken place." (Document 47, *post* p. 482.)

Careful research was made in order to ascertain which families had German blood in their veins. Then measures for re-Germanization were taken under the orders of the district SS and police leader, SS Brigade-Leader Globocnik. In this the local SS and police leader was functioning as a direct emissary of Heinrich Himmler, the German SS and police leader, who was entrusted on October 7, 1939 by Hitler with the fulfilment of Nazi ethnic policy, receiving the title "Reich's Commissar for the Strengthening of the German Nationality"

(*Reichskommissar für die Festigung deutschen Volkstums*).   German school teachers were imported and German BDM groups (Bund Deutscher Mädel, the Nazi girls' organization) were brought into the villages to give instruction "in Germanism and social matters".

As Von Seltmann states the matter:

> "The basic principle for this work of retrieving the Germans is: Those of German origin are to be given pride in their origin, and a consciousness of their origin which is still often present is to be nourished.   They must feel that they are a community amidst a foreign environment.   In order to deepen this feeling of community, the leader of the SS and the police is publishing a small magazine, 'Letters of Colonists', for these villages.   Through the juxtaposition of German and Polish texts, and through the easily comprehensible articles, designed for self-instruction, this magazine moreover facilitates the relearning of German."   (Document 47, *post* p. 484.)

Summing up the success of these endeavors,

> "With regard to language, naturally the descendants of the Zamosc Germans still have much to learn, but their village communal life already exhibits today again the old German colonial spirit, which had been buried.
> "Thus a valuable 'fragment of our people', which through no fault of its own had slid off into a foreign nationality, is being rewon in the Lublin District for the German folk."
> (Document 47, *post* p. 484.)

A report in the *Krakauer Zeitung* of June 15, 1941 of a speech of SS Brigade-Leader Globocnik contains the following with regard to the retrieval of assimilated Germans in the Zamosc District:

> "He announced thereby that at the end the colonists as also their villages shall again receive old German names.   Finally Globocnik outlined a plan according to which all the villages in which those of German race are discovered shall encompass a larger territory which will be determined as a purely German region of settlement. In this new German region of the Lublin District, all those still recognizable as belonging to the German race together with the Germans already settled here shall re-attain the German form of life and attitude of mind, whereby in the course of time also all the institutions of the National Socialistic form of life shall be introduced."   (Document 48, *post* p. 486.)

The following extract from a report of a speech by Andreas Schmidt, leader of the German folk-group in Rumania, which appeared in the *Weltwacht der Deutschen* for March 1941, reveals the employment of the same practices in Rumania:

> "Schmidt described how there are people in this Province [the new Gau Bergland, formed from parts of Transylvania and the Banat], who only speak a few words of German but whose belief in Germanism is unbounded.   'Seek out these people in order to

receive them again in your midst. The question, whether they can speak German now as you, is not decisive, rather that they bear the same blood in their veins, have the same physiognomy, and the same clear eyes. When I appeal today for the comradeship of all folk-members, I do this because it is the duty of every German in this region to help bring back in this new Province the conditions that formerly prevailed here'." (Document 43, *post* p. 475.)

The full implications of Nazi theories and practices for the United States and the real meaning of pronouncements by Nazi-minded spokesmen can only be understood on the background of the actual Nazi *Volksgruppen* and de-assimilation policy in conquered Europe.

The German short-wave radio is accustomed to transmit programs in German designed for Germans abroad. On January 27, 1942 an unnamed radio broadcaster in Berlin spoke to Germans abroad in a special program, recorded in the daily report of January 27, 1942 of the Foreign Broadcast Monitoring Service of the Federal Communications Commission. The blind obedience, fanatical zeal, and absolute allegiance to Hitler and Germany maintained among Nazi Germans abroad, as well as their duplicity toward the country of their residence, are revealed thus in the words of the Berlin radio speaker:

"Only when people abroad had to recognize that National Socialism is a matter of the racial German, that it would not stop because of arbitrary geographical or political boundaries, but only where there are no more German people, only then people began to occupy themselves with the problem of this novel phenomenon, with which no equivalent could be compared in the traditional politics of the parliaments and parties.

"They may accuse us of being the agents of the Fifth Column; they may equate us with spies and saboteurs. Let one thing be said here again: We are not agents in the traditional sense, but every one of us is an exponent of National Socialist philosophy. If today it is essential to win this great and world-wide conflict, to seize the enemy by his roots, then no one knows better than the German National Socialist abroad with whom he has to deal . . . No abuse and no denunciation, neither prison nor internment camp, can make us waver. When the Fuehrer calls, we are at hand . . ."

APPENDIX

LIST OF DOCUMENTS

(German Documents Reproduced Photographically)

PART I

151

DOCUMENT 1

(Summary)

Verfassungsrecht des Grossdeutschen Reiches (Constitutional Law of the Greater German Reich), by Ernst Rudolf Huber: Hamburg, Hanseatische Verlagsanstalt, 1939

Through an analysis of the development of the constitution of the Third Reich and its application in the laws and decrees of Nazi Germany, the author offers an unusually clear presentation of the basic principles of the National Socialist movement.

He begins with a study of the Weimar Constitution and its weaknesses, against which all the early struggles of the National Socialist Party were directed. After the failure of the Munich *Putsch* in 1923, the party, he says, abandoned violence as a means to power and sought to destroy the Republic through its own machinery: "The parliamentary battle of the NSDAP had the single purpose of destroying the parliamentary system from within through its own methods. It was necessary above all to make formal use of the possibilities of the party-state system but to refuse real cooperation and thereby to render the parliamentary system, which is by nature dependent upon the responsible cooperation of the opposition, incapable of action." With its gradual increase in parliamentary strength, the party was able to achieve these aims: "It was in a position to make the formation of any positive majority in the Reichstag impossible . . . Thus the NSDAP was able through its strong position to make the Reichstag powerless as a lawgiving and government-forming body."

The frantic efforts of the governments of Bruning, Von Schleicher, and Von Papen to oppose these tactics by themselves abandoning parliamentary methods and assuming dictatorial powers were unable to stem the rising tide of National Socialism, which swept all parliamentary and popular support from under their feet. When the true nature of the situation had become fully evident, President von Hindenburg finally called the Führer of the National Socialist Party to the chancelorship. This was the culmination of a revolution which was none the less real and far-reaching because it was accomplished within the legal framework of the system which it overthrew. It is therefore ridiculous to maintain, as some do, that the Weimar Constitution is still in force and that the National Socialist regime is merely a sort of temporary emergency order: "It is the nature of revolution that the previous constitution should be destroyed and that a new basic order should take its place. The National Socialist revolution cast aside the entire system of the Weimar Constitution and at the same time established the new Nationalist Constitution."

The first laws of the new regime were enacted under the old legal machinery, but these were the very laws which formed the formal basis of the new constitution. Certain provisions of the Weimar Constitution were found still useful and were consequently taken over, but they took on an entirely new significance in relation to the new system as a whole. The old constitution was never formally renounced, but its renunciation was implied in the seizure of power by National Socialism: "The name Adolf Hitler is in itself a program of which total and deadly war against the Weimar system is the nucleus."

"The new constitution of the German Reich . . . is not a constitution in the formal sense such as was typical of the nineteenth century. The new Reich has no written constitutional declaration, but its constitution exists in the unwritten basic political order of the Reich. One recognizes it in the spiritual powers which fill our people, in the real authority in which our political life is grounded, and in the basic laws regarding the structure of the state which have been proclaimed so far. The advantage of such an unwritten constitution over the formal constitution is that the basic principles do not become rigid but remain in a constant, living movement. Not dead institutions but living principles determine the nature of the new constitutional order."

Part II deals with the formation of the Greater German Reich in the years 1938–39 and attempts to demonstrate the illegality and unconstitutionality of the Austrian and Czechoslovakian states. Austrian history is reviewed from 1918 to 1938 with special emphasis on the Allied Powers' disregard of the right of self-determination, as promised in Wilson's 14 points, and their efforts to prevent Germany and Austria from drawing together, manifested in the Treaties of Versailles and St. Germain, the Geneva Protocol of 1922, and the Lausanne Protocol of 1932. The Austrian Federal Constitution, which was in force from 1920 to 1933 "corresponded in its principal features to the Weimar Constitution of Germany". It was overthrown by the arbitrary power of the Dollfuss regime, the sole purpose of which was to hinder the National Socialist movement and to prevent union with Germany. The Dollfuss regime is pictured as a government without popular support or any claim to legitimacy. The people were given no opportunity to approve or disapprove the constitution which was proclaimed in 1934. Of the 1934 revolt Huber writes: "The unbounded oppression and mistreatment of the German people in Austria by a dictatorial regime led on July 25, 1934 to an attempt to overthrow this illegal power by an uprising of the people. By means of its stronger police and military forces the regime succeeded in maintaining itself. There followed a reign of terror against the participants in the revolt." Schussnigg is pictured as continuing and intensifying the same policy, which reached its culmination in the attempted illegal plebiscite of March 1938 that brought the situation to a head and called forth the occupation of Austria by German troops. The proclamation of Austria's union with the German Reich by the government of Seyss-Inquart is described as "the last sovereign act of the independent state of Austria". It was also proclaimed as a law of the German Reich. This *fait accompli* was submitted to the whole German people for approval in the plebiscite of April 10, 1938. The *Anschluss* was naturally construed as dissolving all treaties and obligations of Austria which were not in the interests of Greater Germany, including the loans which had been made to Austria to help her maintain her independence. Austria became a province of the Greater German Reich and her own constitution at once lost its validity, but her own laws remained in effect and were replaced gradually by German law through single proclamations and decrees. The Führer's representative, Gauleiter Bürckel, was given full authority over state and party during the period of the "reunification" of Austria with Germany.

The overthrow of Czechoslovakia is given a very similar treatment. First Huber writes of the denial of the right of self-determination to the Sudeten Germans after the World War: He tells of the "unconstitutional" suppression of them during the succeeding years through measures affecting their language and schools, denying them self-rule, confiscating their property through land reforms and defense laws, placing border regions under special restrictions, etc. Then he reviews the events leading up to the Munich conference of September 30, 1938, where "the 20-year oppression and distress of the Sudeten Germans were overcome by the strength and unswerving certainty of the German will". In general the reunion of the Sudetenland with the Reich followed the same procedure as in the case of Austria, except that here the old civil organization could not be taken over and modified gradually but an entire new organization had to be built up from nothing. There follows a review of the laws which had been proclaimed for Austria and the Sudetenland up to May 1939, covering social institutions, economic and financial life, the civil services, agriculture and land administration, etc.

The formation of the Protectorate of Bohemia and Moravia was preceded by the complete inner collapse of the rump Czechoslovakia owing to its inability to cope with the problem of its divergent national groups. There was "a renewed terror against the remaining Germans" and the Slovaks found that they were still denied the measure of autonomy which they demanded. On March 14, 1939 Slovakia declared its independence, and on the following day the Germans occupied Bohemia and Moravia in order to "preserve order in central Europe". It was an entirely new sort of protectorate which was set up here: Since the Protectorate is a part of the Reich and fully subject to the authority of the Reich, the protective relation seeks no justification in international law. Theoretically, however, the Protectorate has a good deal of autonomy and the Czech people is supposed to rule itself and develop its own culture. The Reich exercises full control over foreign policy, trade and tariffs, and finance. It can also exercise lawgiving power when deemed necessary for the common good. Representatives of the Reich have the highest administrative and police authority.

Greater Germany, at the time this book was published, also included Memel. Although Memel had been guaranteed autonomy by an international convention in 1924, she had fallen increasingly into the grasp of Lithuania. In view of her recent successes, Germany was now strong and influential enough to impose her will upon Lithuania in the treaty of March 22, 1939, which returned Memel to Germany.

The next three sections of the book develop the three great concepts which underlie the National Socialist state—the people, the Führer, and the movement—as well as the principles which are derived from them and their application in the laws of the Third Reich.

The democracies develop their concept of the people from the wrong approach: They start with the concept of the state and its functions and consider the people as being made up of all the elements which fall within the borders or under the jurisdiction of the state. National Socialism, on the other hand, starts with the concept of the people, which forms a political unity, and builds the state upon this foundation.

> "There is no people without an objective unity, but there is also none without a common consciousness of unity. A people is determined by a number of different factors: by racial derivation and by the character of its land, by language and other forms of life, by religion and history, but also by the common consciousness of its solidarity and by its common will to unity. For the concrete concept of a people, as represented by the various peoples of the earth, it is of decisive significance which of these various factors they regard as determinants for the nature of the people. The new German Reich proceeds from the concept of the political

people, determined by the natural characteristics and by the historical idea of a closed community. The political people is formed through the uniformity of its natural characteristics. Race is the natural basis of the people . . . As a political people the natural community becomes conscious of its solidarity and strives to form itself, to develop itself, to defend itself, to realize itself. 'Nationalism' is essentially this striving of a people which has become conscious of itself toward self-direction and self-realization, toward a deepening and renewing of its natural qualities.

"This consciousness of self, springing from the consciousness of a historical idea, awakens in a people its will to historical formation: the will to action. The political people is no passive, sluggish mass, no mere object for the efforts of the state at government or protective welfare work . . . The great misconception of the democracies is that they can see the active participation of the people only in the form of plebiscites according to the principle of majority. In a democracy the people does not act as a unit but as a complex of unrelated individuals who form themselves into parties . . . The new Reich is based on the principle that real action of a self-determining people is only possible according to the principle of leadership and following."

Geographical considerations play a large part in the shaping of a people: "The people stands in a double relation to its lands; it settles and develops the land, but the land also stamps and determines the people . . . That a certain territory belongs to a certain people is not justified by state authority alone but it is also determined objectively by its historical, political position. Territory is not merely a field for the exercise of state control but it determines the nature of a people and thereby the historical purpose of the state's activity. England's island position, Italy's Mediterranean position, and Germany's central position between east and west are such historical conditions, which unchangeably form the character of the people." But the new Germany is based upon a "unity and entirety of the people" which does not stop at geographical boundaries. "The German people forms a closed community which recognizes no national borders. It is evident that a people has not exhausted its possibilities simply in the formation of a national state but that it represents an independent community which reaches beyond such limits." The state justifies itself only so far as it helps the people to develop itself more fully. In the words of Hitler, quoted from *Mein Kampf*, " 'It is a basic principle, therefore, that the state represents not an end but a means. It is a condition for advanced human culture but not the cause of it . . . Its purpose is in the maintenance and advancement of a community of human beings with common physical and spiritual characteristics.' "

"In the theory of the nationalistic [*völkisch*] Reich, people and state are conceived as an inseparable unity. The people is the prerequisite for the entire political order; the state does not form the people but the people moulds the state out of itself as the form in which it achieves historical permanence . . . The state is a function of the people, but it is not therefore a subordinate, secondary machine which can be used or laid aside at will. It is the form in which the people attains to historical reality. It is the bearer of the historical continuity of the people which remains the same in the center of its being in spite of all changes, revolutions, and transformations."

Citizenship in the National Socialist Reich is dependent first of all upon racial considerations and then upon loyalty. Not all subjects of the state are citizens of the Reich. Persons who are not members of the "race" cannot be citizens. Only citizens can vote in the plebiscites or hold any kind of public office. Anyone who is considered disloyal to the Reich can be deprived of citizenship. Citizenship can be acquired by foreign women of Germanic origin who marry Germans, and persons of Germanic descent may also be naturalized. There follows a review of the laws regarding naturalization or loss of citizenship in the Third Reich, a summary of the anti-Jewish laws, and a discussion of the position of foreign national groups within the Third Reich. With regard to the latter question, the agreement of 1937 between Poland and Germany is held up as a model for the settlement of such problems. German policy in this matter, it is maintained, is based on a recognition of the rights of others which springs from the German's own devotion to his nationality.

This section concludes with a chapter on "the symbols of national unity", their history and significance: the flag; the German eagle; the military and party uniforms; various medals and decorations; the national anthem; etc.

In the next section the National Socialist conception of the Führer and his relation to people, party, and state is developed in great detail:

"The Führer Reich of the [German] people is founded on the recognition that the true will of the people cannot be disclosed through parliamentary votes and plebiscites but that the will of the people in its pure and uncorrupted form can only be expressed through the Führer. Thus a distinction must be drawn between the supposed will of the people in a parliamentary democracy, which merely reflects the conflict of the various social interests, and the true will of the people in the Führer-state, in which the collective will of the real political unit is manifested . . .

"The Führer is the bearer of the people's will; he is independent of all groups, associations, and interests, but he is bound by laws which are inherent in the nature of his people. In this twofold condition: independence of all factional interests but unconditional dependence on the people, is reflected the true nature of the Führer principle. Thus the Führer has nothing in common with the functionary, the agent, or the exponent who exercises a mandate delegated to him and who is bound to the will of those who appoint him. The Führer is no 'representative' of a particular group whose wishes he must carry out. He is no 'organ' of the state in the sense of a mere executive agent. He is rather himself the bearer of the collective will of the people. In his will the will of the people is realized. He transforms the mere feelings of the people into a conscious will . . . Thus it is possible for him, in the name of the true will of the people which he serves, to go against the subjective opinions and convictions of single individuals within the people if these are not in accord with the objective destiny of the people . . . He shapes the collective will of the people within himself and he embodies the political unity and entirety of the people in opposition to individual interests . . .

"But the Führer, even as the bearer of the people's will, is not arbitrary and free of all responsibility. His will is not the subjective, individual will of a single man, but the collective national will is embodied within him in all its objective, historical greatness . . . Such a collective will is not a fiction, as is the collective will of the democracies, but it is a political reality which finds its expression in the Führer. The people's collective will has its foundation in the political idea which is given to a people. It is present in the people, but the Führer raises it to consciousness and discloses it . . .

"In the Führer are manifested also the natural laws inherent in the people: It is he who makes them into a code governing all national activity. In disclosing these natural laws he sets up the great ends which are to be attained and draws up the plans for the utilization of all national powers in the achievement of the common goals. Through his planning and directing he gives the national life its true purpose and value. This directing and planning activity is especially manifested in the lawgiving power which lies in the Führer's hand. The great change in significance which the law has undergone is characterized therein that it no longer sets up the limits of social life, as in liberalistic times, but that it drafts the plans and the aims of the nation's actions . . .

"The Führer principle rests upon unlimited authority but not upon mere outward force. It has often been said, but it must constantly be repeated, that the Führer principle has nothing in common with arbitrary bureaucracy and represents no system of brutal force, but that it can only be maintained by mutual loyalty which must find its expression in a free relation. The Führer-order depends upon the responsibility of the following, just as it counts on the responsibility and loyalty of the Führer to his mission and to his following . . . There is no greater responsibility than that upon which the Führer principle is grounded."

The nature of the plebiscites which are held from time to time in a National Socialist state cannot be understood from a democratic

standpoint. Their purpose is not to give the people an opportunity
to decide some issue but rather to express their unity behind a decision which the Führer, in his capacity as the bearer of the people's
will, has already made:

> "That the will of the people is embodied in the Führer does
> not exclude the possibility that the Führer can summon all
> members of the people to a plebiscite on a certain question. In
> this 'asking of the people' the Führer does not, of course, sur-
> render his decisive power to the voters. The purpose of the
> plebiscite is not to let the people act in the Führer's place or to
> replace the Führer's decision with the result of the plebiscite.
> Its purpose is rather to give the whole people an opportunity
> to demonstrate and proclaim its support of an aim announced
> by the Führer. It is intended to solidify the unity and agree-
> ment between the objective people's will embodied in the Führer
> and the living, subjective conviction of the people as it exists
> in the individual members . . . This approval of the Führer's
> decision is even more clear and effective if the plebiscite is con-
> cerned with an aim which has already been realized rather than
> with a mere intention."

The Reichstag elections in the Third Reich have the same character as the plebiscites. The list of delegates is made up by the
Führer and its approval by the people represents an expression of
renewed and continued faith in him. The Reichstag no longer has
any governing or lawgiving powers but acts merely as a sounding
board for the Führer: "It would be impossible for a law to be
introduced and acted upon in the Reichstag which had not originated
with the Führer or, at least, received his approval. The procedure
is similar to that of the plebiscite: The lawgiving power does not
rest in the Reichstag; it merely proclaims through its decision its
agreement with the will of the Führer, who is the lawgiver of the
German people."

The development of "the office of the Führer" is presented in its
growth from the leadership of the movement to its present position
of absolute control over all national affairs, culminating in the supreme command over the armed forces:

> "The office of the Führer developed out of the National So-
> cialist movement. It was originally not a state office; this fact can
> never be disregarded if one is to understand the present legal
> and political position of the Führer. The office of the Führer
> first took root in the structure of the Reich when the Führer
> took over the powers of the Chancelor, and then when he as-
> sumed the position of the Chief of State. But his primary
> significance is always as leader of the movement; he has ab-
> sorbed within himself the two highest offices of the political
> leadership of the Reich and has created thereby the new office
> of 'Führer of the people and the Reich'. That is not a

superficial grouping together of various offices, functions, and powers . . . It is not a union of offices but a unity of office. The Führer does not unite the old offices of Chancelor and President side by side within himself, but he fills a new, unified office."

There follows a long analysis of the powers of the Führer in the various departments of national life: legal and judicial, diplomatic, military, executive, economic, etc. There is also a list of the various Ministries responsible to the Führer and an outline of their functions. These arrangements are the expression and the application of the Führer-state's unwritten constitution and the entire discussion of them serves simply to demonstrate the universality of the Führer's power within the National Socialist Reich:

"The Führer unites in himself all the sovereign authority of the Reich; all public authority in the state as well as in the movement is derived from the authority of the Führer. We must speak not of the state's authority but of the Führer's authority if we wish to designate the character of the political authority within the Reich correctly. The state does not hold political authority as an impersonal unit but receives it from the Führer as the executor of the national will. The authority of the Führer is complete and all-embracing; it unites in itself all the means of political direction; it extends into all fields of national life; it embraces the entire people, which is bound to the Führer in loyalty and obedience. The authority of the Führer is not limited by checks and controls, by special autonomous bodies or individual rights, but it is free and independent, all-inclusive and unlimited. It is not, however, self-seeking or arbitrary and its ties are within itself. It is derived from the people; that is, it is entrusted to the Führer by the people. It exists for the people and has its justification in the people; it is free of all outward ties because it is in its innermost nature firmly bound up with the fate, the welfare, the mission, and the honor of the people."

A basic principle of the new constitution is the unity between the party and the state. Soon after the rise to power in 1933, steps were taken to establish and insure this unity:

"On July 14, 1933 was issued the law against the formation of new parties which raised the NSDAP to the only political party in Germany . . . The overthrow of the old party-state was accompanied by the construction of the new movement-state [*Bewegungsstaat*]. Out of a political fighting organization the NSDAP grew to a community capable of carrying the state and the nation. This process was accomplished step by step in the first months after the National Socialist seizure of power. The assumption of the office of Chancelor by the Führer of the movement formed the basis for this development. Various party leaders were appointed as *Reichsminister;* the governors of the provinces were national leaders or *Gauleiter* of the party, such

as General von Epp; the Prussian government officials are as a
rule *Gauleiter* of the party; the Prussian police chiefs are mostly
high-ranking SA leaders. By this system of a union of the
personnel of the party and state offices the unity of party and
state was achieved."

These measures were directed against the weaknesses of the Weimar
Republic, "which was founded not on unity of the people but on
internal division, not on a common philosophy but on the deadly
struggle of opposed philosophies, not on a selected Führer-class but
on the leveling process of the functionary system in the party state".
The Third Reich, however, cannot correctly be called a "one-party
state". This term is applicable to a state such as Soviet Russia, in
which a party representing the interests only of one part of the
people imposes itself on the whole nation.

> "The aim of the National Socialist movement is the national-
> istic Reich: that is, a state of which the nature and development
> is determined by the idea of the people, for which the people
> is the substance of political unity, of which the inward and out-
> ward strength is drawn from the whole people, and which is
> supported by the whole people . . . The people and the party
> in the National Socialist Reich are a unit, not in the sense that
> every citizen must be a member of the party, but in the sense
> that the movement is only possible as the visible embodiment and
> realization of the all-embracing unity of the people. The totality
> of National Socialism is not to be explained therein that all fields
> of life are penetrated by the political will of the movement but
> that all members of the people are expected to take part in the
> common political life and to share in the determination of the
> common political fate."

In the nationalistic state certain definite tasks are assigned to the
party. These are described as "the education of the people to a
political people" through awakening the political consciousness of
each individual; the inculcation of a "uniform political philosophy",
that is, of National Socialist principles; "the selection of leaders",
including the choice and training of especially promising boys to be
the Führers of the future; and the shaping of "the political will of
the people" in accordance with the Führer's aims. There follows a
review of the laws covering the relation of the party and its organizations to the state, returning to "the valid constitutional principle
of the Reich that the important state offices should be filled with men
who hold the party offices of the same rank". A special legal status
is granted to party officials, who are regarded as public officials even
if they do not hold state offices.

In the reorganization of the Reich under National Socialism one
of the most important tasks was to remove all traces of the "1000-
year-old federal structure of the Reich" and to strengthen national

unity by destroying all reminders that the various provinces had formerly been independent states. Even under the Weimar Republic a good measure of independence had been left to the provincial governments, but now the entire Reich was brought under a uniform legal and administrative code, with final authority in all matters resting in the central government. Such a process would imply an equal footing for all provinces of the Reich, but there is an evident intention to retain for Prussia her leading position and to Prussianize the rest of the Reich:

> "Prussia and Prussianism are permanent basic concepts of German political theory and practice which will remain strong and influential in the Reich even if Prussia should cease to exist as a unit in a territorial sense. Not the destruction of Prussia but the organic penetration of the Prussian political spirit throughout the whole Reich is the program for the reconstruction of the Reich."

The laws designed to merge certain special territories (the Saar, Hamburg, Austria, and the Sudetenland) into the Reich are analyzed, as well as the position and duties of the provincial governors, who receive their authority directly from the Führer and stand in much the same relation to the province as the Führer does to the nation:

"The provincial governor [*Reichsstatthalter*] is not a functionary of the province but of the Reich . . . It is not his duty to represent the interests of the province as opposed to those of the Reich, but it is his exclusive function to carry out the policies of the central government in his province" and all special interests of the various provinces must be subordinated to and brought into line with the interests of the Reich as a whole.

In a section entitled "The Legal Position of the Individual Citizen [*Volksgenosse*]", Huber develops the concepts with which National Socialism seeks to supplant the democratic conceptions of personal liberty and individual rights:

> "Not until the nationalistic political philosophy had become dominant could the liberalistic idea of basic rights be really overcome. The concept of personal liberties of the individual as opposed to the authority of the state had to disappear; it is not to be reconciled with the principle of the nationalistic Reich. There are no personal liberties of the individual which fall outside of the realm of the state and which must be respected by the state. The member of the people, organically connected with the whole community, has replaced the isolated individual; he is included in the totality of the political people and is drawn into the collective action. There can no longer be any question of a private sphere, free of state influence, which is sacred and untouchable before the political unity. The constitution of the nationalistic Reich is therefore not based upon a system of inborn and inalienable rights of the individual."

In place of these rights the constitution of the Third Reich guarantees to the individual his place in the community of the people:

> "The legal position of the individual member of the people forms an entirely new concept which is indispensable for the construction of a nationalistic order. The legal position of the individual is always related to the community and conditioned by duty. It is developed not for the sake of the individual but for the community, which can only be filled with life, power, and purpose when a suitable field of action is insured for the individual member. Without a concrete determination of the individual's legal position there can be no real community.
>
> "This legal position represents the organic fixation of the individual in the living order. Rights and obligations arise from the application of this legal position to specific individual relationships . . . But all rights must be regarded as duty-bound rights. Their exercise is always dependent upon the fulfilment by the individual of those duties to which all rights are subordinate . . .
>
> "It is a mistake to claim that the citizen of the Reich has no rights but only duties; that there is no right of choice but only a duty of acclamation. There are, of course, no inborn, inalienable political rights which are inherent in the individual himself and which would tend to limit and hamper the leadership of the Reich. But in every true political community the individual has his legal position which he receives from the Führer and which makes him a true follower."

These principles are applied likewise to all groups and associations and to all social institutions: "Marriage and the family . . . are no longer private relationships between individuals but they are the cornerstones in the construction of the nationalistic community and the materials of the basic order of the new Reich."

> " 'Private property' as conceived under the liberalistic economic order was a reversal of the true concept of property. This 'private property' represented the right of the individual to manage and to speculate with inherited or acquired property as he pleased, without regard for the general interests . . . German socialism had to overcome this 'private', that is, unrestrained and irresponsible view of property. All property is common property. The owner is bound by the people and the Reich to the responsible management of his goods. His legal position is only justified when he satisfies this responsibility to the community."

Property may be confiscated whenever the state decides that public management would be in the interests of the community or the owner is found guilty of irresponsible management. In the latter case no compensation is paid.

The legal position of the worker is also conceived from the standpoint of the higher interests of the national community. This has led to a new order in labor relations:

"The labor relation according to nationalistic legal conceptions is not a mere legal relation between the worker and his employer but it is the living arrangement under which the workman becomes a part in the machine of collective national production. His legal position is neither individualistic nor collectivistic but bound up with the community; that is, it is derived neither from a compromise of the opposing interests of the worker and the employer in individual cases nor from the struggle of collective class interests, but it is derived from an order in which the worker and the employer are united as members of the people's community, as powers in the national economy, and as the supporters of their enterprise."

All enterprises are built up on the Führer principle, and the leader has full authority within the limits of the laws and regulations laid down by the state economic and labor organizations. The proprietor of an enterprise may be removed as the leader of his own establishment if he mistreats the workers or if he fails to operate in the interests of the common welfare.

In the new Reich, since all are working primarily for the public good, the old distinctions between private and public service no longer exist. However, employment directly under the state or its agencies demands a special sort of "loyalty", that is, political dependability:

"Whoever is engaged in public service is bound to direct and unconditional loyalty to the Führer. Of course, all members of the people are expected to be loyal to the Führer—not only those engaged in the public service. But the nature of public service is determined by the direct and unconditional loyalty by which the individual is bound to the Führer."

This loyalty is demanded not only in the voluntary state service but also in the compulsory labor service and military service. The laws and regulations governing all of the services are reviewed and analyzed. The first prerequisite for all of them is membership in the people, and they are all organized on the Führer principle:

"The ranks of the public services are regarded as forces organized on the living principle of leadership and following; The authority of command exercised in the labor service, the military service, and the civil service is Führer-authority . . . It has been said of the military and civil services that true leadership is not represented in their organization on the principles of command and obedience. In reality there can be no political leadership which does not have recourse to command and force as the means for the accomplishment of its ends. Command and force do not, of course, constitute the true nature of leadership, but as a means they are indispensable elements of every fully developed Führer-order."

In the Weimar Republic, various bodies within the larger body of the nation enjoyed a measure of autonomy; the individual communities and municipalities, the religious bodies, the universities, certain economic and trade groups, etc., had certain rights and privileges which were guaranteed by the Constitution. But in the Third Reich there can be no such dissociation of local or group interests from the interests of the whole:

"The National Socialist revolution overcame this corporative pluralism. The independent powers of the municipalities were wiped out by making the aims of the national leadership the guiding principle for all municipal administration, by instituting strict state control over the filling of all municipal offices, and discontinuing the municipal representation of the party state. The political influence of the religious bodies, especially of the Catholic Church, was overcome by destroying the Catholic political organizations. The political influence of trade groups was extinguished by dissolving workers and employers unions, by erecting a unified German labor front, and by entrusting the formulation of wage scales to state trustees of labor. The autonomy, the political influence, the constitutional guaranty of the pluralistic corporations—the entire basis of the pluralistic system was thus brought to collapse. But here as everywhere the National Socialist revolution did not stop at the mere negation of old political forms but erected a new system in place of the one which had been destroyed. The goal was not a bureaucratic and centralized system, for qualified bodies within the new Reich had to be given room for self-development, but the component parts could only be granted authority of their own, subject to an understanding of the absolute precedence of the laws for the existence of the whole nation."

Thus the various groups and localities become parts of a unified national organism. They cease to work at cross-purposes and they have no existence outside of the state or in opposition to it. "Their self-administration is coupled with the condition that they should not seek release from the all-embracing unity of the state or try to claim independent autonomy for themselves."

These self-administering bodies are divided by Huber into six groups:

1. The organizations attached to the NSDAP.
2. The various municipalities within the Reich.
3. The labor organizations.
4. The agricultural commissions, waterways commissions, etc.
5. The economic and cultural associations.
6. The religious bodies.

There follows a review of the organization of these various bodies, which, like all things in the Third Reich, follows the Führer principle. Their "self-administration" is conducted in strict accordance with the laws and regulations formulated by the central Government.

The last section deals specifically with the position of religious bodies in the Third Reich, particularly with the Catholic and Evangelical Churches, but it is concerned only with the theoretical side of the picture and not with the actual position and treatment of the churches under National Socialism. Point 24 of the program of the party guarantees religious freedom but not the same unlimited religious freedom which was guaranteed by the Weimar Constitution; religious beliefs in the Third Reich "must not offer offense to the ethical or moral feelings of the German race and they must not endanger the security of the Reich . . . The fact that the party itself stands on a ground of positive Christianity, without associating itself with any special denomination, makes a positive relation of the National Socialist Reich to the Christian Church possible in principle. Whether this possibility becomes a reality depends primarily upon the Christian Church itself. In no sense does point 24 imply a return to the system of a state church." The church enjoys an "autonomy" similar to that of the other bodies within the nation. The state reserves for itself the right to check and control church finances and organizations, and "a right of protest against politically undesirable persons who might be placed in leading church offices. It can also demand that the high church officers execute an oath of loyalty to the Führer, the people, and the Reich."

The book concludes with an analysis of the major agreements establishing the constitutional position of the church in Germany: the concordat of July 20, 1933 with the Roman Catholic Church, and the laws of July 14, 1933 and September 24, 1935 regarding the organization of the German Evangelical Church.

DOCUMENT 2
(Summary)
WESEN UND GESTALT DES NATIONALSOZIALISMUS (THE NATURE AND FORM OF NATIONAL SOCIALISM), BY DR. JOSEPH GOEBBELS: BERLIN, JUNKER UND DUNNHAUPT, 1935

In this lecture, which Goebbels delivered at the German Political Institute (Deutsche Hochschule für Politik) during the first or second year of Nazi rule, he states that the National Socialist movement is still in the process of formation and consequently subject to continual changes and revisions. Nevertheless, National Socialism, like any great philosophy, rests on a few basic concepts which are unchanging and through which the nature of the movement may be studied.

In order to make these concepts clear to the German people, it was necessary first of all to overcome the confusion of thought which had characterized the political life of the foregoing period: "If anyone had taken the trouble 14 years ago, at the beginning of our political disagreements, to clarify the political concepts and to ascertain what the individual really meant by 'democracy', or 'monarchy', 'system', or 'authoritarian state', then it would have become obvious that all Germans agreed upon the basic principles and that we simply called them by different names."

It has been the task of the National Socialist propaganda machine to demonstrate to the Germans that they all want the same thing:

> "National Socialism has simplified the thinking of the German people and led it back to its original primitive formulas. It has presented the complicated processes of political and economic life in their simplest terms. This was done with the well-considered intention of leading the broad masses of the people once again to take part in political life. In order to find understanding among the masses, we consciously practiced a popular [*volksgebundene*] propaganda. We have taken complexes of facts which were formerly accessible only to a few specialists and experts, carried them to the streets, and hammered them into the brain of the little man. All things were presented so simply that even the most primitive mind could grasp them. We refused to work with unclear or insubstantial concepts but we gave all things a clearly defined sense. Here lay the secret of our success."

In this way the National Socialist revolution was prepared from beneath. It cannot be regarded as an arbitrary seizure of power by a special political interest group. It had developed its own legality within itself and had gradually instilled its principles into the people, thus preparing the nation spiritually for the change. By making use of the existent legal forms it was able to transfer its own legality to the state "without bloodshed, barricades, or machine-guns". The seizure of power was not in itself revolution but only the last part of a revolutionary act which had started much earlier, "perhaps at the outbreak of the World War or at the signing of the Versailles Treaty". The seizure of power was merely the point at which "National Socialist authorities assumed the position of state authorities, the laws of the revolution became the laws of the state, and the National Socialist way of thinking transferred itself to the nation. There was nothing in Germany which could escape the legal advance of the historical process . . . National Socialism is now in the act of stabilizing the new legal situation which the revolution has brought about in Germany."

The National Socialist revolution represents the breaking through of a new philosophy, or world-view, in accordance with which all fields of national life must henceforth be regulated. The same aims and ideals and standards must be applied to economics and to politics, to cultural and social development, to education and religion, and to foreign and domestic relations.

Books and programs are not necessary to explain the sense of a revolutionary philosophy. The essential idea can always be expressed in a single word or phrase. The basic idea of Christianity was love for one's fellow man, and all that has been built up around it is the work of theologians. The essence of the National Socialist philosophy is to be found in the concept of the community of the people.

This idea was born out of the community of fighting men which nine million Germans experienced during the World War.

> "For them it was impossible to start again where they had left off four years before. No, these men brought a new way of thinking with them from the trenches. Amid direct distress and danger they had experienced a new kind of community which could never have fallen to their lot in happier circumstances. They learned to know and they experienced the sovereign equalizing power of death which finally strips away all values except those of character. Out there wealth, education, or noble blood were of no importance; such distinctions could not change the course of the bullets which mowed down high and low, rich and poor, great and small alike. Among these men only one distinction remained valid: their personal worth."

It became the mission of the National Socialist movement to transfer to the whole German nation the spirit of the front community— the community in which all existed and worked for the good of the

whole and in which the worth of the individual was measured entirely
by values of character and personality. The establishment of this
community is making the Germans into a people in the fullest sense
of the word; it is giving them that solidarity of ideals the lack of
which resulted in the collapse of the nation and the loss of the war.

In conclusion Goebbels seeks to clarify a few National Socialist
concepts which he says have often been misunderstood:

> "One frequently hears the idea expressed: 'National Social-
> ism wishes to establish a totalitarian state!' This is a great
> mistake, for National Socialism does not strive for the totality
> of the state but for the totality of the idea: that is, a complete
> prevalence of that way of looking at things for which we have
> been fighting during the last decade and which we have brought
> to victory. It is to be applied in the entire public life of the
> nation and will not call a halt before the provinces of economics,
> culture, or religion. In Germany there can no longer be any
> regulation of relations which is not consistent with the National
> Socialist point of view."

Another popular misconception is that the National Socialist
movement will automatically dissolve itself as soon as all Germans
have become National Socialists. Actually only a select few can
be National Socialists in the fullest sense.

> "The party must always continue to represent the hierarchy
> of National Socialist leadership. This minority must always
> insist upon its prerogative to control the state. It must keep
> the way open for the German youth which wishes to take its
> place in this hierarchy. In reality the hierarchy has fewer
> rights than duties! It is responsible for the leadership of the
> state and it solemnly relieves the people of this responsibility.
> It has the duty to control the state in the best interests and to
> the general welfare of the nation."

Finally, the ideological content of the term "National Socialism"
is not to be confused with the old concepts of "national" and
"social": "for the National Socialist, that which characterized the
old 'national' attitude is completely insignificant. He does not care
about outward appearances but he has consecrated his flesh and
blood, his body and soul to his people . . ."

> "The same thing is true regarding the concept of socialism.
> 'I am social' is a phrase usually spoken by the director of a
> bank or a syndicate, a factory owner, or a clerk in a high po-
> sition. They wish to erect hospitals and reform schools in
> order to help the poor people; they admit that 'things can't go
> on this way' and that 'something has to be done about it'. The
> socialist stands high above this plane. He sticks to the stand-
> point: We must all together become a people so that the nation
> can survive its ordeals. No sacrifice is too great for the forma-
> tion of this people. I belong to my people in good days and in

bad and I will share in its joys and sorrows. I know no classes but I feel myself bound wholly and solely to the nation.

"National Socialism does not dream of reducing the whole German people to a common level, and it recognizes every achievement which raises an individual above the mass of his contemporaries. But in the last analysis we are all equal in the face of danger and death and we wish to express this equality by acknowledging our unity and never permitting any cleft to separate us, for the times of danger will one day come when our people will have to depend upon its inner solidarity."

DOCUMENT 3

(Summary)

DER MYTHUS DES 20. JAHRHUNDERTS (THE MYTH OF THE TWENTIETH CENTURY), BY ALFRED ROSENBERG, MUNICH, 1935 [1]

Alfred Rosenberg's *The Myth of the 20th Century* is an elaborate ideological exposition grounded on the Nordic race-theory and proceeding from this standpoint to reconstruct world history, to formulate a pseudo-religious Germanic ideal, and to set down the appropriate structure and policy for a new German racial state.

The "myth of the 20th century", according to Rosenberg, is the "myth of blood", i.e. the *mysterium* of blood. The blood poured in the World War has begun to work, fructifying in the German folk-soul, and the insight is being gained that history is not a strife of class against class, of dogma against dogma, but a struggle between blood and blood, race and race, people and people. The ideals of the "Christianizing of the world" and the "humanizing of mankind" were both buried in the World War experience. Now we are beginning to learn that "values are created and preserved only where the law of blood determines the deeds and ideas of men, whether consciously or subconsciously". "The conflict between blood and surrounding world, between blood and blood represents the final phenomenon within our reach, *behind* which it is impossible for us to probe." The struggles of the blood and the felt *mystique* of life-occurrences are not two different things but represent different aspects of one and the same thing. "Soul means race viewed from within. And, conversely, race is the outer aspect of a soul." The ultimate category in this new world-picture is thus the race-soul (*Rassenseele*).

"Racial history is thus at the same time natural history and soul-*mystique*. The history of the religion of blood is, conversely, the great world-narrative of the rise and decline of peoples, their heroes and thinkers, their inventors and artists."

"The 'meaning of world history' has radiated out from the north over the whole world, borne by a blue-eyed blond race which in several great waves determined the spiritual face of the world . . . These wander-periods were the legendary migration of the Atlantides across north Africa, the migration of the Aryans into India and Persia; the migration of the Dorians, Macedonians, Latins; the migration of the Germanic tribes; the colonization of the world by the Germanic occident."

---

[1] The first edition of this work was published in 1930.

174

Rosenberg presents a detailed interpretation of Indian, Persian, Greek, Roman, and European culture; in each case, the culture is created by the ruling Nordic element and declines through the racial decay of the Nordics in their intermixture with the inferior races.

It has been long accepted, according to Rosenberg, that all the states of the west and their creative values have been generated by Germans; and it follows that, if the Germanic blood were to vanish away completely in Europe, then the whole western culture must also fall to ruin.

> "We stand today before a definitive decision. Either through a new experience and cultivation of the old blood, coupled with an enhanced fighting will, we will rise to a purificatory action, or the last Germanic-western values of morality and state-culture shall sink away in the filthy human masses of the big cities, become stunted on the sterile burning asphalt of a bestialized inhumanity, or trickle away as a morbific agent in the form of emigrants, bastardizing themselves in South America, China, Dutch East India, Africa."

> "A *new* faith is arising today: the myth of the blood, the faith, to defend with the blood the divine essence of man. The faith, embodied in clearest knowledge, that the Nordic blood represents that *mysterium* which has replaced and overcome the old sacraments."

> "The new real struggle today is concerned not so much with external changes in power, along with an internal compromise as hitherto, but, conversely, with the new rebuilding of the soul-cells of the Nordic peoples, for the sake of the re-institution in their sovereign rights [*Herrscherrechte*] of those ideals and values from which originates everything which signifies culture to us, and for the sake of the preservation of the racial substance itself."

Rosenberg propounds as special to Nordic peoples the ideal of *honor and duty* and opposes to them love and compassion. Whenever the latter become dominant, then the epochs of racial and cultural decay begin in the history of all Nordic peoples. The attacks on Christianity, and especially on the Catholic Church, are directed against the Christian propagation of the ideal of love. The person of Jesus is excepted from this attack, his life being given a heroic interpretation, while Matthew and Paul are blamed for the prevalent Christian view.

> "A German religious movement, which would like to develop into a folk-church, will have to declare that the ideal of neighborly love is unconditionally to be subordinated to the idea of national honor, that no act of a German church may be approved which does not primarily serve the safeguarding of the *Volkstum*."

"The idea of honor, national honor, is for us the beginning and end of our entire thinking and doing. It does not admit of any equal-valued center of force alongside of it, no matter of what kind, neither Christian love, nor the Masonic humanity, nor the Roman philosophy."

"The essence of the contemporary world revolution lies in the awakening of the racial types. Not in Europe alone but on the whole planet. This awakening is the organic counter movement against the last chaotic remnants of the liberal economic imperialism, whose object of exploitation out of desperation has fallen into the snare of Bolshevik Marxism, in order to complete what democracy had begun, the extirpation of the racial and national consciousness."

In his discussion of the relation between the state and the folk, Rosenberg unequivocally gives priority to the folk.

"The state is nowadays no longer an independent idol, before which everything must bow down; the state is not even an end but is only a means for the preservation of the folk . . . Forms of the state change, and the laws of the state pass away; the folk remains. From this alone follows that the nation is the first and *last*, that to which everything else has to be subordinated."

"The new thought puts folk and race higher than the state and its forms. It declares protection of the folk more important than protection of a religious denomination, a class, the monarchy, or the republic; it sees in treason against the folk a greater crime than high treason against the state."

"No folk of Europe is racially unified, including Germany. In accordance with the newest researches, we recognize five races, which exhibit noticeably different types. Now it is beyond question true that the Nordic race primarily has borne the genuine cultural fruits of Europe. The great heroes, artists, founders of states have come from this race . . . Nordic blood created *German* life above all others. Even those sections, in which only a small part today is pure Nordic, have their basic stock from the Nordic race. Nordic is German and has functioned so as to shape the culture and human types of the *westisch, dinarisch*, and *ostisch-Baltisch* races. Also a type which is predominantly *dinarisch* has often been innerly formed in a Nordic mode. This emphasis on the Nordic race does not mean a sowing of 'race-hatred' in Germany but, on the contrary, the conscious acknowledgment of a kind of racial cement within our nationality . . . On the day when Nordic blood should completely dry up, Germany would fall to ruin, would decline into a characterless chaos. That many forces are consciously working toward this, has been discussed in detail. For this they rely primarily on the Alpine lower stratum, which, without any value of its own, has remained essentially superstitious and slavish despite all Germanization. Now that the external bond of the old idea of the Reich has fallen away, this blood is active, together with other bastard phenomena, in order to put itself in the service of a magic faith or in the service of the democratic chaos, which finds its herald in the parasitic but energetic Judaism."

"The foundation for the arising of a *new aristocracy* lies in those men who have stood—in a spiritual, political, and military sense —in the foremost positions in the struggle for the coming Reich. It will appear thereby with inner necessity that up to 80 percent of these men will also externally approach the Nordic type, since the fulfilment of the demanded values lies on a line with the highest values of this blood. With the others the inheritance, which exhibits itself in actions, outweighs personal appearance."

Rosenberg's suggestions concerning a German foreign policy follow the lines set down in his earlier work, *The Future Path of a German Foreign Policy*, with the same emphasis on *Lebensraum* and the need for German expansion eastward. "The question of destiny concerning *Lebensraum* and bread was formerly solved by Low Saxons with the sword, which was swung before the plow . . . help will come today only from the will transformed to conscious deed, which acquires land for millions of coming Germans. . . . 'From west to east' is the direction, from the Rhine to the Weichsel, 'from west to east' it must resound, from Moscow to Tomsk. The 'Russian', whom Peter and Catherine cursed, was genuine. Europe ought not to have been imposed on him. But he must be content to move his center of gravity to Asia."

"Europe's states have all been founded and preserved by the Nordic man. This Nordic man through alcohol, the World War, and Marxism has partially degenerated, partially been uprooted . . . In order to preserve Europe, the Nordic energies of Europe must first be revitalized, strengthened. That means then Germany, Scandinavia with Finland, and England."

". . . Nordic Europe is the fated future, with a *German* central Europe. Germany as racial and national state, as central power of the continent, safeguarding the south and southeast; the Scandinavian states with Finland as a second group, safeguarding the northeast; and Great Britain, safeguarding the west and overseas at those places where required in the interest of the Nordic man."

DOCUMENT 4

(Summary)

UNSER AMERIKA (OUR AMERICA), BY COLIN ROSS: LEIPZIG, F. A. BROCKHAUS, 1936

Colin Ross, the German world traveler who is now recognized as one of Nazi Germany's leading lecturers and writers on foreign countries, sets forth in this book the views on the United States which he developed as a result of several extensive trips through this country between 1912 and 1936.

The entire book is devoted to the thesis that America "can never be fully explained from the Anglo-American viewpoint". It is the author's avowed purpose to demonstrate the German share in the physical and spiritual development of America, all recognition of which has, he claims, been wilfully and systematically suppressed by those who wish America to be regarded as an Anglo-Saxon country. "I started this book", he says, "with a conscious one-sidedness, as a history of America which, in contrast to the dozens of Anglo-Saxon ones, would be written from a purely German standpoint. But in the end I succumbed to the German 'vice' of objectivity, to the truly German tendency to be fair to all sides of a question; consequently I could not regard the share of the Germans in the United States as something separate but only as a part of the great America in which and through which alone they are able to live and are justified in their existence."

His treatment of the subject is not, however, as impartial as this statement might lead one to expect. He consistently deprecates all "Anglo-American" traditions, and, although he never denies the essential and potential greatness of America, practically all his observations on the past development and the present form of the nation are derogatory. His viewpoint is summed up as follows in the first chapter: "Because I have felt so deeply what America could be, I am indignant because it is not that. Moreover, I naturally feel an embittered anger over the way in which the Germans in the United States have been treated from the very beginning and in which all that they have done for their American fatherland has been carefully and intentionally allowed to sink into oblivion."

If America is to achieve its potential greatness, it must, he says, be conceived anew, "and this new conception can spring from no other source than the blood of its inhabitants. Half of this blood is

178

non-British. That is a fact which cannot be ignored and which all the Anglification of rising generations cannot overcome." He professes the belief that the Germans in America cannot and should not be regarded as bound to the service of the German homeland: "Germany can derive no advantage from the fact that her sons who have traveled across the sea remain conscious of their German origin; they can only do so as Americans. I cannot warn my countrymen urgently enough never to forget that. The German blood which has flowed out to America is irretrievably lost to the German homeland and not only in a political sense. Even if efforts to preserve the German language should be successful in certain parts of America, these German-speaking Americans will still be nothing else but Americans—no less American than their English-speaking compatriots."

Other passages in the book tend to cast doubt upon the complete good faith of this statement. He is continually calling upon the German element in this country to reassert itself and reestablish its influence. Although he always protests that this should take place not for Germany's sake but for America's, he makes no secret of his distaste for our democracy and his faith in the ideas of National Socialism, and it is implied that German-Americans should lead this country in the realization of similar ideas and eventually toward participation in a new world-order:

> "It is a question whether the millions who have been transplanted from German to American soil will recognize their fateful hour, whether they will be conscious of the arrival of a decisive moment in which they can arise and take upon themselves their share in the responsibility for the future of the United States, not for Germany's sake but for America's . . .
> "I believe in 'America's German Hour'. I have no proof for it and I freely admit that the development of the German element in the United States would seem to indicate the opposite. Still I believe in it. The great historical developments of the world usually prepare themselves below the surface until they suddenly break forth as apparent surprises.
> "I would not be so convinced that the German blood in the United States will once again play a creative and determinant role were it not for the simultaneous appearance of two circumstances: the German rebirth and the collapse of the old American idea."

Ross seeks to justify the claim of German-Americans to a position of leadership in the life of the United States by a long historical survey in which Germans are made to appear responsible for practically every salutory development in American history. Even the spiritual foundations of America are traced back to German origins: "Without Luther's decision and action, America as it developed in the United States—the idea as well as the reality—could never have come into being." He claims that the hard work of actually establishing and protecting the colonies in the early period was performed largely by Germans. He points to the presence of Germans among the Jamestown settlers, and he attributes the success of the Netherlands colony of New Amsterdam to its German founder and governor, Peter Minnewit, who also founded and governed Fort Christina for the Swedes. For the purely English Puritan settlers of Massachusetts he has not a good word, and he traces back many of America's later faults to the "Puritan tradition". All during the colonial period, he claims, it was the German settlers who enabled the colonies to flourish by holding the frontiers against the Indians. The most orderly and the most truly "American" life was developed in regions settled predominantly by Germans, notably in Pennsylvania. That the Germans were nowhere able to rise to a dominant position he attributes to the fact that they had no strong, unified European state behind them. They were never able to found colonies of their own but could come only as subjects, often as virtual slaves, to colonies which were already British.

In spite of their subordinate position the Germans rallied to the American cause at the time of the Revolution. The colonies could not have won their independence without the services of many common soldiers of German blood and of the German generals— Herkimer, De Kalb, Mühlenberg, and, above all, Steuben.

To the Germans who came to this country with the great immigration waves of the nineteenth century, America owes even more than to those of the colonial period: "The thousands, later tens of thousands, and finally hundreds of thousands of Germans who traveled across the Atlantic year upon year after 1830 and made the prairies their second home give to us Germans the right to say 'Our America', for they have made the German heritage as much a part of the American state and nation as is the Anglo-Saxon." Although the America which these Germans found was not at all the Utopia of which they had dreamed, they remained to open up the great areas of the West and to make them the part of the country which came closest to the American dream. Just as at the time of the Revolution, the Germans were the first to embrace any cause which reflected those ideals to which America lays claim. They were the first to protest against slavery. It was their support which elected Abraham Lincoln, and the Union could not have been preserved without their participation in the Civil War.

In the period between the Civil War and the World War, although heavy German immigration continued, the German element in America failed to press its advantage and submitted to the Anglo-American tradition, which regarded all persons of a non-British origin as second-rate Americans. The Anglification of the American people therefore continued unabated, and the German homeland did nothing to keep alive the German consciousness of its children in America. Consequently, when the World War came, the German-Americans were unable to muster enough political influence to determine the country's course. In line with the Puritan tradition, which regarded its own faith as the only right and divinely ordained one, America was swept with a crusade spirit which sought to impose democracy upon the rest of the world. Ross writes very bitterly about the treatment of German-Americans and the attitude toward German language and German culture in this country during the War of 1914–18, but he thinks that these very conditions may prove to have had the same effects upon German-Americans which the loss of the war had upon the German homeland: "Versailles spurred us on to a renewal of our entire nation such as would hardly have been believed possible. There are many signs which indicate that the 'German-American Versailles' will have a similar effect upon the Americans of German blood."

In conclusion Ross contends that America has long since ceased to be a true democracy and that her social order has become a mockery of those ideals for which she is supposed to stand. If she is ever to approach those ideals, if the American dream is ever to be realized, it can only be through an understanding and appreciation of the new ideas which are now abroad in the world:

"If Americans ever give up their empty, self-righteous play with the words 'democracy' and 'dictatorship', they will recognize that the new states, which have arisen from earlier democratic governmental forms, have sprung from the will of the people, which commissioned one man from their midst—in Italy a blacksmith, in Germany a World War corporal—to create a new social order which would bring justice to the whole community of the people.

"'In order to give equal opportunities to all men and, so far as is possible, to insure an equal share of happiness to all, we must proceed from the recognition of their inequality.' That is the basic law of a new form of life and society which is trying to create a new and real democracy through the 'dictatorship' of one who has been commissioned by the people, because the old form, which was based on the alleged equality of man, has failed.

"This basic law will finally establish itself in America also, although perhaps only after violent struggles and troublesome detours. In the United States the conditions are particularly difficult. The new regionalistic order has its origin in a people. In America, however, there is no people but a mixture of peoples . . .

"For a century and a half men of Anglo-Saxon blood have tried to realize the tremendous idea of the equality of all men in the new world and to construct a universal human happiness

upon it.   Germans have helped them faithfully and unselfishly,
even though they had to stand in an obscure position.

"Today the old idea is running down and a new one is being
born.   For Americans of German blood arises the mission of
realizing this new idea, not against, but with, their compatriots
of Anglo-Saxon blood.   The German element in America has
always marched in the second rank.   Now fate is sounding out
the call: 'Germans to the front!'   But just as this cry, when it
was first called out by a British admiral during the Boxer Re-
bellion, did not signify a higher reward but only a better performance, so it must be here too.   The Germans must man the
front not for their own sake but for America's sake—for the
country to which they have bound and consecrated themselves and
which now demands of them not only money and property, not
only sweat and blood, but also creative cooperation in the reconstruction of America, in order to realize that of which they and
their forebears dreamed when they embarked for America   . . .

"One man will arise and gather them together—a German
Thomas Paine.   He will not found a new party or club or association but he will bring together all those who are of German
blood into a natural community.   They will all come to it as soon
as they have become conscious of the simple truth that they are
not 'Americans' but 'Amerikaner', people of German blood on
American soil.   They will drop the hyphen which has been hung
upon them and will no longer call themselves 'German-Americans'
but simply 'Amerikaner', which is an untranslatable word   . . .

"We Germans in the old homeland will then lose the bitter feeling, which formerly came over us so easily, that we had lost millions and millions of our best people to a foreign country.   Then
they will no longer be lost but they will simply be working along
with us on new soil and in a new form to realize the great idea
which now inspires us to create a better, peaceably ordered world
in which every people comes to its rights in accordance with its
gifts and powers and no people is subjected to ideas which are
foreign to its nature."

DOCUMENT 5

(Translation)

REICHSGESETZBLATT (GERMAN BULLETIN OF LAWS), 1942,
PART I, PAGE 247

RESOLUTION OF APRIL 26, 1942 OF THE GERMAN REICHSTAG

In its meeting of April 26, 1942 the Great German Reichstag, on motion of the President of the Reichstag, has unanimously approved, through the following resolution, the rights claimed by the Führer in his address:

"There can be no doubt that in the present period of the war, in which the German people is engaged in a struggle for its very existence, the Führer must possess the right claimed by him, namely, to do everything which serves or contributes to the attainment of victory. In his capacity as leader of the nation, as commander in chief of the army, as head of the government and supreme bearer of the executive authority, as chief judge and as leader of the party, the Führer must therefore—without being bound by existing legal principles—be able at any time, if necessary, to urge any German to fulfil his obligations with all means which appear to him appropriate. It does not matter whether the German is a soldier or an officer, a high or low official or judge, an important or subordinate party official, a manual laborer or an employee. In the case of a dereliction of these duties, after a conscientious investigation he must be able, without regard to so-called 'well acquired' rights, to impose the fitting punishment, in particular, without introducing the prescribed procedure, to remove any man from his office, his rank, and his position."

This resolution is herewith announced for the Führer.

BERLIN, *April 26, 1942*
Reich's Minister and Chief of the Reich's Chancelry
DR. LAMMERS

DOCUMENT 6

(Translation)

DER ANGRIFF (DAILY PAPER OF THE GERMAN LABOR FRONT), BERLIN, ZENTRALVERLAG DER NSDAP, APRIL 9, 1942

THE FORCE OF THE PARTY

BY ROBERT LEY

Germany is fighting for her bare existence. It is necessary to repeat this until every German has grasped it. To bring the war to a successful end, all German forces must be organized. It is not enough to be German, but the German man must become a warrior and carrier-on in the belief in National Socialism.

The nation's life is not easy to govern, since many people may consider themselves employed in capacities for which they are unfitted. But the people must have confidence that someone does the best possible. This confidence should be directed toward the National Socialist Party. To make sure of the people's confidence, one must remember the following: "Right is what serves my people, wrong is what damages it. I am born a German and have, therefore, only one holy mission: work for my people and take care of it." The people has a fine sense for these matters. Whoever acts according to these principles has the people's confidence, but whoever disregards them is condemned by the people, even if a thousand paragraphs speak for him. That is the foundation of confidence.

The people is like a big child. A child believes and has confidence but can also be naughty and cause many troubles. It must be constantly educated and guarded, and likewise the people wants protection, it will not think for itself but wishes somebody to think for it. It will not act for itself but wants to see will-power and energy and deeds. All that is our glorious party's task.

The democracies thought they were safe in laughing at Germany, because she forbade her people to listen to foreign broadcasts, but now they doubtless wish that they had instituted such measures themselves. That the National Socialist Party has acted in the right manner is shown by the increased confidence in the party. The people comes to the party with its sorrows. The party exercises the world's best organization. To organize well is to work with life and nature as models. The secret of organization is to let things grow. Nothing escapes the party, the smallest movement, excitement, discontent, or consent is noted by the party like a never-failing seismograph.

The National Socialist Party is Hitler, and Hitler is the party. The National Socialists believe in Hitler, who embodies their will. Therefore our conscience is clearly and exactly defined. Only what Adolf Hitler, our Führer, commands, allows, or does not allow is our conscience. We have no understanding for him who hides behind an anonymous conscience, behind God, whom everybody conceives according to his own wishes.

We do not recognize it when an individual, whoever he may be, tries to shirk his responsibility to his people and his Führer under the pretext that he is responsible only to his conscience and God. To me, to every National Socialist, to every decent-minded German, our Führer, our party, and our people are our conscience. Adolf Hitler is Germany, and Germany is Adolf Hitler. That is the greatest force of the party and the German people.

DOCUMENT 7

(Translation)

Organisationsbuch der NSDAP (Nazi Party Organization Book),
Munich, Zentralverlag der NSDAP, 1940

(Pages 3–9)

GENERAL BEARING OF THE NATIONAL SOCIALIST

The National Socialist must regard himself as a servant of the movement and of the people. This applies especially to the political leaders, the leaders of all party formations, and the administrative officers and members of the associated organizations.

To keep alive the idea of the people's community and constantly to strengthen it is the highest mission of National Socialism. It is incompatible with this mission for any individual to separate himself from his party comrades and his fellow Germans, to regard himself as better than they, and to open up those chasms which it has cost the heart's blood of the best German men to bridge over. In assuming a higher office, a National Socialist undertakes higher duties. His increased powers are lent to him only so that he will be able to fulfil these higher duties. They do not give him the right to become high and mighty, arrogant, and mysterious. He will never win the confidence and the willing obedience of his followers through threats and aggravating words. On duty he should be a leader and promoter; off duty he should be a good comrade and helper to his sub-leaders, party comrades, and fellow Germans. The more his deeds are in harmony with his words, the more willingly will his party comrades and his fellow Germans follow him.

Every National Socialist should be as simple and modest in his bearing as was customary during National Socialism's struggle for power. He should not wish to appear to be more than he is, and, just as he rejects all "Byzantinism" outside of himself, he should also rule it out where his own person is concerned. A leading party comrade must never be vain or supersensitive, and he must always prefer the honest and candid words of a proved fighter to the honeyed words of those creatures who seek to flatter by agreeing with him. He should always remain in touch with the humblest members of our people and have a willing ear for their needs and their troubles. They will come to him gladly if he is still the same person and if he moves in the same company and the same environment as during the years of struggle.

The political leaders and administrators and the leaders of the organizations should not take part in elaborate banquets nor express their favor by awarding gifts and honors, nor frequent the most expensive places, but on and off duty they should always so act as is to be expected of a representative of the German freedom movement and a participator in the unspeakably hard work of constructing a better Germany. Above all, the excessive indulgence in alcohol should be avoided in a time when many German families still do not have the barest necessities of life and will lose their painfully restored faith if the men of the movement engage in drinking bouts which last beyond the legal hour whenever possible and if they damage the prestige of the movement by appearing publicly in a drunken condition.

A true National Socialist does not boast of his deeds and he demands no thanks. His highest rewards are the consciousness of having fulfilled his duty, the success of his work, and the confidence of his followers. A National Socialist will always act rightly if he daily examines himself and asks himself whether his work and his attitude could stand inspection by the Führer.

THE PARTY MEMBER

1. Admission

Any member of the German people who has a clean record, who is of pure German blood, who does not belong to a Freemason's lodge or any related organization, and who has completed his twenty-first (in some cases his eighteenth) year can become a member of the NSDAP by filling out the admission form and paying the regular admission fee. The party leadership can decree a ban on new admissions at any time or can limit the admissions to certain groups of people. Announcements regarding these matters may only be made by the national treasurer of the NSDAP.

Refusal of membership is made without any explanation of reasons by the local group leader in agreement with the party court for that district. Against this refusal there is no legal redress.

Membership is finally confirmed by the issuance of a membership card or a membership book. Anyone who becomes a party member does not merely join an organization but he becomes a soldier in the German freedom movement and that means much more than just paying his dues and attending the members' meetings. He obligates himself to subordinate his own ego and to place everything he has in the service of the people's cause. Only he who is capable of doing this should become a party member. A selection must be made in accordance with this idea.

Readiness to fight, readiness to sacrifice, and strength of character are the requirements for a good National Socialist. Small blemishes, such as a false step which someone has made in his youth, should be overlooked; the contribution in the struggle for Germany should alone be decisive. The healthy will naturally prevail over the bad if the will to health finds sufficient support in leadership and achievement. Admission to the party should not be controlled by the old bourgeois point of view. The party must always represent the elite of the people. Therefore, care should be taken in the admission of members and all narrow-minded or self-important types who are self-seeking or lacking in true character should be denied admission or cast out. In order to prevent unsuitable elements from slipping in, a person may only be accepted and inducted into the party at his place of residence. Every certificate of admission must pass through the hands of the local *Blockleiter*. If the prospective member has not addressed his application directly to the *Blockleiter* but to the *Zelle*, the *Ortsgruppe*, the *Kreisleitung*, or some other quarter, the certificate of admission is to be forwarded by the speediest route to the local *Blockleiter* for his approval. The *Blockleiter*, who knows every person in his block, should make a copy of this certificate and pass it along to the *Ortsgruppe* as soon as possible. This course should also be followed with regard to candidates for admission into the HJ.

1a. Procedure for the Admission of a New Member

(Extract from the general directions for the national treasurer of the NSDAP)

No individual member of the people has a legal claim to admission into the NSDAP—not even if he fulfils the conditions prescribed for admission. In admitting people into the party, it must be the first principle of all offices which are concerned with admissions that the Führer wishes to be able to count upon the party as a community pledged to a political fighting spirit.

In accordance with the will expressed by the Führer only the best National Socialists should be admitted to membership in the party. The persons in authority should therefore propose such persons for admission as are ready and willing to work and to fight for the Führer and his movement. In admitting new members, the persons in authority are expected always to remain fully conscious of their great obligation to the Führer and the movement. In the selection of new party members, they bear responsibility for the smooth running and the success of our work not only for the next period but also for the more distant future. The admission of new members is of the greatest importance not only for the local spheres of the individual party authorities but also for the party throughout the whole Reich and for the future formation of the political destiny of the German people.

The admission of new members, therefore, presents the party authorities with a difficult task. The forging of individuals into the fighting community of party members will largely determine the development and the effectiveness of the political work in the various larger and smaller divisions of the party during the coming years. The selection of a new party member is therefore an important decision which the responsible authority in the party cannot and must not delegate to someone else and which must be made conscientiously after a thorough investigation. We cannot simply admit anyone who wishes to come to us, but the party authorities must seek out where political talents lie, where the political value and performance of an individual surpass the general standard, in a word, where those men are who are important to us as the embodiment of a very definite value. The induction of a comrade into the party represents a special honor and distinction, since he is thereby admitted into the ranks of the Führer's closest followers.

But the principle of voluntary entrance into the party must never be abandoned or tampered with in any way. This principle of voluntary entrance, which is one of the most valuable and essential features of the movement, must rather be firmly upheld. As natural as it is that the party authorities should wish to enrol as many as possible of those fellow Germans who appear useful to them, force or pressure to make them join the party must never be employed in any form—not even in the threat of a disadvantage for those fellow Germans who do not wish to be admitted to the party.

Personal readiness to serve or to assume responsibility and an irreproachable attitude in political and philosophical matters are the qualities for which the individual applicants should be tested. Decisions regarding admissions should be made wholly impartially and never influenced by personal considerations.

Those party offices which are concerned with admissions are obligated to do all in their power to secure a clear picture of the prospective member. If a party official is unable to form an adequate judgment regarding an applicant because he has not lived for a long enough time in that official's district, then it is up to him to address inquiries to the party authorities at the place where the applicant formerly resided.

The regulations which lay down the general rules for the admission of new members make it the duty of those party offices which are concerned with admissions to conduct an investigation in every single case as to whether the applicant's political dependability, his firmness of character, and his philosophical outlook qualify him for admission into the community of the party. Applications for admission may only be passed along after the officer who has jurisdiction over the case has formed a clear, specific, and unprejudiced judgment of the prospective member's traits of character.

The economic situation and the trade or profession of the individual must not play any part in the decision regarding the application. Admission must rather be open to all who can fulfil the conditions and whose bearing during the last years leads to the belief that they will be valuable party members who are ready to cooperate.

As a matter of principle younger applicants for admission are to be shown preference. In general only persons who have already completed their twenty-first year may be admitted.

Male applicants under 25 years of age must show proof that they have completed their military service before they can be admitted. Persons who have been found unsuited for military service can only be admitted to the party if they are capable and qualified to wear the party uniform—that is, if they are not afflicted with any serious physical or mental incapacity. The party offices which are concerned with admissions are obligated to ascertain the presence of all the necessary qualifications and to confirm them in a report to the national leadership of the party.

The arrangements for the transfer of members of the HJ and the BDM to the NSDAP are not affected by the foregoing regulations.

Only those racial comrades are eligible for admission who possess German citizenship.

In the selection of prospective members the greatest care must be taken to prevent the infusion of religious disagreements into the party. Clergymen and other persons who have strong denominational connections cannot be admitted. Here must also be included professors on the theological faculties of the philosophical theological universities and similar educational institutions for clergymen and theological students. Likewise excluded from admission to the NSDAP are former members of the disbanded Theosophic Society as well as members or former members of the Anthroposophic Society. Former members of the French Foreign Legion also cannot be admitted.

In the investigation of the prospective applicants the information contained in the questionnaire is to be evaluated. The national leadership has restricted the questions to such information as is absolutely necessary, and it is expected of every applicant for admission into the party that he should fill out his questionnaire exactly, completely, conscientiously, and legibly. All party offices are instructed to refuse questionnaires which do not fulfil these requirements. The national leadership will send back unexamined all membership applications with questionnaires which fail to conform to them. The contents of the questionnaires should give the party officers and judges information concerning a few essential matters which in certain cases might furnish grounds for refusal. These questions, however, do not claim to cover all the matters which might be made the basis of a refusal. All the party comrades who participate in refusal proceedings should in every case secure for themselves a complete picture of the entire personality of the applicant and should decide on the basis of this investigation whether he can be counted among the best National Socialists who, according to the will of the Führer, should become party members. The correct filling out of the questionnaire will curtail and alleviate the work of the offices of the party jurisdiction (*Parteigerichtsbarkeit*) and administration.

The application must be refused in all cases where:

(a) The marriage partner of the applicant is not free from Jewish or colored racial admixture;

(b) Such a marriage has been dissolved by divorce or by the death of the partner, but there remain children from this marriage;

(c) The applicant has belonged to a Freemason's lodge or similar organization (Odd Fellows, Druid Order, etc.) or to any secret society;

(d) The applicant has been convicted of defamatory actions—however, undue harshness is to be avoided if special merits are present;

(e) The applicant has not been honorably discharged from the armed forces;

(f) The applicant suffers from a hereditary illness, as defined by the law of July 14, 1933 for the prevention of the procreation of congenitally unhealthy elements. If there is a justified suspicion that the applicant is congenitally unhealthy, the offices concerned with admissions are obliged to assure themselves regarding this question by procuring an official doctor's certificate or through a certification of the proper authorities.

Persons who have voluntarily resigned from the party can only be readmitted if their application has the personal approval of the *Gauleiter*. As a rule only those persons can be readmitted who can be proved to have withdrawn from the party from financial necessity but who have continued to act as National Socialists.

Persons who have been expelled from the party by a decision of the party courts, or persons who have been dishonorably discharged from one of the party formations or associated organizations, can only be readmitted upon the express recommendation of the officer in authority and with the consent of the party courts.

The regulations which are laid down in the Statutes of the NSDAP (division 3, paragraphs 2 and 3) furnish the basis for admission procedure. The admission of an applicant into the party becomes effective only with the presentation of the red membership card which is issued by the national leadership.

The local group leader (*Ortsgruppenleiter*) of the **NSDAP** bears first responsibility for the admission of new members. He must submit all membership applications, whether refused or approved, to his superior district leader (*Kreisleiter*). In the case of an approved application the *Ortsgruppenleiter* confirms his approval by his signature on the application blank, and he thereby pledges his word that he has investigated the applicant's qualifications for admission to the movement. The final decision regarding the admission of an applicant is made in the name of the Führer by the national treasurer in agreement with the Supreme Court of the Party (*Oberster Parteigericht*).

The Führer has decreed that in the future a suitable proportion shall be maintained between the number of party members and the number of racial comrades in the Greater German Reich. The ideal proportion of the number of party members to the number of racial comrades is set at ten percent. This proportion is to apply also to the individual province (*Gau*). The determination of the number of new members who can be admitted in any single *Gau* is made by the *Gauleiter*. The distribution of these new memberships among the various *Ortsgruppen* in any given *Kreis* is made by the *Kreisleiter*. The same function can be exercised by the *Gauleiter* if the approved number of new memberships is not reached by a particular *Kreis*.

Careful but speedy handling of all membership applications in accordance with the prescribed regulations is an absolute requirement.

In the admission of new members all prejudices must be eliminated. No one must be refused because of class or position. The way to cooperation within the party must be open to the leaders of the state and of our economic life as well as to the laborer, the peasant, and the German woman.

2. Pledging

Upon receipt of his membership card the member takes a solemn pledge. This pledge must be taken by all new party comrades, regardless of whether or not they are members of the SA or the SS.

The pledge is administered by the *Ortsgruppenleiter* in a meeting of the members. In a short address he explains the duties of the party member and he points out the significance of the pledge of allegiance. Then he pronounces the pledge of allegiance sentence by sentence. Those who are to be pledged, while facing him, repeat it after him with their right arms raised in the German greeting. The pledge of loyalty is as follows: "I pledge allegiance to my Führer, Adolf Hitler. I promise at all times to respect and obey him and the leaders whom he appoints over me."

The solemn presentation of the membership book is made at the same meeting by the *Ortsgruppenleiter*, with the words: "In the name of the Führer I present to you your membership book. Remain true to the party as you have been in the past."

3. Loss of Membership

Party membership is lost by death, by voluntary resignation, by individual expulsion, or in some cases by the expulsion of whole blocks, *Zellen*, or *Ortsgruppen*. Voluntary resignations, which almost always take place as a result of personal vexations or supposed slights, merely demonstrate that the person in question is not a true National Socialist. The party does not grow poorer but can only gain by such losses. A true National Socialist never resigns voluntarily, because for him National Socialism is the purpose and the content of his life. If the resignation occurs to forestall expulsion, the regular procedure of the party courts is still to be carried out.

In the institution of expulsion proceedings the greatest care and responsibility must prevail. Expulsion is the greatest punishment which is known to the party. While expelled party members, aside from losing their membership, must of course forfeit any positions of leadership which they have held in any office or organization of the party, as well as any honorary offices in the state or municipal governments which they have undertaken by order of the party, it is not generally necessary for the expelled member to be thrown out of his private employment.

Members *will* be expelled:

  (a) Who commit defamatory acts or who, after their admission, are found to have previously committed such acts;
  (b) Whose actions run contrary to the aims of the NSDAP; or
  (c) For lack of interest.
        party or outside of it and who thus damage the prestige of the party.

Members *can* be expelled:

  (a) Who have repeatedly started struggles or quarrels within the *Ortsgruppe*, the *Kreis*, or the *Gau;*
  (b) Who in spite of reminders have failed to pay their dues for three months without giving any excuse; or
  (c) For lack of interest.

If extenuating circumstances are present in the case, a warning may be decided upon in place of expulsion and, in some cases, a suspension of eligibility to hold party offices for a period up to three years.

Expulsion proceedings, on the basis of an authoritative decision of the party courts, may be carried out by (a) the *Ortsgruppenleiter,*

(b) the *Kreisleiter*, (c) the *Gauleiter*, (d) the *Führer*. The expulsion is carried out by the party officer within whose sphere of authority the party court which recommends the expulsion is included.

The party courts can only recommend an expulsion. The recommendation must be delivered both to the accused and to the party officer who has jurisdiction over the case. Either of these has the right to make an appeal within a period of eight days, which has the effect of delaying final action. A party officer may only carry out the court's recommendation for expulsion when he has been informed by the court that the accused has made no use of his right of appeal. In urgent cases the expulsion can be carried out by the party officer in agreement with the chief justice of the party court. Here a protest may be filed within eight days but this protest has no delaying effect. In every case where a protest is made, an investigation is to be conducted by the party court. If the court upholds the expulsion, its decision is final. The highest authority in all cases of expulsion is the Führer. He is empowered, in agreement with the Supreme Court of the Party, to order the expulsion of whole *Ortsgruppen*. Their property, in such cases, becomes the general property of the **NSDAP**.

4. Readmission

In the cases of persons who have lost their membership in the **NSDAP** since January 1, 1932, whether by expulsion or resignation, there can as a rule be no question of a readmission to the **NSDAP**. The reinstatement of a former member who has been expelled on the basis of a decision by the party courts is only possible through a personal pardon of the Führer. Appeals for such pardons must be made as prescribed by the Führer's decree of July 6, 1935 and forwarded by the Supreme Court of the Party to the Chancelry of the Führer, where they will be submitted to the Führer for his decision.

5. Transfers

All party comrades should understand that members of the party are obliged to report every change of address or of legal status, even if only temporary, to the local political office of the party . . .

6. Duties of the Party Comrade

The National Socialist commandments:

> The Führer is always right!
> Never go against discipline!
> Don't waste your time in idle chatter or in self-satisfying criticism, but take hold and do your work!

Be proud but not arrogant!

Let the program be your dogma. It demands of you the greatest devotion to the movement.

You are a representative of the party; control your bearing and your manner accordingly!

Let loyalty and unselfishness be your highest precepts!

Practice true comradeship and you will be a true socialist!

Treat your racial comrades as you wish to be treated by them!

In battle be hard and silent!

Spirit is not unruliness!

That which promotes the movement, Germany, and your people, is right!

If you act according to these commandments, you are a true soldier of your Führer.

7. Guiding Principles for Members of the Ortsgruppen

The following guiding principles are to be made known to all members, and all men and women of the party should impress them upon themselves:

Lighten the work of the political leaders by the punctual performance of your duties.

Women of the party should participate in the activities of the NS Association of Women; there they will find work to do.

Don't buy from Jews!

Spare the health of the party comrades and speakers and refrain voluntarily from smoking at the meetings.

Don't make yourself a mouthpiece for our political opponents by spreading false reports.

To be a National Socialist is to set an example.

8. The Wearing of Insignia and Uniforms by Party Comrades

(1) It is the duty of every party comrade, whether political leader, member of a party formation or an associated organization, to wear his party button at all times.

(2) After two years of membership the member is entitled to wear the brown shirt with his civilian dress.

(3) The wearing of the service dress or parts of the service dress of the political leaders of the SA, the SS, the NSKK, or the HJ, with or without the party button, is only permitted to those who officially belong to the formation in question and who are in possession of the proper identification card.

(4) Party members who are employed in Jewish enterprises may not wear uniforms or insignia of the party or of any of its formations or associated organizations while they are at work.

(5) The wearing of service dress (but not of the brown shirt alone, without any insignia) is forbidden when appearing before the courts (including the labor courts). Witnesses may appear in service dress.

9. Special Instructions for Party Members

Who Can Issue Judgments?

Political judgments and certificates of a clean record, if they have not been requested by a higher party office, may only be issued by the *Kreisleiter* or officers of higher rank.

For official or semi-official purposes and for purposes of work assignment such information is to be given in all cases. In other cases it is up to the party officer to decide whether such information should be given.

Pass Photos on Identification Cards

Members of the NSDAP must not use pass photos which show the holder of any identification card in a uniform of the party or of any of its formations. It is also forbidden to use as pass photos pictures which show the person wearing a party button.

Party Offices and Arbitration Committees

Party offices may not take part in the formation of arbitration committees or be active in them. (Arbitration committees in quarrels over rents and leases, etc.)

Conversations With Foreigners

It is forbidden to all party members to engage in discussions of foreign policy with foreigners. Only such persons as have been designated by the Führer are entitled to do so.

Correspondence With Foreign Countries

All correspondence with foreign groups of the NSDAP, with the associated organizations, the political leaders, or the party members, must pass through the office of the Foreign Organization in Berlin.

Private Correspondence

In private correspondence, especially with persons of German blood in foreign countries, seals or stationery of the party offices or organizations must not be used.

(Pages 93–96)

FÜHRER PRINCIPLE AND SUBORDINATE RELATIONS

The Führer principle represented by the party imposes complete responsibility on all party leaders for their respective spheres of activity.

The party recognizes two fields of responsibility:

(a) Responsibility for complete spheres of activity;
(b) Responsibility for fields of special tasks.

With reference to (a):

The responsibility for all tasks within a major sphere of jurisdiction rests with the respective leader (*Hoheitsträger*) of the NSDAP, i.e. with the Führer for the territory of the Reich, the Gauleiter for the territory of the Gau, the district leader for the territory of the district, the local leader for the territory of the local group, etc.

The party leader has responsibility for the entire territory under his jurisdiction on the one hand and, on the other hand, for all political fields of activity appertaining thereto.

With reference to (b):

To assist the party leaders in the particular fields of work of a professional and specialized nature and in the guidance of the people, office leaders (*Amtsleiter*), etc., are placed under them who are responsible for their respective limited fields of activity within the territory subject to the jurisdiction of the respective party leader.

This responsibility for the complete or partial performance of tasks entails a relation of subordination of the leaders among themselves corresponding to the Führer principle. This relation extends in three directions:

(1) Disciplinary subordination;
(2) Specialized direction;
(3) Supervision.

With reference to (1) *Disciplinary subordination:*

Disciplinary subordination means that the subordinate works under instructions from his disciplinary superior and means personal and political subordination and responsibility of the subordinate in accordance with the Führer principle to his disciplinary superior in all questions concerning the sphere of activity over which he has been given jurisdiction. The disciplinary superior has in especially justifiable cases the right to enter an objection against measures which are to be carried out by his disciplinary subordinate on behalf of the respective special office of a superior jurisdiction.

The same rule applies to the branches and organizations subordinate to the respective party leader.

.   .   .   .

The Führer retains the right to limit the disciplinary prerogatives in individual cases and partially to withdraw them. This occurs, for instance, in the cases of the SA, SS, and the NSKK, which are directly subordinate to him or, in political and ideological matters, to his deputy. The subordinate leaders of these organizations in the various *Gaus*, districts, and local groups are not in a relation of disciplinary subordination to the party leaders.

A limitation or partial withdrawal in certain instances of the principle of subordination also occurs in the case of the party courts and in the sphere of activity of the national treasurer.

With respect to (2) *Specialized direction:*

> In the development of the various fields of activity, the leaders of the offices, etc., are at the disposal of the party leaders.

> These leaders of offices, etc., are disciplinarily subordinate to the respective party leader. With respect to their special field (concerning their sphere of special knowledge, for instance, economy, public welfare, etc.) the leaders of the offices receive directions from the leader of the respective specialized office of the superior party jurisdiction without reference to the party leader.

With respect to (3) *Supervision:*

> With reference to the offices and the associated organizations, central offices and sections are active in the field of *party organization, questions of personnel, indoctrination, propaganda, press policies,* and *public health,* subject to the following regulation:

> The chief of the party organization, personnel, indoctrination, propaganda, press, and public welfare offices of the NSDAP supervises the activity of the respective heads of the comparable services in the party offices and the associated organizations of the same sphere of party jurisdiction.

> Consequently, the head of the Gau press office supervises the activity of the press officers in the associated organizations, etc., of the Gau territory; the district leader of the office for public health supervises the activity of the officer for public health in the associated organizations, etc., of the district; the local chief for indoctrination supervises the activity of the indoctrination officer of the NS Women's League and the associated organizations, etc., of the territory of the local group, etc. . . .

> Through this system a unified direction in the respective specialized fields is achieved, and duplication in the same fields, as well as unfruitful labor without purposeful contact, is avoided, particularly through the supervisory activity of the leaders of the offices (indoctrination, propaganda, etc.)

> Furthermore, only a single competent leader within his sphere of jurisdiction is responsible to the respective competent party leader for each of these specialized internal party activities and he is thereby relieved to that extent of complete responsibility.

(Pages 486–488)

PARTY AND STATE

I. THE STATE

The state is born out of the necessity of ordering the community of the *Volk* in accordance with certain laws. Its characteristic attribute is *power* over *every* branch of the community. The state has the right to demand of every racial comrade (*Volksgenosse*) that he live according to the law. Whoever violates the laws of the state will be punished. The state has officials to execute its laws and regulations. The constitution of the state is the basis for its legislation. *The state embodies power!* In the state men of *different* opinions and different outlook *can* live beside each other. The state cannot demand that all men be of the same opinion. It can, however, demand that all men observe its laws.

II. The Party

In contrast to the state, the party is the community of men *of like opinion*. It is born out of the struggle for an ideology. In order to survive this struggle, it gathered together all men who were prepared to fight for this ideology. The ideology is the basis of the order in accordance with which men live within the party. While in the state laws are considered as pressure, obstacles, and difficulties by many citizens, the laws of the party are no burden but rather signify the will of the community. In the state the characteristic is the *must;* in the party the *I will.*

III. The Functions of the Party and the State

(a) It is conceivable that party and state are one and the same thing. This is the case when all racial comrades are converted to the ideology of the party and the laws of the state are the clear expression of the will of the ideology. Then the *state* becomes the great community of men of like opinion. This ideal situation will only seldom be attained in history. It is, in fact, only conceivable if *this* ideology is the only basis for the inner attitude and takes complete possession of the people.

(b) If the party in power has no ideology whatsoever and is merely an artificial organization for the attainment of a temporary goal, party and state sink to the level of a technical apparatus which is unable to transmit to the *Volk* any spiritual values and merely provides for quiet and order as a nightwatchman- and police-state. We had this state of affairs in the preceding decades.

(c) If the *Volk* in all its branches is not impregnated by the party and its ideology, party and state must remain separated. The party will then be an order in which a select group of leaders and fighters is found. The ideology will be carried to the *Volk* by these fighters. The party shall prepare public opinion and public desire so that the spiritual condition of the *Volk* shall be in accord with the actual legislation of the state.

Therefore it does not suffice for the party to be an elite, a minority which is bound together in unity. The party has rather the task of accomplishing the political education and the political unification of the German *Volk*. It accordingly is charged also with the leadership of its associated organizations. In the course of this leadership the party fulfils its primary task: the ideological conquest of the German *Volk* and the creation of the "Organization of the *Volk*".

The state is a technical instrument to assist in the creation of this community of the people. It is the instrument for the realization of the ideology. The *party* is, therefore, *the primary* which constantly refills dead material with life and the will to life.

The state administrative apparatus functioned before the war and functioned also after the war. Notwithstanding, the German *Volk* experienced the Black Day of November 9, 1918; notwithstanding, it experienced the terrible collapse of the post-war period in all fields of political, cultural, and economic life. Germany could only be saved from sinking into Communistic chaos through the spirit, will, and readiness to sacrifice of the German freedom movement. Its forces of will and spirit alone made reconstruction possible. The party now has the right and the task of again pumping streams of its spirit and will into the state apparatus.

The party must receive this function and take care that it does not become too closely linked with the administration of the state. If it does not do this, it runs the risk of being swallowed by the state bureaucracy and itself degenerating into a party bureaucracy.

We see this struggle for new state forms everywhere in the world. That unspiritual time when parties merely represented a temporary program and the state was a dead machine is past. It was the era of materialism. In the twentieth century, the peoples are fighting for their soul and for a new mode of life which naturally must express itself in the forms of the state. We see this struggle in Italy, Hungary, Germany, and in other states.

After every revolution the bureaucracy fought for its position and generally won. The National Socialist revolution has today already decided the battle between bureaucracy and the party to the party's advantage. A few rear-guard actions will not change this in any way.

In accordance with the will of the Führer the relation between party and state in Germany will be as follows:

With the appointment of the Führer's Deputy as Minister of the Party (*Partei-Minister*) and, of course, through the Führer as Führer of the Party and Reich's Chancelor, the relation between party and state is established at the top. The remainder of the directorate of the party must not be fused with the state. A further connection of the heads of the party and of the state will be provided by the great senate which is planned at a later date. The great senate is a purely party institution which, however, will also be the highest state organ.

The third connection between party and state in Nazi Germany is the union in one person of the offices of *Gauleiter* (Gau leader) and *Reichsstatthalter* (provincial governor).

The reform of the Reich will take this wish of the Führer's into account.

A further liaison between party and state is found in the institution of the party representatives (*Parteibeauftragten*) in the different communities (*Gemeinde*), which was established through the German community order, to whom certain rights are accorded to participate in the structure of the community life.

The state in any form will always be somewhat rigid, but *the party*, on the other hand, *must always and at all times be flexible and vital*. If it wishes to be the conscience of the *Volk*, it must derive its impulses exclusively from its ideology.

(Pages 143–144)

FOREIGN ORGANIZATION OF THE NSDAP

(AUSLANDSORGANISATION DER NSDAP)

The Foreign Organization (AO) of the NSDAP is conducted in an organizational sense, as a Gau. The Director of the Foreign Organization has the rank of a Gauleiter and is directly under the Führer's Deputy. The Foreign Organization has its seat in Berlin. The Director of the Foreign Organization is at the same time the Chief of the Foreign Organization in the Foreign Office and directs the unified care and control of German citizens living abroad.

TASKS AND JURISDICTION

The Foreign Organization has the task of winning the German citizens who live abroad or are engaged in navigation for the National Socialist view of the world and of keeping alive in every single German abroad the principle of the racial community which transcends all classes and religious denominations. The Foreign Organization has nothing at all to do with non-German matters.

The Foreign Organization is the single, qualified party office for all party formations abroad and on board German ships. The Director of the Foreign Organization is responsible for all measures, directives, and instructions issued in this field. Furthermore, he bears the responsibility that the particular instructions of all qualified posts in the main office of the party be altered to conform with conditions abroad, so that an endangering or injury of German interests absolutely be avoided.

MEMBERS

All party comrades who have their domicil in foreign countries, travel abroad to take up permanent residence, or are employed on board seafaring vessels, are under the jurisdiction of the Foreign

Organization and may not be listed as members of Gaus in Germany. Seafaring party comrades who have left their employment on board a ship and have been unemployed for at least a half year, will be transferred to the appropriate German Gau, as will likewise German comrades from abroad who return to take up their permanent residence in the homeland.

The members of the families of German seamen, who reside in the homeland and belong to the National Socialist Women's Organization, will be listed with the National Socialist Women's Organization of the Foreign Organization of the NSDAP, Maritime Division. This concerns all the Gaus in which the Maritime Division of the Foreign Organization has sectional offices, subsectional offices, and branches.

ORGANIZATION

The staff of the Foreign Organization bears the title "Managing Office of the Foreign Organization of the NSDAP".

The Foreign Organization of the NSDAP is divided into country groups or regional sections, sections, local groups, and branches. The designation "country group" (*Landesgruppe*) is employed only for those countries which are of special significance for Germandom abroad. The designation "regional section" (*Landkreis*) applies to all other countries.

The Foreign Organization's bearers of sovereignty are:

(1) The Director with the rank of a Gauleiter,
(2) The deputy director with the rank of a deputy Gauleiter,
(3) The country group leader, given the rank of a Gau office chief, on account of the particular geographic conditions in an organization encompassing almost all the countries of the earth,
(4) Regional section leaders with the rank of a section leader,
(5) The section leaders,
(6) The local group leaders,
(7) The branch leaders.

The office chiefs in the Managing Office of the Foreign Organization, the Foreign Commissars, under whom are placed several country groups and regional sections, in some cases a whole continent, and the country group leaders have the rank of a Gau office chief.

Under the director of the office "Maritime Division of the Foreign Organization of the NSDAP" are:

(1) Divisional chiefs in Bremen, Hamburg, Lübeck, and Stettin with the rank of a Gau divisional chief,
(2) Local group leaders and branch leaders on board German ships.

The Führer has given the members of the Foreign Organization permission to wear a special insignia to designate the political leaders and the party comrades of the Foreign Organization. . . . It is a black diamond, which is worn on the left arm, the lower edge two centimeters above the cuff. Within the black diamond are the two letters A and O, in gold. Members of the party formations, if at the same time they, as party comrades, belong to the Foreign Organization and have the right to wear the AO diamond, have it embroidered in silver. Party comrades wear the insignia *on the brown shirt*. The insignia may only be worn as long as the party comrade concerned is a member of the Foreign Organization. He has to take it off as soon as he returns to the homeland and is transferred to a local group.

The chart shown here (chart 4, *post* p. 494) gives a representation of the organization in detail.

All business communication between all party offices and the organizations of the NSDAP in foreign countries and on board ships is to be forwarded without exception via the Managing Office of the Foreign Organization. Associations affiliated with the party, which intend to include German citizens abroad in their activity, may only do this within the framework of the Foreign Organization.

DOCUMENT 8

(Summary)

RECHTSEINRICHTUNGEN UND RECHTSAUFGABEN DER BEWEGUNG (LEGAL ORGANIZATION AND LEGAL FUNCTIONS OF THE MOVEMENT), BY OTTO GAUWEILER: MUNICH, ZENTRALVERLAG DER NSDAP, FRANZ EHER NACHFOLGER, 1939

The author seeks to present in handbook form a summary of the legal theory and the legal framework of the NSDAP. The book begins with a short presentation of the ideology which underlies Nazi legal concepts and proceeds to a survey of all the party agencies which are designed to impose these concepts upon the legal life and activity of the nation. The second half of the book offers a more particularized discussion of the Nazi ideology in relation to various spheres of national life and explains the legal functions of all offices and organizations attached to the party.

According to Nazi ideology, all authority within the nation is derived ultimately from the people, but it is the party through which the people expresses itself:

> "The will of the German people finds its expression in the party as the political organization of the people. It represents the political conception, the political conscience, and the political will. It is the expression and the organ of the people's creative will to life. It comprises a select part of the German people for 'only the best Germans should be party members' . . . The inner organization of the party must therefore bring the national life which is concentrated within itself to manifestation and development in all the fields of national endeavor in which the party is represented."

Thus the supreme leadership of the party in all phases of national life is justified, and the state becomes merely an administrative machine which the party has set up in accordance with and for the accomplishment of its aims:

> "As the responsible bearer and shaper of the destiny of the whole German nation the party has created an entirely new state, for that which sought to foist itself upon her as a state was simply the product of a deep human confusion. The state of the past and its political ideal had never satisfied the longing of the German people. The National Socialist movement already carried its state within itself at the time of its early struggles. It was able to place the completely formed body of its own state at the disposal of the state which it had taken over."

Thus the party organization runs parallel to the state organization, and the various state agencies are guided and controlled by the corresponding party offices. The study of the legal organization of the NSDAP is largely the study of this system of controls. The higher state offices are usually filled with the corresponding party officers, and the supreme legal authority of the Reich is, of course, the Führer of the NSDAP, who is "Chief of State and head of the Government in one person".

For practical purposes the party has been given the legal status of a "corporate public body" (*Körperschaft des öffentlichen Rechtes*). As such it is clothed with "special rights which are bestowed upon it by the state and performs public duties for the fulfilment of which it is responsible to the state". But this does not define the true nature of the party or its relation to the state:

> "The party stands above and beside the state as the wielder of an authority derived from the people with its own sovereign powers and its own sphere of sovereignty . . . The legal position of the party is therefore that of a completely sovereign authority whose legal supremacy and self-sufficiency rest upon the original independent political authority which the Führer and the movement have attained as a result of their historical achievements."

Full authority in all matters of party leadership has been delegated by the Führer to his so-called "*Stellvertreter*", or Deputy. Although this is purely a party office, the Deputy has also been made a Reich's Minister responsible for "insuring the closest cooperation between the offices of the party and the public offices" and for bringing about "agreement between the state leadership and the principles of the movement". This influence is extended to the legal field by a decree of the Führer that all proposed national laws must be drafted in consultation with his *Stellvertreter* and the completed drafts of all laws must be approved by him before they are submitted to the Führer's Cabinet. He is also to be consulted in connection with the appointment of all state officials who are appointed directly by the Führer. The representatives of the party who are connected with all the municipal governments in the Reich receive their instructions from him. He is responsible for the just application of laws directly concerned with political or ideological matters, such as the laws against attacks on the party and its organizations and the racial laws. He represents the party in all cases of conflict with the Government of the Reich or of the provinces.

The central legal office of the party is the *Reichsrechtsamt*. (The author presents a historical sketch of the development of this office and a brief biography of its leader, Dr. Hans Frank.) "As the chief party office for the legal activity of the movement it deals with all questions which concern the movement as a whole . . . The basic principle of the legal activity of the party as practiced by the *Reichsrechtsamt* is that the interests of the movement as a whole should take precedence over the interests of individual party members or of the separate organizations of the movement." The *Reichsrechtsamt* is divided into seven subordinate offices:

(1) The Central Office, which does the preliminary work for all legal decisions of the party and coordinates the work of all the party's national and local legal agencies.

(2) The Office of Legal Administration, which handles all questions regarding the legal position of the party and its organization, examines and initiates action on petitions which are made to the Führer, and keeps records of criminality within the party ranks.

(3) The Office for Legal Politics, which is responsible for the realization of National Socialist principles in the revision of German law.

(4) The Office for Legal Guidance, which supervises a party organization which offers legal advice and representation to citizens unable to pay lawyers' fees.

(5) The Office for Guardians of the Law (*Rechtswahrer*), which supervises and directs the *NS Rechtswahrerbund*, an organization which is later described in detail.

(6) The Office for Legal Education, which supervises the general inculcation of National Socialist legal conceptions throughout the Reich.

(7) The Office for Legal Publication, which guards the political purity of all literature on legal subjects appearing within the Reich.

In each Gau of the Reich the *Reichsrechtsamt* maintains a branch office which is divided into subordinate offices corresponding to those listed above. Smaller branch offices are maintained in each party district (*Kreis*). Thus a uniform system of legal offices is extended over the whole Reich, the purpose of which is to coordinate legal theory and practice throughout the nation and keep it in line with party principles.

The various bodies attached to the party also have their special fields of legal activity. These bodies are divided into two groups: those designated as party organizations (*Gliederungen der Partei*), which are parts of the party and have no independent administrative, legal, or financial status; and those designated as "attached bodies" (*angeschlossene Verbände*), which have their own administrations and finances, subject, of course, to party supervision. Members of the latter bodies are not necessarily party members. To the former category belong the SA and the SS, the NSKK (the party motorized corps), the HJ (Hitler Youth), the NS Students Association, the NS Womens Union, and the NS Professors Association. Each of these organizations contains a legal division which concerns itself with laws relating to itself or to the group of the people whom it represents. Thus the HJ organization exerts a great influence upon all laws concerning youth training and youthful crime; the NSKK upon traffic laws and regulations, etc. All of the groups are responsible for the National Socialistic legal education of their section of the people.

The same conditions exist with regard to the second group: the NS Physicians Association, the NS Law Guardians Association (*Rechtswahrerbund*), the NS Teachers Association, the NS Welfare Organization, the NS War Victims Assistance Organization, the NS German Technical Association, and the German Labor Front. But several of these organizations play a more far-reaching role in the legal life of the nation. The most important of them from a legal standpoint is the *Rechtswahrerbund*, which is an association of all persons engaged in occupations connected with the nation's legal activity: judges and lawyers of all kinds, notaries, legal administrators and trustees, university professors of law and economics, etc. The purpose of the organization is described as "the realization of the National Socialist program in the entire field of the nation's legal life" and "the establishment of ever-closer bonds between the people and the law". This organization is consequently the party's chief agency for the spreading of its legal theories and methods. By means of it the members of all legal professions are more or less forced into cooperation with the party.

The Labor Front (DAF) also has important legal functions: it is entrusted with the regulation of all legal relations between workers and employers. When conflicts arise, it attempts to settle them without recourse to the courts. It offers its members legal guidance in all matters regarding employment and social insurance. The other organizations also have offices which offer legal guidance in their respective fields; the Welfare Organization (NSV), for example, offers guidance and assistance in all matters regarding claims for state relief. In all legal matters which do not fall within the province of one of these organizations, assistance is offered to any citizen unable to pay lawyers' fees "regardless of his membership in the party", and he will even be represented in court if necessary. This service is offered by the Office for Legal Guidance (a division of the *Reichsrechtsamt*) in cooperation with the *Rechtswahrerbund* and is described as "the most social attempt which has ever been made to strengthen the faith of a whole people in the legal system of its nation".

There are several other party offices concerned with legal matters which are connected neither with the *Reichsrechtsamt* nor with any of the above-named organizations: The national treasurer of the NSDAP has jurisdiction over all legal questions with regard to party administration and party property. The Chancelry of the Führer maintains an office which considers the pardoning of party members convicted of criminal offenses; it also handles petitions of people who are partly of Jewish blood or who have been connected with Freemasonry.

The party maintains an Office for Local Politics (*Kommunalpolitik*) whose function is to guide and influence the municipal governments throughout the Reich and keep them in line with party policies. The Office for Racial Politics has a legal division which assists in the preparation of all laws regarding race, eugenics, and population. The Legal Division of the Foreign Organization concerns itself with the status of Germans living abroad as defined by the laws of the Reich, and it offers legal guidance and assistance to Germans and German firms in foreign countries. The Office for Agrarian Policies cooperates with the National Foods Commission (*Reichsnährstand*) in the formulation of all laws regarding food production and the administration of farming lands.

The party, by means of this extensive machinery, is trying to bring about a "renewal" of German law in accordance with its own ideas. To formulate its aims in the legal field more definitely, it has established the Academy of German Law, which is "a center of research closely associated with the party in its methods and its personnel in which, with academic thoroughness and exactness, new forms and contents are sought within the scope of the movement". It seeks "to assist in the reformation of German legal life and, in close cooperation with all official agencies, to help realize the National Socialist program in the legal and economic fields".

"According to National Socialist legal conceptions, law is the authoritarian order of the life of the national community, which is derived from the people. National Socialist ideology recognizes five basic values and the 'renewal' of the laws of the Reich must have the purpose of establishing and fostering these values:

"1. Race: The legal protection of the race, which has created a new concept of nationality [*Volkszugehörigkeit*], is consciously put in first place, for the most significant historical principle which has been established by the victory of National Socialism is that of the necessity for keeping race and blood pure. All human mistakes and errors can be corrected except one: 'the error regarding the importance of maintaining the basic values of a nation'.

"The purpose of this legal protection of the basic value of *race* must be the prevention for all time of a further mixture of German blood with foreign blood, as well as the prevention of continued procreation of racially unworthy and undesirable members of the people.

"2. Soil [*Boden*]: The living-space and the basis for the food supply of the German people are its territory and soil. The farmer is the first and deepest representative of the people since he nourishes the people from the fertility of the earth and he maintains the nation through the fertility of his own family. Here National Socialism had to accomplish two great legal ends: the reestablishment and the protection of the farmer class and the securing of its land for the farmer family.

"3. Work: The nation's work as a basic national value is grounded on the leading concept of 'work of the hands and of the head' within and for the community of the people and the elevation of work to the only criterion for the value of an individual within the community. In place of the idea of class warfare, National Socialism had to establish the national community legally; in place of the defamation of work and its degradation to an object of barter, National Socialism had to raise it to an ethical duty and the right to work had to become the most clearly defined personal right of the individual. The concept of the honor of work had to be established as the basic concept of the national honor.

"4. The Reich: With the securing of the three basic values of race, soil, and work arises the National Socialist Reich.

"The infusion of foreign cultural and legal influences in Germany was a consequence of the weakening of the central authority of the German Reich since the Middle Ages. The creation and insuring of a strong central authority in contrast to the disorganized, federalistic system of the Weimar Republic became one of the principal lines of National Socialist legal policy. In consequence of the National Socialist revolution, the Reich took on the legal form of a totalitarian state and received a supreme and completely authoritative lawgiver in the person of the Führer. The principle of a division of power could no longer maintain itself: The formulation, the interpretation, and the execution of the law are all performed by the Führer himself or under his authority.

"5. Honor: The fifth great value of the nation is its honor. The honor of the people, the Reich, the party, the Führer, and the individual citizen are all regarded as goods to be protected by law. The basis of national honor is loyalty. National Socialist criminal law is therefore essentially organized as a system of punishment for breaches of faith. Every crime and offense against the community is a breach of faith which must result in loss of honor.

"In accordance with these basic principles and thanks to the dynamics of the National Socialist revolution and the purposeful cooperation of the party in the field of lawmaking, the reformation of the laws of the Reich has already been accomplished in the most important provinces. In a series of basic laws these fundamental national values have been legally secured in all respects . . .

"The party is the organization of the German people, its mouthpiece, and the guardian of its interests. In the party, its organizations, and the associated bodies are included all age, professional, and class strata of the German people. The organization of the party makes it possible for the needs, wishes, and requirements of the people to be made known to the party leadership. Thus the participation of the party in lawgiving really represents the participation of the people and demonstrates the character of the Third Reich as a true democracy."

The party insured the infusion of the entire structure of the state with its ideas through the civil-service law (*Beamtengesetz*) of January 26, 1937, which provides that a person appointed to a civil-service position must be "filled with National Socialist views, since only thus can he be an executor of the will of the state which is carried by the NSDAP. It demands of him that he be ready at all times to exert himself unreservedly in behalf of the National Socialist state and that he be aware of the fact that the NSDAP, as the mouthpiece of the people's will, is the vital force behind the concept of the German state." He is bound to report immediately any occurrences inimicable to the state or to the party.

The party is extremely active in the education of the people in National Socialist legal principles. All of the Nazi propaganda machinery is in the service of this program; political lecturers, the press, the radio, and the films all play a part in helping the people to understand and appreciate the new legal code. The schools and Hitler Youth groups provide instruction for all young people in the fundamentals of National Socialist law, and pupils in those schools which train the carefully selected future leaders are given a specially strong dose of Nazi legal theory and practice. A very intensive educational campaign has been conducted among the members of the *Rechtswahrerbund;* they are subjected to regular courses and classes and they must attend study-camps where they are freed of the old "liberalistic legal conceptions" and steeped in the new legal ideology. "In large cities one cannot speak nearly as easily and understandingly of blood, race, and soil as in the midst of splendid natural scenery." Party membership is not explicitly required of the *Rechtswahrer* but "the experience of National Socialism by a *Rechtswahrer* finds its finest and most militant form in one of the organizations of the movement . . . Here the individual can prove that he has the right spirit, and certainly the people's Führer-state can demand such proof of those who are entrusted with leading state positions."

This book demonstrates very clearly the thoroughness of National Socialism. Not only is the formulation of German law controlled at the source, but all persons connected with the law are kept directly under the thumb of the party and the tentacles of the party's legal machinery reach into every field of national life, exerting pressure to bring the ideas and the activities of the entire people into line with the goals of the movement.

DOCUMENT 9

(Translation)

REICHSGESETZBLATT (GERMAN BULLETIN OF LAWS), 1942, PART I,
PAGE 35

DECREE FOR THE EXECUTION OF THE FÜHRER'S DECREE CONCERNING THE STATUS OF THE DIRECTOR OF THE PARTY CHANCELRY
January 16, 1942

In virtue of the Führer's decree of May 29, 1941, concerning the status of the Director of the Party Chancelry (*Reichsgesetzbl.* I, p. 295), the following is ordained:

§ 1

(1) The party's collaboration in lawmaking takes place exclusively through the Director of the Party Chancelry, so far as the Führer does not determine otherwise. Also, legislative proposals and suggestions from the party, its formations, and associated organizations may be forwarded to the qualified head offices of the Reich only through the Director of the Party Chancelry.

(2) Likewise, the collaboration of the party with regard to personnel matters among public officials takes place exclusively through the Director of the Party Chancelry.

§ 2

In any case of legislative work the Director of the Party Chancelry has the status of a participant Reich's Minister. Consequently the chief offices of the Reich are to grant him from the beginning participation in the preliminary work on laws of the Reich, on decrees and enactments of the Führer, on decrees of the Ministerial Counsel for the Reich's Defense, as well as on decrees of the chief offices of the Reich, including rulings with regard to the execution and enforcement of such decrees. The same applies to approval of laws and decrees made by the provincial governments and to decrees of the provincial governors (*Reichsstatthalter*).

§ 3

In matters of principle and political questions, especially those which pertain to the preparation, change, or enforcement of laws, decrees, and enactments, communication between the chief officials of the Reich and of the provinces, which encompass several Gaus, on

212

the one side, and the offices of the party, its formations, and associated organizations, on the other, takes place only through the Director of the Party Chancelry. Direct communication between the chief offices of the Reich and of the provinces and other party agencies is not permitted in these cases. The same applies to personnel matters regarding public servants, so far as there are not special regulations for these.

THE FÜHRER'S HEADQUARTERS, *January 16, 1942*

Reich's Minister and Chief of the Reich's Chancelry

Dr. LAMMERS

Director of the Party Chancelry

M. BORMANN

DOCUMENT 10

2. September 1923.   Nürnberg.

Source: <u>Das Buch der N.S.D.A.P.</u>, <u>Werden, Kampf</u>
         <u>und Ziel der N.S.D.A.P.</u>, by
         Walter M. Espe. Published by
         G. Schönfeld's Verlagsbuchhandlung,
         Berlin, 1934.

Eine interessante Aufnahme aus den Anfängen der nationalsozialistischen Bewegung. Die
ersten uniformierten Mitglieder der N.S.D.A.P. leisten bei ihrer Vereidigung den Treue=
schwur. Die Windjacke war damals statt des Braunhemdes die Tracht der Nationalsozialisten.

Bild 34.

(Translation: An interesting photograph from the earliest period of the National Socialist Movement. The first uniformed members of the NSDAP, on
taking the oath, are making their pledge of allegiance. At that time the wind-
breaker, rather than the brown shirt, was the garb of the National Socialist.)

214

(Translation)

I

REICHSGESETZBLATT (GERMAN BULLETIN OF LAWS), 1933, PART I,
PAGE 83

DECREE OF THE REICH'S PRESIDENT
FOR THE PROTECTION OF THE PEOPLE AND STATE
February 28, 1933

In virtue of paragraph 2, § 48, of the German Constitution, the following is decreed as a defensive measure against Communist acts of violence, endangering the state:

§ 1

Sections 114, 115, 117, 118, 123, 124, and 153 of the Constitution of the German Reich are suspended until further notice. Thus, restrictions on personal liberty, on the right of free expression of opinion, including freedom of the press, on the right of assembly and the right of association, and violations of the privacy of postal, telegraphic, and telephonic communications, and warrants for house-searches, orders for confiscations as well as restrictions on property, are also permissible beyond the legal limits otherwise prescribed.

.   .   .   .   .   .

§ 6

This decree enters in force on the day of its promulgation.

BERLIN, *February 28, 1933*

Reich's President VON HINDENBURG
Reich's Chancelor ADOLF HITLER
Reich's Minister of the Interior FRICK
Reich's Minister of Justice GÜRTNER

PROVISIONS OF GERMAN CONSTITUTION OF AUGUST 11, 1919
MENTIONED IN ABOVE DECREE

ARTICLE 48, PARAGRAPH 2

If public safety and order in Germany are materially disturbed or endangered, the President may take the necessary measures to restore public safety and order, and, if necessary, to intervene with the help of the armed forces. To this end he may temporarily suspend, in whole or in part, the fundamental rights established in articles 114, 115, 117, 118, 123, 124, and 153.

ARTICLE 114

Personal liberty is inviolable. An interference with or abridgment of personal liberty through official action is permissible only by authority of law. [Cf. the fourth amendment to the Constitution of the United States.]

Persons who are deprived of their liberty shall be informed at the latest on the following day by what authority and on what grounds they have been deprived of liberty, and they shall without delay receive an opportunity to present objections against such loss of liberty. [Cf. the fifth amendment to the Constitution of the United States.]

ARTICLE 115

The house of every German is his sanctuary and is inviolable. Exceptions are permissible only by authority of law. [Cf. the fourth amendment to the Constitution of the United States.]

ARTICLE 117

The secrecy of postal, telegraphic, and telephonic communications is inviolable. Exceptions may be permitted only by national law. [Cf. the fourth amendment to the Constitution of the United States.]

ARTICLE 118

Every German has a right within the limits of the general laws to express his opinion freely by word, in writing, in print, by picture, or in any other way. No relation arising out of his employment may hinder him in the exercise of this right, and no one may discriminate against him if he makes use of this right. [Cf. the first amendment to the Constitution of the United States.]

There is no censorship, although exceptional provisions may be made by law in the case of moving pictures. Legal measures are also permissible for combating obscene and indecent literature as well as for the protection of youth at public plays and spectacles.

ARTICLE 123

All Germans have the right of meeting peaceably and unarmed without notice or special permission.

Previous notice may be required by national law for meetings in the open, and such meetings may be forbidden in case of immediate danger to the public safety. [Cf. the first amendment to the Constitution of the United States.]

ARTICLE 124

All Germans have the right to form associations or societies for purposes not contrary to the criminal law. This right cannot be limited by preventive measures. The same provisions apply to religious associations and societies.

Every association has the right of incorporation in accordance with the civil law. No association may be denied this right on the ground that it pursues a political, social-political, or religious object.

ARTICLE 153

The right of private property is guaranteed by the Constitution. Its nature and limits are defined by law.

Expropriation may be proceeded with only for the benefit of the community and by due process of law. There shall be just compensation so far as is not otherwise provided by national law. If there is a dispute over the amount of the compensation, there shall be a right of appeal to the ordinary courts, so far as not otherwise provided by national law. The property of the states, municipalities, and associations of public utility may be taken by the Commonwealth only upon payment of compensation. [Cf. the fifth amendment to the Constitution of the United States.]

Property-rights imply property-duties. Exercise thereof shall at the same time serve the general welfare.

II

REICHSGESETZBLATT, 1933, PART I, PAGE 141

LAW TO REMOVE THE DISTRESS OF PEOPLE AND STATE
(GESETZ ZUR BEHEBUNG DER NOT VON VOLK UND REICH[1])
[KNOWN AS THE ERMÄCHTIGUNGSGESETZ, ENABLING ACT]

March 24, 1933

The Reichstag has resolved the following law, which is, with the approval of the National Council, herewith promulgated, after it has been established that the requirements have been satisfied for legislation altering the Constitution.

ARTICLE 1. National laws can be enacted by the National Cabinet as well as in accordance with the procedure established in the Constitution. This applies also to the laws referred to in article 85, paragraph 2, and in article 87 of the Constitution.

ARTICLE 2. The national laws enacted by the National Cabinet may deviate from the Constitution so far as they do not affect the position

---

[1] [On Jan. 30, 1937 (*Reichsgesetzblatt* (1937), pt. I, p. 105) the term of the above law was extended to Apr. 1, 1941; on Jan. 30, 1939 (*Reichsgesetzblatt* (1939), pt. I, p. 95) the term was extended to May 10, 1943—EDITOR.]

of the Reichstag and the National Council. The powers of the President remain undisturbed. [²]

ARTICLE 3. The national laws enacted by the National Cabinet are prepared by the Chancelor and published in the *Reichsgesetzblatt*. They come into effect, unless otherwise specified, upon the day following their publication. Articles 68 to 77 of the Constitution do not apply to the laws enacted by the National Cabinet.

ARTICLE 4. Treaties of the Reich with foreign states which concern matters of national legislation do not require the consent of the bodies participating in legislation. The National Cabinet is empowered to issue the necessary provisions for the execution of these treaties.

ARTICLE 5. This law becomes effective on the day of its publication. It becomes invalid on April 1, 1937; it further becomes invalid when the present National Cabinet is replaced by another.

BERLIN, *March 24, 1933*

 Reich's President VON HINDENBURG
 Reich's Chancelor ADOLF HITLER
 Reich's Minister of the Interior FRICK
 Reich's Minister for Foreign Affairs Baron VON NEURATH
 Reich's Minister of Finances Count SCHWERIN VON KROSIGK

PROVISIONS OF GERMAN CONSTITUTION OF AUGUST 11, 1919 MENTIONED IN ABOVE DECREE

ARTICLE 85, §2. The budget is adopted by law before the beginning of the fiscal year.

ARTICLE 87. Funds may be procured by borrowing only in case of extraordinary need and in general for expenditures for productive purposes only. Such procurement of funds as well as the assumption by the state of any financial obligation is permissible only by authority of a national law.

ARTICLE 68. Bills are introduced by the National Cabinet (*Reichsregierung*) or by members of the National Assembly (*Reichstag*).

National laws are enacted by the National Assembly.

ARTICLE 69. The introduction of bills by the National Cabinet requires the concurrence of the National Council (*Reichsrat*). If an agreement between the National Cabinet and the National Council is not reached, the National Cabinet may nevertheless introduce the bill but must state the dissent of the National Council.

If the National Council resolves upon a bill to which the National Cabinet does not assent, the latter must introduce the bill in the National Assembly together with a statement of its attitude.

---

² [Amended by article 4 of the law for reorganization of the Reich, Jan. 30, 1934, giving the Cabinet unrestricted powers to "lay down new constitutional laws"—EDITOR.]

ARTICLE 70. The national President shall compile the laws which have been constitutionally enacted and within one month publish them in the *German Bulletin of Laws* (*Reichsgesetzblatt*).

ARTICLE 71. National laws go into effect, unless otherwise specified, on the fourteenth day following the date of their publication in the *German Bulletin of Laws* at the national capital.

ARTICLE 72. The promulgation of a national law may be deferred for two months, if one third of the National Assembly so demands. Laws which the National Assembly and the National Council declare to be urgent may be promulgated by the national President regardless of this demand.

ARTICLE 73. A law enacted by the National Assembly shall be referred to the people before its promulgation, if the national President so orders within a month.

A law whose promulgation is deferred at the demand of at least one third of the National Assembly shall be submitted to the people, if one twentieth of the qualified voters so petition.

A popular vote shall further be resorted to on a measure initiated by the people if one tenth of the qualified voters so petition. A fully elaborated bill must accompany such petition. The National Cabinet shall lay the bill together with a statement of its attitude before the National Assembly. The popular vote does not take place if the desired bill is enacted without amendment by the National Assembly.

A popular vote may be taken on the budget, tax laws, and laws relating to the classification and payment of public officers only by authority of the national President.

The procedure in connection with the popular referendum and initiative will be regulated by national law.

ARTICLE 74. The National Council has the right to object to laws passed by the National Assembly.

The objection must be filed with the National Cabinet within two weeks after the final vote in the National Assembly and must be supported by reasons within two more weeks at the latest.

In case of objection the law is returned to the National Assembly for reconsideration. If an agreement between the National Assembly and the National Council is not reached, the national President may within three months refer the subject of the dispute to the people. If the President makes no use of this right, the law does not go into effect. If the National Assembly disapproves by a two-thirds majority the objection of the National Council, the President shall promulgate the law in the form enacted by the National Assembly within three months or refer it to the people.

ARTICLE 75. An act of the National Assembly may be annulled by a popular vote only if a majority of those qualified take part in the vote.

ARTICLE 76. The Constitution may be amended by process of legislation. But acts of the National Assembly relating to the amendment of the Constitution are effective only if two thirds of the legal membership are present and at least two thirds of those present give their assent. Acts of the National Council relating to the amendment of the Constitution also require a two-thirds majority of all the votes cast. If an amendment to the Constitution is to be adopted by the people by popular initiative, the assent of a majority of the qualified voters is required.

If the National Assembly adopts an amendment to the Constitution against the objection of the National Council, the President may not promulgate this law if the National Council within two weeks demands a popular vote.

ARTICLE 77. The National Cabinet issues the general administrative regulations necessary for the execution of the national laws so far as the laws do not otherwise provide. It must secure the assent of the National Council if the execution of the national laws is assigned to the state authorities.

III

REICHSGESETZBLATT, 1933, PART I, PAGE 479

LAW AGAINST THE NEW ESTABLISHMENT OF PARTIES
(GESETZ GEGEN DIE NEUBILDUNG VON PARTEIEN)
July 14, 1933

The German Cabinet has resolved the following law, which is herewith promulgated:

§ 1

The National Socialist German Workers' Party [*Nationalsozialistische Deutsche Arbeiterpartei*] constitutes the only political party in Germany.

§ 2

Whoever undertakes to maintain the organizational structure of another political party or to form a new political party will be punished with penal servitude up to three years or with imprisonment of from six months to three years, if the deed is not subject to a greater penalty according to other regulations.

BERLIN, *July 14, 1933*

Reich's Chancelor ADOLF HITLER
Reich's Minister of the Interior FRICK
Reich's Minister of Justice GÜRTNER

IV

REICHSGESETZBLATT, 1933, PART I, PAGE 1016

LAW TO SAFEGUARD THE UNITY OF PARTY AND STATE
(GESETZ ZUR SICHERUNG DER EINHEIT VON PARTEI UND STAAT)

December 1, 1933

The German Cabinet has resolved the following law, which is herewith promulgated:

§ 1

(1) After the victory of the National Socialist revolution, the National Socialist German Workers' Party (NSDAP) is the bearer of the German state-idea and indissolubly joined to the state.

(2) It is a corporation in public law. The Führer determines its statutes.

§ 2

In order to guarantee the closest cooperation of the party and the SA with the public officials, the Führer's Deputy and the Chief of Staff of the SA [3] are made members of the Cabinet.

§ 3

(1) The members of the NSDAP or the SA, including its subordinate formations, as the leading and animating forces of the National Socialist state, have increased obligations toward the Führer, people, and state.

(2) For violation of these obligations they are subject to a special party and SA jurisdiction.

(3) The Führer can extend these regulations to the members of other organizations.

.   .   .   .   .   .

BERLIN, *December 1, 1933*

Reich's Chancelor ADOLF HITLER
Reich's Minister of the Interior FRICK

---

[3] [On July 3, 1934, after the murder of Röhm, the Chief of Staff of the SA, § 2 was amended to the effect that only the Führer's Deputy would be a member of the Cabinet—EDITOR.]

DOCUMENT 12

(Excerpt)

The Programme of the Party of Hitler: The National Socialist German Workers' Party and Its General Conceptions, by Gottfried Feder (Translated by E.T.S. Dugdale): Munich, Franz Eher Nachfolger, G.M.B.H., 1932, Pages 18ff.

2. THE 25 POINTS

The National Socialist German Workers' Party at a great mass-meeting on February 25th, 1920, in the Hofbräuhaus-Festsaal in Munich announced their Programme to the world.

In section 2 of the Constitution of our Party this Programme is declared to be inalterable.

THE PROGRAMME

The Programme of the German Workers' Party is limited as to period. The leaders have no intention, once the aims announced in it have been achieved, of setting up fresh ones, merely in order to increase the discontent of the masses artificially, and so ensure the continued existence of the Party.

1. We demand the union of all Germans to form a Great Germany on the basis of the right of the self-determination enjoyed by nations.

2. We demand equality of rights for the German People in its dealings with other nations, and abolition of the Peace Treaties of Versailles and St. Germain.

3. We demand land and territory (colonies) for the nourishment of our people and for settling our superfluous population.

4. None but members of the nation may be citizens of the State. None but those of German blood, whatever their creed, may be members of the nation. No Jew, therefore, may be a member of the nation.

5. Anyone who is not a citizen of the State may live in Germany only as a guest and must be regarded as being subject to foreign laws.

6. The right of voting on the State's government and legislation is to be enjoyed by the citizen of the State alone. We demand therefore that all official appointments, of whatever kind, whether in the Reich, in the country, or in the smaller localities, shall be granted to citizens of the State alone.

We oppose the corrupting custom of Parliament of filling posts merely with a view to party considerations, and without reference to character or capability.

222

7. We demand that the State shall make it its first duty to promote the industry and livelihood of citizens of the State. If it is not possible to nourish the entire population of the State, foreign nationals (non-citizens of the State) must be excluded from the Reich.

8. All non-German immigration must be prevented. We demand that all non-Germans, who entered Germany subsequent to August 2nd, 1914, shall be required forthwith to depart from the Reich.

9. All citizens of the State shall be equal as regards rights and duties.

10. It must be the first duty of each citizen of the State to work with his mind or with his body. The activities of the individual may not clash with the interests of the whole, but must proceed within the frame of the community and be for the general good.

We demand therefore :

11. Abolition of incomes unearned by work.

ABOLITION OF THE THRALDOM OF INTEREST

12. In view of the enormous sacrifice of life and property demanded of a nation by every war, personal enrichment due to a war must be regarded as a crime against the nation. We demand therefore ruthless confiscation of all war gains.

13. We demand nationalisation of all businesses which have been up to the present formed into companies (Trusts).

14. We demand that the profits from wholesale trade shall be shared out.

15. We demand extensive development of provision for old age.

16. We demand creation and maintenance of a healthy middle class, immediate communalisation of wholesale business premises, and their lease at a cheap rate to small traders, and that extreme consideration shall be shown to all small purveyors to the State, district authorities and smaller localities.

17. We demand land-reform suitable to our national requirements, passing of a law for confiscation without compensation of land for communal purposes; abolition of interest on land loans, and prevention of all speculation in land.[1]

---

[1] On April 13th, 1928, Adolf Hitler made the following declaration :

It is necessary to reply to the false interpretation on the part of our opponents of Point 17 of the Programme of the N.S.D.A.P.

Since the N.S.D.A.P. admits the principle of private property, it is obvious that the expression "confiscation without compensation" merely refers to possible legal powers to confiscate, if necessary, land illegally acquired, or not administered in accordance with national welfare. It is directed in accordance with national welfare. It is directed in the first instance against the Jewish companies which speculate in land.

MUNICH, *April 13th, 1928.*

(signed)   ADOLF HITLER.

We demand ruthless prosecution of those whose activities are injurious to the common interest. Sordid criminals against the nation, usurers, profiteers, etc. must be punished with death, whatever their creed or race.

19. We demand that the Roman Law, which serves the materialistic world order, shall be replaced by a legal system for all Germany.

20. With the aim of opening to every capable and industrious German the possibility of higher education and of thus obtaining advancement, the State must consider a thorough re-construction of our national system of education. The curriculum of all educational establishments must be brought into line with the requirements of practical life. Comprehension of the State idea (State sociology) must be the school objective, beginning with the first dawn of intelligence in the pupil. We demand development of the gifted children of poor parents, whatever their class or occupation, at the expense of the State.

21. The State must see to raising the standard of health in the nation by protecting mothers and infants, prohibiting child labour, increasing bodily efficiency by obligatory gymnastics and sports laid down by law, and by extensive support of clubs engaged in the bodily development of the young.

22. We demand abolition of a paid army and formation of a national army.

23. We demand legal warfare against conscious political lying and its dissemination in the Press. In order to facilitate creation of a German national Press we demand:

(a) that all editors of newspapers and their assistants, employing the German language, must be members of the nation;

(b) that special permission from the State shall be necessary before non-German newspapers may appear. These are not necessarily printed in the German language;

(c) that non-Germans shall be prohibited by law from participation financially in or influencing German newspapers, and that the penalty for contravention of the law shall be suppression of any such newspaper, and immediate deportation of the non-German concerned in it.

It must be forbidden to publish papers which do not conduce to the national welfare. We demand legal prosecution of all tendencies in art and literature of a kind likely to disintegrate our life as a nation, and the suppression of institutions which militate against the requirements above-mentioned.

24. We demand liberty for all religious denominations in the State, so far as they are not a danger to it and do not militate against the moral feelings of the German race.

The Party, as such, stands for positive Christianity, but does not bind itself in the matter of creed to any particular confession. It combats the Jewish-materialist spirit within us and without us, and is convinced that our nation can only achieve permanent health from within on the principle:

THE COMMON INTEREST BEFORE SELF.

25. That all the fore-going may be realised we demand the creation of a strong central power of the State. Unquestioned authority of the politically centralised Parliament over the entire Reich and its organisations; and formation of Chambers for classes and occupations for the purpose of carrying out the general laws promulgated by the Reich in the various States of the confederation.

The leaders of the Party swear to go straight forward—if necessary to sacrifice their lives—in securing fulfilment of the fore-going Points.

MUNICH, *February 24th, 1920.*

DOCUMENT 13

(Translation)

MEIN KAMPF, BY ADOLF HITLER: MUNICH, VERLAG FRANZ EHER NACHFOLGER, G.M.B.H., 1933 (COPYRIGHT 1925)

I

I wish, moreover, to state the following general premises:

If by foreign policy we understand the regulation of the relations of a people to the rest of the world, then the nature of this regulation will be determined by very definite facts. As National Socialists we can further set forth the following principle with regard to the nature of the foreign policy of a folk-state:

It is the task of the foreign policy of a folk-state to secure the existence on this planet of the race which is encompassed by the state and at the same time to establish a healthy, viable, natural relation between the number and growth of the folk on the one hand and the size and quality of its soil and territory on the other hand.

In this connection only that condition may be regarded as a healthy relation which insures the nourishment of the people from its own soil and territory. Any other condition, even though it may endure for hundreds or even thousands of years, is none the less unhealthy and will lead sooner or later to the damaging, if not to the destruction, of the people in question.

(pp. 727–728)

We National Socialists must never at any time join in the distasteful hurrah-patriotism of the present-day bourgeois world. It would be particularly deadly to regard the last developments before the war as in any way binding upon our present course. Not a single obligation from the whole historical period of the nineteenth century can be followed up by us. In contrast to the representatives of that period we have again proclaimed ourselves the representatives of the supreme historical viewpoint of all foreign policy, namely: *to bring the territory into harmony with the size of the population.* Yes, we can only learn from the past that we must undertake the setting of aims for our political activity in two directions: *Soil and territory as the goal of our foreign policy, and a new, philosophically firm and uniform foundation as the goal of our domestic political activity.*
(pp. 735–736)

226

*Our task, the mission of the National Socialist movement, how-
ever, is to lead our folk to such political insight that it will see its
future goal fulfilled not in the intoxicating impression of a new
Alexandrian campaign but rather in the industrious work of the
German plow, which waits only to be given land by the sword.*
(p. 743)

If the National Socialist movement, in view of this greatest and
most important task, frees itself of all illusions and lets reason
prevail as its sole guide, then the catastrophe of the year 1918 can
one day turn into an infinite blessing for the future of our folk.   As
a result of this collapse our people can achieve a complete re-
orientation of its foreign political activity, and, furthermore,
inwardly strengthened by its new philosophy, it can arrive externally
at a final stabilization of its foreign policy.   It can then, at last,
attain that which England has, which even Russia used to have, and
which enabled France always to make uniform decisions which were
in the last analysis best for her interests, namely: *a political
testament.*

But the political testament of the German nation for its outwardly
directed activity should and must always have the following import:

> *Never tolerate the establishment of two continental powers
> in Europe.   See an attack against Germany in every attempt
> to organize a second military power on the German borders,
> even if it is only in the form of the establishment of a state
> which is a potential military power, and see therein not only
> the right but also the duty to prevent the formation of such a
> state with all means, even to the use of force, or if it has already
> been established, to destroy it again.   See to it that the strength
> of our folk has its foundations not in colonies but in the soil of
> the European homeland.   Never regard the foundations of the
> Reich as secure, if it is not able to give every off-shoot of our
> folk its own bit of soil and territory for centuries to come.
> Never forget that the most sacred right in the world is the right
> to the soil which a man wishes to till himself, and the most
> sacred sacrifice is the blood which he spills for this soil.*

(pp. 753–755)

The basic racial elements are differently situated, not only territorially but also in individual cases within the same territory.
Nordic men exist side by side with Eastern types; Easterners, with
Dinarics; both of these types, with Westerners; and everywhere
among them are mixed types.   On the one hand this is a great disadvantage: The German folk lacks that sure instinct of the herd
which has its roots in the unity of blood and, especially in moments
when great danger threatens, preserves the nation from collapse,
in as much as with such a folk all small internal distinctions will
then immediately disappear and the common enemy will be faced

with the closed front of the uniform herd. In the existence side by side of our most varied component racial elements, which have remained unmixed, lies the foundation of that which we designate with the word *superindividualism*. In peaceful times it may sometimes perform good services for us, but, considered all in all, it has deprived us of world supremacy. If the German folk, in its historical development, had possessed that herdlike unity which other peoples have enjoyed, the German Reich would today be mistress of the globe. World history would have taken another course, and no one can tell whether in this way that might not have been attained which so many deluded pacifists are hoping today to wheedle by moaning and whining: *A peace supported not by the palm branches of tearful pacifistic female mourners but founded by the victorious sword of a master race* (Herrenvolk) *which places the world in the service of a higher culture.* (pp. 437–438)

II

In this regard one proceeded from the very correct principle that the size of the lie always involves a certain factor of credibility, since the great mass of a people will be more spoiled in the innermost depths of its heart, rather than consciously and deliberately bad. Consequently, in view of the primitive simplicity of its mind it is more readily captivated by a big lie than by a small one, since it itself often uses small lies but would be, nevertheless, too ashamed to make use of big lies. Such an untruth will not even occur to it, and it will not even believe that others are capable of the enormous insolence of the most vile distortions. Why, even when enlightened, it will still vacillate and be in doubt about the matter and will nevertheless accept as true at least some cause or other. Consequently, even from the most impudent lie something will always stick . . . (pp. 252–253)

To whom must propaganda appeal? To the scientific mind or to the less educated masses? (p. 196)

The task of propaganda does not lie in a scientific education of the individual but in pointing out to the masses definite facts, processes, necessities, etc., the significance of which in this way is first to be brought within the masses' range of vision.

The art lies exclusively therein, to do this in such an excellent way that a universal conviction arises of the reality of a fact, of the necessity of a process, of the correctness of something necessary, etc. Since it is not and cannot be necessary in itself, since its task, just as in the case of a placard, consists of bringing something before the attention of the crowd and not in the instruction of those who are scientifically trained or are seeking education and insight, its efficacy must always be oriented more to the emotions and only in a very restricted way to the so-called "intellect".

All propaganda has to appeal to the people and its intellectual level has to be set in accordance with the receptive capacities of the most-limited persons among those to whom it intends to address itself. The larger the mass of men to be reached, the lower its purely intellectual level will have to be set.
(p. 197)

The more modest, then, its scientific ballast, and the more it exclusively takes account of the emotions of the masses, the more decisive will be its success. This, however, is the best proof of the accuracy or non-accuracy of propaganda and not the successful satisfaction of a few scholars or youthful esthetes.

The art of propaganda lies precisely therein, that, comprehending the great masses' world of emotions and imagination, it finds the way, in a psychologically correct form, to the attention and, further, to the hearts of the great masses.
(p. 198)

The receptive capacity of the great masses is very restricted, its understanding small. On the other hand, however, its forgetfulness is great. On account of these facts all effective propaganda must restrict itself to very few points and impress these by slogans, until even the last person is able to bring to mind what is meant by such a word. (p. 198)

The task of propaganda is, for instance, not to evaluate diverse rights but to emphasize exclusively the single right of that which it is representing. It does not have to investigate objectively the truth, so far as this is favorable to the others, in order then to present it to the masses in strict honesty, but rather to serve its own side ceaselessly. (p. 200)

If one's own propaganda even once accords just the shimmer of right to the other side, then the basis is therewith laid for doubt regarding one's own cause. The masses are not able to distinguish where the error of the other side ends and the error of one's own side begins. (p. 200–201)

But all talent in presentation of propaganda will lead to no success if a fundamental principle is not always strictly followed. Propaganda has to restrict itself to a few matters and to repeat these eternally. Persistence is here, as with so many other things in the world, the first and most important presupposition for success. (p. 202)

Propaganda is, however, not designed to furnish jaded gentlemen currently with interesting diversions but rather to convince, and, indeed, to convince the masses. In view of their slowness of mind, they require always, however, a certain period before they are ready even to take cognizance of a matter, and only after a thousandfold repetition of the most simple concept will they finally retain it.

Any variation ought never to affect the content of that which the propaganda seeks to present, rather the same thing must always be said at the end. Thus the catchword must be elucidated from various sides, but the end of every consideration must always reiterate anew the catchword itself. Only in this way can and will the propaganda have a unified and concentrated effect.

(p. 203)

In general the art of all truly great popular leaders at all times consists primarily in not scattering the attention of a people but rather in concentrating it always on one single opponent. The more unified this use of the fighting will of a people, the greater will be the magnetic attractive force of a movement and the more powerful the force of its push. It is a part of the genius of a great leader to make even quite different opponents appear as if they belonged only to one category, because the recognition of different enemies leads weak and unsure persons only too readily to begin doubting their own cause.

When the vacillating masses see themselves fighting against too many enemies, objectivity at once sets in and raises the question whether really all the others are wrong and only one's own people or one's own movement is right.

Therewith, however, appears already the first weakening of one's own force. Consequently, a number of intrinsically different opponents must always be comprehended together, so that in the view of the masses of one's own adherents the fight is only being carried on against one enemy alone. This strengthens the faith in one's own cause and increases the bitterness toward the aggressor against this cause.

(p. 129)

In all cases in which there is a question of the fulfilment of apparently impossible demands or tasks, the entire attention of a people must be concentrated only on this one question, in such a way as if being or non-being actually depends on its solution. Only in this way will one make a people willing and capable of really great accomplishments and exertions.

This principle is also true for the individual man, if he wants to attain high goals. He also will be able to accomplish this only

in steplike stages. He also will have to concentrate his entire exertions toward the attainment of a definitely restricted task until
this one appears to be fulfilled, and the determination of a new segment can be undertaken. If he does not undertake to divide in
separate stages the path to be mastered and does not seek to accomplish
these one by one, systematically, by means of the greatest concentration
of all energies, he will never be able to arrive at the final goal but rather
will remain somewhere on the way, perhaps indeed somewhere off on a
tangent. This slow approach to the goal is an art and always requires
the use of all energies in order thus to accomplish the way step by step.
The most primary prerequisite, accordingly, which is necessary for
the attack on a very difficult partial segment of the human path is
this, that the leadership succeeds in presenting to the mass of the
people precisely that partial goal, which is now to be attained, better,
to be fought for, as the only goal worthy of attention, on whose attainment everything depends. The great mass of the people can
never see the entire way before them, without tiring and doubting
the task. It will to a certain extent keep the goal in mind; in general, however, it is only able to survey the path in small partial
segments, just as the hiker, who likewise knows the destination of
his journey but who proceeds better along the endless road if he
divides it up for himself in segments and marches in each single one
as if it were the desired goal itself. Only in this way does he get
ahead without despairing.

   (pp. 273–274)

DOCUMENT 14

Source: <u>London</u> <u>Times</u>, September 26, 1939, p. 9.

EXTRACTS
FROM ADOLF HITLER'S
PUBLIC SPEECHES

February 10, 1933 to September 1, 1939

BERLIN, FEBRUARY 10, 1933.

"The first and best point of the Government's program is that <u>we won't lie and we won't swindle.</u>"

POTSDAM, MARCH 21, 1933.

"Weighing the sacrifices of the last war, we want to be true friends of a peace which will at last heal the wounds from which all have suffered."

BERLIN, MAY 17, 1933.

"Germany, France, and Poland will continue to exist. Germany wants nothing that she is not ready to give to others. . . .

"<u>No fresh European war is capable of putting</u> something better in the place of unsatisfactory conditions which exist to-day. . . . The outbreak of such madness without end would lead to the collapse of existing social order in Europe. . . . The German Government are convinced that to-day there can be only one great task, and that is to assure the peace of the world. . . . <u>The German Government wish to settle all difficult questions with other Governments by peaceful methods.</u> They know that any military action in Europe, even if completely successful, would, in view of the sacrifice, bear no relation to the profit to be obtained. . . .

"Germany will tread no other path than that laid down by the Treaties. The German Government will discuss all political and economic questions only within the framework of, and through, the Treaties.

"The German people have no thought of invading any country."

ON THE RADIO, MAY 27, 1933.

"We do not want a war merely for the purpose of bringing to Germany people who simply do not want to be, or cannot be, Germans."

On October 14, *1933,* Germany left the League of Nations

ON THE RADIO, OCTOBER 14, 1933.

"The history of the last 150 years should, in its changing course, have taught France and Germany that essential and enduring changes are no longer to be gained by the sacrifice of blood. As a National-Socialist I, with all my followers, refuse on the basis of our national principles to win for ourselves the members of other nations, who will never love us, at the cost of the blood and lives of those who are dear to us. It would be a mighty happening for all humanity if these two nations of Europe would banish, once and for all, force from their common life. The German people is ready to do so. . . . No one could demand that millions of men in the flower of youth should be annihilated for the sake of a readjustment of indefinite scope of our present frontier."

KELHEIM, OCTOBER 22, 1933.

"There is no better guarantee for the peace of the world than the fanatical unity of the German people."

BERLIN, OCTOBER 24, 1933.

"There are Germans and Poles in Europe, and they ought to live together in agreement. The Poles cannot think of Europe without the Germans and the Germans cannot think of Europe without the Poles."

BERLIN, NOVEMBER 10, 1933.

"I am not crazy enough to want a war. . . . The German people have but one wish—to be happy in their own way and to be left in peace. They do not interfere in other peoples' business, and others should not interfere in theirs. . . .

"When has the German people ever broken its word?"

BERLIN, JANUARY 13, 1934.

"The National-Socialist racial idea and the science underlying it does not lead to scorn or contempt for other nations, but rather to the natural respect for the life and character of other people. It frees foreign political activity from any attempt to dominate foreigners in order to rule them or to incorporate them as a mere numerical mass in one's own nation. . . . The new German Reich has fundamentally no other wish in its attitude towards other peoples and States than to live in peace and friendship with them. We are convinced that it must be again possible in this world to talk over differences in the lives of nations without always at once thinking of a resort to force.

"Germans and Poles must reconcile themselves as to the fact of each others' existence. It has seemed to me necessary to demonstrate by an example that it is possible for two nations to talk over their differences without giving the task to a third or a fourth. . . .

"The assertion that the German Reich plans to coerce the Austrian State is absurd and cannot be substantiated or proved. . . . The assertion of the Austrian Government that from the side of the Reich an attack would be undertaken or planned I must emphatically reject. . . . The German Reich is always ready to hold out a hand for a real understanding, with full respect for the free will of Austrian Germans. . . .

"After the Saar question has been settled the German Government is ready to accept not only the letter but the spirit of the Locarno Pact. . . .

"I can give the assurance that this sovereign nation has no other wish than to apply joyfully the strength and weight of her political, moral, and economic resources, not only for the healing of wounds which the past has inflicted on the human kind, but towards the cooperation of all cultured and civilized nations. After a year of the National-Socialist Revolution, Germany is fitter and more prepared than before to play her part among the nations in the preservation of happiness and prosperity."

LIPPE, JANUARY 14, 1934.

"We do not wish to interfere with the rights of others, to restrict the lives of other peoples, to oppress or subjugate other people."

GERA, JUNE 17, 1934.

"A nation has awakened to the consciousness of its strength. When the rest of the world asks what it all means, what we want, we can answer: 'At home everything; abroad, only to be left in peace.' We have a great aim before us; a mighty work of reform of ourselves, of our lives, of our life in common, of our economy, of our culture. This work does not disturb the rest of the world. We have enough to do in our own house."

HAMBURG, AUGUST 17, 1934.

"The German Government, like the German people, are filled with the unconditional wish to make the greatest possible contribution to the preservation of peace in this world."

On March 16, 1935, Germany announced conscription

BERLIN, MAY 21, 1935.

"The German Government intend not to sign any treaty which seems to them incapable of fulfilment, but will scrupulously observe every treaty voluntarily concluded, even if it was drawn up before their assumption of power and office. In particular they will hold to all obligations arising out of Locarno so long as other parties are ready to stand by that treaty. . . .

"Germany has concluded a non-aggression pact with Poland which is more than a valuable contribution to European peace, and she will adhere to it unconditionally. . . . . We recognize the Polish State as the home of a great patriotic nation with the understanding and the cordial friendship of candid nationalists. . . .

"The German Reich, and in particular the present German Government, has no other wish than to live on friendly and peaceable terms with all neighboring states—not only the larger states but the neighboring smaller states. . . .

"Both we National-Socialists and the Bolshevists are convinced that there is a gulf between us which can never be bridged. . . . So far as ever this Bolshevism draws Germany into its clutches we are the deadliest and most fanatical enemies. . . .

"Germany neither intends nor wishes to interfere in the internal affairs of Austria, to annex Austria, or to conclude an Anschluss."

BERLIN, NOVEMBER 29, 1935.

"Germany is the bulwark of the West against Bolshevism, and, in combating it, will meet terror with terror and violence with violence."

BERLIN, JANUARY 30, 1936.

"We want to be a peace-loving element among the nations. We cannot repeat that often enough."

On March 7, 1936, Germany reoccupied the Rhineland and denounced Locarno

BERLIN, MARCH 7, 1936.

"I should like the German nation to see in the other nations historical realities which the visionary might like to wish away, but which cannot be wished away. For this reason I should like the German people to understand the inner motives of National-Socialist foreign policy. We feel, for instance, that it is very unpleasant that the access to the sea of a nation of 33,000,000 should cut through former territory of the Reich, but we recognize that it is unreasonable, because impossible, simply to wish to deny so great a state access to the sea. . . .

"I shall demand from history confirmation of the fact that in no moment of my work for the German nation have I ever forgotten the obligation incumbent on me and on us all for the maintenance of European culture and civilization. . . .

"France, before Locarno, had made pacts of mutual assistance with both Czecho-Slovakia and Poland. Germany did not take offence at these, not only because, unlike the Franco-Soviet Pact, they were subordinated to the provisions of the League Covenant, but because at that time Czecho-Slovakia, and especially Poland, always pursued a policy governed by their own national interests. Germany has no desire to attack these States, and does not believe they have any interest in attacking her. Above all, however, Poland will remain Poland and France will remain France, but Soviet Russia is the exponent, organized into a State, of a revolutionary philosophy. The introduction into Central Europe of this mighty military factor destroys any real European balance of power. . . .

"After three years I believe that I can regard the struggle for German equality as concluded to-day. I believe, moreover, that thereby the first and foremost reason for our withdrawal from European collective collaboration has ceased to exist. We have no territorial demands to make in Europe."

KARLSRUHE, MARCH 12, 1936.

"I want to have a monument in the hearts of my people. A 30-centimeter shell costs two thousand marks. If I have another thousand marks I could build a workman's house."

MUNICH, MARCH 15, 1936.

"The German people do not wish to continue waging war to readjust frontiers. Each readjustment is bought by sacrifices out of proportion to what is to be gained."

BRESLAU, MARCH 22, 1936.

"I have been guided always by the principle that German freedom has nothing to do with injury to others. . . . It is one of the most elementary principles that nations should allow each other to live within their own territories as they wish to live."

COLOGNE, MARCH 28, 1936.

"Germany has no claims to make against the European nations except to live exactly like the others. . . . What we have in mind is a legal order of European national states with equal rights."

BERLIN, MAY 1, 1936.

"The lie goes forth again that Germany to-morrow or the day after will fall upon Austria or Czecho-Slovakia. I ask myself always: Who can these elements be who will have no peace, who incite continually, who must so distrust, and want no understanding? Who are they? I know they are not the millions who, if these inciters had their way, would have to take up arms."

NUREMBERG, SEPTEMBER 13, 1936.

"We see in Bolshevism a bestial, mad doctrine which is a threat to us. . . . I cannot make a pact with a regime whose first act is not the liberation of workmen but of the inmates of jails. . . . We cannot negotiate with Jewish Communist leaders. . . .

"These are two worlds. In Bolshevist Russia there is devastation, grim murder, and ruin. Here is laughter, happiness, and beauty."

BERLIN, JANUARY 11, 1937.

"The anxieties of the present should be for all nations a warning and a stimulus to recognize without delay the dangers which threaten the peace and therewith the development of Europe, and to work determinedly for international understanding and conciliation, giving all countries the possibility of an individual economic existence and thereby the surest guarantee for the welfare and progress of all mankind."

BERLIN, JANUARY 30, 1937.

"I do not want to leave any doubt as to the following: We look upon Bolshevism as upon an intolerable danger to the world; we shall try to keep this danger away from the German people by every means at our command; we are therefore endeavoring to make the German people as immune as possible from this contagion. For this it is necessary that we should avoid all close contacts with the bearers of these poisonous bacilli. . . . Any treaty links between Germany and present-day Bolshevist Russia would be without any value whatsoever. . . .

"The period of so-called surprises is now over."

NUREMBERG, SEPTEMBER 7, 1937.

"Our relations with Fascist Italy are a community of wills which it will be impossible for any party to ignore in future in any question of international politics. The agreement with Japan serves the same purpose—a standing together in defense against attacks on the civilized world such as are taking place to-day in Spain and could to-morrow or the day after to-morrow begin in the East or elsewhere."

NUREMBERG, SEPTEMBER 10, 1937.

"Germany is a guarantor of peace because she warns all those who from Moscow endeavor to set the world in flames."

NUREMBERG, SEPTEMBER 13, 1937.

"Nothing binds us closer to National-Socialism than the mere realization that we are in the midst of a world which is kept in a state of decomposition and spiritual uproar by Jewish Bolshevists in Moscow."

NUREMBERG, SEPTEMBER 14, 1937.

"I refuse most emphatically to be joined with those whose program is the destruction of Europe and who do not even try to conceal this program."

BERLIN, FEBRUARY 20, 1938.

"Shall I remind you of the Bolshevist Revolution which slaughtered millions upon millions of people, but whose blood-stained murderers still occupy high places? . . . With one single country alone we have detested to enter into relationships. That state is Soviet Russia. We see in Bolshevism more now than before the incarnation of human destructive forces.

" "I may say that since the League of Nations has abandoned its continuous attempts at disturbance in Danzig and since the advent of the new Commissioner this most dangerous place for European peace has entirely lost its menace.

"I fear that a Japanese defeat in East Asia would never be to the advantage of Europe or America, but exclusively to that of Bolshevist Russia. But the greatest victory of Japan would be much less dangerous for the general peace of the world than a Bolshevist victory would be. . . .

"The Polish State respects the national conditions in this country, and Danzig and Germany respect Polish rights. Thus it has been possible to find the way to an understanding which, emanating from Danzig, in spite of the assertions of many mischiefmakers, has succeeded in removing all friction between Germany and Poland, and made it possible to work together in true amity."

MUNICH, FEBRUARY 24, 1938.

"The genuineness of Germany's desire for peace and international understanding is demonstrated by her large-scale building schemes."

1938

On March 11, Germany invaded Austria

BERLIN, MAY 1, 1938.

"The motto must be, 'Never war again.' "

BERLIN, SEPTEMBER 26, 1938.

"We are not interested in suppressing other nations. We do not want to see other nations among us. We want to live our own life, and we want other peoples to do the same. . . .

"Germany and Poland are two nations, and these nations will live, and neither of them will be able to do away with the other. I recognized all of this, and we all must recognize that a people of 33,000,000 will always strive for an outlet to the sea. . . .

"We have assured all our immediate neighbors of the integrity of their territory as far as Germany is concerned. That is no hollow phrase; it is our sacred will. . . .

"The Sudetenland is the last territorial claim which I have to make in Europe. . . . I have assured Mr. Chamberlain, and I emphasize it now, that when this problem is solved Germany has no more territorial problems in Europe. I have further assured him that at the moment when Czecho-Slovakia has solved its other problems—that is, when the Czechs shall have come to an understanding with their other minorities—I shall not be interested in the Czech State any more, and that, so far as I am concerned, I can guarantee it."

SAARBRUCKEN, OCTOBER 9, 1938.

"Now as a strong State, we can be ready to pursue a policy of understanding with surrounding states. We want nothing from them. We have no wishes or demands; we desire peace. . . . No people can need peace more than we."

WEIMAR, NOVEMBER 6, 1938.

"As a peace-loving man, I have made every effort to give the German nation the defence and the weapons which are appropriate to persuade others also for peace. A hedgehog never attacks another animal except when it is attacked. No one should come near us. We want only our quiet and the right to live."

REICHENBERG, DECEMBER 2, 1938.

"We have undertaken very great limitations of the aims of our foreign policy."

BERCHTESGADEN, JANUARY 1, 1939.

"In general we have but one wish—that in the coming year we may be able to make our contribution to this general pacification of the whole world."

BERLIN, JANUARY 30, 1939.

"Only the war-mongers think there will be a war. I think there will be a long period of peace."

On March 15, 1939, Germany seized Czecho-Slovakia and March 21 annexed Memel

WILHELMSHAVEN, APRIL 1, 1939.

"We are rearming, but do not dream of attacking other nations, providing they leave us alone. . . .

"We have given Central Europe a great fortune—namely, peace, which is protected by the German might."

BERLIN, APRIL 28, 1939.

"As the National Leader of the German people I have never left any doubt that, wherever the national interests of the European comity were at stake, national interests must, if necessary, be relegated to second place in certain cases. And—as I have already emphasized—this is not for tactical reasons, for I have never left any doubt that I am absolutely earnest in this attitude of mind. . . . I have given binding declarations to a large number of states. None of these states can complain that even a trace of a demand contrary thereto has ever been made to them by Germany. . . .

"The Czech nation, with the sum total of its skill and ability, its industry, its diligence, its love of its native soil and of its own national heritage, deserves our respect. . . . That which the best and wisest Czechs have struggled for decades to attain is as a matter of course granted to this people in the National-Socialist German Reich—namely, the right to their own nationality and the right to foster this nationality and to revive it. . . .

"I have never ceased to uphold the view that the necessity of a free access to the sea for the Polish State cannot be ignored. . . .

"If the sub-human forces of Bolshevism had proved victorious in Spain they might easily have spread across the whole of Europe. . . . Since 1918 Soviet Russia has engaged in 10 wars and military actions involving force and bloodshed. Germany was concerned in none of these. . . .

"Mr. Roosevelt expresses the belief that every major war, even if it were to be confined to other continents, must have serious consequences while it lasts, and also for generations to come. No one knows this better than the German people. . . . Mr. Roosevelt believes that the 'tide of events' is once more bringing the threat of arms, and that if this threat of arms continues a large part of the world is condemned to a common ruin. As far as Germany is concerned I know nothing of this kind of threat to other nations. . . . Mr. Roosevelt then speaks of the reports that he admittedly does not believe to be correct but which state that further acts of aggression are contemplated against independent nations. I consider every such unfounded insinuation as an offence against the tranquility, and consequently the peace, of the world. I also see therein something which tends to frighten smaller nations or at least make them nervous. If Mr. Roosevelt really has any specific instances in mind in this connection I would ask him to name the states who are threatened with aggression and to name the aggressor in question. It will then be possible to refute these monstrous general accusations by brief statements. . . . All states bordering on Germany have received much more binding assurances, and above all suggestions, than Mr. Roosevelt has asked from me in his curious telegram."

On August 21, 1939, Germany signed a pact with Russia and on September 1 invaded Poland

In a speech delivered after the outbreak of war the Fuehrer said:

BERLIN, SEPTEMBER 1, 1939.
"I will not war against women and children. I have ordered my air force to restrict itself to attacks on military objectives."

The bombing of Polish open towns began on the first day of the war.

DOCUMENT 15

Die Vereidigung der Marlene Dietrich

Stürmer-Archiv

Marlene Dietrich, berühmter Filmstar, wird amerikanische Bürgerin. Man sieht sie hier
in Los Angeles mit einem Naturalisationsbeamten

Die aus Deutschland stammende Filmschauspielerin Marlene Dietrich hat so viele Jahre bei den Kino-Juden von Hollywood verbracht, daß sie nun amerikanische Staatsbürgerin geworden ist. Der viele Umgang mit Juden hat ihr ganzes Wesen undeutsch gestaltet. Auf dem Bilde sehen wir sie bei einer Vereidigungsszene in Los Angeles. Was der jüdische „Richter" von dem gesetzlich vorgeschriebenen Eid hält, ergibt sich aus seiner Haltung: in Hemdärmeln (!) nimmt er der Marlene Dietrich den Eid ab, auf daß sie ihr Vaterland verrate!

244

DOCUMENT 15–A

(Translation)

DER STÜRMER (PUBLISHED BY JULIUS STREICHER, NAZI GAULEITER OF FRANCONIA), NUREMBERG, OCTOBER 1937

ADMINISTERING OF OATH TO MARLENE DIETRICH

Marlene Dietrich, famous film star, becomes American citizen. She is here seen in Los Angeles with a naturalization official.

The film actress Marlene Dietrich, who hails from Germany, has spent so many years with the movie-Jews of Hollywood that she has now become an American citizen. Much association with Jews has made her entire nature un-German. In the picture we see her in an oath-scene in Los Angeles. What the Jewish "judge" thinks of the legally prescribed oath may be seen from his attitude: in shirtsleeves (!) he administers to Marlene Dietrich the oath that she betray her fatherland!

DOCUMENT 16

Vertraulicher Abdruck

aus einem noch nicht veröffentlichten
politischen Tagebuch eines
Deutsch-Amerikaners.

Wann erhält Deutschland von Amerika einen deutschstämmigen Botschafter?

Die kürzliche Ankunft des neuen amerikanischen Botschafters, Professor Dodd, wirft diese Frage wieder einmal auf.

Diesmal bin ich daran ganz besonders interessiert, weil ich mich sehr ernsthaft bei der neuen Roosevelt-Regierung bemüht hatte, daß den Deutschamerikanern wichtige politische Ämter gegeben würden, denn der überwältigende Sieg Roosevelts ist in hohem Maße den deutschen Stimmen zuzuschreiben, die alle für die Aufhebung der Prohibition und eine 100prozentig amerikanische Politik, die man nach der überheblichen Einmischungspolitik des Prosperity-Hoover von Roosevelt erhoffte, abgegeben wurden. Ich hatte den demokratischen Politikern gesagt, daß jetzt die Zeit gekommen wäre, die Dankbarkeit des deutschamerikanischen Elementes zu erwerben und dieses für die nächste Wahl mit der demokratischen Sache zu verknüpfen. Es dürften nicht die Fehler von Harding und Hoover wiederholt werden, die die deutschen Stimmen durch Versprechungen geködert hatten, die dann später nicht eingelöst wurden.

Nun besteht da natürlich nach einer großen amerikanischen Wahlschlacht, wo eine Partei die andere ablöst, ein unheimlicher Andrang zu den Stellungen. Diesmal haben die Demokraten acht Jahre lang nicht mehr ihre Suppe am öffentlichen Feuer kochen können und waren deshalb ausgehungert. Trotzdem war der Anspruch auf einen Teil der Beute, den das deutsche Element erhob, berechtigt. Ich habe viele Briefe in diesem Sinne geschrieben und viele politische Führer persönlich ganz energisch bearbeitet, und im vertraulichen Zwiegespräch ist die Berechtigung meiner Forderung vielfach weitgehend anerkannt worden. Ich habe dann auch noch von Deutschland aus, meiner alten Heimat, wo ich meine Sommerfrische verlebe, den Vorschlag gemacht, wenigstens einen deutschstämmigen Botschafter nach Deutschland zu schicken, nachdem die Yankees unter dem Eindruck der Deutschenhetze sich offenbar nicht zu diesem Posten drängten.

Ich mußte aus Gesundheitsrücksichten Amerika schon verlassen, als die Roosevelt-Regierung das Steuer übernahm, und so brachte mir der Draht und die Post die Meldungen über die fortlaufenden Ernennungen, und ich mußte allmählich bemerken, daß meine ganzen Bemühungen umsonst gewesen sind. Wenn wir auch vielleicht augenblicklich keinen Mann haben, der für das Kabinett qualifiziert gewesen wäre, da Charles Nagel aus St. Louis, der schon Mitglied des Taft-Kabinetts war, Republikaner ist und eine Berufung ins Kabinett auch garnicht angenommen hätte, so hatten wir doch unzählige würdige Männer, die zu Richtern, zum Collector of Customs and Revenue, Postmaster usw. hätten ernannt werden können. Aber die Demokraten gingen nach dem alten, um nicht zu sagen veralteten Grundsatz vor, daß nur verdiente Demokraten sich überhaupt bewerben sollten, denn nur sie hätten Aussicht auf Berücksichtigung.

Ich ließ mich natürlich hierdurch nicht im geringsten abschrecken, sondern im Gegenteil fühle ich mich dadurch nur angefeuert, denn angesichts die Ungerechtigkeit wird immer schreiender.

Bisher habe ich unseren Botschafter noch nicht kennen gelernt; er soll ja ein sehr sympathischer Herr sein, der sehr gut Deutsch spricht. Er hat die deutsche Sprache als Student in Leipzig gelernt und sagt selbst von sich, daß er sich eng mit der deutschen Kultur verbunden fühlt.

Worauf ich hinaus will und was ich zur Kenntnis einflußreicher deutscher Kreise bringen will, ist, daß Deutschland selbst den Schlüssel zu der hier behandelten Frage in der Hand hält. Das kaiserliche Deutschland hat uns nämlich nach meiner Meinung nicht anerkannt; es gab nur Deutsche oder Amerikaner, aber keine Deutschamerikaner. Man kann aber doch nicht

246

leugnen, daß es amerikanische Bürger deutscher Abkunft gibt, deren Zahl viele viele Millionen beträgt, und wenn uns der Vorwurf gemacht worden ist, daß wir politisch so schwach sind, so kommt das zum Teil daher, daß Berlin immer einen geborenen Amerikaner haben wollte, und ein Deutschamerikaner nie persona grata gewesen wäre. Ein richtiger Amerikaner mußte nach reichsdeutscher Auffassung englischer Abstammung sein.

Die ganze Kriegsgeschichte hat bewiesen, daß der amerikanische Bürger deutscher Abstammung der einzige wirklich 100prozentige Amerikaner gewesen ist, loyal gegen Amerika und viel zuverlässiger als der englischbürtige Amerikaner, der nichts besseres wußte, als Amerika in den europäischen Krieg hineinzuzerren, in dem Amerika nichts zu suchen hatte. Wir Deutsch-amerikaner kämpften mit unseren irischen Bundesgenossen darum, daß der Friede für Amerika erhalten bliebe. Die Anglo-Amerikaner haben vollkommen versagt. Man braucht nur an die veröffentlichten Briefe des amerikanischen Botschafters in London, Page, zu denken oder an die Rolle, die Herrick in Paris spielte, als im August 1914 eine deutsche Fliegerbombe in der Nähe der amerikanischen Botschaft einschlug. Herrick tat damals die berühmte Äußerung, er bedauerte, nicht von der Bombe getötet worden zu sein, denn: „Ein von den Deutschen getöteter Botschafter ist für Frankreich mehr wert als ein lebender". Dies war eine so flagrante Verletzung der Neutralität des Landes, das er vertrat, daß er unbedingt hätte abberufen werden müssen. Er hatte die Vereinigten Staaten geradezu kompromittiert, und genau so machten es alle die Millionen englisch-stämmiger Amerikaner mit wenigen Ausnahmen, die sich einbilden, das Rückgrat der Nation zu sein, die aber in Wirklichkeit die Bannerträger der britischen Weltherrschaft sind. Sie wissen nichts von der alten Tradition Amerikas und dem Vermächtnis George Washington's, der der jungen Republik den Rat mit auf den Weg gab, als er das Steuer aus der Hand gab, "to keep free from entangling European alliances".

Deutschlands Aufgabe in dem Kampf um die Anerkennung des Deutschamerikaners in der amerikanischen Politik ist es, dem Deutschen, der nach Amerika ausgewandert ist, eine staatsrechtliche Stellung zu geben, die sein Ansehen in Amerika stärkt. Er darf nicht mehr als Auswurf der Nation von Deutschland betrachtet werden, sondern der in Deutschland Geborene soll Zeit seines Lebens ungeachtet des Erwerbs der fremden Bürgereigenschaft deutscher Staatsangehöriger bleiben, wie dies entsprechend bei dem Schweizerbürger der Fall ist, der in Amerika eine hochgeachtete Stellung einnimmt, gerade weil er seine Schweizerbürgereigenschaft neben der neuerworbenen amerikanischen beibehält.

Es käme also darauf an, die Bestimmungen des deutschen Staatsangehörigkeitsgesetzes in diesem Sinne abzuändern. Ich habe diese Idee schon dem sozialistischen Deutschland vorgetragen und im Jahre 1919 auf meine Kosten einen sachverständigen Universitätsmann nach Weimar geschickt, um die Sache wirksam zu fördern, aber die Anregung wurde weder in der Weimarer Verfassung noch im deutschen Staatsangehörigkeitsgesetz berücksichtigt.

Dem deutschen Element in den Vereinigten Staaten würde durch ein solches Gesetz das politische Rückgrat ungeheuer gestärkt und ein neuer Sieg wäre errungen in dem langjährigen Kampf für die politische Gleichberechtigung des Deutschamerikaners, den ich seit zwei Jahrzehnten mit Hingabe und Zähigkeit führe.

Mit Erlaubnis des Verfassers
als Manuskript gedruckt

HAMBURG, im September 1933.   **Paul Strasser jr.**

DOCUMENT 16–A

(Extract)

WHEN WILL GERMANY RECEIVE A GERMAN-BLOODED AMBASSADOR FROM AMERICA?

In 1933 this leaflet was sent to a member of the German-American Steuben Society by one Ferdinand Hansen, a fellow member who was at that time sojourning in Germany. The leaflet, which is signed by Paul Strasser, Jr., is entitled "When Will Germany Receive a German-blooded Ambassador From America?", and bears a note explaining that it is a confidential extract from the still-unpublished political diary of a German-American.

The leaflet expressed dissatisfaction that President Roosevelt, in spite of the fact that his overwhelming victory in the election could be ascribed to a great extent to German votes, had given no important political appointments to German-Americans. The leaflet concludes as follows:

> "It is Germany's task in the struggle for the recognition of the German-American in American political life to give the German who has emigrated to America a definite position in constitutional law which will strengthen his prestige in America. He should no longer be regarded by Germany as the cast-off scum of the nation, but he who has been born in Germany should remain a German citizen his whole life long regardless of the acquisition of foreign citizenship, as is the case with the citizen of Switzerland, who occupies a position of high esteem in America precisely because he retains his Swiss citizenship along with his newly won American citizenship.
>
> "It would be necessary, therefore, to modify the provisions of the German citizenship law in this sense. . . . Such a law would immeasurably strengthen the political backbone of the German element in the United States, and a new victory would be won in the long struggle for political equality of the German-American, which I have been waging wholeheartedly and determinedly for the last two decades.

"HAMBURG, *September 1933*. PAUL STRASSER, JR."

248

(Translation)

ZEITSCHRIFT FÜR GEOPOLITIK (MONTHLY MAGAZINE EDITED BY PRO-
FESSOR KARL HAUSHOFER), SEPTEMBER 1941, PAGE 534

THE LEADER OF THE GERMANIC PEOPLES

The *Deutsche Zeitung* in Norway (Oslo, June 14, 1941) published a decree protecting the positions of Norwegian SS men, in which among other things it was stated, "workers who have been engaged in a position for one month may not be discharged, or removed in any other way, because they serve in the Norwegian SS", etc. In the explanation of this, issued on the order of the Supreme Leader of the Norwegians, Vidkun Quisling, it was stated, "the twenty-first of May 1941 will stand as a memorable day in Norway's history. On this day the work was continued which had begun in the establishment of the regiment 'Nordland'. With this work the honor of the Norwegian people is being reestablished. It is receiving again an honor to which a people has a claim, namely, to be allowed to bear weapons. The Norwegian SS will be Norway's protection, guarding the common Germanic interests and taking care that the consciousness of race and of the community of destiny lives ever strong and awake in the people. May 21 is the day in which the first division of the Norwegian SS took the solemn oath of allegiance. If in some quarters unclarity concerning the significance of this oath of allegiance has reigned, this can only imply an ignorance of the content and the range of the oath. Every good Norwegian will be able to approve and take the oath, which is made in Norway. It is taken to the man Adolf Hitler, not in his capacity as head of the German state and leader of the German people, but as Supreme Leader of the community of Germanic peoples, and to the man Vidkun Quisling as leader of the Norwegian people. May 21 is therefore more than a memorable day merely in the history of our fatherland. It will be a memorable day in the history of the community of Germanic peoples and in the history of our race. On this day for the first time expression was given to the association (*Gleichordnung*) among the Germanic peoples on a free and equal basis. The Norwegian SS ought to have an eminent place in the consciousness of the Norwegian people, and the authorities will see that no injustice occurs to the men who enter in their ranks."

An article published in the German press under the dateline, Brussels, July 20, 1941, stated similarly: "In the very near future the Flemish Volunteer Legion will be engaged in the struggle against Bolshevism. They will wear the uniforms of the military SS (*Waffen SS*), not, however, with the insignia of the eagle but with that of a sundial. The Volunteers will take an oath to Adolf Hitler as the leader of all Germans and at the same time a pledge of allegiance to the Flemish people. Like the Flemish troops who in the Middle Ages fought in innumerable campaigns for the Reich and the cause of the Occident, the Flemish Corps of today has received permission also to bear as its banner the Flemish lion-flag. The Flemish Volunteers will be led by Flemish officers."

DOCUMENT 18

(Translation)

REICHSGESETZBLATT (GERMAN BULLETIN OF LAWS), 1939, PART I,
PAGE 1741

DECREE OF SEPTEMBER 4, 1939
CONCERNING THE NATURALIZATION OF VOLUNTEERS [1]

With regard to naturalization of persons who intend to enter the German Army as volunteers, the Ministerial Council for the Reich's Defense decrees, with force of law for the territory of the Great German Reich:

§ 1

If the person receiving naturalization has completed his eighteenth year, then the approval of his legal guardian is not required for the application and naturalization.

§ 2

If the applicant has not established a domicil in Germany, residence in Germany suffices.

§ 3

The following requirements can be disregarded:

(a) that the applicant in case of the acquisition of German citizenship give up his previous citizenship;
(b) that the applicant at the place of his residence has his own dwelling or lodgings;
(c) that he is able in this place to provide for himself and his dependents.

BERLIN, *September 4, 1939*

Chairman of the Ministerial Council for the Reich's Defense
GÖRING
General Field Marshal

Controller General for the Reich's Administration
FRICK

Reich's Minister and Chief of the Reich's Chancelry
Dr. LAMMERS

---

[1] Does not apply to Danzig.

DOCUMENT 19

Reichsgesetzblatt, Jahrgang 1942, Teil I

Verordnung zur Regelung von Staatsangehörigkeitsfragen.
Vom 20. Januar 1942.

Der Ministerrat für die Reichsverteidigung verordnet mit Gesetzeskraft:

§ 1

(1) Ein Ausländer kann — abgesehen von den §§ 13, 15 Abs. 2, §§ 33 und 34 des Reichs- und Staatsangehörigkeitsgesetzes vom 22. Juli 1913 (Reichsgesetzbl. S. 583) — auch ohne Begründung einer Niederlassung im Inland eingebürgert werden. Für die Verleihung der deutschen Staatsangehörigkeit gelten im übrigen die Vorschriften des Reichs- und Staatsangehörigkeitsgesetzes vom 22. Juli 1913 (Reichsgesetzbl. S. 583), der Verordnung über die deutsche Staatsangehörigkeit vom 5. Februar 1934 (Reichsgesetzbl. I S. 85) und des Gesetzes zur Änderung des Reichs- und Staatsangehörigkeitsgesetzes vom 15. Mai 1935 (Reichsgesetzbl. I S. 593).

(2) Der Reichsminister des Innern bestimmt die für die Einbürgerung zuständige Behörde.

(3) Der Reichsminister des Innern kann Gruppen von Ausländern, die in einem unter deutscher Hoheit stehenden Gebiet ihre Niederlassung haben oder aus einem solchen Gebiet stammen, durch allgemeine Anordnung die Staatsangehörigkeit verleihen. Er kann anordnen, daß die Verleihung im Einzelfall binnen zehn Jahren widerrufen werden kann.

§ 2

Der Reichsminister des Innern kann Länder bezeichnen, deren Staatsangehörigkeit auf eigenen Antrag oder auf Antrag des Ehemanns oder des gesetzlichen Vertreters erworben werden kann, ohne daß ein Verlust der deutschen Staatsangehörigkeit damit verbunden ist.

§ 3

Ein unter elterlicher Gewalt oder unter Vormundschaft stehender deutscher Volkszugehöriger, der auf Grund einer zwischenstaatlichen Vereinbarung selbständig den Wunsch nach Umsiedlung in das Deutsche Reich äußern kann oder konnte, kann nach der Umsiedlung auf seinen Antrag eingebürgert werden, auch ohne daß der gesetzliche Vertreter für ihn den Antrag stellt

oder der Stellung des Antrags zustimmt. Sind solche Einbürgerungen bereits vorgenommen worden, obwohl die nach den bisherigen Vorschriften erforderliche Beteiligung des gesetzlichen Vertreters unterblieben ist, so sind sie mit Rückwirkung vom Tage der Aushändigung der Einbürgerungsurkunde an rechtswirksam.

§ 4

(1) Ein deutscher Staatsangehöriger fremder Volkszugehörigkeit, der auf Grund einer zwischenstaatlichen Vereinbarung in ein anderes Land umgesiedelt wird, verliert die deutsche Staatsangehörigkeit mit dem Tage, an dem er das Deutsche Reich im Zuge der Umsiedlung verläßt. Ist in der zwischenstaatlichen Vereinbarung ein anderer Zeitpunkt für den Verlust der deutschen Staatsangehörigkeit vorgesehen, so ist dieser Zeitpunkt maßgebend.

(2) In den Fällen, in denen eine Umsiedlung deutscher Staatsangehöriger fremder Volkszugehörigkeit bereits durchgeführt ist, ist der Verlust der deutschen Staatsangehörigkeit mit dem Tage eingetreten, an dem der Umsiedler das Deutsche Reich verlassen hat.

§ 5

(1) Der § 26 des Reichs- und Staatsangehörigkeitsgesetzes vom 22. Juli 1913 (Reichsgesetzbl. S. 583) tritt außer Kraft.

(2) Soweit der Verlust der Staatsangehörigkeit auf Grund des § 26 Abs. 1 des Reichs- und Staatsangehörigkeitsgesetzes nach Wiedereinführung der allgemeinen Wehrpflicht durch das Wehrgesetz vom 21. Mai 1935 (Reichsgesetzbl. I S. 609) eingetreten ist, gilt er als nicht erfolgt.

§ 6

Der Reichsminister des Innern erläßt die zur Durchführung und Ergänzung dieser Verordnung erforderlichen Rechts- und Verwaltungsvorschriften.

Berlin, den 20. Januar 1942.

Der Vorsitzende
des Ministerrats für die Reichsverteidigung
Göring
Reichsmarschall

Der Generalbevollmächtigte für die Reichsverwaltung
Frick

Der Reichsminister und Chef der Reichskanzlei
Dr. Lammers

Herausgegeben vom Reichsministerium des Innern — Verlag: Reichsverlagsamt — Druck: Reichsdruckerei

DOCUMENT 19-A

(Translation)

Reichsgesetzblatt (German Bulletin of Laws), 1942, Part I,
Page 40

DECREE OF JANUARY 20, 1942
REGULATING MATTERS OF CITIZENSHIP

The Ministerial Council for the Reich's Defense decrees with force
of law:

§ 1

(1) Apart from §§ 13, 15 (paragraph 2), §§ 33 and 34 of the German citizenship law of July 22, 1913 (*Reichsgesetzblatt*, p. 583), a foreigner can also be naturalized without the establishment of a domicil in Germany. Otherwise, the following regulations are applicable in the conferring of German citizenship: the regulations of the German citizenship law of July 22, 1913 (*Reichsgesetzblatt*, p. 583), of the decree concerning German citizenship of February 5, 1934 (*Reichsgesetzblatt* I, p. 85), and of the law of May 15, 1935 changing the German citizenship law (*Reichsgesetzblatt* I, p. 593).

(2) The Reich's Minister of the Interior determines the authority qualified to perform the naturalization.

(3) The Reich's Minister of the Interior can by a general decree confer citizenship upon groups of foreigners, who have their residence in a territory under German sway or who originate from such territory. He can ordain that the citizenship in individual cases can be revoked within ten years.

§ 2

The Reich's Minister of the Interior can designate the countries for which citizenship can be acquired on petition, or on petition of the husband or of the legal guardian, without the loss of German citizenship therewith being involved.

§ 3

A member of the German folk under parental authority or guardianship, who can or could independently express the wish for resettlement into the German Reich in virtue of an interstate agreement, can after such resettlement be naturalized on his own petition, even if his legal guardian does not present the petition for him nor

253

approve of the petition. If naturalization in such cases has already taken place, although the participation of the legal guardian required by former regulations has been lacking, nevertheless the naturalization has legal validity, as of the date of the naturalization certificate.

§ 4

(1) A German citizen of an alien race, who is resettled to another country in virtue of an interstate agreement, loses German citizenship on the day when he leaves the German Reich in the course of resettlement. If the interstate agreement has provided another date for the loss of German citizenship, then this date has precedence.

(2) In the cases in which a resettlement of German citizens of an alien race has already taken place, the loss of German citizenship has ensued, on the day when the resettled person left the German Reich.

§ 5

(1) §26 [1] of the German citizenship law of July 22, 1913 (*Reichsgesetzblatt*, p. 583) is annulled.

(2) If the loss of citizenship in virtue of paragraph 1, §26, of the German citizenship law has taken place after the reintroduction of universal military service through the military-service law of May 21, 1935 (*Reichsgesetzblatt* I, p. 609), such loss is herewith declared null and void.

§ 6

The Reich's Minister of the Interior issues the legal and administrative measures required to enforce and supplement this decree.

BERLIN, *January 20, 1942*

Chairman of the Ministerial Council for the Reich's Defense
GÖRING
Reich's Marshal

Controller General for the Reich's Administration
FRICK

Reich's Minister and Chief of the Reich's Chancelry
Dr. LAMMERS.

---

[1] [§26 deprives German deserters of their citizenship—EDITOR.]

DOCUMENT 20

(Translation)

RECHTSEINRICHTUNGEN UND RECHTSAUFGABEN DER BEWEGUNG, BY OTTO GAUWEILER: MUNICH, ZENTRALVERLAG DER NSDAP, FRANZ EHER NACHFOLGER, 1939, PAGES 71ff.

THE LEGAL OFFICE IN THE FOREIGN ORGANIZATION

The Foreign Organization of the NSDAP includes all party members living abroad or traveling at sea. In addition, it offers guidance and protection to all German citizens residing in foreign territory. It does not concern itself with citizens of other states but only with German citizens living abroad. A basic principle of the activity of the Foreign Organization is respect for the laws of those countries where Germans are living as guests; the struggles of German minority groups beyond the borders of the Reich are carried on in other organizational forms. Like the NSDAP itself, the Foreign Organization is divided into country groups (*Landesgruppen*), regional sections (*Landeskreise*), local groups (*Ortsgruppen*), and community centers (*Stützpunkte*).

The offices of the Foreign Organization of the NSDAP or of its representatives in foreign countries take a position beside the official representatives of the Reich, to whom they furnish a necessary and valuable complement. A party representative in a foreign land becomes the leader of all German people within his district. The political and ideological guidance of Germans living abroad is the exclusive province of the Foreign Organization or of its representatives.

The unity of party and state in matters concerning the guidance and protection of German citizens living abroad finds visible expression in the Führer's decree of January 30, 1937, regarding appointment of a chief of the Foreign Organization in the Foreign Office, in which it is provided that a chief of the Foreign Organization shall be appointed in the Foreign Office for the uniform guidance and protection of all Germans living abroad and that the direction and disposal of all matters concerning German citizens abroad which come within the sphere of the Foreign Office shall be entrusted to him. The leader of the Foreign Organization of the NSDAP, Gauleiter Ernst Wilhelm Bohle, has been appointed Chief of the Foreign Organization in the Foreign Office.

He is directly and personally responsible to the Foreign Minister. His field of activity as leader of the Foreign Organization and his responsibility as such to the Deputy of the Führer remain unchanged. His official title is Chief of the Foreign Organization in the Foreign Office.

The directors of the Foreign Organization are directly responsible to the Deputy of the Führer and form a part of his staff. Nevertheless, the Foreign Organization is also a Gau of the NSDAP. With regard to organizational form, therefore, it has a double status.

The present legal position of foreign Germans and of the foreign groups of the NSDAP has been decidedly influenced by the historical fact of the seizure of power by the party. It stands in close relation to political developments within the Reich, just as the development of German communities abroad has always been strongly influenced by the political development in the homeland. The basic change in the legal position of foreign Germans has found expression in a series of laws which give a new definition of their legal position, for example, the law regarding the annulment of naturalization and the revocation of German citizenship of July 14, 1933 . . . The loyalty which German citizens residing in foreign countries owe to the Reich finds its expression here in the exclusion of faithless Germans.

The increased duties which the German Reich and the National Socialist movement have imposed upon Germans living abroad are balanced, on the other hand, by the increased security of the foreign Germans, by an increased protection of them from the Reich, and by the creation of social and welfare organizations within foreign German communities.

II

In the direction of the Foreign Organization of the NSDAP there has been set up a Legal Office of the Foreign Organization, the functions of which extend into the fields of legal administration, legal politics, and legal protection.

Legal administration: The status of the offices of the Foreign Organization or of its representatives in foreign countries in relation to the foreign states and their governments is such as to make necessary a system of legal advice and evaluation of these legal relations with regard to national and international law. The danger is especially great in those countries whose governments are hostile or unfriendly to National Socialism and the German Reich. In this case, a special legal protection must be afforded to the officers of the Foreign Organization, usually honorary officers, who are active in foreign countries. The legal status of these representatives in foreign countries and of the groups of foreign Germans gives rise to so many other questions of legal nature that these must be given a uniform classification by a central office, namely, the Legal Office of the Foreign Organization.

Legal politics: From the character of the Foreign Organization as the unified body of all German citizens residing abroad who are conscious of their bond of loyalty to the Reich, arises the special nature of its legal political functions. The Foreign Organization, as the highest party office authorized to deal with all questions concerning the movement in foreign countries, must recognize not only the legal political necessities of the Reich in this field but also the wishes and the necessities of the foreign Germans themselves.

It is therefore called upon by the Deputy of the Führer to cooperate in the field of the revision of the law wherever questions arise which are directly or indirectly connected with the legal status of Germans in foreign countries. Since the Chief of the Foreign Organization in this capacity, as provided in the decree of January 30, 1937, also takes part in the meetings of the Reich Cabinet whenever his field of activity is touched upon, the possibility is opened for the realization of those legal political necessities which have been recognized by the Foreign Organization.

Legal protection: The Foreign Organization of the NSDAP and its offices in foreign countries stand ready to offer legal guidance in personal matters to individual German citizens living abroad. The National Socialistic legal guidance of the German people is thus extended to all foreign Germans, as well as to German seamen. In an agreement of January 12, 1934 between the Legal Office of the Foreign Organization and the Office for Legal Guidance of the German People, the forms and the manner of the accomplishment of this legal guidance were set forth.

The cooperation between Germans at home and abroad has been secured and regulated in such a way that, on the one hand, Germans in foreign countries who are without funds can ask for help of the NS legal-guidance offices within the Reich, and these offices, on the other hand, can claim the help of the Legal Office of the Foreign Organization and of the party offices in foreign countries. The legal-guidance service of the Legal Office of the Foreign Organization has been called upon extensively by Germans living abroad in all fields of foreign and domestic law. A considerable part of this legal-guidance work consists in the transmitting and, in certain cases, in the support of petitions, especially in connection with naturalization cases.

THE FOREIGN GAU OF THE RECHTSWAHRERBUND

All *Rechtswahrer* living abroad are collected in the foreign Gau of the NSRB, which, through a union of personnel, is directed by the leader of the Legal Office of the Foreign Organization. The foreign

Gau of the NSRB comprises all *Rechtswahrer* active in foreign countries and maintains their connections with the legal community in the Reich.   In order to prevent the unworthy occurrence that German firms or individuals should engage Jewish attorneys for legal representation in foreign countries, the foreign Gau of the NSRB has prepared a world-wide index of Aryan attorneys and patent lawyers. This index represents a collection of all Aryan lawyers and patent attorneys active in foreign countries and otherwise qualified who may be engaged by Germans for legal representation in court or for the protection of patent interests.

DOCUMENT 21

(Translation)

REICHSGESETZBLATT (GERMAN BULLETIN OF LAWS), 1940, PART I, PAGE 754

DECREE CONCERNING THE JURISDICTION OF CRIMINAL LAW

The Ministerial Council for the Defense of the Reich decrees for the territory of the Greater German Reich, with force of law:

ARTICLE 1
Field of Application of Criminal Law

In the place of sections 3 to 5, 8, and 37 of the Reich's code of criminal law, the following provisions become effective:

§ 3

German criminal law applies to the act of a German national regardless of whether it is committed in the Reich or abroad.

German criminal law does not apply to an act committed abroad which is not subject to punishment under the law of the place where committed if, in the sound judgment of the German people, on the basis of the particular conditions applying, the act is not a crime justifying punishment.

An act is committed at that place in which the person committing the act has operated or would have operated, in case the action was not completed, or in which the result has occurred or would have occurred.

§ 4

German criminal law also applies to acts committed by a foreigner in the Reich.

German criminal law applies to criminal acts committed by a foreigner abroad if they are subject to punishment under the law of the place where committed, or no penal authority has jurisdiction over the place where committed, and if

    (1) The person committing the act acquires German nationality after committing the act, or

    (2) The criminal act is directed against the German people or against a German national, or

    (3) The person committing the act is apprehended in the Reich and not extradited, although extradition would be permissible on the basis of the nature of the crime.

Regardless of the law of the place where the act is committed, German criminal law applies to the following crimes committed by a foreigner abroad:

    (1) Crimes committed in the capacity of a German official, a German soldier, or a member of the Reich's Labor Service, or committed against the holder of a German office of the state or the party, against a German soldier, or against a member of the Reich's Labor Service during the exercise of their duties or in connection with their duties;

    (2) High treason or treasonable acts against the German Reich;

    (3) Bomb outrages;

    (4) Traffic in women and children;

    (5) Betrayal of the industrial or the business secrets of a German enterprise;

    (6) Perjury in proceedings before a German court or any other German office competent to take oaths;

    (7) Counterfeiting;

    (8) Unauthorized traffic in narcotics;

    (9) Traffic in obscene publications.

§ 5

The German criminal law applies, regardless of the law of the place where an act is committed, to acts committed on a German ship or airplane.

ARTICLE 2

Supplementary Regulations Concerning Criminal Procedure

(1) The following regulation is added as section 8a of the Reich's order of criminal procedure:

"§ 8a

"Jurisdiction rests with the court in whose district the accused is held in custody at the time the charge is entered at the direction of the competent authorities."

(2) The following regulation is added as section 153a of the Reich's order of criminal procedure:

"§ 153a

"The state prosecutor can decline to prosecute an act committed by a German national abroad or a foreign national on a foreign ship or airplane within Germany if the prosecution is not essential in the interests of the national community or if it would be unreasonably difficult.

"An act committed by a foreigner abroad is prosecuted by the state prosecutor only on instructions from the Reich's Minister of Justice.

"The state prosecutor can decline to prosecute an act if punishment has already been imposed on the accused abroad for the same act and the penalty which might be expected in the Reich does not exceed that imposed abroad."

Article 3

Final Provisions

(1) The provisions of this decree as well as sections 7 and 9 of the Reich's code of criminal law apply likewise in the *Reichsgauen* of the Ostmark (Austria). Sections 36 to 41, 234, and 235 of the Austrian criminal law, so far as they have not already lost their effect, as well as section 34, subsection 2, line 3, of the Austrian order of criminal procedure, are canceled. Section 2 of the Austrian administrative criminal law of July 21, 1925 (BGBl. no. 275) remains in effect.

(2) So far as German criminal law is applicable in the Protectorate of Bohemia and Moravia, this decree applies, with the condition that crimes committed by nationals of the Protectorate of Bohemia and Moravia are treated on the same basis as crimes committed by German nationals.

(3) This decree enters into effect one week after its promulgation. It is likewise applicable to crimes committed before it enters into effect.

(4) The Reich's Minister of Justice will issue the necessary legal and administrative regulations for the execution and application of this decree. So far as it concerns the Protectorate of Bohemia and Moravia they will be issued in conjunction with the Reich's Protector in Bohemia and Moravia.

BERLIN, *May 6, 1940*

Chairman of the Ministerial Council for the Reich's Defense
Göring
General Field Marshal

Controller General for the Reich's Administration

Frick
Reich's Minister and Chief of the Reich's Chancelry
Dr. Lammers

1.

Mitteilungsblatt
der
Kameradſchaft U.S.A.

Nr. 1   Stuttgart-S, Haus des Deutschtums   Januar 1941

ZUR BEACHTUNG :

> Diese Mitteilungen tragen einen
> vertraulichen Charakter.Sie sind
> ausschliesslich für die Ange-
> hörigen der Kameradschaft USA.
> bestimmt. Jeder Verstoss dagegen
> wird die Entziehung des Rund-
> briefes zur Folge haben.

2.

An die

Kameradschaft USA.

Das Jahr 1939 mit seinen grossen politischen und
militärischen Ereignissen hat die engen Bande, die
die Kameradschaft umschloss, teilweise gelöst. Gar
mancher verliess als Soldat seinen bisherigen Wir-
kungskreis oder ist inzwischen in einem der neuen
Gebiete eingesetzt. Eine Zusammenkunft in Stuttgart
ist die Veranlassung gewesen, nunmehr die Verbindung
mit allen Kameraden von der Zentrale aus wieder aufzunehmen. Zu diesem Zweck wird Pg. Walter K a p p e,
der inzwischen von den Soldaten zurückgekehrt ist,
die Führung der Kameradschaft übernehmen und durch
diesen Rundbrief die Bande wieder neu knüpfen. Ich
bitte jeden Einzelnen,wieder aktiv an der Arbeit
seiner zuständigen Kameradschaft teilzunehmen, denn
ich bin überzeugt, dass unser Einsatz in Zukunft von
Bedeutung sein wird.
In alter Treue
                        Heil Hitler!
                    (gez.) Fritz G i s s i b l

Wenn ich die Leitung der Kameradschaft USA. nach Rück-
sprache mit Fritz Gissibl und dem inzwischen zur Wehrmacht einberufenen Sepp Schuster übernommen habe, so
aus der Erwägung heraus, dass auch in Kriegszeiten
eine Zentralstelle der Kameradschaft USA. vorhanden
sein muss. Dieser Rundbrief soll dazu beitragen, die
Verbindung mit allen Kameraden und Kameradinnen von
Stuttgart aus wieder aufzunehmen. Ich stütze mich
dabei auf die Mitarbeit aller.

                        Heil Hitler!
                    (gez.) Walter K a p p e

3.

R u n d b r i e f a n a l l e K a m e r a d e n

Liebe Kameraden!

Als wir im Jahre 1938 daran gingen, die Idee Sepp Schusters,
der schon früher in München einen stattlichen Kreis einstiger
Mitkämpfer aus dem Bund "Freunde des Neuen Deutschlands" um
sich geschart hatte, auf das Reichsgebiet zu erweitern und
die "Kameradschaft USA." zu gründen, bewogen uns dazu
drei Gesichtspunkte :

> einmal wollten wir die Kameradschaft, die uns drüben
> alle Hindernisse und Schwierigkeiten bewältigen liess
> und in der wir unser höchstes Erlebnis fanden, hier
> im Vaterlande fortsetzen, uns gegenseitig helfen,
> im Austausch unserer Erinnerungen an die Kampfzeit
> in USA. uns Kraft und Mut für den Alltag holen,

> zum anderen aber wollten wir durch Bildung dieser
> Kameradschaft uns selbst und unsere drüben gesammel-
> ten Erfahrungen unserem Vaterland zur Verfügung
> stellen

> und schliesslich erhofften wir, irgendwie unseren
> kämpfenden Brüdern drüben einen moralischen Rück-
> halt zu geben und sei es nur durch die Tatsache,dass
> wir, die Rückgewanderten, in Treue jener tapferen
> Kämpfer gedachten, mit denen wir Jahre hindurch in
> einer Front gestanden hatten.

So wurden in Stuttgart, Berlin, Hamburg, Hannover Kamerad-
schaften gegründet und kurz vor Kriegsbeginn konnte durch
Entgegenkommen des Deutschen Ausland-Instituts und der
Stadt Stuttgart das erste Reichstreffen der Kameradschaft
USA. verbunden mit der Eröffnung der Ausstellung "Amerikadeutschtum im Kampf" abgehalten werden, ein unvergess-
liches Erlebnis für alle Teilnehmer!

Der Krieg machte durch unsere weiteren Zukunftspläne einen
dicken Strich, auch hörte die weitere Rückwanderung so
gut wie auf. Ein grosser Teil unserer Kameraden eilte
zu den Fahnen, einzelne Kameradschaftsgruppen verwaisten
völlig. Dazu kam, dass Fritz Gissibl im Osten, in Litzmannstadt, eingesetzt wurde, Sepp Schuster nach Berlin
ging, Ernst Vennekohl und ich schon vom ersten Kriegstage
an den Schreibtisch mit der Waffe vertauschten.

4.

So ist denn heute unsere Anschriftenliste zum Teil
veraltet, viele Kameraden sind verzogen, ohne uns ihre
neue Anschrift hinterlassen zu haben. Eine Reihe von
Briefen, die ich in letzter Zeit in dem Bemühen schrieb,
unsere Kameradschaft neu zu beleben, blieb ohne Antwort.

Trotzdem aber lebt die Kameradschaft USA., das spürt
man aus der Arbeit unserer Berliner Gruppe, die inzwischen die weitaus grösste geworden ist, das wissen
auch die im Felde stehenden Kameraden, die auch zum
letzten Weihnachtsfest mit einem Päckchen bedacht wurden, das klingt auch aus allen Feldpostbriefen und
das hört man aus den oft ungeduldigen Anfragen, was
denn eigentlich die Kameradschaft mache.

Es kommt also nur darauf an, den ersten Anstoss zur
Wiederaufnahme unserer Tätigkeit zu geben.

Das soll dieser erste Rundbrief besorgen.

(Walter Kappe)

- -

Diesem Rundbrief beigefügt ist ein als
streng vertraulich zu betrachtender Bericht über die Lage des Deutschtums in
USA., der die Kameraden auf dem Laufenden
halten soll.

                D.O.

5.

Eberhard von N a s s e gefallen

Wenige Tage vor Abschluss des Waffenstillstands mit
Frankreich fiel bei einem Sturmangriff auf die
Maginotlinie

der Gefreite Eberhard von Nasse,

der erste Landesjugendführer des Bundes "Freunde des
Neuen Deutschland" und langjährige Ortsgruppenleiter
von Buffalo.
Eberhard von Nasse gehörte zu den ältesten Vor-
kämpfern der völkischen Bewegung in den Vereinigten
Staaten und war der Gründer der amerikadeutschen
Jugendbewegung in den zwanziger Jahren.
Dem Amerikadeutschtum war er nicht nur das Vorbild
eines nationalsozialistischen Führers, sondern auch
des stets einsatzbereiten Kameraden. Seinen Einsatz
für Führer und Volk hat er an der Front mit dem Tode
besiegelt.
Eberhard von N a s s e wird in unseren Reihen
weiterleben !

––––––––––

6.

Anordnungen der Kameradschaftsleitung:

Sitz der Kameradschaftsleitung ist Stuttgart,

Anschrift: Kameradschaft USA.
                 Stuttgart-S,
                 Danziger Freiheit 17.

Mitgliedsbeitrag:

Von jedem Mitglied der Kameradschaft USA. wird ein Jahresbeitrag in Höhe von RM 1.-- erhoben. Die Beiträge sind unter
Verwendung der beiliegenden Zahlkarte auf das Postscheckkonto
142 64 Stuttgart einzuzahlen.

Diese Beitragserhebung erfolgt ausschliesslich aus dem Grunde,
um festzustellen, wer Interesse an der Kameradschaft hat und
wer nicht. Wem die Zahlung von RM 1.-- zuviel ist, der möge
ruhig fernbleiben.

Das Geld wird für besondere Fälle und Deckung besonderer
Ausgaben (z.B. Vorbereitung einer Tagung usw,) zur Verfügung gehalten.

Es wird verwaltet vom Sekretär der Kameradschaft USA.,
Kamerad J.K.Leibl (Chikago).

Sammlung von Dokumenten aus der Bewegung:

Die von mir im Frühjahr 1939 eingeleitete Sammlung von
Bildern, Fotos, Flugblättern, Broschüren, Zeitungsbe-
richten und Plakaten aus der völkischen Bewegung in USA.
wird fortgesetzt.

Mit dem bereits vorhandenen Material soll es zu einer
lückenlosen Sammlung ausgestaltet werden, die später
einmal dem Deutschen Ausland-Institut sowie dem Zentral-
archiv der NSDAP. in München als ewiges Dokument unseres
Kampfes in USA. einverleibt werden soll.

Die Originalstücke werden nach Bearbeitung an jeden
Kameraden zurückgegeben werden, sodass eine Einbusse
an persönlichen Andenken nicht erfolgt. Nur bitte ich,
Geduld zu haben.

Sammlung von Filmen der Bewegung:

Aus dem gleichen Grunde wollen sich bitte alle Kameraden
melden, die im Besitz von Filmen aus der Bewegung sind.
Ich bin in der Lage, aus solchen Filmen einen guten Ge-
samtfilm in mehreren Kopien kostenlos herstellen zu
lassen.

Die Filme brauchen vorläufig noch nicht eingesandt zu werden, es genügt mir vorerst Meldung und Beschreibung sowie
ungefähre Länge der Filme.

5003860—43——18

7.   - 2 -

Verbindung mit USA:

Es ist von grösstem Interesse, dass die Kameraden ihre
brieflichen Beziehungen zu ihren Bekannten in USA. auf-
recht erhalten, bzw. diese Beziehungen bei Beobachtung
der gebotenen Vorsicht neu aufnehmen. Hierbei ist besonders zu beachten, dass der Empfänger nicht durch un-
vorsichtige Bemerkungen unsererseits blossgestellt wird.
So hat jede Kritik oder Einmischung in inneramerikanische
Verhältnisse zu unterbleiben. Aus unseren Briefen soll
die feste Siegeszuversicht Grossdeutschlands heraus-
klingen.
Die Briefe werden am besten "Via Sibirien" versandt,
unter genauer Beachtung der postalischen Vorschriften.

Für uns von Wichtigkeit sind Stimmungsberichte aus USA.,
aus denen hervorgeht, wie es um die Haltung des Deutschtums bestellt ist, welche Vereine zu Kreuze gekrochen
sind, wie der Durchschnittsamerikaner die Lage beurteilt,
wie die Stimmung gegenüber den Juden ist, usw. Es muss
aber auf jeden Fall unterlassen werden, diese Fragen
direkt an die Empfänger der Briefe zu stellen.

Ich bitte alle Kameraden, mir Auszüge aus ihren Briefen
aus USA. zu geben, sofern darin Mitteilungen über die
oben angedeuteten Themen enthalten sind.

- - -

Neue USA.-Kameraden:

Jeder Kamerad, der Adressen von unseren einstigen Kampfgenossen im Reich besitzt, die noch nicht von der Kameradschaft USA. erfasst sind, wird gebeten, diese an die Zentrale
in Stuttgart zu senden.

- - -

Einbürgerung:

In allen Fragen der Einbürgerung wollen sich die Kameraden
wenden an:
Kamerad Georg N e b b e, Volksdeutsche Mittelstelle,
                         Berlin W 62,
                         Keithstr.27

- - -

Genaue Anschriften:

Jede Adressenänderung bitte ich sofort der Zentrale
mitteilen zu wollen.

                         (gez.) Walter K a p p e

8.

Berichte aus den Kameradschafts-
kreisen

Bericht der Kameradschaft B e r l i n :

Die Kameradschaft Berlin, bestehend aus ca. 120 Mitgliedern,
kommt jeden ersten Sonntag im Monat nachmittags zu einem
Treffen zusammen. Wir versuchen, diese Zusammenkünfte so
gemütlich wie irgend möglich zu machen; durch Unterhaltung,
Vorträge,musikalische Unterhaltung usw. tun wir unser Mög-
lichstes. Die Versammlungen sind sehr rege besucht.
Zur Einleitung werden allgemeine Fragen erörtert, die gerade
für die meisten Kameraden von Interesse sind, z.B. Einbür-
gerungsangelegenheiten, die von einem Vertreter der Volksdeutschen Mittelstelle-Berlin, besprochen werden, was zur
Folge hat, dass die Wiedereinbürgerung der meisten Kameraden
bisher reibungslos vonstatten ging.
Die Besten in der Kameradschaft haben sich geschlossen das
SA-Sportabzeichen erworben und wir müssen sagen, die Resul-
tate waren, trotz der fehlenden Möglichkeit, sich durch
Training auf die einzelnen Übungen vorzubereiten, sehr gut.

Auch haben wir seit ca. 16 Monaten eine Kleinkaliberbüchsen-
mannschaft aufgestellt, die sich reger Anteilnahme erfreut.
Das Schiessen findet jeden zweiten Sonntagvormittag statt;
auch werden Preisschiessen veranstaltet. In Zukunft wollen
wir aus dieser Mannschaft die 6 Besten herausziehen, um
gegen andere Organisationen in Schiesswettbewerb zu treten.
Der erste Versuch in dieser Richtung war besser, als wir
erwarteten, denn wir konnten mit 8 Mann gegen den SA-Sturm,
dessen Gäste wir waren, mit einem Plus für uns abschliessen.
Bemerken möchte ich noch, dass es sich hierbei nicht um
Kleinkaliber, sondern um das 98er Gewehr handelt. Die
meisten von uns hatten erstmalig dieses 98er Gewehr in
den Händen. -
Auch werden die Kameraden, die im Felde stehen, von uns
regelmässig mit Zeitschriften, Zigaretten usw. betreut;
eine einmalige Sammlung im Dezember ergab RM 165.15.

9.

Bericht der Kameradschaft S t u t t g a r t :

Die Kameradschaft Stuttgart trifft sich jeden zweiten Sonntag im Monat nachmittags um 3 Uhr im Hotel "König von Württemberg". So war eine überaus grosse Anzahl unserer Stuttgarter Kameradinnen und Kameraden am Sonntag, 12. Januar, in dem
bis auf den letzten Platz gefüllten Saal zu einem recht
lebhaft und stimmungsvoll verlaufenen Nachmittag zusammen-
gekommen. Kameradschaftsführer Leutnant Walter Kappe, der
vor einigen Monaten aus Frankreich zurückkehrte und zeit-
weilig "in mufti" im Deutschen Ausland-Institut tätig ist,
begrüsste in herzlichen Worten die Anwesenden, deren Zahl
inzwischen auf rund 100 gestiegen war, so dass weitere
Tische und Stühle bereitgestellt werden mussten. Ein grosser Teil der Kameradinnen und Kameraden hatte es sich nicht
nehmen lassen, trotz der empfindlichen Kälte und der nicht
immer einwandfreien Zugverbindungen auch aus der Umgebung
Stuttgarts und weiteren Entfernungen zu kommen - ein Zeichen,
dass der alte Geist noch in voller Frische lebt, und das
konnte man auch auf allen Gesichtern lesen.
Nach Bekanntgabe der Dankesschreiben unserer Kameraden an
der Front und deren Weihnachts- und Neujahrswünsche an die
Kameradschaft, die selbstredend auch in diesem Jahre viele
"zünftige Weihnachtspäckle" hinausgeschickt hatte, ergriff
Kam.Walter Kappe das Wort zu einem kurzen Vortrag über die
kommende Gemeinschaft aller Deutschen, so wie sie der
Führer am Anfang des Programmes der NSDAP. vor langen
Jahren bereits gefordert hatte. In seiner gewohnten knappen und verständlichen Art gab der Redner seinen aufmerk-
sam lauschenden Zuhörern ein klar umrissenes Bild von dem,
was in diesem Zusammenhang kommen wird. Und dass alle ein-
verstanden waren, das bewies der spontane Beifall, der dem
Redner für seine aufschlussreichen Ausführungen dankte.

Zum Schluss wurde noch bekanntgegeben, dass die regel-
mässigen Zusammenkünfte der Stuttgarter Kameradschaft
von jetzt ab nunmehr jeden zweiten Sonntag im Monat stattfinden werden, auch soll an diesem Nachmittage von nun an
jeweils ein Kamerad oder Kameradin von seinen oder ihren

10.

Erinnerungen an die Kampfzeit in USA. und der Tätigkeit
der betreffenden Ortsgruppe ungezwungen berichten, damit
durch diese Wiedergabe alter Erinnerungen die "vom Osten"
auch einmal erfahren sollen, was die "vom Mittelwesten"
und Westen getan haben und umgekehrt - mehr aber noch,
um den Geist von drüben auch hier in unserem grossen
deutschen Vaterlande geziemend weiterzupflegen.

Alles in allem - die Stuttgarter Kameradschaft kann in
der Tat einen ganz trefflich verlaufenen Sonntagnachmittag
verbuchen.

11.

Aufstellung der einzelnen USA-Kameradschaften

1. **Stuttgart**
   Kameradschaftsführer:
   Walter Kappe,
   Stuttgart-S,
   Haus des Deutschtums
   Danziger Freiheit 17
   a) Württ.-Hohenz.
   b) Baden
   c) Schwaben

2. **München**
   Kameradschaftsführer:
   Sepp Schuster
   Vertretung:

   noch nicht
   bestimmt
   a) Mchn.-Oberbayern
   b) Bayr. Ostmark
   c) Kärnten
   d) Oberdonau
   e) Niederdonau
   f) Steiermark
   g) Tirol
   h) Wien
   i) Salzburg
   k) Franken

3. **Berlin**
   Kameradschaftsführer:
   Felix Wagner,
   Berlin-Halensee,
   Westfälische-Str.69
   a) Gross-Bln.
   b) Ostpreussen
   c) Danzig
   d) Pommern
   e) Kurmark
   f) Halle-Mersebg.
   g) Magdebg.-Anh.

4. **Hamburg**
   Kameradschaftsführer:
   Emil Goppelt,
   Hamburg-Poppenbüttel,
   Lützowstr.23
   a) Hamburg
   b) Schlesw.-Holstein
   c) Weser-Ems
   d) Mecklenburg-Lübeck

5. **Hannover**
   Kameradschaftsführer:
   Dipl.-Ing.R.A.
   Piekenbrock
   Misburg b.Hannover
   Am alten Schützenplatz 12
   (Tel. 57 175 Hannover)
   a) Westfalen-Nord
   b) Westfalen-Süd
   c) Kurhessen
   d) Ost-Hannover
   e) Süd-Hannover-Braunschweig

6. **Düsseldorf**
   Kameradschaftsführer:
   Walter Rankenburg
   Köln-Sülz
   Mommsenstr.16
   a) Düsseldorf
   b) Essen
   c) Köln-Aachen

7. **Leipzig**
   Kameradschaftsführer:
   P.S. Urban,
   Leipzig 05
   Kohlgartenstr.21
   a) Sachsen
   b) Schlesien
   c) Sudetengau
   d) Thüringen

8. **Braunschweig**
   Kameradschaftsführer:
   Heinz Heinck,
   Braunschweig
   Kärntenstr.10

9. **Frankfurt a.M.**
   Kameradschaftsführer:
   Ing.Heinrich Edling,
   Frankfurt a.M.
   Im Prüfling 33
   a) Hessen-Nassau
   b) Main-Franken
   c) Koblenz-Trier

hätte erwarten können.

So hat denn die deutschfeindliche Propaganda ein verhältnis-
mässig leichtes Spiel, da die grosse Masse des in Tausende
und Abertausende von Vereinen und Vereinchen, Logen und Kirchen-
organisationen zersplitterten Deutschtums jegliche Hetze und
Schmähung geduldig über sich ergehen lässt und noch dazu in dem
Wahn lebt - in dem es von der deutschsprachigen Presse noch bestärkt wird - , da jetzt Ruhe die erste Bürgerpflicht sei und
man sich ganz aus der Politik heraushalte und sich strikt damit
begnüge, seinem Vereinsprogramm oder seiner kirchlichen Über-
zeugung zu leben, müsse ja die Welle des Hasses an ihnen vorüber-
gehen. Dass dies ein Trugschluss war, dürfte man inzwischen wohl
eingesehen haben, denn ganz gleich, ob es sich um Kundgebungen
der grösseren Zentralverbände, um Heimatabende der Reichsdeutschen oder um Veranstaltungen landsmannschaftlicher Vereinigungen
handelte, sie wurden gestört, aus ihrem beabsichtigten Rahmen
gedrängt oder gänzlich unterbunden. Wie denn ja auch kein Unterschied gemacht wurde, wenn es galt, das Kampfprogramm des Amerikadeutschen Volksbundes zu diffamieren oder gegen einen sich gegen
die britische Propaganda in USA wendenden Beschluss der Steuben
Society of America Sturm zu laufen.

Natürlich steht der Amerikadeutsche Volksbund als die weitaus ak-
tivste und kampfgeschulteste Gruppe des Amerikadeutschtums nach
wie vor im Brennpunkt der Deutschenhetze. Obwohl er völlig legal
arbeitet und eine rein amerikanische Angelegenheit ist, in der
nur naturalisierte oder gebürtige Amerikaner aufgenommen werden
können, ist er zusammen mit den Kommunisten (die amerikanische
Presse schreibt seit dem deutsch-russischen Abkommen nur noch von
den "Communazis") unter Ausnahmegesetz gestellt und werden seine
führenden Männer immer wieder vor die Schranken des Kongressaus-
schusses zur Untersuchung "unamerikanischer Umtriebe" gezerrt. Mitglieder des Bundes (der Name "Bund" und die Bezeichnung "Bundist"
für Bundesmitglied sind inzwischen in den amerikanischen Sprach-
schatz aufgenommen worden) dürfen in keinem kriegswichtigen oder
Rüstungsbetrieb angestellt werden und unterliegen auch sonst
einer scharfen Überwachung. Razzien der Polizeiorgane auf die
Sommerlager des Bundes, die sogenannten "Camps", sind an der Tages-
ordnung, obwohl sie immer ergebnislos verlaufen und in keinem

falls die angeblich vorhandenen Waffen oder sonstiges aus
Deutschland zum Zweck eines gewaltsamen Umsturzes importiertes
"Kriegsmaterial" gefunden worden ist.

Zwar hat der Bund seit Kriegsbeginn in diesem ungleichen Kampf
gegen eine die öffentliche Meinung des Landes beherrschende und
über unermessliche Geldmittel verfügende Übermacht Haare und
Zähne lassen müssen. Der Mitgliederstand ist gesunken, und einige
gleich Aussenforts in einer feindlichen Umwelt liegende Ortsgruppen mussten aufgegeben werden, aber er verfügt auch heute
noch über rund 40 Ortsgruppen, die sich um die drei Zentren
Neuyork, Chikago und San Franzisko schaaren, und mit berechtig-
tem Stolz konnte der neue Bundesführer, der amerikabürtige Wilhelm Kunze, auf der Chikagoer Landestagung im Spätsommer des Jahres
1940 die Feststellung machen: "Wir bestehen immer noch, mitten
in der giftigsten Kriegshetze! Wir bestehen in einer Lage, in
der während des letzten Krieges sämtliche Deutschtumsorganisationen
zusammenbrachen. Das ist schon der Beweis, dass wir die Voraussetzung zum Durchhalten in unserer Bewegung haben!"

Ähnlichen Anfeindungen ausgesetzt sind die Reichsvertretungen
in USA, sowie andere amtlichen deutschen Stellen. Ständig von
Geheimbeamten, Spitzeln und Provokateuren überwacht, bildet ihre
Tätigkeit immer wieder den Gegenstand sensationeller Pressear-
tikel und sogenannter "Untersuchungen".

Vor allem sind es das Deutsche Generalkonsulat in Neuyork, die
diesem Konsulat angegliederte Informationsbibliothek, das Neu-
yrker Büro der Deutschen Reichsbahn und der deutsche Transocean-
dienst, die immer wieder in der Presse als "Zentren der Nazi-
Propaganda in USA" genannt werden und deren Tätigkeit neuerdings in einem "Weissbuch" der vom Abgeordneten Martin Dies
geleiteten Untersuchungskommission als 'umstürzlerisch" ange-
prangert worden ist.

Fernerhin ist auch die Arbeit des "Kyffhäuserbundes deutscher
Kriegervereine" in USA neuerdings in der Presse heftig ange-
griffen worden.

Es wäre indessen falsch, aus dem in diesem Bericht Gesagten zu
dem Urteil zu kommen, das Amerikadeutschtum habe in dieser Schick-
salswende im grossen und ganzen versagt. Allerdings fehlt ihm der
organisatorische Zusammenschluss, mangelt ihm in vielen Fällen die
völkische Kraft und Disziplin, aber im Herzen empfinden die Deutschen
Amerikas zutiefst den gewaltigen Umbruch in Europa, verfolgen sie doch
am Kurzwellenompfänger atemlos jede Phase des deutschen Ringens, und
stets fühlen sie sich durch d Heldentum des deutschen Soldaten
in ihrem Stolz auf ihr Deutsc tum bestärkt.   K..

DOCUMENT 22–A

(Translation)

[p. 1]

INFORMATION SHEET
OF THE
COMRADESHIP U. S. A.

No. 1   **Stuttgart-S, House of Germandom**   **January 1941**

NOTICE:

This communication has a confidential character. It is meant exclusively for the members of the Comradeship USA. Any violation of this rule will result in the suspension of the circular letter.

[p. 2]   TO THE
          COMRADESHIP USA.

The year 1939 with its great political and military events has partially dissolved the close bands which bound the Comradeship together. Many left their former circles of activity to become soldiers or have been transferred in the meantime to one of the new territories. A meeting in Stuttgart provided the incentive to resume contact by the Central Office with all comrades. To this end Party Member *Walter Kappe*, who meanwhile has returned from the Army, will take over the *leadership of the Comradeship* and will renew the bonds through this circular letter. I beg each individual to resume active participation in the work of his respective group for I am convinced that our work in the future will be of significance.

In old loyalty

Heil Hitler !
(Signed)   FRITZ GISSIBL

I have accepted the leadership of the Comradeship USA after a discussion with Fritz Gissibl and Sepp Schuster, who meanwhile has been called up for military service, on the ground that a Central Office of the Comradeship USA must also exist in time of war. This circular letter from Stuttgart is to assist in renewing contact with all comrades, men and women. I depend upon the cooperation of everyone.

Heil Hitler !
(Signed)   WALTER KAPPE

[p. 3]   CIRCULAR LETTER TO ALL COMRADES
Dear Comrades !

When in 1938 we undertook the task of extending throughout the Reich the idea of Sepp Schuster, who earlier had gathered about him in Munich a numerous circle of former fighters from the Bund "Friends of the New Germany", and of establishing the "Comradeship USA", we were moved by three reasons:

first, we wished to continue here in the fatherland the comradeship which enabled us to overcome all obstacles and difficulties over there [in the United States], to help each other and, by the exchange of our experiences during the period of struggle in the United States, to gather strength and courage for our daily work,

second, we wished also through the establishment of this Comradeship to place at the disposal of our fatherland ourselves and the experience which we gained over there,

and, finally, we hoped in some manner to give our fighting brothers over there moral support, even if only through the fact that we, who had returned, loyally remembered the brave fighters at whose side we stood through the years at the front.

Accordingly, Comradeship groups were established in Stuttgart, Berlin, Hamburg, and Hanover; and shortly before the beginning of the war it was possible, through the cooperation of the German Foreign Institute and the city of Stuttgart, to hold the first national meeting of the Comradeship USA in conjunction with the opening of the exposition "American Germanism in Combat", an unforgettable experience for all who participated!

The war drew a heavy line through our extensive plans for the future, and further repatriation practically stopped. The greater part of our comrades hastened to the flag, some Comradeship groups were completely orphaned. Furthermore, Fritz Gissibl was transferred to the east to Litzmannstadt [Lodz, Poland], Sepp Schuster went to Berlin, and, in the first days of the war, Ernst Vennekohl and I exchanged the desk for weapons.

[p. 4]   Consequently, at present our list of addresses is partly out of date. Many comrades have moved without furnishing us with their new addresses. A number of letters which I have written recently in an effort to revive our Comradeship remain unanswered.

Nevertheless, the Comradeship USA still lives. That is evident from the work of our Berlin group, which, in the meantime, has become by far the largest. That is also known to the comrades in the field who were remembered last Christmas with a package. That is apparent in all letters from the front and is also heard in the often impatient inquiries as to what the Comradeship is actually doing.

It is, therefore, only necessary to give the first stimulus to the resumption of our activity. That is to be provided by this first circular letter.   WALTER KAPPE

Attached to this letter is a report concerning the position of Germandom in the United States, which is to be considered as strictly confidential and which is to keep the comrades *au courant*.

                                                                W. K.

[p. 5]   EBERHARD VON NASSE HAS FALLEN

A few days before the signature of the Armistice with France, there fell, during an attack on the Maginot Line,

                    Corporal Eberhard von Nasse,

the first National Youth Leader of the Bund "Friends of the New Germany" and for many years local group leader in Buffalo.

Eberhard von Nasse was one of the oldest front fighters in the German racial movement in the United States and was the founder of the American "German Youth Movement" in the twenties.

For American Germandom he was not only the model of a National Socialist Führer but also a comrade who was always ready for service. His service for Führer and people was sealed by death at the front.

Eberhard von Nasse will live on in our ranks!

———

[p. 6] INSTRUCTIONS OF THE LEADERSHIP OF THE COMRADESHIP:
The headquarters of the Comradeship leadership is at Stuttgart,

Address: Kameradschaft USA.
Stuttgart–S,
Danziger Freiheit 17.

Membership Fees:

An annual contribution in the amount of one mark is collected from every member of the Comradeship USA. The fees should be sent to Postal Account 142 64 at Stuttgart by using the attached payment card.

This collection of fees is being made exclusively for the purpose of determining who has interest in the Comradeship and who does not. Anyone for whom the payment of one mark is too much may quietly remain outside.

The funds will be used for special cases and to cover special expenditures (for example, the preparation of a conference, etc.)

They will be administered by the secretary of the Comradeship USA, Comrade *J. K. Leibl* (Chicago).

Collection of Documents Concerning the Movement:

The collection of pictures, photos, handbills, pamphlets, newspaper clippings, and posters of the German national movement in the United States, which was begun by me in the spring of 1939, will be *continued.*

The material already at hand is to be built up to a complete collection, which later is to be incorporated into the German Foreign Institute, as well as the Central Archives of the NSDAP in Munich, as an eternal record of our struggle in the United States.

The original documents will be returned to each comrade after recording, so that no sacrifice of personal souvenirs will occur. I only ask you to have patience.

Collection of Films of the Movement:

For the same reasons we wish to hear from all comrades who are in possession of films concerning the movement. I am in a position to have a *good complete film in several copies* prepared from such films.

The films do not need to be sent in yet. It is sufficient at present to inform me and to describe the film and indicate its approximate length.

[p. 7]   **Contact With the United States:**

It is of the greatest interest that the comrades maintain relations by letter with their acquaintances in the United States or renew these relations while observing the prescribed caution. In this respect it should be particularly noted that the recipient should not be endangered by careless remarks on our part. Any criticism or interference in internal American affairs should be avoided. Firm confidence in the victory of Greater Germany should ring out in our letters.

Letters may best be sent "Via Siberia" with exact observance of postal regulations.

Important to us are reports concerning public opinion in the United States, such as the nature of the attitude of Germans, which clubs have disbanded, how the average American considers the situation, how anti-Jewish sentiment is developing, etc. But in every case asking these questions directly of the recipient of the letters must be avoided.

I request all comrades to furnish me with excerpts from their letters from the United States, so far as they contain *information* on the *subjects* mentioned above.

New USA Comrades:

Every comrade who knows addresses of our former fighters in the Reich who are not yet members of the Comradeship USA, is requested to send them to the Central Office in Stuttgart.

Naturalization:

In all questions concerning naturalization, the comrades should communicate with:

Comrade *Georg Nebbe*,   Volksdeutsche Mittelstelle,
                          Berlin W 62,
                          Keithstr. 27.

Exact Addresses:

I request that the Central Office be informed immediately of every change of address.

(signed)   WALTER KAPPE

[p. 8]   NEWS FROM COMRADESHIP CIRCLES

News From the Berlin Group:

The Berlin group, consisting of approximately 120 members, meets the first Sunday afternoon of every month. We try to make these meetings as pleasant as possible through conversation, lectures, musical programs, etc. The meetings are very well attended. First, all general questions are discussed which are of interest to most of the comrades. For example, naturalization affairs were discussed by a representative of the Volksdeutsche Mittelstelle—Berlin, with the result that the re-naturalization of most of the comrades has so far occurred without friction.

The best men in the group have all won the SA sport insignia, and we must say that, in spite of the absence of opportunities to train for the individual events, the results were very good.

About 16 months ago we organized a small-bore rifle team, which is extremely popular. Target practice takes place every second Sunday forenoon; prize events are also organized. In the future we will choose the six best marksmen from this team, in order to enter contests against other organizations. The first attempt in this direction was better than we expected, since we were able, with an eight-man team, to get the best of the SA Storm Troopers, whose guests we were. I should like to note in passing that this contest was not conducted with small-bore rifles but with the 98 rifle. For most of us this was the first time that we had handled this 98 rifle.

Furthermore, the comrades at the front are regularly provided by us with magazines, cigarettes, etc.; a single collection in December yielded RM 165.15.

[p. 9]   **News From the Stuttgart Group**

The Stuttgart group meets every second Sunday afternoon in the month at three o'clock in the König von Württemberg Hotel. A particularly large number of our Stuttgart comrades, men and women, met on Sunday, January 12, in the hall, which was filled to the last seat, for a very lively and enthusiastic afternoon. The leader of the Comradeship, Lieutenant Walter Kappe, who returned from France several months ago and at present is "in mufti" at work in the German Foreign Institute, greeted the audience, which in the meantime had increased to about 100, so that additional tables and chairs had to be brought in, with hearty words. A greater part of the comrades were not deterred from attending, despite the bitter cold and the train connections from points in the vicinity of Stuttgart and farther away, which are not always too good—a sign that the old spirit still lives in full freshness, and that could also be seen in the faces of all members of the audience.

After the reading of a message of thanks from our comrades at the front and their Christmas and New Year's wishes to the Comradeship, which naturally had sent many Christmas packages this year also, Comrade Walter Kappe delivered a short lecture concerning the coming community of all Germans which had already been demanded by the Führer years ago at the beginning of the program of the NSDAP. In his usual incisive and understanding way, the speaker gave his attentive listeners a clearly drawn picture of what would develop in this direction. That everyone was in agreement with his remarks was evident from the spontaneous applause which greeted the speaker at the end of his inspiring address.

Finally, it was announced that the regular meetings of the Stuttgart group from now on would take place every second Sunday in the month and that on these afternoons a comrade would speak voluntarily about his or her [p. 10] experiences during the time of struggle in the United States and the activity of his respective local group, in order that, through the repetition of old experiences, those "from the East" might also know what those "in the Middle West" and the West have done and vice versa—but still more in order to cultivate further the spirit from over there here in our great German fatherland.

All in all, the Stuttgart group can record a very satisfactory Sunday afternoon.

———

[p. 11] LIST OF THE INDIVIDUAL GROUPS OF THE COMRADESHIP USA

1. *Stuttgart*
   Group Leader:
   Walter Kappe,
   Stuttgart-S,
   House of Germandom
   Danziger Freiheit 17
   (a) Württ.-Hohenz.
   (b) Baden
   (c) Schwaben

2. *Munich*
   Group Leader:
   Sepp Schuster
   Representatives:
   not yet determined.

(a) Mchn.-Oberbayern
(b) Bayr. Ostmark
(c) Kärnten
(d) Oberdonau
(e) Niederdonau
(f) Steiermark
(g) Tirol
(h) Wien
(i) Salzburg
(k) Franken

3. *Berlin*
   Group Leader:
   Felix Wagner,
   Berlin-Halensee,
   Westfälische-Str. 69

(a) Gross-Bln.
(b) Ostpreussen
(c) Danzig
(d) Pommern
(e) Kurmark
(f) Halle-Mersebg.
(g) Magdebg.-Anh.

4. *Hamburg*
Group Leader:
Emil Goppelt,
Hamburg-Poppenbüttel,
Lützowstr. 23
(a) Hamburg
(b) Schlesw.-Holstein
(c) Weser-Ems
(d) Mecklenburg-Lübeck

5. *Hannover*
Group Leader:
Dipl.-Ing. R.A.
Piekenbrock
Misburg b. Hannover
Am alten Schützenplatz 12
(Tel. 57 175 Hannover)
(a) Westfalen-Nord
(b) Westfalen-Süd
(c) Kurhessen
(d) Ost-Hannover
(e) Süd-Hannover-
Braunschweig

6. *Düsseldorf*
Group Leader:
Walter Rankenburg
Köln-Sülz
Mommsenstr. 16
(a) Düsseldorf
(b) Essen
(c) Köln-Aachen

7. *Leipzig*
Group Leader:
P.S. Urban,
Leipzig 05
Kohlgartenstr. 21
(a) Sachsen
(b) Schlesien
(c) Sudetengau
(d) Thüringen

8. *Braunschweig*
Group Leader:
Heinz Heinck, [1]
Braunschweig
Kärntenstr. 10

9. *Frankfurt-am-Main*
Group Leader:
Ing. Heinrich Edling,
Frankfurt-am-Main
Im Prüfling 33
(a) Hessen-Nassau
(b) Main-Franken
(c) Koblenz-Trier

[Pages I and II of the *Supplement* to the *Information Sheet* are miss-
ing; pages III and IV follow.]

[p. 12 (III)]

. . . . . . Accordingly, anti-German propaganda had a comparatively easy time, since the great mass of the thousands and thousands of societies and little groups, lodges, and people's organizations
in which Germandom was split up patiently permitted all agitation
and defamation to pass over it and furthermore lived under the mad
delusion—in which it was strengthened even more by the German-

---

[1] [Believed to be identical with Heinrich Heinck, who was executed as one
of the eight Nazi saboteurs landed by submarine on American shores in June
1942—EDITOR.]

language press—that a quiet attitude was now the first duty of citizenship and that one should hold aloof from politics and limit oneself strictly to one's club program or one's denominational persuasions and the wave of hate would pass by. That this was a false conclusion must have been apparent in the meantime, for, regardless of whether it was a matter of proclamations of the large central organizations, of German social gatherings of German nationals, or of the programs organized by German-American associations, they were disturbed, forced out of their intended framework, or suppressed entirely. No difference was made between defaming the combat program of the American-German Volksbund and opposing a resolution of the Steuben Society of America directed against British propaganda in the United States.

Naturally, the *American-German Volksbund,* which is by far the most active and most indoctrinated combat group in American Germandom, always stands in the *forefront of the anti-German agitation.* Although it operates on a fully legal basis and is a purely American affair in which only naturalized or native-born Americans can be accepted as members, it is given exceptional legal treatment (*Ausnahmegesetz*) together with the Communists (since the German-Russian pact the American press writes only about the "Communazis"), and its leaders are constantly called before the Congressional Committee for the Investigation of "Un-American Activities". Members of the Bund (the name "Bund" and the designation "Bundist" for members of the Bund have in the meantime been included in the American vocabulary) may not be employed in any strategic or armament industry and are also subject to strict surveillance. Police raids on the summer places of the Bund, the so-called "camps", are common, although they are always without result, and in no [p. 13 (IV)] case have the alleged stocks of weapons or other "war material" imported from Germany for the purpose of a revolution by force been found.

It is true that since the beginning of the war the Bund has suffered losses in its unequal fight against a superior power, which controls the public opinion of the country and has at its disposal unlimited funds. Membership has dropped and some local groups which were like fortified outposts in enemy country have had to be given up, but there are today still about 40 local groups ranged around the three centers at New York, Chicago, and San Francisco, and the new leader of the Bund, the American-born Wilhelm Kunze, could state with justified pride at the Chicago National Congress in the late summer of 1940, "We still exist in the midst of the poisonous war propaganda ! We exist in a situation in which during the last war all German organizations broke up. That is proof enough that we have the prerequisites in our movement to hold out !"

The official representatives of the Reich in the United States are subject to similar hostile attacks, as well as other official German agencies. Constantly under surveillance by secret agents, plain clothesmen, and *agents provocateurs*, their activity is continually the subject of sensational press articles and so-called "investigations".

In particular, it is the *German Consulate General* in New York, *the Library of Information* which is a part of this Consulate, the New York office of the *German Railways* and the *German Transocean Service* which are constantly named in the press as "centers of Nazi propaganda in the United States" and whose activity recently was denounced as "revolutionary" in a "White Book" of the investigating committee headed by Representative Martin Dies.

Furthermore, the work of the *"Kyffhäuserbund of German War Veterans' Societies"* has also recently been strongly attacked in the press.

It would be a mistake, however, to conclude from what has been said in this report that American Germandom has in this fateful hour entirely failed. To be sure, it lacks organizational structure, in many cases it lacks folk strength and discipline, but in their hearts the Germans of America experience very deeply the powerful revolution in Europe. They follow breathlessly on their short-wave receivers every phase of the German struggle, and they always feel themselves strengthened in their pride in their Germandom through the heroism of the German soldiers.

K.

DOCUMENT 23

(Translation)

THE FOREIGN ORGANIZATION
OF THE
NATIONAL SOCIALIST PARTY

(Die Auslandsorganisation der NSDAP)

BY

DR. EMIL EHRICH, GAUAMTSLEITER

Personal Adviser to the Gauleiter of the Foreign Organization of the Nazi Party

[Published as no. 13 in vol. II of a series of monographs concerning National Socialism, a series including contributions by Goebbels, Alfred Rosenberg, and other prominent Nazi officials and authoritative spokesmen]

JUNKER UND DÜNNHAUPT VERLAG
BERLIN
1937

PREFACE

The following short pamphlet attempts to describe through its activities the present status of the youngest division (Gau) of the Nazi Party and thus the youngest branch of the German people. An objective effort is made, on the basis of the actual development of German organizations and institutions abroad, to make political Germany conscious of the *rapprochement* of the German folk-community abroad to the people at home, by a sober presentation of the many-sided activities and accomplishments of the AO[1] of the NSDAP, which has been working under the most difficult conditions. May the pamphlet fulfil this aim and spread the conviction that the Führer has won for the Reich millions of its citizens, for whom life and prosperity are a reward for service and sacrifice! May it also for the first time testify in ringing tones to the return to the fatherland of foreign Germandom, through whose year-long, selfless share in honorary work—at the expense of its leisure and recreation—alone an AO has become possible.

THE AUTHOR

BERLIN, *February 4, 1937, on the first anniversary of the murder of the national group leader, Wilhelm Gustloff.*

---

[1] [*Auslandsorganisation*, Foreign Organization—EDITOR.]

CHAPTER I

History and Aim

All persons of German blood residing outside of the boundaries of the Reich, conscious of their German origin, and possessing German citizenship are foreign Germans (*Auslandsdeutsche*). The AO of the NSDAP concerns itself only with such German citizens abroad. Their exact number (estimates vary between two and three million) cannot be determined in the absence of consular registers. As understood by the AO for purposes of organization, foreign Germans also include approximately 70,000 persons following the calling of seamen.

The principal characteristics of pre-Nazi Germany, division into small states (*Kleinstaaterei*) and the political party system, also left their mark on Germandom abroad before the World War and after it again until 1933. It is true that, except for a few miserable attempts, the countless political parties which were tearing apart the body of the German people and represented various political philosophies and special interests were unable to obtain a foothold abroad. The Germans abroad were too far removed from party bickering at home to permit the parties to recruit sympathizers or supporters among them. But either their point of view was determined naturally by the confusion of ideas and organization in the Reich, or they turned away in disgust from all this activity and were content to pursue their own interests in their own particular ways. With a dismembered and powerless Germany behind them, which was unable to follow the thinking and feeling of Germans abroad and which displayed only slight understanding for their difficult position and for their German mission, those who still sought a community life and were drawn toward it in many ways for their mutual advantage (for example: schools, churches, sport, welfare) grouped themselves together in clubs and societies of a "non-political" character. So far as they were united by common aims these organizations, notwithstanding the unfavorable circumstances and conditions under which they worked, produced astonishing results and in some measure justified their existence. Other organizations, however, wasted their energies in empty social functions in a patriotic setting—with careful distinctions based on class and income—and thereby hardly helped to provide for the individual a substitute for his far-off fatherland or even to form a worthy representative of the Reich. They existed only for external appearance, and, therefore, after the seizure of power in Germany by the Nazi Party they failed to understand the essence of National Socialist demands. They knew nothing about the obligations of the individual to the whole group; they misunderstood the meaning of the natural duty of loyalty to folk and Reich—to them this was all "political" and illegal and hateful. By taking this attitude they relinquished all claim to community leadership and sank into insignificance when National Socialism knocked on the doors of Germans abroad.

The first National Socialist organizations among Germans abroad were founded without encouragement from the fatherland. Their establishment sprang from the need of our German compatriots abroad to announce their support for Adolf Hitler's freedom movement through membership in the Nazi Party or through the voluntary proclamation of their goals. Nevertheless, the Nazi success at the polls on September 14, 1930 came as a great surprise to the great mass of Germans abroad. They had no personal idea either of the uneconomic policies of the November Republic and the dangerous growth of Communism or of the rise of a new and better Germany under the leadership of the Nazi movement, concerning which they had been informed only by tendentious or derogatory news carried in the foreign press or in the German papers circulating abroad.

The task of systematically remedying this lack of information was assumed by a few men who even at that time were conscious of the needs of Germans abroad and who met at Hamburg in the fall of 1930, preparatory to establishing an office which, by an order of the Reich's Organization Directorate of May 1, 1931, was designated as the "Foreign Section of the Reich's Directorate of the NSDAP" with headquarters in Hamburg. The same order provided that every party member who was abroad or who changed his permanent residence to a foreign country was without exception under the supervision of the Foreign Section. In addition to the consolidation of the Nazi groups which were already in existence and which now obtained a firm basis in the fatherland, it was possible during 1931 by tireless, careful work to establish numerous new branches and local groups (*Stützpunkte* and *Ortsgruppen*), which made the establishment of the first country groups (*Landesgruppen*) necessary in 1932.

In the first months after the party's accession to power, when all the energies of the fatherland were required for internal development and the question arose whether the existence of a Foreign Section was at all justified and necessary, the office for a time was called the "Section for Germans Abroad Attached to the Supreme Directorate of the PO[2]", until it was placed directly under the Führer's Deputy, on October 3, 1933, with its former name. Its leader, Ernst Wilhelm Bohle,[3] who has been in charge since May 8, 1933, was appointed to

---

[2] [Politische Organisation (Political Organization)—EDITOR.]

[3] Ernst Wilhelm Bohle was born of German parents July 28, 1903 in Bradford, England. Three years later his father, Dr. Ing. E.H. Hermann Bohle, became a professor at the University of Capetown. E.W. Bohle graduated from the English high school there, then studied political science and commerce at the Universities of Cologne and Berlin and the Commercial College at Berlin, and in 1923 passed

the staff of the Führer's Deputy with the rank of Gauleiter. On February 17, 1934 the Führer's Deputy ordered the new designation, "Foreign Organization of the NSDAP". At the same time, in regulations issued pursuant to this order, the competence of the AO was set forth. Party members abroad are subject to the AO and may not be carried as members of Gaus in Germany; the AO is the only competent party liaison office for all party branches abroad; official communications from all party groups in Germany with the party organization abroad go through the AO; National Socialist occupational societies which intend to include German nationals (*Reichsdeutsche*) abroad in their activities may do so only within the framework of the AO. In a supplementary decree of March 16, 1934 the Deputy of the Führer ordered that all party members in possession of a seaman's registration book who had not left the sea for an occupation on land, as well as German pilots, were likewise subject to the AO.

These decrees ended all uncertainty concerning the work for Germans abroad. They created the presupposition and confirmed the necessity for a stronger development of the central office which, in its organic growth up to the time of its unavoidable transfer to Berlin in the middle of March 1935, had increased its staff to 170 employees. The determination of the specialized work of the branches and associated societies permitted intensive activity, which extended to all phases of the life of Germans abroad and, together with the development of the remaining departments, was of decisive significance for the subsequent expansion to a total staff at the present time (beginning of 1937) of more than 700 persons. The organizational status of the AO was fixed for the present by a decree of the Führer's Deputy dated April 15, 1935, which, because of its very favorable numerical and organizational development, raised the AO from a "Section of the Reich's Directorate" to the status of an independent Gau with the designation "Foreign Organization of the NSDAP". (For details, see chapter II.)

The membership campaign among Germans abroad and at sea experienced a noticeable improvement after the party's accession to power, which was obvious in view of the fact that previously the possibilities for promotional activities for the party had been only slight. In the same degree the membership of branches and associated societies increased. Today 548 local groups and branches (*Ortsgruppen* and *Stützpunkte*) abroad, which, excepting a large number of independent groups, are united in 45 country groups and regional sections,

the commercial examination. After several years' activity in the import and export business in the Rhineland and at Hamburg, he entered the Foreign Section of the NSDAP in November 1931 as an honorary collaborator. On January 30, 1937 he was decorated by the Führer with the highest order of the Third Reich, the Gold Decoration of Honor of the NSDAP.

and 1097 groups among seamen constitute the AO, the "youngest Gau" of the NSDAP, and guarantee that every German (*Volksgenosse*) abroad can feel bound to the fatherland through the NSDAP whenever he so desires.

*
* *

As early as 1931 the principles were formulated which were distributed as commandments to every party member of the AO on the foreign certificate (*Auslandsausweis*) of the party membership card. After the conquest of the German people by National Socialism they became fundamental obligations for all Germans abroad through the Führer's decree of January 30, 1937 (see Conclusion) ; they read as follows:

(1) Observe the laws of the country whose guest you are.
(2) Leave the politics of the country where you reside to its inhabitants. You are not concerned with the internal politics of a foreign country. Take no part in them, even in conversation.
(3) Acknowledge yourself as a party member at all times and in all places.
(4) Always speak and act in such a way that you bring honor to the National Socialist movement and thereby to the new Germany. Be upright, honorable, fearless, and loyal.
(5) Recognize every German abroad as your compatriot, a man of your blood and your kind. Extend your hand to him regardless of his position. We are all "creators" of our people.
(6) Help your German compatriots gladly and voluntarily when they get in difficulty through no fault of their own.
(7) Do not be merely a member but also a fighter in the foremost line. Inform yourself thoroughly of the methods, content, and aims of our movement.
(8) Work and fight day after day for the entry of every honorable German into our movement. Convince him of the superiority and justness of our movement, of the necessity of our victory in order that Germany may live on ! Fight with spiritual weapons !
(9) Read our party publication, our pamphlets and books.
(10) Associate yourself with party members in your place of residence. If a local or city group exists there, be a disciplined and active worker. Not only should you not support dissension but you should also make every effort to settle disputes which arise.

These ten commandments, for the realization of which National Leader Wilhelm Gustloff fell, reveal the new significance which National Socialist Germany has given to the work among Germans abroad and the great value which it attaches thereto. It is no longer a question of participation alone, but of duty, of accomplishment that is expected, of behavior which is prescribed. Formerly the work for Germans abroad consisted of an appeal to the sympathetic heart of the citizen sitting at home by his fire; it was a diligent labor of building up files and collections which, however, in periods of difficulty and struggle was considered of secondary importance; it was at best material support which often was satisfied when the files could be filled with sentimental letters of thanks from distant colonies. Under the ideas and form imposed by National Socialism the work for Germans abroad means the conversion of the living man, his enlistment and employment for the German community. It recognizes as the highest law solely the right of the folk-community, of which foreign Germandom is only a part. It emphasizes the fundamental principle that the Reich and the people in the Reich do not exist for the benefit of Germans abroad, but demands the contrary—that foreign Germandom shall accept and be responsible for that share of the nation's tasks which is assigned to it by Providence. The task of the AO of the NSDAP is to prepare foreign Germandom for this role and to inculcate this concept of foreign Germandom in the Reich by sweeping away outmoded ideas. The goal of its work is a community of destiny (*Schicksalsgemeinschaft*) at home and abroad which can defy all storms.

The realization of this concept is conditioned upon the existence of a true people's community abroad. It can only be National Socialist and be maintained by convinced National Socialists. It must be able to raise the individual regardless of his person or position, to stiffen his back for the struggle of life, and in cases of need to assist him. The German abroad is denied the help and guidance of the state which give to the German at home the feeling of being a cog in the great national machine and place upon him restraints when these are necessary. Certain advisory and official functions of German consular representatives abroad are not pertinent in this respect. The AO fills the gap. It should provide for the German abroad a substitute for the state's control at home. In the first place it unites in voluntary association those whose lives are dedicated to cooperation in accomplishing German tasks and in realizing the aims of the Führer. In addition it also enlists and inspires as the core of the people's community—in accordance with the totalitarian ideas which are inherent in every National Socialist organization and on the basis of the primacy which the decree of the Führer's Deputy accords to it and which the position of the NSDAP as the national political movement guarantees by virtue of the fundamental law of December 1, 1933 establishing the identity of the party and the state—all nonparty members belonging to the old societies and colonial associations, so far as they consider it of importance to be regarded as Germans. Yes, the consciousness in some manner of belonging thereto and the deep ethical demands of National Socialism allow each individual foreign German for the first time to renew his faith in the future and once more give meaning to his life. That a struggle is necessary to achieve this people's community is founded in human nature and is good. Struggle produces life; but it leads to decay when idealism or healthy stubbornness are dissipated in the realm of insignificant personal dissension or when such disputes are carried on publicly abroad. For this reason the struggle of Germans abroad requires a large measure of internal discipline and strong character from its supporters. The responsibility of the Central Office of the AO in the selection of leaders is therefore particularly great—quite apart from the requirements of political clarity and technical competence which must be demanded of the workers, who almost without exception function without remuneration.

Such a people's community in a foreign German colony or aboard a German ship, rooted in itself and based on voluntary association in the service of an idea, is capable of appearing before the foreign country and the world as a unified whole. It displays abroad the external features of the movement and the Reich, gives to the individual a feeling of assurance such as a great and able people should have, and, through the good-will thereby created, is enabled to build strong bridges to the foreign (native) community. It is not an outpost of plotting imperialism only awaiting an opportunity to bring decay into the land—as the AO is continually accused of being by certain hostile interests which formerly could not do enough to deride Germans abroad because of their lack of dignity—but instead is the personification of order and understanding. The rule against participation in the politics of the country and the National Socialist concept of the dignity of foreign peoples refute all attacks of this kind on the AO. No state can be denied the right to fill its citizens residing abroad with the wealth of its ideas—nor can the Third Reich be so denied. And no power in the world can withdraw from a German abroad the obligation which he bears to his people and his Reich. The legality of the AO is based on the innermost law of the National Socialistic political philosophy, which exists only for the German people. To recognize this and to allow the strength of foreign Germandom to become effective signifies for the foreign state the knowledge that a compact community of disciplined and loyal guests resides within its borders.

The AO would accomplish only half its task and in a certain sense would stamp its work as for selfish ends if it did not also set for itself the goal of attacking sharply the widespread aping of foreign customs by the German people, an unholy heritage of the century-long national division and people's weakness which has often made Germany's name despised in the world, notwithstanding all the exceptional achievements of our people for mankind. The National Socialist leadership of the Reich and the movement have recognized this defect and are determined to remedy it. Among many other measures it is enough to mention the success of the national political institutions of learning, which stand at the head of the students' exchange, and that the Youth Leader of the German Reich recently made obligatory the requirement of a period of residence abroad for the higher officials of the Hitler Youth.

The AO, which is also the agency for pooling the experience of millions of German men and women with knowledge of foreign countries, will not fail in the solution of this great task, which is so unusually important for the proper evaluation of the German people by the rest of the world.

CHAPTER II

STRUCTURE AND CONSTITUENT ORGANIZATIONS

The Foreign Organization of the NSDAP is conducted as a Gau from the point of view of organization and is divided accordingly—notwithstanding certain differences which are required by special conditions abroad and at sea. As in the case of Gaus within Germany, the basic units are the local and city groups (*Stützpunkte* and *Ortsgruppen*) abroad and on board ship. Their leaders hold the same rank in the party as the lowest bearers of sovereignty (*Hoheitsträger*) in Germany. Between them and the *Gauleiter*, in the case of foreign countries, stand the country leaders (*Landesgruppenleiter*) or the regional section leaders (*Landeskreisleiter*), who are wholly responsible to the *Gauleiter* for the leadership of Germandom in their respective countries. The country leaders are equivalent to *Gauamtsleiter* (department heads of the Gau) and the regional section leaders to *Kreisleiter*. The larger national groups may, if necessary, be divided into regions with a regional leader in charge. The regions are subdivided only into city or local groups (*Ortsgruppen* or *Stützpunkte*). There is no intermediate bearer of sovereignty between the *Gauleiter* and the leaders of groups on ships. The section leaders (*Abschnittsleiter*) of the Seamen's Department (see below) are vested with the duties and rights of sovereigns for purposes of party discipline and are equivalent in rank to directors of the principal offices of the Gau (*Gauhauptstellenleiter*).

The bearers of sovereignty in the AO may accordingly be listed as follows:

(1) The *Gauleiter*. Assisting him:
    (a) The Staff Office (*Stabsamt*)
    (b) The Personal Adviser (*Persönliche Referat*)
    (c) The Adjutant's Office (*Adjutantur*)
(2) The *Deputy Gauleiter*
(3) The country leaders (rank, Gau department head)
(4) Regional section leaders (rank, section leader)
(5) Section leaders
(6) Local group leaders abroad and on board ship
(7) Branch leaders abroad and on board ship.

The staff of the *Gauleiter*—the "Central Office of the Gau"—is designated as "The Managing Office of the Foreign Organization of the NSDAP" (location: Berlin W 35, Tiergartenstrasse 4–4a, several other buildings in Berlin, and branches outside of Berlin, as well as the offices of sections and subsections of the Seamen's Department). The department heads, among whom are the Director of the Staff Office and the Personal Adviser, have the rank of heads of Gau departments. Their associates include the directors of principal offices (*Hauptstellenleiter*), the directors of ordinary offices (*Stellenleiter*).

etc., in the Gau management. The staffs of country leaders are organized on the same basis. The associates of the regional section leaders, section leaders, and leaders of local groups and branches are classified according to the rank of their sovereigns.

To identify the political leaders of the Foreign Organization the Führer has approved a special insignia, the so-called "AO diamond" (*Raute*). The black diamond in the form of a rhombus standing on its point is worn on the left arm two centimeters above the cuff. The letters "AO" in the diamond are embroidered in yellow for the bearers of sovereignty and in white for the other political leaders. The insignia may only be worn as long as the party member belongs to the AO and must be removed as soon as he returns to the Reich and is assigned to a local group within Germany.

The diversity of conditions abroad requires that the Central Office of the Foreign Organization have offices which, on the one hand, are continuously and precisely informed concerning all events abroad that are in any way connected with and exert influence upon the existence of foreign Germandom, and which, on the other hand, must be in a position politically to determine and carry out the work of the party divisions and organizations associated in the AO and the activities of the departments which are charged with functions not limited to specific geographic regions.

This task falls to the eight regional departments (*Länderämter*). They constitute the actual political foundation of the AO and are responsible to the *Gauleiter* for the entire development of the country groups and regional sections assigned to them and of the independent local groups existing in certain countries. They are:

(1) Regional Dept. I, northern and eastern Europe.
(2) Regional Dept. II, western Europe (excluding Great Britain and Ireland).
(3) Regional Dept. III, southeastern Europe, Austria, and the Near East.
(4) Regional Dept. IV, Italy, Switzerland, and Hungary.
(5) Regional Dept. V, Africa.
(6) Regional Dept. VI, North America.
(7) Regional Dept. VII, Latin America.
(8) Regional Dept. VIII, the Far East, Australia, Great Britain, and Ireland.

In addition—with the same tasks and with competence over all seafaring party members and over the development of conditions in German maritime shipping in all fields of social and general policy:

(9) The Seamen's Department, with its subordinate sectional offices:
    (a) Weser-Ems (Bremen)
    (b) Elbe (Hamburg)
    (c) Western Baltic (Kiel)

(d) Eastern Baltic (Stettin) and wherever necessary, subsections organized as local groups. In order to insure orderly cooperation with the coastal Gaus the section and subsection leaders belong to the respective Gau or section offices of their territories in the capacity of "maritime shipping" advisers.

The party organizations for the leadership and guidance of the people, which are associated with the AO or which work in close cooperation with it, guarantee that foreign Germans beyond the circle of party membership will all be reached through their occupational and social interests, regardless of age and sex, and that the creative ideas of National Socialism which are released through organization will also become effective abroad in all branches of life. It is part of the tactics of the work among foreign Germans that the constituent organizations of the party must fit their activities even more closely into the whole picture than those in Germany. In view of the oftentimes close relations in German colonies abroad, the personal and absolute responsibility of the respective bearer of sovereignty must be very strongly developed. Furthermore, the heavy demands on the material wealth and time of compatriots who participate in the community life of German colonies abroad exclude all special claims which have only a purely organizational basis and every superficial differentiation in the working methods of individual organizations. It is an important task of the sovereign to see that this principle is carefully observed under all circumstances in order that a sound and influential organization may result.

The departments and organizations of the AO which may be listed in this connection are (numbering continued):

(10) The German Labor Front of the AO: This includes all members of the DAF (German Labor Front) abroad and at sea; it conducts the social and occupational work of the AO. In order to insure a unified leadership on board ship the sovereigns on board are likewise commissioned by the DAFAO (Foreign Organization of the Labor Front) and by the Reich Occupational Group for Ocean Shipping in Reich Industrial Community #10 of the DAF.

(11) The Department for Government Employees (Foreign Gau of the Reich Union of German Government Employees, Inc.): This office handles all occupational affairs of employees in the Foreign Service of the Reich, of frontier officials (police, railroad, customs, etc.) who reside abroad, as well as of pilots in the employ of the state.

(12) The Department for Teachers (Foreign Gau of the National Socialist Teachers Union, Inc.): This includes men and women teachers abroad, namely, German nationals on leave from schools in Germany who are serving in German schools abroad, as well as teachers in seamen's and shipping engineers' schools.

(13) The Office of the Foreign Gau of the Instructors Union.

(14) The Office of the Foreign Gau of the Students Union: All students of German nationality abroad and student groups in seamen's and shipping engineers' schools.

(15) The Gau Overseer of the NS Culture Community (without organization).

> With reference to 12–15: The leader of the Foreign Gau of the Instructors Union and the Gau Overseer of the NS Culture Community are at present personally associated with the Director of the Culture Department. The officials of the Department for Teachers and of the Office of the Foreign Gau for Students hold at the same time the respective principal offices of the Culture Department (principal office for school methods and principal office for academic work abroad).

(16) The Gau Office of the Nazi Legal Association.

(17) The Labor Community of the German Woman Abroad: The organization recognized by the Reich's Women's Führer, under direction of a Gauleiter for Women. In case of their return to Germany the members are transferred to the Nazi Women's Organization.

(18) The Youth Department ("Foreign" region of the Hitler Youth): The department head is at the same time leader of the Foreign Department of the Youth Directorate of the German Reich. The bearers of sovereignty of the AO have the right to supervise the youth work in their territories. —The law of January 12, 1936 with respect to the Hitler Youth is limited in its application specifically to the youth within the borders of the Reich.

*
* *

The remaining offices of the Directorate of the AO—to which reference is generally made under the expression "functional offices" (*Sachämter*)—have sometimes a more administrative, sometimes a more functional character. They determine by and large the external image of the AO, provide the means whereby the needs of foreign Germandom are presented to the party and official authorities in the Reich. They also are intended to enable foreign Germandom to profit by the progress and changes made in the Third Reich. It is also their function to make the forces of foreign Germandom available to the Reich. These offices (arranged in alphabetical order and with the numbering continued), together with a very brief summary of their functions so far as they differ basically from internal conditions in Germany, are as listed below:

(19) The Office for Foreign Trade: This office is under the direction of the Gauleiter's deputy, who is at the same time the Commissioner of the AO for Economic Questions, and is subdivided on a regional and functional basis and handles all questions of foreign trade.

(20) The Inspection Department. This department prepares organizational statistics on foreign Germandom, its char-

acteristics and institutions. The preparation of mail and registration also fall within its functions. Furthermore, this department is responsible for transportation, for the control and reporting service in the Directorate of the AO, for the supervision of German seamen and traveling co-nationals in foreign ports, and for the representation of groups from aboard ship at ceremonial functions ashore.

(21) The Department for Culture. This department is divided functionally and cooperates on an organizational basis with the Gau administration of the NSLB (Nazi Teachers Union), the Foreign Gau Office of the Instructors Union and the Foreign Gau Office of the Students Union. The head of the department is also Gau Overseer of the Nazi Culture Community. (See nos. 12–15.) The Department for Culture observes and supervises German cultural institutions abroad. It discovers and places those who are able to engage abroad in cultural work derived from the National Socialist spirit, and will prepare and execute from the cultural angle the use of foreign Germandom to further popular understanding between the German people and other nations. In the last analysis it is the central office for all the numerous organizations and bureaus which are aiming at a spiritual and cultural exchange with Germandom abroad.

(22) The Personnel Department.

(23) The Press Department: The principal functions of this department are the observation and evaluation of the German and foreign press concerning all developments in foreign Germandom and the servicing of the Reich's press and the foreign German press with information and articles.

(24) The Gau Tribunal (standing outside of the framework of this structure both from the point of view of party organization and of functions but included here for reference purposes): It is divided into two chambers. No party tribunal but only the arbitrator (*Schlichter*) is at the disposal of sovereigns abroad. Dismissals from the party can only be made by the Gau Tribunal of the AO. The section offices of the Seamen's Department of the AO include a "seamen's section tribunal" of the first instance in which the section leaders exercise the functions of party sovereigns.

(25) The Legal Department. The directorate and staff of this department cooperate personally with the Gau Tribunal and are divided regionally and functionally. Its principal duties are legal protection, legal administration, and legal policy (cooperation in working out legislation which concerns foreign Germandom and seamen). It is recognized as a training school for court and Government advisers.

(26) The Speakers Department. This department directs the use of speakers in general and in particular for the celebration of national holidays in other European countries, and endeavors also on occasion to furnish overseas groups with speakers. It supervises the organization of festivals in German colonies abroad and is responsible for their Na-

tional Socialist complexion through inspiration and control. This department also handles film and radio work.

(27) The Department for Returning Germans. Through the examination of personal details concerning co-nationals who, as a result of economic pressure or for other reasons, have returned to take up residence in the Reich, and through the issuance of a passport, this department insures the systematic and purposeful insertion of these co-nationals in the domestic economy. At the same time it prevents the re-insertion of doubtful and undesirable returning Germans and the unjustified demands of such persons upon welfare institutions. It works in closest cooperation with the corresponding official offices. The Department for Returning Germans maintains branches in Breslau, Dresden, Düsseldorf, Hamburg, Munich, Schneidemühl, and Stuttgart. An excellent home for returning Germans in Berlin-Tegel serves as a first receiving station for needy co-nationals.

(28) The Finance Department, under the direction of a Gau treasurer.

(29) The Instruction Department. The national school for foreign Germans and seamen (*Reichsschule für Auslandsdeutsche und Seefahrer im Donnerschloss in Altona*) is at the disposal of this department.

(30) The Department for People's Welfare: This department is also the managing office for winter relief work for Germans abroad (no branch of the NSV exists abroad). Existing local relief societies and the women's organization are included in the scope of the activities of the NSV.

(31) The Technical Department. This department works in closest cooperation with the Office for Foreign Trade and, like the latter, is subject to the Office of the Commissioner of the AO for Economic Questions.

(32) The Hamburg office of the AO.

*
* *

In addition to the foregoing departments the staff of the Central Office of the AO includes a number of department heads and principal-office directors who provide a close personal and functional relation with the Government and party offices whose work may in part be of benefit to foreign Germandom.

It is hardly necessary to point out in addition that—with very few exceptions—all department heads and principal-office directors of the Central Office of the AO are Germans who formerly resided abroad; in fact most of them have risen in recent years as political leaders abroad through their industry and established reliability. This fact is a guaranty that the tasks of the AO will never be directed from a purely theoretical standpoint. It is, however, also, together with the untiring zeal of the party members abroad, really the principal cause of the rapid development of the AO and the considerable success which may already be accredited to it.

CHAPTER III

FOREIGN GERMANDOM AND THE FATHERLAND

Foreign Germandom has grasped the meaning of the National Socialist movement, represented abroad by the AO, surprisingly fast. After overcoming the initial difficulties it has attacked the prescribed tasks with typical thoroughness and with idealistic enthusiasm. From the standard bearers of the National Socialist idea in foreign Germandom have developed, in the years following the party's accession to power in Germany, the creators of new forms and of a National Socialist comradeship of action. Out of the formless mass of foreign Germandom has grown—after the example of the fatherland even though the external details were often different—a disciplined community prepared and ready for work and sacrifice. Foreign Germandom has now rediscovered the fatherland in the truest meaning of the word, has discovered the great widespread German folk-community of which it feels itself to be the most advanced post—with all the hardship and advantages which this lot entails. Wherever it has been possible, since the accession to power, to accomplish work for the benefit of the folk-community or to affirm the community spirit, foreign Germandom has, in ever increasing measure, succeeded in keeping pace with the fatherland. Thereby it has not only given evidence of its own reaction to the Reich of Adolf Hitler but has also demonstrated before the entire world that National Socialism bases its supremacy not only upon control of the power of state but also on the conviction of all German citizens. There is no better witness nor more convincing evidence of the correctness of our idea.

The effect of the new German people's community abroad on the individual can hardly be comprehended in its reality as an essential psychic phenomenon and is only occasionally apparent to the distant eye through revealing occurrences: when here and there, without material assistance from the fatherland, new German houses, homes, and schools arise; when employer and employees in the large overseas business houses create playing fields and recreation resorts through voluntary labor; when we see the lonesome solitary settlers riding by the hour through the jungle to attend a party group meeting; when even difficult and expensive journeys of several days do not prevent participation in an election for the Führer; when we are informed of comradely evenings in the great ports of the world at which our seamen meet in comradely communion with foreign Germans; when one experiences the typical national celebrations abroad.

The German colonies abroad which in recent years have placed themselves under National Socialist leadership almost without exception are now closed communities which are still striving everywhere to achieve their final form. Their structure is characterized by the will of self-maintenance. The community assists the weak and demands sacrifices from the strong. It endows and advances the worthy and rejects the quarrelsome and the parasites. Wherever assistance, advice, and advancement fail or are insufficient, where vital matters are at stake, where the prestige of the Reich is endangered, and its reputation must be saved, the leadership of the AO takes hold by stimulating and pointing out proper courses and thus places the fatherland with its whole power behind foreign Germandom.

Winter relief work, one-course meals on Sundays, sales, women's social work, and community welfare are also important activities abroad. In the winter of 1934–35 the winter relief work of the Foreign Organization contributed RM. 1,100,000 in addition to individual contributions; in the winter of 1935–36, RM. 1,800,000; and the figures for the present year which are available to date indicate a further increase in the contributions by more than one third. It should be noted that the actual contributions, measured by the rate of exchange and the purchase power of the funds abroad, is considerably higher. The Managing Office of the AO supervises the distribution of funds, allots a portion to the winter relief work in the Reich, and insures that German "emergency territories" abroad receive particular consideration. The contributor in China, for example, assists his unemployed German compatriot in eastern Upper Silesia or in Luxembourg to obtain a warm room in order that he may hold out longer and not give up a German advance position through premature return to the Reich. Eight hundred and eighty German mothers abroad were able to come to the fatherland in 1936 for one month's vacation, and more than 350 persons from all parts of the world were helped during the same period to return to Germany for medical treatment, including free return transportation. Ten thousand German children abroad passed their vacations in the Reich, and at the present time there are 170 children from needy families in National Socialist youth homes for schooling and subsequent assignments as apprentices.

The social situation of foreign Germandom at work will generally be freed from its former isolation through measures which are already in preparation and will be placed on a footing with conditions in the fatherland. In the field of free legal advice the social position of the German seamen has from the beginning received the particular attention of the AO. Through a wage agreement, which was adopted as a result of its influential collaboration, the greatest hardships were first eliminated. In 1936 the first bonuses for children and Christmas gifts outside of the wage agreement were introduced, and the beneficial results of the "Foundation for Sacrifice in Maritime Labor", which was founded in December 1935 on the initiative of the AO, for which over

RM. 200,000 have been collected—of which RM. 80,000 have already been distributed—became apparent. The establishment of settlements of privately owned homes for the families of seamen and the vacation work of the student union in the seamen's and shipping engineers' schools constitute further evidence of a new social policy for seamen.

The best proof to date of the social ties between the fatherland and foreign Germandom is given by the great relief work for the 8500 compatriots who were obliged to flee from the terror of the Spanish Civil War. A single appeal on July 29, 1936 from the Gauleiter of the Foreign Organization in his capacity as chairman of a quickly founded "Assistance Committee for Germans in Spain" produced RM. 2,400,000 in currency up to the end of that year. The regular assistance and advice which was given to the exiles through the branches of the party in Germany and through the authorities, particularly in the areas where they were received, cannot be estimated in figures. That German Socialism was capable of military protection in contrast to the Marxism of the November Republic became clear when naval vessels were sent to Spanish waters for the protection of the Germans who were being evacuated. In this manner, for the first time in years, an example was again given to foreign Germandom that the community without and within was not merely a wishful image or theory but an incontrovertible fact that is supported by the regular visits of German naval vessels in foreign waters, which contribute especially toward arousing a feeling of national patriotism and thereby strengthen the community spirit of Germandom.

Nothing binds a community more than a common experience. The center of the community life of foreign Germans abroad is the national celebration. The AO insures that the 30th of January and 1st of May, the Thanksgiving festival, the Führer's birthday, and the 9th of November are not observed in the old style of patriotic celebrations. In the course of years it has made up a list of approximately 100 speakers, which is composed, in addition to a number of Reich speakers and men from the Central Office of the AO, of leading personalities of the movement and its branches, of the state, of the labor service, from cultural life, and from industry. In close cooperation with the Foreign Office these speakers are sent at only slight cost to the national celebrations of German colonies abroad, and even the smallest groups are not forgotten. From their intimate knowledge of developments they give to their compatriots an accurate picture of the foundations of the Third Reich and through the weight of their personalities exert a truly revealing and attractive effect. On May 1, 1936, for example, 58 speakers from the fatherland addressed 177 meetings of foreign Germans in various countries of Europe. Except for occasional opportunities Germandom overseas is still dependent on its own resources, which does not mean, however, that its national celebrations are less worthy or powerful; on the contrary, the largest assemblies which have been held to date were organized in the great German areas of South America. On May 1, 1936, for example, in São Paulo, Brazil, 25,000 Germans marched in the open; and in Rio de Janeiro a splendid picture was presented on the same day, as the proudest work of German technology, the Zeppelin, cruised over the heads of Germans gathered in a national memorial celebration. In the future an increased supply of speakers from the AO in the Reich will carry the message of the life and works of Germans abroad to the widest circles of our folk.

Wherever actual personal contact is not possible to forge the bands between fatherland and foreign Germandom, other means of revelation and communication are adopted. About 40 party and colonial papers of all kinds (from the typewritten "circular letter" of the regional section of Angola to the *West Coast Observer* published at Santiago, Chile, or the *East Asiatic Observer* of Shanghai, which long ago outgrew the frame of colonial periodicals) help to accomplish this task. Through regular rapid delivery by the special "Nazi Service for German Papers Abroad" of pictures and miscellaneous press material, the editors of these papers are kept informed concerning the latest developments in the Reich. The Central Office of the AO for its part keeps the home press informed through a comprehensive service of articles and pictures and through the distribution of brief notices concerning foreign Germandom. A series of instructive articles, which appeared in *Arbeitsmann* during the last half of 1936 concerning the AO and perhaps 25 of its branches abroad, received much attention. Up to the present time the obvious plan for an important AO newspaper of our own could not be realized. Its realization will grow out of our further work. In the meantime the AO of the German Labor Front continues to publish the monthly *The German Abroad (Der Deutsche im Auslande)*. The richly illustrated monthly *Seafaring Is Necessary (Seefahrt ist not)* is published under the supervision of the Seamen's Department of the AO, and the occupational journal *The German Seaman (Der Deutsche Seemann)* is published by the Reich Occupational Group for Ocean Shipping in Reich Industrial Community #10. The Alliance of German Societies Abroad (Verband Deutscher Vereine im Ausland) distributes once a month the "home letter" (*Heimatbrief*) and in 1935 and 1936 published an excellent yearbook *We Germans in the World (Wir Deutsche in der Welt)*.[4]

---

[4] The Alliance of German Societies Abroad (Verband Deutscher Vereine im Ausland, Inc.), with headquarters in Berlin, has the task, in which it has now succeeded almost without exception, of uniting all German societies, alliances, and

The AO makes wide use of radio and films, the most modern means of publicity, in order to advance the understanding and the patriotic feeling of foreign Germans. The stacks of letters from foreign Germans which are received daily give eloquent testimony to the popularity of the German short-wave stations which permit them to participate in the great events in the Reich and offer evidence of the creative activity of the National Socialist German. The Foreign Organization has often made use of these facilities in order to transmit good wishes and speeches from the fatherland to Germandom overseas on special occasions. The Christmas greetings of the Führer's Deputy have already become a tradition. The problem of a short-wave receiving set of German origin which meets all requirements still awaits solution. As a supplement and partially as a substitute for the radio, the AO records, the quantity of which has been tripled since 1935–36, serve the groups abroad. The record library has become indispensable for the instruction of the party and for ceremonial functions, particularly in remote groups overseas. They serve likewise in many countries in the organization of "German Hours" through the local transmitting station and assist in making the population of the foreign country familiar with the achievements of German culture. The sound film is probably the most highly regarded and sought-after means of publicity which can be supplied to foreign Germandom. In it the fatherland really comes to life. In addition to the most important national film productions, the AO sends regular instalments of its own "Echo of the Fatherland", a newsreel prepared for its own purposes and consisting of a collection of cuts from weekly newsreels which cover a longer period. In order that these films may be shown independently of the local motion-picture houses in closed German circles, most groups of the AO have their own sound-film projectors. Wherever lack of space or the absence of such projectors does not permit the presentation of regular sound films, silent films are substituted. As early as 1936 the untiring film work of the AO received cordial recognition abroad: The national group for Argentina produced the talking film "Winter Solstice"—a record of the celebration of the solstice by the Germans in Argentina—which was made available to all other national groups and to the Gau film office in the Reich and in the future is certain to be frequently imitated.

Without justifying the accusation of "propaganda" in the foreign country, the creative German abroad is naturally also a link between the fatherland and the foreign country, particularly from a cultural

colonial associations under one head in the Reich, of avoiding through advice and counsel the unhealthy formation of too many societies (*Vereinsmeierei*) in foreign Germandom and of giving to such societies, so far as they are justified and necessary through the awakening of the available worthwhile forces, a National Socialist direction in form and content.

and economic point of view. Since his blameless activity in this direction determines in part the reputation of the Reich, his work in both
these fields leads to an improvement in international relations, in the
service of which the Foreign Organization deliberately participates.
For example, it participated in the organization of short tours of
Germany by groups of Latin American students. The arrangements
for the book week made by it in recent years in conjunction with the
Foreign Office with the cooperation of well-known poets—which in
1935, furthermore, led to the large donations of the SS for books for
AO groups—have produced exceptional success for the advancement
of German culture abroad and have even attracted the heads of foreign states. It must further be emphasized that almost all German
schools abroad and likewise their teaching staffs are important factors for the advancement of German culture. In the economic field
German chambers of commerce abroad are of particular service to international relations. The reorganization of the network of German
chambers of commerce (20 chambers), after the party's accession to
power in Germany, and its completion through the establishment of
new branches in London, Amsterdam, Stockholm, Copenhagen, and
Lima can be traced to the initiative of the AO.

The German people has never been so alert to the needs of foreign
Germandom as at the present time. A foreign German has never been
so greatly honored as the great Wilhelm Gustloff, for the return of
whose remains from Davos the whole united German people formed
a lane from Singen to Schwerin, where the Führer himself paid the
last tribute at his grave. Nor has the foreign German participated so
joyfully nor been so filled with homesickness as since 1933. Now
this homesickness of millions of foreign Germans has also found a
symbolic outlet in the Reich: On August 27, 1936 the Führer designated Stuttgart as the "City of Foreign Germans" and the Gauleiter
of the Foreign Organization of the NSDAP assumed the protection
of this beautiful city, which also houses within its walls the German
Foreign Institute (Deutsches Ausland-Institut), which works in
hearty cooperation with the AO, and the "Memorial to German
Achievement Abroad". Here in the future the great national assemblies of foreign Germans will take place in the late summer. The
national assemblies already held, which have been arranged by the
AO and which have already found their place in the history of foreign
Germandom (Nuremberg 1933–34, Erlangen 1935–36), the assemblies
of foreign teachers in 1934–36 in Potsdam, Braunschweig, and Stuttgart, the Day of the German Seamen in Hamburg in 1935, were only
an overture to the forthcoming great gatherings of foreign Germandom in Stuttgart. Thousands of foreign Germans and seamen will
absorb here the point of view of the new leadership and position of

the Reich and will be able to orient themselves from the words of the
responsible men of the movement. They will feel the concentrated
strength of the new Germany and will always leave with new strength
as men to whom National Socialism is something just as natural as
their Germanism. They will embody and continually build up the
new type of foreign German who is recognized and respected everywhere as a worthy representative of the new Germany. They will
go abroad with the will to forge communities which can stand on their
own feet and still belong to a great whole; and the Gauleiter of the
Foreign Organization and his co-workers will stand as one with them
in the service to a National Socialist folk-community which is based
on the word and the acts of the Führer, but for which boundaries and
separating oceans no longer exist.

CONCLUSION

On the fourth anniversary of the accession to power the Führer and Chancelor of the Reich issued a decree providing that a chief of the Foreign Organization be placed in the Foreign Office. This decree leaves the position and methods of the Foreign Organization of the NSDAP fundamentally unchanged but gives it a state character in the person of the Gauleiter. Through the grant to the Gauleiter of full state authority, the law concerning the unity of party and state receives a logical application to German nationals abroad. The decree, the provisions of which are given below, constitutes evidence that the German Reich is actually a people's state comprising all Germans, which accepts its responsibility for the all-inclusive protection of all citizens but which in the same measure demands cooperation from all in achieving the goals which have been placed before the German people:

I. For the unified care and control (*Betreuung*) of the German citizens in foreign countries, a chief of the Foreign Organization is appointed to the Foreign Office, who will be charged with the direction and handling of all matters concerning German nationals abroad.

II. (1) Gauleiter Ernst Wilhelm Bohle, the leader of the Foreign Organization of the NSDAP, is named Chief of the Foreign Organization in the Foreign Office.

(2) He is responsible personally and directly to the Reich's Minister for Foreign Affairs. His jurisdiction as leader of the Foreign Organization of the NSDAP and his responsibility as such under the Führer's Deputy remain unchanged.

(3) His official title is: Chief of the Foreign Organization in the Foreign Office.

III. The Chief of the Foreign Organization in the Foreign Office participates in all meetings of the Reich Cabinet in which matters under his jurisdiction are under discussion.

IV. The Reich's Minister for Foreign Affairs, in agreement with the Führer's Deputy, will issue the pertinent regulations to place this decree in effect.

BERLIN, *January 30, 1937*

The Führer and Chancelor of the Reich
    ADOLF HITLER

                The Minister of Foreign Affairs
                    Baron VON NEURATH

DOCUMENT 24

(Translation)

ALMANACH DER NATIONALSOZIALISTISCHEN REVOLUTION, BERLIN, 1934,
PAGES 90ff.

THE FOREIGN ORGANIZATION OF THE NSDAP

BY ERNST WILHELM BOHLE

LEADER OF THE FOREIGN SECTION OF THE NSDAP

It was no accident that the idea of recruiting Germans abroad for
the idea of National Socialism was first conceived in Hamburg. The
old Hanseatic city has maintained for centuries a multiplicity of relations with all parts of the world, and in particular with the large
German colonies overseas. As in hardly any other city of Germany
one repeatedly finds in Hamburg threads which lead to the most remote corners of the earth.

It was not surprising, therefore, that after the unparalleled success
at the polls on September 14, 1930 the National Socialists in Hamburg
began discussion of the plan to recruit German nationals abroad for
the National Socialist idea. At the beginning of 1931 several foreign German party members residing in Hamburg approached Party
Member Dr. Hans Rieland,[1] a member of the Reichstag, with a proposal to this effect, which shortly thereafter was presented to the
Reich's Organization Directorate at Munich, with the result that on
May 1, 1931 the Foreign Section of the NSDAP was established, with
headquarters at Hamburg, under the direction of Party Member
Dr. Rieland.[1]

There were only a few party members who at the outset took upon
themselves.the difficult task of building up the movement outside of
the boundaries of the Reich. As in all branches of the party, there
was a lack of the necessary means for an immediate planned development of the organization. At first, therefore, the recruiting could only
be carried on through the activities of cooperative party members—
all of whom served without remuneration—who conscientiously gathered together lists of foreign addresses and sent personal letters
abroad. All obtainable propaganda material was begged and bor-
rowed and the necessary measures were discussed at meetings which
at first were held once or twice a week. In the course of the following

---

[1] ["Rieland" is believed to be a typographical error. The correct name is Hans
Nieland—EDITOR.]

months the number of collaborators was steadily increased, so that toward the end of the year an imposing apparatus with its own small offices had already been established and further development was now assured.

The aim of the Foreign Section was the winning over of persons of German origin abroad according to plan, and the establishment of party groups wherever the number of party members justified the formation of an organization. Before the establishment of the Foreign Section, small groups had already arisen in various countries which corresponded directly with the Reich's Directorate and which could be regarded primarily as the basis for the present widely spread organization abroad. The fact that the Foreign Section could expect no financial support except from the contributions of party members abroad was responsible for the very modest limits within which the proselyting was carried on during the first year. This unfortunate condition was remedied proportionately as the number of party members grew, so that during the course of 1932 a substantially stronger propaganda could be carried on. In considering the development of our Foreign Organization, one should not forget that our racial comrades beyond the borders of the Reich were only rarely acquainted with the National Socialist newspapers. The German abroad either subscribed to well-known economic journals or to those of pronounced liberal tendencies. For the rest he was dependent on the newspapers of his own country, which either failed to report on National Socialism at all or rejected it hostilely.

A further difficulty was the fact that the official representatives of the Reich were in almost all instances hostile to what was then the strongest party in opposition.

These factors prove how very difficult it was to transmit the ideas of National Socialism to the Germans abroad. Our party members abroad did not hesitate to risk either danger to their economic existence or personal sacrifice if necessary to propagate the idea of their Führer, not only in opposition to the hostility of foreign public opinion, which was usually influenced by the Jews, but also in the struggle against their own countrymen who regarded them with hate and scorn. For those who, from their own experience, do not know postwar conditions abroad it is difficult to envisage the desperate situation in which those of our party comrades found themselves who day by day courageously stood up for our cause amid a world of foes. The foreign Germans lacked almost everything which here in the Reich was able to strengthen the backs of the party comrades in their difficult struggle. They never heard the Führer himself speak. They could never attend a mass meeting with all its incomparable enthusiasm. They could never take courage from the sight of the Brown Shirts. On the contrary, every day they had to listen in powerless rage to the most disreputable insults to the Führer and the movement, and every day to see in German and foreign newspapers the lowest reports and the foulest caricatures of our leaders.

In spite of all this, the organization grew from day to day, so that in the fall of 1932 more than 150 city and local groups were already organized. The foreign German had proved that, in the struggle for the attainment of a goal which was recognized once for all as right, he was able to accomplish things just like his brothers and sisters in the homeland.

That the Foreign Section today supervises over 230 national, city, and local groups which are scattered over the entire globe, is thanks to the willingness to sacrifice of its party members abroad. In full consideration of this, the Foreign Section has fixed as its primary task the creation of an apparatus which can give every conceivable support to our racial comrades far from the homeland in their hard struggle. As far as possible the divisions for the various countries, of which the Foreign Organization naturally has a considerable number, are staffed by party members who know the respective country from their own experience and, consequently, have the necessary understanding of the wishes and needs of our groups.

A constantly expanding propaganda service provides daily material concerning our movement and the new Germany to all parts of the world.

The press office follows with particular attention press reports received daily from all over the world and takes the necessary action. Furthermore, care is taken that the press office places suitable articles at the disposal of the groups' own newspapers, of which there are already a considerable number.

A reference service for questions concerning the labor service, in which there is tremendous interest among foreign Germans, is already extremely busy. The same is true of the youth reference service which serves as a liaison office with the Foreign Section of the Youth Leadership of the German Reich. Furthermore, liaison with the Reich's Women's Leadership is now being worked out in order that the numerous inquiries received from our foreign German women may be competently answered.

A division for school and church questions, which is headed by an expert, advises our party members in these questions, which are particularly important toward the maintenance of our nationality abroad, and endeavors to effect changes when necessary.

A legal office headed by a jurist is available to foreign party members for advice in legal matters.

A harbor service which has been built up to the minutest detail takes care of party members on all vessels leaving and entering the port of Hamburg. The harbor service devotes itself particularly to the usually completely penniless arriving repatriates and endeavors within the limits of its means, which are still unfortunately limited, to be of assistance to these racial comrades, who are deserving of sympathy on their return to their homeland. The harbor service especially maintains liaison with the subsection for seamen in which almost 10,000 seagoing party members are organized. The harbor service is of particular importance from the mere fact that it maintains intimate relations with the commanding officers and crews of the ships and arranges for party members abroad to have an opportunity as far as possible to pass homelike hours on German ships. It also undertakes liaison with the leader of the Reich's Schooling Office of the NSDAP and with the German Labor Front, with the result that several foreign party members have already been given an opportunity to attend the instruction courses at Bernau.

The remaining purely organizational branches of the Foreign Section also have very complicated tasks resulting from the variety of conditions in the different countries, so that specialized knowledge is also required here.

Every party member residing abroad receives a foreign certificate, on the back of which the following lines of conduct are set forth:

What you must observe abroad as a National Socialist:

(1) Observe the laws of the country whose guest you are.
(2) Leave the politics of the country where you reside to its inhabitants. You are not concerned with the internal politics of a foreign country. Take no part in them, even in conversation.
(3) Acknowledge yourself as a party member at all times and in all places.
(4) Always speak and act in such a way that you bring honor to the National Socialist movement and thereby to the new Germany. Be upright, honorable, fearless, and loyal.
(5) Recognize every German abroad as your compatriot, a man of your blood and your kind. Extend your hand to him regardless of his position. We are all "creators" of our people.
(6) Help your German compatriots gladly and voluntarily when they are innocently in difficulty.
(7) Do not be merely a member but also a fighter in the foremost line. Inform yourself thoroughly of the methods, content, and aims of our movement.
(8) Work and fight day after day for the entry of every honorable German into our movement. Convince him of the superiority and justness of our movement, of the necessity of our victory in order that Germany may live on! Fight with spiritual weapons!
(9) Read our party publication, our pamphlets, and books.

> (10) Associate yourself with party members in your place of
> residence.   If a local or city group exists there, be a dis-
> ciplined and active worker.   Not only should you not sup-
> port dissension but you should also make every effort to
> settle disputes which arise.

The assumption of power by our Führer on January 30 of this year
caused indescribable jubilation among our party members abroad,
which found eloquent expression in countless dispatches and letters of
rejoicing.   It was probably thought abroad too that the period of hate,
of scorn, and of hostility was past.   But it turned out otherwise.   The
measures adopted by the national Government for the raising of our
people led immediately in all foreign countries to an ugly and unrestricted agitation against everything Nazi.   Our party members
were boycotted, in many countries actually attacked in the lowest manner, and often expelled from the country and deprived of their existence.   It is a beautiful sign of the loyalty of our party members abroad
that in no single case did they complain on their own account.   Today
our fighters abroad are standing at posts which are often desperate.
They know, however, that just as at home, so also abroad, only National Socialism can prepare the way for a solid Germandom.   Only
National Socialists who are ideologically well grounded can unite the
German colonies, which outside of the homeland are often still divided,
and create a unity in which alone the guaranty for support of the homeland by foreign Germandom can be given.   The point of view of Germans abroad contributes substantially to the formation of public opinion in foreign countries themselves.   A failure in National Socialist
influence on foreign Germandom would lead, without any doubt, to
an increasing misunderstanding by Germans of the measures taken by
the new Germany.

Therefore, we need party members abroad who have mastered our
ideology and who are able to communicate it to other Germans.
We know that Germans abroad are still in part cool to the movement
because they do not know what they want.   The education of racial
comrades who still stand apart has, therefore, been made a special task
of the group leaders abroad, and it is pointed out to them that there are
still many Germans abroad who are not friendly toward us because
they have not understood the will of our Führer, although otherwise
they are often valuable German comrades.

From this, one will be able to understand that the Foreign Organization, notwithstanding the expansion achieved to date, still faces
tremendous tasks, which places a particularly heavy responsibility on
the National Socialist group leader.   He must know that the National Socialist abroad is today regarded in foreign countries as an
exponent of the state power in Germany and must, therefore, repeatedly and emphatically impress on his party members that they must
conduct themselves irreproachably in all matters.

Our party members abroad without exception act in honorary capacities and perform their work in the few free hours at their disposal. Anyone who reads the files of the Foreign Section will be shaken by the boundless love for Führer and country which springs from the lines.

The victory of the National Socialist idea among the Germans abroad, which must, and will, come, means a strengthening of the homeland in the struggle against the current campaign of slander which should not be underestimated. In many countries the skill and vision of our group leaders have already succeeded in persuading German societies and bunds of the most valuable character, which were still standing apart, of the necessity for a positive position toward the National Socialist state. The word *"Gleichschaltung"* (conformity) cannot, because of the absence of the instruments of force of the state, find the same application abroad as in Germany. It is only thanks to the conscientious work of enlightenment carried on by our party members abroad, often under great personal sacrifices, that in many places the solidarity of Germandom in our sense of the word has already been established.

The homeland, however, must stand by them, for they do pioneer work for their fatherland.

At this time we also do not wish to fail to mention that in many countries our party members have been shown the greatest understanding by foreigners and foreign government offices, whereas, in certain countries where the Jewish might dominates, our party members are still faced today with a boundless hate.

To those racial comrades who are still not actively cooperating in a National Socialist foreign Germandom, the call therefore goes out to support our fighters with all their experience and connections in order that in the future those shall no longer be constantly persecuted and slandered who for years, in spite of need and hatred, have already assured that among Germans abroad, even in the remotest corner of the world, the cry shall always ring out: Heil Hitler!

DOCUMENT 25

(Translation)

DER PARTEITAG DER EHRE (THE PARTY CONGRESS OF HONOR) (OFFICIAL REPORT OF THE PROCEEDINGS OF THE REICH'S PARTY CONGRESS, WITH ALL SPEECHES), SEPTEMBER 8–14, 1936: MUNICH, CENTRAL PUBLISHING HOUSE OF THE NSDAP, FRANZ EHER, 1936, PAGES 124–131

The ceremonial hour of the Foreign Organization on Friday morning in the festively decorated hall of the Hercules Building. On this occasion the Führer's Deputy honored forty-eight flags of local groups of the Foreign Organization.

RUDOLF HESS:
"THE PROTECTION OF THE FATHERLAND IS STRONGER THAN EVER."

The ceremonial hour of the Foreign Organization took place on Friday morning in the ceremonially decorated hall of the Hercules Building in the presence of many guests of honor.

In his opening address Gauleiter Bohle first paid tribute to the heavy sacrifices of property and blood which National Socialist Germans abroad had made for the Reich in the year since the previous party congress (The Reich's Party Congress of Freedom) and emphasized that the many sacrifices obligate all of us to recognize the necessity of this struggle which German National Socialists have been carrying on abroad for many years on behalf of the Reich. This obligation is, in a very particular measure, that of the Foreign Organization of the National Socialist movement, since it is the organization in the Reich which takes hold of German citizens outside of its borders and has been able by long years of hard labor to incorporate them in the great people's community of Adolf Hitler. When sacrifice of life is made in the struggle for the realization of an idea, the question necessarily arises whether this struggle is necessary and whether the right course is being followed. As the responsible Gauleiter of the German National Socialists abroad, Bohle stated he would make an effort to explain the meaning of the struggle for the Third Reich and Adolf Hitler and at the same time answer the question concerning the absolute necessity for the work of the Foreign Organization. Gauleiter Bohle continued in part as follows:

We German National Socialists abroad start in our work from the basic premise that there is no "question" of foreign Germanism, but that our Germanism abroad is composed of individual Germans who can only live as Germans if they form among themselves an *indestructible community* and if this community is incorporated in the community which Adolf Hitler has given the racial comrades in the Reich. *We believe in the eternal value of the race and the blood* and

314

we feel ourselves the appointed *protectors of these values in foreign Germanism*. A state which is built on the iron laws of blood and race, like the National Socialist Reich, cannot do other than accept its own blood always and everywhere even in the remotest corner of the earth. The Foreign Organization is, therefore, the gathering place for every single racial comrade of the Reich, who—otherwise dependent on himself alone—would be lost to the Reich. The Foreign Organization wishes to preserve for the Reich every German wherever he may be in the world, be he rich or poor, young or old, in the knowledge that no sin is greater than that of *voluntarily* abandoning German blood.

Gauleiter Bohle referred to the situation of Germanism abroad before the Nazi seizure of power, which manifested the same disunity as had the Germans in the Reich itself and which, because of the collapse of the old fatherland, was little respected abroad; and he emphasized that, only a few years before the seizure of power, an immense change began through the formation of local groups of the NSDAP, which at that time was still unknown or unmentioned abroad. Everywhere abroad there were a few enthusiastic men and women who believed in Adolf Hitler regardless of all slander and who began the struggle to win their German compatriots for the ideology of the new movement.

Today, barely four years after the seizure of power, we can proudly and joyfully declare that our party comrades abroad have conquered foreign Germanism—conquered it for the National Socialist idea—conquered it without any external pressure—conquered it *through the strength of persuasion—conquered it through the deeds of the Führer in the Reich!* The Führer had to come in order to hammer into all of us the fact that the German cannot choose and may not choose whether or not he will be German but that he was sent into this world by God as a German and that God thereby had laid upon him as a German duties of which he cannot divest himself without committing treason to Providence. *Therefore, we believe and we know that the German everywhere is a German*—whether he lives in the Reich or in Japan, in France or in China, or anywhere else in the world. *Not countries or continents, not climate or environment but blood and race determine the world of ideas of the German.*

The wonderful thing about our new Reich is that this Reich will not voluntarily release a single one of its citizens from his holy duties to his people.

Therefore, it depends on each German citizen to think German, to act German, and to remain German; wherever he may be, he will know that Germany stands beside him and that his new Germany is determined to protect every single one of its citizens outside of its boundaries. When the Bolshevik terror broke out in Spain and threatened the lives and property of German citizens, German warships appeared in Spanish waters. The Führer looked out for his German racial comrades abroad. *Unconditional loyalty to the nation must also be axiomatic for the very last citizen of our new state outside in the world.* This loyalty is nothing but the *loyalty to his own life* and thereby loyalty to the *Almighty.* To make every racial comrade of the Reich outside of its borders understand this concept as the *penetrating voice of the blood* is the deepest sense of our work in the Foreign Organization. *Our task is, therefore, a purely German one. The Foreign Organization can never forsake this path. It will never concern itself with people or matters which are not those of the Reich.*

If certain circles abroad believe that they must denounce and oppose our work abroad before the world, we know that thereby they only manifest the anger and the disillusionment of those who hope in their dreams to be able to keep the Germans abroad away from National Socialism. They have failed to recognize the *strength and the will of the National Socialist Reich to embrace* all its racial comrades just as they have misunderstood the healthy urge of Germanism abroad to return to the Reich in order to remain with this new Reich for all time.

The world will have to accustom itself to the fact that Germany has again taken its place among the great nations and peoples of this earth. Whoever today insults or attacks a racial comrade of German nationality must know that he also insults the Reich. That is the proudest and finest feeling that National Socialism can give to citizens of the Reich abroad. If the Foreign Organization strives by intensive labor to make our fellow citizens abroad acquainted in ever greater measure with the ideology of the new Germany, it is only being the tool of the will of Adolf Hitler: for—*whoever acknowledges himself to belong to the Reich and enjoys the protection of this new Reich must be a follower of our Führer.*

It is not necessary for the new Reich to permit its racial comrades abroad inactively to fall prey to foreign and un-German ideas so that they may then become estranged from the Reich itself. *That* German abroad will always be the best guest of the foreign country who himself is firmly rooted in the land of his fathers and who observes foreign laws and viewpoints with National Socialist discipline, as we demand from all countries of the world that they should respect the National Socialist persuasion of our citizens. The Führer has given foreign Germans this one thing in rich measure—*the certainty that their new Reich can demand respect everywhere.*

Full of pride in the Führer and in their Germanism, our racial comrades abroad under the leadership of the party comrades of the Foreign Organization will pursue this way. We have the holy conviction that a task must be right and good to which Wilhelm Gustloff dedicated himself for many years and for which he gave his life.

Our murdered Germans in Spain are likewise witnesses to the unbending will of our foreign Germans, *who will not let themselves be turned aside from their fanatical allegiance to the new Reich by any terror or any Bolshevik threats of murder.* The almost five thousand party comrades, men and women, who in the past days have come back to the fatherland from all over the world in order to give expression to their love and their allegiance to the Führer and to their people, and who fear no sacrifice in order to be able to take part in this greatest assembly of National Socialist foreign Germanism to date, are proof to the Reich *that its citizens abroad are determined to follow the Reich always and forever.*

In Schwerin, where Wilhelm Gustloff rests, ancient German oaks whisper their eternal song over his grave. *It is the song of German loyalty, the song that every German in the Reich and abroad knows today, a song that will never more cease, for Adolf Hitler has given it eternal strength. It is the pledge of German National Socialists abroad in this hour of dedication that they will always remain true to their Führer and to their Reich.*

At the close of Gauleiter Bohle's speech the Führer's Deputy rose to transmit to the foreign Germans on behalf of the Führer the thanks of the fatherland and of the man who today symbolizes it:

THE SPEECH OF CONSECRATION OF THE FÜHRER'S DEPUTY

For the first time since the establishment of the Foreign Organization, for the first time, in fact, since the establishment of the NSDAP, we must *remember in the ceremonial hour of the foreign Germans the dead who fell far from the fatherland.* We must remember the dead who gave up their lives because they were National Socialists or supporters of the new Germany. For this reason, and for this reason alone, they had to sacrifice their lives.

The struggle which was once carried on against us inside of our borders and which, thanks to the Führer, we concluded victoriously, has now been carried abroad by our enemies.

These enemies know that they can take revenge on our racial comrades abroad without fear of the certain death which would await them as punishment at home—they can take revenge because they are no longer able to give vent to their political passions here. We dip the flags and remember in sorrow those who have fought for us outside of German borders.

I should like particularly to pay tribute for all the others to one man whom many of us knew not only by name but also in person: *Wilhelm Gustloff.* Those who knew him know that he was a man of very special qualities: an *idealist* like few others, who died in the service of the territory for which he had been made responsible. He died in the service of the Führer. Those who knew him know how he was loved by those who worked under him, by those who came under his care. They know that he enjoyed the highest respect of foreigners who knew him personally. He was above reproach and not subject to attack by his enemies.

But because he was beyond attack in his activity and his attitude, because as a man he was the best advocate of National Socialism and the new Germany, he fell in a *ritual murder* committed by the hands of a Jew. *He was the victim of the bullet of a hate which becomes all the stronger in the world as the German people has become more reasonable.*

The bullets of the same hate struck the Germans in Spain, for they had committed no other crime than to be Germans, Germans of the National Socialist Reich of Adolf Hitler, which was sufficient to have them murdered by the executionary organs of Bolshevistic Jewry.

In memory of those who have fought we want to promise—we Germans at home—even more than before to remember the lot of our racial comrades abroad and to do everything in our power to make things easier for them. And we want to make them feel constantly that we consider ourselves bound with them in a community of fate.

We want to tell them that we know how hard they have to struggle in order to establish themselves and to hold out abroad, that we know how great are the sacrifices which the fatherland demands from them, that many of them have to lead a life of hard work without receiving the just reward therefor.

We know that many Germans who follow their professions abroad, German merchants, etc., just manage to hold out, no matter how hard it may be not to surrender. They remain at their posts only because they are certain that they abroad—yes, particularly there abroad— work *for the German community*, for the fatherland, that they contribute to the maintenance of shrunken German foreign trade, to the sale of German goods and the production of materials which the fatherland needs, as much as possible.

The Germans abroad wish to be convinced that the fatherland knows how hard it is to acknowledge themselves supporters of this National Socialist Germany in a world which for the most part still has no understanding for National Socialists, that this hate, enmity, slander, and persecution mean—yes, can mean ruin and death! *And, notwithstanding, those abroad joyfully acknowledge themselves to be supporters of the new Germany and of the Führer*, our German national racial comrades, although few of them know this Führer by sight, yes, although most of them do not even know the feeling of the new fatherland.

Of course, the results of the new spirit in the fatherland have reached even them. With astonishment, and in the end also with wonder, the foreign countries have seen that the foreign Germans have bound themselves together more closely than ever, that they create German people's communities everywhere abroad in which they reach an understanding in spite of all former disruptive differences of wealth, education, and position!

That they still feel themselves to be only Germans and support each other when they are in difficulties like the Germans in the fatherland who have become a model for them. If love has not grown in the hearts of the others, at least *respect for Germany* and its achievements has increased! For Germany and its strength, for Germany and its Führer.

After the events in Spain the Germans abroad know, as well as the foreign countries where they reside, that Germans abroad are no longer defenseless but that, when they are in difficulties, *powerful new battleships with proudly waving swastika flags appear to give them protection!*

Many of you here at this festive hour are probably experiencing for the first time the Reich's party congress which has become a celebration not only for party comrades but for the entire German people, even as the party has grown from the NSDAP to the party of Germany!

You know that in these days not only those who are assembled here in Nuremberg but the *entire German people takes part*, that the foreign Germans participate—and thereby *all Germanism!* For just as we do here at home, the Germans abroad also let the speeches of the Führer speak to their understanding and their hearts over the radio. They hear the description of the marching, they hear the applause of the participants, they are present themselves!

The Germans at home can scarcely estimate what it means far away in the world across continents and seas *to hear the voice of the Führer of the Germans,* which has already become so familiar, and to hear *how the enthusiasm of the racial comrades inspires him; and how happy it makes one to be able to say that that is also my Führer who is speaking and that those who are celebrating are the people of my blood.*

Only one thing is not transmitted by the radio. That is this nebulous something which flows from the Führer to the people who stand before him during his speeches, that flows into the people whom he passes— *that binding stream from the Führer to the people!*

But I know that you who are fortunate enough to take part here in Nuremberg feel it like everyone else. And that which is not transmitted by the radio, that which you have felt here in your hearts you will carry with you out into the world to our racial comrades! You will communicate it somehow through your reports to those abroad by describing what you saw, heard, and felt here. Report to them of the experience of being a German among Germans in contemporary

Germany. *Report to them what it means after years of internal dissension, of disturbance, to be among hundreds, thousands, hundreds of thousands of Germans who feel themselves to be a great community and who have a great love and a common reverence: the love and reverence for their Führer.*

And report, too, that the Führer cleaves to his people with the same love; yes, report that he thinks of Germans abroad with special love, that he—who himself was a foreign German—knows only too well what it means as a German *to hold his Germanism high outside of the borders of Germany.* He wishes through me to transmit to Germans abroad his thanks and his recognition and therewith the thanks and recognition of the fatherland.

Report abroad what you saw in the new Germany, tell of the Germans who *again march to one command*—regardless of whether it is the SA and the SS, the political leaders, youth, men of the labor service, or soldiers of the Army—march to the command of the Führer.

And tell them also of all that you will see on Army Day next Monday, of this new Army that is worthy of the old. Tell them of all the ultramodern weapons, the tanks, the heavy artillery, the antiaircraft, and tell them how squadrons of your young *Luftwaffe* roam the heavens; tell them also of the particular friends of Germans abroad, the blue-clad youths who take part in the parade before the Führer, whose ships, moreover, are ready to protect German racial comrades abroad.

Tell them: The defense of the fatherland is stronger than ever!

My party comrades!

From this Reich's party congress some of you are taking your flags back with you to forty-eight local groups of the Foreign Organization as a special greeting from the fatherland and as a symbol of the unity of Germans throughout the world. I will now consecrate them.

Flags up!

You, symbols of the new faith and of the new Reich, who will wave in Chile, Brazil, Argentina, in Manchuria, in the Netherlands East Indies, as well as in Poland, England, and Italy, and in many other places in the world, who will wave over German ships which travel around the earth, I consecrate you with the words which have become traditional as the *consecration ritual of the fatherland* for the flags of the Foreign Organization:

"Flags of National Socialism, wave for the honor of Germany and of its Führer!

"Wave in the distant world as a symbol of the greater united Germany which Adolf Hitler created.

"We greet the Führer, Adolf Hitler—Sieg Heil!"

DOCUMENT 26

Erste Morgen=Ausgabe.
Deutsches Nachrichtenbüro G.m.b.H.

(Als Manuskript gedruckt, Nachdruck und jede Art Verbreitung
ohne Vereinbarung untersagt. Ohne alle Gewähr.)

4. Jahrg. 1937	Berlin, Montag, 30. August	Nr. 1157

Die Tagung der Auslandsdeutschen.

Stuttgart, 29. August. Die Stadt der Auslandsdeutschen hat ihre Gäste aus aller Welt empfangen. Am
Sonnabend trafen die Sonderzüge aus Berlin, Hamburg
und Mailand ein. Dem Mailänder Sonderzug entstiegen
über 600 Reichsdeutsche aus Italien. Auch Botschafter
von Ribbentrop ist in Stuttgart eingetroffen.

Rudolf Heß trifft ein.

Rudolf Heß traf gegen 18 Uhr auf dem Flughafen
Böblingen ein, wo er von Gauleiter Reichsstatthalter
Murr und Gauleiter Bohle herzlich willkommen ge-
heißen wurde. Geleitet von den beiden Gauleitern begab
sich der Stellvertreter des Führers im Kraftwagen nach
Stuttgart.

Schon stundenlang vor der Ankunft des Stellvertreters
des Führers warteten Tausende vor dem Hotel, in dem
Rudolf Heß während seines Stuttgarter Aufenthaltes
Wohnung genommen hat. Immer wieder erschollen die
Heilrufe, und der Jubel wollte kein Ende nehmen, als
Rudolf Heß sich am Fenster zeigte.

Einläutung des Festes.

Pünktlich um 19 Uhr wurde das Fest von den Glocken
sämtlicher Stuttgarter Kirchen eingeläutet. Damit hatte
die V. Reichstagung der Auslandsdeutschen ihren Anfang
genommen.

Auf allen öffentlichen Plätzen der festlich geschmückten
und illuminierten Stadt konzertierten die Kapellen der
Wehrmacht und die Musikzüge der Bewegung.

321

Presseempfang der Auslandsorganisation.

Abends veranstaltete die Auslandsorganisation der NSDAP. im ehemaligen Landtag einen Presseempfang. Der Presseamtsleiter der AO., Veinhauer, hieß die Pressevertreter im Namen des Leiters der Auslandsorganisation der NSDAP., Gauleiters B o h l e , auf der V. Reichstagung der Auslandsdeutschen willkommen. Der Redner stellte fest, daß die AO. seit ihrem Bestehen für ihre Angehörigen als Richtschnur ausgegeben habe: „Die Politik Deines Gastlandes lasse deren Bewohner machen. Dich geht die Politik eines fremden Landes nichts an. Mische Dich nicht in diese, auch nicht gesprächsweise."

Diese Richtlinien seien geeignet, völlige Klarheit über die Auffassung der AO. zu geben. Die Aufgabe der AO. sei die Betreuung der Auslandsdeutschen, d. h. der Deutschen im Ausland, die die deutsche Staatsbürgerschaft besitzen; denn es sei selbstverständlich, daß der deutsche Staatsbürger jenseits der Grenzen von der deutschen Heimat nicht vergessen werden dürfe.

Der Empfang schloß mit Dankesworten von Reichshauptamtsleiter Dr. Dreßler von der Reichspressestelle der NSDAP. Er bezeichnete die Presse als eines der wichtigsten Bindeglieder von Heimat und Auslandsdeutschtum und wünschte der V. Reichstagung einen vollen Erfolg.

Machtvolle Eröffnungskundgebung.

Die V. Reichstagung der Auslandsdeutschen in Stuttgart wurde am Sontag vormittag in festlicher Weise eröffnet.

Die riesige Halle vermochte die gewaltige Zahl der Teilnehmer kaum zu fassen. Die Bedeutung der V. Reichstagung wurde besonders unterstrichen durch die Anwesenheit einer überaus großen Zahl von Ehrengästen, an ihrer Spitze des Stellvertreters des Führers, Reichsministers Rudolf H e ß , der, als er mit Reichsaußenminister v o n N e u r a t h , dem Leiter der Auslands=Organisation, Gauleiter B o h l e , und dem Gauleiter Reichsstatthalter M u r r die Halle betrat, von den Massen durch minutenlange Heilrufe begrüßt wurde.

Unter den Ehrengästen sah man die Witwe des ermordeten Landesgruppenleiters Schweiz, Wilhelm G u s t l o f f , Botschafter v o n R i b b e n t r o p und den größten Teil der deutschen Botschafter und Gesandten, Staatssekretär v o n M a c k e n s e n , den Kommandeur des 5. Armeekorps, General der Infanterie G e y e r , den stellvertretenden Gauleiter und Leiter des Hauptschulungsamtes der NSDAP., S c h m i d t , die Mitglieder der württembergischen Staatsregierung, Vertreter der Partei und ihrer Gliederungen, Oberbürgermeister S t r ö l i n = Stuttgart sowie die Hoheitsträger und Amtsleiter der A. O.

Nach dem Fahneneinmarsch und einem von HJ. und BdM. unter Mitwirkung des Landessinfonie=Orchesters vorgetragenen Chorwerk „Lang war die Nacht, lang war die Not", nahm Gauleiter

Reichsstatthalter Murr

das Wort.

Er wies darauf hin, daß es das erste Mal sei, daß sich die Mitglieder der Auslandsorganisation der NSDAP. in Stuttgart, der Stadt der Auslandsdeutschen, versammelt hätten. Der Gauleiter gab seiner Freude darüber Ausdruck, daß es gerade die Schwaben sein dürften, die die Auslandsdeutschen willkommen heißen könnten.

Der Redner dankte Gauleiter Bohle dafür, daß er sich entschlossen habe, die großen Treffen der A. O. künftig stets in Stuttgart abzuhalten. Stuttgart trete damit nicht zum ersten Male in Beziehung zum Auslandsdeutschtum. Die Verbindung zu den Deutschen in aller Welt sei vielmehr von Stuttgart und Württemberg aus stets in besonderem Maße gepflegt worden.

Gauleiter Murr sprach den Wunsch aus, daß die arbeitsreichen und festlichen Tage unseren Brüdern und Schwestern aus aller Welt zum großen Erlebnis werden möchten, damit sie alle die Gewißheit mit nach Hause nehmen könnten, daß die Kinder der Mutter Germania noch niemals mit größerem Stolz bekennen durften, Deutsche zu sein, als heute unter der Führung Adolf Hitlers.

Oberbürgermeister Dr. Strölin,

der Präsident des Deutschen Auslandsinstituts, begrüßte darauf die Ehrengäste und die zu der Tagung nach Stuttgart gekommenen Auslandsdeutschen auf das herzlichste. In seiner Ansprache wies der Redner darauf hin, daß der Führer Stuttgart zur Stadt der Auslandsdeutschen bestimmt habe. Die Stadt sei sich der daraus ergebenden hohen Verpflichtung im Innersten bewußt. Die Stuttgarter würden alles daran setzen, daß diese Stadt in Wahrheit für die Auslandsdeutschen zum Sinnbild der Verbundenheit mit der heimatlichen Erde und zum Inbegriff alles wahrhaft Deutschen werde.

In diesem Zeichen grüßten sie hier in der Stadt der Auslandsdeutschen die Fahnen des Dritten Reiches.

Es grüßten sie aber auch die Flaggen der Länder, in denen sie eine Heimat gefunden haben. Es solle damit bekundet werden, daß die Reichsdeutschen im Ausland den ehrlichen und aufrichtigen Willen haben, in loyalen Beziehungen zu ihren Gastländern zu stehen.

Oberbürgermeister Strölin wandte sich dann mit herzlichen Grußworten an den Stellvertreter des Führers, Reichsaußenminister Freiherrn von Neurath und Gauleiter Bohle und schloß mit dem Wunsche, daß Gastgeber und Gäste in diesen Tagen zu einer Einheit völkischen Wollens verschmelzen mögen: "Ein deutsches Bewußtsein, ein fester Wille, eine heiße Liebe für unseren Führer möge uns umschließen. Das ist unser Wunsch für diese Tage, das ist mein Willkommgruß an die deutschen Volksgenossen aus aller Welt!"

Hierauf betrat, stürmisch begrüßt,

Gauleiter Bohle

das Rednerpult und führte folgendes aus:

„Einmal im Jahre ruft die Auslands-Organisation der Nationalsozialistischen Partei zur Reichstagung der Auslandsdeutschen auf. Einmal im Jahre will das ganze Auslandsdeutschtum und mit ihm die deutsche Seefahrt ein Bekenntnis zum Führer und seinem Reich ablegen.

„Die 5. Reichstagung, die wir heute festlich beginnen, wird in diesem Jahre erstmalig in unserer Stadt, „Der Stadt der Auslandsdeutschen", abgehalten. Wir sind uns dieser Verpflichtung zutiefst bewußt und wir wollen damit dem Führer unseren Dank abstatten, indem wir diese Tage in der „Stadt der Auslandsdeutschen" würdig und in deutscher Art begehen."

Nach Worten der Begrüßung und des Dankes, besonders an die Reichsminister Rudolf Heß und Freiherrn von Neurath, fuhr Gauleiter Bohle fort:

„Es ist für uns alle ein beglückendes und zugleich stärkendes Gefühl, zu sehen, daß wir heute mit unseren Sorgen, Nöten und Wünschen nicht mehr allein sind, sondern daß führende Männer aus Partei und Staat und aus der neu erstandenen Wehrmacht hier unter uns weilen, um mit uns zusammen zu sein und uns so zu zeigen, daß wir zu der großen Einheit gehören, die Deutschland heißt.

„An solchen Tagen müssen unsere Gedanken in die Vergangenheit zurückgehen. Weder vor dem Weltkrieg, noch danach gab es eine Einheit oder auch nur den Versuch einer einheitlichen Ausrichtung des Deutschtums draußen; und es gab ebensowenig Verständnis der Menschen daheim für diejenigen, die ihr Vaterland verlassen hatten und überall in der weiten Welt als aufrechte Deutsche zu ihrem Deutschtum standen.

„Obwohl wir vor dem Krieg ein starkes und mächtiges Reich hatten und der Name Deutschland Gewicht in der Welt besaß, waren die Auslandsdeutschen und die Seefahrer nicht nur nicht vollberechtigt, sondern oft Deutsche zweiter Klasse. Das wußten nicht nur die Auslandsdeutschen selbst, sondern das empfanden vor allem die Angehörigen fremder Staaten, in denen diese Auslandsdeutschen lebten.

„Es gibt hierfür nur die Erklärung, daß damals in dieser Beziehung eine heute unvorstellbare politische Kurzsichtigkeit herrschte.

„Noch viel trostloser war es um die Auslandsdeutschen bestellt, als der große Krieg sein Ende fand, und als im Reiche das Chaos und der Verrat am Deutschtum regierten. Konnte man sich vor 1914 immerhin als Angehöriger einer großen Macht fühlen, so war dies in der Zeit der Weimarer Republik vorbei. Die moralisch, machtpolitisch und geistig zerrüttete Heimat war kein Begriff, an den sich die Deutschen im Ausland stolz klammern konnten.

„Es war deshalb nicht verwunderlich, daß unendlich viele
Deutsche sich vom alten Vaterland abwandten und in eine
stumpfe Gleichgültigkeit verfielen. Unbefriedigend war auch
der Zustand innerhalb des Auslandsdeutschtums selbst.
Sicherlich gab es zahllose Vereine, Verbände und sonstige
Zusammenfassungen von Auslandsdeutschen. Aber diese
standen stets unter der Devise, die der einzelne Verein jeweils auf seine Fahne geschrieben hatte, und nicht unter
der Devise „Deutschland". Man kegelte, turnte, spielte
Skat und pflegte Geselligkeit, aber man pflegte in den
wenigsten Fällen das alle Volksgenossen verbindende
Deutschtum.

„Man kann mir auch nicht entgegenhalten, daß bei dieser Geselligkeit deutsch gesprochen und hier und da in patrio-
tischer Weise des Reiches gedacht wurde. Dieser Patriotis-
mus war nicht nur oft gedankenlos, sondern krankte insbesondere und in erster Linie daran, daß die Patrioten
säuberlich nach Klassen oder Geldsack getrennt unter sich
blieben. Ueber die Aeußerlichkeiten vergaß man den deutschen Menschen.

„Das ist der V o r w u r f, den wir erheben müssen,
und der um so größer ist, weil die Nichtachtung des
deutschen Menschen sich unter den Augen der Ausländer abspielte. Die Zahl dieser Deutschen, die durch Klassen- und
Geldarroganz ihrer lieben Mitbürger d e m R e i c h e v e r -
l o r e n g i n g e n, ist ungeheuer groß. Die damaligen
deutschen Vertretungen im Auslande hätten in vielen Fällen
die Möglichkeit gehabt, hier einzugreifen.

„Es waren die e r s t e n P a r t e i g e n o s s e n im Auslande, die im Jahre 1931 den Versuch unternahmen, in diese
Zustände einzugreifen. Ich glaube, sagen zu können, daß die
Auslands-Organisation in den sechs Jahren, die seit dem
Beginn unserer Tätigkeit im Auslande verflossen sind, auf
allen Gebieten g r u n d l e g e n d e n W a n d e l geschaffen
hat, auch wenn, wie wir wissen, noch sehr viel Arbeit vor
uns liegt. Unser ganzes Tun wurde erst möglich auf
der G r u n d l a g e d e r W e l t a n s c h a u u n g d e s
F ü h r e r s.

„Ohne den Führer und seine alle Deutschen erfassende
und umspannende Idee wäre es sinnlos gewesen, an eine
Einigung des Auslandsdeutschtums heranzugehen. Die
von Adolf Hitler gepredigte deutsche Volksgemeinschaft war
die einzige Basis, auf der eine Zusammenfassung des Auslandsdeutschtums überhaupt erfolgen konnte. Es ist notwendig, sich diese Tatsache vor Augen zu halten, wenn wir
rückblickend feststellen, wie anders es heute draußen gegenüber früher aussieht.

„Die Partei hat durch ihre Auslandsorganisation ver-
mocht, unzählige deutsche Menschen im Auslande an die
Heimat heranzubringen und diesen Menschen zu zeigen, daß
sie zu dieser Heimat gehören, ihr verbunden und ihr verpflichtet sind.

„Wenn heute Festtage der Nation im Reiche begangen werden, so wissen wir, daß die Deutschen im Auslande im gleichen Geist diese Tage begehen, und daß alle Deutschen hieran teilnehmen.

„Das Winterhilfswerk des deutschen Volkes ist gerade im Auslandsdeutschtum von einem vorbildlichen Erfolg gekrönt worden und hat vielleicht besser als irgendetwas anderes den nationalen Opfersinn und das soziale Verständnis unserer Auslandsdeutschen unter Beweis gestellt.

„Die Auslandsdeutschen helfen sich heute selbst, sie kümmern sich um die Armen und Kranken in ihren Reihen und geben damit ein schönes Beispiel wahrer nationalsozialistischer Volksgemeinschaft.

„Kraft durch Freude" ist ebenfalls im Auslandsdeutschtum heute ein geläufiger und nicht mehr fortzudenkender Begriff, sei es unter dem Auslandsdeutschtum selbst oder in Verbindung mit unseren deutschen Seeleuten, denen beim Liegen im Hafen in kameradschaftlicher Weise dazu verholfen wird, diese Stunden in gemeinsamer Freude mit ihren Landsleuten zu verleben.

„Heute braucht kein Deutscher im Auslande das Gefühl zu haben, daß er verlassen ist.

„In kameradschaftlicher Zusammenarbeit mit den amtlichen Vertretungen sorgt sich die Auslandsorganisation nach besten Kräften um jeden einzelnen Volksgenossen und gibt somit der ganzen Welt den untrüglichen Beweis dafür, daß die Deutschen im Auslande die Idee nationalsozialistischer Verbundenheit untereinander ebenso begriffen und in die Tat umgesetzt haben, wie dies im Reich der Fall ist.

„Bei Ausbruch der Wirren in Spanien hat die Auslandsorganisation sofort einen Hilfsausschuß für die Spanienflüchtlinge ins Leben gerufen und in Zusammenarbeit mit den amtlichen Stellen die gesamte Betreuung bis auf den heutigen Tag durchgeführt. Mein Aufruf an die Volksgenossen im Reich, Spenden für unsere SpanienDeutschen zu geben, fand größten Widerhall.

„In neuester Zeit hat der Chef der Auslandsorganisation im Auswärtigen Amt, gestützt auf die AO. der NSDAP. und ihre Gruppen draußen, alle Maßnahmen getroffen, um den China-Deutschen zu helfen, die oft unter Zurücklassung von Hab und Gut abtransportiert werden müssen.

„Diese beiden Beispiele zeugen einmal von der heute selbstverständlichen Fürsorge der Partei und des Reiches für die Auslandsdeutschen und insbesondere für das starke Zusammengehörigkeitsgefühl unter den Auslandsdeutschen selbst.

„Der Geist der Kameradschaft bei unseren Auslandsdeutschen ersetzt die Machtmittel, die anderen Nationen draußen zur Verfügung stehen, und dieser Geist ist der sprechendste Zeuge für die neue Haltung des Auslandsdeutschtums, auf die wir so stolz sind.

„Die Arbeit der vielen Vereine und Verbände hat durch die alle umspannende Tätigkeit der Auslandsgruppen der Partei einen neuen Sinn erfahren und diese Arbeit fruchtbringender für die Gemeinschaft gestaltet.

„Es kann heute praktisch kaum noch vorkommen, daß die Mitglieder des deutschen Vereins X mit den Angehörigen des deutschen Vereins Y bis aufs Messer verfeindet sind, weil etwa die Mitglieder X in denjenigen des Vereins Y ihre Klassen- oder Berufsgegner sehen.

„Unter dieser Voraussetzung bilden unsere Vereine im Auslande, die zum Teil jahrzehntelang bestehen und, wie nicht verkannt werden darf, in vielen Fällen hervorragende Deutschtumsarbeit geleistet haben, eine überaus wertvolle Unterstützung der Gesamtarbeit im Auslandsdeutschtum.

„Ich habe deshalb Wert darauf gelegt, festzustellen, daß wir nicht Gegner der Vereine sind, sondern nur unerbittliche Gegner aller Bestrebungen, die Auslandsdeutschen in Klassen oder Berufe aufzuteilen.

„Wenn heute führende Männer von Partei und Staat an den nationalen Feiertagen zu unseren Volksgenossen im Auslande sprechen, dann finden sie schon in den meisten Fällen einen Geist der Zusammengehörigkeit, der in Anbetracht der oft schwierigen Verhältnisse überraschen muß.

„Das Bild, das sich Ihnen heute bietet, gibt im Ganzen wohl den besten Ueberblick über die Erfolge der Arbeit unserer Parteigenossen draußen, die trotz starker beruflicher Ueberlastung, trotz ungünstiger klimatischer Verhältnisse und trotz vielfacher Anfeindungen unbeirrt tätig sind, um auch den letzten Bürger dieses Reiches in die Volksgemeinschaft einzufügen.

„Wenn in Südamerika oder in Afrika Deutsche stundenlange und oft Tagesreisen unternehmen, um einen Film aus Deutschland zu sehen oder einer Zusammenkunft beizuwohnen, dann wird man die Tatsache anerkennen müssen, daß Adolf Hitler auch im Auslandsdeutschtum gesiegt hat. Wenn der Deutsche von draußen ins Reich zurückkehrt, sei es auf Urlaub oder für längere Zeit, dann wird er auch feststellen, daß hier im Reich eine andere Meinung über die Auslandsdeutschen herrscht, als dies früher der Fall war.

(Fortsetzung auf Nr. 1158.)

Verantwortlich: Kurt Schwartzkopff, Berlin-Wilmersdorf. Druck und Verlag: Deutsches Nachrichtenbüro G. m. b. H., Berlin.

Zweite Morgen-Ausgabe.
Deutsches Nachrichtenbüro G.m.b.H.

(Als Manuskript gedruckt, Nachdruck und jede Art Verbreitung
ohne Vereinbarung untersagt. Ohne alle Gewähr.)

4. Jahrg. 1937	Berlin, Montag, 30. August	Nr. 1158

Die Tagung der Auslandsdeutschen.
(Fortsetzung.)

„Der Führer hat durch seinen Erlaß am vierten Jahres-
tage der Machtergreifung, mit dem er einen Chef der Auslands-Organisation im Auswärtigen Amt einsetzte, dem
ganzen Auslandsdeutschtum gezeigt, wie groß und um-
fassend sein Verständnis für ihre Belange und ihre Sorgen
ist. Dieser Erlaß bedeutet aber auch eine Anerkennung für
die Arbeit, die unsere Parteigenossen im und am Auslandsdeutschtum in den letzten Jahren geleistet haben.

„Ich bin mir darüber klar, daß die Auslands-Organisation noch sehr große Aufgaben vor sich hat, und daß es
geraume Zeit dauern wird, bis unsere Reichsbürger im
Auslande so nationalsozialistisch ausgerichtet sind, wie wir
es wünschen und wie es sein muß. Es ist kein Wunder,
daß viele alte liberalistische Auffassungen draußen noch nicht
überstanden sind. Wir werden immer wieder Front gegen
derartige Auffassungen machen und ich weiß, daß die Auslands-Organisation hier und draußen Erfolg damit haben
wird.

„Wer als deutscher Wirtschaftler oder als Kaufherr im
Auslande lebt, arbeitet nicht nur für sich selbst und seine
Familie, sondern nach der Auffassung des neuen Deutsch-
lands in erster Linie für sein Volk.

„Er sollte nicht vergessen, daß sich unter den wenigen
Tausend Volksgenossen, die sich vor der Machtergreifung für
Adolf Hitler draußen einsetzten, sehr sehr viele Kaufmanns-
gehilfen und Arbeiter befanden. Wenn wir von unseren

Auslandsdeutschen, d. h. von unseren Reichsdeutschen im Auslande, sprechen, so verstehen wir darunter ausschließlich die Nationalsozialisten im Auslande. Unter den Nationalsozialisten im Auslande verstehen wir aber keineswegs nur die Parteigenossen, sondern alle Deutschen, die dem Reiche treu sind. Es wäre auch nicht möglich, einen Unterschied zwischen Deutschen im Auslande und Nationalsozialisten machen, weil beide heute einen Begriff darstellen.

„Es gibt immer noch einige wenige Deutsche im Auslande, die keine Nationalsozialisten sein wollen und sich irrtümlich immer noch als Deutsche bezeichnen. Diese sogenannten Deutschen äußern sich sogar in deutschgeschriebenen Zeitungen und in Zeitschriften in einer Weise gegen das Dritte Reich, die an die übelsten Blüten der Emigrantenliteratur erinnert. Es lohnt nicht, sich mit diesen Menschen des längeren auseinanderzusetzen. Wir haben für diese Sorte von sogenannten Deutschen, die nicht müde werden, ihr nationales deutsches Herz zu bekunden und trotzdem bewußt den Gegner des Reiches helfen, nur den Ausdruck „Landesverräter".

„Wir auslandsdeutschen Nationalsozialisten lehnen den Begriff des universalen Deutschen ab, dessen vornehmstes Bestreben es ist, sich überall anzupassen, weil dieser universale Deutsche sich nicht nur damit bei den Ausländern lächerlich macht, sondern bewußt oder unbewußt mit dieser Selbstaufgabe sein Deutschtum verleugnet.

„Wir kennen nur den Begriff des totalen Deutschen, der als Bürger seines Reiches immer und überall deutsch und nichts als deutsch ist, und damit Nationalsozialist.

„In früheren Zeiten war die Welt gewohnt, bei den Deutschen etwas weniger Nationalgefühl als bei den anderen großen Nationen vorauszusetzen. Es hat den Anschein, daß man in einigen Ländern lebhaft bedauert, heute von dieser Voraussetzung nicht mehr ausgehen zu können und alles versuchen möchte, um durch Entstellungen und unwahre Behauptungen der verschiedensten Art ein allgemeines Mißtrauen gegen uns Auslandsdeutsche zu säen.

„Wir nehmen die vollkommen irrsinnigen Mitteilungen über das Auslandsdeutschtum und insbesondere über die Auslands-Oganisation schon lange nicht mehr ernst, weil diese Veröffentlichungen selbst für den Dümmsten den Stempel der Lügen tragen und sich daher selbst widerlegen.

„Die Versuche, es so hinzustellen, als ob Nationalsozialisten im Auslande ausschließlich Spione oder politische Agenten wären, findet man aber wohl als letzten Versuch einer Diskriminierung neuerdings sogar in den Zeitungen, die selbst Wert darauf legen, ernst genommen zu werden.

Es ist deshalb amüsant zu lesen, daß Deutschland alle weiblichen Hausangestellten im Auslande zu Spionen ausbildet,
und daß die Nazimänner selbst den hauptsächlichen Auftrag
hätten, das jeweilige fremde Land in eine Hitler-Kolonie zu
verwandeln.

„Weil es aber doch noch Leute im Auslande gibt, die so
etwas glauben, möchte ich hier ausdrücklich versichern, daß
wir die weiblichen Hausangestellten nicht zu Spionen aus-
bilden und keine Nazis im Auslande beauftragt haben,
fremde Länder zu erobern.

„Wir sind nicht nur auf diesen Gedanken niemals gekommen, sondern ich glaube, daß die Hausangestellten selbst
und unsere Männer draußen berechtigte Zweifel an unserer
Zurechnungsfähigkeit hegen würden, wenn Derartiges verlangt werden sollte. Man kann geradezu eine gewisse Be-
sessenheit in einigen Redaktionen feststellen, ihren Lesern
glaubhaft zu machen, daß alle Nationalsozialisten im Auslande Spitzel seien, Menschen, die, wie es eine bekannte
Zeitung schrieb, nur eine irreguläre Aktivität entfalten.
Diese unsinnigen Behauptungen brauchte man überhaupt
nicht ernst zu nehmen, wenn sie nicht dazu beitrügen, die
internationale Atmosphäre zu vergiften
und die Beziehungen zwischen Deutschland und fremden
Ländern zu trüben.

„Die Welt weiß heute nach vier Jahren nationalsozialistischer Herrschaft und gibt es gern oder widerwillig zu,
daß Adolf Hitler und sein Land keinen sehn-
licheren Wunsch haben, als in Frieden und in
Eintracht mit allen Völkern zu leben.   Die
Auslandsdeutschen teilen diesen Wunsch aus tiefstem Herzen.

„Ich möchte daher eindeutig feststellen, daß die Aufgaben und die Tätigkeit der Auslands-Organisation vollkommen klar vor aller Augen liegen. Was für andere
große Nationen selbstverständlich ist, machen wir auch. Wir
kümmern uns um unsere Bürger im Auslande und nur um
diese und wir sorgen für ihre Verbindung zum Reich und
für die Erhaltung ihres Deutschtums.

„Daß diese Betreuung eine umfassende ist, liegt in den
neuen Idealen begründet, die Adolf Hitler dem deutschen
Volke gegeben hat. Das erste Gesetz für die auslandsdeutschen Nationalsozialisten schreibt ihnen die genaue Respek-
tierung der Gesetze ihrer Gastländer vor, und Partei und
Reich wachen sorgfältig darüber, daß dieses Gesetz eingehal-
ten wird.

„Ebenso sehr aber müssen wir verlangen, daß auch
der Deutsche im Auslande sein eigenes Leben nach den
Grundsätzen einrichten darf, die in seiner Heimat gelten.

„Wenn Franzosen, Engländer, Schweizer und andere treu zu ihrem Lande stehen, wundert sich darüber niemand.

Und wir beanspruchen dasselbe und nicht mehr und nicht weniger für uns. Ein Reichsbürger im Auslande ist heute ein Nationalsozialist, und keine Redaktion der Welt wird diese Tatsache beseitigen. Für keinen Menschen ist es eine Sensation, wenn ein Engländer im Auslande seinem König und seinem Empire treu ist, sondern man setzt diese Treue voraus. Für den Nationalsozialisten im Auslande gilt genau dasselbe, nämlich daß er seinem Führer und seinem Reich die Treue hält.

„Nationalgefühl ist eine internationale Erscheinung und nicht von einzelnen Nationen gepachtet. Wer hinsichtlich Deutschlands hieran zweifelt, hat die letzten Jahre verschlafen.

„Meine auslandsdeutschen Volksgenossen und Volksgenossinnen! Kameraden der Seefahrt!

„Sie sind nach Stuttgart gekommen, um sich vor aller Welt zu diesem Deutschland zu bekennen. Das Reich freut sich über dieses Bekenntnis und dankt Ihnen und darüber hinaus allen, die draußen in der Welt leben, für die Treue, die Sie dem Reich halten. Ich weiß, daß diese Treue zur Heimat nicht plötzlich oder erst im Jahre 1933 entstanden ist. Sie war schon seit vielen Jahrzehnten in den Herzen der Deutschen draußen.

„**Aber erst, seitdem Adolf Hitler die Geschicke des Reiches lenkt, kann diese Treue ihren wirksamsten und schönsten Ausdruck finden, der sich mit dem Gefühl des Stolzes mischt, Angehöriger einer großen und geachteten Nation zu sein. Für diese Treue bürgen alle Deutschen draußen, die deutsch geblieben sind, unter ihnen besonders die Eltern unserer auslandsdeutschen Jugend.**

„Niemals hätte die Auslands-Organisation ihre Arbeit mit Erfolg leisten können, wenn nicht schon Jahre und Jahrzehnte zuvor deutsche Kinder von deutschen Eltern deutsch erzogen worden wären. Wir Jüngeren, die das Glück hatten, im Auslande solche deutschen Eltern zu besitzen, die auch in schwerster Zeit deutsch blieben, können heute unseren Dank nur dadurch abtragen, daß wir im Dienste Adolf Hitlers für Deutschland arbeiten. In diesem Dienst ist unter unvergeßlicher Landesgruppenleiter Wilhelm Gustloff gefallen. Für seine Treue fand er den Tod. Wilhelm Gustloff und mit ihm die in Spanien ermordeten Deutschen mahnen uns alle an unsere Pflicht gegenüber dem Reich.

„Dies soll der Sinn unserer Reichstagung sein: Die Auslandsdeutschen sind der Welt gegenüber die wirkungsvollsten und selbstverständlichsten Zeugen für das stolzeste und heiligste Bekenntnis, das wir kennen, für das Bekenntnis: **Ich bin ein Deutscher.** Damit erkläre ich die 5. Reichstagung der Auslandsdeutschen 1937 in der „Stadt der Auslandsdeutschen" für eröffnet."

In das dreifache Sieg=Heil auf den Führer und Reichs=
kanzler A d o l f H i t l e r stimmten die Tausende begeistert
ein. Der Gesang der nationalen Lieder bildete den Ab=
schluß der machtvollen Kundgebung.

Im Anschluß an die Feier fanden am Ehrenmal für die
Gefallenen des Weltkrieges und an drei Gedenktafeln er=
mordeter SA=Männer in Stuttgart Kranzniederlegungen
durch Gauleiter Bohle und die Landesgruppenleiter der
AO. statt.

Empfang zu Ehren des Stellvertreters des Führers.

Auf Einladung des Oberbürgermeisters Dr. Strölin
fand am Sonntag mittag in der Villa Berg zu Ehren des
Stellvertreters des Führers, Reichsministers Rudolf Heß,
ein Empfang statt. An diesem nahmen außer dem Stell=
vertreter des Führers Reichsaußenminister Freiherr v o n
N e u r a t h, Botschafter v o n R i b b e n t r o p, Gauleiter
Reichsstatthalter M u r r, Gauleiter B o h l e, Minister=
präsident M e r g e n t h a l e r, die Mitglieder der württem=
bergischen Regierung, die Spitzen der Partei und ihrer
Gliederungen, sowie die übrigen anläßlich der Reichstagung in
Stuttgart weilenden Ehrengäste, darunter zahlreiche Ver=
treter des Auswärtigen Amtes mit Staatssekretär v o n
M a c k e n s e n an der Spitze, und die Mitglieder der Aus=
lands=Organisation teil.

Großkundgebung in der Adolf=Hitler=Kampfbahn.

Zu einem eindrucksvollen Erlebnis des Zusammen=
gehörigkeitsgefühls aller Deutschen diesseits und jenseits der
Reichsgrenzen wurde die erste Großkundgebung, die am
Sonntag nachmittag in der Adolf=Hitler=Kampfbahn statt=
fand. Nicht weniger als 80 000 Volksgenossen, darunter
Tausende von Auslandsdeutschen, waren in der Kampfbahn
zusammengeströmt, um Rudolf Heß sprechen zu hören.

Schon eine Stunde vor Beginn der Kundgebung war
die riesige Anlage fast besetzt. Kurz vor 16 Uhr erschien
Reichsaußenminister Freiherr v o n N e u r a t h. Ferner
bemerkte man Botschafter v o n R i b b e n t r o p mit weite=
ren deutschen Botschaftern und Gesandten, Staatssekretär
v o n M a c k e n s e n und Vertreter des Auswärtigen Amtes,
den Kommandeur des V. Armeekorps, General der Infan=
terie G e y e r, den stellvertretenden Gauleiter und Leiter
des Hauptschulungsamtes der NSDAP., Schmidt,
Ministerpräsident und Kultusminister M e r g e n t h a l e r
mit den Ministern Dr. S c h m i d und Dr. D e h l i n g e r,
Staatssekretär W a l d m a n n, SS.=Gruppenführer K a u l,
Oberbürgermeister Dr. S t r ö l i n, sowie weitere führende
Männer von Partei, Staat und Wehrmacht und Hoheits=
träger und Mitglieder der Auslands=Organisation.

Dann begann der Einmarsch der Formationen unter den
Klängen eines Musikzuges des Reichsarbeitsdienstes. Vor
der Hauptttribüne stellten sich 60 Fahnen unserer auslands=
deutschen Gruppen auf.

Rudolf Heß kommt.

Kurz nach 16 Uhr ertönte das Kommando: Stillgestanden! Wie eine eherne Mauer standen die Formationen, als der Stellvertreter des Führers, Reichsminister Rudolf Heß, umtost von minutenlangen stürmischen Heil=Rufen, die Ehrentribüne betrat. Im Paradeschritt marschierte eine Ehrenkompanie eines Infanterieregiments ein. Der Vorbeimarsch wurde von General der Infanterie Geyer abgenommen. Dann nahm ein Ehrensturm der Ellwanger SS.=Standarte „Deutschland" Aufstellung vor der Mitteltribüne. Knappe Kommandos: Die Truppe präsentierte zum Einmarsch der Standarten und Fahnen. SA.=Standartenführer **Himpel** meldete dem Stellvertreter des Führers 400 Fahnen und 8000 Mann der Gliederungen des Standortes Stuttgart.

Von Jubel begrüßt, betrat dann der Leiter der Auslandsorganisation, Gauleiter **Bohle**, das Rednerpult und eröffnete die Großkundgebung mit dem Gedenken an die im Auslande gefallenen auslandsdeutschen Volksgenossen. Mit Freude wies er auf die Anwesenheit vieler führender Männer des neuen Deutschlands hin und dankte besonders dem Stellvertreter des Führers für sein Kommen. Seine Worte fanden mit einem begeistert aufgenommenen Sieg-Heil auf Rudolf Heß ihre vieltausendstimmige Bekräftigung. In dem Reichsminister des Auswärtigen hieß Gauleiter Bohle dann einen Mann willkommen, der aus jahrzehntelanger Erfahrung heraus die Sorgen und den Wert der Auslandsdeutschen kenne.

Telegramm an den Führer.

Schließlich gab Gauleiter Bohle zwei T e l e g r a m m e an den F ü h r e r und vom Reichskriegsminister Generalfeldmarschall v o n B l o m b e r g bekannt. Das Telegramm an den Führer hat folgenden Wortlaut:

„Mein Führer! Zu Beginn der 5. Reichstagung der Auslandsdeutschen entbieten Ihnen die in Stuttgart versammelten Deutschen aus aller Welt stolzen und freudigen Gruß. Dieser bisher größte Appell der Auslandsdeutschen steht im Zeichen der bedingungslosen Treue zu Ihnen, mein Führer, und Ihrem Reich. Wir Auslandsdeutschen schließen in unser Bekenntnis zum Nationalsozialismus in der unbegrenzten Liebe zur neuerstandenen Heimat jene Achtung vor den fremden Nationen ein, die den unumstößlichen deutschen Friedenswillen unter Beweis stellt."

Telegramm Blombergs.

Das Telegramm des Reichskriegsministers v o n B l o m b e r g hat den folgenden Wortlaut:

„Ich grüße die deutschen Volksgenossen, die anläßlich der 5. Reichstagung der Auslandsdeutschen vom 28. August bis 5. September in Stuttgart versammelt sind, und wünsche ihrer weiteren Arbeit für das Deutschtum im Auslande vollen Erfolg."

Mit lebhaftem Beifall begrüßt, nahm dann

Reichsaußenminister Freiherr von Neurath

das Wort:

„Es ist für mich ein erhebender Gedanke, daß ich bei dieser feierlichen Kundgebung als Außenminister des neuen Deutschland einmal unmittelbar an Sie, meine lieben Volksgenossen und Volksgenossinnen aus dem Ausland, das Wort richten kann.

„Wer von Außenpolitik und auswärtigem Dienst hört, hat zunächst alle möglichen Bilder von den diplomatischen Auseinandersetzungen zwischen den Regierungen über die großen Fragen des Weltgeschehens vor Augen. Der Unkundige übersieht dabei aber leicht, welche bedeutsame Rolle in unseren Beziehungen zum Ausland und in der Verwaltung des auswärtigen Dienstes die Tatsache spielt, daß Millionen deutscher Reichsbürger jenseits der Grenzen des Reiches in fremden Staaten leben. Und zwar eine Rolle in mehrfacher Hinsicht:

„Die Auslandsdeutschen sind überall, vor allem in überseeischen Ländern, die stets sichtbaren Vertreter deutscher Art und deutscher Kultur und tragen deshalb eine besondere Verantwortung für das Ansehen Deutschlands in der Welt. Darüber hinaus sind sie in vielen, wenn nicht den meisten Fällen unmittelbar als Förderer materieller deutscher Interessen tätig. Alles das macht sie zu einem wertvollen, ja unentbehrlichen Faktor für die Gestaltung unserer Beziehungen zu den einzelnen fremden Völkern und ihren Regierungen.

„Dem steht auf der anderen Seite die Notwendigkeit gegenüber, das persönliche Schicksal der Auslandsdeutschen und ihr Verhältnis zur Heimat von dieser aus so zu betreuen und zu sichern, daß sie ihr Wirken für Deutschland in natürlicher und gedeihlicher Weise entfalten können.

„Ebenso offen liegt aber zutage, daß die Erfüllung aller der Aufgaben, die uns durch die Existenz des Auslandsdeutschtums gestellt sind, von einer Grundvoraussetzung abhängt, derselben Voraussetzung, die überhaupt für die gesamte Außenpolitik entscheidend ist:

„**Deutschland, der deutsche Staat, die deutsche Volksgemeinschaft, müssen als eine fest geschlossene, unerschütterliche, von dem gleichen starken Willen beseelte Einheit dastehen, wenn wir uns als Volk und Staat im Kräftespiel der Weltpolitik behaupten und durchsetzen wollen. Und nur auf dieser Grundlage kann auch das Auslandsdeutschtum seine besondere Mission erfüllen, sich fest in sich zusammenschließen und seiner Verbundenheit mit der Heimat gewiß sein.**

(Fortsetzung auf Nr. 1159)

Verantwortlich: Kurt Schwartzkopff, Berlin-Wilmersdorf.
Druck und Verlag: Deutsches Nachrichtenbüro G. m. b. H., Berlin.

Dritte Morgen=Ausgabe.

Deutsches Nachrichtenbüro G.m.b.H.

(Als Manuskript gedruckt. Nachdruck und jede Art Verbreitung
ohne Vereinbarung untersagt. Ohne alle Gewähr.)

4. Jahrg. 1937	Berlin, Montag, 30. August	Nr. 1159

Die Tagung der Auslandsdeutschen.
(Fortsetzung.)

„Sie alle, die zu unserer Freude in so großer Zahl aus
den verschiedensten Ländern der Welt hierher gekommen
sind, könnten es, wenn Sie es nicht schon wüßten, mit Händen greifen, welcher ungeheure Wandel sich während der
letzten Jahre im deutschen Volke vollzogen hat.

„Die vom Nationalsozialismus mit beispiellosem Elan
geschaffene Einheit des Volks- und Staats-
willens hat eine Außenpolitik ermöglicht, deren Erfolge
Ihnen allen bekannt sind. Die unerträglichen Fesseln
des Versailler Diktats sind gesprengt. Wir
haben unsere Wehrfreiheit wiedergewonnen. Wir
haben die Souveränität im ganzen Staatsgebiet wie-
derhergestellt. Wir sind überhaupt wieder Herr im
eigenen Hause geworden und haben uns die Machtmittel geschaffen, das nun auch in aller Zukunft zu
bleiben.

„Alles dessen können wir uns vor der Welt offen und
mit ruhigem Stolze rühmen. Denn wir haben ein gutes
außenpolitisches Gewissen. Wir haben mit
unseren außenpolitischen Aktionen niemandem etwas genommen, was ihm gehört; wir haben kein fremdes Land
verletzt, kein fremdes Volk bedroht. Das werden wir
auch in Zukunft nicht tun. Wir haben uns lediglich von den Ketten befreit, die kurzsichtige, von Haß geblen-
dete Staatsmänner glaubten einem 65=Millionen=Volk für
alle Ewigkeit anlegen zu können.

„In den Jahren nach dem Krieg, als Deutschland wehrlos und ohnmächtig zwischen hochgerüsteten Nachbarn und ernährt von geborgten fremden Geldern lebte, konnte wohl der Eindruck entstehen, als habe es endgültig resigniert. Und wer damals diesem Irrtum unterlag, mag dann dem neuen Irrtum verfallen sein, als werde unsere Wiedererstarkung von gefährlichen imperialistischen Absichten getragen.

„Aber die Welt sollte aus den Taten und Worten Adolf Hitlers erkannt haben, daß seine Ziele keine aggresiven sind. Die unnachgiebige Verständnislosigkeit gegenüber unserem unverzichtbaren Anspruch auf Gleichberechtigung hat dazu beigetragen, uns zum schnelleren Erwachen zu verhelfen, und da, wo man uns ungerecht behandeln oder gar angreifen will, üben wir nicht mehr die schwächliche Geduld einer vergangenen Nachkriegsperiode.

„Aber diese Haltung des neuen Deutschland ist in Wahrheit das stärkste Bollwerk für die Sicherung des Friedens und wird sich in einer unruhig bewegten Umwelt immer mehr als ein solches erweisen

„Gerade weil wir die Gefahr bestimmter zersetzender Tendenzen, wie sie sich in Europa geltend zu machen suchen, klar erkannt haben, suchen wir nicht nach dem Trennenden, sondern nach dem Verbindenden zwischen den Staaten und Völkern. Wir denken nicht an politische Isolierung. Wir erstreben eine politische Zusammenarbeit der Regierungen, eine Zusammenarbeit, die, wenn sie Erfolg haben soll, allerdings nicht auf theoretischen Kollektivitätsideen, sondern auf der lebendigen Realität beruhen und sich den konkreten Aufgaben der Gegenwart zuwenden muß.

„Mit Genugtuung können wir feststellen, daß wir in der Verfolgung einer solchen realen Friedenspolitik Hand in Hand mit dem uns befreundeten Italien gehen. Das rechtfertigt die Hoffnung, daß wir auch mit den anderen Regierungen zu einer freundschaftlichen Verständigung über die wichtigen aktuellen Fragen der Außenpolitik gelangen.

„Mit den Grundsätzen unserer inneren und äußeren Politik sind auch alle Fragen des Auslandsdeutschtums ein für allemal geklärt. Nun weiß jeder Auslandsdeutsche, daß er auch im fremden Lande ein lebendiges Mitglied der deutschen Volksgemeinschaft bleibt. Er weiß, daß er für sich und seine Interessen auf den sicheren Schutz seines Heimatstaates vertrauen kann. Er wird dafür auch die Verpflichtung in sich fühlen, Teil seines Volkes zu bleiben und ihm nach Kräften zu dienen.

„Da ihm infolge der räumlichen Trennung die unmittelbare Teilnahme am innerstaatlichen Leben in
Deutschland versagt ist, soll und wird er umso stärker von
dem Bedürfnis getragen werden, den inneren Zusammenhang mit dem völkischen Leben zu
wahren, das sich in der Heimat entfaltet.

„Wenn es so eine Selbstverständlichkeit war, daß das
gewaltige Geschehen in Deutschland, die Neugestaltung unseres innenpolitischen Lebens, nicht ohne Rückwirkung auf
die jenseits unserer Grenzen lebenden Reichsdeutschen
bleiben konnte, ist es kaum begreiflich, wie man in gewissen
Teilen des Auslandes Anstoß daran hat nehmen können,
daß auch unter den Auslandsdeutschen der Wunsch lebendig
wurde, an der Neugestaltung der Dinge im Reich innerlich
Anteil zu nehmen und diese Anteilnahme durch einen Zusammenschluß mit anderen gleichgesinnten Volksgenossen
Ausdruck zu geben.

„Es ist, wenn auch nur in einzelnen Ländern, dazu gekommen, daß man den dort lebenden Reichsangehörigen
jede Bekundung ihrer nationalsozialistischen Gesinnung hat
verbieten, und daß man sie daran hat verhindern wollen,
sich auf der Grundlage ihrer gemeinsamen politischen
Ueberzeugung als Vereinigungen zu konstituieren.

„Ein solches Vorgehen läßt sich nur aus einer völligen
Verkennung der Absichten und Ziele erklären, die von den
örtlichen Organisationen der Deutschen im Ausland selbst,
wie auch von den für ihre Betreuung zuständigen heimischen
Stellen verfolgt werden. Wir wissen selbstverständlich und
sind die Letzten, daran deuteln zu wollen, daß das Gastrecht,
das fremden Staatsangehörigen in einem Lande gewährt
wird, sie verpflichtet, sich jeder Einmischung in die inneren
Verhältnisse des Gastlandes auf das strikteste zu enthalten
und die dort geltenden allgemeinen Gesetze zu beobachten.

„Geschieht das aber, so kann ihnen nicht versagt werden,
sich auf der Grundlage und zum Zwecke der Bekundung gemeinsamer nationaler Einstellung zu Gemeinschaften zu-
sammenzuschließen und mit den heimischen Organisationen
in Verbindung zu treten.

„Die Einsetzung eines Chefs der Auslands-
organisation im Auswärtigen Amt, die der
Führer zu Beginn dieses Jahres verordnet hat, ist nicht
nur ein sichtbares Zeichen für die Einheit von Partei und Staat, sondern auch eine Gewähr dafür, daß
die von den verantwortlichen innerdeutschen Stellen für die
Pflege des Auslandsdeutschtums aufgestellten Grundsätze
und Richtlinien sich in den von mir soeben angegebenen
Grenzen halten und von den auslandsdeutschen Organisationen selbst genau respektiert werden.

„Ich hoffe deshalb auf das bestimmteste, daß die
Schwierigkeiten, die in dieser Beziehung hier und da im
Ausland entstanden sind, nun bald für immer verschwinden.

So wenig wie wir daran denken, uns über die allgemein
anerkannten Regeln des Fremdenrechts hinwegzusetzen,
ebensowenig werden wir zulassen, daß Auslandsdeutsche
wegen ihrer nationalsozialistischen Einstellung von fremden
Regierungen unter eine Art von Ausnahmerecht gestellt
werden.

„Wenn Sie, meine lieben Auslandsdeutschen, jetzt in
das Land Ihres Aufenthalts zurückkehren, werden Sie, des
bin ich sicher, die in Deutschland und vor allem hier in
Stuttgart empfangenen Eindrücke sowohl den anderen
Volksgenossen dort draußen, als auch den Ihnen zugäng-
lichen Ausländern übermitteln. Seien Sie dort draußen
Zeugen für das große Geschehen in Deutschland, für den
Neuaufbau des Reichs, für seine Wiedererstarkung und zugleich für seinen unverbrüchlichen Friedenswillen.

„Bleiben Sie immer der Ehre bewußt, Mitglied der
deutschen Volksgemeinschaft, und jeder Einzelne von Ihnen
ihr Repräsentant in der Fremde zu sein. Seien Sie einig
unter sich, und erweisen Sie Ihrem Gastland dieselbe Achtung, die wir selbst überall für Deutschland fordern.
Dann werden Sie wichtige und wertvolle Mitarbeit leisten
an dem Werke unseres Führers Adolf Hitler und an unserem unter ihm geeinten geliebten deutschen Vaterland."

Reichsaußenminister von Neurath, der bereits während
seiner Rede wiederholt lebhaften Beifall und weiteste Zustimmung gefunden hatte, wurde zum Schluß mit stürmischen Heilrufen gefeiert.

Fanfaren der Hitler-Jugend leiteten über zu der Rede
des Stellvertreters des Führers,

Rudolf Heß,

der bei seinem Erscheinen auf der Rednertribüne mit minutenlangen, stürmischen Heilrufen empfangen wurde.

Rudolf Heß führte aus:

„Meine deutschen Volksgenossen und Volksgenossinnen!
Deutsche Seefahrer!

„Ihr steht vor mir als Ausschnitt der großen deutschen
Volksgemeinschaft — der Volksgemeinschaft, die sich über
die Grenzen unseres Reiches hinaus erstreckt, denn der
Nationalsozialismus hat nicht nur im Inlande über alle
Klassen und Stände hinweg eine Volksgemeinschaft geschaffen, wie sie vordem unbekannt war, sondern er hat einbezogen die deutschen Volksgenossen im Auslande. Er hat
sie zu bewußten und stolzen Gliedern dieser Volksgemeinschaft gemacht! Und der Inlandsdeutsche rechnet die
Deutschen draußen heute selbstverständlich zu sich gehörig,
obwohl noch wenige Jahre vordem die große Masse unseres
Volkes kaum etwas von ihnen wußte.

„Es gab einst eine Zeit, da der Auslandsdeutsche in der
Heimat auf ein geradezu verletzendes Unverständnis stieß
ob der Mission, die er in der Fremde erfüllt. Mit so vielen
Wandlungen ist auch hier eine Wandlung eingetreten: die
alte Heimat, die zum neuen Deutschland geworden ist, hat
Euch, meine auslandsdeutschen Volksgenossen, empfangen
mit offenen Armen, mit offenen Herzen. Sie heißt Euch
willkommen als Angehörige nicht nur der deutschen Volksgemeinschaft, sondern der großen Schicksalsgemeinschaft.
Denn gemeinsam ist unser Schicksal. Mit Deutschlands
Niedergang sank auch Euer Stern. Da Deutschland der
Verachtung anheimfiel, schwand auch Euer Ansehen. Jetzt
aber, da das neue Deutschland stolz und stark vor der Welt
steht, jetzt könnt auch Ihr wieder Euer Haupt hoch tragen,
wenn Ihr Euch zu Deutschland bekennt. Deutschlands Ehre
ist auch Eure Ehre!

„Mit gleichem Selbstbewußtsein dürft Ihr Euch hier in
der Heimat als A u s l a n d s deutsche bekennen. Wo Ihr
auch hinkommt, überall weiß man in diesem neuen Deutschland, daß unter denen, die einst hinausgingen, die besten
waren. Sie gingen hinaus in eine ungewisse Fremde, ein
ungewisses Schicksal auf sich zu nehmen, weil der Raum zu
eng war in der Heimat. Und draußen mußten sie sich wiederum in schwerem Daseinskampf durchringen. Viele gingen
unter, viele aber siegten. Sie und ihre Nachkommen wurden
bewußt oder unbewußt zur Stütze des Deutschtums, rangen
der Welt Anerkennung für sich und damit für Deutschland
ab. Manche machten ihr Glück, brachten es zu Ansehen und
Wohlhabenheit.

„Bis dann die furchtbare Katastrophe des Weltkrieges
mit ihren Folgen über Deutschland kam; bis unzählige von
ihnen verloren, was sie so schwer erkämpften, und zugleich
verloren die Achtung der anderen. Es war damals bitter
schwer, Deutscher zu sein und sich Deutscher zu nennen! Wir
wissen, daß die meisten von Euch, meine Auslandsdeutschen,
trotzdem zu Deutschland hielten oder gerade deshalb zu
Deutschland hielten, weil Deutschland arm und verachtet war.
Und das danken wir diesen Auslandsdeutschen, daß sie „im
Unglück erst recht" zu Deutschland standen, trotz aller Schmä-
hungen, oft trotz Verfolgungen und Entrechtungen!

„Ich weiß, was auch Ihr deutschen Seefahrer in den
Zeiten der Schmach gelitten, wenn Ihr als Sendboten der
Heimat in der Fremde weiltet.

„Wie leicht ist es demgegenüber heute, sich Deutscher zu
nennen! Mögen sie uns da und dort noch hassen — wenn
der Haß nur gepaart ist mit Achtung!

„Schlimmer als Haß ist Mitleid, denn das Schlimmste,
was sie uns einst draußen in der Welt entgegenbringen
konnten, war das Mitleid. Heute brauchen sie kein
Mitleid mehr mit uns zu haben: das Mitleid ist in weiten
Teilen dieser gleichen Welt gewandelt in Neid und Bewunderung für den Führer, für sein Deutschland und seine
Leistungen!

„Eines wissen heute alle: das Hoffen auf den Zusammenbruch des nationalsozialistischen Regiments war vergeblich. Einst trösteten sich unsere Gegner damit: Laßt nur einige Monate, schlimmsten Falls Jahre vergehen, dann haben sie sich abgewirtschaftet! Dann ist es vorbei mit aller Hitlerei! Heute weiß die Welt: **Das nationalsozialistische Deutschland steht und wird stehen!**

„Nach der nationalsozialistischen Revolution wagten sich nur wenige Fremde in unser Land, in dieses Land, das angeblich völlig der Barbarei verfallen, in dem niemand mehr seines Lebens sicher sein sollte, in dem der Hunger wüten sollte. Und die Freunde dieser Waghalse, die zu uns kamen, waren nur erstaunt, daß diese überhaupt zurückkehrten. Und heute: die Besucher aus anderen Nationen kommen gern in unser nationalsozialistisches Deutschland. Für viele gilt es bereits als das sicherste Land der Erde — und zugleich als eines der schönsten Länder der Erde.

„**So, wie die Lügen über den kommenden Zusammenbruch, die Lügen über die Barbarei in Deutschland, sich als Lügen herausstellten, so werden sich auch die anderen Lügen über das nationalsozialistische Deutschland als Lügen entblößen. So wird auch einst die Verdächtigung, Deutschland habe kriegerische Absichten, als Lüge erkannt werden.**

„Will man in der Welt wirklich behaupten, daß allein der Besitz von Kanonen, Tanks, Flugzeugen gleichbedeutend mit kriegerischen Absichten ist? Wenn das so wäre, dann müßte die ganze übrige Welt ständig mit kriegerischen Absichten erfüllt sein. Denn die übrige Welt rüstete unausgesetzt, als Deutschland gutgläubig seine Waffen ablieferte oder zerstörte. Sicher ist: Trotz unserer Abrüstung kam der ewige Friede nicht! So wenig wie die anderen trotz aller Versprechungen selbst abrüsteten! Welcher Fairdenkende will uns verübeln, daß wir auf alle Fälle — der Sicherheit halber — uns a u c h wieder eine Rüstung zu unserem Schutz zugelegt haben?

„Und diese Rüstung dient auch der Sicherheit der Auslandsdeutschen. Ich weiß, was es für einsame Volksgenossen in der Fremde bedeutet, wenn Unruhen ihr Leben und ihre Habe bedrohen, und ein Kriegsschiff erscheint unter Deutschlands Flagge, um zu dokumentieren: h i n t e r u n s e r e m P r o t e s t s t e h t n ö t i g e n f a l l s u n s e r e M a c h t.

„Als die Bomben internationaler Friedensstörer auf unser Panzerschiff „Deutschland" fielen, hat der Führer der Welt gezeigt: Die Beleidigung des Symbols unserer Macht, die Beleidigung der Flagge und das Blut deutscher Seeleute werden gesühnt. Seit Almeria weiß die Welt, daß sie endgültig ein neues Deutschland vor sich hat! Und Ihr, meine Auslandsdeutschen, werdet die Wirkung verspürt haben und weiterhin verspüren. Die Welt hat zur Kenntnis genommen: als Parias lassen wir uns nicht wieder behandeln.

„Unter dem starken Schutz der Heimat festigt sich das Auslandsdeutschtum immer mehr. Unter der Einwirkung der Heimat schließt es sich immer mehr zusammen.

„Unter der Führung der Auslands=Organisation wird auch das Auslandsdeutschtum immer mehr von nationalsozialistischem Geist erfüllt. Die Auslands=Organisation der NSDAP. hat die noch lange nach der Machtübernahme in sich zersplitterten, in Klassengegensätzen auseinanderklaffenden Deutschen draußen zusammengeführt und sie verbunden mit dem Reiche Adolf Hitlers. Die Betreuung des Auslandsdeutschtums im nationalsozialistischen Geist erhält eine Unzahl von Deutschen der Nation, die sonst als Kulturdünger in anderen Nationen aufgingen.

„Von Zeit zu Zeit erfreut sich die Auslands=Organisation der NSDAP. der besonders liebevollen Aufmerksamkeit fremder Politiker. Nämlich der Politiker, die es gerade einmal wieder für zweckmäßig halten, wegen irgendwelcher politischer Geschäfte das Schreckgespinst der „deutschen Gefahr" an die Wand der internationalen Oeffentlichkeit zu malen. Und wie sie malen! Unser jüngster Gau der NSDAP. wird zu einer finsteren, geheimnisvollen Organisation.

„Ihr, meine Parteigenossen draußen, werdet zu Spinnen eines gewaltigen Spionagenetzes. Es ist geradezu gruselig zu hören, wie Ihr das Gift tödlicher Lehren in fremde Völker tragt und große Weltreiche von ihnen bedroht. Und es ist erschütternd zu hören, wie Ihr Armen Euch dauernd in den Zentralen der NSDAP. — morgens, mittags, abends — melden müßt, um Rechenschaft abzulegen, ich möchte fast sagen, ob Ihr gut oder schlecht geträumt habt vom Nationalsozialismus. Ganz zu schweigen von all den anderen geheimnisvollen Dingen, von denen wir selbst auch nichts wissen, die aber diese Politiker wissen, ohne sie bisher preisgegeben zu haben. Doch das wird alles noch kommen, verlaßt Euch darauf!

„Im Ernst: Scheint es auch lächerlich, so hat es doch Methode. Durch die ewig wiederholten Lügen — die schließlich dann auch manch ein ehrlich um den Frieden besorgter Mann nachspricht — soll immer von neuem das Gift des Mißtrauens zwischen die anderen Nationen und uns geträufelt werden. Die Drahtzieher wollen um den Preis jeder Lüge verhindern, daß das Vertrauen zum neuen Deutschland auch weiterhin wächst, wie es zu ihrem Leidwesen in den letzten Jahren gewachsen ist.

(Schluß auf Nr. 1160)

Verantwortlich: Kurt Schwartzkopff, Berlin-Wilmersdorf.
Druck und Verlag: Deutsches Nachrichtenbüro G. m. b. H., Berlin.

Erste Vormittags-Ausgabe.
Deutsches Nachrichtenbüro G.m.b.H.

(Als Manuskript gedruckt, Nachdruck und jede Art Verbreitung
ohne Vereinbarung untersagt. Ohne alle Gewähr.)

4. Jahrg. 1937	Berlin, Montag, 30. August	Nr. 1160

Die Tagung der Auslandsdeutschen.
(Schluß.)

„Sie wollen den Völkern einreden: Die guten Kommunisten und die harmlosen Juden, ja, die wollen Völkerverbrüderung, Freundschaft der Nationen, Freiheit der schaffenden Menschen und Frieden auf Erden! Aber die verfluchten Nazis, die haben sich verschworen, mit ihrer geheimnisvollen Organisation einen neuen Krieg zu führen, die wollen die Völker aufeinander hetzen und Mord und Brand über die Erde tragen.

„Natürlich wollen die Drahtzieher nichts anderes, als von denen ablenken, die wirklich den Frieden der Völker bedrohen. Denn wir sind es ja nicht, die Handelsvertretungen zu Zentralen der Zersetzungen der Gastvölker machen. Wir schmuggeln nicht Hetzartikel in fremden Sprachen in andere Länder. Wir organisieren nicht die Unterwelt anderer Staaten zu Stoßtrupps des Bürgerkrieges.

„Mit reinem Gewissen können wir die Erklärung abgeben: Wir wollen den Nationalsozialismus nicht anderen Völkern als Gift einträufeln! Wir wollen ihn ebensowenig anderen Völkern aufzwingen. Wir wollen ihn nicht einmal an andere Völker verschenken. Im Gegenteil: Wir sind eifersüchtig darauf bedacht, den Nationalsozialismus für uns zu behalten.

„Und glaubt man wirklich, daß wir so dumm sind, daß, wenn wir schon eine Spionageorganisation aufziehen wollten, wir dann unsere so sichtbaren Stützpunkte, Ortsgruppen und Landesgruppen draußen dazu benutzen würden?

„Wollten wir wirklich einen geheimen Nachrichtendienst in anderen Ländern uns schaffen, dann würden wir klugerweise uns Bestehendes zum Vorbild nehmen, zum Beispiel den so ausgezeichnet arbeitenden weltumspannenden Geheimdienst eines Landes, in dem unsere A. O. besonders oft dunkler Absichten verdächtigt wird.

„Die wirklichen Aufgaben der Gruppen unserer Auslands-Organisation haben sich dieser Tage erst an einem Beispiel gezeigt: In Schanghai fuhren die Angehörigen des dortigen NSKK. unter Todesverachtung in die unter Granatfeuer liegenden Stadtteile und retteten Leben und Gut vieler unserer Landsleute. Das Einstehen für einander, die Hilfe in der Not — wie sie auch in den Winterhilfsaktionen draußen zum Ausdruck kommt — das sind die Ergebnisse des Organisierens innerhalb der Auslandsdeutschen.

„Was wir durch die Auslands-Organisation weiter tun, ist nichts anderes, als was jede andere Nation auch tut: nämlich die Zusammengehörigkeit zwischen der Heimat und ihren Angehörigen draußen betonen und stärken. Wir machen das organisatorisch vielleicht gründlicher als andere — wir sind nun mal Deutsche. Aber das Ziel ist nichts anderes, als die Einheit der Söhne und Töchter unseres Reiches diesseits und jenseits der Grenze. Wenn andere auch noch so gewaltige Zeitungsartikel schreiben und noch so gewaltige Reden halten.

„Die nationalsozialistischen Deutschen sind ihren Gastländern gegenüber loyal, ebenso wie sie loyale Bürger i h r e r   e i g e n e n   H e i m a t sind.

„Wir zitieren unsere Funktionäre, die im Ausland Dienst tun, nicht nach Hause, um sie vor Gericht zu stellen, weil sie angeblich mit den Feinden „konspirierten". Unsere auslandsdeutschen Vertreter brauchen nicht zu fürchten, wenn sie nach Deutschland gerufen werden, daß die Befolgung dieses Rufes ihnen den Kopf kostet. Mit welchen Gefühlen mögen bolschewistische Auslandsvertreter die Reise in ihr gelobtes Land antreten! Und mit welchen Gefühlen kommt I h r , meine auslandsdeutschen Volksgenossen, zu uns!

„Ich weiß, wie glücklich Ihr seid, wenn Ihr kommen könnt, wenn Euch die Reise ermöglicht wird. Ich weiß, wie Ihr draußen Euch sehnt, einmal wieder gerufen oder ungerufen den Boden der Heimat zu betreten. Und ich weiß, daß jeder, der nun hier ist im neuen Deutschland, innerlich angefüllt ist von Stolz auf alles, was er an Neuem und Großem sieht, daß alle seine Erwartungen übertroffen werden. Ich weiß, daß die meisten von Euch am liebsten hier blieben, weil Euch zum Bewußtsein kommt, daß kein anderes Land der Welt so schön ist wie unser Deutschland.

„Und Ihr werdet den Reichsparteitag erleben als Kundgebung des reinsten und geballtesten Nationalsozialismus; Ihr werdet sie marschieren sehen, die SA.- und SS.-Männer, die Politischen Leiter, die Jugend, die Arbeitsdienstmänner; Ihr werdet einen Begriff bekommen von der stolzen neuen Wehrmacht. Und wenn das Glück Euch freundlich ist, werdet Ihr den Mann sehen, der Deutschland hochriß, als die Welt glaubte, Deutschland sei verloren. Ihr werdet den Mann sehen, der Deutschland rettete.

„Ihr werdet den Mann sehen, der den Führerbegriff schuf und selbst als der erste Führer mit diesem Begriff die stärkste Klammer um Deutschland und alle Deutschen der Welt legte. Ihr werdet von Angesicht sehen den Mann, der eingehen wird als einer der ganz Großen in die Geschichte.

„Auf seinen Namen weihe ich jetzt die Fahnen, die von diesem Parteitag als besonderer Gruß der Heimat, als Symbole der Verbundenheit der Deutschen auf der Welt zu unseren Parteigenossen hinausgehen.

(Kommando: „Stillgestanden! Die Fahnen hoch!")

„Euch, Symbole des neuen Glaubens und des neuen Reiches, die ihr in Kanada, in Iran, in Syrien und Paraguay, in der Schweiz und in Abessinien, in Spanien und Australien, in Bolivien und in Italien und in vielen anderen Ländern und Erdteilen wehen werdet, die ihr wehen werdet auf deutschen Schiffen, ich weihe euch:

„Fahnen des Nationalsozialismus, weht für die Ehre Deutschlands und seines Führers!

„Weht nun in der fernen Welt als Symbole des großen einigen Reiches, das Adolf Hitler schuf!

„Fahnen, ihr seid geweiht!

(Kommando: Fahnen ab!)

„Ihr, meine auslandsdeutschen Volksgenossen, und Ihr Seefahrer, wenn Ihr nun wieder an Eure Arbeit geht, wenn Ihr wieder zurückkehrt in die fremden Lande und auf Eure Schiffe, dann sagt denen draußen: Die Heimat gedenkt aller Deutschen in der Welt. Die Heimat nimmt Anteil an ihrem Schicksal, nimmt Anteil an ihrem Leid, an ihrer Not, — wo immer sie als Deutsche stehen.

„Nehmt die Gewißheit mit hinaus: Die Heimat vergißt Euch draußen nicht; denn Ihr seid ein Teil von uns! Sagt draußen, daß Ihr das Land Eurer Väter gesehen, und daß es größer und stolzer ist, als Ihr es erträumtet. Geht hinaus und berichtet: Deutschland lebt und wird leben, weil ein Adolf Hitler lebt und weil ein Gott im Himmel lebt, der mit Deutschland ist.

„Wir grüßen den Führer:

„Adolf Hitler — Sieg-Heil!"

Von 80 000 Volksgenossen diesseits und jenseits der Grenzen jubelnd aufgenommen, ertönte der Gruß und das Gelöbnis an den Führer.

Die größte bisherige Kundgebung des Auslandsdeutschtums hatte damit ihr Ende erreicht.

DOCUMENT 26–A

(Translation)

DEUTSCHES NACHRICHTENBÜRO (OFFICIAL GERMAN NEWS AGENCY), FIRST, SECOND, AND THIRD MORNING BULLETINS, AND FIRST FORE-NOON BULLETIN, BERLIN, AUGUST 30, 1937

ANNUAL ASSEMBLY OF GERMANS LIVING ABROAD

Stuttgart, August 29. The City of Germans Abroad has been receiving its guests from all over the world. On Saturday special trains arrived from Berlin, Hamburg, and Milan.

. . . . . .

In the evening the Foreign Organization of the NSDAP held a reception for the press in the former Parliament Building. The Director of the Foreign Organization's Press Office, *Beinhauer*, welcomed the members of the press to the Fifth Annual Assembly of Germans Living Abroad, in the name of the Director of the NSDAP's Foreign Organization, Gauleiter *Bohle*. The speaker stated that since its beginning the Foreign Organization has issued to its members the following guide for conduct: "Let the politics of the country where you are residing be determined by its inhabitants; the politics of a foreign country don't concern you at all. Don't meddle in them, even in conversation."

These principles are suited to clarify completely the view of the Foreign Organization. The task of the Foreign Organization involves the care of Germans abroad, i.e. of Germans in foreign countries who possess German citizenship. And it is self-evident that the German citizen living outside of the German borders ought not to be forgotten by the German homeland.

The reception was closed with expressions of gratitude from Dr. *Dresler*, national office chief in the NSDAP's Press Office. He characterized the press as one of the most important connecting links between the homeland and Germandom abroad and wished the Fifth Assembly complete success.

. . . . . .

. . . The significance of the Fifth Assembly was especially emphasized by the presence of an extremely large number of guests of honor, at their head the Führer's Deputy, Reich's Minister *Rudolf Hess*, who, as he entered the hall with Reich's Foreign Minister *von Neurath*, Director of the Foreign Organization Gauleiter *Bohle*, and

Governor and Gauleiter *Murr*, was greeted by the masses with cries of "Heil" for several minutes.

Among the guests of honor was the widow of *Wilhelm Gustloff*, the murdered leader of the Switzerland party group; Ambassador *von Ribbentrop*, and a majority of the German Ambassadors and Ministers; State-Secretary *Mackensen;* the Commander of the Fifth Army Corps, Infantry General *Geyer;* Deputy Gauleiter and Director of the NSDAP's Main Schooling Office, *Schmidt;* the members of the Württemberg government; representatives of the party and its formations; the Chief Mayor of Stuttgart, *Strölin;* as well as leaders and officers of the Foreign Organization.

Gauleiter and Governor *Murr* pointed out that it was the first time that the members of the NSDAP's Foreign Organization had met in Stuttgart, the City of Germans Abroad. . . .

He thanked Gauleiter Bohle for having decided to hold the great meetings of the Foreign Organization always in Stuttgart in the future. Stuttgart does not thereby come into contact with Germandom abroad for the first time. Rather the ties to Germans all over the world have been cultivated to a special degree from Stuttgart and Württemberg.

Gauleiter Murr expressed the wish that these days, full of work and fetes, of our brothers and sisters from all over the world might become a great experience so that they could all take back home the certainty that the children of Mother Germania have never been able to profess with such great pride as now under Adolf Hitler's leadership the fact of being German.

Chief Mayor Dr. Strölin, the President of the Deutsches Ausland-Institut, thereupon welcomed most cordially the guests of honor and the Germans from abroad who had come to Stuttgart for the meeting. In his address, he pointed out that the Führer had designated Stuttgart as the City of Germans Abroad. The city is deeply conscious of the great obligations ensuing therefrom. The people of Stuttgart will do everything so that this city may truly become for Germans abroad the image of solidarity with the home soil and the epitome of everything which is truly German.

In this sense the flags of the Third Reich greeted them here in the City of Germans Abroad.

But the flags of the country, in which they have found a home, also greeted them. It is therewith to be emphasized that the German citizens abroad have the honest and sincere will to stand in loyal relations to their host countries.

Chief Mayor Dr. Strölin . . . concluded with the wish that guests and hosts might be fused in these days into a unity of national will:

"May a German consciousness, a German will, an ardent love of our Führer encompass us. That is our wish for these days, that is my greeting of welcome to the German racial comrades from all over the world!"

Gauleiter Bohle, greeted with great applause, then stepped on the platform and spoke as follows:

"Once a year the Foreign Organization of the National Socialist Party holds a Reich's Assembly for Germans Living Abroad. Once a year the entire Germandom abroad, and with it German navigation, wants to make *a pledge of allegiance to the Führer and his Reich.*

"The Fifth Assembly, which we solemnly begin today, is being held this year for the first time in our city, 'the City of Germans Abroad'. We are deeply conscious of this obligation, and we want therewith to express our gratitude to the Führer, while we celebrate these days in the 'City of Germans Abroad' in a worthy and German way.

.   .   .   .   .   .

"It is for us all a gratifying and at the same time fortifying feeling to see that we today are no longer alone with our cares, needs, and wishes but rather that leading men from the party and the state and from the newly created army have come here among us in order to be together with us and to show us thus that we belong to the great unity which is called 'Germany'.

"On such days our thoughts must reach back into the past. Neither before the World War, nor thereafter, was there a unity, or even an attempt at a unified direction, of Germandom abroad. And there was just as little understanding from people at home for those who had left their fatherland and everywhere in the wide world stood as sincere Germans.

"Although before the war we had a strong and mighty Reich, and the name of Germany had weight in the world, the Germans abroad and the seamen not only did not have full rights but were also Germans of second class. Not only the Germans abroad themselves knew this, but above all the citizens of the foreign states in which these Germans abroad lived felt this as well."

[An account is then given of the conditions among Germans abroad after the war, characterized by class differences, innumerable social clubs, and scant consciousness of their homeland.]

"*It was the first party comrades abroad, who made the attempt in 1931 to alter these conditions. I believe myself able to say that the Foreign Organization, in the six years which have passed since the beginning of our activity in foreign countries, has brought about a thorough change in all spheres, even if, as we know, there is still very much work ahead of us. Our entire activity is only possible on the basis of the Führer's idea* [Weltanschauung].

"Without the Führer and his conception, which takes hold of and encompasses all Germans, it would be senseless to attempt unification of Germandom abroad. The German racial community [*Volksgemeinschaft*], preached by Adolf Hitler, was the only basis on which a unification of Germandom abroad could have taken place.   It is necessary to keep this fact in mind, when on looking back we confirm how differently it looks today out there in comparison with the previous period.

"Through its Foreign Organization the party has been able to bring innumerable Germans abroad to the homeland and to show these Germans that they belong to this homeland, are bound and obligated to it.

"*When national holidays are celebrated in the Reich today, then we know that the Germans in foreign countries are celebrating these days in the same spirit, and that all Germans are taking part therein.*"

[Mention is then made of the success of the Winter Relief collections among Germans abroad, of the charitable activities within the German colonies, and of the "Strength Through Joy" activities.]

"In a cordial collaboration with the official representatives, the Foreign Organization devotes its best energies for every single racial comrade and therewith gives the whole world the indubitable proof that the Germans in foreign countries have comprehended and transformed into the deed, among one another, the idea of National Socialist solidarity, just as is the case in the Reich.

.   .   .   .

"The work of the many groups and societies has taken on a *new significance* through the all-encompassing activity of the party's groups abroad, and this work has been shaped in a more fruitful way for the community.

.   .   .   .

"With this presupposition, our societies in foreign countries, which in part have existed for decades and, as one ought to acknowledge, have in many cases performed excellent work for Germandom, constitute an extremely valuable support of the entire work in Germandom abroad.

.   .   .   .

"The picture, which is offered you today, by and large gives the best survey of the successful work of our party comrades abroad, who, despite the burdens of their occupations, despite unfavorable climatic conditions, and despite much hostility, are calmly engaged in bringing even the last citizen of this Reich *into the national community* [Volksgemeinschaft].

.   .   .   .

"*By his decree on the fourth anniversary of the seizure of power, through which a chief of the Foreign Organization was installed in the Foreign Office, the Führer has shown to the whole Germandom abroad how great and all-encompassing is his understanding for their affairs and their concerns.   This decree, however, also means a recognition of the work which our party comrades have accomplished in and on Germandom abroad in the past years.*

.   .   .   .

"Whoever lives in foreign countries as a German businessman, is working not only for himself and his family but, according to the conception of the new Germany, primarily for his people.

". . . If we speak of our Germans abroad, i.e. of our German citizens in foreign countries, we understand thereby exclusively the National Socialists living abroad. Among the National Socialists living abroad, however, we do not at all mean merely the party comrades but rather *all Germans who are loyal to the Reich.* It will also not be possible to make a difference between Germans in foreign countries and National Socialists, because today both represent one concept.

. . . .

"We foreign German National Socialists reject the conception of the universal German, whose prime endeavor is to adapt himself everywhere, because this universal German not only makes himself ridiculous among the foreigners but also consciously or unconsciously repudiates his Germanism with this self-abandonment.

"We acknowledge only the concept of the total German, who as a citizen of his country is always and everywhere German and nothing but German and therewith National Socialist.

. . . .

"The attempts to make it appear as if National Socialists abroad were exclusively spies or political agents—principally as the last attempt at a discrimination—one sees recently even in newspapers which want to be taken seriously. It is amusing to read that Germany is training all housemaids abroad as spies and that the Nazi men themselves have as their chief task to transform the foreign countries concerned into Hitler-colonies.

"Because there are still people in foreign countries who believe such things, I should like here especially to assure them that we are not training the housemaids as spies and that we have not ordered the Nazis living abroad to conquer foreign countries.

. . . .

"After four years of National Socialist rule, the world knows today, whether it admits it gladly or not, that Adolf Hitler and his country have no more ardent wish than to live in peace and harmony with all peoples. The Germans living abroad share this wish in their innermost hearts.

"I should like therefore to state clearly that the tasks and the activities of the Foreign Organization lie with complete clarity before the eyes of everyone. What is self-evident for other great nations we are doing also. We concern ourselves with our citizens in foreign countries and only with our citizens, and we care for their connection with the Reich and for the maintenance of their Germanism.

"That this care is a comprehensive one lies grounded in the new ideas which Adolf Hitler has given to the German people. The first law for the German National Socialists abroad prescribes an exact respect for the laws of the country where they are residing, and the party and the Reich wish carefully to see that this law is kept.

"We must demand, however, just as strongly, that the German in a foreign country may organize his own life according to the principles which are valid in his own land.

.   .   .   .

"My German racial comrades from abroad, men and women! Comrades of the sea!

"You have come to Stuttgart in order to show the whole world your allegiance to this Germany. The Reich is happy about this allegiance and thanks you and furthermore all those, who live out there in the world, for the loyalty which they maintain toward the Reich.

.   .   .   .

"This is to be the meaning of our assembly: The Germans living abroad are, before the world, the most effective and self-evident witnesses for the most proud and sacred profession of faith that we know, for the profession, *I am a German*. I therewith declare the Fifth Assembly of Germans Living Abroad opened in 1937 in the 'City of Germans Living Abroad'."

With a threefold "Sieg Heil" to the Führer and Reich's Chancelor Adolf Hitler, the thousands concurred with enthusiasm. The singing of the national anthems concluded the impressive ceremony.

.   .   .   .

The first great demonstration, which was held Sunday afternoon in the Adolf Hitler Stadium, was an impressive experience of the feeling of solidarity of all Germans, within and without the borders of the Reich. Not less than 80,000 racial comrades, among them thousands of Germans from abroad, had gathered together in the stadium to hear Rudolf Hess speak.

[In his opening words at the demonstration, Gauleiter Bohle read a telegram which had been sent to the Führer. Its wording was as follows:]

"My Führer! At the beginning of the Fifth Assembly of Germans Living Abroad, the Germans from all over the world gathered here in Stuttgart render you a proud and joyous greeting. This, the largest meeting of Germans living abroad, is animated by an unqualified loyalty to you, my Führer, and to your Reich. In our allegiance to National Socialism, in the unlimited love of our newly arisen homeland, we Germans living abroad include that respect for foreign traditions which proves the incontrovertible German will for peace."

[In his address at this meeting, the German Foreign Minister, Baron von Neurath, stated in part:]

"All of the questions of Germandom abroad have been clarified once and for all by the principles of our internal and foreign policy. Every German living abroad now knows that even in a foreign country he remains a living member of the German national community. He knows that he can count on the sure protection of his home state for himself and his interests. He will in return also feel within himself the obligation to remain a part of his people and to serve it according to his powers.

"Since on account of the physical separation he is denied direct participation in the internal political life of Germany, he ought to and will feel all the more strongly the need to maintain an inner *connection with the national life* which is unfolding in the homeland.

.   .   .   .

"It has occurred, although only in a few countries, that German citizens living abroad have been forbidden any manifestation of their National Socialist convictions, and that men have sought to prevent them from forming associations on the basis of their political views.

"Such a proceeding may only be explained by a complete misunderstanding of the purposes and goals which are pursued by the local organizations of Germans in foreign countries and also by the home offices dealing with their affairs.   We know, of course, and we are the last to seek to put any false interpretation on it, that the hospitality which is granted foreign citizens in a country obligates them to abstain strictly from any meddling in the internal affairs of the foreign country and obligates them to observe the general laws prevailing there.

.   .   .   .

"The installation of a chief of the Foreign Organization in the Foreign Office, which the Führer decreed at the beginning of this year, is not only a visible sign of the unity of party and state but also a guaranty for the fact that the principles and directives issued by the responsible German offices attending to matters of Germandom abroad will keep within the above-mentioned bounds and will be exactly observed by the organizations of Germans abroad.

.   .   .   .

"When you, my dear Germans from abroad, return now to the countries in which you reside, you will, I am sure, transmit the impressions received in Germany, and above all here in Stuttgart, both to the other racial comrades out there as well as to the foreigners to whom you have access.   Bear testimony out there for the great events in Germany, for the reconstruction of the Reich, for its restrengthening, and at the same time for its inviolable will for peace.

"Remain always conscious of the honor of being a member of the German national community, and let every single one of you be a representative of it in the foreign world.   Be united among yourselves, and show the country where you live the same respect which we ourselves everywhere demand for Germany.   Then you will be accomplishing important and valuable collaboration in the work of our Führer, Adolf Hitler, and for our beloved fatherland united by him."

[In the subsequent address Rudolf Hess, the Führer's Deputy, stated in part:]

"My German racial comrades, men and women!   German seamen!

"You stand before me as a slice of the great German racial community, the racial community which extends beyond the borders of our Reich, for National Socialism has not only at home created a national community transcending all classes and groups in a way previously unknown, but it has also included German racial comrades in foreign countries. It has made them conscious and proud members of this racial community! And the Germans within Germany today take for granted that the Germans out there belong to them, although only a few years ago the great mass of our people hardly knew anything about them.

.   .   .   .   .   .

"Under the leadership of the Foreign Organization, Germandom abroad is also becoming more and more *filled with the National Socialist spirit.* The Foreign Organization of the NSDAP has brought together the Germans out there, who even long after the seizure of power were disunited and split by class differences, and joined them with Adolf Hitler's Reich. The National Socialist care for Germandom abroad is maintaining an enormous number of Germans for the nation, who otherwise would be absorbed as cultural fertilizer for other nations.

"From time to time the Foreign Organization of the NSDAP enjoys the especially loving attention of foreign politicians. . . . Our youngest party Gau is made to appear a sinister secret organization.

"You, my party comrades abroad, become spiders in the enormous network of espionage. It is really frightening to hear how you bear the poison of fatal doctrines to foreign peoples and how great world empires are threatened by you, and it is terrifying to hear how you poor fellows must constantly report at the central offices of the NSDAP, morning, afternoon, and evening, in order to report, I would almost like to say, whether you have had a good or bad dream about National Socialism. Not to speak of all the other secret things, of which we ourselves know nothing, but which these politicians know, although they have not yet told them.

.   .   .   .   .   .

". . . The good Communists and the harmless Jews, why, they want brotherhood among the peoples, the friendship of nations, freedom of the working-man, and peace on earth! But the accursed Nazis, they have sworn with their secret organization to carry on a new war, they want to stir the peoples up against one another and carry fire and murder over all the earth.

"Naturally the wirepullers want nothing else than to divert attention from those who really threaten the peace of the nations. For it is not *we* who use our commercial offices as agencies for the disintegration of the nations who are our hosts. *We* do not smuggle inflammatory articles in foreign languages into other countries. *We* are not organizing the underworld of other states as the storm troops of civil war.

"*We can declare with a pure conscience: We do not want National Socialism to trickle into other peoples as poison! We likewise do not wish to force it on other peoples. We do not even want to give it away to other peoples. On the contrary: We are jealously concerned to keep National Socialism for ourselves.*

"Does one really believe that we are so dumb, that if we wanted to set up an organization for espionage, we would then use for this purpose our so visible branches, local groups, and country groups abroad?

.   .   .   .   .   .

"The National Socialist Germans are loyal to the country where they reside just as they are loyal citizens *of their own homeland.*

.   .   .   .   .

"I know how happy you were when you were able to come, when the trip was made possible for you. I know how you out there yearn, summoned or unsummoned, to tread once again the soil of the homeland. And I know that each one who is now here in the new Germany is innerly filled with pride about everything new and great which he sees; I know that all his expectations are being surpassed. I know that most of you would prefer to remain here, because you become cognizant of the fact that no other country of the world is as beautiful as our Germany.

"And you will experience the Reich's party congress as a demonstration of the purest and most concentrated National Socialism. You will see them march, the SA and SS, the political leaders, the youth, the labor service. You will get an idea of the proud new Army. And if you are lucky enough, you will see the man who has raised up Germany, when the world believed that Germany was lost. You will see the man who saved Germany.

"You will see the man who created the idea of the Führer, and who himself as the first Führer has put with this idea the strongest clamp around Germany and all the Germans of the world. You will see the face of the man who will count as one of the few great figures in history.

In his name I now consecrate the flags which go out to our party comrades from this party meeting as a special greeting of the homeland, as a symbol of the solidarity of the Germans of the world."

(Command: "Halt! Up with the flags!")

"You, symbols of the new faith and of the new Reich, which will wave in Canada, in Iran, in Syria, in Paraguay, in Switzerland, and in Abyssinia, in Spain and Australia, in Bolivia and in Italy, and in many other countries and continents, you that will wave on German ships, I consecrate you!

"Flags of National Socialism, wave for the honor of Germany and its Führer!

"Wave now far off in the world as a symbol of the great united Reich which Adolf Hitler created!

"Flags, you are consecrated!"

(Command: "Flags down!")

"You, my German racial comrades from abroad, and you seamen, when you now return to your work, when you again return

*to the foreign countries and to your ships, then say to those out
there: The homeland is thinking of all the Germans in the world.
The homeland participates in your destiny, participates in your
suffering, in your need—wherever you stand as Germans.*

*"Take this certainty along with you out there: The homeland
does not forget you out there, for you are a part of us! Say out
there that you have seen the land of your fathers and that it is
greater and prouder than you had dreamed. Go abroad and report: Germany lives and will live, because an Adolf Hitler lives
and because a God lives in Heaven who is with Germany.*

"We greet the Führer:

"Adolf Hitler—Sieg Heil!"

The *greeting* and the *pledge of allegiance to the Führer* resounded,
jubilantly received by the 80,000 racial comrades from this side of and
beyond our borders.

The greatest demonstration hitherto held of Germandom abroad
was therewith concluded.

DOCUMENT 27
(Translation)

Wir Deutsche in der Welt (We Germans in the World), Published by the VDVA (League of German Societies Abroad): Berlin, 1937

EVERY GERMAN NATIONAL ABROAD IS A FULLY OBLIGATED SERVANT OF THE NATION AND OF THE FÜHRER

By Gauleiter E. W. Bohle

The address delivered by the leader of the Foreign Organization of the Nazi Party, Gauleiter E. W. Bohle, at the Harvest Festival of the German colony at Vienna on October 24, 1936, is directed to all German nationals abroad. Gauleiter E. W. Bohle has made the text of the address available for inclusion in the yearbook *Wir Deutsche in der Welt* (*We Germans in the World*).

It has always been a special pleasure for me to be able to speak in the Reich and abroad about my German brothers and sisters in foreign countries.

I must confess, however, that it is difficult for me to tell you today how extraordinarily I rejoice from the depths of my heart to be able to speak to you all today for the first time in this beautiful German city.

I can immediately return your hearty welcome with a pleasure for you; Adolf Hitler has commissioned me to transmit to all of you his particularly hearty greetings and best wishes.

In these greetings of the Führer, the greetings and best wishes of the entire Reich are included.

Particularly to us German nationals who live outside of the borders of our fatherland, the most wonderful thing about this new Reich is that the Führer and his state feel themselves bound to every single citizen of the Reich, including those abroad, and constantly give expression to this community of fate by word and deed.

Today things are different from formerly. Today the German abroad has been firmly placed in the great structure of destiny of the united nation which Adolf Hitler has created in long years of struggle for the German man.

Today every German national abroad knows that he is not abandoned and forgotten, that he does not hold a lost outpost, but is valued as a worthy member of a great community. *Today every German national abroad is a wholly equal and fully obligated servant of his nation and his Führer.*

355

As we celebrate the Harvest Festival of the German people here in Vienna, we are filled with a deep gratitude to Providence, which gave an Adolf Hitler to the German people. As in all other fields it is also thanks exclusively to the work of the Führer that today in Germany the German peasant has again become the respected nourisher of his people and has been able to insure this nourishment of the nation.

Today German peasants again work on German soil for their German nation. They harvest the blessing which the Almighty bestowed on the will of Adolf Hitler.

In the deep faith in Adolf Hitler and his movement, German peasants bow down in gratitude to the goodness of the Almighty. That is the meaning of the Thanksgiving Festival of the new Germany. The joy which is evidenced by such a holiday of the people is greater, particularly here in Vienna, by the fact that a few months ago the Führer of the Reich and the Chancelor of the Austrian brother state gave visible expression to the community of fate of both countries.

That we can be together here today to celebrate in so ceremonious and happy a manner an honored day of the nation is thanks to the agreement of July 11 of this year.

Our thanks are due particularly to the statesmen of Austria for proclaiming to all the world the German character of their country and thereby preparing the end of an unholy fraternal strife.

Just as deep and great, however, as the joy in the Reich and in Austria about this was the disappointment, and one can fairly say the anger, of those for whom the strife between the two German countries was a condition for the success of their dark political intrigues. And so once again in the very rich and agitated history of German men, the German method could not fail and proved itself victorious for the welfare of the German way.

It seems to me that it would be quite incidental to have to speak here in Vienna of the friendly feelings of the people of the Reich for our Austrian racial comrades.

As German nationals we have friendly feelings toward, and a benevolent understanding of, foreign peoples close to us politically, economically, and ideologically. But what stirs us German nationals in our deepest thoughts about the German people in Austria is not friendship but love. I know, therefore, that you, my German nationals in Austria, feel so well and so at home here as nowhere else outside of the borders of the Reich. It is true that you are guests in another country, but the same pulse beat of the German heart binds you to your hosts, and many Germans abroad are very jealous of you for this reason.

Today's celebration of the German nationals in Vienna gives me a welcome opportunity to explain to the whole world the tasks which have been assigned to the Foreign Organization of the National Socialist movement by the Führer, and for which I am responsible as the responsible Gauleiter of the millions of German nationals abroad.

In view of the complexity of foreign Germandom, it is naturally extraordinarily difficult to formulate regulations and rules of conduct which are applicable to all German nationals abroad.

Such uniformity in the work of the Foreign Organization is not simple because, in the first place, the first requirement of our work is based always and everywhere on the necessity and on our serious determination to observe most strictly the laws of the host countries. Just as I have repeatedly announced this basic principle of my organization, so I will declare unambiguously here today in Vienna that every German national abroad, regardless of whether he is a member of the party or not, has the primary duty of keeping out of things which do not concern the Reich. I never permit our German nationals abroad to become involved in the internal political affairs of other countries. Whoever violates this rule is removed without further consideration from our ranks. This position is not based merely on the self-evident respect for the laws of other countries, for we Nazis place great emphasis on being considered model guests in all countries.

I mean that the Nazi ideology, as the bearer of the new German state, is suited as hardly any other to promote and to deepen consideration and respect for the views of others.

The new Germany has announced countless times to the world that we National Socialists desire nothing more than to be able to build up our new state in quiet and peace.

In view of the overwhelming volume of tasks faced by our country, which for 15 years was despised, humbled, and practically plundered, it is not surprising that this wish dominates everyone.

Adolf Hitler has raised the new Germany in a great political march of victory which is without precedent in the history of the world.

Amazing things have been achieved in all fields of public and private life.

We in the Reich know, however, very well that the unheard-of sins of the past cannot be entirely overcome in a few years and that in the future also, therefore, we require all our strength in order to establish the new German nation to the final detail.

German unity, which Adolf Hitler gave us, is the wonderful realization of the old dream of German men for hundreds and thousands of years.

Today the people of the Reich already stand as a single bloc of confidence and faith before our eyes.

In contrast to the internal dissension which formerly existed, as with no other nation on the earth, we can today say with unrestrained pride that a united German people stands behind a German flag for a single great Führer and his historic leadership to the end.

Where formerly countless small states with their conflicting interests, their petty jealousies, and their complete helplessness existed, today we have a Reich. This Reich represents our entire yearning, our entire will, and our eternal loyalty.

This Reich, however, is something which affects every single citizen of the Reich. Millions of these citizens, however, live outside of the boundaries of the Reich but are no less obligated to the Reich and are also no less loyal to it. For just as the foreign Germans can justly demand that Germany accept them forever and everywhere, the Reich can expect that its citizens abroad do not consider themselves on furlough from their duties of citizenship.

The political philosophy which made National Socialism the foundation of the new state-structure prescribes that every single racial comrade of the Reich place himself in the service of the nation for his entire life. One cannot represent the view that certain persons in the Government or in the administration or in the party will achieve the development of the new Germany, for this new Germany has only arisen because a great German has called the whole people to cooperate. The world has repeatedly been able to establish unquestionably with what passion and what deep faith the German people has joyfully followed the call of its Führer. For the Foreign Organization of the NSDAP and for me, as its responsible leader, it is a particular pleasure to be able to say after only a few years that the unconditional will to cooperation with the new state has overcome and swept along every single German national regardless of all boundaries and unto the farthest corners of the earth.

In this way the Foreign Organization has found the correct synthesis between the duties of the homeland in respect to Germans abroad and the duties of the Germans abroad in respect to the fatherland.

In this, the Foreign Organization has followed wholly new paths; it has deliberately turned aside from the old unsuitable idea of the pure protection of foreign Germandom, a protection which is of no use to the Reich and in one way or another must give Germans abroad the feeling of not belonging to the people of the Reich in the same measure as a racial comrade in the Reich itself.

For a master race, however, a protection of this kind would be humiliating. The Foreign Organization has, therefore, deliberately begun its work by placing upon foreign Germandom obligations to the new Reich, and it is a cause of pride for our German nationals beyond the borders that almost all of them have joyfully accepted these obligations.

Not all circles of Germans abroad were sympathetic to the establishment of the Foreign Organization.

But we did not allow ourselves for that reason to be misled in our work for a single second and have consoled ourselves with the thought that Adolf Hitler and the National Socialist movement in the Reich were not desired and were burdensome to many people for many years.

In the Fourth Reich's Congress of Foreign Germans in Erlangen I characterized the Foreign Organization as the dynamic force which pumped fresh air into foreign Germandom, and I believe that the success of our work in recent years has proved the correctness of our action.

Today one can no longer quarrel about the necessity of a Foreign Organization and say that formerly there was nothing of this nature; for, in the first place, the Foreign Organization exists and will continue to exist and, in the second place, many things were lacking which exist today and which have worked out in a most wondrous way for the welfare of Germany.

When in the history of Germandom abroad was there so close and vibrant a tie with the Reich as there is today? Which of the societies, associations, or unions was able in the old days to bring together, aside from its own members, all the German nationals in one center abroad many times each year?

Never in the past was the German national abroad able to cast his vote in elections. Never before could he see about him such a close community and such readiness for mutual assistance as today in the Winter Relief work of German nationals abroad.

Never before were there 500 and even more groups of German nationals abroad in all parts of the world who were of one mind with the homeland.

We have only been able to achieve these incontestable successes in foreign Germandom through the principle of converting the individual German abroad without regard for position, profession, denomination, or education. We have said to him: You, German racial comrade, are not an isolated phenomenon in the world. You belong to your people and your people needs you.

Not only do you have the passport of a German national in your pocket, not only are you a citizen, but you are, in the first place, a racial comrade (Volksgenosse)—*a racial comrade of the German Reich,* which Adolf Hitler raised from the deepest need and despair in spite of a world of foes and powerfully placed in the ranks of the great and proud nations of the world. You can have the consciousness of belonging to this nation.

You can say proudly, I am a German. All this Adolf Hitler gave you!

But this obliges you through good and evil days to give him the same loyalty which he gave your people and you in Germany's saddest hour.

Just as in the Reich, we of the Foreign Organization, notwithstanding all the difficulties and distances, have shaken foreign Germandom awake and led it to the new Germany. Thereby we only fulfil an obvious national duty, for no sovereign state, and certainly not the new Germany, can neglect to hold for the state its citizens abroad.

For our work we are cursed as Nazi spies, as Gestapo agents, as Hitler spies, and as Brown *provocateurs*. This has never bothered us; for these designations always come from those who cry out to all the world that they recognize no fatherland called Germany, who believe that they can live from daily prophesies of the collapse of the Third Reich. These prophets have become somewhat more silent recently; for now little business can be made by predicting the fall of Hitler Germany, and even the dumbest person abroad has noticed slowly but surely that today Germany stands more firmly, more immovably, and more strongly than ever before.

I, myself, who was born and brought up abroad, am filled with immeasurable pride that the overwhelming majority of our German nationals abroad, regardless of whether they live in Austria, or in China, or in Japan, or in Brazil, have never succumbed to the lies about the new Germany. This has shown the whole world that our German nationals abroad are not the worst Nazis.

Today has brought me incontestable proof that likewise the German nationals in Vienna and in Austria will permit themselves to be excelled by no one in their deep loyalty and their boundless support of Adolf Hitler and his Reich.

I will take back to Germany the splendid feeling that in the German colony at Vienna National Socialism has been accepted, to remain forever.

Our holiday joy today, the feeling of happiness that we can be together, that we may feel so boundlessly proud of our membership in the Reich—all this, my German racial comrades, we owe to the Führer.

Only future historians will be able to evaluate his work in its entire, almost unbelievable, significance. History will speak of a man who created a great nation from nothing and freed it from uncounted foes. Adolf Hitler repeatedly emphasizes that he was only able to do this because he had deep faith in the decency and the loyalty of the German people and because German men and women gave him the same faith and the same loyalty to the National Socialist movement.

A kind Providence gave Adolf Hitler to the Reich, and Providence has blessed his work as that of no one else. Let all of us who are National Socialists abroad recognize that this Reich can never fall or be shaken as long as each one of us remains true to Adolf Hitler, for whom Wilhelm Gustloff laid down his life as a foreign German "blood witness" to the National Socialist idea.

Let that also be our solemn avowal today, that at no time as long as we live will we ever lack the loyalty which Wilhelm Gustloff gave to his Führer.

DOCUMENT 28

(Translation)

DER PARTEITAG DER FREIHEIT (THE PARTY CONGRESS OF FREEDOM) (OFFICIAL REPORT OF THE PROCEEDINGS OF THE REICH'S PARTY CONGRESS, WITH ALL SPEECHES), SEPTEMBER 10–16, 1935: MUNICH, CENTRAL PUBLISHING HOUSE OF THE NSDAP, FRANZ EHER, 1935, PAGES 119–123

THE FÜHRER BEFORE THE FOREIGN GERMANS

The political leaders of the NSDAP from foreign countries who were present at the party congress in Nürnberg and the representatives of German citizens (*Reichsdeutsche*) in all parts of the world met together on Friday for a great meeting of the Foreign Organization in the Apollo Theater. This meeting derived its significance from the fact that it was addressed by the Führer and his Deputy.

On the stage and all around the stage there was a forest of swastika banners which bore names from all parts of the earth. From everywhere the representatives of the Foreign Organization have come to Germany in order to deepen their experience of the community of National Socialism in the motherland through hours of work and of thoughtful deliberation. Many of them have traveled for weeks to come to Germany. Many of these German citizens have not seen the motherland for many years, some of them have never seen it before. One can understand therefore what it meant to them—what it must have meant to them to see and to hear the Führer of all Germans and his Deputy.

Gauleiter Bohle, the leader of the Foreign Organization, expressed this idea in his introductory address. In it he afforded the political leaders an insight into the manifold fields of work of the offices of the Foreign Organization, and he emphasized that the successes which had so far been won had only been made possible through the service of the individual man, regardless of what class he belonged to or what occupation he engaged in. Common to all of them was the unrelenting will to make the groups in foreign countries true carriers of the National Socialist ideology. This will found its visible expression in the outstanding success of the Winter Relief collection of 1934–35.

In conclusion, Gauleiter Bohle thanked all those German men and women who have been preserving their Germandom in foreign countries for decades and have taught their children to be German, and

362

he thanked all those who had added to the esteem and influence of the German name and who, in many parts of the world, created the organizations to which alone thanks are due that Germandom in foreign countries did not disintegrate before the war and during the war.

Cries of "Heil!" from outside proclaimed the arrival of the Führer. When the Führer entered the hall, minutes went by before Gauleiter Bohle was able to greet the Führer and announce his address.

Then the Führer mounted the podium amid a powerful roar of voices. He spoke of the necessity for those German citizens who were members of the NSDAP in foreign countries to feel themselves living members of the community of the German people even while they were out in the world. The possibility for this is given them by National Socialism, which during these days at Nürnberg is shown to be the incarnation of the German nature. What they were having an opportunity to see here in Nürnberg was so great and so significant for the German future that every single German citizen and racial comrade abroad could feel a deep inner satisfaction in being a member of such a community.

The Führer then expressed the idea that the German people is today not merely a state but that it has become a racial corpus (*Volkskörper*) which is pulsing with a vital and inner life. This is the great thing which National Socialism has given to the German people: that the German who goes to a foreign country nowadays is not a lost member but remains a living member of the people's community. The individual knows then that his life for the community is not in any sense a lost life but that he can be somehow useful and helpful for the totality of the people even though he may remain abroad. That is the miracle of the National Socialist organization and leadership of the people.

From this, however, are derived duties for every single individual. It is not enough that he should know that he still retains German citizenship—it is his duty to make up for the lost possibility of taking part in the inner life of the state through an inner participation in the life of our people as it is today revealed in the National Socialist movement. It is his duty, always, everywhere and at every hour, to feel himself a member of the people.

Even if he is not a participant in the living community in a legal sense, nevertheless he is still a participant in the community of the people, which is manifested everywhere in the Foreign Organization of the NSDAP. He is a member of the National Socialist movement, of the National Socialist Party, and he is therewith a German racial comrade who is just as much duty-bound to live according to the principles of our new conception as is everyone in the homeland.

He cannot say that he is relieved of the obligations imposed by the National Socialist conception of the community, but, on the contrary, while he is abroad, since he has no opportunity to take part in the formation of the national destiny, he should support the community of the people and cooperate with it all the more.

It is assumed, of course, that he should do everything which National Socialism demands of the individual man. Above all considerations of class and clan he should give first place to the feeling that he is a member of a people. This is perhaps almost made easier for the German who is living abroad, for the farther he is removed from the homeland, the more will all disintegrating influences be dissolved into their true lack of reality and so much the more will the greater German Reich emerge from the old tangle of local interests, group interests, party interests, and the interests of churches and societies.

The farther he is removed from the homeland, the more does he lose the ability to discern these countless subdivisions and the more quickly does all of that grow together into a unity.

The Führer spoke of the miracle of the National Socialist movement, which always seeks the German simply as a man, regardless of where he comes from, regardless of his education, his knowledge, or his ability, simply the individual German of flesh and blood, not only in the present but also in the future.

The Führer closed his address, which was continually interrupted by wild applause, with a touching appeal to the foreign Germans to penetrate through to all Germandom in foreign countries and to fulfil its duties, regardless of where the individual might be working.

After the Führer had left the hall, the Deputy Führer, Pg. Rudolf Hess, likewise amid wild acclaim, began to deliver his address in consecration of the 68 flags of the local groups, which will be carried before German citizens all over the world, and preliminary to administering the oath to the political leaders. He said in part:

"Always be aware of the honor which is derived from being a member of this people's community or a member of the National Socialist corps of leaders. Always prove yourselves worthy of this honor. Never forget that from now on all your public deeds and words will be judged as the deeds and words of an official representative of Germany. The picture which foreign countries form of the new Germany will be influenced by your bearing. Always preserve manly dignity. Don't angle for the favor of foreign countries any more than you would display a provocative attitude. Follow the laws of the country where you are living just as you demand of it that you be protected by its law and order. Respect the country where you are living, just as you expect it to show respect for the new Germany.

"You are swearing loyalty and obedience to the man who for us Germans and for the whole world represents the essence of Germany, the man who snatched Germany from its deepest distress and brought it to new flower, who welded a torn people together into a greater unity, who led Germany from sheer hopeless weakness to new power, who won back freedom for Germany, who restored honor to Germany. You are pledging yourselves to the man whom we can thank that we can again proudly profess our Germanity while we are out in the world, and that we can live among the citizens of other nations with our heads high. You are pledging yourselves to the man whom you can thank that Germany is again worthy of taking the part of Germans in all the world. Consider well what duties you are taking upon yourselves with this oath. As the Führer will never demand anything of you and will never give you any command which cannot be reconciled with the laws of the country where you are living, therefore he must expect of you that you will preserve your loyalty and faith in him come what may, and that you will never go against your oath because of personal advantages or disadvantages."

It was a gripping moment when these German citizens from abroad, touched to their innermost being, arose and repeated the oath through which they pledged their allegiance to the Führer. Their inward excitement released itself in the *Horst Wessel* song, which has seldom been sung with such feeling.

DOCUMENT 29

(Translation)

JAHRBUCH FÜR AUSWÄRTIGE POLITIK (YEARBOOK FOR FOREIGN POLITICS), EDITED BY PROFESSOR DR. FRITZ BERBER, DIRECTOR OF GERMAN INSTITUTE FOR FOREIGN POLICY RESEARCH: BERLIN, AUGUST GROSS PUBLISHING HOUSE, 1938, PAGE 14

THE FOREIGN ORGANIZATION OF THE NSDAP

BY GAULEITER BOHLE
SECRETARY OF STATE AND HEAD OF THE FOREIGN
ORGANIZATION IN THE FOREIGN OFFICE

(Lecture delivered before the Hungarian Society for Foreign Policy in Budapest, January 24, 1938)

Very Honorable Excellencies, Ladies and Gentlemen!

In the first place, I feel a sincere urge to express my heartiest thanks to the Hungarian Society for Foreign Policy and to its very honorable president for the invitation to speak to the Hungarian public before this high group. I associate herewith also my deepest thanks for the friendly words of greeting which your Mr. President has had the kindness to address to me.

Right at the beginning let me dispose of the honorable task of conveying the sincere greetings of the Führer's Deputy, Reich's Minister Rudolf Hess, and the Reich's Minister for Foreign Affairs, Freiherr von Neurath. Both Reich's Ministers noted with thankful satisfaction that I have an opportunity to speak to you about my work both in the party and within the official framework of the Foreign Office.

Allow me a few words of a general nature before I reach the real theme of my address. When a German who is active in the political life of the new Germany travels abroad in order to make an official visit to a friendly government, the impressions which he receives on such occasions as a German National Socialist are extremely varied. I mean thereby that for the German Reich today the general term "foreign country" does not exist; rather, from the German national point of view, one is inclined on the basis of his feelings to divide foreign countries into three categories. On the one hand we see a foreign world which, for many different reasons not under discussion here, views the German Reich with strongly emphasized hostility, particularly in the press—a foreign world, therefore, in which a German from the Reich in no sense has the feeling of being a particularly welcome guest. In other parts of the foreign world the general rela-

366

tions both in politics and in international affairs are strictly normal without evidencing a definite character either positive or negative. In these countries the German feels exactly like every person who is outside of the borders of his own country. There are, however, for German National Socialists countries with which the Reich feels a particularly close connection politically, culturally, and economically, countries which, either as a result of a century-long tradition or through particular events in recent history, stand in close relation to the German people, of which the German is likewise sensible, even if this relation is not expressed in words.

I know I do not have to give you the expressed assurance that it is these latter thoughts and sentiments which every German feels who visits Hungary. Here in the land of St. Stephen's Crown we Germans find a people and a state leadership which has a sincere sympathy for us and which can be assured that it enjoys the same sympathy and friendship from us in the Reich. The recent visit of their Excellencies Premier von Daranyi and Foreign Minister von Kanya to the Reich presented clear evidence to both peoples and to the world beyond not only of the friendship of the two states but also of the friendship of the two peoples. We can also note with particular satisfaction that this friendship between the two peoples is an old tradition which I might characterize as one of the good traditions in the life of European peoples.

The statesmen of the Kingdom of Hungary received new evidence in Berlin of the sympathies which the Führer and the German people, and therewith the German Reich, have for Hungary. The union of destiny of the two peoples in the great struggle of the World War has continued beyond the brotherhood of arms and has also become a union of destiny in the post-war period.

If I began with these words it was because it was necessary in order to show that we in Germany just as in Hungary, and also oftentimes in other territories, demand understanding for things which are obvious in the protection of our just interests. I now come to the theme which I will discuss today. I speak to you in my capacity as head of the Foreign Organization of the NSDAP as well as in my capacity of Secretary of State and head of the Foreign Organization in the Foreign Office.

The Foreign Organization of the Nazi Party is in the limited sense a union of all citizens of the Reich abroad who are members of the NSDAP. Since the Nazi Party in the new Reich possesses the exclusive right to determine the philosophical and political views of the entire people, the Foreign Organization has logically been established for the leadership of all German citizens abroad. The NSDAP has conquered the German people in a philosophical and political sense and has become thereby the only bearer of political initiative in the

Reich.   The law of December 1933 concerning the unity of party and state gives official expression to this fact.   Through my appointment as Chief of the Foreign Organization in the Foreign Office on January 30, 1937 this union of party and state received clear expression also in the supervision of foreign Germandom.

This appointment means that I as Gauleiter, i.e. as deputy of the Führer for German citizens abroad, at the same time become responsible for the official protection of foreign Germandom, a protection which is always considered among the foremost tasks of the Minister of Foreign Affairs.   It is also, as the Reich's Foreign Minister emphasized in his speech at Stuttgart at the Fifth Congress of Foreign Germans last year, a guaranty that the principles and directions set up by the responsible internal German authorities for the care of foreign Germandom will be observed within the limits fixed by the Foreign Office and will be carefully respected by German organizations abroad as well.

It is indispensable to point out at this point the concepts which we in the Reich, after careful thought, consider desirable for Germans abroad.   Clear views and concepts in this field prevent misunderstandings—particularly those in the field of foreign policy.   In the past a clarity of this kind could not be achieved because in the old Germany everyone was allowed to formulate definitions which appeared correct to him personally.   It can also be understood that even today new concepts require time before they are adopted in everyday terminology.

When we speak in general of foreign Germandom we understand thereby not only German nationals abroad but also persons of German origin.   However, we know how to distinguish very clearly between Germans abroad, i.e. German nationals abroad and persons of German extraction who in speech and culture are of German origin but who are not citizens of the German Reich.

In the speech which I delivered last autumn before the German colony in London, I pointed out repeatedly and with great emphasis that the Foreign Organization of the NSDAP does not have the task of organizing persons of German origin abroad.   I wish here formally to repeat this declaration not only in my official capacity but also as Gauleiter of the Nazi Party.   All assertions to the contrary, which from time to time may be made by a hostile press often subsidized for this purpose, are gratuitous inventions and can only have the purpose of sowing mistrust and evoking political difficulties.   It is the fundamental principle of my organization never and under no circumstances to mix in the internal political affairs of foreign countries.   On the contrary, the Reich and the party expect from all German nationals abroad that they be exemplary and loyal guests of the country in which they reside.   I personally have the ambition of achieving a state of affairs in which our Germans abroad throughout the world, by their conduct, their attitude, and their observance of the laws, will be respected in every foreign country as the best-loved foreigners. It is an old and for us flattering remark that we Germans are the best organizers in the world. When we therefore also organize our nationals abroad, although this word—willingly or unwillingly—is often given a false meaning, then I can give the assurance that this fact alone offers to all foreign governments the strongest guaranty for a loyal attitude on the part of our Germans abroad. The German discipline which rules in our local, city, and national groups provides a guaranty that my orders will be strictly followed. A party member abroad who concerns himself with things which are exclusively the affairs of the country of his residence will be punished by the party and the Reich without regard to his previous record. The new Germany will not permit its citizens abroad to arouse hostility and to disturb the relations between the Reich and the foreign country. This rule, which was adopted by the Foreign Organization of the party back in 1931 and which may be read on every certificate of a party member abroad since that time, applies likewise, through the unity of party and state, to all German nationals abroad.

National Socialism is the world philosophy and the political persuasion of all German nationals. Whoever as a German national asserts that he is not or does not wish to be a National Socialist is at odds with his nation, which time and again has by overwhelming majorities approved the Führer and his doctrine—odds which cannot be overcome. He has ceased to be a member of the German folk community even though on paper he may still be a German national. Whoever places himself in opposition to the man who has saved Germany from chaos and complete collapse commits high treason against his people. That is our position and this position is not a subject for international debate since it is an internal German question. It is the logical result of this view, which is shared by the entire German people in the Reich, that the movement and therewith the Reich has the right to instruct its citizens abroad in the philosophy of National Socialism. The great national congresses of foreign Germans which have been held annually by my organization since 1933 have proved without dispute that our foreign Germandom is National Socialist by just as large a majority and stands true to the new Germany.

When a few German nationals abroad join together as party members, they constitute a local group of the NSDAP. If they are more numerous, they constitute a city group; if there are several local and city groups in a country, these groups are combined in a regional group, and in the case of a further development the regional group is replaced by a national group. This structure is wholly clear and without any hidden aspects. When, as often occurs, certain circles abroad break forth in sensational cries about local groups of the NSDAP and try to impress upon frightened citizens that a local group represents a secret military organization, it is sufficient proof that these persons either have no knowledge of the structure of the NSDAP or are consciously hostile. In most instances the latter is the case, for there are throughout Germany local groups of the NSDAP, which are unions of party members not having the slightest concern with military affairs. I am convinced, however, that these hostile persons would raise exactly the same cries in the world if we should call our local groups something like "subordinate groups" (*Unter-Klubs*) and the city groups "upper clubs" (*Ober-Klubs*). I can establish to my satisfaction, however, that serious and objective persons in many countries as a result of their experiences with our groups no longer give any credence to such tendentious reports. Not only the structure of our organization but likewise its entire work is carried on so clearly and openly before the whole world that it would be simply childish stupidity on our part to engage in, for example, espionage through such channels. One does not place spies and similar agents in the light of publicity; also one does not publish books and pamphlets on this subject. Our groups, however, are so evident that every foreign state has an opportunity to convince itself of their loyalty and correct activity within the limits of local laws. Our groups are likewise not diplomatic or consular agencies. Privileges of this kind are never expected or demanded for them. The national leader or the national regional leader in a country is the spokesman of the German nationals in that particular land. He is responsible for the National Socialist training of his co-nationals. In conjunction with the Consulates he is concerned with providing assistance for fellow Germans who are in difficulty. Our winter assistance work, the greatest social achievement of the new Germany, is also conducted by the party abroad. That is convincing proof that the spirit of the people's community has also become effective in foreign Germandom. In conjunction with the official representatives of the Reich, the party organizes the great national celebrations to which prominent speakers are sent from the Reich in order to tell our citizens abroad about the Führer and Germany. Just as in Germany the groups abroad are the organizational expression of the new concept of the people's community which in the Reich constitutes the basis for our community life.

Every German national abroad who is a true follower of his Führer has the understandable wish to pattern his life on National Socialist lines. The citizens in the Reich cannot have one view of life and those outside of our borders another. Every Hungarian abroad desires to remain in vital contact with his country and his people. He does not become less Hungarian because he lives outside of the boundaries of the Kingdom. This fact applies to all persons abroad who wish to remain true to their way of life, their culture, and their language. The times are past, however, in which men believed that they had the right to grant citizens of the German Reich fewer privileges than those of other states. The demand that our citizens abroad may organize their lives within the German colony on National Socialist principles is obvious. Every sovereign state considers it of the greatest importance that its citizens abroad are unrestricted in their personal and community life so long as that life is within the limits fixed by the laws of the foreign country. The Third Reich demands exactly the same rights for its citizens—no more, but also no less. That in certain countries the impression also arose after the seizure of power by Adolf Hitler that it was not necessary in this connection to grant Germans full equality with other aliens may certainly be attributed to the apparent belief that Germans had less national feeling. Whoever formerly accepted this point of view, however, must have been persuaded, the sooner the better, of the fact that these times are definitely over.

Moreover, one should not attempt to convince the world that the idea of organizing our citizens abroad and looking after them is something novel or even an intrusion in the sovereign rights of foreign countries. The obvious desire of the Fascist Government in Italy to make Italians living abroad aware of Fascism as the new mode of life in their fatherland led very soon after the "march on Rome" to the foundation of the Italian Foreign Organization. It was asserted in Italy with complete right that it is better to instruct Italians abroad from Italy concerning Fascism, its aim and purpose, rather than leave this instruction to the foreign press. In Poland also the position has been very much emphasized that the Polish state has a right to concern itself with Poles abroad. "The World Union of Poles Abroad" is a very great and very well conceived organization which, I am convinced, has accomplished splendid work in looking after Poles throughout the world.

Likewise France, which, in the "Alliance Française", possesses a very aggressive institute for spreading its culture, gives particular attention to the intensive cultivation of relations to its nationals abroad. This was clearly indicated by the October meeting of the "Union of Frenchmen Abroad" in Paris last year, which left nothing undone in its splendid and hearty welcome to participants from all over the world, and the political significance of which was emphasized by the official presence of the President of the Republic. In Sweden there has existed for 30 years a "National Association for the Protection of Swedes Abroad", which, according to recent reports, is to be supplemented by a special central organization for all Swedes abroad. The proposal by a member of the Swedish Parliament to this end demands the determination of the rights and duties of Swedes abroad by Parliament, with a view to tightening the bonds between the fatherland and the Swedish community abroad.

There is also, to cite a further example, a Secretariat for Swiss Abroad in Bern, of which the group in Germany today consists of 37 chief groups and 31 subordinate groups. The President of the Swiss Federation belongs to the Patrons' Committee of this Secretariat and emphasized in a speech the significance of the last meeting of Swiss abroad. In London I have already pointed out, furthermore, that England with perfect right and very actively has also concerned itself with the question of British subjects abroad.

It will be seen, therefore, that the fundamental principles of our Foreign Organization contain absolutely nothing new or even secret. In certain circles there is always a sensation when the German Reich permits itself to enjoy the same rights which other states consider customary. The exercise of this same right by the Germans is characterized as German agitation or pan-Germanism.

Last year a foreign diplomat, in the course of a general political conversation with me, felt obliged to say that we Germans today are supersensitive. I replied that, in fact, we are particularly sensitive in all matters which concern the national order and the dignity of the German Reich and will always remain so. Every state which in the truest sense of the word is a national state will be very sensitive in such questions. Every lack of such sensitivity means an equal lack of national pride. National pride, however, is not a quality which is limited to a few countries but is one which is usually found in all peoples who are proud of their history.

The numerous attacks which have been directed against the Foreign Organization in the course of the last few years have not been able to withstand a serious investigation. I do not believe, furthermore, that it was intended to injure German nationals abroad with this slander but that on political grounds the possibility was seen herein to arouse opposition to National Socialist Germany. There is found, therefore, a very definite system in these attacks, although the system has not displayed in any sense the advantage of logic. In London I discounted the very transparent tales about spying maids. Every observer of these matters must have noted that for the most part the Germans abroad today, who are characterized as organized Gestapo agents, are the same who were resident abroad before 1933, although at that time it was not considered necessary to suspect them in this way.

When, on the one hand, the assertion is made that the Foreign Organization terrorizes German nationals abroad and intends to force them to become National Socialists, and, on the other hand, it is stated that these foreign Germans are all in the secret service of a great central espionage agency, it must be admitted that one assertion directly contradicts the other. The recent fantastic lies about a secret fund of 20,000,000 pounds sterling with which, among others also, my so-called "agents" abroad were financed is, apart from its baseness, not without a certain humor. Overlooking the fact that the British Empire will not be shaken with 20,000,000 pounds, the authors of this kind of inciting report seem to have heard very little about the foreign-exchange system of the German Reich. I might also point out that the foreign Germans themselves who have been provided with these funds for such dark purposes, and would certainly be in the best position to provide information about them, have not yet heard of them. It would be at least amazing, moreover, if a country like England should permit such activity if the financial operations were so precisely known. However, we have far too high an opinion of the intelligence and the competence of the English secret service to be able to make such an assumption.

Even though we know that responsible circles in England give no attention to such reports, it is nevertheless necessary to point out that in the interest of good relations between the two countries they must at least be regarded as regrettable and unfair.

After the extensive possibilities of a systematic slander campaign against the Third Reich at the cost of our Germans abroad are exhausted, one falls back on a word which, presented against a suitably sensationally prepared background, is expected to produce something like an international panic. It is the word "pan-Germanism".

Since it is very difficult even for our opponents to explain what they mean by pan-Germanism, we ourselves must admit that we are not able to define this word, which was invented outside of our borders. I am convinced that the attempt to paint on the wall in the different countries a German threat to the world as a final means of discriminating against the Reich will be shattered against the sound human understanding of contemporary statesmen. We National Socialists can give the fervent assurance that we have no greater wish than to be left in quiet and peace to rebuild our Reich. The respect of our former enemies for the achievements of the German Army in the war, even though unspoken, appears to have given a great American newspaper, through the pen of its Berlin correspondent, cause for a loud cry of fear of the German threat to the world. In the Reich we have ceased to become excited about such outpourings of agitation from journalists, although we, nevertheless, note the respect for the Germans with a certain satisfaction. Today one can no longer harm the German Reich with newspaper articles of this kind. We will not even bother to deny outbursts of such fantastic nature since they refute themselves through their groundless stupidity.

More serious are the attacks in which an effort is made to prove that the Foreign Organization or the German Reich is trying to agitate among persons of German origin. Here in Hungary I can speak publicly of a practical example, in as much as there is a large German element in your country. The basis for the treatment of this question, which, in our opinion is no longer a problem, is the exchange of important declarations in July of last year between the Hungarian Minister of the Interior, Von Szell, and the Führer's Deputy, Reich's Minister Rudolf Hess. Anyone who reads these declarations in the spirit of the traditional friendship between our countries must recognize that such principles can serve as examples for all countries in which similar questions exist. The German Reich has never expected or wished that the Germans of Hungarian nationality should be anything but a true and loyal part of the Hungarian state. If attempts are made by individuals or irresponsible organizations to arouse Germans of Hungarian nationality against the Hungarian state, I can give the emphatic assurance that such plots will be most sharply condemned on the part of Germany. The Reich has no intention of permitting its relations with Hungary to be disturbed in the least by unofficial excursions of political fantasies. The interest of the German Reich in Germans of Hungarian nationality is not political but purely cultural. As a result of its natural feeling of cultural and national relationship, Germany has noted with grateful joy not only the declaration of the Hungarian Minister of the Interior in July of last year but also the New Year's message of Prime Minister von Daranyi to the German minority.

I think that as a result of these declarations this question has ceased to serve certain hostile circles as a welcome pretext for the disturbance of relations between Germany and Hungary; and the German group of Hungarian nationality can in tested loyalty give no better expression of its German culture to the Hungarian state than through its endeavor in the relations between the two states to be a bridge between the two peoples—as Rudolf Hess has expressed it. I think I may also say that the Germans of Hungarian nationality are the last who would wish to serve as a pretext for the assertion that the German Reich has designs on the integrity of the Hungarian state.

History will serve as the best proof that German soldiers, when they have appeared in Hungary, never came as conquerors or attackers or aggressors but always as friends and allies.

In all periods of world history conscious lies have been a weapon in political affairs. Without the slightest fear of honorable contradiction I can make the assertion that no single country in the world has since 1914, and particularly since 1933, been the subject of so many lies as Germany. From the standpoint of international relations the lie about pan-Germanism is certainly the most infamous. Anyone who has concerned himself even superficially with the doctrines of National Socialism in Germany must know that this philosophy is a purely internal point of view which we jealously protect and never expect to export. Whoever knows the Germans knows that while they are a highly competent military people—and on this point we have every reason to be particularly proud—they are not militaristic in an aggressive sense. The Germans, however, are not only a peace-loving people but they have a strong feeling for justice. That which has happened to Germany through many centuries is without any doubt the greatest injustice of world history. Today for the first time we have not only a united Reich, which Adolf Hitler has created for us, but also a Reich which is defended by a great and strong army against being a plaything for envious enemies, as it has been so often in the past. If we note after five years of National Socialistic development work in Germany that our Reich is a world power in the largest sense of the word, we come to this conclusion without any arrogance but with great pride and deep gratitude to the Führer. Those forces which we have recognized with perfect clarity, which have the mad belief that they can injure the German people with lies of all kinds, have not kept pace with recent history. These methods were able to injure the unpopular Republic and likewise the Germany of the Kaiser but can never harm the leader-state of the German nation united in National Socialism. We can understand the sigh of a foreign politician which was emitted in my presence a few months ago, that he preferred the Germany of before 1933 to that of the present. This statement in itself shows the powerful German accomplishment of Adolf Hitler, for it is of no concern whether Germany pleases our enemies or former enemies but whether it pleases the Germans.

When during the great war we were described everywhere by enemy propaganda as barbarians and as a degenerate people in every respect, this assertion certainly aroused our anger at that time. On looking back we must say, as citizens of the Third Reich, that these lies had only a single cause, namely the powerful respect for Germany and Germans and particularly for the achievements of the unconquered German Army. If, therefore, I give expression to my joy over this cause, I can be sure that you here in this country, in which soldierly qualities and national heroism are cultivated in the same degree, will understand me.

If I have established that people cannot disrupt the new German Reich by hate and lies, then it will certainly be clear to you that they would like to find compensation for this by getting at our German citizens abroad. These foreign Germans who go about their peaceful work in all civilized states throughout the world are naturally exponents of the National Socialist Reich. When attempts are made to defame and cast suspicion on them, the Reich is also criticized, and

at the same time the suspicions of foreign governments are aroused.
From this train of thought the attacks against the Foreign Organization of the NSDAP result.   It is desired to damage German prestige
by seeking to ruin the lives of apparently unprotected German citizens
abroad.   It is desired to brand our legal associations as obscure bands
of plotters.   It is desired to destroy Germans who have been peaceful
and loyal residents of foreign countries for years and often for decades
and concerning whom the foreign country never had occasion to
complain.   Such tactics condemn themselves.   As long as there are
international relations and trade, there will be those who live outside
of the borders of their own country.   Such persons contribute in a
high degree to the preservation and intensification of such relations.
They do not desire to be politicians or agents but wish to go about
their daily work as merchants, technicians, laborers, or scientists.
Even if this is not expressed, they are involuntary links between one
people and another and contribute to mutual understanding.   Certainly there are spies and agents in all countries in the world.   In
making this statement I am saying nothing new.   It is, however, a
particularly repulsive form of infamy to accuse whole communities
of foreign nationals living abroad of activities of this nature.   Anyone who doubts the complete legality of the Foreign Organization and
its branches abroad has, according to the most primitive principles of
justice, the duty of producing evidence, even the smallest amount.
That has never occurred because the originators of these slanders are
not men who have the slightest serious concern but only those who
seek pretexts for international agitation and propaganda against the
German Reich.

Ladies and gentlemen!   In the few days I have been here I have
already been able to see to my great joy that our German nationals
here in Hungary feel themselves well off and live in friendly harmony
with your people.   I did not expect otherwise, for Hungary belongs
to the countries in which Germans always feel well off.   Be persuaded that the colonies of German nationals in Hungary, which are
led by the Foreign Organization, merely through the National Socialist discipline which unites them, never will give cause for com-
plaint.   Our German nationals are heartily grateful to the Hungarian
state for the hospitality which is reserved for them in this country
related to us by destiny and for which I, as Chief of the Foreign
Organization, may express on their behalf my most cordial thanks.
The time will come, I am convinced, in which foreign Germans in
all other countries will also enjoy the same decent treatment accorded
to foreigners in Germany.   It is even our aim in the Reich to receive
with particular politeness aliens temporarily in our midst, for we
consider this politeness to be a national virtue.   It is all the same to
us whatever the philosophy and whatever the political persuasion

of individual foreigners in Germany may be. We do not believe that those aliens in Germany who are democrats can constitute a danger to the existence of our Reich. Our state is so firmly established internally and so well protected against foreign attack that we have no cause for anxiety, and in the second place we really have more serious concerns. As long as the alien in Germany remains within the framework of the laws and within the circle of his compatriots, he can think what he will for himself. I must assume that the members of the French or English or American colonies in Berlin are good and convinced democrats and that in their associations they express this democratic persuasion with all earnestness. As long as they praise democracy before their own compatriots and do not harm the Reich, whose hospitality they enjoy, we are quite indifferent; however, we expect the same right for our citizens abroad, and the Foreign Organization of the NSDAP is built on this right. On the basis of this right, the new Reich protects every one of its citizens abroad and is not willing to allow a German citizen to be persecuted merely because he is a National Socialist. Whoever persecutes German citizens abroad on such grounds attacks the German Reich. Those to whom this fact means something sensational must have been asleep for the last five years.

If we Germans everywhere in the world again acknowledge ourselves proudly and with raised heads as members of the German Reich, then each one of us knows that we owe our thanks therefor to a single man and his work. Adolf Hitler has in a few years extinguished the injustice which was done to the German people. He has saved Germany and with it Europe as well from the Bolshevist chaos and is building with his Reich the strongest wall against this international scourge. You here in Hungary who were freed from a Bela Kun and his Communist assistants by the Protector of the Nation—who is highly respected by us all—particularly you, I think, will understand the German people's seeing in Adolf Hitler not only the builder of a united Reich but in equal measure the savior from destruction.

My Hungarian friends! I have tried to show you on large lines the fundamental ideas which have guided me from the beginning in my work for foreign Germandom. I was moved to point out that the German national abroad is today a citizen of a great and proud nation whose splendid history has been taken over by the reliable hands of a young, strong generation and has been united with the powerful impulse of the great National Socialist movement for the assurance of Germany's future.

In this inspiring consciousness the foreign German will constitute a valuable link between the Reich and the other peoples of the earth— he will participate as a missionary of German good-will in the great work of peace and therewith in the elimination of international hate, which has brought so much unrest into the life of humanity.

We Germans are fortunate to know that Hungary and Germany will follow together this way of peace in traditional comradely association.

In this sense I ask the German nationals present to greet His Excellency, the Protector of the Kingdom of Hungary and the great Hungarian nation, with the cry of the new Germany: Sieg Heil! Sieg Heil! Sieg Heil!

2. Ausgabe Berlin
29. August 1938
Nr. 33

Bilder und Sport vom Sonntag

Der Montag

10 Pf.
auswärts
15 Pf.

Heß: Mission der Auslandsdeutschen

Tschechen überfallen sudetendeutsches Dorf
Wüste Tumulte gegen Konrad Henlein

70 000 auf der Adolf-Hitler-Kampfbahn

Großkundgebung in Stuttgart

Stürmische Begeisterung um den Stellvertreter des Führers

Drahtmeldung unseres Sonderberichterstatters

wgk Stuttgart, 28. August. Ein erhebendes Bild politischer Geschlossenheit, gläubigen Bekenntnisses und begeisterter Hingabe an das neue Deutschland und seinen Führer bot die erste Großkundgebung der VI. Reichstagung der Auslandsdeutschen, die am Sonntagnachmittag mit 70 000 Teilnehmern in der Stuttgarter Adolf-Hitler-Kampfbahn stattfand. Wie im letzten Jahre, so hatte sich auch diesmal der Stellvertreter des Führers, Reichsminister Rudolf Heß, wieder bereit gefunden, den ihm besonders verbundenen und an das Herz gewachsenen Deutschen in aller Welt den ersten Willkomgruß der Partei und des Führers zu überbringen.

Mit Stürmen jubelnder Begeisterung wurde Rudolf Heß bei seiner Ankunft Sonnabend nacht und bei seiner Fahrt zu den einzelnen Veranstaltungen empfangen. In der überfüllten, würdig ausgeschmückten Stuttgarter Stadthalle fand Sonntag mittag die feierliche Eröffnung der Auslandsdeutschentagung statt, die ihre besondere Note durch die Teilnahme des Stellvertreters des Führers, Reichsminister Rudolf Heß, und durch eine Ansprache des Reichsinnenministers Dr. Frick erhielt. Unter den zahlreichen Ehrengästen bemerkte man die Mutter von Rudolf Heß, dessen Familie seit sieben Jahrzehnten im Auslande ihr Deutschtum hochgehalten hat, ferner die Reichsminister von Neurath und Dr. Frick.

Gauleiter und Reichsstatthalter von Württemberg, Murr, und Oberbürgermeister Dr. Strölin-Stuttgart betonten in ihren Begrüßungs-

worten die auslandsdeutsche Sendung dieser Stadt und des gesamten Schwabenlandes. Reichsinnenminister Dr. Frick, der die Grüße und den herzlichen Willkommensgruß der Reichsregierung an alle Auslandsdeutschen überbrachte, ging in seiner Ansprache vor allem auf die Aufgaben der Auslandsdeutschen ein, wobei er insbesondere drei Punkte hervorhob: Die Pflege des Bewußtseins der Zusammengehörigkeit unter allen Auslandsdeutschen, die Wahrung und Vertiefung des lebendigen Geistes nationalsozialistischer Volksgemeinschaft und als drittes, Träger zu sein der Verständigung mit den anderen Völkern und damit Diener der Verständigung selbst.

Anschließend eröffnete der Leiter der Auslandsorganisation, Gauleiter Bohle, die 6. Reichstagung mit einem besonderen Gruß an den Stellvertreter des Führers und die Reichsminister, in den die Anwesenden begeistert einstimmten. Gauleiter Bohle brachte sodann in seiner Eröffnungsansprache zum Ausdruck, daß dieses Treffen im wahrsten Sinne eine Reichstagung der großdeutschen Volksgemeinschaft im Auslandsdeutschtum sei. Der Treueschwur der vielen tausende Auslandsdeutschen auf den Führer und die nationalen Lieder beschlossen die eindrucksvolle Feierstunde.

Die mit den Bannern des Dritten Reiches und dem Wahrzeichen der Auslandsorganisation festlich geschmückte mächtige Sportarena war schon lange vor Beginn der Massenkundgebung ringsum gefüllt mit zehntausenden Teilnehmern. Stürmisch bejubelt wurde der Einmarsch der Parteigliederungen und besonders die Ehrenformation der Auslandsorganisation in weißen Hemden mit der Hakenkreuzbinde. Vor den Tribünen haben die 34 neuen Ortsgruppenfahnen der Auslandsorganisation Aufstellung genommen. Mit brausenden Heilrufen wurde Rudolf Heß empfangen, als er in Begleitung von Gauleiter Bohle und Gauleiter Reichsstatthalter Murr auf der Kampfbahn eintraf.

Ergreifende Totenehrung

Dann erlebten die Auslandsdeutschen ein Schauspiel deutscher Macht und Größe. Unter Vorantritt des Musikzuges hielten eine Ehrenkompanie des Heeres und der SS ihren Einzug in das Stadion. Neuer Jubel brauste auf, als die vier Standarten und fünfhundert Fahnen der Stuttgarter Parteigliederungen hereingetragen wurden. Gauleiter Bohle eröffnete die erste Großkundgebung der Auslandsorganisation auf dieser Reichstagung mit einem weihevollen Gedenken an die Blutopfer der Auslandsdeutschen.

Unter den Klängen des Liedes vom Guten Kameraden senkten sich die Fahnen, und in die feierliche Stille wurde Name um Name der auslandsdeutschen Blutzeugen für das Großdeutsche Reich aufgerufen. Mit besonderer Freude begrüßte sodann Gauleiter Bohle auf dieser Ersten Großdeutschen Reichstagung der Auslandsdeutschen die anwesenden Gauleiter und Minister aus der deutschen Ostmark, er begrüßte weiter Reichsminister Freiherrn v. Neurath und ganz besonders herzlich Rudolf Heß. Gauleiter Bohle übergab hierauf die Fahne der ehemaligen Landesgruppe Oesterreich als Traditionsfahne an die Auslandsorganisation der NSDAP, die er als ein Symbol der Treue aller Auslandsdeutschen bezeichnete. Unter begeisterten Zustimmungskundgebungen verlas er ein Grußtelegramm an den Führer, in dem er Adolf Hitler die Treue und Ergebenheit aller hier versammelten Auslandsdeutschen übermittelt.

Rudolf Heß spricht

Minutenlanger Jubel und Heilrufe brausten über das riesige Oval, als dann der Stellvertreter des Führers, Rudolf Heß, an das Podium trat und das Wort ergriff. Seine große Rede zu den Auslandsdeutschen begann Rudolf Heß mit den Worten der Erinnerung an die Größe der Ereignisse und der Entwicklung, die sich im Laufe des seit der letzten Stuttgarter Kundgebung des Auslandsdeutschtums vergangenen Jahres im Reiche vollzogen haben.

Es sei ein Jahr schwerer Entscheidungen des Führers und vertrauensvoller Erwartung des deutschen Volkes gewesen. Die Rückkehr der Ostmark habe die glücklichste und schönste Erfüllung eines alten deutschen Traumes gebracht. In unermüdlicher Arbeit habe das deutsche Volk das Jahr genutzt, seine wirtschaftliche Kraft zu stärken und seine Sicherheit vor feindlichem Angriff so weit zu erhöhen, daß es in Ruhe jeder Entwicklung entgegensehe, die Böswillige gegen Deutschland hervorrufen können. War es so ein arbeitsames und im Innern glückliches Jahr, so war es zugleich ein Jahr der Stärkung der Freundschaften, die das wiedererstarkte Reich mit anderen großen Nationen geschlossen hat. Die Tage der Gastfreundschaft und Kameradschaft, die wir Deutsche auf der Führerreise nach Italien erlebten, sind uns symbolisch für die große Gemeinschaft zwischen Großdeutschland und dem Imperium am Mittelmeer, und der Empfang, den Deutschland dem Reichsverweser Ungarns und zugleich dem wagemutigen, so verdienten Admiral bot — er war der Ausdruck herzlicher und erprobter Freundschaft! Unendlich stolz und glücklich sei das deutsche

Volk darüber, daß der Führer der Welt erneut gezeigt habe, welche Leistungsfähigkeit, welche Stärke, welches Selbstbewußtsein und welche Leidenschaft der Selbsterhaltung dem deutschen Volk innewohne, wenn die richtige Hand es leitet.

"So meine Parteigenossen", so fuhr Rudolf Heß unter brausendem Beifall fort, "wie wir in Dankbarkeit und Liebe des Führers gedenken, so gedenkt er euer, und er läßt euch durch mich seine Grüße sagen! Ihr, die ihr wieder hinausgeht auf eure Arbeitsplätze in fremden Ländern und inmitten fremden Volkstums, ihr deutschen Seefahrer, die ihr zurückkehrt auf eure Schiffe, tragt diese Grüße mit hinaus an eure Volksgenossen und eure Parteigenossen, tragt sie mit hinaus, denn sie sind die Grüße eures Volkes, sie sind die Grüße Großdeutschlands!

Der Stellvertreter des Führers spricht von Kampf und Treue der Deutschen draußen. Er gedenkt der Entwicklung, die später für das Auslandsdeutschtum kam, im Kriege und im Zwischenreich. "Was es in den Jahren des Zwischenreiches bedeutete", so rief er aus, "unter der Verachtung der Welt draußen als Deutscher zu leben, für Deutschland zu wirken und trotz allem zu Deutschland zu stehen, das kann nur der ermessen, der selbst draußen war — bis dann endlich das neue Reich Adolf Hitlers erstand. Gewiß, wohl wuchs damit der Haß noch in weiten Teilen der Welt, aber zugleich mit diesem Haß erstand doch auch wieder die Achtung, die sie uns allmählich zollen mußten, wenn sie es manchmal auch noch so widerwillig taten. Die Achtung wuchs wieder, und heute könnt ihr euch, meine Volksgenossen, stolzer denn je als Deutsche bekennen." (Brausender Beifall.)

Abwehr der Verdächtigungen

Rudolf Heß unterstreicht mit eindringlichen Worten den Zusammenschluß, zu dem sich die Deutschen draußen zu gleicher Gemeinschaft zusammengefunden haben wie im Innern. Mit klaren Worten kennzeichnet er die Aufgabe der Auslandsorganisation der NSDAP und tritt damit den Verdächtigungen entgegen, die gegen die nationalsozialistischen Deutschen im Ausland immer wieder aus durchsichtigen Gründen erhoben wurden:

„In der Auslands-Organisation der NSDAP habt ihr euch zusammengeschlossen. Euer Deutschtum zu pflegen, gute Nationalsozialisten zu sein. Euer Deutschtum und euer Nationalsozialismus, das ist eure eigenste Angelegenheit. Ihr betreibt keine „Pénétration pacifique", ihr denkt gar nicht daran, die Gastvölker mit dem Nationalsozialismus „friedlich zu durchdringen". Nein, euer Deutschtum und euer Nationalsozialismus ist eure persönliche Angelegenheit und bleibt auch eure eigenste Angelegenheit.

Daran ändert auch nichts, wenn ihr da und dort dunkler Aufgaben und Ziele verdächtigt werdet, oder wenn man glaubt, euch den Nationalsozialismus etwa nehmen zu können, indem man willkürlich eure äußere Gemeinschaftsform verbietet. Eure Ortsgruppen kann man schließen, eure Abzeichen kann man euch verbieten, aber nicht euren nationalsozialistischen Geist und euer deutsches Herz. (Minutenlanger Beifallssturm.)

Wir und unsere Auslandsdeutschen drängen uns nicht in die Verhältnisse anderer Länder. Mögen sie nach ihrer Fasson selig werden! Wir müssen freilich aber auch erwarten, daß sich andere Länder nicht in unsere Angelegenheiten zu mischen suchen und daß sie uns nach unserer Fasson selig werden lassen.

Mögen sie die „Freiheit des Individuums" zum Idol erheben, so wie sie es verstehen. Mögen sie dem Individuum die Freiheit geben, immer mehr in Arbeitslosigkeit, Hunger und Verzweiflung zu verfallen — mögen sie ihm die Freiheit geben, sich gegen die eigene Ordnung zu organisieren, um damit die größte Unfreiheit, die stärkste Unterdrückung des Individuums zum Prinzip zu erheben — es ist ihre eigene Angelegenheit.

Mit sarkastischen Worten befaßt sich Rudolf Heß mit dem Begriff der wahren und der falschen Freiheit, der Freiheit bei uns und dieser sogenannten „Freiheit des Individuums" in den Demokratien: „Mögen die Parteien anderer Länder die Massen des Volkes gegeneinander aktivieren — — bei uns aktiviert eine Partei das Volk für eine Gemeinschaft. Mag in den Demokratien von der Freiheit des Individuums noch soviel geschrieben und geredet werden — in den sogenannten autoritären Staaten vollbringt das Individuum Leistungen wie nirgends sonst." Rudolf Heß erinnerte dabei an die vielen deutschen Höchstleistungen auf allen Gebieten.

„Man frage doch unsere Arbeiter, so tief der Stellvertreter des Führers aus, die mit Kraft durch Freude aus dem Ausland zurückkehren, ob sie etwa sich als Individuum unfrei fühlen, ob sie etwa tauschen wollen mit ihren Arbeitsgenossen in angeblich liberalen Ländern. Jeder sagt: Gott sei Dank, daß Deutschland meine Heimat ist. Keiner würde diese Heimat jemals hingeben. Wir Deutsche sind alle freie Bürger eines freien Reiches, auf das wir unendlich stolz sind."

Die Heimkehr der Ostmark

Rudolf Heß erinnerte daran, daß das frühere Oesterreich einst ein besonderer Günstling der Demokratien auf der ganzen Welt gewesen sei. „Und in diesem Günstlingsland der Demokratie, da wurden 6½ Millionen deutscher Menschen terrorisiert durch eine kleine politische Minderheit. Aber wie hat man sich draußen aufgeregt, als das deutsche Volk aus wirklich freiem Entschluß und in freiem Selbstbestimmungsrecht die 6½ Millionen Deutscher im früheren Oesterreich heimführte in die große Heimat, zurückführte in das große deutsche Volk. Nicht die Demokratien, nicht die Länder mit den feierlichen Versprechungen des Selbstbestimmungsrechts: Wir, die „Diktatur", wir, das Land mit dem „autoritären Regime", wir haben eines freien Volkes Willen zum Gesetz erhoben, wir haben die demokratischste Tat vollbracht."

Rudolf Heß weist weiter darauf hin, daß erst in den autoritären Staaten der wahre Begriff der Volkswirtschaft als eine Wirtschaft für das Volk praktische Wirklichkeit geworden ist. Niemand könne bestreiten, daß nicht nur ein neues soziales, sondern auch neues wirtschaftliches Leben in den autoritären Staaten kommt und viele in der Welt zum Nachdenken veranlaßt.

Ja, es kommt vor, daß ein fremder Politiker unter leidenschaftlichen Anklagen gegen den Faschismus und den Nationalsozialismus soziale Ideen vertritt und Forderungen erhebt, die wir alle in fast ganz gleicher Form schon einmal, nur etwas klarer, knapper und begreiflicher, gelesen haben, und zwar gelesen haben in Adolf Hitlers „Mein Kampf".

Wir haben bestimmt nichts dagegen einzuwenden, wenn andere Völker neue Wege beschreiten, die sie als Fortschritt bezeichnen. Aber wir nehmen uns das Recht festzustellen, daß diese Fortschritte sich mit unseren Errungenschaften decken — Errungenschaften, die man einst nur zu oft glaubte, uns zum Vorwurf machen zu können.

Seid Vermittler der Wahrheit!

Vorwürfe und Kritik, mögen sie noch so gehässig sein, lassen uns völlig kalt. Wir tun, was wir für richtig halten. Wir tun, was unserem Volke nützt, gleichgültig, was man draußen darüber denkt oder sagt.

Wir wissen aus Erfahrung, daß solche Kritik meist gar nicht einer besseren Ueberzeugung oder gar dem Wunsche entspricht, uns helfend zu beraten, sondern es ist lediglich die Absicht, uns in der Weltmeinung Schaden zuzufügen, koste es, was es wolle. Es ist die Absicht, kein Verständnis für das Tun und Lassen der sogenannten autoritären Staaten aufkommen zu lassen und dadurch die Verständigung zwischen den Völkern zu erschweren. Weil wir dies wissen, weil wir den Hintergrund der Kritik an uns durchschauen, deshalb zeigen wir auf die Beweise der Unwahrhaftigkeit der Kritiker.

Erfreulicherweise kommen alljährlich in immer wachsender Zahl Angehörige fremder Staaten in unser Land, Fremde, die mit eigenen Augen sehen wollen, wie es bei uns in Wirklichkeit aussieht und welches nun tatsächlich die Ergebnisse der nationalsozialistischen Herrschaft sind. Ueber diese Besucher freuen wir uns ehrlich. Wir freuen uns, weil wir wissen, daß, gleich welcher politischen Anschauung sie angehören und gleich welchem Stand und welcher Klasse sie sich zurechnen, sie bald anerkennen müssen, welche Leistungen im Reich Adolf Hitlers vollbracht wurden und vollbracht werden. Wir wissen, daß alle, die guten Willens sind, Deutschland einst wieder verlassen als Träger des Verstehens und als Träger der Verständigung zwischen uns und dem Lande, dem sie angehören.

Auch ihr, meine auslandsdeutschen Volksgenossen", so fuhr der Stellvertreter des Führers mit besonderer Betonung fort, „geht wieder zurück in eure Gastländer als Vermittler der Wahrheit über eure große Heimat, über das neue Deutschland. Wir wissen, daß ihr draußen an eurem Teil der Wahrheit zum Siege verhelfen werdet.

Weihe neuer Fahnen

Als Sinnzeichen des Nationalsozialismus und als Symbole der Verpflichtung auf den Mann, der ihn schuf, werden auch in diesem Jahre wieder 24 Haken-kreuzfahnen hier von Stuttgart aus mit euch hinausgehen in alle Welt. Ihr tragt diese Fahnen der nationalsozialistischen Gemeinschaft mit euch hinaus, nicht zum Sturmangriff auf fremde Ueberzeugungen und Weltanschauungen! Ihr nehmt sie mit euch als eure eigensten, nur für euch allein bestimmten friedlichen Symbole eurer Heimat.

Es sollen die Fahnen, die wir jetzt weihen, euch ein Stück Heimat in der Fremde sein. Sie sollen wehen als Mittelpunkt des Deutschtums, und sie sollen euch mahnen und euch die Kraft geben, euer Leben dem Gedanken unterzuordnen: Alles für Deutschland!"

Es beginnt nun die feierliche Weihe der neuer Fahnen. Das Kommando: „Stillgestanden! Fahnen hoch!" schallt über die Arena. Rudolf Heß nimmt die Weihe mit folgenden Worten vor:

„Euch Symbole des neuen Glaubens und des neuen Reiches, die ihr in Niederländisch-Indien, in Südafrika, in Rumänien, in Polen, in den Niederlanden, in der Schweiz, in Großbritannien und im Sudetenland wehen werdet, die ihr wehen werdet auf deutschen Schiffen, ich weihe euch: Fahnen des Nationalsozialismus, weht für die Ehre Deutschlands und seines Führers. Weht nun in der fernen Welt als Symbol des großen Reiches, das Adolf Hitler schuf! Fahnen, ihr seid geweiht!"

Rudolf Heß gedenkt zum Abschluß seiner Rede der Stuttgarter Tage des vergangenen Jahres, als hier in Stuttgart deutsche Männer und Frauen, deutsche Buben und Mädel in ihren heimischen Trachten erschienen waren, glühend beseelt vom großdeutschen Gedanken, leidenschaftlich bewegt vom Nationalsozialismus, aber doch eben äußerlich Volksdeutsche, Deutsche fremder Staatsangehörigkeit.

„Heute", so fuhr Rudolf Heß fort, „stehen sie auch äußerlich in unseren Reihen. Sie werden stolz und glücklich in den Formationen der nationalsozialistischen Bewegung an ihrem Führer in Nürnberg vorbeimarschieren — diesmal als Reichsdeutsche! Und wir alle sind von Herzen glücklich, wenn wir sie sehen. Sie haben einen langen und zähen Kampf gekämpft, einen Kampf mit einem hinterhältigen und verlogenen Gegner. Sie haben sich ihre Heimat erkämpft, und sie haben sich zu der Liebe, die ihnen Deutschland immer entgegenbrachte, die stolze Anerkennung des ganzen Volkes errungen."

Der Kampf der Sudetendeutschen

Rudolf Heß gedenkt hier des ähnlichen Ringens in einer anderen deutschen Volksgruppe um ihr nationales Lebensrecht: „Mit tiefster Anteilnahme für ihre Leiden sieht das deutsche Volk auf die deutschen Volksgenossen in der Tschecho-Slowakei. Niemand auf der Welt, der sein eigenes Volk liebt und stolz auf sein Volk ist, wird es uns verdenken, wenn wir auch hier von dieser Stelle aus unsere Gedanken zu den Sudetendeutschen wenden, wenn wir ihnen sagen, daß wir voller Bewunderung sehen, wie sie trotz schlimmster Schikane, trotz Terror und Mord eiserne Disziplin wahren. Hätte es überhaupt eines Beweises bedurft, daß beste deutsche Tugenden sich im Sudetendeutschtum verkörpern, dann ist es diese eiserne Disziplin und die unerschütterliche Ruhe, die aus dem Gefühl des eigenen Rechts kommt. Ihr wißt es im Sudetenland: Wir sind mit heißem Herzen bei euch. (Mit jubelnder Begeisterung unterstreichen die Massen diesen Gruß des Stellvertreters des Führers an die Sudetendeutschen). Bei euch liegt das Recht von 3½ Millionen deutscher Menschen, das Recht von Millionen Angehörigen eines großen Volkes, ihr Leben so zu führen und so zu gestalten, wie es die Zugehörigkeit zu diesem Kulturvolk gebietet."

Der Stellvertreter des Führers schließt seine Rede mit den Worten: „Nach den Stunden des Feierns hier führen uns unsere Lebenswege wieder auseinander. Wir kehren zurück an jene Plätze, auf denen wir arbeiten dürfen für unser Volk, unser Reich und unseren Führer. So wie wir hier sichtbar eine geschlossene Einheit gebildet haben, so bleiben wir auch im Alltag eine unzertrennbare Gemeinschaft, eine Gemeinschaft deutscher Herzen und des deutschen Willens. Unser politischer Glaube auf dieser Welt ist der Glaube an die Sendung des Führers für Deutschland. In diesem Glauben grüßen wir den Mann, der Deutschlands Schicksal ist: Adolf Hitler Sieg-Heil!"

Nicht endenwollender Jubel dankte dem Stellvertreter des Führers als er seine von großer Liebe zum gesamten Deutschtum im Auslande zeugende Rede beendete. Mächtig hallen das Sieg-Heil auf den Führer und die Nationalhymnen empor. Mit dem Fahnenausmarsch und dem Vorbeimarsch der Ehrenkompanie vor dem Stellvertreter des Führers schloß die denkwürdige Großkundgebung.

Am Abend nahmen die zahlreichen Ehrengäste an einer Festaufführung des „Rosenkavalier" im Großen Hause der Württembergischen Staatstheater teil, das aus diesem Anlaß ein besonders festliches Gewand angelegt hatte.

DOCUMENT 30–A

(Translation)

DER MONTAG (DAILY NEWSPAPER OF BERLIN), SECOND EDITION, AUGUST 29, 1938

70,000 in the Adolf Hitler Stadium

BIG DEMONSTRATION IN STUTTGART

Great Enthusiasm for the Führer's Deputy
Telegraphed by Our Special Correspondent

Stuttgart, August 28. The first big demonstration of the Sixth Reich's Assembly of Germans Living Abroad, in which 70,000 persons participated Sunday afternoon in Stuttgart's Adolf Hitler Stadium, offered a moving picture of political unity, a devout profession of faith, and enthusiastic devotion to the new Germany and its Führer. As in the previous year, the Führer's Deputy, Reich's Minister Rudolf Hess, appeared again this year to transmit to the Germans all over the world, who are especially close and dear to him, the first greeting of welcome from the party and the Führer.

. . . .

The Gauleiter and Governor of Württemberg, Murr, and the Chief Mayor of Stuttgart, Dr. Strölin, stressed in their remarks the mission of this city and of all Swabia toward Germans living abroad. The Reich's Minister of the Interior, Dr. Frick, who transmitted the greetings and the hearty welcome of the German Government to all Germans abroad, discussed in his talk primarily the tasks of the Germans abroad. In particular he emphasized three points: the cultivation of the consciousness of solidarity among all Germans abroad, the maintenance and deepening of the living spirit of the National Socialist racial community, and, thirdly, acting as the intermediaries for an understanding with other peoples and, therewith, as agents of the understanding itself.

Next, the Director of the Foreign Organization, Gauleiter Bohle, opened the Sixth Assembly with a special greeting to the Führer's Deputy and the Reich's Ministers in which those present joined with enthusiasm. Gauleiter Bohle then asserted in his opening remarks that this meeting is in the truest sense a Reich's Assembly of the Great German racial community in Germandom abroad. The pledge of allegiance to the Führer of the many thousands of Germans from abroad and the national anthems concluded the impressive ceremony.

. . . . . .

. . . With special joy Gauleiter Bohle then welcomed at this First Great German Assembly of Germans Abroad the Gauleiters and Ministers present from the German Ostmark (Austria) ; he welcomed further Reich's Minister Baron von Neurath and, with especial cordiality, Rudolf Hess. Gauleiter Bohle then gave the flag of the former national party group of Austria to the Foreign Organization of the NSDAP as a *flag of its tradition*, which he designated as a symbol of the loyalty of all Germans abroad. Receiving enthusiastic demonstrations of agreement, he read a *telegram of greetings to the Führer*, in which he transmitted to Adolf Hitler the loyalty and devotion of all the Germans from abroad who were assembled here.

[In his address Rudolf Hess stated in part:]

"You have joined up in the Foreign Organization of the NSDAP in order to cultivate your Germanism and in order to be good National Socialists. Your Germanism and your National Socialism are your own private concern. You are not engaged in any *'pénétration pacifique'*, you do not at all seek 'in a peaceful way to permeate' the host peoples with National Socialism. No, your Germanism and your National Socialism are your own private concern and remain also your most private concern.

"Nothing in this is changed, if here and there you are suspected of sinister tasks and aims, or if men believe that your National Socialism can be taken from you through the arbitrary prohibition of your external communal form. They can close your local groups, they can forbid you to wear your insignia, but they cannot forbid your National Socialist spirit and your German heart."

Rudolf Hess then recalls that the former Austria had previously been a special favorite of the democracies throughout the whole world:

"And in this favorite land of democracy, six and one-half million Germans were terrorized by a small political minority. But how excited people all over the world became, when the German people, with a really free decision and in the free exercise of self-determination, brought home the six and one-half million Germans of the former Austria into the great homeland, led them back into the great German people."

"As a visible sign of National Socialism and as a symbol of duty to the man who created it, this year also 24 *swastika flags* will again *go out* here from Stuttgart with you *to all parts of the world*. You bear these flags of the National Socialist community with you not for an attack by storm on foreign convictions and ideals! You take them with you as your own private symbols of your homeland, symbols meant for you alone.

"The flags, which we are now consecrating, are to be for you a piece of the homeland out in the foreign world. They are to wave as centers of Germandom, and they are to admonish you and give you the strength to subordinate your life to the principle: Everything for Germany!"

Now begins the solemn consecration of the new flags. The command, "Halt! Up with the flags!" resounds through the arena. Rudolf Hess performs the consecration with the following words:

"You symbols of the new faith and of the new Reich, which will wave in the Netherlands East Indies, in South Africa, in Rumania, in Poland, in the Netherlands, in Switzerland, in Great Britain, and in Sudetenland, and you which will wave on German ships, I consecrate you: Flags of National Socialism, wave for the honor of Germany and its Führer. Wave now far off in the world as the symbols of the great Reich that Adolf Hitler created! Flags, you are consecrated!"

At the close of his talk, Rudolf Hess recalls the day last year in Stuttgart when German men and women, German boys and girls, in their native costumes, had appeared here in Stuttgart, completely animated by the great German idea, passionately moved by National Socialism but nevertheless outwardly *Volksdeutsche*, Germans of foreign citizenship.

"Today", Rudolf Hess continued, "they also stand openly in our ranks. They will be proud and happy to march in the formations of the National Socialist movement past their Führer in Nuremberg—this time as German citizens! . . ."

Rudolf Hess then recalls the similar struggle of another German folk-group for its natural right to live:

"The German people looks at the German racial comrades in Czechoslovakia with the profoundest sympathy for their suffering. No one in the world, who loves his own people and is proud of his own people, will find fault with us, if from this place here we also turn our thoughts to the Sudeten Germans, if we say to them that we see with complete admiration how they are maintaining an iron discipline, despite the worst chicanery, despite terror and murder. If it had in general required a proof, that the best German virtues are embodied in Sudeten Germandom, then it is proved by this iron discipline and this steadfast calm, which comes from the feeling of one's own right. You in Sudetenland know: We stand by you, with passionate hearts. (The masses emphasize this greeting of the Führer's Deputy to the Sudeten Germans with jubilant enthusiasm.) *The right of three and one-half million German men lies with you, the right of millions of members of a great people to conduct their life and so to shape it as adherence to this people of culture demands."*

The Führer's Deputy closes his speech with the words:

"After the hours of celebration here, our paths again lead apart. We return to those places at which we are permitted to work *for our people, our Reich,* and *our Führer.* Just as we have visibly formed here a unity, so we remain an inseparable community in everyday life also, a community of German hearts and of German will. Our political faith in this world is faith in the Führer's mission for Germany. In this faith we greet the man who is Germany's destiny: Adolf Hitler, *Sieg Heil!"*

DOCUMENT 31

GERMANY SPEAKS (CONTAINING ARTICLES BY TWENTY-ONE LEADING MEMBERS OF THE NAZI PARTY AND GERMAN GOVERNMENT; PREFACE BY JOACHIM VON RIBBENTROP, REICH'S MINISTER FOR FOREIGN AFFAIRS): LONDON, THORNTON BUTTERWORTH LIMITED, 1938, PAGES 326ff.

GERMANS ABROAD

BY E. W. BOHLE

HEAD OF THE FOREIGN ORGANISATION OF THE NATIONAL SOCIALIST PARTY AND SECRETARY OF STATE IN THE FOREIGN OFFICE.

(Address delivered in London on October 1, 1937 before members of the German Colony.)

I was born at Bradford in Yorkshire, and spent the whole of my youth within the British Empire, partly in England and partly in South Africa. It is generally agreed that the impressions we receive during the first sixteen or seventeen years of our lives are particularly lasting in their effects upon our subsequent development. It is but natural, therefore, that my knowledge of Great Britain and the British should be more intimate and deeper than it would be had I acquired it in later life. In like manner, a British boy born and educated in Germany is certain to have a far better understanding of that country, and the national traits of the German people, than one born and bred in England, even though he may have made a profound study of our country and people when grown up.

My reason for thus prefacing the following is that as Head of the Foreign Organisation I have been subjected to a great deal of criticism, and my critics have entirely failed to appreciate the significance of the facts indicated.

I would like, therefore, to give a clear and straightforward account of the work done by that Organisation and to put right a few mistaken ideas about it, not by way of parrying the attacks made upon us— for our conscience is quite clear—but rather to explain the profound change that has come over the minds of Germans resident abroad with the transformation that has been effected in the Reich itself.

That transformation has attracted the attention of the whole world for the past five years with the result that—broadly speaking—people are now beginning to understand the new order of things in Germany. It stands to reason that so far-reaching a change in the mother country could not but greatly affect all Germans living beyond its borders,

387

and the responsible body guiding the changing trend in the right direction is the Foreign Organisation of the National Socialist Party, of which I am the Head.

On January 30th, 1933, Herr Hitler took over the government of Germany. Everybody knows that this step was much more than a mere change of government. It was the definite assumption of supreme political power.

Anyone who failed to realise that difference at the time has had ample opportunity since then to convince himself that the Leader of the National Socialist Party has not only changed the whole form of government but has entirely transformed every other aspect of public life in Germany. What could be more natural than that the Germans abroad should watch these tremendous developments with an interest unprecedented in its intensity? And, having grasped what has been done at home, they have become as fervent National Socialists as the people in the Reich.

That is nothing surprising; it is, in fact, a natural and logical development. For Germans living abroad are no different from those at home; they belong to each other, and they must know of the happenings in the Reich. After five years of effort in maintaining this contact I am proud to be able to state that perfect harmony between the Reich and its nationals abroad has been established—a harmony that will never be shattered.

Anyone who witnessed the enthusiasm of the 10,000 Germans who came from all parts of the world to attend the Fifth Congress held at Stuttgart in 1937 will endorse this statement.

If it be argued that there are Germans resident in other countries who are still opposed to the Third Reich, the answer is that they are a negligible factor. Their existence is no more important than the fact that in the Reich, too, there are still some people who object to National Socialism.

What is of importance, however, is that the National Socialist views on the values of life and citizenship have now been accepted by the vast majority of Germans within and without the Reich. This fact cannot be questioned by any fair-minded person. The inference is that the German element abroad is, as a matter of course, completely National Socialist minded, and that to be a German is the same thing as being a National Socialist.

Once people realise that the terms "Nazi" and "German" are synonymous the former will no longer be used to designate some exceptional type of German. To ensure this must be one of our principal aims if an honest attempt at a friendly understanding is to be made on both sides.

By way of explanation: if a London paper announces "A German speaks in London," this may be of interest or it may not, but there is nothing sensational in it.   If, on the other hand, the heading reads "A Nazi speaks in London," it would probably cause quite a flutter, many English people committing the mistake of thinking of a "Nazi" as something out of the ordinary, mysterious, although a Nazi is *ipso facto* a German and a German a Nazi.

When an Englishman addresses a Berlin audience, he does so as an Englishman and not as a Conservative, Liberal, Socialist or Independent.   The fact that we have only one party in Germany is a characteristic peculiar to ourselves.

And another eloquent illustration : supposing a Reich German goes abroad and says he is not a Nazi; similarly an Italian on his travels says he is not a Fascist, nobody would seriously take them to be representatives of their country.

If these things were properly understood in England as the home of common sense, we might cheerfully look forward to the disappearance of many obstacles tending to keep apart two great nations that have so much in common.   And if people would only grasp the fact that Germans in the Reich are National Socialists by conviction, they would realise that Germans abroad must likewise be regarded as National Socialists.

This brings me to the object of the Party's Foreign Organisation in Berlin, which is to unite these National Socialist Germans resident abroad by setting up local and divisional groups to foster and strengthen their love of the homeland, that is their National Socialist homeland, and their feeling of national solidarity.

These National Socialist groups in foreign countries are nothing more than voluntary associations of German citizens who believe in National Socialism as the instrument of their country's salvation and who, by joining these groups, want to show their readiness to contribute their share towards building up the new Germany.   They are not members of various political parties, but of the only political movement that exists in present-day Germany, and one that has taken a sure hold of the whole nation.

It is no part of their task to propagate National Socialist ideas among the citizens of other countries.   Their only function is to encourage their members to conform to these ideas and ideals as closely as their fellow-citizens in the Reich have done and are doing.

It is downright nonsense, therefore, to talk of the members of our Party abroad as "Nazi agitators" or "agents of the German Secret Police" (to mention only two of the many misleading terms that have been used), whose aim it is to infect foreign nations with what is called "Nazi poison".

The truth is that National Socialists abroad are expressly forbidden to interfere in any way with the domestic politics of other countries, and the much maligned Party discipline is perhaps the surest guarantee that this injunction is strictly obeyed. When other countries organise their nationals abroad in clubs, societies, associations and the like, nobody takes exception to it, and no country would consider its security thereby menaced.

The same is claimed for the organisations of German residents abroad being similarly a menace to nobody. Not one instance to the contrary has ever been brought to my notice.

It is more than ridiculous when certain persons and certain newspapers persist in raising the bogy of such a menace. The only result of insinuations of this kind is to disturb the relations between Germany and the country involved. And those disturbances are bound to occur if, for instance, young German women employed in foreign households are denounced as "spies," and if every National Socialist is referred to as a "political agent". The point that matters here is not whether the editors of those papers are pleased or displeased at the thought that German citizens abroad are National Socialists, but that they *are* National Socialists.

In Germany we do not trouble ourselves about the political views of British subjects residing in our midst. There are thousands and thousands of them, and I assume that they are good Democrats. But it has never occurred to us that they might be a source of danger to the existence of the Third Reich. Nor have we the slightest objection to their gathering together as often as they like in appreciations of the benefits of Democracy. We should be justly entitled, however, to put a stop to their activities if they attempted to impose their Democratic ideas upon us on the ground that they were suitable for our country. And with the same right the British people would be justified in prohibiting the propagation of National Socialist ideas in their own country.

But as nothing of the kind has ever happened, the attempts recently made in certain quarters to arouse feelings of hostility against National Socialists living abroad can only be regarded as acts of interference with the internal affairs of Germany. The ideology of Germans living abroad is nobody's concern but their own, just as the ideology of British residents abroad is exclusively their own affair. To take up any other stand on this question would imply a denial of Germany's equality of status; and we all know that the time for such a denial is definitely past.

It is one of the foremost duties of every government to look after its nationals abroad, to help them and to protect them whenever protection is needed. The British Government has always been a model to all as regards the fulfillment of this duty. That truth is so universally recognised that a passing reference to it is all that is needed here. In like manner, the solidarity shown by the British all over the world has always been exemplary.

The official representatives of the British Government have at all times protected the interests of their fellow nationals abroad in the most admirable fashion. They take every care (and rightly so) that His Majesty's subjects abroad shall remain loyal to their King and Country wherever they are. Every other country conscious of its national responsibilities takes the same view as a matter of course.

Some time ago, a Congress of French residents abroad was held in Paris under the chairmanship of the President of the Republic. It was attended by a large number of Frenchmen from the colonies, mandated territories and foreign countries; and several Cabinet Ministers were among the speakers.

Similarly a Congress of Swiss residents abroad was held at Berne. It was organised by the New Helvetian Society, and its importance was underlined by the fact that M. Motta, the Federal President, delivered one of the addresses on that occasion. Many of those attending the Congress used that opportunity of suggesting that the Secretariat of the Swiss foreign groups should be transformed into a Department of State. The Federal President himself is a member of the Committee of Patrons under whom the Secretariat conducts its activities. In Germany alone the Society has at present 37 principal groups and 31 sub-groups.

It is well known that Fascist Italy has had its Foreign Organisation for the past sixteen years. Poland, too, has a World League of Polish residents abroad, with branches all over the globe. It concerns itself in great detail with all questions that may affect its members in any way. It is presided over by a Cabinet Minister. Congresses attended by Poles from all parts of the world are held at regular intervals, and this League has undoubtedly achieved a great deal in keeping the national spirit alive among Poles in foreign countries.

We Germans do not look upon this as a matter for surprise, and we see nothing sensational in it. And strange to say, all other countries feel the same way. It is regarded as the natural thing to do. But as soon as Germany creates a similar organisation for her nationals abroad, limitless sensational charges are made against her and all sorts of ulterior motives attributed to her.

Thus, in outlining the work of our Foreign Organisation it must be understood that there is nothing out of the ordinary about it. As its Head my position was very clearly defined by the Führer when appointing me. Within the scope of the Foreign Office I am responsible for all questions that concern citizens of the Reich living abroad. The fact that I have nothing whatever to do with non-German nationals—either in my capacity as a member of the National Socialist Party or owing to my connection with the Foreign Office—has been emphasised so often as to require no further reference. All statements to the effect, for instance, that I make it my business to organise the German minorities in foreign countries are pure inventions; and nobody knows this better than the governments of the countries concerned. I am here referring, of course, to those of German origin abroad who are citizens of the countries in which they live.

I should like to state categorically that we neither desire nor expect any special privileges from foreign governments for those of our leading men abroad who are not connected with the diplomatic or consular service. This gives the lie to the rumours which would have it that the Foreign Organisation is thinking of appointing so-called cultural attachés abroad.

Great Britain, too, takes a lively interest in all matters affecting British residents abroad, than which nothing could be more justified. In 1920 a very interesting official report entitled, "Report of the Foreign Office Committee on British Communities Abroad", was presented to Parliament by command of His Majesty. The purpose for which the Committee was appointed was to discuss ways and means whereby His Majesty's Government can:

(1) foster a greater spirit of solidarity among British communities abroad, and
(2) make British ideals more generally known and appreciated by foreign nations.

Anyone who has read this Report, and who is in any way acquainted with the work done by our own Foreign Organisation, can see at a glance that we pursue exactly the same aims. And it should be noted that the Report was drawn up by a Committee appointed by the Foreign Office.

We consider it extremely important (the Report says) that His Majesty's Government should make it known without delay that they take a sympathetic interest in the activities of British communities in foreign countries, and that they are prepared in certain cases to afford practical support.

It is also suggested that British nationals abroad should be induced to register their names with the consular offices competent for their district. It is emphasised that every British child living abroad should be given the opportunity of receiving an English education. The Government is urged to support all associations and societies of British residents abroad that serve to promote British ideals. Stress is also laid on the desirability of establishing British Chambers of Commerce abroad, of organising trade propaganda, of providing English libraries, and of maintaining English schools.

Can the above go by the name of agitation, political or economic espionage? The British Government, and the special associations concerned with British communities abroad, have a perfect right to interest themselves in the affairs of their nationals, provided—of course—that they do not come into conflict with the laws of the countries in question.

Moreover, British residents abroad are perfectly entitled to promote the commercial interests of their country whenever they have a chance of doing so.   Similarly, no one can possibly object to our claims to exercise exactly the same rights on behalf of our German communities in foreign countries.   This is a birthright, as it were, which we do not wish to relinquish any more than the British people would think of relinquishing theirs.

Cosmopolitan sentiments will never take the place of national sentiment so long as there are different nations.   There will always be a British, French and an Italian national sentiment—and there will always be a German national sentiment.   Incidentally, the time has passed when people could count on a weaker national sentiment among Germans than among the members of other nations. We Germans of today, who are National Socialists, demand the same rights for ourselves as do other nations. We do not ask for special privileges, but we feel equally disinclined to put up with discrimination against us.

No fair-minded person can deny that many countries have derived untold benefits, more especially in the cultural sphere, from the German communities that have existed in their midst for a number of decades.   Besides, it cannot be questioned that these Germans are peaceful and respectable citizens who have always abided by the law and for whose presence no country has been the worse.

For this reason, surely, the unfortunate practice of suspecting and reviling Germans in other countries, that has lately been indulged in, should definitely cease.

When the Führer appointed me Head of the Foreign Organisation, numerous foreign papers seized the opportunity of designating me as the head of a widespread system of espionage; and no one was more surprised at the absurd charges levelled against me by a clique of irresponsible journalists than I was myself.   These outbursts came to a climax when they called me the "Chief of the Nazintern", an imaginary organisation whose existence, I suppose, is confined to their own fertile brains.   That such wild accusations could be raised is all the more remarkable as the work done by the numerous groups controlled by our Foreign Organisation must have made it plain to everybody that we Germans look upon National Socialism as something which we jealously treasure as our own property.

These false accusations make it extremely difficult for me to achieve an object which I am most anxious to see realised with the aid of our Foreign Organisation, namely to make the German communities the most popular among the foreign residents of each country in which they are domiciled.

We believe, and every reasonable critic will agree with our views, that the well-disciplined German nationals residing abroad constitute a special element of security for the country in which they live because their own country expects them to conduct themselves in a particularly decent and loyal manner whilst abroad, and because the National Socialist Government will hold each of them answerable for any attempt they may make to interfere in the domestic affairs of other nations, and thus impair Germany's chances of living in harmony with them. Moreover, those of our nationals abroad who may become destitute can never become as heavy a charge upon the country's revenue as the citizens of many another country, as we have a well-organised Relief Scheme for such cases, and resort to self-help as much as possible. We never tire of reminding our compatriots abroad that they must have the highest regard for the nationals of other countries. The very reason why we understand and respect other peoples' ways and traditions is that we love our own.

German residents abroad can surely be trusted when they say that they are staunch upholders of the cause of peace, as it is they who stand to lose most—if not everything—in the event of a war breaking out between their home country and their country of residence. It is therefore particularly infamous to represent them as warmongers.

Ever since the dawn of civilisation people have at times left their homeland to settle among strangers. Indeed, this is likely to continue so long as there is peaceful intercourse among nations. Instead of treating these foreign communities with suspicion and distrust, they ought to be regarded—in my opinion—as the best possible emissaries in the cause of international peace. They know the country from which they come and they get to know the country of their adoption. Who could be better qualified than they to create mutual understanding?

British residents in Germany are the welcome guests of the Third Reich, and not one of them—I am sure—can honestly say that there is such a thing as anti-British propaganda in our country. It is not usual for German newspapers to slander them or to accuse them of being spies. Nobody molests them, either privately or officially, because of their Democratic principles or because of their faith in the parliamentary system; and I think I may say that we treat our foreign guests with exemplary courtesy.

And even if we should have to arrest one or two on occasion because they happen to be spies, we should never think of generalising from such isolated cases and accusing all British residents in Germany of being spies. We should regard such an attitude as exceedingly unfair and, besides, we have no reason to entertain any apprehension for the security of our National Socialist régime.

There is an English word that has found its way into numerous languages in its original form and that is more appropriate than any other to serve as a basis for approaching all questions connected with our Foreign Organisation and the German communities. That word is "fairness".

It is not fair to reproach German residents abroad for being loyal to the Reich and for being National Socialists.

Nor is it fair to hold them responsible for the establishment of the National Socialist régime in Germany, because that is the régime desired by the German people and they want no other. This is known to every Englishman, however slight his knowledge of German affairs may be.

The form of government that exists in Great Britain is a matter of complete indifference to us; and we should never think of giving advice on this subject to any British nationals, whether living at home or among us. That is their own affair, just as it is exclusively ours to select a régime we consider best suited to ourselves.

Some time ago an article appeared in a London paper entitled, "Germany To-day". That article appealed to me and I would like to cite a few passages in support of my contentions.

> Germany's system of government is Germany's affair; Britain's is Britain's. And there is no sound reason why these two countries, each governed in the manner that its people prefer, should not live side by side in a spirit of friendly cooperation and human understanding. Such a change in their relationships would be immensely beneficial to themselves, and an incalculable contribution to the peace of the world.

That, of course, has always been Germany's view of the problem. It is the only suitable basis for all attempts at removing the endless series of misunderstandings that have unfortunately grown up in the relations between the two countries.

We Germans in foreign countries have declared over and over again that we desire nothing better than permission to assist in bringing about a fair and decent understanding among nations. The groups affiliated to our Foreign Organisation are representatives of the new Germany in the truest sense of the term, and are, therefore, admirably qualified to render most useful work in that domain.

But this can only be done if a stop is put to the practice of discriminating against them merely because they have completely identified themselves with the National Socialist Party.

And to this end I would direct an appeal to the British, and I do so not as an absolute outsider. After all, my whole childhood was spent among British boys and girls, and I was educated with them. During the terrible war years I attended an English grammar school and was the only German boy at the school. These facts, I think, enable me to see both sides of the question.

Anyone who knows Great Britain, the British people, and more especially British history, cannot but admire this great nation with its grit and foresight. Similarly, I think that every Britisher who has had the chance of studying German character and the epic history of Germany will be equally impressed with the imposing spectacle presented by the heroic struggle towards national unity which our people have waged for a thousand years, a struggle made all the more difficult by our geographical position. No power in the world has ever been able permanently to dismember our country, though there has certainly been no lack of effort to do so.

Surely, the time has come for these two great and proud nations to grasp each other's hands in friendship and to try to arrive at a sincere understanding even on matters concerning which their views must necessarily differ. They have so many things in common that these differences—which are part of their national characteristics—ought not to stand in the way of a *rapprochement*.

The Führer has often expressed a desire for such an understanding; and we Germans have noted with much gratification that his suggestions have been received with an increasing measure of approval on the part of the British people. Our Foreign Organisation will do everything in its power to support any such attempt, because we cherish the hope that German residents in Great Britain will be regarded by our British friends as what they really are—the Messengers of German Goodwill.

The National Socialists do not disseminate hatred and discord, but are anxious to deliver the messages of goodwill emanating from a country whose Leader loves peace because he loves his people and wants to make them happy.

The man who raised one of the world's great nations from the depths of misery and despair and made it great and united again, did not do so as a prelude to another war that would throw sixty-five million people back into the abyss from which he had rescued them.

He stands for the cause of peace—peace for Germany and peace for the world.

We National Socialists from foreign countries do the work that the Führer wants us to do. We are his loyal and devoted followers because we know that by carrying out his instructions we shall ensure the peace and happiness of our own country, and assist in healing the wounds inflicted upon a distracted world that knows no peace.

Sinn und Wesen

des

V. D. A.

Volksbundes für das Deutschtum im Auslande

von

Dr. phil. Otto Schäfer,
V. D. A.-Bezirksführer

**2. verbess. Auflage
5.—14. Tausend**

———

Herausgegeben von der

Ortsgruppe Wermelskirchen
und dem
Landesverband Niederrhein.

———

Druck: Müller & Co., Opladen (Pressehaus)
Generalvertrieb: Ludwig Schäfer, Frankfurt/Main

Vorwort

Die Volksbewegung unserer Tage ist nicht von irgendwo dahergeweht. Sie wurzelt zutiefst im Besten, was deutsche Nation je schuf,
im glaubenserfüllten Katholizismus deutscher Prägung wie in reiner
und klarer Wahrheit des Protestantismus, im Einheits-, Freiheits-
und Machtsehnen deutschen Volkes seit den Tagen eines Barbarossa
und Heinrichs d. VI., in edelster Dienstverpflichtung unserer großen
Preußenherrscher, ebenso wie in tiefster und geistigster Leistung unserer
Großen von Weimar. Sie wuchs im Leidensweg unserer österreichischen
Brüder, die dynastischer Verrat an slavischen Uebermut verkaufte, im
Kampfe der deutschesten Deutschen, der Kulturbringer des gesamten
slavischen Ostens um ihr Daseins- und Lebensrecht, ebenso wie in der
sozialen Gesetzgebung und Staatskunst eines Bismarck. Sie ergriff das
Reichsvolk im Volks- und Brudererleben des Weltkrieges und schlief
unter der Decke des Schuttes, den Verrat und Knechtung über deutscher
Volksseele aufhäufte. Den Nationalsozialismus oder das deutsche Volk
befreit, geweckt und zu sich selbst geführt zu haben, ist das Verdienst
Adolf Hitlers, die Hoffnung darauf in bitterster und schwerster Pflichterfüllung erhielt Paul von Hindenburg, der Ehrenvorsitzende des Volksbundes für das Deutschtum im Auslande. Unter seiner Führung hat
der Volksbund an seinem Platze gekämpft für die nationale und soziale
Umsinnung, für die Erhaltung unserer kostbarsten Erkenntnisse aus
dem Weltkriege. Dafür mag dies Büchlein, das mit Ausnahme der
letzten Seiten in den bewegten Julitagen 1932 entstand, Zeuge sein.
Darum gehört es auch den beiden Deutschen

Paul von Hindenburg
Adolf Hitler.

Alles für unser Volk!

Wermelskirchen (Rhld.), Mai 1933.

Dr. Otto Schäfer.

Vom Reichsdeutschtum und Auslandsdeutschtum zum Volksdeutschtum.

1. Deutsches Staatsdenken und seine Wurzeln — Eine Wandlung im Denken des deutschen Volkes

Wenn wir vom deutschen Volke sprechen, so pflegt sich fast stets das in der Kriegszeit aufgekommene Wort vom 60 = Millionenvolk einzustellen. Im Laufe des letzten Jahrzehntes erleben wir es jedoch immer häufiger, daß diese stolze Bezeichnung durch die noch stolzere eines 100-Millionenvolkes*) ersetzt oder wenigstens durch sie ergänzt wird. In diesem Vorgange verkörpert sich schlicht und unauffällig die Tatsache, daß das Denken des deutschen Volkes über sich selbst einer entscheidenden Umwandlung unterworfen ist, an der immer weitere Kreise teilnahmen. Sie bedeutet nicht mehr und weniger als den großen Fortschritt vom staatsdeutschen zum volksdeutschen Denken.

Was staatsdeutsches Denken heißt, erkennen wir am besten, wenn wir die betreffenden Abschnitte der Verfassung des deutschen Reiches, die sich das deutsche Volk**) gegeben hat und die zugehörigen Ausführungsgesetze ansehen***).

*) Deutsche befinden sich schätzungsweise in:

Dänemark (einschl. Nordschleswig) rund		60 000
Belgien (einschl. Eupen=Malmedy)	„	150 000
Luxemburg	„	250 000
Niederlande	„	80 000
Elsaß=Lothringen	„	1 600 000
Italien (einschl. Südtirol)	„	300 000
Polen	„	1 350 000
Danzig	„	360 000
Estland	„	30 000
Lettland	„	75 000
Litauen und Memelland	„	130 000
Rußland	„	1 000 000
Deutsch=Oesterreich	„	6 300 000
Tschecho=Slowakei	„	3 500 000
Südslawien	„	700 000
Ungarn	„	600 000
Rumänien	„	800 000
Schweiz	„	2 860 000
Vereinigte Staaten	„	10 000 000
Kanada	„	300 000
Süd= und Mittelamerika	„	800 000
Australien	„	160 000
Asien	„	197 000
Afrika	„	125 000
Deutsches Reich (1925)	„	63 339 000

**) R. V. Vorspruch;

***) A. 109—112; Reichsstaatsangehörigkeitsgesetz v. 22. Juli 1913 R.=G.=Bl. 538.

Wir machen dann die merkwürdige Entdeckung, daß das deutsche Volk nicht aus Deutschen besteht, wie wir annehmen sollten, sondern aus Reichsdeutschen, d. h. Angehörigen eines Bundesstaates oder unmittelbaren Reichsangehörigen, Auslandsdeutschen, d. h. im Auslande lebenden Reichsdeutschen und Deutschausländern, d. h. deutschstämmigen Ausländern. Der mehr als 30 Millionen starken Gruppe der Deutschausländern wird also der Name der Deutschen als die sie sich empfinden, von seiten des deutschen Staates vorenthalten. Sie sind ihm bestenfalls Deutschamerikaner, Deutschrussen, Deutschpolen, Deutschdänen, Deutschösterreicher, Deutschungarn usw., und die deutsche Oeffentlichkeit spricht dem Staate und seiner Behörde gedankenlos nach. Erst wenn von Deutschfranzosen, Deutschtschechen oder Deutschitalienern die Rede ist, wird sie stutzig. Das Gefühl erwacht, daß ein Angehöriger des deutschen Volkes nicht als Franzose, Italiener oder Tscheche bezeichnet werden kann.

Wer sich bei diesem Gefühle des Unbehagens nicht beruhigt und weiterdenkt, der findet dann nicht unschwer, daß ein Angehöriger des deutschen Volkes ein Deutscher ist, und daß die deutsche Volkszugehörigkeit und die Zugehörigkeit zu einem bestimmten Staate im Grunde garnichts miteinander zu tun haben. Weder hindert die fremde Staatsangehörigkeit den Deutschen an seinem deutschen Denken und Fühlen und in dem Gebrauche der deutschen Sprache, noch hindert umgekehrt sein Deutschtum ihn, ein treuer Bürger des fremden Staates zu sein. Volks- und Staatsangehörigkeit erweisen sich als zwei verschiedene Dinge. Man sollte sie deshalb auch sprachlich, d. h. im Ausdruck streng auseinander halten.

Woher stammt das staatsdeutsche Denken?

Die Ursache dieser Begriffsunklarheiten und ihrer verderblichen Folgen liegt in den noch heute gewaltig nachwirkenden Denkgewohnheiten des ausgehenden 18ten und 19ten Jahrhunderts. In jener Zeit geistiger Vorherrschaft der Westmächte, Frankreich und England, waren in Europa die Ideen von Staat, Nation und Volk ganz andersartig als die heute werdenden. Sie entstammten vorzüglich französischem Boden und waren für französische Verhältnisse geprägt worden. Sehen wir uns deshalb einmal den französischen Staats- und Volksbegriff näher an. Das französische Nationalgefühl erwächst aus der mittelalterlich=ritterlichen Vorstellung „la

5

douce France" (das liebliche Frankreich) und der Gedankenwelt, die durch die Begriffe des Gallikanismus (unabhängige Sonderstellung Frankreichs im päpstlichen Herrschaftsystem) und des rex christianissimus (allerchristlichsten Königs) bezeichnet wurde. In der Forderung der Grenzen des cäsarischen Galliens (Rheingrenze) gewann dies Nationalgefühl im 14. Jahrhundert geopolitische Form und angreiferischen Inhalt. Unter den Bourbonen, besonders Ludwig XIV., nahm das französische Nationalgefühl die Missionsidee der Zivilisation auf und fand in dem Begriffe „la grande nation" sein werbendes Schlagwort.

Dieser absolutistische-missionistische Nationsbegriff verband sich in der Revolution mit dem individualistisch-liberalistischen Staatsbegriffe eines Rousseau und Montesquieu. Sie sahen im Staate nicht eine höchste Ausdrucksform der Kräfte eines Volkes und seiner Wesenheit, sondern hielten ihn nur für eine Sicherheitseinrichtung, die von den Menschen zum Zweck des geregelten Zusammenlebens ersonnen, jederzeit wieder von ihnen abgeändert oder aufgehoben werden konnte.

„Le contrat social und la grande nation" sind somit die Wurzelbegriffe des heutigen französischen und damit des europäischen Nations- und Staatsbegriffes. Unter Betonung des ersten erscheint die Nation als eine politische Einheit, die auf Grund eines Willensentschlusses einer größeren Zahl Einzelpersonen entsteht. Die völkische Verschiedenheit dieser Einzelpersonen wird dabei völlig außer Acht gelassen. Willensmäßige, wirtschaftliche und politische Verknüpfung genügen, um Deutsche, Flamen, Italiener, Basken und Bretonen als ebenso zur Nation gehörig zu empfinden wie die Angehörigen des Kernvolkes der Franzosen selbst. Wir sehen deutlich, Staat und Nation, Staatsbürger und Volksbürger werden gleichgesetzt. Decken sich aber Staat und Nation, so hat der Staat — und damit wird der zweite Teil des französischen Nationsbegriffes führend — die Pflicht, das nationale Wesen zur höchsten Entfaltung zu bringen; es dort aber, wo es in seinen bedeutsamen Ausprägungen der Sitte, Zivilisation und Sprache noch nicht vorhanden ist, zu wecken und zu entwickeln. Diese Aufsaugung (Assimilation) der fremdvölkischen Bestandteile der französischen Nation bedeutet keineswegs eine Entnationalisierung und Unterdrückung eines bodenständigen Volkstums, denn zeigen alle Völkerschaften den Wunsch „de former un corps politique" (mit den Franzosen einen Staat zu bilden), so kann ihnen erst recht nichts lieber sein, als ganz und gar im Franzosentum aufzugehen, unter Hingabe ihrer alten Volkskultur.

Ob dieser Schluß in der Theorie und erst recht gegenüber der Wirklichkeit als richtig aufrechterhalten werden kann, muß füglich bezweifelt werden. Allein Frankreich hat ihn gezogen und die meisten Völker Europas haben ihn lange für richtig gehalten und vielleicht hat Frankreich gerade seiner Unbedingtheit die Erfolge in der Assimilationspolitik zu danken.

Dieser französische Staats- und Nationsbegriff hat das deutsche Denken und das der andern europäischen Festlandsvölker lange Zeit beherrscht. Völlig ungeeignet den volklich so verwickelten Verhältnissen in Mittel- und Osteuropa gerecht zu werden, war er eine der Hauptursachen des Weltkrieges und rief auch in Deutschland jene unklare Denk- und Ausdrucksweise in völkischen und staatlichen Dingen hervor, die wir oben kennen lernten. Wie verhängnisvoll diese Begriffsverwirrung, die französischer Einfluß in uns schuf, für das Deutschtum, vor allem im Auslande, beinahe hätte werden können, mögen die folgenden Zeilen zeigen.

2. Folgen der Uebernahme des französischen Volkstumsbegriffes für das deutsche Volksdenken

a) bei der Regierung:

Staat ist gleich Nation und wer in gleichen Grenzen wohnt, hat sich dem Mehrheitsvolke anzupassen. Ohne diese Grundsätze im eigenen Gebiete durchzuführen, erkannte sie die deutsche Regierung und mit ihr weite Kreise des deutschen Volkes dem Auslande gegenüber als unbedingt richtig an. Auf die Hilferufe der Deutschen in Ungarn hatten Kaiser Wilhelm I und sein Kanzler Bismarck keine Antwort. Man kümmerte sich nicht um den Bruch der zugesicherten Einwanderungsvorrechte in Rußland, unterstützte nicht die deutschen Ansiedler in Brasilien bei der Besitztitelbereinigung und sah der Zurückdrängung des deutschen Einflusses im Habsburgerreiche tatenlos zu. Während England dafür bekannt war, daß es für seine Volksangehörigen bis zum letzten eintrat und die Bevölkerung der Vereinigten Staaten zum englischen Volkstum rechnete, ließ Deutschland selbst seinen Reichsangehörigen im Ausland nur mäßige oder keine Unterstützung. Gerade in den Zeiten seiner größten Macht und seines stärksten Einflusses auf die Politik anderer Staaten, hat sich das deutsche Reich vom Auslandsdeutschtum abgekehrt und die eigenen Volksinteressen hinter den fremden Staatsinteressen zurückgestellt. Man hielt dies einerseits für politische Klugheit, denn man hoffte so die Anmeldung von Ansprüchen der Volksminderheiten im Reiche zu vermeiden, andererseits für eine Loyalitätspflicht (Treue- und Anstandspflicht) den fremden Staaten gegenüber. Ob diese Staaten nicht auch Loyalitätspflichten gegenüber ihren deutschstämmigen Untertanen hatten, wurde überhaupt nicht gefragt. Dazu kam die Furcht, daß durch eine Fürsorge für die Ausgewanderten die Auswanderungsbewegung stärker werde. Das war der Regierung nicht erwünscht, denn sie hatte längst erkannt, daß die Auswanderer in ihrer Mehrzahl nicht Taugenichtse, sondern tüchtige, wohlhabende Leute waren, deren Auswanderung einen großen Verlust für das Reich bedeutete.

Vor allem aber verursachte diese Zurückhaltung in völkischen Dingen, die auch heute noch im deutschen Volke lebendige aber irrige Meinung, daß der Deutsche nicht imstande sei, seine Nationalität festzuhalten. Dies trifft wohl öfters für die Gebiete zu, in denen der Deutsche einer höheren oder gleichgearteten Zivilisation oder Kultur gegenüber steht. Doch unterscheidet er sich dabei keineswegs von Engländern oder Franzosen, die beispielsweise genau so im Amerikanertum aufgehen wie die Deutschen, obwohl sie einen ganz anderen staatlichen Rückhalt besessen haben und besitzen. Zudem ist keines dieser Völker so sehr auf die Probe gestellt worden wie das deutsche und in alle Welt hinausgezogen. War es aber doch der Fall war, hatten die anderen Völker fast stets das Glück, in verhältnismäßig leeren Räumen mit kulturell tiefstehender Bevölkerung zu siedeln. Dort waren sie unter sich und konnten ihr Volkstum mit Leichtigkeit behalten, festigen und entwickeln. Das gilt von den Franzosen und Engländern in Nordamerika, aber schon nur teilweise von den Spaniern im Süden und den Russen in Asien.

Gegenüber unterlegenen Kulturen haben die Deutschen ihr Volkstum stets genau so wie die Engländer zähe bewahrt, während das romanischen Völker sich hier als viel weniger widerstandsfähig erwiesen. Wir brauchen nur in den Osten Europas oder nach Südamerika zu blicken, um für beides die Bestätigung unserer Ansicht zu finden. Zweifellos hätte der Deutsche dem Engländertum Amerikas gegenüber eine größere Widerstandskraft besessen, wenn eine starke deutsche Regierung hinter ihm gestanden und ihn in seinen ersten Maßnahmen zur Erhaltung und Pflege des Deutschtums unterstützt hätte, wie dies die englische Regierung mit ihren Einwanderern tat. Keinesfalls dürfen aber die aus schließlich in den Vereinigten Staaten gemachten Beobachtungen zu dem Satze verallgemeinert werden. „Wer auswandert, der gibt sein Vaterland auf und geht ihm verloren." (F r i e d r i c h K a p p Geschichte der Deutschen im Staate Newyork 1868/69 3. Auflage.) Denn gerade auch aus diesem, dem Untergang geweihten Deutschtum, klangen Stimmen wie die Fr i e d r i c h L e r o w s, „das deutsche Element kann und muß sich erhalten, Hand in Hand werden die Deutschen diesseits und jenseits des Weltmeeres gehen, nicht nur als Brüder, sondern als eine Einheit werden sie einander betrachten, sie werden ein organisches Ganzes werden, für dessen geistigen Verkehr das Weltmeer keine Schranke mehr sein wird."

b) bei dem Volk:

Waren es tatsachenfernes Denken, falsche Begriffsbildung und unpolitische Politik die Regierung und Gebildete dem Auslandsdeutschtum gleichgültig gegenüber stehen ließen, so war es bei der Masse des Volkes die Vorstellung, daß jeder Auswanderer ein Taugenichts sei. Man war froh, ihn loszuwerden, und mußte sich hüten, draußen seine Zugehörigkeit zum deutschen Volke gelten zu lassen. Niemand bemerkte, daß am Ende nicht jeder dritte Deutsche ein Taugenichts sein konnte, und daß jeder Deutsche in der nächsten Verwandtschaft dann deren mehrere hätte. Tau

genichtse waren stets die Verwandten der anderen, nie die eigenen. Den reichen Onkel in Amerika oder Rußland ließ sich jeder gern gefallen. Kam aber einmal die Nachricht, daß der oder jener sein Volkstum verleugnete, zum Ueberläufer geworden war, dann hieß es: „Da sieht man es ja, so machen's alle." Erwies sich dieser oder jener Verwandte oder Bekannte als bedenkenloser Geldverdiener und grober Materialist, der vielleicht dem Vertreter des Binnendeutschtums rücksichtslos und herrisch gegenübertrat, so hatte man gleich die Nase voll von diesen abgefeimten, rein kaufmännisch eingestellten Gesellen, bei denen man doch eben selber seinen Vorteil gesucht hatte. Erzählte man irgendwo von dem Vertreter eines Geschäftshauses oder einem Auslandslehrer, der von den materiell denkenden Auslandsdeutschen schlecht behandelt worden war, so vergaß man meist hinzuzufügen, daß diese Auslandsdeutschen Reichsdeutsche waren, die womöglich die Heimat noch nicht allzu lange verlassen hatten. In den Notjahren 1846—50, 1873—87 des vorigen Jahrhunderts und der Inflationszeit, sah man gar die Auswanderung als etwas durchaus Natürliches und Begrüßenswertes an. Schuf sie doch Raum für die Zurückgebliebenen und bedeutete so eine willkommene Erleichterung der eigenen bedrängten Lage. Noch weniger als seitens der Regierung erkannte man die gewaltigen Verluste, die das Volksganze und mit ihm der Einzelne an Arbeitskraft, Unternehmer- und Erfindergeist, an Geld und Gut, Ansehen, kultureller und politischer Geltung durch die Auswanderung und ihr Aufgehen im fremden Volkstum erlitt; ein Verlust, der umso schwerer wog, da er bei den anderen als Gewinn erschien. Macaulays Ausspruch, daß die Auswanderung eine der größten Taten der Nation sei und Schlözers Meinung, daß Emigranten gleich große und meist wohltätigere Revolutionen angerichtet haben als Eroberer, galt in England, aber nicht in Deutschland.

c) bei den Parteien und Auslands-Reichsdeutschen:

Materialistisch und liberalistisch dachte man in allen Teilen des deutschen Volkes, und staatliches Empfinden verdrängte auch hier mehr und mehr das völkische. Die Hoheitsrechte anderer Völker wurden unbedingt geachtet. Das Streben nach völliger Verbundenheit über die Grenzen hinweg, erschien als schwerer Eingriff in fremde Rechte. Rechtsstehende, nationale Kreise sahen in der Hilfstätigkeit für das Auslandsdeutschtum die Unterstützung fremder Staatsbürger gegen ihre Regierung und fürchteten unnötige Konflikte aus dieser Einmischung in fremde Angelegenheiten. Die Politiker der Linken wandten sich gegen solche Einbrüche in fremde Gerechtsame, da sie nichts anderes als der Versuch einer machtpolitischen, imperialistischen Ausdehnung sehen und verkannten ganz, daß diese Einbrüche ja gegen den Willen der von ihnen bekämpften Reichsregierung erfolgten.

Diese weitgehende Ueberwucherung völkischen Denkens durch die liberale Staatsidee bewirkte

7

endlich, daß der Reichsdeutsche, der hinauszog,
in dauernder Gefahr war, durch Unachtsamkeit
seine Staatsangehörigkeit und damit sein Volkstum zu verlieren. Die deutschen Gesetze zwangen
ihn zu lästigen, selten recht erfüllten Formalitä-
ten, widrigenfalls er schon nach 10 Jahren Aus-
landsaufenthalt das deutsche Staatsbürgerrecht
verlor. Wie man schließlich vom Auslandsdeutschen dachte, zeigt ein Vorfall aus dem Jahre
1913. der sich in der deutschen Kolonie in Chile
abspielte. „Dort haben es einige Reichsdeutsche
glücklich fertig gebracht, in der Presse einen
Streit über die Frage zu entfesseln, wer sich
Deutscher nennen durfte. Die Herren wollen
den in Chile geborenen Nachkommen der deutschen Einwanderer das Recht absprechen, sich
Deutsche zu nennen. Diesen wird empfohlen,
unter Teutonen, Teutochilenen, Germanen,
Deutschländern und ähnlichem mehr sich etwas
ihnen Wohlgefälliges auszusuchen; Deutscher ist
der Reichsdeutsche allein", so schrieb eine deutsche Zeitung.

d) bei dem Auslandsdeutschen.

War es noch ein Wunder, wenn angesichts
solcher Vorkommnisse die Auslandsdeutschen sich
zum Teil bewußt vom Deutschtume abwandten?
Lange war die Heimat machtlos und ohne Ansehen gewesen. Ohne Rückhalt hatten manche
im Kampfe um die angestammte Kultur die
Waffen gestreckt, die meisten umso treuer aus-
gehalten. Nun aber, da die Heimat die Macht
hatte, wollte sie von ihren treuesten Söhnen
nichts wissen. Die Frauenabordnung der Siebenbürger Sachsen, die das Reich um Unterstützung
in dem Kampfe um altangestammte Rechte, um
die deutsche Schule und deutsche Universität bat,
wurde vom Kaiser nicht empfangen. Der Tätigkeit des V.D.A. wurde, wo sie nicht wesentlich
den Reichsdeutschen zugute kam, die Unterstützung versagt, Hindernisse in den Weg gelegt.
Die verhängnisvolle Neigung des politisch un-
geschulten Deutschen, auf Stammesgenossen mit-
leidig, ja verächtlich herabzusehen und alles
Fremde kritiklos zu verehren, führte dazu, daß
der Reichsdeutsche im Auslande vielfach den
Angehörigen des Gastvolkes näherstand als den
eigenen Volksgenossen, von denen natürlich auch
umgekehrt der neuangekommene Reichsdeutsche,
der nicht wie sie siedelte, weniger freundlich aufgenommen wurde. Was hatte es da noch für
einen Sinn, zu dem alten Mutterlande zu halten, ihm zu Liebe Benachteiligungen im neuen
Staatsverbande in Kauf zu nehmen? War es
nicht am Ende richtig, daß Staat und Nation
eins waren und eins sein mußten? Wie manchen wertvollen Deutschen hat die Bitterkeit solcher Erlebnisse und Ueberlegungen, haben mate-
rielle Lockungen zur Aufgabe seines Deutschtums
veranlaßt.

3. Entfremdung und Umschwung.

So tat sich zwischen dem Reichsdeutschtum und
Auslandsdeutschtum eine immer größere Kluft
auf und die wenigen auslandsdeutschen und

reichsdeutschen Führer, die die drohende Gefahr
erkannten, mühten sich vergebens, das deutsche
Volk aufzurütteln, es zu völkischem Denken zu
erziehen, das Verhängnis abzuwenden. So lange
nicht die Reichsregierung oder ein Großteil des
deutschen Volkes hinter ihnen stand, waren sie
machtlos. In diesen Jahren gingen dem deutschen Volkstum zum späteren ungeheuren Schaden Deutschlands 20 Millionen Menschen in den Vereinigten Staaten verloren.
Im Bereiche der österreichischen Monarchie und
Rußlands erlitten wir ebenfalls gewaltige Ein-
bußen. Zu Beginn des neuen Jahrhunderts war
lich, war das deutsche Volk im Begriffe, weitre
35 Millionen Brüder, d. h. mehr als ein Drittel
seiner Gesamtzahl zu verlieren, denn es schien
zwischen Reichsdeutschen und Auslandsdeutschen
nichts Gemeinsames, sondern nur noch Trennen-
des zu geben.

Ehe aber noch Reichsdeutsche und Auslandsdeutsche recht begriffen, was vor sich ging, wohin
sie in ihrer Verblendung, deutschen Eigenbröde-
lei und Dickköpfigkeit gerieten, brach über die
deutsche Volks- und Kulturgemeinschaft der große
Krieg herein. Im Nu war alles Trennende,
alles Kleine, alles Verbitternde hinweggespült
von der gewaltigen Flut an Haß und Neid,
Schmach und Schande, Gewalt und Roheit, die
über alles dahinbrauste, was deutscher Zunge
war. Die Liebe zur Heimat, zur Sprache, zum
deutschen Menschen, zur deutschen Sitte und Kultur brannte auf in Millionen deutschen Herzen,
glühte sie frei von allem Kleinen und Bedenk-
lichen, allem Mißmut und aller Verbitterung.
Wie im und nach dem dreißigjährigen Kriege
Kulturdeutschland die Führung in der Philosophie (Comenius, Leibniz, Spinoza), Kunst
(Bach, Händel, Neumann, Pöppelmann) und
Rechtswissenschaft (de Grotius und Pufendorf)
übernahm, wie Preußen-Deutschland 1807 seine
Not durch innere geistige Wiedergeburt über-
wand, so entdeckte das deutsche Volk im Jahre
1914 sich selber. Im Augenblicke der größten
Bedrängnis fand es die größte innere Kraft-
quelle, die ein Volk als Ganzes und in seinen
Teilen über jede Not hinwegträgt, es fand das
Bewußtsein seiner selbst. Volk kam zu Volk,
Bruder zum Bruder, aus Deutschen in aller Herren Länder wurde ein einiges, deutsches Volk,
das alles in diesem Volksbewußtsein tat, das
alles in diesem Volksbewußtsein opferte, das
keine Macht der Erde mehr auseinanderreißen
konnte, das sich in den Tagen voll Schmach und
Unterdrückung, in den Tagen der Verfälschung
deutschen Volksgeistes selber treu blieb, daß es
unter der Führung seiner Besten wieder in herr-
lichstem Glanze erstehe.

Aus dieser Erkenntnis seiner selbst floß dem
deutschen Volke doppeltes Wissen. Es erkannte,
daß der bisher von ihm verwandte Staats- und
Nationsbegriff falsch, dem deutschen Volke nicht
wesensgemäß war. Nation und Staat, Nations-
gefühl und Staatsgefühl fielen dem deutschen
Volke in ihrer Begriffsdeutung wieder auseinander. Die Unterscheidung der Regierung zwischen Reichsdeutschen, Auslandsdeutschen und

Deutschausländern wurde aufgegeben. Es gab nur noch Deutsche schlechthin, Menschen deutscher Abstammung, Sprache und Sitte. So wünschenswert der Staat, der Nationalstaat als höchste Ausdrucksform reifen Volkstums blieb, er trat in der Schätzung hinter dem Volkstum und Volksbewußtsein, der Nation und dem Nationalgefühl zurück. Volkstum wurde wieder als das Naturhafte und Ewige gewertet, das vor dem Staate ist und nach ihm sein wird, das weit über seine Grenzen hinausreichen kann, ohne deshalb seine Echtheit und Ursprünglichkeit zu verlieren.

Zugleich aber erfuhr das deutsche Volk, daß solch urhaftes Volkstum nichts Starres, Lebloses, ein für alle Mal Feststellbares, sondern etwas Lebendiges, Wachsendes, Gedeihendes, Krankendes und Schwindendes ist, das vom Staate wohl geschützt, aber nicht von ihm geschaffen oder erhalten werden kann, etwas, das nur der Wille aller Glieder eines Volkes hervorbringt und am Leben erhält. Nur wenn sich alle entscheiden, deutsches Volk zu sein, im vollen Bewußtsein der Bedeutung dieser Entscheidung, dann ist das deutsche Volk eine Lebensmacht. Nur wenn alle willentlich um die Gestaltung der deutschen Volksgemeinschaft ringen, formt und erhält sich die deutsche Volkspersönlichkeit. Denn wie jede Einzelpersönlichkeit im Lebensstrome, ist auch sie nichts Seiendes, nichts Absolutes, sondern muß immer wieder aufs Neue geschaffen und verlebendigt werden in der Auseinandersetzung ihrer Glieder unter sich und mit anderen Völkern

Wenn aber das deutsche Volk mit solchem Gewinn, mit so glückhaftem Wissen aus dem großen Kriege heraustrat, wenn es sich endlich als Volk gefunden hatte und diese Erkenntnis immer schneller als seine Glieder ergreift, so ist das nicht zuletzt das Verdienst des Vereins für das Deutschtum im Auslande. Er hat das volksdeutsche Denken wachgehalten, als allein das staatsdeutsche galt. Während Regierung und Volk glaubten, sie könnten die deutschen Brüder im Auslande entbehren, hat er Verbindung mit ihnen unterhalten und alles vorbereitet für die Ueberwindung des staatsdeutschen Denkens durch das volksdeutsche. Möge im Gefolge seiner Arbeit sich diese Umsinnung im deutschen Volke ausbreiten und mit Gottes Hilfe Frucht tragen in alle Zeit.

Entstehung und Entwicklung des V. D. A.

1. Der Gründungsanlaß.

Ursache und Anlaß zur Gründung des V. D. A. waren die innenpolitische und völkische Entwicklung in Oesterreich-Ungarn seit den 70er Jahren. Von 1867—79 hatte in Oesterreich eine liberale, von deutschgesonnenen Ministern geführte Regierung das Deutschtum gestützt und als führende Staatsnation erhalten.

Als im Jahre 1879 das Ministerium T a a f f e ans Ruder kam, das mit kleinlichen Mittelchen durch 14 Jahre seine Regierungszeit immerwährend verlängerte, die Slaven gegen die Deutschen ausspielte und umgekehrt, wurde die Vormachtstellung der Deutschen in Oesterreich schwer erschüttert. Das Haus Habsburg hatte seine Herkunft und die Leistungen der deutschen Völker für seine Größe vergessen. Es glaubte, besser mit Tschechen, Polen und Ungarn zu fahren und benachteiligte die Deutschen überall. Deutsche Führer hatten in Kundgebungen schon mehrfach auf die systematische Verdrängung der Deutschen aus Schule und Amt hingewiesen. Man erkannte, daß das Deutschtum überall im Zurückweichen war. Tschechen und Ungarn, Slovenen und Italiener, griffen es unter Duldung oder gar Beihilfe der Regierung aufs heftigste an. Besonders kam ihnen dabei zustatten, daß sie die größere Kinderzahl, die stärkere Bevölkerungsvermehrung aufzuweisen hatten und zugleich bedeutend geringere kulturelle Ansprüche machten, als die Angehörigen des deutschen Volkes. Der Selbsterhaltungstrieb und der Stolz des deutschen Volkes auf seine Vergangenheit, seine Leistungen im Osten und das Bewußtsein auf den Rückhalt im Reiche, verlangten gebieterisch eine energische Gegenwehr. Verlassen von Regierung und Herrscherhaus, vollzog das deutsche Volk Oesterreichs einen bedeutsamen Wandel seiner Gesinnung und seines Denkens. Es unterschied endgültig und klar zwischen Staat und Volk, zwischen Staatsbürger und Volksbürger. Dem Staate galt nur noch seine Pflicht, dem Volke seine Liebe. Ihm in der Verteidigung seines Besitzes auch gegen die Bestrebungen einer parteiisch eingestellten Regierung zu helfen, wurde zur Selbstverständlichkeit für jeden Einzelnen (vergl. A. Hitler „Mein Kampf", S. 80 bis 83, S. 9—11, S. 102—108).

Diesem n a t i o n a l e n E r w a c h e n des österreichischen Volkes entsprach eine ähnliche, fast gleichzeitige Bewegung im deutschen Reiche. Ihre letzten Wurzeln liegen in der Entdeckung des siebenbürgisch-deutschen Volkstums durch Schlözer im Jahre 1791, der Forderung Lists in den 30-er und 40-er Jahren auf Ausbau eines deutschen Donaureiches, das seinen Einfluß bis zum persischen Golf erstrecken sollte, eine kühne Vorwegnahme des Berlin-Bagdad-Gedankens — und den verschiedenen Einwanderer- und Kolonialgesellschaften, die um die Mitte des Jahrhunderts ebenso schnell verschwanden, wie sie entstanden, da sie alle mehr oder weniger imperialistische oder wirtschaftlich-egoistische Ziele verfolgten, denen die reale Grundlage eines mächtigen Reiches fehlte. Viel bedeutsamer waren die gleichzeitigen und späteren Leistungen deutscher Gelehrter. In Frankfurt a. M. gab Wilhelm Stricker seine „Germania, Archiv zur Kenntnis des deutschen Elements in allen Ländern der Erde" (1847—50), heraus, forderte der Hamburger L a p p e n b e r g 1846 auf dem Germanistentage vom Reiche die Errichtung und Unterstützung von Kirchen und Schulen für Auslandsdeutsche, trug Heinrich N a b e r t in langer Arbeit die Grundlagen seiner Karte der Verbreitung der Deutschen in Europa zusammen, leistete A u g u s t L o t z eine umfangreiche Betreuungsarbeit in fast allen auslandsdeutschen Grenzgebieten. In weiten Wanderungen durch Frankreich, Belgien, die Zips, Bukowina, Gottschee, Südtirol, hatte er sich mit allen einschlägigen Fragen vertraut gemacht und aus der Praxis heraus die Grundsätze der Betreuungsarbeit entwickelt, die noch heute maßgebend sind. Allerdings dachte auch er noch nicht volksdeutsch, sondern staatsdeutsch, und die Stärkung der südösterreichischen Volkssplitter sollte vor allem der Gewinnung des Adriazuganges dienen. Die Betreuung der Grenzdeutschen schien ihm von größerer Bedeutung als die des Inseldeutschtums in Ungarn.

In ähnlicher Weise und ebenfalls völlig selbständig arbeitete in Stuttgart Dr. H e d i n g e r, in Baden Dr. Wilhelm Groos. Später trat noch in München Dr. Wilhelm Rohmeder, in Großenhain in Sachsen Dr. Gehre hinzu. Diesen Praktikern der Volkstumsbewegung trat der Berliner Richard B ö c h als Schöpfer der Gedankenwelt des Schulvereins zur Seite. Im Jahre 1863 brachte er seine „Sprachenkarte für den preußischen Staat" heraus, 1869 folgte sein Buch „Der Deutschen Volkszahl und Sprachgebiet in den europäischen Staaten". In diesem legte er den für die spätere Zeit, ja heute noch geltenden Volkstumsbegriff fest und trennte Volk und Staat als zwei völlig verschiedene Wesenheiten. Unter diesen Umständen bedurfte es in Deutschland und ebenso in Oesterreich nur eines äußeren Anstoßes, um eine große, erfolgreiche Volksbewegung auszulösen.

23

2. Die Gründung und Entwicklung in Oesterreich

In Wien hatte sich inzwischen eine politische Organisation national gesinnter Deutscher gebildet, die sich mit der Lage des Deutschtums in Oesterreich befaßte. Am 20. Dezember 1879 lenkte dort der Abgeordnete Max Unger die Aufmerksamkeit der anwesenden Vereinsmitglieder auf die Lage der Deutschen an der Sprachgrenze. Ein Ausschuß trat zusammen, dessen Mitglieder es übernahmen, die Verluste des Deutschtums in einzelnen Gebieten der Monarchie zu überprüfen und gelegentlich darüber zu berichten.

Unter diesen Berichterstattern befand sich auch ein Student, Engelbert Pernerstorfer, der spätere Mitbegründer der österreichischen Sozialdemokratie. Er nahm seinen Auftrag, über das Deutschtum in Südtirol zu berichten, besonders ernst. Während seiner Arbeit kam ihm eine Schrift des Frankfurter Arztes Dr. Aug. Lotz, „Aus den Bergen an der deutschen Sprachgrenze in Südtirol", in die Hände. Darin wurde über die Arbeit des Kuraten Franz Xaver Mitterer in Proveis berichtet, die er im Kampfe mit den wirtschaftlichen Schwierigkeiten und den italienisch gesonnenen Behörden Südtirols geleistet hatte.

Aus dieser Schrift entnahm Pernerstorfer wohl die Anregung zur Gründung eines Schutzvereins. Am 13. Mai 1880 benutzte er die Gelegenheit in einem studentischen Leseverein, in dem auch Altakademiker zugegen waren, diesen Gedanken einem größeren Kreise deutsch-gesonnener Männer vorzutragen. Seinem Antrage auf Gründung eines „Deutschen Schulvereins" stimmten die Anwesenden begeistert zu. Die deutsche Schutzbewegung war damit endlich zur Tat geschritten. Ein aus dem Kreise der Anwesenden gewählter Ausschuß, dem auch Dr. Viktor Adler, der spätere Führer der österreichischen Sozialdemokratie angehörte, arbeitete Satzungen aus und erließ einen Aufruf, der von fast allen bedeutenden deutschen Persönlichkeiten des damaligen politischen Lebens unterzeichnet wurde. Nur die Namen der deutschen Bischöfe fehlten, ohne daß die Veranlasser des Aufrufs hierfür verantwortlich zu machen wären. Die katholisch-konservative Partei jener Zeit war noch sehr klein, und so verstand es sich von selbst, daß die führenden Liberalen und Radikalen die größte Zahl der Unterschriften stellten, woran die Bischöfe Anstoß nahmen.

Um möglichst weite Kreise zu erfassen, setzte man den Mitgliedsbeitrag auf 1 Gulden fest. Eine kleine Kanzlei wurde eingerichtet, und als das Ministerium die Satzungen genehmigt hatte, fand die Gründungsversammlung am 2. Juli 1880 statt. In diesem Augenblick lagen 3150 Mitgliedsanmeldungen vor, weitere waren zu erwarten. Unter ihnen befanden sich erfreulicher Weise auch zahlreiche Meldungen deutscher Priester. Einen engeren Ausschuß bildeten Dr. M. Weitlof als Obmann, Dr. v. Kraus

als Obmannsstellvertreter, Pernerstorfer und Bondy als Schriftführer, Dr. Maresch als Zahlmeister, ferner Dr. V. Adler und Dr. Steinwender als Beisitzer. Am Jahresende betrug die Zahl der Mitglieder 20 000, die Einnahme 55 000 Gulden, 41 Schulen waren gegründet bzw. unterstützt worden, die Aufgliederung des Vereines in Ortsgruppen wurde notwendig. Ihre Zahl stieg 1886 auf 980, senkte sich leicht bis 1902, um dann weiter kräftig anzusteigen. Seit 1893 wurden sie in Gaue, später, als sich auch zahlreiche ländliche Gemeinden anschlossen, in Bezirksverbände eingeteilt, wobei die städtische Ortsgruppe den Mittelpunkt eines Bezirkes bildete. Von 1910 an drang die Bewegung auch in die Schulen vor und bis Februar 1920 waren 37 Schulgruppen gegründet. Zahlreiche Gemeinden hatten sich als solche dem Vereine angeschlossen, seine jährlichen Hauptversammlungen fanden einen immer größeren Widerhall im ganzen Lande.

Während sich der deutsche Schulverein so entwickelte, stellte sich für Teile der Monarchie doch heraus, daß seine auf das kulturelle Gebiet beschränkte Arbeit nicht genüge. In Böhmen und Mähren waren schon früher Zusammenschlüsse der in ihrem Deutschtum bedrohten Bevölkerung erfolgt. Das erwies sich jetzt auch für den Volkstumskampf im Süden als notwendig. Am 24. November 1889 wurde auf Anregung des Grazer Privatschulbesitzers Josef Feichtinger nach langen, mühevollen Vorbereitungen der Verein „Südmark" gegründet, der es sich zur Aufgabe machte, die in den gemischtsprachigen Gebieten Steiermarks, Kärntens, Krains, des Küstenlandes und später auch Tirols, bereits wohnenden oder sich niederlassenden Deutschen wirtschaftlich zu unterstützen.

Den äußeren Anlaß zur Gründung des Vereins gab die wirtschaftliche Bedrängnis des deutschen Bauern Franz in St. Egydi in den Windischen Büheln (Hügeln) bei Marburg. Er stand vor der Notwendigkeit, seinen schönen Besitz einem slavischen Bewerber zu überlassen. Eine einzige Mißernte genügte oft, um den von fremdem Leihgelde abhängigen deutschen Bauern zu vertreiben. An seine Stelle trat dann in der Regel ein von seinen Volksgenossen weitgehend unterstützter Slovene.

In den meisten Gebieten des Südlandes, in dem über ein Jahrtausend Slovenen und Deutsche friedlich nebeneinander gesessen hatten, wurde der Uebergang deutschen Besitzes in fremde Hände immer häufiger. Dieser steigenden slovenischen Flut wollte der Verein einen wirksamen Damm entgegensetzen. Es sollten alle bedrängten deutschen Bauern gerettet und ihre Scholle für das deutsche Volk erhalten werden, wie es im Falle des Franz durch Feichtingers tatkräftiges Eingreifen geschehen war. Im ersten Tätigkeitsjahr gewann der Verein 2 500 Mitglieder, Ende des Jahres 1899 waren es 20 000, die sich in 170 Ortsgruppen zum Abwehrkampfe vereinigt hatten. Die Einnahmen waren auf

24

90 000 Kronen gestiegen, 1914 waren die entsprechenden Zahlen 90 000 und 600 000.

Die Arbeit der beiden Vereine war so verteilt, daß sie sich nicht gegenseitig störten, sondern ergänzten. Der deutsche Schulverein übernahm vor allem die kulturelle Betreuungsarbeit, während die „Südmark" vorzugsweise bo-
den- und wirtschaftspolitisch tätig war, die Arbeit des Schulvereins erfaßte das gesamte ge-
fährdete deutsch-österreichische Gebiet, während
die „Südmark" ihre Tätigkeit auf die obenge-
nannten Gebiete beschränkte. In beiden Vereinen fiel den Ortsgruppen in erster Linie die
Werbe- und Sammeltätigkeit zu. Die Hauptleitung, ihre Vertrauensleute und besonders
beauftragte Ortsgruppen, leisteten die eigent-
liche Betreuungsarbeit.

Die Erfolge dieser Arbeit waren recht groß.
So wurde das in dem Gebiete zwischen Sa-
lurn und Bozen durch die Einwanderung
italienischer kinderreicher Tagelöhnerfamilien
schwer bedrohte Deutschtum durch die Einrichtung von Kindergärten und Schulen gekräftigt
und gestärkt, das Deutschtum der südlich gelege-
nen Sprachinseln im Fleimstal, Fersen-
tal und auf dem Hochlande von Vielge-
reuth zu neuem Leben erweckt. In Kärnten
trat man der Wühlarbeit slowenischer Lehrer
und Pfarrer unter der deutschgesinnten, windischen Bevölkerung entgegen und erfüllte ihre
Forderungen nach zweisprachigen Schulen.
Deutsche Büchereien wurden errichtet und deutsche Lehrer und Pfarrer herangezogen, die der
slowenischen Sprache mächtig waren. Der Lohn
dieser Bemühungen war das treue Einstehen
der windischen Bevölkerung für ihre kärntische
Heimat, als sich Jugoslavien 1919 dieser Gebiete
zu bemächtigen suchte.

Die bedeutende Arbeit, die in der Gott-
scheer Sprachinsel mit etwa 18 000 Deutschen, in Laibach, im Küstenlande geleistet
wurde, ist heute vernichtet. Besondere Erfolge
hatte die Arbeit in dem gemischtsprachigen Gebiet zwischen Mur und Drau erzielt. Ueberall
wurden verläßliche deutsche Bauern angesetzt,
mit Hilfe der Roseggerstiftung alle Schul- und
Büchereiwünsche erfüllt. Besonders das wichtige
und zu 90 Prozent deutsche Marburg kam so
wieder in fast unmittelbare Verbindung mit
dem deutschen Volksboden. Die Zahl der deutschen Stimmen nahm bei den Wahlen ständig
zu, ein großer Teil der Slowenen entschied sich
für die deutsche Kultur, trennte sich von den
slowenisch-nationalen Parteien und gründete
die steirische Staerc-Partei. Das
Land zwischen Mur und Drau schien wieder
deutsch zu sein, als der Zusammenbruch erfolgte
und jugoslavisches Militär einrückte. Da sich die
Steiermärker nicht wie die Kärntner zu be-
waffnetem Widerstand entschließen konnten, fand
hier keine Volksabstimmung statt, und das Land
blieb in jugoslavischen Händen. Wie die Betreuungsarbeit in Südtirol, so war auch die
in Böhmen im Unterschiede zu der Arbeit

in Kärnten und Steiermark rein abwehrend.
Sie erstreckte sich vor allem auf die Orte an der
Sprachgrenze und des Inseldeutschtums. Die
Hauptgebiete waren hier im Süden die Neu-
bistritzer- und Budweiser-Sprachinsel
und das Böhmerwaldgebiet; im Westen und
Norden lag das Hauptkampfgebiet im Be-
rauntal und im Mittelgebirge in Richtung
auf Leitmeritz und den Höhen des Iser-
tales.

Besonders schwer war der Kampf in den
Industriegebieten der Kohle, wo
der anspruchslose, kinderreiche, tschechische Arbeiter schnell die Mehrheit erlangte. Im Riesen-
gebirgsgebiet war die Bedrohung am größten;
hier hatten die Tschechen fast alle Täler besetzt
und die Hauptorte tschechisiert, so daß fast das
ganze Gebiet in die Betreuung einbezogen werden mußte. Gleiches galt von dem wirtschaftlich
schwachen und sehr armen Gebiete des Adler-
gebirges und den anschließenden nordmährischen
Sprachinseln. Auch in Prag war die Errichtung von Vereinsschulen notwendig, da die seit
den 70-er Jahren bestehende tschechische Ge-
meindemehrheit den Kindern der immer noch
40 000 Köpfe betragenden deutschen Bevölkerung
hartnäckig deutsche Schulen und Klassen verwei-
gerte. Die Prager Ortsgruppe übernahm diese
Arbeit und brachte Jahr für Jahr 70 000 Kronen für die Zwecke der deutschen Schule auf.
In Mähren wurden ferner vor allem die
Sprachinseln Iglau, Olmütz und Brünn
und die südmährischen Randgebiete geschützt.

Die gleiche Arbeit war auch in den Randge-
bieten Oesterreichisch-Schlesiens zu
leisten, während im Innern die Bauernschaft
genügend Widerstandskraft gegen alle Tscheki-
sierungsversuche besaß. Auch das galizische
Deutschtum und das des Buchenlandes (Bukowina) wurde im weiteren Fortgange erfaßt.
Ueberall, wo der Schulverein tätig war, zeigte
sich ein rasches Erstarken des deutschen Volksteiles und in manchen Gebieten, wie Ostschle-
sien, sogar eine Zunahme seiner Bedeutung. Vor
Ausbruch des Krieges schien der seit einem
halben Jahrhundert andauernde Rückgang des
deutschen Volksteiles in der Monarchie stillzu-
stehen. Man hoffte sogar, das deutsche Volk
werde die alte, durch Jahrhunderte besessene
Bedeutung wieder erlangen.

3. Die Gründung und Entwicklung im Reich bis zum Weltkrieg

Eine ähnliche, wenn auch nicht so glanzvolle
Entwicklung nahm die Volkstumsbewegung im Reiche. Wir sehen, daß auch dort
sich um das Jahr 1880 die Erkenntnis Bahn
brach, daß das deutsche Volk einen viel größeren Raum als den des neuen Deutschland aus-
füllte und daß dieser Raum ebenfalls vertei-
digt werden mußte. Es bedurfte nun noch des
Anstoßes, der Gefährdung des Deutschtums in
der österreichischen Monarchie und seiner Bedrohung in Ungarn, um überall in Deutschland
den Anschluß von Einzelpersonen und loser

25

Gruppen an den eben gegründeten österreichischen Schulverein oder doch ihre Mitarbeit an den gleichen Aufgaben zu veranlassen. Diese Urplötzlichkeit der Gründungen in allen Teilen des Reiches führte jedoch zu einer starken Zersplitterung der Arbeit und mußte auch auf die Dauer die Stoßkraft der Bewegung lähmen. Daran war der österreichische Verein nicht ganz schuldlos, da er nach österreichischen Gesetzen in Deutschland keine festen Ortsgruppen bilden konnte und deshalb lose Zusammenschlüsse unter der Führung von Vertrauensleuten bevorzugte. Auf diese Weise waren ihm außerdem die in Deutschland gesammelten Mittel sicherer, als wenn sie ein selbständiger Verein verwaltete, der auch das übrige Grenzdeutschtum in seinen Arbeitskreis einbezog. Tatsächlich wurde auch dieser Gedanke immer gewichtiger und trieb nun erst recht, da so die Gefahr der Zersplitterung ins Unendliche wuchs, zum Zusammenschluß. Ihn hatte die Ortsgruppe Berlin des Allgemeinen Deutschen Schulvereins, wie sich der dortige Verein unter Führung von Falkenstein, Böch, Bernard und Vormeng nannte, am 15. August 1881 zuerst ins Auge gefaßt und beschlossen. Doch bedurfte es noch langer Verhandlungen, bis im Jahre 1883 der endgültige Zusammenschluß aller Gruppen zu einem Verein mit 9000 Mitgliedern gesichert war Der Verein war unabhängig von dem österreichischen Verband, stand aber in engen, freundschaftlichen Beziehungen zu ihm, bis das Erstarken des Reichsgedankens und der immer maßgebendere Einfluß des staatlichen Denkens eine gewisse Entfremdung herbeiführte. Da der Verein noch zu klein war, um das gesamte Auslandsdeutschtum zu betreuen, nahm er sich zunächst der ungarländischen Deutschen an, die damals gerade auf das Schmählichste entrechtet und bedrückt wurden, und unterstützte den österreichischen Verein gelegentlich im Kampfe gegen die Tschechen.

Der Kampf gegen die ungarischen Regierungsmaßnahmen, die darauf hinausliefen, das gesamte deutsche Schulwesen in Ungarn zu vernichten, dauerte von 1881—87. Er spielte sich vor allem in der Presse und im ungarischen Abgeordnetenhause ab. Die Absichten der ungarischen Magyarisierungsvereine und der Regierung wurden enthüllt, auf die Schließung von 365 deutschen Volksschulen von 1869—80 hingewiesen. In Budapest war die Zahl der magyarisch-deutschen Schulen von 28 auf 6 gesunken, die rein deutschen waren völlig verschwunden, ein Ergebnis, das im Abgeordnetenhaus mit den Rufen: So ist's recht! Fort mit ihnen! begrüßt wurde. Den siebenbürgischen Sachsen waren nicht nur die Schulen, sondern auch das Privatvermögen, die Stiftungen, aus denen sie erhalten wurden, genommen worden.

Bismarck meinte: „Der Verlust der hergebrachten Selbständigkeit der Sachsen in Siebenbürgen hat in weiten Kreisen Aufsehen erregt. Wir haben indessen niemals auch nur durch die leiseste Regung dem Verdacht Nahrung gegeben, als wollten wir irgendwo über fremde Untertanen deutscher Abstammung irgendeine Art von Interventions- oder Schutzrecht beanspruchen. Haben die Deutschen in Ungarn oder Siebenbürgen Grund sich zu beklagen, so können wir das bedauern, werden uns aber dadurch in unseren politischen Beziehungen zu der Regierung des Landes so wenig wie in der vollständigen Enthaltung jeder Einmischung in dessen innere Angelegenheit irre machen lassen". Er hoffte, die Ungarn würden schon einsehen, wie sehr sie auf die Deutschen im Kampfe mit den Rumänen und Slaven angewiesen seien, erkennen. Bismarck dachte nur staatsdeutsch, nicht volksdeutsch. Ja, er sah noch nicht einmal, daß diese Deutschen eines Tages wie im Mutterland von unschätzbarem Werte werden konnten.

Weniger kühl blieb das deutsche Volk und die nationale Presse. Infolgedessen strömten dem Vereine in diesen Jahren immer neue Mitglieder zu. Ihre Zahl belief sich 1887, als die zweite große Tagung in Wiesbaden stattfand, auf 30 000 in 249 Gruppen. Die Einnahmen betrugen 54 000 Mark, 1890 waren es 40 000 Mitglieder. Man gewann überall Vertrauensleute, faßte in den Kreisen der Auslandsdeutschen selbst und in den Vereinigten Staaten festen Fuß. Um 1890 wurde es wieder stiller in Ungarn, die Regierung hatte im Wesentlichen erreicht, was sie wollte. Was der deutsche Schulverein gerettet hatte, war mit der Zeit schon zu beseitigen.

In Deutschland nahmen gleichzeitig eine Reihe staatlich denkender Vereine, wie die Kolonialvereine und der Alldeutsche Verband, von der Regierung unterstützt, die Aufmerksamkeit der Oeffentlichkeit in Anspruch. Dennoch beschloß der Verein die Werbetätigkeit der Hauptleitung zu beschränken. So war es kein Wunder, daß ein weiteres Wachstum der Mitgliederzahl nicht mehr zu verzeichnen war, vielmehr ganze Gruppen und Landesverbände das neutrale, anscheinend weniger aktive Lager des Schulvereins verließen und zu jenen neuentstehenden Verbänden überschwenkten. Bereits nach einem Jahre war ein Viertel des Mitgliederbestandes verloren, der Rest hätte gerne eine stärkere Beteiligung im staatsdeutschen Sinne gesehen. Dennoch hielt die Hauptleitung an der einmal angenommenen Einstellung fest. Der Verein beschränkte sich nach wie vor seine Tätigkeit auf das kulturelle Gebiet, auf Schule, Kindergarten und Volksbücherei. Politische Forderungen und parteimäßige oder konfessionelle Einstellung wurden abgelehnt, die Kritik an Regierungsmaßnahmen weiterhin vermieden. Da auch die deutsche Presse mehr und mehr in den Bann staatsdeutschen Denkens geriet, die Regierungsstellen sich in Schweigen hüllten und es meisterhaft verstanden, das nationale Wollen des Vereins nicht einmal durch einen Schein von Wohlwollen zu unterstützen, wurde die Lage immer schwieriger. So konnte die leidenschaftliche Arbeit eines Karl Pröll, der sich an Lehrer, Schriftsteller und

26

Abgeordnete wandte, ein Aufruf der Burschenschaft an die deutsche Jugend, nur wenig nützen. Auch vermehrte Werbung brachte wenig Erfolg. Es blieb nichts anderes übrig, als den Verein und seine Idee in eine bessere Zeit hinüberzuführen.

Indes lebte sich das deutsche Volk mehr und mehr in seinen Staat ein. Die gefühlsmäßige Trennung des deutschen Volkes in Inland- und Auslandsdeutsche vertiefte sich. Das Interesse an den Volksgenossen draußen schwand zuse..s. Das öffentliche Leben war eingestellt a..staatliche Geschehnisse. Innenpolitische Fragen, außenpolitische Gefahren für das Reich erfüllten das Denken der Reichsdeutschen. Vaterländische Feste, der Geburtstag des Kaisers, die Feier des Sedantages, waren Stunden der Erhebung. Die sozialen Unterschiede vertieften sich. Die Arbeiter sammelten sich in der sozialdemokratischen Partei, die Gewerkschaften wurden ausgebaut, heftige Auseinandersetzungen zwischen den Ständen drohten, während Deutschlands Waffenmacht und Weltgeltung wuchsen, die Kolonien aufblühten. Parteien und Konfessionen, Kapital und Arbeit dachten nur noch im Rahmen des Staates, und dennoch lag gerade auch in dieser Uebersteigerung staatlichen Denkens die Vorbereitung des Wandels zum volksdeutschen Denken, der sich so stürmisch im Kriegserlebnis vollzog.

Schon führte 1897 das Vorgehen der Regierung Badeni gegen die Deutschen in ihrer Sprachenverordnung für Böhmen und Mähren und die erneuten Angriffe der Ungarn auf das kulturelle Leben der nicht-magyarischen Nationalitäten zu einem Aufhorchen der reichsdeutschen Oeffentlichkeit. Neue Werbungen hatten Erfolg. Die Mitgliederzahl überstieg wieder 30.000. Im Jahre 1901 gelang es endlich, die Rechtsfähigkeit des Vereins zu erwirken, um die man sich seit 1885 bemühte. Der Arbeitskreis erweiterte sich, die reichsdeutschen Auslandsschulen wurden in die Betreuung einbezogen. In Baden und in Württemberg wurde eine starke Berücksichtigung des Auslandsdeutschtums im geschichtlichen und geographischen Unterricht angeordnet, in Preußen die Errichtung und Erhaltung deutscher Schulen im Auslande nachdrückliche Förderung zugelaßt. Das Reich regelte die Unterbringung von Auslandslehrern im deutschen Schuldienste bei ihrer Rückkehr, und erhöhte den Schulfonds auf 300.000 Mark. 1904 wurde ein Handbuch des Deutschtums im Auslande herausgegeben, die Errichtung eines Reichsschulamtes erbeten.

Obwohl diese Anregung nicht vom Reiche aufgenommen wurde, begann es doch eigene Kulturpolitik im Auslande zu treiben. 1905 fand der erste deutsch-amerikanische Professorenaustausch statt. Im Vorderen Orient und Ostasien wurde eine Reihe von Schulen und Hochschulen errichtet, die deutsches Geistesleben in der Welt bekannt machen sollten und den Deutschen dieser Gebiete dienen. Die Bestrebun-

gen des Reiches begannen sich erstmalig mit denen des Vereins zu berühren. In den folgenden Jahren nahm das deutsche Schulwesen und die Tätigkeit der deutschen Vereine einen gewaltigen Aufschwung. Der nordamerikanische Turnerbund schloß 400 000 Deutsche zusammen, der deutsche Tag in St. Louis 1904 sah die Vertretungen von 2500 deutschen Vereinen. In Kanada und Ungarn traten die Deutschen politisch auf und wählten Abgeordnete in das Parlament.

Die Zentralstelle, die alle diese Vorgänge beobachtete und unterstützte, war der Allgemeine Deutsche Schulverein. Er kam damit selbst allmählich in das Fahrwasser staatsdeutschen Denkens. Aber während ihm infolgedessen die Unterstützung der Behörden allmählich zu gute kam, vergaß er doch nicht den volkstümlichen Gedanken, sondern rettete ihn lebenskräftig in die kommende schwere Zeit. 1908 nahm er den Namen „Verein für das Deutschtum im Auslande (V. D. A.)" an. 1913 hatte die Mitgliederzahl 50 000 überschritten, der Gesamtumsatz belief sich auf über 500 000 Mark. So trat der Verein in den Krieg ein als ein mächtiges Gebilde, als der Zentralverein innerhalb der großen Schar der inzwischen entstandenen Deutschtumsvereine weitesten Sinnes, als Träger des deutschen Gedankens der Zukunft. Er war berufen, um des deutschen Volkes und seiner seit willen in seiner weiteren Entwicklung den Ausgleich zwischen den beiden Möglichkeiten deutschen Werdens zu suchen, der staatspolitischen, des Wachstums zum deutschen Weltvolk, das alle Volksgenossen einmal in seinen Bann ziehen mußte, und der volkspolitischen, des Werdens einer großen, freiwilligen, seelischen Schicksalsgemeinschaft aller deutschen Menschen.

4. Die Entwicklung vom Beginn des Weltkrieges bis heute.

Der Ausbruch des Weltkrieges schien den Verein auf die Bahn der Weltpolitik zu drängen und seinen Aufgabenkreis im staatsdeutschen Sinne unendlich zu erweitern. Er mußte sich der vielen vertriebenen Auslandsreichsdeutschen annehmen, sie unterstützen und ihre Entschädigungsansprüche bei der Reichsregierung vertreten, den Staatenlosen bei der Wiedererlangung ihres reichsdeutschen Bürgerrechts behilflich sein, daß sie einer bloßen Formalität halber verloren hatten. Man half den fliehenden Bewohnern der südtiroler Sprachinseln und sammelte für die kämpfenden Söhne des ganzen Volkes.

Bis 1916 waren für diese Zwecke rund 1 Million Mark aufgebracht. Nun fand der Verein auch endlich die Anerkennung der obersten Reichsbehörden und der Regierenden, die sie ihm bisher in einseitigem Staatsdenken vorenthalten hatten. Im weiteren Verlauf des Krieges suchte er die Meinung des Auslandes zu beeinflussen, sammelte die Deutschland freundlichen Stimmen und gab die Gewaltmaßnahmen der fremden Regierungen gegen ihre deutsch-

27

stämmigen Untertanen bekannt. In Polen
und Oesterreich beobachtete er die Haltung
der Nationalitäten, suchte die Lage der ungari=
schen Rumänen zu bessern und warb um Ver=
ständnis für die zunächst deutschgesonnenen
Polen. Seit 1916 hatten die Tschechen alle
Brücken zum österreichischen Gesamtstaate abge=
brochen. Auch hierfür wurden die Belege ge=
sammelt. In Brasilien, der Schweiz und
Polen gab es deutschfeindliche Vor=
gänge, die der Regierung zur Kenntnis gebracht
werden mußten. In den eroberten Gebieten
ging man an den Bau von Schulen und Lehrer=
seminaren, wenn deutsche Minderheiten vorhan=
den waren, so in Warschau, in Lodz, im
Baltenlande und der verbündeten Tür=
kei.

Der vor dem Kriege aufgenommene Gedanke
der Reisegemeinschaften zum Besuche auslands=
deutscher Siedlungen wurde weiter gepflegt.
Vor allem aber ging der Verein auch den Wand=
lungen in der deutschen Volksseele nach, die
das Kriegserlebnis hervorrief. Er erkannte zu=
erst, daß hinter dem scheinbaren Versagen des
Auslandsdeutschtums angesichts der Gewaltmaß=
nahmen der Feindstaaten in Wahrheit der große,
ernste Wille zur Volksgemeinschaft aufstand,
daß der Krieg das Deutschbewußtsein vieler Ge=
meinden und Bezirke Osteuropas zu ungeahnter
Stärke entfachte, in denen es vordem erloschen
schien. Und die Antwort all der Kundgebungen,
Spenden und Liebe zum deutschen Volkstum,
die aus den verlorensten Winkeln Europas und
der Welt kamen, war die Durchsetzung volks=
deutschen Denkens im Reichsvolke, die sich im=
mer stärker vollzog. Mitten in der kriegsnot=
wendigen Uebersteigerung des Staats= und
Machtgedankens, rang sich der volk=deutsche Ge=
danke zum Lichte empor.

Diese beglückende Erkenntnis half dem Ver=
ein wie dem deutschen Volke die Tage des Zu=
sammenbruchs überwinden. Sie gab die Ge=
wißheit, daß all die Not der Schmachverträge
nur vorübergehend sein werde, daß das deutsche
Volk Kräfte in sich trägt, die oon niemand auf
die Dauer niedergehalten werden. In dem Be=
wußtsein des Ewigen in unserem Volke,
ging der Volksbund in dem politischen
Wirrwarr der Zeit seinen Weg, erfüllte die
Aufgaben, die ihm gestellt waren. Er forderte die
Vereinigung mit Deutsch=Oesterreich, die Siche=
rung der deutschen Sprache und Kultur auf
Grund des von Wilson so laut verkündeten
Selbstbestimmungsrechtes, des Völker= und Min=
derheitenschutzes, und die Uebertragung des ak=
tiven und passiven Wahlrechtes zur National=
versammlung auf die Reichsauslandsdeutschen.
Aus dem Beschützer im Auslande wollte er zum
Bannerträger des Deutschtums im Auslande
und im Reiche werden. Er wußte sich, Hort
völkischen Denkens, frei von allem Imperialis=
mus, Sammelbecken aller Deutschen im Geiste
und Sein, Schützer deutscher Kultur, Verteidiger
der dem Parteienstreit vorzuenthaltenden Le=
bensbezirke des Volkes, Verkünder volksdeut=
schen Wesens, Lehrer volksdeutschen Denkens.

Vorsichtig wollte er seinen Weg auch weiter=
hin suchen zwischen all den vielen Vereinigun=
gen mit einseitig gefärbten Zielen, helfend, wo
es galt, große, gemeinsame Interessen zu ver=
treten, zurückhaltend, wo seine Neutralität nicht
geachtet wurde, vorsichtig mahnend und bittend
in den großen Lebensfragen unseres Volkes, un=
ter Verzicht auf alle Eingriffe in die Fragen
der Innen= und Außenpolitik, die nur seine
helfende Wirksamkeit draußen im Auslande
ten stören könnte. Das gelang dem Verein
so vollkommen, daß er lange Zeit bei den links=
gerichteten Parteien im Geruche imperialisti=
scher oder wenigstens nationalistischer Gesinnung
stand, während die rechtsgerichteten Kreise ihn
für unnational und zu wenig aktiv hielten.
Erst allmählich vermochte er auch in diesen, den
unbedingt national gesonnenen Kreisen des Vol=
kes Fuß zu fassen. Daß es ihm aber gelang,
daß ihm heute der Weg frei ist zu allen deutschen
Menschen, das beweist, daß seine Haltung die
richtige ist.

Indem der Verein so den Sinn deutscher
Volkheit zu seinem Sinne machte, übernahm er
eine Menge von Aufgaben materieller und ide=
eller Art, deren Umkreis und Form allein von
der Verwirklichungsweise des Sinnes deutscher
Volkheit bestimmt wird und daher hier nicht ge=
schildert werden soll.[1] Der Arbeitsbereich
dehnte sich auf das Gesamtlebensgebiet deutschen
Volkstums aus. Das verlangte von dem Verein
eine unerhörte Verstärkung seiner Mittel und
eine strafere Zusammenfassung und Neuorgani=
sation. Sie erfolgte in den Jahren 1919 bis
1925. Das Ortsgruppennetz wurde weiter aus=
gebaut und vor allem die deutsche Jugend durch
die Schulgruppen erfaßt, die Hauptleitung des
Vereins mit der Erweiterung seines Aufgaben=
kreises und der Einrichtung wirtschaftlicher Be=
triebe ausgebaut. Sie besteht heute aus den
Abteilungen: Geschäftsführung, Werbung und
Ausbau, Presse und Zeitschrift, Jugendarbeit,
akademische Arbeit, Stipendien, Ferienfahrten
und Wanderungswesen, Leibesübungen, Schul=
abteilung, Auslandsbüchereien, Bücherei und
Archiv, geschäftliche Abteilung.

Das Jahr 1921 brachte den Anschluß des deut=
schen Schulvereins als Verband Oesterreich an
den V. D. A. Am 29. März 1925 verschmolz
die „Südmark" mit dem Schwesterverein und
dem „Deutschen Schulverein Südmark", Verband
Oesterreich des V. D. A.", nachdem sie sich vor=
her mit dem „Bund der Deutschen in Nieder=
österreich", dem „Verein zur Erhaltung des
Deutschtums in Ungarn" u. a. österreichischen
Deutschtumsvereinen vereinigt hatte. Was unsere
Feinde verhindern wollten, war doch erreicht.
Das deutsche Volk bekundete seine Einheit über
die künstlich aufrechterhaltenen Staatsgrenzen

[1] Wir verweisen auf die Aufsätze „Vom
Sinn des V. D. A." und „Die Arbeit des
V. D. A."

28

hinweg, die fallen müssen und fallen werden, so bald die Fesseln von Versailles fallen und der Deutschtumsgedanke auch die regierenden Kreise Oesterreichs überwältigt hat.

Im Reiche selber entstanden unter Führung und Mitwirkung des so mächtig gewordenen B. D. A. in diesen Jahren eine Anzahl von Tochter- und Schwesterorganisationen, die die Erfüllung besonderer Aufgaben übernahmen, wie der „Deutsche Schutzbund" das „Deutsche Ausland-Institut" u. a. Die Mehrzahl der Deutschtumsvereine (über 90 Prozent) wurden Oich zu einem großen „Verband der freien Deutschtumsvereine" zusammengeschlossen, dessen Geschäftsführung vom B. D. A. besorgt wird. Er soll einerseits eine wirksame Zusammenarbeit und gegenseitige Ergänzung herbeiführen, andererseits Reibungen und unnötige Doppelarbeit vermeiden helfen. Seine bedeutsamsten Mitglieder sind der „Deutsche Schutzbund", das deutsche Auslandsinstitut, der „Bund der Auslandsdeutschen", die „Deutsche Kolonialgesellschaft", die „Vereinigung für Siedlung und Wanderung", der „Reichsverband für die katholischen Auslandsdeutschen", und die „Vereinigung Deutsch Evangelisch im Auslande". In den letzten Monaten ging der deutsche Schutzbund im B. D. A. auf, schloß sich ihm der Vereinsverband deutscher Auslandslehrer an, der durch seine Darmstädter Tagungen unter der Führung von Herrn Staatsrat Block mehr und mehr Bedeutung gewann, trat das deutsche Auslandsinstitut unter Führung des Siebenbürger Sachsen Dr. Richard Csaki in engere Verbindung mit ihm. Im Volksbunde selbst fand unter Vorgang des neuen Reichsführers, des Kärntners Dr. Hans Steinacker eine Umorganisation auf der Grundlage des Führerprinzips statt. Die Ortsgruppen wurden zu Bezirken, diese zu Landesverbänden unter Leitung national zuverlässiger Männer vereinigt.

So glänzend diese Entwicklung des B. D. A. der heute über 2 000 000 Mitglieder umfaßt, und der gesamten Deutschtumsbewegung auch erscheint, sie ist noch nicht zu Ende und darf nicht zu Ende sein, bevor sie nicht das gesamte deutsche Volk ergriffen, den letzten verlorenen Sohn in das Vaterhaus zurückgeführt, den letzten von deutschem Schweiß und Blut gedüngten Acker gesichert hat.

29

Die Arbeit des V.D.A.

1. Arbeitsziel und Arbeitsgrundsätze.

Das Arbeitsziel des V.D.A. im weiteren Sinne ist die Verwirklichung des Sinnes deutscher Volkheit, die Durchdringung aller Deutschen mit dem Volksgedanken, im engeren Sinne die erfolgreiche Schutzarbeit zur Erhaltung des Deutschtums in allen Ländern der Erde und zwar vorzugsweise durch die Pflege der Werk- und Ausdrucksformen deutscher Kultur. Er betrachtet sich dabei nur als Mitarbeiter, niemals als Wohltäter oder Fürsorger der in ihrem Abwehrkampfe unterstützten Volksbrüder. Als gleichberechtigte Kämpfer treten er und seine Mitglieder in die Volksfront der Auslandsdeutschen.

Die Erreichung dieser Ziele wird durch die Arbeitsgrundsätze, die sich der V.D.A. zu eigen gemacht hat, gewährleistet. Sein erster Grundsatz ist die unbedingte Neutralität in allen Fragen, die das Volkstum nicht unmittelbar und in seiner Gesamtheit angehen. Er stellt sich innenpolitisch bewußt über alle Parteien, Konfessionen und Gruppen. Für ihn gilt nur das Deutsche Wollen des Menschen, das aus seiner Deutschheit fließt. Ihm sind deutsche Menschen aller Parteirichtungen und jeder Weltanschauung willkommen, sofern sie darauf verzichten, innerhalb des Vereins ihre Sonderinteressen zu verfolgen. Die gleiche Neutralität bewahrt er in außenpolitischen Dingen. Er macht keinerlei Versuche, die Außenpolitik der Regierung zu beeinflussen, noch greift er in die Politik der fremden Staaten ein. Die politische Vertretung ihrer Interessen überläßt er ausschließlich den Minderheiten selbst.

Sein zweiter Grundsatz ist die strengste Rechtlichkeit. Gerade weil er auf die Mitarbeit jeder Regierung in Deutschland, die Volksregierung ist, unabhängig von ihrer Form, Wert legt, tut er alles, um mit seinem Gebaren in dem Rahmen der Rechtsnormen zu bleiben. Erst recht aber sucht er sich dem Rechte der fremden Staaten, in deren Gebiet er seine Schutzarbeit leisten muß, anzupassen, denn der Boden des Rechtes ist der einzige zuverlässige Grund für den Aufbau seiner Arbeit. Sein dritter Arbeitsgrundsatz ist der unbedingter Sachlichkeit. Gerade die den ganzen Menschen erfassende und erregende Volkstumsarbeit muß diesen Grundsatz immer wieder betonen, um die Leidenschaften, die sich so leicht einstellen, zu bannen, um Hilfe nicht dort zu gewähren, wo sie zwar menschlich erwünscht, dem Volksganzen aber schädlich ist, um die allzu geringen Mittel an der richtigen Stelle einzusetzen, die den größten Gesamterfolg verspricht. Sachlichkeit muß gewahrt werden in allen Aeuzerungen des Vereins, auch dann, wenn bittere Gefühle wegen Fehlern oder Nachlässigkeiten der Regierungen oder der Gleichgültigkeit vieler Volksgenossen die Herzen erfüllen. Sie muß erhalten werden im Meinungskampfe um den Gedanken des Bundes, für den Gedanken deutschen Volkstums, denn der Andersdenkende, der auch Deutscher ist, kann wohl auf falsche, aber nie auf böswillige Weise seinem Vaterlande dienen wollen. In der Anerkennung des guten Willens aller Deutscher liegt die einzige Voraussetzung für die Gewinnung der noch Abseitsstehenden. Darin muß der Bund und seine Mitglieder gerade in den Zeiten nationaler Zersplitterung vorbildlich sein.

Mit dem Grundsatz strengster Sachlichkeit ist der Grundsatz der Uneigennützigkeit eng verknüpft. Sie muß vor allem von denen gefordert werden, die der Sache des Volkstums durch ihre regelmäßigen oder gelegentlichen Geldbeiträge helfen, von denen, die ihre Arbeit zur Verfügung stellen, von denen in amtlichen Stellen, die um Förderung dieses großen Gedankens gebeten und nicht gebeten werden. Der V.D.A. kann nichts bieten, denn er muß seine Mittel möglichst uneingeschränkt den Schutzzwecken zuführen, oder er kann nur bieten, was die Helfer meist schon besitzen, die Liebe zum deutschen Volkstum. Wer vom deutschen Volke durch den Bund um seine Hilfe gebeten wird, wird letzten Endes auch um seine selbst willen gebeten. Darum müssen im Dienst dieses Gedankens alle persönlichen Wünsche verstummen, darf es keine Eitelkeiten, Zurücksetzungen und Rücksichtnahmen geben. Das Volk wird jeden rufen, wo und wann es ihn braucht. Nichts gilt hier als der gute Wille und die Sache des Volksganzen.

Der fünfte und sechste Arbeitsgrundsatz betreffen die Schutzarbeit des Bundes. Er gewährt seine Hilfe nur dort, wo sie verlangt wird, vor allem niemals gegen den Willen der Betroffenen. Er gewährt sie so, daß er zunächst die nötigen Anregungen zur Selbsthilfe gibt, ihre Formen ins Leben ruft und organisiert. Ist dies nicht möglich, so mahnt er die politischen Körperschaften an die rechte Erfüllung ihrer Aufgaben und sucht sie sonst irgendwie dazu zu veranlassen. So hat er z. B. viele Schulen zunächst selbst gegründet, und nachdem ihre Notwendigkeit erwiesen war, ihre Uebernahme durch die entsprechenden Gemeinde- oder Staatskörperschaften erwirkt. Nur wo Selbst-

Hilfe und Staatshilfe versagen, greift der Verein mit einmaliger oder dauernder materieller Hilfe ein. In jedem Falle zielt er aber darauf ab, dieser Hilfe Dauer zu verleihen und die Verwendung der gegebenen Mittel im nationalen Sinne unbedingt zu sichern. Damit die Hilfe schnell und wirksam gegeben werden kann, ist für jedes bedrohte Deutschtumsgebiet ein besonderer Berichterstatter vorhanden, der es beobachtet, Mitteilungen über seine Lage und Vorschläge zur Hilfeleistung macht. Im Kern aller Hilfsarbeit soll endlich stets in erster Linie das Gebiet der Kultur bilden, denn es ist durch Menschen- und Völkerrecht am besten geschützt, hat den zuverlässigsten Rechtsboden und ist für die Erhaltung des Volkstums von ausschlaggebender Bedeutung.

2. Das Arbeitsgebiet.

Das Arbeitsgebiet des B.D.A. ist naturgemäß das gesamte Gebiet des deutschen Volkes.

Ueberall wirkt er an der Verbreitung und Vertiefung des Volkstumsgedankens. Die praktische Arbeit gilt in Kerndeutschland wesentlich der Bereitstellung der Mittel, im Ausl nde ist sie dagegen vorzugsweise Schutzarbeit. Heute erfaßt sie alle auslandsdeutschen Gebiete, zu denen ihr der Zugang überhaupt möglich ist. Diese Gebiete werden eingeteilt in die des Grenz- und Inseldeutschtums. Zum Grenzdeutschtum gehören die Deutschen in: Nordschleswig, holländ. Limburg, Eupen-Malmedy, Luxemburg, Ostbelgien, Elsaß-Lothringen, der Schweiz, Südtirol, Kärnten, Steiermark zwischen Mur und Drau, den ungarischen Teilen des Burgenlandes, in Süd- und Nordmähren, in Böhmen, Schlesien, Polen und dem Memellande. In holländisch Limburg braucht im allgemeinen keine Betreuungsarbeit geleistet zu werden, da Holland das Deutschtum der Bevölkerung nicht bedroht, ähnlich liegen die Dinge in Luxemburg, obwohl die französische Einstellung der gebildeten Oberschicht eine gewisse Gefahr mit sich bringt. In Belgien versucht man leider in letzter Zeit immer mehr deutsches Volkstum zu unterdrücken, obwohl die amtlichen Stellen das Gegenteil behaupten, dies gilt besonders von dem durch eine Scheinabstimmung um sein Recht betrogenen Eupen-Malmedy—St. Vieth.

In Elsaß-Lothringen ist heute eine Schutzarbeit nicht möglich, da dies die Lage der Bevölkerung nur verschlimmerte und der französische Staat sie nicht zuläßt. Allein auch Frankreich muß sich darüber klar sein, daß der Locarnopakt erst dann lebendig wird, wenn es die systematischen Unterdrückungsversuche deutschen Volkstums aufgibt und den Willen der Bevölkerung achtet, die ihre deutsche Kultur nicht aufgeben will. Auch die Schweiz bildet ein Arbeitsfeld des B.D.A. Der deutsche Schweizer muß sein Volkstum dort, wo es notwendig ist, selbst verteidigen und ist dazu auch durchaus in der Lage. Am schlimmsten ist die Lage der 250 000 Südtiroler. Ihnen ist jeder deutsche Unterricht, jede Aeußerung ihres deutschen Volksbewußtseins verboten. Man zwingt

sie ihre Namen zu italienisieren, verbietet ihnen deutsche Auf- und Inschriften sogar auf den Grabsteinen und den Gebrauch der deutschen Sprache im öffentlichen Verkehr. Ihren Kindern wird jetzt sogar die letzte Zuflucht der deutschen Sprache, der deutsche Religionsunterricht, geraubt. In dem von Kärnten abgetrennten Kanaltal und im Mießtal liegen die Verhältnisse nicht besser. Hier ist die Schutzarbeit außerordentlich erschwert, wenn nicht ganz unmöglich gemacht. Ebenso sind die Deutschen der Südsteiermark großen Bedrückungen ausgesetzt und ihres öffentlichen Schulwesens zum großen Teil beraubt.

In Oedenburg, das durch den Terror der ungarischen Banden und eine verfälschte Volksabstimmung vom Burgenlande getrennt wurde, gibt sich Ungarn alle Mühe, mit der Entdeutschung der Einwohner. In Böhmen, Mähren und Schlesien sind auch die geschlossenen deutschen Sprachgebiete, die mehr als ein Drittel der Bewohner (3,6 Mill.) des tschechoslowakischen Staates bilden, in ihrer Gänze zu Betreuungsgebieten geworden. Deutsche Beamte werden überall entlassen und durch Tschechen ersetzt, deutsche Arbeiter und Angestellte aus den verstaatlichten Betrieben entfernt, so daß sie eine Arbeitslosenziffer von 54 Prozent aufzuweisen haben, während der Durchschnitt der Arbeitslosen in der Tschechoslowakei 23 Prozent beträgt. Deutsche Großgrundbesitzer werden enteignet und das Land wird an tschechische Bauern verteilt. Bis heute sind 311 Volksschulen, 34 Mittel-, 37 höhere Schulen und 2911 Klassen geschlossen worden unter dem Vorwande der Sparsamkeit. Dafür hat man aber 812 tschechische Schulen im deutschen Sprachgebiet neu erbaut, die geraubten deutschen Schulen selbstverständlich in tschechische umgewandelt. Die Deutschen dieser Gebiete haben sich zu dem „Deutschen Kulturverband" (Prag) zusammengeschlossen, der die Arbeit des österreichischen deutschen Schulvereins fortsetzt, seinen Besitz verwaltet und für die Zwecke des deutschen Volkstums verwendet. Ihm ist es zu danken, wenn das deutsche Volk hier wenigstens noch die notwendigsten Kultureinrichtungen besitzt.

Wie Polen, das zu 48 Prozent deutsche Oberschlesien in ein rein polnisches Land umzuwandeln bestrebt ist, davon berichten unsere Zeitungen oft genug. Aus Polen und Westpreußen sind etwa 2 Millionen deutscher Menschen vertrieben worden, der Rest ist den schlimmsten Verfolgungen ausgesetzt. In Bromberg wurde z. B. eine deutsche Fachschule, deren Errichtung genehmigt worden war, wegen zu kleiner Klassen geschlossen. Nach einiger Zeit wurde darin eine polnische Schule errichtet. Nun waren die Klassen nicht mehr zu klein. Danzig soll mit allen Mitteln zugrunde gerichtet werden, bis es seine Selbständigkeit aufgeben und sich Polen unterordnen muß. In dem Landstreifen innerhalb 50 km von der polnisch-deutschen Grenze darf kein Deutscher mehr wohnen das deutet die völlige Entdeutschung des sogenannten Korridors. Zu gleicher Zeit errichtet aber

Polen in Oberschlesien und Ostpreußen polnische Gymnasien und Volksschulen und kauft Land von deutschen Großgrundbesitzern für die Ansiedlung polnischer Bauern, denn es will die Odergrenze erreichen. Auch in dem unter der Verwaltung des Völkerbundes von Litauen geraubten Memellande hat die Litauisierung durch Verfolgung deutschgesinnter Führer und die planmäßig betriebene Einwanderung von Litauern bereits gewisse Fortschritte gemacht, so daß das deutsche Reich alle Ursache hat, die Sache der Memelländer kräftig bei dem Völkerbunde zu vertreten.

Verhältnismäßig am besten ist die Lage der Deutschen in Dänemark. Hier wird der Grenzkampf mit anständigen, ritterlichen Mitteln ausgefochten. Er trägt hier am ehesten den naturgemäßen Charakter des Messens zweier Kulturen. Nur die Schulwünsche der deutschen Bevölkerung wurden nicht genügend erfüllt. Da haben die schleswig-holsteinischen Volks-, Mittel- und höheren Schulen durch Pfennigsammlungen geholfen, die die großen Beträge von 70- und 80 000 Mark erbrachten. Dieser Grenzkampf wäre überhaupt unnötig, wenn Dänemark nicht der Versuchung des französischen Angebotes der Aneignung deutschen Volksbodens erlegen wäre, denn gerade in diesen Gegenden wäre die Ziehung einer gerechten Grenze besonders leicht gewesen.

So legt sich um die gesamte deutsche Grenze heute ein Wall von deutschem Elend und deutscher Not, der das deutsche Kernland augenblicklich vor weiteren Angriffen schützt. Umsomehr hat aber dieser Teil unseres Volkes ein Recht darauf, daß seine Not von uns gelindert, sein Kampf von uns mitgekämpft wird.

Weiter hinaus liegen dann wie große Wellenbrecher und einsame, von der alten Küste abgesprengte Blöcke, die deutschen Sprachinseln in der uns umbrandenden Völkerflut. Den Bewohnern dieser Sprachinseln geschieht von den Mehrheitsvölkern nicht geringeres Unrecht als den Deutschen an den Grenzen, und ihre Lage ist dabei unvergleichlich viel schwerer. Mehr noch als jene sind sie auf sich selber angewiesen und seltener fast dringt ihr Ruf zu uns. Dabei sind sie alle in früheren Jahrhunderten von diesen Völkern und ihren Herrschern eingeladen worden, sich in ihrem Lande anzusiedeln. Sie haben ihnen ihre Städte gebaut, sie die Kunst deutschen Handwerks und deutschen Ackerbaues gelehrt, brachten ihnen das Vorbild deutschen Rechts und deutscher Sitte, trockneten die Sümpfe ihrer Länder aus, rodeten die Wälder und schufen überall blühendes Land und Leben. Was sie im Schweiße ihres Angesichts erwarben, will man ihnen heute wieder nehmen. Zum Dank für ihr Wirken und Lehren sucht man sie zu vertreiben. Zu diesen Gebieten gehören vor allem das Deutschtum um Laibach in Krain, in Gottschee, Bosnien, im Banat, der Batschka, Syrmien und im Bakonjer Wald. Kaum besser als die Lage in diesen Gebieten ist die Lage der Deutschen Siebenbürgens, des rumänischen Banates, der Dobrudscha, Bukowina und Bessarabiens. Immerhin kommt ihnen die Führung der im Minderheitenkampfe aus der ungarischen Zeit erfahrenen Siebenbürger Sachsen zu statten. In der Errichtung eines rumänischen Minderheitenamtes liegt außerdem eine gewisse Bürgschaft für die Zukunft.

Das Deutschtum in Rußland hat zwar in der Wolgarepublik einen eigenen Staat, doch wird es in der Krim, Südrußland, dem Kaukasus und Sibirien hart verfolgt, da es auf Grund seiner Tüchtigkeit und individualistischen Veranlagung leicht in die Schicht der Kulaken einrückt und sich überhaupt für die Bestrebungen des russischen Kollektivismus als ungeeignet erweist. Die Deutschen der Zips, Prags und Brünns leben unter den gleichen Bedingungen wie die Grenzdeutschen Böhmens, denn ihr Gebiet fällt ja auch in den Bereich der tschechoslowakischen Republik. In Polen werden die Deutschen Wolhyniens, Lodzs und Warschaus naturgemäß ebenso verfolgt wie die an der Westgrenze wohnenden. Von den baltischen Staaten erfüllt nur Estland bis zu einem gewissen Grade die Pflichten eines Kulturstaates gegenüber seinen Minderheiten. Die zur Zeit der Gründung dieses Staatswesens gewährte Kulturautonomie hat in der Praxis leider manche Einschränkung erfahren. In Lettland und Litauen dagegen sucht man systematisch die deutschen Schulen aufzuheben. Vor allem im letzteren sind infolgedessen heute fast die Hälfte der deutschen Kinder dem Analphabetentum ausgeliefert, da die litauischen Schulen fehlen und die Erteilung deutschen Unterrichtes aufs äußerste erschwert wird.

Im Vergleich mit diesen europäischen Kulturstaaten überaus würdigen Verhältnissen ist die Lage des Deutschtums in Kanada, den Verein. Staaten, Mexiko, Brasilien, Argentinien, Chile, Deutsch-Süd-West-Afrika und Deutsch-Ostafrika geradezu paradiesisch. Dort wird ihnen wenigstens erlaubt, deutsche Schulen unter betonter Pflege der Landessprache zu errichten, was bis zu einem gewissen Grade notwendig und begrüßenswert ist. In manchen Staaten leistet die Regierung sogar Zuschüsse, was überall eine Selbstverständlichkeit sein sollte, da die Deutschen ja auch die Landessteuern in vollem Umfange mittragen müssen. Dort blüht auch das deutsche Vereinsleben, das in den europäischen Staaten mit Ausnahme Rumäniens ebenfalls verboten oder starken Beschränkungen und Verfolgungen ausgesetzt ist. Endlich ist noch aller der Deutschen zu gedenken, die in aller Welt verstreut sind und, immer wieder in Not geratend, die Hilfe des V. D. A. in Anspruch nehmen. Unter seiner Führung errichten sie in den stärkeren Kolonien deutsche Klassen und Schulen.

Wir sehen, das Arbeitsgebiet des V. D. A. ist übergroß geworden, es umspannt den ganzen Erdball und es vermag den Anforderungen, die an ihn gestellt werden, bei weitem nicht Genüge zu leisten. Auch darum muß sein Ziel bleiben: die Vereinigung aller Deutschen zu einer großen Gefahren- und Schicksalsgemeinschaft, zu einem Volk.

32

Die Arbeitsformen (drinnen)

Damit berühren wir aber bereits die Frage nach den Formen der Schutzarbeit. In Kerndeutschland, im Reiche also, hat sie vor allem die Aufgabe, den Volkstumsgedanken zu fördern, d. h. die Geistesverfassung vorzubereiten, die allein zu wahrer Hilfsbereitschaft und damit zur Bereitstellung der notwendigen materiellen Mittel überhaupt führt. Die Verbreitung des Gedankens deutscher Volkheit und die Werbung um die äußeren Mittel sind also eng verkn... Diesen Arbeiten unterziehen sich die Schulgruppen, Jugendgruppen und Erwachsenengruppen oder Ortsgruppen. Die Schulgruppen stehen unter einem aus den Reihen der Schüler gewählten Jungführer und seinen Gehilfen, dem Vorstande, dessen Tätigkeit wieder von einem Lehrer, dem Gruppenführer, beraten, geleitet und beaufsichtigt wird. Sie veranstalten Vorträge unterhaltender und belehrender Art, kleine vaterländische oder volkstümliche Feiern, bei denen deutsches Brauchtum besondere Pflege erfährt. Die Aelteren sammeln sich in Arbeitsgemeinschaften, in denen sie das notwendige Wissen über das Volkstum zu erwerben suchen. Diese Arbeitsgemeinschaften bilden den Kern der Schulgruppen. Seinen Höhepunkt findet das Schulgruppenleben in der Teilnahme an Treffen und vor allem den jährlichen Pfingsttagungen des B.D.A., die wechselnd vorzugsweise in Grenzgebieten stattfinden. Diese Tagungen weisen, wenn auch nicht absolut, so doch relativ steigende Besucherzahlen auf. 1925 Kufstein: 15 000; 1926 Hirschberg: 10 400; 1927 Goslar: 20 000; 1928 Gmünden: 16 000; 1929 Kiel: 15 000; 1930 Salzburg: 15 000; 1931 Aachen: 10 000; 1932 Elbing: 10 000; 1933 Klagenfurt-Passau: 11 000. Sie stellen für alle Beteiligten das größte Erlebnis deutschen Volkstums dar, wer sie einmal mitgemacht hat, ist der Sache des B.D.A. für immer gewonnen. Die Führer der Schulgruppen, die Obleute und sonst hervorragende Mitglieder werden außerdem noch in besonderen Schulungstagungen zusammengefaßt, auf denen sie die Pflichten ihrer Stellung und die wesentlichen Gedanken des Bundes näher kennen lernen. Was sie erfahren haben, sollen sie dann weitergeben, damit der Gedanke des B.D.A. allmählich in die weitesten Volksschichten dringt. Neuerdings wetteifern alle Schulen und Schulgruppen in dem Fest der deutschen Schule darum, ihrer innigen Verbundenheit mit den auslandsdeutschen Schulen, mit der deutschen Jugend insgesamt erhebenden Ausdruck zu geben. Mit den auslandsdeutschen Gebieten, in denen die Staatsregierungen nicht der Verbindung mit dem Reiche Schwierigkeiten in den Weg legen oder sie gänzlich verhindern, pflegen Mitglieder der Gruppen Briefwechsel. Leider müssen immer wieder Warnungen ergehen: Schreibt nicht nach Polen, nicht nach Südtirol, nicht nach Böhmen! Der Empfang deutscher Briefe ist eine Belastung für unsere Volksbrüder, bedeutet unter Umständen die Bedrohung ihrer wirtschaftlichen Existenz! Die Schulgruppen verfügen über zwei Zeitschriften, den Jung Roland für die jüngeren, die Rolandblätter für die älteren Schüler. Außerdem besitzen die meisten eine mehr oder weniger große Bücherei. Die Schulgruppen im Bereiche eines Landesverbandes sind wieder in einem oder mehreren eigenen Schulgruppenverbänden zusammengefaßt.

Wie die Schüler und Schülerinnen in Schulgruppen, so sind die Erwachsenen in Ortsgruppen, Männer- und Frauengruppen organisiert. Ihre Aufgabe ist es, den Volkstumsgedanken in die breite Oeffentlichkeit hineinzutragen. Zu diesem Zwecke veranstalten sie Werbeabende mit einheimischen und auslandsdeutschen Rednern, Volkstumsabende, die die Kenntnis volksdeutscher Kulturformen vermitteln sollen, volksdeutsche Kundgebungen, zu denen Vereine und Verbände auf breitester Grundlage herangezogen werden. Die Zeitschriften der Ortsgruppen sind der monatlich erscheinende „Volksdeutsche" (Jahresbezug 1,20 Mk.) für Mitglieder frei, die mit schönen Bildern geschmückte Monatsschrift „Deutsche Welt" und die Führerzeitschrift „Deutsche Arbeit". Außerdem verfügen die meisten Ortsgruppen über Büchereien, und werden von der verantwortungsbewußten Presse in ihrer Arbeit weitgehend unterstützt. Sie treten zu Gauen und Landesverbänden zusammen, deren Vorstand unmittelbar unter der Hauptleitung steht. Die Landesverbände sind:

1. Verband Oesterreich (Deutscher Schulverein Südmark).
2. Landesverband Baden.
3. Landesverband Bayern.
4. Landesverband Brandenburg.
5. Landesverband Freie Stadt Danzig.
6. Landesverband Grenzmark.
7. Landesverband Hamburg.
8. Landesverband Niedersachsen.
9. Landesverband Hessen-Darmstadt.
10. Landesverband Hessen-Nassau.
11. Landesverband Mecklenburg.
12. Landesverband Mittelrhein.
13. Landesverband Niederrhein.
14. Landesverband Ostpreußen.
15. Landesverband Niederschlesien.
16. Landesverband Oberschlesien.
17. Landesverband Pommern.
18. Landesverband Sachsen.
19. Landesverband Sachsen-Anhalt.
20. Landesverband Schleswig-Holstein.
21. Landesverband Thüringen.
22. Landesverband Weser-Ems.
23. Landesverband Westfalen.
24. Landesverband Westpreußen.
25. Landesverband Württemberg.

Alle Veranstaltungen der Schul- und Ortsgruppen sollen nach Möglichkeit der Bereitstellung von Mitteln für die Schutzarbeit dienen. Am bedeutsamsten, weil am sichersten verfügbar, sind die regelmäßigen Mitgliedsbeiträge. Dazu kommen die Sammlungen, die gelegentlich der

Veranstaltungen stattfinden, Straßen- und Haussammlungen in den Werbewochen und Büchersammlungen. Auch durch den Verkauf von Postkarten, Abzeichen, Blumen usw., wird manches Sümmchen hereingebracht. Erfreulicherweise mehrt sich auch die Zahl derjenigen, die den Bund mit größeren Stiftungen, sei es zu Lebzeiten, sei es für den Todesfall, bedenken. Aus ihnen werden in erster Linie die Mittel zur Errichtung volksdeutscher Heime gewonnen.

Die Arbeitsformen (draußen)

Diese Arbeit im Innern findet ihr Gegenstück in der Betreuungsarbeit im Auslande.

Ihr Kernstück stellt die Errichtung und Erhaltung deutscher Kindergärten und Schulen dar, denn die ersten 14 Lebensjahre sind in der Regel entscheidend für die Volkszugehörigkeit, wenn nicht ein ganz starker nationaler Wille vorhanden ist. In der Regel werden die Zahl der Kinder und die besonderen Verhältnisse der Gegend festgestellt und dann die Lösung der Frage in Angriff genommen. Leben die deutschen Kinder in national stark gemischter Gegend, so wird bereits die Errichtung eines deutschen Kindergartens notwendig. In einsprachigen Gegenden genügt die Errichtung deutscher Klassen und Schulen. In den meisten Fällen wird versucht, die Behörden zur Erfüllung ihrer Pflichten zu veranlassen; gelingt es nicht, so greift der Verein ein, und veranlaßt den Bau eines Schulhauses, indem er Unterstützungsgelder gibt oder die Schule selbst baut. Ueberläßt er sie einer Gemeinde später gegen die Verpflichtung der Unterhaltung, so bedingt er sich den Rückfall des Gebäudes und Grundes in sein Eigentum aus, falls sie nicht mehr nationalen Zwecken dienen können. An andern Orten übernimmt er die Besoldung der Lehrer, gibt Zuschüsse, um tüchtige Lehrer und Pfarrer in der bedrohten Gegend zu halten. Ist die Errichtung einer Schule unmöglich, so versucht er guten Privatunterricht zu vermitteln oder einzurichten, und stellt auch hierbei Zuschüsse zur Verfügung.

Eine ähnliche Einrichtung stellen die im Friedensvertrag für die Deutschen in Polen gewährleisteten sogenannten Mutterschulen dar. Sie erfassen die Kinder der ersten vier Schuljahre. Lehrerin oder Lehrer ist irgendeine geeignete Persönlichkeit aus dem Orte, die in einem Hause, einer Scheune oder einem Schuppen die Kinder der deutschen Familien sammelt und unterrichtet. Oft genug wohnt diesem Unterricht der Ortsgendarm oder sonst eine „Behörde" bei, um staatsverräterische Gesinnung festzustellen, und so einen Vorwand zur Schließung der Schule zu finden. Die eigentlichen Träger der Schulen sind Wanderlehrer, die mit dem Rucksack und Fahrrad von Dorf zu Dorf ziehen, die Mütter der Kinder und Helfer um sich versammeln, sie lehren, wie man die noch nicht Schulpflichtigen beschäftigt, ihnen die notwendige Kenntnis der Muttersprache vermittelt, festigt und erhält, wie die Schulpflichtigen unterrichtet werden müssen. Andere Wanderlehrer halten selbst Schule ab. Dann kommen die Kinder oft weit her, bleiben 3—4 Wochen am Orte, besuchen die Schule, nehmen Bücher in Empfang, aus denen sie weiter lernen können und kehren wieder heim. Das wiederholt sich vielleicht 2—3 Mal im Jahre. Im Vergleich zu diesen Kindern sind jene, die täglich einen 4—6stündigen Schulweg machen müssen oder jede Woche für zwei Tage kommen, noch verhältnismäßig günstig dran.

Alle diese Schwierigkeiten werden aber von der deutschen Bevölkerung gern in Kauf genommen, da sie weiß, daß mit der Aufgabe ihres Volkstums auch die Aufgabe ihrer Kulturstufe verbunden ist. Die Regierungen aller dieser Staatsvölker streben oft nur deshalb dahin, die deutsche Kultur zu zerstören, weil sie ihren Angehörigen eine so große Ueberlegenheit gibt, während sie selbst nicht im Stande sind, ihr Volk zur gleichen Höhe emporzuführen.

In den Ländern, in denen das Deutschtum geringerer Verfolgung ausgesetzt ist bestehen auch private höhere Schulen und Fachschulen. Da sie die Schüler aus weiten Gebieten des Landes sammeln, sind sie oft mit Schülerheimen verknüpft, die vielfach sogar nur aus den Mitteln einer Selbstbesteuerung der Deutschen oder mit Zuschüssen des V. D. A. errichtet sind.

Neben der Fürsorge für die Kindergärten und Schulen steht die Errichtung von Seminaren für die Ausbildung von Lehrern. Ihre Zahl ist infolge der Unduldsamkeit der Mehrheitsvölker heute sehr gering. Man sucht deshalb auch reichsdeutsche Lehrer heranzuziehen, schickt Angehörige der Minderheiten zum Studium nach Deutschland, gewährt Unterstützungen und veranstaltet Kurse zur Weiterbildung, die dann gewöhnlich ebenfalls in Deutschland stattfinden müssen.

Dem Erwachsenen dient dann vor allem das deutsche Schrifttum. Die Zahl guter, die Durchschnittshöhe der reichsdeutschen Zeitungen erreichender Blätter ist gar nicht so klein, wie man vielleicht annehmen sollte. Die deutschen Minderheiten wissen, welches Bindemittel sie an ihren Zeitungen besitzen und haben große Opfer gebracht, um sie ins Leben zu rufen und zu erhalten. Da und dort sendet der V. D. A. auch deutsche Zeitungen hin, doch ist es nicht überall angängig, da das Halten und der Empfang reichsdeutscher Zeitungen, in denen vielleicht einmal das zweite Vaterland kritisiert wird, leicht Anstoß erregt und Verfolgungen auslöst. Infolgedessen ist heute die Verteilung guter Bücher und die Einrichtung von stehenden und wandernden Volksbüchereien bedeutend wichtiger. Darum ist es auch so erwünscht, daß das deutsche Volk immer wieder Bücher aus seinen Beständen schenkt.

Alles das kann aber nichts helfen, wenn die deutschen Minderheiten ohne Führer aus ihren eigenen Reihen bleiben. Die Frage des volksdeutschen Führers ist die wichtigste im Leben

34

der Minderheit. Darum bemüht sich der B. D. A. die gebildeten Kreise der deutschen Minderheit für die Mitarbeit zu gewinnen, sie auf ihre Pflichten gegenüber ihrem Volke hinzuweisen. Er zieht möglichst viel Studierende durch Gewährung von Unterstützungen nach Deutschland, ermöglicht ihnen später immer wieder den Aufenthalt in Deutschland und schickt seine Abgesandten hinaus, damit die Verbindung niemals abreißt. In seinen Heimen nimmt er auslandsdeutsche Kinder für Monate und Jahre auf, um ihnen eine geeignete Erziehung geben zu lassen. Darum unterstützt er auch den Bau von Volkshäusern, die als Mittelpunkt für alle deutschtümlichen Bestrebungen eines Volksteiles dienen, sucht er an andern Orten das Pfarrhaus und die Schule durch entsprechende Einrichtungen dafür in Stand zu setzen. Wenn sich die Verhältnisse wieder bessern sollten, so wird es auch wieder möglich sein, größere Besuchs-

reisen Reichsdeutscher bei Auslandsdeutschen einzurichten und reichsdeutsche Redner auf Vortragsreisen zu senden. Augenblicklich können diese Formen des Austausches und der Gemeinschaft fast nur von seiten der Auslandsdeutschen bei uns gepflegt werden.

Blicken wir zurück, so ergibt sich, daß die volksdeutsche Arbeit sehr mannigfaltig ist und mit recht großen, manchmal schier unüberwindlichen Schwierigkeiten zu kämpfen hat. Zugleich dürfen wir aber auch feststellen, daß sie in stetem Fortschreiten auf dem weiten Wege zu ihrem großen Ziele ist. Möge sich jeder, der dies liest, sagen, daß er viel dazu beitragen kann, wenn er sich ungesäumt in die Reihen des B. D. A. stellt, dorthin stellt, wo wir früher oder später einmal stehen müssen, wenn wir nicht unsere Volks- und damit auch unsere Lebensrechte preisgeben wollen.

Nationalsozialismus und V. D. A.

Das Ergebnis einer Tagung.

Passau ist Schicksalsstadt in der deutschen Geschichte. Von hier ging der Nibelungenzug ins Hunnenland hinein, hier blühte der Minnesang unter kunstfreudigen Bischöfen, hier sammelten sich die Scharen deutscher Auswanderer und Kolonisatoren des europäischen Südostens, von hier aus trugen deutsche Mönche und Geistliche das Christentum nach Ungarn, von hier brachen die Heere auf, um die Türken von Wien zu vertreiben, Europa den christlichen Charakter zu erhalten.

Und wiederum hat sich Passau als Schicksalsstadt der Gegenwart erwiesen. In Passau wurde über die Vergangenheit des V.D.A. geurteilt, mußte er sich in der Gegenwart bewähren, wurde seine Zukunft bestimmt. Nicht darin, daß der Volksbund zum ersten Male die restlose Unterstützung der Behörden fand, daß die Tagung in ganz Deutschland in Europa widerklang, sondern in dieser geistigen Schau liegt die Bedeutung der Tagung.

In Passau wurde gültig anerkannt, was der Volksbund in den vergangenen 53 Jahren für die Erhaltung deutschen Volkstums in unermüdlicher, stiller, treuer, zäher und hingebender Arbeit geleistet hat. Ohne ihn wäre heute bodenständiges deutsches Volkstum in weiten Gebieten längst vergangen oder doch dem Untergange nahe. Mit dieser Anerkennung verknüpft sich zugleich die Einsicht in die grundlegenden Leistungen des Volksbundes für die Erziehung zur Volksgemeinschaft, für die Ueberwindung des Partikularismus, des alten deutschen Erbübels, und die Erziehung zum Volksdenken. Wenn es dem Nationalsozialismus heute in weiten Kreisen gelingt, gerade diesen Teil seines Programms reibungslos zu verwirklichen, so verdankt er es vor allem der Vorarbeit des Volksbundes. In diesem Sinne ist der Volksbund auch der Wegbereiter nationalsozialistischer Gesinnung im Auslandsdeutschtum selbst gewesen.

Was die Gegenwart aber vom Volksbunde forderte, war vielleicht die beste Probe auf seine Daseinsberechtigung und Daseinsnotwendigkeit. Urplötzlich sah er sich vor die Aufgabe gestellt, an Stelle der Regierung die rechte Lösung des deutsch-österreichischen Gegensatzes zu finden. Er

fand sie selbstverständlich aus der Tiefe seiner volksdeutschen Ueberlieferung, vor deren Würde eine Regierung Dollfuß klein und winzig erscheint. Was kleine Männer an Typen und Typchen ersinnen, an Posten und Pöstchen im politischen Geschehen schaffen, hat vor dem Stuhle echten Volksgeistes keine Geltung, wird nicht beachtet. So ward die Kundgebung auf dem Passauer Domplatze keine Trutzkundgebung, wie schadenfrohe Geister erhofft hatten, sondern der Ausdruck einer tiefernsten Schicksalsverbundenheit und ewigen Gemeinschaft mit dem Oesterreichischen Bruderstamm, die nicht Klüfte aufriß, sondern alle kleinen Gegenstände ohne Unterschied beseitigte, vor der nichts blieb als deutsches Volk.

Aus diesem Geiste heraus gelang ein zweites. Dem Auslande wurde vor London und während Genf klar und deutlich gezeigt, daß das deutsche Volk nicht gezwungen, sondern freiwillig, nicht teilweise, sondern ganz hinter seiner Regierung steht, daß es nicht offizieller Anordnungen bedarf, um das zum Ausdruck zu bringen. Hier sprach Volk, hier sprach ein Volksbund, der mit der Regierung nichts zu tun hat, der vollkommen frei ist und doch zu ihr steht.

Das dritte, was aber zur Klärung kam, war das Verhältnis des VDA zur Regierung und NSDAP. Es zeigt sich deutlich, daß das Gedankengut des Volksbundes aus der gleichen Wurzel kommt, wie das des Nationalsozialismus. Nicht umsonst ist beider Geist aus dem Volkstumskampfe, aus dem Ringen deutschen Volkes um seine Erhaltung und seinen Fortbestand geboren, nicht umsonst hat ein Adolf Hitler in den Reihen des Volksbundes als Knabe die erste völkische Schulung erhalten. Darum war auch keine Gleichschaltung und Umschaltung notwendig und konnte die hier oder dort notwendige Reinigung getrost dem Volksbunde selbst überlassen bleiben. Sein Geist bürgte dafür, daß sie richtig erfolgte.

Er hatte sich ja von jeher als einer der wichtigsten, wenn nicht der einzige Träger einer wahren Volkspolitik im nationalsozialistischem Sinne mit aller notwendigen Mäßigung gegenüber andern Völkern aber auch aller Unerbittlichkeit in der Verteidigung des eigenen Volkstums erwiesen. Diese Lage der Dinge kam in dem Schreiben des stellvertretenden Führers der NSDAP, Rudolf Heß und dem Freundschaftsabkommen mit der Hitlerjugend deutlich zum Ausdruck. Zugleich erwies sich darin auch der hohe staatsmännische Sinn unseres Führers, der sofort erkannt hatte, welches wichtige Instrument für eine erfolgreiche volksdeutsche Politik dem deutschen Volke in einem unabhängigen V.D.A. zur Verfügung steht. Diese Anerkennung, die der Volksbund durch unseren Führer fand, löste naturgemäß eine gewaltige Welle freudigen Vertrauens und hohen Dankes aus und wirkte auf seine Arbeit ungemein befruchtend und tragend zurück. Das ward vor allem deutlich in der völligen und richtigen Erfassung des Führergedankens, der niemals blinde Unterwerfung unter irgendeinen Ernannten, sondern freiwillige Unterordnung unter den vom Vertrauen aller getragenen, vor dem Schicksal durch Leistungen und Taten bewährten Manne, bedeutet. In diesem Sinne wurde Dr. Hans Steinacher zum Reichsführer erwählt, in diesem Sinne den Führern der Nation gehuldigt, in diesem Sinne fanden sich in Passau nicht Vereinsmitglieder, sondern alte disziplinierte Mitarbeiter zusammen.

Für die Zukunft bedeutete aber Passau die klare Erkenntnis, daß wir niemals Nationalstaat im Sinne westlicher Völker werden können, daß wir in erster Linie Volk sind und bleiben müssen, daß weder der Volksbund noch der neue deutsche Staat diesem Lebens- und Schicksalsgesetz deutscher Nation ausweichen kann. Die letzte Zielsetzung des Volksbundes und der NSDAP stimmen darum auch überein. Es geht um die Eroberung des letzten deutschen Menschen, um die Gewährleistung einer unzerstörbaren deutschen Volkseinheit, die tief bewußt und tief verankert in der Brust eines jeden deutschen Menschen sein höchstes und letztes Gut darstellt, es geht um das Selber-Ueberflüssigwerden. Aus dieser Zielsetzung zieht der Volksbund augenblicklich die Folgerung. Er sprengt den Rahmen des Vereins, der ihm längst zu eng worden ist und trägt seine alte Idee in neuer Form und neuer Organisation ins Volk. Er weitet seinen Arbeitsbereich über das gesamte deutsche Volk hin. Nicht mehr nur Betreuer und Helfer, Verteidiger und Kämpfer, sondern Mittler wird er in Zukunft sein, Mittler zwischen dem Binnen- und Außendeutschtum, Mittler zwischen Deutsch- und Welschtum, Mittler zwischen Regierung und Volk. Er wird der Führer sein einer Volkspolitik, die weit hinausgeht über die Politik einer offiziellen Regierung, er wird ein Führer sein zur Einordnung aller deutschen Staaten und deutschen Menschen in die gemeinsame, einige, große deutsche Volksfront.

So steht er hinter, so steht er vor der Regierung, in vollkommener Freiheit aber tiefinnerer Verbundenheit. Mag in Zukunft Regierungspolitik und Volkspolitik auf verschiedenen Gleisen laufen und notwendig laufen müssen, sie werden dennoch Hand in Hand gehen und nur das eine Ziel kennen: „Deutsches Volk".

42

Warum ein ſtarker V. D. A.?

Weil unſere Volksbrüder im Auslande ſich zu uns und zum Reiche und wir uns zu ihnen bekennen und darum ein national= ſozialiſtiſches Reich die V.D.A.=Aufgaben niemals vernachläſſigen darf, wenn es ſich nicht ſelbſt aufgeben will.

2. Weil wir einen Volksbund brauchen, der als nicht regierungsamtliche und nicht par= teiamtliche Organiſation auch dort für ſeine Volksbrüder einzutreten vermag, wo Re= gierung und Partei dies aus politiſchen Gründen nicht tun können und dürfen, d. h. weil Volkspolitik und Regierungspolitik zwei ganz verſchiedene Dinge ſind, die zwar den gleichen Ausgangspunkt und das gleiche Ziel haben, aber notwendig ganz verſchie= dene Wege gehen müſſen.

3. Weil nur eine ſtarke, weitgeſpannte Or= ganiſation die großen Aufgaben der Volks= politik löſen kann.

4. Weil das Ausland ſich nicht täuſchen läßt und eine ſchwache Organiſation für eine ſtarke, eine Regierungs= und Parteiorgani= ſation für eine Volksorganiſation nimmt.

5. Weil ſonſt Partei und Hitlerjugend in ſich beſondere Gruppen bilden müßten für die Löſung der V.D.A.=Aufgaben.

6. Weil das Ausland die Volkstumsarbeit in dieſer Form am eheſten ablehnt, der Na=

tionalſozialiſt aber gerade die Volkstums= arbeit in jeder Form unterſtützen und durch= ſetzen muß.

7. Weil unter den heutigen Verhältniſſen nur durch den V.D.A. der Volkstumsgedanke in alle Kreiſe unſeres Volkes getragen werden kann.

8. Weil der V.D.A. unbedingt auf dem Boden deutſchen Volksdenkens, d. h. auf national= ſozialiſtiſchem Boden ſteht.

9. Weil die Führer des V.D.A. ohne Ausnahme Nationalſozialiſten des Geiſtes und nicht nur der Partei ſind.

10. Weil das wahre V.D.A.=Mitglied ein wah= rer Nationalſozialiſt iſt, d. h. der V.D.A. zu= verläſſig zum Nationalſozialismus hinführt.

11. Weil unſer Führer und Volkskanzler Adolf Hitler einen ſtarken V.D.A. will:

a) zur Durchdringung des ganzen Volkes und der Partei mit dem Volkstumsge= danken, dem Kerngedanken des Natio= nalſozialismus,

b) für die Zwecke einer ſtarken und erfolg= reichen Volkstumspolitik.

12. Weil kein Nationalſozialiſt gegen den Wil= len ſeines oberſten Führers handelt, ſondern ihn ausführt, indem er ſelbſt Mitglied des V.D.A. wird.

45

Urteile von Sachkennern über die Schrift.

Ich habe geradezu aufgeatmet, als ich Ihre Schrift in die Hände bekam, weil sie seit langem die erste größere Veröffentlichung ist, die der inneren Haltung, und dem Rang unserer volksdeutschen Arbeit Ausdruck gibt. Ihre Schrift müßte doch tatsächlich jeder irgendwie im B. D. A. führende Mann bis zum Jungführer herab nicht nur in die Hand bekommen, sondern auch durcharbeiten. Ich werde mich jedenfalls aufs nachdrücklichste für die Verbreitung Ihrer Schrift einsetzen. . . . . Landesgeschäftsführer im B. D. A.

Ihre Schrift „Sinn und Wesen des B. D. A." gefällt uns so gut, daß wir sofort 1000 Stück bestellen.
„Etwas was uns noch fehlt"
X, Hauptleitung d. B. D. A.

. . . . So habe ich sie einer gründlichen Durchsicht unterzogen und freue mich über die tiefgründigen Darlegungen über deutsche Volkheit, sowie überhaupt über die allgemeine Zielsetzung unserer Arbeit. In diesen Darlegungen wird doch eine ganze Reihe von Gedanken entwickelt, die man sonst nicht findet. X, Hauptleitung i. B. D. A.

Die Schrift gefällt uns recht gut und wären wir darum bereit 3000 Stück zu übernehmen . . . .
Landesverband . . . .

Wir nehmen sofort 1000 Stück. Das suchen wir gerade.
Landesverband . . . .

Wenn Sie uns . . . . geeignete Einzelabschnitte Ihrer Ausführungen . . . . zur Verfügung stellen würden, wären wir Ihnen sehr dankbar. X, Presseabteilung.

. . . . wie wichtig ein solches Schriftchen für uns wäre. Ich brauche es jetzt fast jeden Tag. Können Sie mir nicht sagen, wo ich Ihr Schriftchen bekommen könnte?
X, Hauptleitung i. B. D. A.

Ich habe vorgeschlagen 2000 Stück sofort zu bestellen für B. D. A.-Schulgruppen, Ortsgruppen und Volksschulen des Landesverbandes. X, Landesgeschäftsführer.

Stichproben, die ich gemacht habe, gaben mir die Ueberzeugung, daß wir es in Ihrem Werk mit einem vorzüglichen Schulungsmittel zu tun haben.
X, Führer des Landesverbandes.

Ich habe mit Interesse davon Kenntnis genommen und möchte wünschen, daß die Schrift recht zahlreich gelesen wird. X, Oberpräsident.

Aus dem flüchtigen Ueberblick möchte ich die Notwendigkeit der Schrift unbedingt bejahen. X, Reichsführer.

Eine erfreulich reiche und tiefgründige Arbeit! Echt deutsche Gründlichkeit und wahrhaft nationale Arbeit sprechen aus diesem Heft, welches sich gewiß viele Freunde erwerben wird. Ein Mitglied.

. . . . Der Führer dankt . . . . Ihnen. Er hat sich sehr darüber gefreut.
X, Adjutant d. Reichskanzlers.

Ich habe Ihre Schrift befürwortend weitergegeben. Der L. V. wird sie selbstverständlich gern in seinem Kreis verbreiten. X, Landesführer.

Ich wäre Ihnen dankbar, wenn Sie mir etwa 10 Exemplare a conto unserer Bestellung zusenden würden. Einzelne Sachbearbeiter, ferner Gau- und Ortsgruppenleiter, die mich besuchen, legen für Ihr Buch ein so großes Interesse an den Tag, daß ich Ihnen immer die Schrift sofort mitgeben muß und nicht bis zum allgemeinen Vertrieb warten möchte. X, Landesgeschäftsführer.

Das Buch ist seines Gedankenreichtums wegen ein ganz ausgezeichneter Wegweiser in das Wesen des B. D. A. und ich habe die Geschäftsstelle ersucht, sofort 2000 Stück in Bestellung zu geben. X, Landesführer.

Ihr schönes Schriftchen hat durchschlagenden Erfolg gehabt. Es füllt eine längst empfundene Lücke aus. Wir verdanken ihm die Gründung von etwa 50 Volksschulgruppen an Orten, wo früher unsere sämtlichen Bemühungen erfolglos blieben.
X, Gauschulgruppenführer.

DOCUMENT 32–A

(Extracts)

SINN UND WESEN DES VDA, VOLKSBUNDES FÜR DAS DEUTSCHTUM IM AUSLANDE (NATURE AND SIGNIFICANCE OF THE VDA, LEAGUE FOR GERMANDOM IN FOREIGN COUNTRIES), BY OTTO SCHÄFER, VDA DISTRICT LEADER: PUBLISHED BY THE WERMELSKIRCHEN LOCAL GROUP AND THE LANDESVERBAND NIEDERRHEIN (LOWER RHINE SOCIETY), FRANKFURT-AM-MAIN, SECOND EDITION, MAY 1933 [1]

(Pages 5–9)

"FROM REICH GERMANDOM AND GERMANDOM ABROAD TO RACIAL GERMANDOM

"1. THE GERMAN CONCEPTION OF THE STATE AND ITS ROOTS—A TRANSFORMATION IN THE GERMAN PEOPLE'S WAY OF THINKING

"When we speak of the German people, then the phrase which arose during the war, *a people of 60 millions*, is almost always inserted. In the course of the last decade, however, we have experienced more and more frequently that this proud designation is being replaced or at least supplemented by the still prouder one of 'a people of 100 millions'.[2] This proceeding embodies simply and unobtrusively the fact that the German people's conception of itself has undergone a decisive transformation, in which *larger and larger circles have participated*. It means neither more nor less than the great progress from thinking in terms of the German state to thinking in terms of the German race.

---

[1] In the foreword Schäfer states that this pamphlet was written in July 1932 with the exception of the closing pages.

[2] Estimates of the Germans in the following countries are as follows:

Denmark (incl.			German-Austria	approx.	6,300,000
North Schleswig)	approx.	60,000	Czechoslovakia	"	3,500,000
Belgium (incl.			Yugoslavia	"	700,000
Eupen-Malmedy)	"	150,000	Hungary	"	600,000
Luxembourg	"	250,000	Rumania	"	800,000
Netherlands	"	80,000	Switzerland	"	2,860,000
Alsace-Lorraine	"	1,600,000	United States	"	10,000,000
Italy (incl. Tyrol)	"	300,000	Canada	"	300,000
Poland	"	1,350,000	South & Central		
Danzig	"	360,000	America	"	800,000
Estonia	"	30,000	Australia	"	160,000
Latvia	"	75,000	Asia	"	197,000
Lithuania & Memel	"	130,000	Africa	"	125,000
Russia	"	1,000,000	Germany (1925)	"	63,339,000

421

"What thinking in terms of the German state means, we best recognize if we consider the pertinent sections of the Constitution of the German Reich,[3] which the German people has made for itself, and associated enactments.[4] We then make the remarkable discovery that the German people does not comprise Germans, as we should expect, but German citizens [*Reichsdeutsche*], i.e. citizens of a federal state or citizens of the Reich directly; Germans abroad [*Auslandsdeutsche*], i.e. German citizens living in foreign countries; and German foreigners [*Deutschausländer*], i.e. foreigners of German extraction. The more than 30 million German foreigners are withheld by the German state from the use of the name of Germans, although they feel themselves to be such. They are at best German-Americans, German-Russians, German-Poles, German-Danes, German-Austrians, German-Hungarians, etc., and the German public follows the state and its authorities unthinkingly. Only if German-Frenchmen, German-Czechs, or German-Italians are mentioned are they disturbed. The feeling awakens that a member of the German race cannot be termed a Frenchman, Italian, or Czech.

"Whoever does not remain content with this feeling of discomfort and thinks the matter out further, then readily finds that a member of the German race is a German and that membership in the German race and membership in a particular state basically have nothing at all to do with one another. Neither does the foreign citizenship hinder the German in his German thinking and feeling and in the use of the German language, nor, conversely, does his Germanism hinder him from being a loyal citizen of the foreign state. Racial alliance and citizenship prove themselves to be two different things. Consequently, one should also separate them rigorously in linguistic usage."

The author then states that the usual opinion that the German abroad is not able to maintain his nationality is false. "Against inferior cultures the Germans have always preserved their national characteristics just as tenaciously as the English, while the Latin peoples have shown themselves of much less resistance. We need only look to the European East and to South America, in order to see in both the confirmation of our view. Doubtless the Germans would have possessed greater powers of resistance against America's Anglo-Saxonism, if a strong German Government had stood behind them and supported them in their first measures toward the maintenance and cultivation of Germanism, as did the English Government for its emigrants."

". . . As long as the German Government or a great part of the German people did not stand behind them [the German emi-

---

[3] Preamble to the Constitution of the Reich.
[4] A. 109–112; German citizenship law of July 22, 1913, *Reichsgesetzblatt*, p. 538.

grants], they were powerless. In these years the German nationality lost 20 million persons in the United States, to the great detriment of Germany later. In the realms of the Austrian monarchy and Russia we suffered likewise enormous losses. At the beginning of the new century, finally, the German people was in the process of losing 35,000,000 more of its brothers, i.e. more than one third of its whole number, since it seemed that Germans in the Reich and Germans in foreign countries had nothing in common."

The war, it is stated, changed the situation entirely, breaking down the barriers between the Germans scattered throughout the world and uniting the Germans in a common German sentiment. "German came to German, brother to brother—out of the Germans in all the countries of the world emerged a unified German people, which did everything and made all its sacrifices in this consciousness of its German nature. . . .

"Out of this knowledge of itself, the German people acquired a double insight. It recognized that the concept of the state and nation hitherto used by it was wrong, not in conformity with the essential nature of the German people. Nation and state, national feelings and state feelings, again became separated for the German. A distinction of the Government between German citizens, German citizens abroad, and German foreigners was given up. There are now just simply Germans, men of German extraction, language, and customs. Desirable as the state, the national state, remained as the highest form of a mature nationality, its esteem receded behind that of nationality and national consciousness, the nation and national sentiments. Nationality [*Volkstum*] was again regarded as the natural and eternal, which is prior to the state and will be after it, which can extend far beyond its borders without thereby losing its genuineness. If the German people has emerged from the Great War with such a gain, with such a happy insight, if it has finally found itself as a people and this knowledge is more and more quickly penetrating all its branches, then this is not due least to the Association for Germandom in Foreign Countries. It kept the racial-German thinking alive, at a time when thinking in terms of the state was validated. While the Government and the people believed they could dispense with the German brothers in foreign countries, it has maintained connections with them and prepared everything for the overcoming of thinking in terms of the state, by thinking in terms of the race."

(Pages 23–29)

"ORIGIN AND DEVELOPMENT OF THE VDA

"The internal political ethnic development in Austria-Hungary after the 1870's was the cause and occasion for the foundation of the VDA." The author states that in 1879 an administration headed by

Taaffe came into power, which for 14 years sought to play off the Slavs against the Germans and considerably disturbed the privileged position of the Germans in Austria.

Through the activities of Engelbert Pernerstorfer, who was later one of the founders of the Austrian Social Democratic Party, a "German School League" (Deutscher Schulverein) was founded on July 2, 1880, with the purpose of supporting endangered German schools in areas of mixed nationality. Dr. Viktor Adler, who was later leader of the Austrian Social Democrats, was on the committee which wrote the statutes for the League. The League started with 3,150 members. At the end of the first year the number of members amounted to 20,000; the income, 55,000 gulden; 41 schools had been founded or supported. The division of the League into local groups became necessary. The number of local groups rose by 1886 to 980, decreased a little up to 1902, and then increased greatly. After 1893 these were organized in Gaus and later, as numerous rural groups arose, were divided into district associations, in which the urban local groups formed the center of a district. From 1910 on, the movement entered into the schools, and, by February 1920, 37 school groups had been founded.

On November 24, 1889, on the initiative of Josef Feichtinger, a private-school teacher in Graz, the association "Südmark" was founded, the aim of which was to support economically Germans residing or settling in the mixed-language areas of Styria, Carinthia, Carniola, and the Tyrol. The two associations supplemented one another in their work.

A similar popular movement was taking place in Germany. In 1883 the various local groups were united in the "Universal German School League", with a membership of 9,000. This League was independent of the Austrian one but in close contact with it. In 1887 the membership was already 80,000, divided into 239 groups; in 1890 there were 40,000 members. "Trusted agents were acquired everywhere, and a firm footing was established in the circles of Germans abroad, and in the United States." In 1908 this League assumed the name "League for Germandom in Foreign Countries" (Verein für das Deutschtum im Auslande, VDA). In 1913 it had a membership of 50,000, and its revenue amounted to over 500,000 marks. As a result of the ethnic problems arising after the war the VDA expanded considerably and reorganized its groups. "The sphere of activity became extended to the entire realm of life of the German race." The reorganization took place during the years 1919 and 1925. The network of local groups was further developed, and above all the German youth was reached by means of school groups. The main office itself was divided into the following departments, still existing: Business Management, Publicity and Organizations, Press and Periodicals, Youth Work, Academic Work, Scholarships, Vacation Trips and Hiking, Physical

Training, School Department, Libraries Abroad, Library and Archives, Business Department.

In 1921 the "German School League" joined the VDA as the "Austrian Association" (Verband Oesterreich). On March 29, 1925 the association "Südmark" was also amalgamated with the Austrian branch of the VDA, after it had previously been united with several smaller Austrian societies doing similar work.

"In the Reich itself, under the leadership and collaboration of the VDA, which had become so powerful, a number of affiliated organizations arose in these years, which undertook special tasks, such as the 'German Protective Association' (Deutscher Schutzbund), the 'German Foreign Institute' (Deutsches Ausland-Institut), and others. The majority of Germandom's associations, over 90 percent, finally united into a large 'Alliance of Free Germandom Associations', whose management is attended to by the VDA. It aims on the one hand to bring about extensive collaboration and mutual supplementation, and on the other hand to help avoid friction and unnecessary double work. Its most important members are the 'Deutscher Schutzbund', the Deutsches Auslandsinstitut, the 'Bund der Auslandsdeutschen', the 'Deutsche Kolonialgesellschaft', the 'Vereinigung für Siedlung und Wanderung', the 'Reichsverband für die katholischen Auslandsdeutschen', and the 'Vereinigung Deutsch Evangelisch im Auslande'. In recent months the Deutscher Schutzbund was absorbed by the VDA; the Alliance of Associations of German Teachers Abroad, which has acquired more and more significance through its Darmstadt meetings under the leadership of State Councilor Block, joined the VDA; and the Deutsches Auslandsinstitut, under the leadership of the Transylvanian Saxon, Dr. Richard Csaki, has entered into a closer connection with the VDA. In the VDA itself, under the guidance of the new Reich's leader, the Carinthian Dr. Hans Steinacher, a reorganization has taken place on the basis of the Führer principle. The local groups were united into districts, these into provincial alliances under the leadership of nationally reliable men.

"Brilliant as this development of the VDA, which encompasses today over 2,000,000 members, and of the whole Germandom movement appears, it is not yet at an end, and ought not to come to an end, until it has reached the entire German race, led the last lost son back into his father's house, has secured the last field fertilized by German sweat and blood."

(Pages 30–35)

"THE WORK OF THE VDA

"1. AIMS AND PRINCIPLES OF THE WORK

"The *aim* of the VDA's *work, in its broadest sense,* is the fulfilment of the meaning of German racial unity, the permeation of all Germans with the racial idea; *the aim in the more restricted sense* is the successful work of maintaining and protecting Germandom in all countries of the earth, and especially by the cultivation of German cultural forms of activity and expression. It considers itself in this only as a fellow worker, never as a benefactor or a relief agency for the racial brothers supported in their defensive struggle. It and its members enter the national front of the Germans abroad as equal fighters.

"The attainment of these goals is guaranteed by the principles of work which the VDA has adopted. Its first principle is absolute neutrality in all questions which do not concern Germandom directly nor in its totality. With regard to internal politics it places itself deliberately over all parties, religious denominations, and groups. It only validates the German will of a man, the will which follows from his Germanness. . . ."

"2. The Sphere of Work

"The sphere of the VDA's work is naturally the entire realm of the German race."

"We see that the sphere of the VDA's work has become very great, it encompasses the entire planet, and it is by far not able to satisfy the demands made upon it. Also for this reason its aim must remain: the unification of all Germans to one great community of destiny, to a nation.

"The Forms of Work (Within Germany)

". . . The periodicals of the local groups are the monthly appearing '*Volksdeutsche*' (yearly subscription 1.20 marks, for members, free), the handsomely ill strated monthly '*Deutsche Welt*', and the leaders' magazine '*Deutsche Arbeit*'. Moreover, most of the local groups have their own libraries and are considerably supported in their work by the responsible press. They are organized in Gaus and provincial associations, whose directors are directly under the main office. The provincial associations are:

1. Verband Oesterreich (Deutscher Schulverein Südmark).
2. Landesverband Baden.
3. Landesverband Bayern.
4. Landesverband Brandenburg.
5. Landesverband Freie Stadt Danzig.
6. Landesverband Grenzmark.
7. Landesverband Hamburg.
8. Landesverband Niedersachsen.
9. Landesverband Hessen-Darmstadt.
10. Landesverband Hessen-Nassau.
11. Landesverband Mecklenburg.
12. Landesverband Mittelrhein.
13. Landesverband Niederrhein.
14. Landesverband Ostpreussen.

15. Landesverband Niederschlesien.
16. Landesverband Oberschlesien.
17. Landesverband Pommern.
18. Landesverband Sachsen.
19. Landesverband Sachsen-Anhalt.
20. Landesverband Schleswig-Holstein.
21. Landesverband Thüringen.
22. Landesverband Weser-Ems.
23. Landesverband Westfalen.
24. Landesverband Westpreussen.
25. Landesverband Württemberg.

"All the events of the school groups and local groups are designed wherever possible to raise means for the VDA's protective work. The regular membership dues are most important because most surely at our disposal. To these are added the collections which take place on the occasion of fetes, street and house collections during publicity weeks, and collections for books. Also, goodly sums are brought in by the sale of postcards, insignias, flowers, etc. Fortunately the number of those persons is increasing who remember the VDA with large gifts, during their lifetime or at their death. The means for founding *Volksdeutsche* homes have been obtained primarily in this way.

"THE FORMS OF WORK (ABROAD)

"This work within Germany finds its counterpart in the welfare work within foreign countries.

"Its major feature lies in the establishment and maintenance of German kindergartens and schools, for the first 14 years are usually decisive with regard to national allegiance, if an especially strong national will is not at hand. Usually the number of children and the particular conditions of the neighborhood are ascertained and then the solution of the matter is begun. If the German children live in a region of very mixed nationality, then the establishment of a German kindergarten is necessary. In unilingual areas, the establishment of German schools suffices. In most cases attempts are made to induce the authorities to fulfil their obligations; if this does not succeed, the VDA acts and arranges for the building of a schoolhouse, in that it either furnishes a subsidy or itself builds the school . . . In other localities it pays for the teachers, or gives subsidies so that able teachers and pastors may be kept in the endangered areas. If the establishment of a school is impossible, then it attempts to arrange for good private instruction and grants subsidies for this also."

". . . The question of the *Volksdeutsche* leaders is the most important in the life of the minorities. Consequently the VDA seeks to gain the collaboration of the cultivated circles of the German minority, pointing out to them their obligations toward their people. It brings as many students as possible to Germany through granting scholarships, enables them later again and again to visit Germany, and sends its own representatives abroad so that the connection is never broken. In its own homes it takes German children from abroad for months and years in order to give them a proper education. For this reason also it subsidizes the erection of "German Houses" which serve as a center for all the German endeavors of a racial fragment, or in other places by appropriate alterations it seeks to put the parish house or the school in condition to serve this purpose. If conditions should improve, then it will again be possible to arrange extensive visiting trips of Germans from the Reich among the Germans abroad and to send German speakers from the Reich on lecture tours. At present this form of exchange and community can be carried on almost only from the side of the Germans abroad, who come among us."

(Pages 41–42)

"NATIONAL SOCIALISM AND THE VDA
"THE RESULT OF A MEETING"

This article, concerning the VDA meeting at Passau early in 1933, closes with the following paragraphs:

"The third matter which became clarified was the relation of the VDA to the Government and to the NSDAP. It appears clear that the ideas of the VDA come from the same root as those of National Socialism. Not in vain is the spirit of both born of the racial strife, from the struggle of the German people for its maintenance and continued existence; not in vain has an Adolf Hitler received his first ethnic schooling as a boy in the ranks of the VDA. Consequently, no coordination [Gleichschaltung] nor transformation was necessary, and the cleansing, which was here and there necessary, could be entrusted to the VDA itself. Its spirit was a guaranty that this would take place properly.

"It had shown itself from the beginning as one of the most important if not the only bearer of a true National Socialist policy in the racial sense, with all necessary moderation toward all peoples but with all pitilessness in defense of its own race. This state of affairs was clearly expressed in the letter of Rudolf Hess, the Deputy Leader of the NSDAP, and in the agreement of friendship with the Hitler Youth. At the same time the high political talent of our Führer was exhibited in the fact that he had recognized at once what an important instrument for a successful racial-German [Volksdeutsche] policy stands at the German people's disposal in the form of an independent VDA. This recognition, which the VDA received from our Führer, naturally released an enormous wave of great thanks and joyful confidence which reacted on its work in an unusually fructifying and supporting way. This was above all clear in the full and proper comprehension of the Führer idea, which never means blind subjugation under any appointee, but voluntary subordination to the man, who is borne by the confidence of all, and who has shown his merit in the face of fate by deeds and accomplishments. In this sense, Dr. Hans Steinacher was elected Reich's Führer, in this sense homage was accorded to the leaders of the nation, in this sense not mere League members met in Passau but old disciplined collaborators.

"For the future, however, Passau meant the clear knowledge that we can never become a national state in the sense of the western nations, that we are and must remain primarily a people, that neither the VDA nor the new German state can evade this vital and fateful law of the German nature. The ultimate goals of the VDA and the NSDAP consequently agree. It is a matter of the conquest of the last German person, the guaranteeing of an indestructible German racial unity, which deeply conscious and deeply anchored in the breast of every single German represents his highest and ultimate goal; it is a matter of the abandonment of self. From this goal the VDA is drawing the consequences at present. It is bursting the framework of the League, which for a long time has been too narrow, and it is carrying its old idea in a new form and a new organization out into the world. It is extending its sphere of work over the entire German race. No longer merely sustainer and helper, defender and champion, in the future it will be a mediator, a mediator between Germandom at home and Germandom abroad, a mediator between the government and the people. It will be the leader in a racial policy which extends far beyond the policy of an official government, it will be the leader in the organization of all German states and German men, in the common united great German racial front.

"Thus it stands behind, thus it stands ahead of the government, in complete freedom, but in deepest solidarity. If, in the future, government policy and racial policy may and must necessarily take different courses, nevertheless they will go hand in hand and have only the one goal: 'German *Volk*'."

(Page 45)

"WHY A STRONG VDA?

"(1) Because our racial brothers in foreign countries acknowledge their adherence to us and to the Reich and we ours to them, and therefore a National Socialist Reich ought never to neglect VDA tasks, if it does not want to abandon itself.

"(2) Because we need a racial league, which not being an official government nor official party organization is able to work for its racial fellows, where the government and the party are not able and may not do this on account of political reasons, i. e. because racial policy and government policy are two different things, which it is true have the same point of departure and the same goal but must necessarily proceed along entirely different paths.

"(3) Because only a strong far-reaching organization can solve the great problems of racial policy.

"(4) Because the foreign countries do not let themselves be deceived and do not take a weak organization for a strong one, a government and party organization for a racial organization.

"(5) Because otherwise the party and the Hitler Youth must form special groups in their own organizations for the solution of the VDA's tasks.

"(6) Because the foreign countries most readily reject racial work in this form, but the National Socialist, however, must support and push through precisely racial work in every form.

"(7) Because under present conditions the racial idea can be carried to *all* sections of our German race only through the VDA.

"(8) Because the VDA rests unconditionally on the foundation of German racial thinking, i. e. on the National Socialist foundation.

"(9) Because the leaders of the VDA are without exception National Socialists of the spirit and not just of the party.

"(10) Because the true VDA member is the true National Socialist, i.e. the VDA leads surely to National Socialism.

"(11) Because our Führer and Chancelor, Adolf Hitler, wants a strong VDA:

"(a) to permeate the entire people and the party with the racial ideas, the central ideas of National Socialism;
"(b) for the purpose of a strong and successful racial policy.

"(12) Because no National Socialist acts against the will of his Supreme Führer, but rather is executing it when he himself becomes a member of the VDA."

(Page 48)

". . . The Führer thanks . . . you. He took very much pleasure in it.

"Signed X.—*Adjutant of the Reich's Chancelor*"

DOCUMENT 33

Volksbund für das Deutschtum im Ausland
Wirtschaftsunternehmen G. m. b. H.

Berlin W 30, VDA-Haus · Postschließfach Nr. 25 · Drahtanschrift: „Volksdeutsch"

Fernsprecher: B5 Barbarossa 3026

Postscheckkonto: Berlin 43 30
Bankkto.: Dresdner Bank, Dep.
Kasse 9, Berlin W 30, Mohstr. 37
Porto- u. spesenfreie Überweisung
durch Berliner Stadtbank, Giro-
kasse 123 Konto 4400
(Einzahlung bei einer Stadtbank)

Ihr Zeichen	Ihr Schreiben vom	Unser Zeichen	Berlin W 30, den

Betr.:

Lieber Volksgenosse!

Zu unserer Freude ist es uns möglich, auch Ihnen als Treuegruss
der alten Heimat zum kommenden Weihnachtsfest einen VDA-Abreiss-
kalender "Deutsche in aller Welt" 1937 zu senden. Unserer Anregung entsprechend haben zahlreiche Firmen im Reich uns eine grosse Anzahl Jahrweiser für Auslanddeutsche zur Verfügung gestellt,
um damit ihre enge Verbundenheit mit diesen Volksgenossen zu be-
kundigen.

Wir bitten herzlich, den Kalender so zu verwenden, dass er möglichst vielen vor Augen führt, wie unser 100 Millionenvolk über
die ganze Erde zerstreut lebt und trotz oft jahrhundertelanger
Trennung vom Reich an deutscher Sitte,Sprache und Kultur in un-
wandelbarer Treue festgehalten hat und ungeachtet massloser Un-
terdrückungen in vielen Staaten auch weiterhin festhält.

Recht sehr würden wir uns freuen, gelegentlich zu hören, ob der
Kalender angekommen ist und ob Ihnen auch in Zukunft mit Schriften aus dem Reich Freude bereitet werden kann. Vor allen Dingen
ist uns aber daran gelegen, dass die Firma, die unter anderen
auch den beigefügten Jahrweiser stiftete, den Empfang mit ein
paar Zeilen bestätigt erhält.Wir sind davon überzeugt,dass solch
ein Brief bei dem Spender, dessen Anschrift unten angeführt ist,
grosse Freude hervorrufen würde.

Mit deutschem Gruss!
und den besten Wünschen zum
Weihnachtsfest und neuem Jahr.
Volksbund für das Deutschtum im Ausland
Wirtschaftsunternehmen G. m. b. H.

Den Kalender stiftete die Firma:

An die ....-
u. .... "Rheinmetall"

..... b. Erfurt

Thüringen

431

DOCUMENT 33–A

(Translation)

LEAGUE FOR GERMANDOM IN FOREIGN COUNTRIES
Incorporated Commercial Enterprise

DEAR RACIAL COMRADE:

It is a great pleasure for us to be able to send to you, as a greeting of loyalty from the old homeland for the coming Christmas, a VDA detachable-leaf calendar, "Germans All Over the World", for 1937. In response to our suggestion many firms in the Reich have put at our disposal a large number of almanacs for Germans in foreign lands in order to demonstrate thereby their close connection with these racial comrades.

We beg you to use this calendar so that it will bring to the attention of as many people as possible how our hundred million people live scattered over the whole earth, and often, in spite of centuries of separation from the Reich, still hold to German customs, language, and culture in unchangeable loyalty and despite endless suppressions in many countries.

We should be very glad to hear at your convenience whether the calendar reached you and whether you would enjoy hearing more from the Reich in the future. We are especially anxious that the firm, which among other things provided the enclosed almanac, should receive a few lines of acknowledgment from you. We are sure that such a letter would greatly please the donor, whose address appears below.

With German Greeting!
and best wishes for
Christmas and the New Year.

LEAGUE FOR GERMANDOM IN FOREIGN COUNTRIES

This calendar was given by the firm:

Rhenish Metal Goods and
"Rheinmetall" Machine Factory
Sömmerda near Erfurt

Thüringen

432

DOCUMENT 34

(Translation)

DER NATIONALSOZIALISTISCHE STAAT (THE NATIONAL SOCIALIST STATE) (PART I: FROM MAY 2 TO NOVEMBER 12, 1933), EDITED BY DR. WALTHER GEHL: BRESLAU, 1933, PAGES 215ff.

GERMANDOM IN THE BORDER COUNTRIES AND GERMANDOM IN FOREIGN COUNTRIES

[The explanatory note at the beginning of the chapter states in part as follows:]

There has been a Germandom in foreign countries since the 13th century, when German settlers migrated to the European east and southeast, and since the 17th century, when these isolated German settlements were increased and strengthened, and when Germans as farmers and as artisans migrated to North America. The small German Reich of Bismarck left millions of Germans outside of its borders, and the Treaty of Versailles separated from the Reich still further territory inhabited by Germans.

To the pure state-thinking of the 19th century, Germans in foreign countries, who were not citizens of the Reich, were counted as foreigners. . . . One spoke of German-Russians, instead of Russian-Germans, of German-Bohemians, instead of Sudeten-Germans, etc. The Reich did not concern itself about them, in order to avoid political complications. Merely the VDA, the "Volksbund (formerly Verein) für das Deutschtum im Ausland", maintained the connection between Germandom in the Reich and Germandom in foreign countries. Its slogan was "Germans of all countries. unite !"

[The following extracts are from an address by the Reich's leader of the VDA, Dr. Steinacher, at the meeting of the VDA in Passau, Whitsuntide 1933:]

The movement arises from the depths of the German race. Because it does so, it is no purely state movement and is therefore not limited by the borders of the state. It affects the entire extent of our racial corpus. The present moment is decisive, since the revolution has terminated within the Reich and the entire life is in a state of transformation. . . .

And over there beyond our borders: from the Baltic down to the mouth of the Danube, from Upper Silesia to Egerland, from Burgenland to Tyrol and to Eupen-Malmedy, we see everywhere how the young generation is being seized by this movement. We observe it also beyond the seas in North America, in Brazil, and in South Africa, where with unique ardor precisely the simple classes have gained in self-consciousness and are proceeding along their way everywhere more full of faith and stronger. The entire German racial corpus has become actually fluid. Whatever belongs to it is being newly formed. A new aspect of German life has begun. . . .

The fight of the Germans abroad has taken on an entirely new significance . . . Between the Germans within and those outside of the state center there is no difference of rank but only a difference of function. Every German folk-group in the world, out of its own particular life, out of its own special geographic and cultural situation, will in the future have to collaborate in a common European task and a world task of Germandom. These functions will be very different. In one place, the German folk-group and German states will have to be a wall against foreign claims. In another place, they will be bridges, and, in a third place, factors bringing about an alliance . . .

The aim of our work is the maintenance of the race outside of our borders. This work cannot be isolated from the life of the Germans within our borders. Borders can separate the life of states but not the life of a people. No matter if the state be forced here and there to give up its claims and to endure borders which lie on this side of our ethnic borders, the race does not admit any such resignation of race! On the contrary, the brotherliness and imperishable community of the race has to prove itself precisely where the state is no longer in a position to support and fulfil the race . . . We are the intermediaries of this exchange between the fight out there and the renewal here within. To be sure, there is still a long and difficult path to be traversed, in order really to arrive at this great goal, the truly entire German nation . . . It is necessary to see all important vital occurrences and results of our being in the whole extent of our racial corpus [*überstaatlichen Volkskörpers*], a racial corpus which extends beyond and is superior to the state. We do not want German culture, German sentiments, German obligations to be any longer restricted by the sphere of state borders.

DOCUMENT 35
BERLINER BOERSEN ZEITUNG
of February 22, 1934.

435

DOCUMENT 35-A

(Translation)

Berliner Börsen Zeitung, Berlin, February 22, 1934

The Germans are a people of 100 millions!

VDA

Canada	Estonia
United States	Latvia
Mexico	Lithuania
Central America	Siberia
Colombia	Volga
Chile	Poland
Argentina	Ukraine
Brazil	Bucovina
South Africa	Caucasia
South-West Africa	Crimea
Australia	Transylvania
North Schleswig	Banat
Eupen-Malmedy	Czechoslovakia
Luxembourg	Hungary
Alsace-Lorraine	Sudetenland
South Tyrol	Lower Styria

Every Third German Lives Outside of the Reich's Borders!

The great German racial community is fighting all over the whole planet.

The VDA is the trustee of the 30 million Germans in foreign countries!

Friday, February 23, is its

DAY OF SACRIFICE FOR THE WINTER RELIEF!

Do Your Duty!

Nur 5 Minuten Besinnung!

Das weißt Du?

Deutschland hat durch das Diktat von Versailles viele Millionen Volksgenossen verloren. Was soll nach dem Willen der fremden Völker aus diesen abgetrennten deutschen Volksgenossen werden? In Nordschleswig: Dänen! In Elsaß-Lothringen: Franzosen! In Eupen-Malmedy: wallonische Belgier! Im Korridor, in Ostoberschlesien: Polen! In Memel: Litauer!

Weitere fünf Millionen deutsche Volksgenossen sind durch den Zusammenbruch des alten Oesterreich an fremde Staaten gefallen. Was will man aus ihnen machen? In Südtirol: Italiener! In der Tschechoslowakei: Tschechen! In Ungarn: Magyaren! In Südslawien: Serben! In Siebenbürgen und im Banat: Rumänen!

Das ist so! Darüber ist kein Zweifel! Das weißt Du!

Es gibt eine Organisation, die all diesen Millionen deutscher Volksgenossen im Ausland großzügige Hilfe leistet:
Der Volksbund für das Deutschtum im Ausland (V.D.A.) erhält die deutsche Schule und damit die deutsche Jugend außerhalb der Grenzen deutsch.

Das weißt Du bestimmt auch!

Auf dem ganzen Erdball gibt es Deutsche. Wieviel? Das ist schwer zu sagen. Zahllose davon haben infolge der Gleichgültigkeit der alten Heimat ihre deutsche Sprache und Art längst vergessen. Millionen allein sind in dem Völkergemisch der Vereinigten Staaten ertrunken. Die Zahl der Deutschen in der Welt beträgt aber bestimmt noch nahezu

hundert Millionen!

Denke sie Dir mit einheitlichem Willen erfüllt. Das wäre eine gewaltige Kraft, ein unerschütterlicher Unterbau für unsere Zukunft, für deutsche Wirtschaft, Industrie und Weltgeltung, Lebensraum für unser heranwachsendes Geschlecht, Grundlage unserer Ausfuhr und damit Quelle der Arbeitsmöglichkeit für uns alle. Wir wollen diesen Willen schaffen! Hilf mit!

Jeder dritte Deutsche lebt im Ausland!

437

DEUTSCHE IN EUROPA | DEUTSCH-ÖSTERREICH 6 300 000 | TSCHECHOSLOWAKEI 3 500 000 | SCHWEIZ 2 860 000 | ELSASS-LOTHRINGEN 1 600 000 | POLEN 1 350 000 | RUSSLAND 1 000 000 | RUMÄNIEN 800 000 | SÜDSLAWIEN 700 000 | UNGARN 600 000 | DANZIG 360 000 | ITALIEN (DEUTSCH-SÜDTIROL) 300 000 | LUXEMBURG 250 000 | BELGIEN (EUPEN-MALMEDY) 150 000 | LITAUEN U. MEMELLAND 130 000 | LETTLAND 75 000 | DÄNEMARK (NORDSCHLESWIG) 50 000 | ESTLAND 30 000

rund 20 MILLIONEN

33 Mill. Deutsche wohn

Euben-Malmedy

Belgien 150000

Durch das Diktat von Versailles sind an der Westgrenze des Rheinlandes, dicht bei Aachen, die beiden rein deutschen Kreise Eupen und Malmedy vom Deutschen Reich losgerissen und gegen den Willen der Bevölkerung an Belgien gegeben. Aber auch jenseits der ehemaligen Reichsgrenze gibt es deutsche Siedlungen in Altbelgien und außerdem zahllose Reichsdeutsche in den großen Städten Belgiens. In Belgien ist man sich dessen bewußt, daß Eupen-Malmedy ohne irgend einen Rechtsgrund vom deutschen Mutterland losgerissen worden ist. Das beweist die Tatsache, daß Belgien es nicht wagte, eine ehrliche Abstimmung unter der Bevölkerung über die Zugehörigkeit des Gebietes zuzulassen. Das beweist die rücksichtslose Unterdrückung des deutschen Kulturwillens, das beweisen die Verbote deutscher Veranstaltungen und die Ausweisung bewußt deutschgesinnter Persönlichkeiten.

Elsaß-Lothringen 1600000

Elsaß-Lothringen ist altes deutsches Kulturland, das seit mehr als anderthalb Jahrtausenden von deutscher Bevölkerung bewohnt ist und das schon im Mittelalter Brennpunkt deutschen Kulturlebens und Heimat zahlreicher deutscher Dichter, Künstler und Geisteshelden gewesen ist: Hier hat der deutsche Meister Erwin von Steinbach das herrliche Münster geschaffen und Gottfried von Straßburg das Lied von Tristan und Isolde gesungen. Hier ist Jahrhunderte später der junge Goethe nach seinem eigenen Geständnis erst seines Deutschtums bewußt geworden.

Die Bevölkerung von Elsaß-Lothringen ist auch heute ihrer Sprache und ihrem ganzen Volkstum nach zum weit überwiegenden Teil deutsch und auch gewillt, an ihrer Muttersprache festzuhalten. Das beweist der hartnäckige Kampf, den die Elsässer um die deutsche Unterrichtssprache in der Schule und die Doppelsprachigkeit der Behörden führen. Das beweisen die von Jahr zu Jahr steigenden Erfolge der elsässischen Heimatbewegung. Frankreich hat erfahren müssen, daß man in heutiger Zeit ein Volk gegen seinen Willen nicht mehr seiner Sprache und seiner Art berauben kann.

Das Münster zu Straßburg

Elsaß-Lothringen

DEUTSCHE IN ÜBERSEE

VEREINIGTE STAATEN 10-12 000 000

SÜD- UND MITTEL-AMERIKA 800 000

KANADA 300 000

ASIEN 197 000

AUSTRALIEN 160 000

AFRIKA 125 000

rund 13 MILLIONEN

en außerhalb des Reichs

Dänemark 60 000

Davon etwa 50 000 im verlorenen Nordschleswig. Unsere Volksgenossen im verlorenen Land. Sie müssen ihre Erhaltung in schweren wirtschaftlichen Kämpfen und in kulturellem Ringen durchsetzen. Es geschieht vornehmlich dadurch, daß ausgezeichnete Schulen eingerichtet und Büchereien geschaffen werden. Deutsche Vereine suchen unsere Volksgenossen zusammenzuhalten. Der Volksbund für das Deutschtum im Ausland (V.D.A.) hat in den abgetrennten Gebiet Nordschleswigs in den letzten Jahren überaus segensreich gewirkt. Die Zahl der Schulen stieg in wenigen Jahren von 9 auf 20; die Zahl der deutschen Schüler von 249 auf 815; die Zahl der Lehrer von 17 auf 49.

Nordschleswig

Polen 1 350 000, Danzig 360 000
Litauen und Memelland 130 000

Das Deutschtum im Osten befindet sich in größter Not und Gefahr

Ostpreußen ist vom deutschen Volkskörper losgerissen und so von ihm getrennt, daß es nur nach Überwindung großer Verkehrsschwierigkeiten zu erreichen ist. Ein breiter „Korridor" wurde mitten durch deutsches Land gelegt. Dort, wo deutsche Siedler in vergangenen Jahrhunderten Land erst geschaffen haben, hat man unsere Volksgenossen zu Hunderttausenden vertrieben. Trotzdem ist die Zahl der Deutschen in Polen immer noch sehr beträchtlich. Sie führen einen unendlich schweren Kampf und sind in ständiger Gefahr, wenn sie für das Recht ihres Volkstums eintreten. Tausende von Deutschen sind in die Gefängnisse geworfen, unzählig schwer mißhandelt worden. Auch hier sucht man durch Vernichtung der deutschen Schulen das Land endgültig polnisch zu machen. Das politische Ziel der Polen geht weiter. Es ist eine offenkundige Tatsache, daß sie nicht nur danach streben, Litauen sich anzugliedern, sondern auch Danzig und das von der polnischen Flut schwer bedrohte deutsche Ostpreußen an sich zu reißen.

Rathaus in Thorn

Die Ostmark

Öfterreich mit Südtirol

Deutſch-Öſterreich 6 300 000

Staatsgeſetz der deutſch-öſterreichiſchen Nationalverſammlung
vom 12. Nov. 1918:

„Deutſchöſterreich iſt ein Beſtandteil der Deutſchen Republik.
Beſondere Geſetze regeln die Teilnahme Deutſchöſterreichs an der
Geſetzgebung und Verwaltung der Deutſchen Republik, ſowie die
Ausdehnung des Geltungsbereiches von Geſetzen und Einrichtungen
der Deutſchen Republik und Deutſchöſterreichs.“

Dieſer von der deutſchöſterreichiſchen Nationalverſammlung be-
ſchloſſene Anſchluß an das Deutſche Reich iſt unſeren Volksgenoſſen
in Deutſchöſterreich verboten worden.

Wo bleibt das Selbſtbeſtimmungsrecht der Völker?

Tſchechoſlowakei 3 500 000

Gegen 3½ Millionen Deutſche wohnen in der Tſchechoſlowakei: im Böhmer-
wald, an den Südhängen des Erzgebirges und im Rieſengebirge. Ein breiter
Gürtel iſt längs der Grenzen des Reiches mit Deutſchen beſiedelt. Ihre
Forderung, mit Oeſterreich zu Deutſchland zu kommen, wurde nicht erfüllt.
Das herrſchende Staatsvolk der Tſchechen ſucht auch hier die Deutſchen von
ihrem angeſtammten Volkstum abzudrängen, ſie durch Gewaltmaßnahmen
mürbe zu machen und ihrer Führer zu berauben, indem ſie dieſe ins Ge-
fängnis wirft.

Sudetendeutſchland

Südſlawien 700 000, Ungarn 600 000
Rumänien 800 000, Rußland 1 000 000

Bis an die Küſten des Schwarzen Meeres verklingt die deutſche Sprache
nicht. Zahlloſe deutſche Sprachinſeln folgen einander. Stätten hoher Kultur
ſind von Deutſchen geſchaffen worden, zumal in Siebenbürgen. Sümpfe
wurden urbar gemacht, verwildertes Land wurde gerodet, blühende Dörfer
entſtanden. In vergangenen Jahrhunderten waren ſie dem völkiſchen Untergang ausgeſetzt. In der Gegenwart hat das ſchwere Schickſal der Deutſchen
und die dadurch hervorgerufene Beſinnung überall zu einem Erwachen
deutſchen Kulturwillens geführt.

Die Brücke nach dem Oſten

Mittelamerika, Südamerika, Aſien, Auſtralien, Afrika 1 572 000

Wie mit einem Netz ſind die Deutſchen über den Erdball geſpannt. Es gibt keine Stadt der Erde, wo Deutſche nicht
als Kaufleute Fuß gefaßt haben, kaum ein Land, in dem ſie nicht als Siedler wohnen. Der deutſche Name erklingt auf
der ganzen Welt. Es fehlt uns nur eins: der Wille, überall zuſammenzuſtehen, ſo wie es die anderen tun. Wenn er einmal
vorhanden iſt, wird die deutſche Sprache nie verklingen, deutſches Weſen nicht vergehen und deutſche Wirtſchaft immer blühen.

Deutſche Auswanderung.

Immer noch ziehen deutſche Menſchen hinaus in die Welt. So ging es Jahrhunderte hindurch, ſo geht es heute noch.
Die Vergangenheit hat deutſches Blut vertan, verſchenkt an fremdes Volk. Das iſt vorbei! Wir wollen endlich
auch ein Volk ſein wie alle Völker der Erde. Helft, daß die Deutſchen draußen deutſch bleiben und mit
uns gemeinſam die deutſche Zukunft geſtalten!

Hier abtrennen!

Hierdurch melde ich mich als Mitglied im

Volksbund für das Deutſchtum
im Ausland (V.D.A.)

Ortsgruppe: ————————————

mit einem Jahresbeitrag von ———————— RM. an
und bitte um Ueberſendung eines Aufnahmeſcheines.

Name: ————————————————

Beruf: ————————————————

Wohnung: ————————————————

300000. V. 33. T6.

DOCUMENT 36–A

(A VDA Pamphlet: Partial Translation)

CONSIDER THIS FOR ONLY 5 MINUTES!

DO YOU KNOW THIS?

Through the dictated peace of Versailles, Germany has *lost many millions of racial comrades*. According to the intentions of foreign peoples, what are these separated German racial comrades to become? In North Schleswig: Danes! In Alsace-Lorraine: Frenchmen! In Eupen-Malmedy: Walloon Belgians! In the Corridor, in East Upper Silesia: Poles! In Memel: Lithuanians!

A further five million German racial comrades have fallen to foreign states through the destruction of old Austria. What does one want to make of them? In the South Tyrol: Italians! In Czechoslovakia: Czechs! In Hungary: Magyars! In Yugoslavia: Serbs! In Transylvania and in Banat: Rumanians!

THAT'S THE TRUTH! THERE'S NO DOUBT ABOUT IT! YOU KNOW IT!

There is one organization which is furnishing extensive aid to all these millions of German racial comrades in foreign countries:

THE LEAGUE FOR GERMANDOM IN FOREIGN COUNTRIES (Volksbund für das Deutschtum im Ausland, VDA), is keeping the German school, and therewith the German youth outside of our borders, German.

YOU CERTAINLY KNOW THIS ALSO!

There are Germans on the whole planet. How many? That's hard to say. As a result of the indifference of the old homeland countless numbers of these have long since forgotten their German language and German ways. Millions have drowned in the melting pot of the United States alone. The number of Germans in the world, however, certainly still amounts to nearly ONE HUNDRED MILLION!

Think of these animated by a unified will. They would be an enormous energy, a firm foundation for our future, for the German economy, industry, and prestige in the world, *Lebensraum* for our growing generation, basis for our export trade, and therewith *source of employment opportunity* for us all. We want to create this will! Help us!

441

EVERY THIRD GERMAN LIVES IN A FOREIGN COUNTRY!

Germans in Europe		Germans Overseas	
German-Austria	6, 300, 000	United States	10—12, 000, 000
Czechoslovakia	3, 500, 000	South and Central	
Switzerland	2, 860, 000	America	800, 000
Alsace-Lorraine	1, 600, 000	Canada	300, 000
Poland	1, 350, 000	Asia	197, 000
Russia	1, 000, 000	Australia	160, 000
Rumania	800, 000	Africa	125, 000
Yugoslavia	700, 000	**About 13 Million**	
Hungary	600, 000		
Danzig	360, 000		
Italy (incl. South Tyrol)	300, 000		
Luxembourg	250, 000		
Belgium			
(incl. Eupen-Malmedy)	150, 000		
Lithuania & Memel	130, 000		
Latvia	75, 000		
Denmark & North Schleswig	60, 000		
Estonia	30, 000		

About 20 Million

33 MILLION GERMANS LIVE OUTSIDE OF THE REICH

. . . .

Germans are stretched over the planet like a net. There is no
city on earth where Germans have not gotten a foothold as businessmen, scarcely a country in which they do not dwell as settlers.
The German name rings out throughout the whole world. We lack
only one thing: the will to stand together everywhere, as the others
do. If this will is once at hand, the German language will never die
out, German characteristics will never slip away, and the German
economy will always flourish.

GERMAN EMIGRATION

Germans are still migrating out into the world. Thus it was for
centuries, so it still is today. The past has cast away German blood,
donated it to foreign peoples. This is all over! We also want finally
to be a people like all the peoples of the earth. Lend your aid, so that

the Germans out there remain German and shape the German future together with us!

. . . . *Cut off here* . . . .

I enroll herewith as a member in the LEAGUE FOR GERMANDOM IN FOREIGN COUNTRIES (VDA)

Local group: . . . .

with an annual contribution of . . . .

. . . . RM

and request the forwarding of a Certificate of Admission.

NAME: . . . .

OCCUPATION: . . . .

RESIDENCE: . . . .

. . . .

Verein für das Deutschtum im Ausland

Berlin W 30, Martin-Luther-Straße 97

Der Reichsinnenminister für die V. D. A.=Arbeit!

Abschrift II B 7855/27. 4.   Berlin, den 24. Februar 1933.
Der Reichsminister des Innern.
II B 7855/4. 2.

  An die Landesregierungen.

Betrifft: Verein für das Deutschtum im Ausland,
    Deutscher Schulverein e. V.

  Bei der Pflege der nationalen Aufgaben hat mein Ministerium in besonderem Maße den Schutz und die Förderung des Grenz= und Auslanddeutschtums ausgeübt. Eine größere Zahl mit Sonderaufgaben auf diesem Gebiete betrauter Einrichtungen wird aus mir zur Verfügung stehenden Mitteln so weit möglich unterstützt. Unter allen diesen nimmt der Verein für das Deutschtum im Ausland, Deutscher Schulverein e. V., Berlin, eine bevorzugte Stellung ein. Seiner durch ein halbes Jahrhundert hindurchgeführten Arbeit ist die Erhaltung so mancher deutschen Schule, Kirche, Zeitung oder sonstigen Einrichtung in den Volkssiedlungen deutscher Abstimmung im Ausland zu verdanken. Ohne die Erhaltung dieser Einrichtungen wären große deutsche Volksgruppen vor allem unter dem Druck der Nachkriegszeit als Kulturdünger fremden Volkstums untergegangen. Leider war in den vergangenen Jahren eine gewisse Zurückhaltung weiter Volkskreise gegenüber der Werbearbeit des genannten Volksvereins festzustellen und auch behördliche Einengungen seiner Tätigkeit sind nicht unterblieben. Es erscheint mir jedoch als dringende Pflicht des Reichs und der Länder, nicht nur solche Hemmungen zu beseitigen, sondern dem Verein für das Deutschtum im Ausland auf allen von ihm gewünschten Gebieten eine größere Entfaltung der Werbung zu ermöglichen. Es darf auch die Rücksicht auf die Not und das Elend der Zeit, auf den Mangel an Arbeit und Brot im Binnendeutschland den Blick nicht davon ablenken, daß die rund 30 Millionen Auslanddeutschen außerhalb der verengerten gegenwärtigen Reichsgrenzen ein Bestandteil des deutschen Gesamtvolkes sind, ein Bestandteil, dem die Reichsregierung zwar wirtschaftlich keine Hilfe zu bringen vermag, dem sie jedoch die kulturelle Stützung durch den in erster Linie hiermit befaßten Verein für das Deutschtum im Ausland zu ermöglichen sich verpflichtet hält.

  Ich möchte daher die besondere Aufmerksamkeit der Regierungen der Länder auf die Tätigkeit des Vereins für das Deutschtum im Ausland mit dem Ziele lenken, daß ihm eine bevorzugte Behandlung zuteil werde. Vornehmlich sind es die Schulgruppen, die die Werbung des Vereins tragen, in denen sich zugleich eine überkonfessionelle und überparteiliche Erziehung der Jugend zum vaterländischen Denken vollzieht. Ich würde daher größten Wert darauf legen, daß seinen Schulsammlungen weitester Spielraum gewährt wird und daß auch den Schülern und Schülerinnen das Tragen von Abzeichen des Vereins innerhalb der Schule gestattet wird. Eine wirksame Belebung dieser Arbeit würde ich mir davon versprechen, wenn die Leitung aller Schulen in ihren Jahresberichten über den Schulbetrieb auch über die Förderung des Vereins für das Deutschtum durch die Schulgruppen jeder Schule den vorgesetzten Behörden gegenüber sich zu äußern angehalten würden.

Zur Weitung des gesamtdeutschen Bewußtseins der Jugend über die Reichsgrenzen hinweg hat im vergangenen Jahre, von besonderen Wünschen des Herrn Reichspräsidenten geleitet, im Berliner Stadion das „Fest der deutschen Schule" mit großem Erfolge abgehalten werden können. Im laufenden Kalenderjahr soll das „Fest der deutschen Schule" außerdem in Beuthen, Breslau, Erfurt, Düsseldorf, Gera, Gladbeck, Köslin, Köln, München, Nürnberg, Karlsruhe, Stettin u. a. stattfinden. Ich würde es begrüßen, wenn das „Fest der deutschen Schule" in weiten Kreisen des Reichs zur Einführung käme, da kein Vorhaben geeigneter ist, alle Schulen, somit auch gerade die Volksschulen, in den Dienst des Auslanddeutschtums zu stellen, während die große Reichstagung des VDA. stets nur Gruppen, vor allem solche der höheren Schulen, erfaßt. Ich beehre mich daher, die Regierungen der Länder besonders auf die Einführung des „Festes der deutschen Schule" hinzuweisen, damit die Schulbehörden veranlaßt werden, sich hinter die Veranstaltung zu stellen, und durch besondere Erlasse, wie es in Berlin geschehen ist, die Vorbereitungen des Festes erleichtern.

Neben der Schularbeit des Vereins für das Deutschtum im Ausland hat seine allgemeine Werbung in der Oeffentlichkeit an ernster Bedeutung für das Weiterbestehen der deutschen Volksgruppen im Ausland in demselben Ausmaße gewonnen, in dem angesichts der Finanzlage von Reich und Ländern die Möglichkeit aus Etatsmitteln unmittelbare Zuschüsse zu gewähren, geringer geworden ist. Im vergangenen Jahre hat mit Genehmigung des Preuß. Staatskommissars für die Regelung der Wohlfahrtspflege in ganz Preußen eine Landessammlung stattgefunden, die trotz der schlechten Wirtschaftslage angesichts des nationalen Erwachens des deutschen Volkes einen erfreulichen Erfolg gehabt hat, so daß es dem Verein gelungen ist, die erhebliche Verringerung seiner sonstigen Einnahmen durch die neuen Sammlungen annähernd auszugleichen. Die Bitte des Vereins, ihm durch Fürsprache bei den Regierungen der Länder die Durchführung dieser Landessammlung im ganzen Reichsgebiet zu ermöglichen, wird daher von mir lebhaft befürwortet. Der Erfolg der vorjährigen Sammlung war darauf zurückzuführen, daß in Preußen die Oberpräsidenten, die Regierungspräsidenten und die Landräte sich dankenswerterweise selbst in den Dienst der Sache gestellt haben. Ich wäre dankbar, wenn nunmehr alle Länderregierungen die Landessammlung zuließen und in gleicher Weise förderten.

Für eine zustimmende Aeußerung zu meinen vorstehenden Ausführungen, gegebenenfalls für eine Mitteilung über das bereits Veranlaßte wäre ich dankbar.

Dem Auswärtigen Amt habe ich Abschrift übersandt.

gez. **Frick**

DOCUMENT 37-A

(Translation)

VEREIN FÜR DAS DEUTSCHTUM IM AUSLAND
(LEAGUE FOR GERMANDOM IN FOREIGN COUNTRIES)
BERLIN W 30, MARTIN LUTHER STREET 97

THE REICH'S MINISTER OF THE INTERIOR IS FOR THE VDA WORK!

TRANSCRIPT II B 7855/27.4
THE REICH'S MINISTER OF THE INTERIOR   BERLIN, *February 24, 1933*
II B 7855/4.2

To the Governments of the Federal States
(*Landesregierungen*)

Re: Verein für das Deutschtum in Ausland,
   (League for Germandom in Foreign Countries)
   Deutscher Schulverein e.V.
   (German School League, Inc.)

My Ministry in its attention to national tasks has to a special degree exercised protection over and furtherance of Germandom in the border countries and Germandom in foreign countries. A large number of institutions concerned with special tasks in this sphere are being supported as far as possible by means at my disposal. Among all these the *League for Germandom in Foreign Countries*, German School League, Inc., Berlin, enjoys an *especially favored position.* To its work carried on for half a century is due the maintenance of so many German schools, churches, newspapers, or other institutions in the German settlements in foreign countries. Without such maintenance of these institutions large German folk-groups, especially under the pressure of the post-war period, would have perished as cultural fertilizer for foreign peoples. Unfortunately in past years a certain reserve among wide circles of the population was noticeable with regard to the propaganda work of the above-named national League, and also administrative restrictions on its activities have not been left undone. It appears to me, therefore, as an urgent duty of the Reich and of the federal states not only to set aside such hindrances but also to enable the League for Germandom in Foreign Countries to unfold the increased propaganda work in all spheres which it desires. Also, regard for the needs and misery of the time, and for the lack of work and bread within Germany, ought not to divert attention from the fact that the around 30 million Germans in foreign countries (*Auslanddeutschen*) outside of the present contracted borders of the Reich are an integral part of the entire German people. They are an integral part, which the Reich's Government is not able to help economically, but whose cultural support through the league primarily concerned with this, the League for Germandom in Foreign Countries, it considers it is obligated to make possible.

I should like accordingly to direct the special attention of the governments of the federal states to the activity of the League for Germandom in Foreign Countries with the idea that it *be accorded privileged treatment.* It is primarily the school groups which carry on the propaganda work of the League, in which at the same time the education of the youth to patriotic thinking takes place, an education which is above denominational and party differences. I will, therefore, attach the greatest value to the fact that its school meetings be accorded the greatest freedom of action and that the pupils be allowed to wear the insignia of the League in the schools. I would expect an effective enlivenment of this work, *if the supervisors of all the schools, in their annual reports to their superior authorities concerning the school activities, will be urged to report the furtherance of the League by the school groups of each school.*

Last year, in accordance with the particular desire of the Reich's President, the "German School Celebration", aiming to extend the pan-German consciousness of our youth beyond the borders of the Reich, was held with great success in the Berlin Stadium. Moreover, in the current year the "German School Celebration" is to take place in Beuthen, Breslau, Erfurt, Düsseldorf, Gera, Gladbeck, Köslin, Cologne, Munich, Nuremberg, Karlsruhe, and Stettin, among others. I would welcome it, if the "German School Celebration" could be introduced extensively through the Reich, since no project is more suited to put *all* the schools, and especially the *elementary* schools, in the service of Germandom in foreign countries, while the big national assembly of the VDA always affects only groups, primarily those from the higher schools. I am honored, therefore, to refer the governments of the federal states especially to the introduction of the "German School Celebration", so that the school authorities may be induced to support this event and to facilitate the preparations for the celebration by special orders, as has occurred in Berlin.

Along with the school work of the League for Germandom in Foreign Countries, its general propaganda work among the public has assumed greater significance for the continuance of the German folk-groups in foreign countries in the same measure in which, in view of the financial situation of the Reich and of the federal states, the possibility of granting direct subsidies from the budget has become smaller. In the last year, with the approval of the Prussian State Commissar for the Regulation of Relief Work, a collection has taken place in all Prussia and, despite the poor economic situation, has had gratifying results in view of the national awakening of the German people, so that the League has approximately succeeded through the new collections in compensating for the considerable decrease of its other income. The request of the League, by intercession with the governments of the federal states to enable it to carry out this collection throughout the whole of the Reich, is accordingly most cordially seconded by me. The success of last year's collection was due to the fact that in Prussia the Senior Presidents, the Governing Presidents, and the State Councilors have devoted themselves to the service of the cause in the most commendable way. I would be grateful if all the governments of the federal states permit this collection and further it in the same way.

I would appreciate an answer approving my preceding remarks, and in the given case a report concerning what has already been done.

I have sent a copy to the Foreign Office.

Signed, FRICK

Verein für das Deutschtum im Ausland

Berlin W 30, Martin-Luther-Straße 97

Abkommen

mit der Reichsjugendführung

der Hitlerjugend.

Zwischen der Hitlerjugend und dem B. D. A. wurde folgende grundsätzliche Einstellung beider Organisationen vereinbart:

1. In voller Würdigung der bedeutsamen volkspolitischen Aufgaben empfiehlt die Hitlerjugend ihren Mitgliedern auch die Mitgliedschaft und Mitarbeit im B.D.A.

2. Die Arbeit der B.D.A.-Gruppen bleibt in den bisherigen Formen bestehen. Der B.D.A. verzichtet aber auf wehrsportliche Ausbildung.

3. Die Schulgruppen des B.D.A. (volksdeutsche Arbeitszellen) stehen der Hitlerjugend mit ihrer Arbeit zur Seite.

4. Die B.D.A.-Gruppenobleute arbeiten deshalb in engster Fühlung mit der Hitlerjugendführung und nehmen mit ihren Gruppen an den Veranstaltungen der Hitlerjugend teil, wie auch umgekehrt die Hitlerjugend an den volksdeutschen Veranstaltungen des B.D.A. teilnehmen kann.

5. Der B.D.A. führt als sichtbares Zeichen seiner Verbundenheit mit der Hitlerjugend eine B.D.A.-Armbinde mit dem Hakenkreuz.

6. Von der Reichsjugendführung der N.S.D.A.P. tritt Referendar Nabersberg in den Führerrat des B.D.A. Vom B.D.A. gehört Dr. H. Schoeneich zum Führerrat beim Reichsausschuß der deutschen Jugendverbände. Die gleiche gegenseitige Vertretung ist auch bei den Landesausschüssen herzustellen.

Karlsruhe, den 6. Mai 1933.

Für den B.D.A.
gez. Dr. H. Schoeneich
i. A.: E. Klinghammer

Für die Hitlerjugend
Der Reichsjugendführer
gez. Baldur v. Schirach

DOCUMENT 38–A

(Translation)

VEREIN FÜR DAS DEUTSCHTUM IM AUSLAND
(LEAGUE FOR GERMANDOM IN FOREIGN COUNTRIES)
BERLIN W 30, MARTIN LUTHER STREET 97

AGREEMENT

With the National Office of the Hitler Youth

Between the Hitler Youth and the VDA the following fundamental arrangement has been agreed upon:

(1) With a complete respect for the important racial-political tasks the Hitler Youth recommends to its members membership in and collaboration with the VDA.

(2) The work of the VDA group continues in its previous forms. The VDA, however, discontinues its military and physical training.

(3) The school groups of the VDA (racial-German work-cells) assist the Hitler Youth in their work.

(4) The VDA group chiefs work consequently in closest contact with the Hitler Youth leaders and participate with their groups in the events of the Hitler Youth, as conversely the Hitler Youth can also take part in the racial-German fetes of the VDA.

(5) As a visible sign of his solidarity with the Hitler Youth, the VDA member wears a VDA armband with the swastika.

(6) Solicitor Nabersberg of the NSDAP's National Youth Office becomes a member of the VDA's Council of Leaders. Dr. H. Schoeneich of the VDA becomes a member of the Council of Leaders in the Reich's Board of German Youth Societies. The same reciprocal representation is also to be established in the provincial boards.

KARLSRUHE, *May 6, 1933*

For the VDA	For the Hitler Youth
Signed: Dr. H. SCHOENEICH	*The Reich's Youth Leader*
Per E. KLINGHAMMER	Signed: BALDUR VON SCHIRACH

450

STUTTGARTER NEUES TAGBLATT,
Stuttgart, Germany

Setember 21,1933.
Morning Edition.

Im Dienst des Ausland-Deutschtums

Jahresversammlung des DAI vom neugewählten

Vorsitzenden Oberbürgermeister Dr. Strölin eröffnet

* Stuttgart, 20. September.

Die diesjährige Jahrestagung des Deutschen Ausland-Instituts stand ganz im Zeichen des neuen nationalsozialistischen Reiches. Erst die nationalsozialistische Weltanschauung vermag es, dem Gedanken der Arbeit für das Auslanddeutschtum die hohe Bedeutung zuzuweisen, die ihr gebührt. Die volksdeutsche Idee ist heute zum Durchbruch gelangt. So war es selbstverständlich, daß der diesjährigen Jahrestagung des Deutschen Ausland-Instituts auch von den maßgebenden Regierungsstellen stärkste Anteilnahme entgegengebracht wurde. Die Vertreter der Behörden und der volksdeutschen Organisationen waren bei der Jahresversammlung und der Kundgebung in großer Zahl vertreten.

Die Jahresversammlung

Die Jahresversammlung fand am Mittwoch nachmittag im festlich geschmückten kleinen Saal des Hauses des Deutschtums statt. Oberbürgermeister Dr. Strölin, der in einer Ausschußsitzung zum neuen Vorsitzenden des DAI gewählt wurde, eröffnete die Versammlung und begrüßte die Anwesenden, unter denen man hervorragende Vertreter der auslanddeutschen Arbeit bemerkte. Oberbürgermeister Dr. Strölin begrüßte besonders den Danziger Senatspräsidenten Dr. Rauschning, General a.D. Professor Haushofer, Geheimrat Dr. Rüdiger als Vertreter des Reichsaußen- und Reichsinnenministeriums, den stv. württembergischen Reichspropagandaleiter und Gauleiter Schmidt als Vertreter des Reichspropagandaministers Dr. Goebbels, Oberregierungsrat Dr. Drück vom Kultusministerium als Vertreter der Aufsichtsbehörde, Senator Kaspar Muth-Rumänien und Geheimrat Professor Dr. von Müller.

Der neue Vorsitzende OBM. Dr. Strölin spricht

Oberbürgermeister Dr. Strölin betonte, daß er sich nur schwer hätte entschließen können, den Vorsitz des Instituts zu übernehmen, daß er es aber getan habe im Hinblick auf die enge Verbundenheit, die zwischen der Landeshauptstadt und dem Deutschen Ausland-Institut bestünden. Nach einigen grundsätzlichen Ausführungen über die Arbeit des Instituts und die besonderen Beziehungen der Schwaben zu dem Auslanddeutschen kam Oberbürgermeister Dr. Strölin auf die Neuordnung des Instituts und im besonderen auf die Neubildung des Vorstands zu sprechen.

Zum Stellvertreter des Vorsitzenden wurde Landtagsdirektor Dr. Eisenmann bestellt. Weiter gehören dem Vorstand an: Oberregierungsrat Dr. Drück vom Innenministerium, Dr. Robert Ernst, Universitätsprofessor Dr. Göring, Oberstudiendirektor Dr. Krehl, Dr. Hans Steinacher, Universitätsprofessor Dr. Mannhardt und Universitätsprofessor Dr. Uhlig. Berater des Vorstands in Wirtschaftsfragen ist Fabrikant Kiehn, juristischer Berater Ministerialdirektor Dr. Dill. Die Zusammensetzung des Vorstands wurde vornehmlich unter dem Gesichtspunkt der Vereinheitlichung der Deutschtumsarbeit vorgenommen.

Die Leitung des Instituts wurde Herrn Professor Dr. Csaki übertragen. Bei der Suche nach einem geeigneten Leiter ging man davon aus, eine Persönlichkeit zu finden, die selbst in der Deutschtumsarbeit wurzelt und sich dieser Arbeit draußen in der Welt schon gewidmet hat. Der neue Leiter, Professor Dr. Csaki, der Siebenbürger Sachse ist, stand in vorderster Linie unter den Auslandspionieren. Oberbürgermeister Dr. Strölin dankte Dr. Steinacher, Dr. Krehl und Dr. Ernst für ihre erfolgreiche Tätigkeit im DAI während des Uebergangszustandes der vergangenen Monate.

Im Folgenden sprach der Redner kurz über die künftigen Aufgaben der Deutschtumsarbeit in organisatorischer und wirtschaftlicher Beziehung, die auf eine Zusammenfassung und Intensivierung hingleiten müßten. Ein Punkt, so betonte Oberbürgermeister Dr. Strölin, liege ihm vor allem am Herzen: Ein Volk, das wie das deutsche der Welt das Beispiel einer gewaltigen Wiederauferstehung, eines Aufbruchs der Nation zu den alten und ewigen Quellen seiner Kraft darbiete, habe es schwer, bei den Völkern draußen Verständnis zu finden. An dieser Stelle habe das DAI seine volle Kraft einzusetzen:

Ausnützung aller Möglichkeiten zur Abwehr von Mißtrauen und Mißverständnissen, zur Aufklärung des Auslanddeutschtums und Ausrüstung des Auslanddeutschen zur Werbung um Verständnis für deutsches Geschehen und deutsches Wesen.

Oberbürgermeister Dr. Strölin schloß seine Rede mit dem Appell zur Mitarbeit.

Der Bericht über ein Jahr DAI

Anschließend gab Dr. Csaki, der neue Leiter des

Instituts, einen Bericht über die Tätigkeit des Instituts im Jahr 1932/33. Während in den früher erstatteten Jahresberichten mehr eine Rechenschaft über den inneren Betrieb gegeben wurde, sprach Dr. Csaki gewissermaßen mit dem Blickpunkt von außen her. Als Mann, der von der vordersten Front der Deutschtumsarbeit im Ausland selbst in das Reich berufen wurde, konnte er wichtige Ausführungen darüber machen, wie sich die Arbeit des DAI. nach außen hin auswirkt und welches Echo ihr aus dem bodenständigen Auslanddeutschtum entgegenhallt. Die Pünktlichkeit und Zuverlässigkeit, mit der das DAI. seine Aufgaben erfüllt hat, wirkte sich auch im Auslanddeutschtum im erzieherischen Sinn aus. Die Auslanddeutschen hatten, wie Dr. Csaki betonte, stets den Eindruck, daß in Stuttgart alle den Auslanddeutschen interessierenden Arbeits- und Lebensgebiete behandelt würden.

Wenn das DAI. seine wirtschaftlichen Aufgaben nicht voll erfüllen konnte, so lag das an der Unzulänglichkeit des bisherigen politischen Regimes, dem der Blick für die Bedeutung der volksdeutschen Arbeit fehlte. Jetzt, wo der Weg freigegeben ist, muß sich das DAI. mit doppelter Verantwortung dessen bewußt sein, daß es seinen zentralen Anteil zu nehmen hat an dem großen Aufklärungs- und Propagandafeldzug, der im Sinn einer fruchtbaren wirtschaftlichen Verknüpfung des Mutterlandes mit den Auslanddeutschen zu führen ist. Alle deutschen Volksgruppen im Ausland ohne Ausnahme erwarten heute vom neuen Deutschland und vor allem vom Deutschen Ausland-Institut, daß es sich wirksam in den Dienst einer ihr Wirtschaftsleben tatsächlich ankurbelnden Vermittlung stellte. Wir haben die tiefste Verpflichtung, zu helfen. Almosen zu empfangen, verbittert.

Es handelt sich für uns um eine unbedingte volksdeutsche Pflicht, nicht um Wohltätigkeit. Das deutsche Volkstum im Ausland muß in den Blutkreislauf des deutschen Volkes organisch einbezogen werden.

In ausführlichen Darlegungen sprach dann Dr. Csaki über die Tätigkeit der einzelnen Abteilungen des Instituts. Wenn das Institut nicht schon bestände, meinte er, so müßte es sofort gegründet werden. Die Arbeit, die hier geleistet werde, müsse unmittelbar im Dienst der deutschen Volksgenossen im Ausland stehen und dürfe nicht in archivalische Erstarrung und museale Unbeweglichkeit verfallen. Es muß damit ein Denkmal des unbekannten auslanddeutschen Soldaten, der für uns an der Front ist, in einer der Würde des deutschen Volkes entsprechenden Weise ausgestaltet werden. Der Ueberblick über die Arbeit der einzelnen Abteilungen des Instituts brachte viel Wissenswertes und Wichtiges.

Die erste Spanne der Entwicklung des DAI. ist abgeschlossen. Die zweite Stufe, die jetzt betreten wird, muß getragen sein durch den großen seelischen Erfülltheit der gesamtdeutschen Volksgemeinschaft. Dr. Csaki betonte, daß er selbst sich mit allen Fasern seines Wesens zum Dienst am Volkstum bekenne und er gelobte, sie im Geist des neuen Staates und im Sinn der nationalsozialistischen Weltanschauung zu führen. Er dankte zum Schluß den Vertretern der Regierung für ihr Interesse und Oberbürgermeister Dr. Strölin für die Uebernahme des Vorsitzes.

Nach der Erstattung des Jahresberichts durch Dr. Csaki nahm Oberbürgermeister Dr. Strölin nochmals das Wort zu einigen Ausführungen. Er faßte seine Auffassung über die künftige Gestaltung der Arbeit des DAI. in einer kurzen Erklärung zusammen und verlas den Wortlaut zweier Telegramme, die an den Reichspräsidenten und den Reichskanzler abgeschickt wurden.

Die Sitzung klang aus in einem Siegheil auf das ... Volk innerhalb und außerhalb der Grenzen, auf den Reichspräsidenten und den Führer Adolf Hitler.

STUTTGARTER NEUES TAGBLATT,   September 21,1933.
Stuttgart ,Germany.   Morning Edition.

Große volksdeutsche Kundgebung

Ein begeisterter und begeisterndes Bekenntnis zu Alldeutschland

Der großen volksdeutschen Kundgebung war von der Stuttgarter Bevölkerung erfreulicherweise großes Interesse entgegengebracht worden. Der Festsaal der Liederhalle war schon geraume Zeit vor Beginn der Versammlung überfüllt. An der Estrade des Saales waren die Wappen einiger wichtiger auslandsdeutscher Städte, so von Memel, Hermannstadt, Thorn, Eupen, Eger, Kattowitz, Danzig, Straßburg und Tondern, angebracht. Vor dem Podium hatte SA Aufstellung genommen, hinter der Musikkapelle Hitler-Jugend und DWA-Gruppen mit ihren Wimpeln.

Unter den Anwesenden bemerkte man u. a. Finanzminister Dr. Dehlinger, Professor Dr. Martin Spahn, M.d.R., Präsident Dr. Kilpper vom Industrie- und Handelstag, Dr. v. Stauß-Berlin, Oberbürgermeister a. D. Dr. Lautenschlager, Polizeipräsident Klaiber, Landtagsdirektor Eisenmann, General Liebmann und die Vertreter der Reichswehr, die Spitzen der staatlichen und städtischen Behörden.

Die Kundgebung wurde mit dem Vorspiel zu den „Meistersingern" eingeleitet, das von der SA-Standartenkapelle 119 unter Leitung von Obertruppführer Hanfer ausdrucksvoll vorgetragen wurde.

Begrüßung der Ehrengäste

Der Vorsitzende des Deutschen Ausland-Instituts, Oberbürgermeister Dr. Strölin, eröffnete die Kundgebung. Er begrüßte unter den Anwesenden besonders den Ministerpräsidenten Kultminister Mergenthaler als den Vertreter der Aufsichtsbehörde, General Haushofer-München als den Bevollmächtigten von Rudolf Heß, der vom Führer mit der obersten Leitung aller auslandsdeutschen Angelegenheiten beauftragt wurde, den stb. Gauleiter Schmidt als den württembergischen Vertreter von Reichspropagandaminister Dr. Goebbels, Herrn Ruberg als den Vertreter des außenpolitischen Amtes und seines Leiters Alfred Rosenberg. Mit lebhaftem Beifall wurde der Danziger Senatspräsident Dr. Rauschning als der Vertreter der kerndeutschen, gegen ihren Willen vom Mutterland getrennten Danziger Bevölkerung begrüßt. Ferner begrüßte Oberbürgermeister Dr. Strölin Geheimrat Dr. Röbiger als Vertreter des Reichsaußen- und Reichsinnenministeriums, dessen Anwesenheit als ein Zeichen der besonderen Interessennahme des Reiches an der Arbeit des Instituts gewertet werden müsse, sowie Senator Dr. Muth, den kampferprobten Führer des Banater Deutschtums, und Geheimrat Professor Dr. von Müller, den Präsidenten der Deutschen Akademie. Im weiteren führte

Oberbürgermeister Dr. Strölin

aus: In der Jahresversammlung ist mir heute das Amt des Vorsitzenden des DAI übertragen worden. Ich habe dies als eine Kundgebung des Vertrauens und der Ehrung der Landeshauptstadt Stuttgart aufgefaßt, die es schon immer zu würdigen gewußt hat, daß ein für das Deutschtum im Ausland und die deutsche Weltgeltung so bedeutungsvolles Institut in ihren Mauern beheimatet ist. Diesen Entschluß hat mir die Tatsache erleichtert, daß ich der Mitarbeit zuverlässiger und erprobter Männer sicher bin. Für das Amt des Leiters des DAI ist in Herrn Professor Dr. Csaki ein Mann gefunden worden, der als Siebenbürger Sachse selbst im Auslanddeutschtum wurzelt, der sich aus eigener Arbeit draußen am Auslanddeutschen die für sein Amt erforderliche Erfahrung erworben hat. Ich begrüße ihn aufs herzlichste in Stuttgart.

Außen- und Innenpolitisches

Das DAI hat die Aufgabe, die Beziehungen zwischen den Deutschen im Ausland und dem Mutterlande zu erhalten und enger zu knüpfen. Zur Durchführung dieser Aufgabe bedarf es des Einsatzes aller Kräfte.

Es ist in ganz Deutschland auf das lebhafteste begrüßt worden, daß vor einigen Tagen unser schwäbischer Landsmann, der Reichsaußenminister von Neurath, vor der Weltöffentlichkeit so mannhafte deutsche Worte gegen die politischen Brunnenvergifter gefunden hat.

Die außenpolitischen Grundgedanken, die der Reichsaußenminister in dieser bedeutungsvollen Rede entwickelt hat, bilden auch die Richtlinien für die Einstellung des DAI. Wir sind von tiefem Friedenswillen beseelt. Aber wir wissen auch, daß es für ein Volk nichts Höheres, nichts Heiligeres geben kann als die Verteidigung seiner Ehre, seiner Freiheit und seiner völkischen Einheit. Und so werden wir Deutsche nicht ruhen und rasten, bis wir neben der inneren Freiheit, die wir uns durch die deutsche Revolution eroberten, auch die äußere Freiheit wieder gewonnen haben. Dieser Kampf um Ehre und Freiheit muß geführt werden nicht nur innerhalb der Grenzen unseres Vaterlandes, sondern gerade auch von unseren Brüdern und Schwestern draußen in der Welt.

Und so rufe ich von dieser Stelle in meiner Eigenschaft als Vorsitzender des Deutschen Ausland-Instituts allen Auslanddeutschen in Nord und Süd, in Ost und West, in Ueberland und Uebersee zu:

Arbeitet mit uns für die Erhaltung des Friedens, kämpft mit uns gegen den Ungeist von Versailles, gegen die Zerstörung und Unterdrückung des deutschen Volkstums, für die Gleichberechtigung des deutschen Volkes, für die Durchsetzung des Volkstumsgedankens und für die Wiedererlangung unserer Ehre und Freiheit.

In diesem Geiste rufen wir unseren deutschen Bluts-, Schicksals- und Kampfgenossen in allen Ländern der Welt ein dreifaches Sieg-Heil zu.

Anschließend sprach

Ministerpräsident, Kultminister Mergenthaler

Die nationalsozialistische Bewegung hat auf allen Lebensgebieten befruchtend gewirkt. Sie hat auch der Deutschtumsarbeit ganz neue Impulse gegeben. Die Arbeit für das Auslanddeutschtum hat erst dadurch die rechte Weihe und Tiefe erhalten. Es hat uns in den letzten Jahren des Kampfes oft mit Sorge erfüllt, daß die Arbeit für das Auslanddeutschtum nicht in enger Verbindung mit den braunen Kämpfern des Nationalsozialismus geführt werden konnte. Die überwundene liberalistische Weltanschauung arbeitete mit dem formalen Begriff des Staatsbürgers. Wir haben damit aufgeräumt. Heute steht im Mittelpunkt der blutmäßige deutsche Volksgenosse. Das ist das neue Fundament, auf dem wir aufbauen müssen.

Es ist kein Zufall, daß gerade die Stämme besonders bodenverwurzelt und völkisch sind, die, wie zum Beispiel die Schwaben, ihr Volkstum draußen in der Welt unter den schwierigsten Umständen gehalten haben.

Die Deutschtumsarbeit muß in Zukunft auf rassischer Grundlage geschehen, sonst hat sie den Boden unter den Füßen verloren.

Wenn wir diese rassische Bedingtheit erkennen, müssen wir auch die Folgerungen daraus ziehen. Das konnte gewisse Härten mit sich bringen, aber es mußte sein, um des Volkes willen.

Wir begrüßen es, daß mit dem neuen Leiter ein Auslanddeutscher an die Spitze der Arbeit für das Auslanddeutschtum getreten ist. Von der neuen Auffassung aus werden der Deutschtumsarbeit neue Wege erschlossen.

Die neue Auffassung wird ein Schutzwall gegen das kulturelle und rassische Aufgehen unserer Volksgenossen in anderen Völkern sein.

Der Nationalsozialismus wird den deutschen Volksgenossen Kraft geben. Damit geben wir den Ausland-deutschen etwas ungeheuer Großes. Wir dürfen auch nicht vergessen, daß die Auslanddeutschen gewissermaßen als Wächter um uns stehen. So will ich dem Deutschen Auslandinstitut warm ans Herz legen: Sorgt mit uns dafür, daß auch bei den deutschen Volksgenossen im Ausland der Geist des Nationalsozialismus lebendig wird, daß von ihm Kraftströme ausgehen! Ihr Jungen und Mädchen, ihr sollt stolz sein darauf, daß ihr bei dieser Aufgabe mitarbeiten dürft. Ihr sollt für deutsche Art und Sitte einstehen und zeigen, daß dieses Volk das Recht hat, gleichberechtigt mit anderen Völkern dazustehen. Ihr sollt stolz darauf sein, Deutsche zu sein. Wir sehen nicht mit Ueberheblichkeit auf andere Rassen und Völker herab, aber wir wollen den Platz erhalten, der uns gebührt. So soll uns diese Kundgebung Mahnung sein, für unser Volk zu arbeiten und auf unsere Volksgenossen jenseits der Grenzen Kraft auszuströmen. Nur wenn das deutsche Volk wie ein Fels zusammensteht, wird das neue Reich erstehen, ein Reich der Gerechtigkeit und Freiheit, das Reich, das fähig ist, seinen Kindern Arbeit und Brot zu geben.

Der Vertreter der Reichsregierung

Als Vertreter des Reichsinnen- und Außenministeriums sprach Geheimrat Dr. Rödiger. Er überbrachte die Grüße der Reichshauptstadt und die persönlichen Grüße des Reichsaußenministers Freiherr von Neurath, der es sehr bedauert habe, wegen der Vorarbeiten zur Genfer Konferenz nicht anwesend sein zu können. Die beiden Ministerien hätten stets mit vollem Interesse die Arbeit des Deutschen Auslandinstituts verfolgt.

Der Redner fand warme Worte für die Aufgabe des Instituts. Auch das deutsche Muttervolk könne viel von den deutschen Volksgenossen im Ausland lernen. Die Wahl von Professor Csaki dürfe man als Gewähr für eine Zusammenarbeit aller beteiligten Kreise auffassen. Zu seinem Amt bedürfe es einer glühenden Begeisterung und eines umfassenden Wissens. — Nun nahm der

stv. Gauleiter Schmidt

das Wort. Er überbrachte als der württembergische Reichspropagandaleiter die Grüße von Reichsminister Dr. Goebbels. Die Gauleitung der NSDAP, so sagte er, ist bereit, mit der neuen Leitung des DAI durch dick und dünn zusammen zu gehen und mit ihr zusammenzuarbeiten. Der Nationalsozialismus will die völkische Gemeinschaft aller Deutschen als geschichtliches Recht fordern. Unsere Blutszusammengehörigkeit sei das große Geschenk, dessen wir uns immer bewußt sein müssen.

Nun ergriff der neue Leiter des DAI,

Professor Dr. Csaki

das Wort zu einer immer wieder von Beifall unterbrochenen Ansprache, in der er u.a. ausführte: Wenn meine Volksgenossen im Ausland heute abend hier sein könnten, so würden sie ihren Augen und Ohren kaum trauen. Auch wir im Ausland arbeiten aus innerstem deutschen Wesen heraus, aber wir sind geknebelt. Wenn wir die deutsche Grenze überschreiten, öffnet sich uns ein neues großes Erleben. Es ist unbeschreiblich, welches Erzittern durch uns im Ausland ging, als wir zum erstenmal im Rundfunk deutsches Leben miterleben durften. Wir verfolgten mit tiefem Schmerz die innere Zerrissenheit des deutschen Volkes.

Nun, da all das überwunden ist, da wir sehen, daß alle volksdeutschen Organisationen in einer Linie stehen, erfüllt uns ein Gefühl des Stolzes auf unser deutsches Mutterland,

ein Gefühl des Glücks: Deutschland ist eins.

Ich komme zu Ihnen von meinen Schicksalsgenossen da draußen und sie bitten mich, Künder ihres Wesens, ihrer Einstellung zu Deutschland und Künder auch ihrer Not zu sein. Ich bringe Kunde von einem Boden, der erfüllt ist von Kampf. Was wir immer wieder in den Vordergrund stellen müssen, ist das:

Zu uns wird von früh auf das Bewußtsein erzogen: Du stehst vielen gegenüber in hartem Kampf um dein deutsches Volkstum.

So haben wir immer das Gefühl, alles was wir wollen, im Kampf gegen die Behörden erreichen zu müssen. Aber das Gefühl der Zugehörigkeit zum deutschen Volk gibt uns ein glückliches Bewußtsein. Im Lauf der Jahrhunderte ist diese oder jene Position verloren gegangen. Wir müssen es verhindern, daß noch mehr verloren geht. Es gibt uns ein Gefühl des Stolzes und des Selbstbewußtseins, daß wir Brücken sind für den deutschen Lebensraum.

Daß bisher nur wenig getan wurde für die Erhaltung des deutschen Bodens im Ausland weist uns den Blick auf die Zukunft. Wir lernen aus der Vergangenheit für die Zukunft. Wir kämpfen für höchste Dinge. Es ist kein Zufall, daß das Deutsche Ausland-Institut in Stuttgart steht. Die Bauern im Banat und in der Dobrudscha und in anderen Gebieten sind zum großen Teil Schwaben, und von Stuttgart aus gehen Fäden in alle Welt. So ist es für mich ein Gefühl des Glücks, für meine Volksgenossen arbeiten zu können, für die unbekannten Soldaten auf dem Schlachtfeld jenseits der Grenzen. Ihrer zu gedenken bitte ich auch Sie. Ihnen fühle ich mich zeitlebens zugehörig, wenn ich mich auch jetzt bemühe, hier heimisch zu werden, vielleicht auch bald ein guter Schwabe zu werden.

Anschließend sprach Dr. Ernst als Vertreter der Deutschtumsorganisationen. Es geht nicht dahin, daß wir aus sentimentalen Gefühlen heraus für unsere Volksgenossen arbeiten. Es geht um die . . . unseres Volkes. In den Jahren der tiefsten . . . macht ist sich unser Volk seiner völkischen . . .keit bewußt . . . leben. Wenn wir uns aus den Tiefen unseres Volkes . . . unsere Kräfte holen, dann können wir niemals überwunden werden. Wenn unser Kampf von Erfolg gekrönt ist, dann werden uns die anderen Nationen beneiden, daß wir 30 Millionen Volksgenossen außerhalb der Grenzen haben. Im Wort Deutschland sind wir jedem deutschen Volksgenossen in der Welt verbunden.

Oberbürgermeister Dr. Strölin verlas zum Schluß folgendes Antworttelegramm des Reichskanzlers, das soeben eingelaufen war:

„Für das mir übersandte Treuegelöbnis danke ich aufrichtig und entbiete den zur Jahrestagung des DAI versammelten Teilnehmern meinen herzlichsten Gruß.   Adolf Hitler."

Die begeisternde Kundgebung wurde mit dem Deutschland- und dem Horst-Wessel-Lied geschlossen.

(Bh)

N.S. KURIER.   September 21,1933.
Stuttgart, Germany.   Morning Edition.

Das Hilfswerk an den Auslandsdeutschen

Jahrestagung des Deutschen Auslandsinstituts
Dr. Strölin der neue Führer

Stuttgart.

Am Mittwoch, den 20. September, nachmittags 4 Uhr fand die Jahrestagung des Deutschen Ausland-Instituts statt, zu der eine große Anzahl der bisherigen Verwaltungskörperschaften, eine Reihe geladener Mitglieder sowie Vertreter der Reichs- und Länderregierungen, führender Deutschtumsorganisationen und Wirtschaftsverbände erschienen waren.

In einer vorbereitenden Sitzung, in der eine Anzahl Mitglieder des bisherigen Ausschusses zugegen waren, gab zunächst Oberregierungsrat Dr. Drück im Namen des Ministerpräsidenten und Kultministers Mergenthaler eine Erklärung ab: Im Verlauf des revolutionären Umschwungs habe sich ein Notstand ergeben, der die Oberaufsichtsbehörde der Württ. Regierung nötigte, zur Erhaltung der Arbeitsfähigkeit einen Reorganisationsausschuß einzusetzen, an den alle Befugnisse übergingen. Dieser Zustand wurde von der Versammlung nachträglich als zurechtbestehend anerkannt. Der Ausschuß hatte den Auftrag, den neuen Vorsitzenden des Instituts zu berufen, der dann von sich aus den neuen Vorstand ernennen und im Einvernehmen mit den Regierungsstellen die neuen Satzungen ausarbeiten sollte.

Der Sprecher des Dreierausschusses, Reichsführer des VDA., Dr. Steinacher, erklärte, daß man in Oberbürgermeister Dr. Strölin den Mann gefunden habe, der nach Lage der Verhältnisse und seiner Persönlichkeit nach am geeignetsten erscheine, das verantwortungsvolle Amt zu übernehmen. Mit dieser Berufung habe der Auftrag des Dreierausschusses sein Ende gefunden.

Nachdem sich Oberbürgermeister Dr. Strölin zur Uebernahme des Amtes bereit erklärt hat, stellte Dr. Drück namens des Kultministers fest, daß

Dr. Strölin in rechtsgültiger Form zum neuen Vorsitzenden des Instituts berufen

sei und das Recht zur Berufung der übrigen Vorstandsmitglieder habe. Dem neuen Vorsitzenden sprach er den Dank für die Annahme des Vorsitzes aus, zugleich die besten Wünsche für die Arbeit und reiche Erfolge für das Gesamtdeutschtum, ferner die Versicherung, daß seine Person die Gewähr für gedeihliche Arbeit biete.

Die anschließende Jahrestagung wurde von dem neuen Vorsitzenden, Oberbürgermeister Dr. Strölin, eröffnet, der die zahlreich erschienenen Mitglieder und Ehrengäste begrüßte, unter ihnen den Vertreter des Auswärtigen Amtes der NSDAP., als Vertreter des Reichspropagandaministers den württembergischen Reichspropagandaleiter, ferner den Danziger Senatspräsidenten, Dr. Rauschning, als Vertreter des Reichsaußen- und Reichsinnenministeriums Geheimrat Dr. Roediger. und als Vertreter der Aufsichtsbehörde Oberregierungsrat Dr. Drück, und führte sodann aus:

Die Neuordnung des Instituts habe sich als gebieterische Aufgabe erwiesen. Zur Vorbereitung dieser Aufgabe sei vor Monaten im Einvernehmen mit den zuständigen Behörden ein Dreierausschuß bestellt worden, dem die Herren Dr. Steinacher, Dr. Ernst und Oberstudiendirektor Dr. Krehl als Vertreter der volksdeutschen Organisationen angehörten und der ihm unter Zustimmung der satzungsmäßigen Organe das Amt des Vorsitzenden des DAI. angetragen habe. Er habe sich entschlossen, das verantwortungsvolle Amt zu übernehmen im Hinblick auf die Tatsache, daß die schwäbische Landeshauptstadt zu dem in ihren Mauern beheimateten DAI. besonders enge Beziehungen habe. Schwaben seien in aller Welt und das DAI. sei die Stätte, durch die wir mit unseren zahllosen schwäbischen Landsleuten draußen in enger Verbindung blieben. Er hoffe deshalb, bei der Ausübung seines Amtes nicht nur dem deutschen Volk, sondern auch seiner engeren schwäbischen Heimat dienen zu können.

Zur

Neubildung des Vorstandes

übergehend, berief Oberbürgermeister Dr. Strölin zu seinem Stellvertreter Landtagsdirektor Dr. Eisenmann. Als Vertreter der Aufsichtsbehörde gehört auch Oberreg.-Rat Dr. Drück vom Kultministerium dem Vorstand an. Des Weiteren wurden zu Vorstandsmitgliedern berufen: die Herren Dr. Robert Ernst-Berlin, Univ.-Prof. Dr. Göring, Oberstudiendirektor Dr. Krehl-Stuttgart, Univ.-Prof. Dr. Mannhardt-Marburg, Dr. Hans Steinacher-Berlin, Univ.-Prof. Dr. Uhlig-Tübingen und als Leiter des DAI. Prof. Dr. Csaki. Weiter werden dem Vorstand angehören als Berater in Wirtschaftsfragen Fabrikant Riehn-

Troſſingen und als juriſtiſcher Berater Miniſterial-
direktor Dr. Dill.

OBM. Dr. Strölin betonte, daß die Zuſammen-
ſetzung des Vorſtandes vornehmlich unter dem Geſichtspunkt der Vereinheitlichung der Deutſchtums-
arbeit vorgenommen worden ſei; er würdigte im einzelnen die neuen Vorſtandsmitglieder und ſtellte ins-
beſondere den neuen Leiter des Auslandsinſtituts
vor als eine Perſönlichkeit, die ſelbſt in der Deutſch-
tumsarbeit wurzele und ſich draußen in der Welt der
Arbeit im Auslandsdeutſchtum gewidmet hat. Als
Siebenbürger Sachſe habe Dr. Cſaki in vorderſter
Linie unter den Auslandspionieren geſtanden; im
Intereſſe des deutſchen Volkes wünſche er ihm für
ſeine Arbeit vollen Erfolg. — Zur

künftigen materiellen Arbeit

des Inſtituts übergehend, ſtrich Dr. Strölin die Möglichkeiten ſtärkerer Aktivität heraus und trat für Zuſammenfaſſung aller Verbände und Gruppen, die ſich
mit Auslandsdeutſchtum beſchäftigen, Vereinheitlichung des Apparates und ſchärfere praktiſch
brauchbare Abgrenzung der Arbeitsbe-
reiche der verſchiedenen Organiſationen ein. Auf
wirtſchaftlichem Gebiete ſehe er die Möglichkeit einer ſtärkeren Auswertung des im Inſtitut
vorhandenen Fonds an Material und Erfahrung zur
Anknüpfung und Feſtigung wirtſchaftlicher Beziehungen zwiſchen dem Deutſchtum im Ausland und der
Wirtſchaft des Mutterlandes. Das Auswanderungs-
und Siedlungsweſen müſſe vorwiegend unter dem
Geſichtspunkt der Erhaltung des deutſchen Volkstums
geſtellt werden. Bei der Ausnützung aller Möglichkeiten zur Abwehr von Mißtrauen und Mißverſtänd-
niſſen, die zur Aufklärung des Auslandsdeutſchtums
und Ausrüſtung des Auslandsdeutſchen zur Werbung
um Verſtändnis für deutſches Geſchehen und deutſches
Weſen dienen, ſei das DAI. mit voller Kraft einzu-
ſetzen. Mit der Aufforderung zu tatkräftiger Mitarbeit und Unterſtützung ſchloß OBM. Dr. Strölin
ſeine mit Beifall aufgenommenen Ausführungen.

Der neue Leiter des DAI.

Prof. Cſaki,

nahm hierauf das Wort zur Erſtattung des Berichtes
über die Tätigkeit des Inſtituts im Jahre 1932/33.
Seit Weltkrieg und Zuſammenbruch hätten ſich die
Lebens- und Arbeitsbeziehungen des deutſchen Volksgruppen im Ausland mit dem Reich mindeſtens ver-
zehnfacht. Mit Pünktlichkeit und ſachlicher Zuverläſ-
ſigkeit habe das DAI. mit ſeiner Arbeit inmitten dieſer Beziehungen geſtanden und durch das Beiſpiel
ſeines techniſch tabelloſen Betriebes im geſamten Auslandsdeutſchtum eine wertvolle erzieheriſche
Arbeit geleiſtet. Wenn dem DAI. die Erfüllung ſeiner wirtſchaftlichen Aufgaben für die deutſchen
Volksgenoſſen im Ausland nicht voll gelungen ſei, ſo
könne man hieraus nicht einer einzelnen Stelle Vorwürfe machen,

ſondern die Fehlerquellen ſeien in dem früheren
Syſtem, in der Unzulänglichkeit eines politiſchen
Regimes zu ſuchen.

Der Redner ging dann näher auf die muſeale
archivaliſche und ſammelnd-wiſſen-
ſchaftliche Tätigkeit des Inſtitutes ein,
deren Bedeutung er damit kennzeichnete: Wenn das
DAI. nicht ſchon beſtände, ſo müßte unverzüglich eine
Anſtalt gegründet werden, die den Zweck hat, das
Leben der Auslandsdeutſchen in all ſeinen Erſcheinun-
gen feſtzuhalten und darzuſtellen. Dieſe ganze Arbeit
habe nicht ſtimmungsmäßiges als vielmehr wiſſen-
ſchaftliches Intereſſe, das die lückenloſe Materialſammlung zur
Pflicht mache, ſondern es ſpiele auch ein ſachliches
Moment von größter Tragweite mit. Das Volkstum
im Ausland, das mitten in ſeinem ſchweren völkiſchen
und wirtſchaftlichen Daſeinskampf nicht die Muße ge-
winnt, ſich ſelbſt und ſein Schickſal darzuſtellen, begrüßt, daß dieſe Darſtellung ſeiner ſelbſt, ſeiner Lei-
ſtung und ſeines Kampfes im Mutterlande erfolge.
Das DAI. habe nicht mit dem Unterfangen, in ſeinen
Sammlungen ein Nationaldenkmal des Grenz- und
Auslandsdeutſchtums anzubahnen, ſich den Dank der-
ſelben verdient, und deshalb ſei es heute notwendig,
wo uns eine freiere Gaſſe gebahnt iſt,

alle mit um ſo größerem Nachdruck aufzurufen,
dieſes Denkmal des unbekannten auslandsdeutſchen Soldaten, der für uns an der Front iſt, in
einer der Würde des deutſchen Volkes entſprechen-
den Weiſe auszugeſtalten zu helfen.

Anſchließend daran gab Dr. Cſaki einen knappen
Ueberblick über die Arbeit der einzelnen Abteilungen des DAI. im Geſchäftsjahr 1932/33 und
zeigte, wie in Zukunft eine ſteigende Verlebendigung
der Beziehungen und wechſelſeitigen Wirkungen zwiſchen Reich und Auslandsdeutſchtum geplant und
möglich ſei. Dr. Cſaki erklärte zum Schluß: Das
DAI. ſchließt nach 16jährigem Beſtehen die erſte große
Spanne ſeiner inneren Entwicklung ab. Die zweite Stufe,
die wir betreten, ſteht unter der Wirkung der großen Geſchehniſſe im deutſchen Vater-
land und der großen ſeeliſchen Erfülltheit der geſamtdeutſchen Volksgemein-
ſchaft. Sie muß und wird getragen ſein durch den
großen Gedanken der Erziehung und Sendung unſerer Nation im Auslande. Mit
allen Faſern ſeines Weſens bekenne er ſich zu dem
Dienſt am Volkstum und zu der Arbeit am Inſtitut
und gelobe, daß ſie

im Geiſte des neuen Staates und im Sinne der
nationalſozialiſtiſchen Weltanſchauung geleiſtet
werden wird.

Oberbürgermeiſter Dr. Strölin dankte hierauf
dem Leiter des DAI. für die Erſtattung des Jahres-
berichtes und gab ſeiner Auffaſſung über die künftige
Geſtaltung der Arbeit des DAI. in der folgenden

Kundgebung

Ausdruck:

Das DAI. wird in ſtärkſter Auswertung der ihm
zur Verfügung ſtehenden Möglichkeiten ſich zu einem
aktiven Träger der volksdeutſchen Bewegung aus-
geſtalten.

Angeſichts der Zuſammenfaſſung der mit dem
Auslandsdeutſchtum befaßten Organiſationen wird

das DAJ. mit allen seinen Kräften an dem gemeinsamen Ziel der Arbeit am Deutschtum draußen und
daheim mitarbeiten.

Dem Auswanderungs- und Siedlungswesen wird
das DAJ. vom Standpunkt des auslandsdeutschen
Volkstums aus Rechnung tragen. Daraus ergibt sich
ein Zusammenwirken mit den kolonialen Verbänden.

Mit seinem wertvollen Material und seiner reichen
Erfahrung wird das DAJ. in den Dienst der Wirtschaft treten als Vermittlungsstelle zur Anknüpfung
und Unterhaltung von Beziehungen zwischen dem
Deutschtum im Ausland und der heimischen Wirtschaft. Seine vordringlichste Aufgabe sieht es in der
Aufklärung des Auslandsdeutschtums über die geistige Haltung und die neuen Wesensformen des zum
vollen Gemeinschaftsbewußtsein erwachten deutschen
Volkes, nicht zuletzt aber auch in der Abwehr jeder
Grenzpropaganda.

Das DAJ. weiß sich bei der Erfüllung seiner Aufgabe nach diesen Gesichtspunkten eins mit dem klaren
und festen **Willen der nationalen Bewegung.** Das
DAJ. erwartet Mitarbeit und die **Mithilfe** jedes
einzelnen deutschen Volksgenossen im Inland **und**
Ausland zum großen letzten Ziel seiner **Arbeit:**
Deutschland.

OBM. Dr. S t r ö l i n gab dann noch die mit **Bei-**
fall aufgenommene Absendung zweier Begrü-
ßungstelegramme an den Reichspräsidenten
von Hindenburg und Reichskanzler Adolf Hitler bekannt. Das

Telegramm an den Reichspräsidenten
lautet: „30 Millionen Auslandsdeutsche erblicken in
Ihnen die Verkörperung der Einheit des deutschen
Volkes. Das Deutsche Ausland-Institut entbietet
Ihnen aus Anlaß der Jahrestagung, der Neuordnung und des ersten Zusammentritts des neuen Vor-
standes ehrerbietigste Grüße und bittet Sie,
auch künftighin Ihre Hand über unsere Arbeit schir-
mend zu halten."

An Reichskanzler Adolf Hitler
wurde folgendes Telegramm gesandt: „Die zur Jahrestagung des Deutschen Ausland-Instituts versammelten Teilnehmer und der neugebildete Vorstand
des Instituts grüßen den Führer des deutschen Volkes. Das gesamte Auslandsdeutschtum,
kampfgewohnt in der Verteidigung seiner Kulturgü-
ter, verehrt in Ihnen den Erneuerer deutschen
Volkstums und sieht in Ihrer Führerschaft die
Gewähr für die untrennbare Verbundenheit des Auslandsdeutschtums mit dem Mutterland und für den Ausbau der gesamten volksdeutschen
Arbeit."

Die Jahresversammlung wurde beschlossen mit
einem von Oberbürgermeister Dr. Strölin ausge-
brachten dreifachen S i e g - H e i l auf Reichs-
präsident von Hindenburg und Reichskanzler Adolf Hitler.

N.S.KUPIER,   September 21, 1933.
Stuttgart, Germany   Morning Edition.

Volksdeutsche Kundgebung

Gestern abend fand aus Anlaß der diesjährigen Jahrestagung des DAI. und aus Anlaß der Ernennung von Pg. Oberbürgermeister Dr. Strölin zum Vorsitzenden des DAI. im überfüllten Festsaal der Liederhalle, eine volksdeutsche Kundgebung statt, die sich zu einem gewaltigen Bekenntnis für das bedrohte und um seine Scholle kämpfenden Deutschtum im Ausland gestaltete. Die Kundgebung war umrahmt von flotten Marschweisen der SA.-Standartenkapelle 119 unter Leitung von Kapellmeister Hanker. Unter den Ehrengästen bemerkte man u. a. Ministerpräsident Prof. Mergenthaler, Oberbürgermeister Dr. Strölin, stellv. Gauleiter Schmidt, den Danziger Senatspräsidenten Dr. Rauschning, Geheimrat Dr. Roediger, Senator Dr. Muth als Führer des Banats, Prof. Dr. v. Müller als Vertreter der Deutschen Akademie, Verwaltungsdirektor Habizel, Prof. Martin Spahn und General Liebermann. Die Galerie der Liederhalle war mit den Wappen von außerdeutschen Gebieten geschmückt, die vorwiegend von Volksgenossen bewohnt sind.

Der neuernannte Vorsitzende des DAI., Pg. Oberbürgermeister Dr. Strölin, eröffnete die Kundgebung und begrüßte die zahlreichen Vertreter der Ministerien und volksdeutschen Organisationen. Pg. Oberbürgermeister Dr. Strölin betonte, daß er seine Ernennung als eine Kundgebung des Vertrauens und der Ehrung der Landeshauptstadt Stuttgart ansehe, die es schon immer zu würdigen gewußt habe, daß ein für das Deutschtum im Ausland und die deutsche Weltgeltung so bedeutungsvolle Institut in ihren Mauern beheimatet sei. Das DAI. habe die Aufgabe, die Beziehungen zwischen den Deutschen im Auslande und dem Mutterlande zu erhalten und enger zu knüpfen. In einem Augenblicke, in dem die Welt von Mißverständnissen über das deutsche Geschehen erfüllt sei, bedürfe es des Einsatzes aller Kräfte. Die außenpolitischen Grundgedanken, die unser schwäbischer Landsmann, Reichsaußenminister von Neurath, gegenüber der Weltöffentlichkeit gefunden habe, bildeten die Richtlinien für die Einstellung des DAI. Wir Deutschen würden nicht ruhen noch rasten, bis wir neben der inneren Freiheit, die wir uns durch die deutsche Revolution erobert haben, die äußere Freiheit, die für uns in der Anerkennung der deutschen Gleichberechtigung mit den anderen Völkern verkörpert sei, wiedergewonnen wäre. Seine Ausführungen schlossen mit den Worten:

Arbeitet mit uns für die Erhaltung des Friedens, kämpft mit uns gegen den Ungeist von Versailles, gegen die Zerstörung und Unterdrückung des deutschen Volkstums, für die Gleichberechtigung des deutschen Volkes, für die Durchsetzung des Volkstumsgedankens und für die Wiedererlangung unserer Ehre und Freiheit.

Nach der oft durch starken Beifall unterbrochenen Rede des neuen Vorsitzenden des DAI. sprach Ministerpräsident Prof. Mergenthaler. Der Ministerpräsident wies darauf hin, daß die nationalsozialistische Erhebung auf allen Lebensgebieten befruchtend gewirkt habe und auch der Deutschtumsarbeit neue Impulse gegeben habe. Die Arbeit des Deutschen Ausland-Institutes und der anderen Verbände, die die Betreuung der deutschen Brüder und Schwestern übernommen hätten, habe sich dadurch die richtige Weise erfahren, daß die braune Front jetzt mit ihnen verschmolzen sei. (Beifall.) In den letzten Jahren habe es uns mit Sorge erfüllt, daß die Betreuung der Auslandsdeutschen nicht die notwendige enge Verbindung hatte mit den braunen Kämpfern des deutschen Nationalsozialismus. Früher arbeitete man mit dem formalen Begriff des Staatsbürgers. Die deutsche Revolution habe mit diesem formalen Staatsbürgerbegriff aufgeräumt. Der blutsmäßig begründete Volksgenosse sei das Fundament, auf dem das Deutsche Auslandinstitut und die ganze Arbeit der Betreuung des Deutschtums im Auslande aufgebaut sei. Gerade die Schwaben seien es gewesen, die unter den schwierigsten Umständen im Auslande ihr Deutschtum gewahrt hätten. Die Deutschtumsarbeit müsse in Zukunft auf rassischer Grundlage stehen, wie sie das nicht, so verliere sie den Boden unter den Füßen. Er begrüßte es im Namen der württembergischen Staatsregierung auf das freudigste, daß der Leiter des Deutschen Auslandinstitutes selber ein Auslandsdeutscher ist und dem Not und Sorgen der Auslandsdeutschen am eigenen Leibe erfahren habe. Der Geist, der in der nationalsozialistischen Bewegung lebendig sei, sei geradezu ein Schutzwall gegen das kulturelle und rassische Aufgehen des deutschen Volkstums innerhalb der fremden Völker.

Als Vertreter des Reichskanzlei- und Reichsinnenministeriums sprach sodann Geheimrat Dr. Roediger. Er überbrachte die Grüße des Reichsinnenministeriums und des Außenministers Freiherrn von Neurath, der leider durch die vorbereitenden Arbeiten für die Genfer Abrüstungskonferenz am Erscheinen verhindert worden sei. Ganz besonders grüßte er den neuen Vorsitzenden des DAI., Pg. Oberbürgermeister Dr. Strölin und wünsche dem DAI. für alle Zukunft eine segensreiche Arbeit.

In seiner Eigenschaft als Reichspropagandaleiter für Württemberg sprach sodann stellvertr. Gauleiter Schmidt. Er überbrachte die Grüße des Reichsministers Dr. Goebbels. Die Gauleitung Württemberg sei stolz darauf, in ihrem Gaubereich das Deutsche Auslandinstitut zu wissen, ein Organ, das ungeheuer schwere, aber auch wertvolle Aufgaben zu leisten habe. Die Gauleitung sei bereit, mit dem Deutschen Auslandinstitut durch dick und dünn zusammenzuarbeiten und seine Arbeit in jeder Weise zu unterstützen und zu fördern.

Prof. Dr. Csaki sprach dann aus der Praxis seiner Deutschtumsarbeit im Ausland. Er fühle sich als Verbindungsoffizier zwischen der Heimat und den Volksgenossen draußen, denen Kräfte mit der Aufgabe wachsen. Er sei Künder ihres Wesens, ihrer Einstellung zu Deutschland und ihrer Not. Wo auch immer ein deutscher Bauer pflüge, sei deutscher Boden. Der Auswanderer Ziel heißt: Boden.

Zum Schluss der Kundgebung sprach der Führer des Schutzbundes, Dr. Ernst, Berlin, für den Reichsführer des Volksbundes für das Deutschtum im Ausland, Dr. Steinacher. Er stellte sein Elsässertum bewußt in den Vordergrund und betont als lebenswichtiges Element aller Deutscher die Kräfte, die aus deutschem Volkstum heraufsteigen. Im Kampfe seien die Auslandsdeutschen die Frontkämpfer. — Mit dem Deutschlandlied und dem Horst-Wessel-Lied schloß die bedeutsame Kundgebung, nachdem OBM. Dr. Strölin folgendes Telegramm des Reichskanzlers Adolf Hitler verlesen hatte:

"Für das mir übersandte Treuegelöbnis danke ich aufrichtig und entbiete den zur Jahrestagung des DAI. versammelten Teilnehmern meinen herzlichsten Gruß. Adolf Hitler."

DOCUMENT 39–A

(Extracts)

STUTTGARTER NEUES TAGBLATT (DAILY NEWSPAPER OF STUTTGART), SEPTEMBER 21, 1933 (TWO ARTICLES)

N. S. KURIER (DAILY NEWSPAPER OF STUTTGART), SEPTEMBER 21, 1933 (TWO ARTICLES)

ARTICLE 1
(Stuttgarter Neues Tagblatt, September 21, 1933)

"IN THE SERVICE OF GERMANDOM ABROAD

"ANNUAL MEETING OF THE DAI OPENED BY THE NEWLY ELECTED CHAIRMAN, CHIEF MAYOR DR. STRÖLIN

"STUTTGART, *September 20*

"This year's annual meeting of the Deutsches Ausland-Institut stood entirely under the sign of the new National Socialist Germany. Only the National Socialist world-view is able to give to the idea of the work for Germandom abroad the great significance which is due it. The racial-German idea has today finally won through. Hence it was to be taken for granted that this year's annual meeting of the Deutsches Ausland-Institut would be participated in by the authoritative Government offices. Representatives of the authorities and of pan-German organizations were present in great numbers at the annual meeting and the demonstration.

". . . Chief Mayor Dr. Strölin, who was appointed by a committee to be the new chairman of the DAI, opened the annual meeting . . .

.   .   .   .

"Dr. Eisenmann, director of the provincial parliament, was appointed vice chairman. On the Board of Directors belong also: Senior Government Councilor Dr. Drück from the Ministry of the Interior; Dr. Robert Ernst [leader of the Schutzbund, Berlin]; University Professor Dr. Göring; Senior Director of Education Dr. Krehl; Dr. Hans Steinacher [national leader of the Volksbund für das Deutschtum im Ausland]; University Professor Dr. Mannhardt; and University Professor Dr. Uhlig. The manufacturer Kiehn is the Economic Adviser to the board, Ministerial Director Dill is the Legal Adviser. The composition of the board was formed primarily with the aim of unifying Germanism activities.

"The direction of the Institute is entrusted to Professor Dr. Csaki [a Transylvanian Saxon who had previously devoted himself to Germanism activities outside of Germany]."

In his report concerning the activity during the year 1932–33, Dr. Csaki stated, "If the DAI was not able to accomplish its unique tasks fully this was caused by the inadequacy of the previous political regime, which failed to appreciate the significance of the racial-German work. Now, when the way has been freed, the DAI must with increased responsibility be conscious of the fact that it has to play an essential role in the great campaign of propaganda and enlightenment, which is to be carried on in favor of a fruitful economic connection of the mother country with the Germans in foreign countries. All the German folk-groups in foreign countries, without exception, today expect the new Germany, and above all the Deutsches Ausland-Institut, to work effectively toward an exchange which will greatly stimulate their economic life. We have the deepest obligation to help. Receiving alms creates bitterness. It is a question for us of the absolute racial-German obligation, not of charity. The German racial element in foreign countries must be organically included in the vital processes of the German people."

In the course of the meeting, Dr. Strölin read a telegram which had been sent to Reich's Chancelor Hitler:

"The assembled participants of the annual meeting of the Deutsches Ausland-Institut and the newly formed Board of Directors of the Institute *greet the Führer of the German people*. The entire Germandom abroad, accustomed to struggle in the defense of its cultural goods, reveres in you *the renovator of Germandom* and sees in your leadership *the guaranty for the inseparable unity* of Germandom abroad with the mother-country and for the expansion of all racial-German work [text taken from the *N.S. Kurier*, Sept. 21, 1933 (*ante* p. 458)]."

In the pan-German celebration Dr. Strölin read the following telegram of response from the Reich's Chancelor:

"I sincerely thank the assembled participants of the DAI's annual meeting for the pledge of allegiance transmitted to me, and send my most cordial greeting. Signed, Adolf Hitler [*Stuttgarter Neues Tagblatt*, Sept. 21, 1933 (*ante* p. 455)]."

ARTICLE 2

(*Stuttgarter Neues Tagblatt*, September 21, 1933)

"PAN-GERMAN CELEBRATION

"The Chairman of the Deutsches Ausland-Institut, Chief Mayor Dr. Strölin, opened the celebration. He greeted among those present, in particular, Minister-President and Minister of Religion in Württemberg Mergenthaler as the representative of the supervisory authorities; General Haushofer of Munich as the representative of Rudolf Hess, who has been entrusted by the Führer with the supreme direction of all matters concerning Germans in foreign countries; the Deputy Gauleiter Schmidt as the Württemberg representative of Reich's Propaganda Minister Dr. Goebbels; Herr Ruberg as the representative of the NSDAP's Foreign Policy Office and its Director Alfred Rosenberg. The President of the Danzig Senate, Dr. Rauschning, was greeted with great applause as the representative of the purely German population of Danzig which has been separated from the mother-country against its will. Chief Mayor Dr. Strölin further greeted Privy Councilor Dr. Rödiger as the representative of the Reich's Ministry of Foreign Affairs and the Reich's Ministry of the Interior, whose presence must be taken as the sign of the Reich's special interest in the work of the Institute. He also greeted Senator Dr. Muth, the tried Führer of the Banat Germandom, and Privy Councilor Professor Dr. von Müller, the President of the German Academy."

Geheimrat Dr. Rödiger, as representative of the Ministry of Foreign Affairs and Ministry of the Interior at the session, brought greetings from Foreign Minister von Neurath, and stated that "both Ministries had always followed with great interest the work of the DAI".

Deputy Gauleiter Schmidt, representing Dr. Goebbels, stated, "The local party leadership [*Gauleitung*] is prepared to cooperate through thick and thin with the new officers of the DAI. National Socialism will demand the blood community of all Germans as its historic right. Our blood relationship is a great gift of which we must always be conscious."

In his address Dr. Strölin stated, "The DAI has the task of maintaining and tightening the connections between the Germans in foreign countries and the mother-country."

In his address Minister-President Mergenthaler stated, "The National Socialist movement has had a fructifying effect in all spheres of life. It has also given an entirely new impulse to the work for Germandom. The work for Germandom in foreign countries has thereby received the proper consecration and depth. In the past years of struggle it has often filled us with concern that the work for Germandom in foreign countries could not be carried on in close connection with the Brown fighters of National Socialism. The liberalistic ideology which has been overcome dealt with the formal concept of the citizen. We have gotten rid of that. Today the blood-united German racial-comrade stands in the center. That is the new foundation upon which we must build."

"The work for foreign Germandom must in the future proceed on a racial basis; otherwise it has lost the ground under its feet.

". . . New paths will be opened up for the work of Germandom by the new conception. The new conception will be a protective wall against the cultural and racial absorption of our comrades in other peoples. National Socialism will give energy to the German racial comrades. We are giving the Germans abroad therewith something enormously great. We also ought not to forget that the Germans abroad in a certain sense stand as guardians around us. Hence I want to impress on the Deutsches Ausland-Institut: Join us therefore in taking care that the spirit of National Socialism also become alive among the German racial-comrades in foreign countries, so that streams of energy may emanate from it!"

In his address the new Director of the DAI, Dr. Csaki, stated, "We followed with deep pain the inner disunity of the German people. Now since all that has been overcome, since we see that all the German folk (*Volksdeutsche*) organizations are standing in one line, we are filled with a feeling of pride for our German mother-country, a feeling of happiness: Germany is united."

"The feeling of adherence to the German people gives us a happy consciousness. In the course of centuries this or that position has been lost. We must prevent any more from being lost. It gives us a feeling of pride and of self-consciousness that we are bridges for the German *Lebensraum*."

ARTICLE 3

(*N.S. Kurier*, September 21, 1933)

In this article, concerning the reorganization of the Deutsches Ausland-Institut, it is stated, "In the course of the revolutionary turn of events, an emergency has ensued, which required the chief supervisory authorities of the Württemberg government to install for the maintenance of the work a Committee of Reorganization, to which were transferred all powers. This condition was subsequently recognized as proper by the Assembly. The committee had the task of appointing the new chairman of the Institute, who then himself was to appoint the new Board of Directors, and in agreement with the Government offices work out the new statutes."

"The head of the Committee of Three, Dr. Steinacher, Reich's Führer of the VDA, declared that they have found the right man in Chief Mayor Dr. Strölin, who in view of the situation and his personality appeared most suited to assume this responsible post. The task of the committee had concluded with this." The other two members of this Committee of Three were Dr. Robert Ernst of Berlin, the leader of the Schutzbund, and Dr. Krehl, Senior Director of Education; all three functioned as representatives of pan-German (*Volksdeutsche*) organizations.

The end of Dr. Csaki's annual report included the following remarks: "After sixteen years of its existence the DAI is concluding
the first great span of its development. *The second stage*, upon which
we are entering, stands under the influence of the *great happenings in
the German fatherland and the great psychic fulfilment of the entire
German racial community.* It must and will be borne by the great
ideas of the *education and mission of our Nation in foreign countries.*
With every part of his [Dr. Csaki's] being he pledges himself to service for Germandom and to the work of the Institute, and *he vows* that
it will be *accomplished in the spirit of the new state and in the sense
of the National Socialist ideology.*"

ARTICLE 4
(*N.S. Kurier*, September 21, 1933)

In this article a passage of Minister-President Mergenthaler's speech
at the 1933 session of the DAI is quoted as follows: "The rise of National Socialism has had fruitful results in all fields of activity and
has also given new strength to the work of Germanism. The work
of the DAI and other organizations which have undertaken the protection of Germans has for the first time experienced a proper appreciation since they have become united with the Brown Front. In recent years we have been concerned because the protection of Germans
abroad did not enjoy the necessary close ties with the Brown warriors
of German National Socialism. Previously only a formal concept of
citizenship has been current. The German revolution has dispensed
with this formal concept of citizenship. Racial relationship based
on blood ties is the foundation on which the DAI and the entire task
of protecting Germanism abroad is erected."

DOCUMENT 40

(Translation)

BÖHMEN UND MÄHREN (OFFICIAL PERIODICAL OF THE REICH'S PROTEC-
TOR OF BOHEMIA AND MORAVIA), PUBLISHED BY STATE-SECRETARY
SS GROUP LEADER K. H. FRANK: PRAGUE, MAY 1941, PAGE 179

SS Group Leader State-Secretary
K. H. FRANK:

THE SS ON MARCH 15, 1939

A modern people and a modern state are today unthinkable without
political troops. To these are allotted the special task of being the
advance guard of the political will and the guarantor of its unity.
This is especially true of the German folk-groups, which have their
home in some other people's state. Accordingly the Sudeten German Party had formerly also organized its political troop, the Voluntary Vigilantes (*Freiwilliger Selbstschutz*), called "FS" for short.
This troop was trained essentially in accordance with the principles
of the SS, so far as these could be used in this region at that time.
The troop was likewise assigned here the special task of protecting
the homeland actively, if necessary. It stood up well everywhere in
its first test in this connection, when in the fall crisis of 1938 it had
to assume the protection of the homeland, arms in hand.

After the annexation of the Sudeten Gau, the tasks of the FS were
transferred essentially to the German student organizations as compact troop formations in Prague and Brünn, aside from the isolated
German settlements which remained in the second republic. This was
also natural because many active students from the Sudeten Gau
were already members of the SS. The student organizations then
had to endure this test, in common with other Germans, during the
crisis of March 1939. The calm of German men is to be thanked
for the fact that there were no greater disturbances, which would
have at least made more difficult the peaceful solution of March 15.
Thus the educational work of the SS already found its expression in
the course of the preliminary events. The Führer himself has com-
mended the conduct of the German students. After they had marched
up in formation to the first gathering in the Burg yard on March 16,
he strode down the line and gave his hand to each wounded student.

In the early morning hours of March 15, after the announcement of
the planned entry of German troops in various localities, German
men had to act in order to assure a quiet course of events, either by

assumption of the police authority, as for instance in Brünn, or by corresponding instruction of the police president, etc. In some Czech offices, men had likewise, in the early hours of the morning, begun to burn valuable archives and the material of political files. It was also necessary to take measures here in order to prevent foolish destruction . . . How significant the many-sided and comprehensive measures of the qualified German posts were considered, follows from the fact that many of the men either on March 15 itself or on the following days were admitted into the SS with fitting acknowledgment, in part even through the Reich's leader of the SS himself or through SS Group Leader Heydrich. The activities and deeds of these men were thereby designated as accomplished in the interest of the SS.

Immediately after the corresponding divisions of the SS had marched in with the first columns of the German Army and had assumed responsibility in the appropriate sectors, the men here placed themselves at once at their further disposition and became valuable auxiliaries and collaborators.

Much had to be done quickly but nevertheless thoroughly. This was possible, however, only because many of the SS men were not completely unfamiliar with this region. They had already in many cases been interested in the conditions here and had carefully studied all questions in connection with the problems here.

DOCUMENT 41

(Translation)

DEUTSCHES WOLLEN (MAGAZINE OF THE FOREIGN ORGANIZATION OF THE NSDAP) BERLIN, JULY 1941, PAGE 1

INTERNED FOR TWENTY-ONE DAYS IN ATHENS

The following war diary of the *Landesgruppe* of the Foreign Organization of the NSDAP in Greece furnishes a straightforward testimony of the truly National Socialist behavior of our Germans abroad in this greatest struggle of destiny of the Reich. A lively community spirit, a strong national feeling and, before everything else, the unshakable belief in the Führer are the characteristics of this attitude. In Greece, as everywhere else in the countries of the New Order, the *Landesgruppe* of the party, hardened by the experience of war, is conscious of the great task of leading our German comrades outside of the borders of the Reich in the National Socialist sense and thereby contributing their part to the establishment of a happier world.

E. W. BOHLE, *Gauleiter.*

OUR WAR DIARY

On April 6 at 5:20 a.m. German troops began their march over the Greek border in order to drive the British from this corner of the European Continent. On April 27 they entered Athens. The Germans in Athens passed these 21 days in internment. The training and organizational work of the AO made it possible not only to make their condition bearable but to provide a test of foreign German community life.

Through the entire winter of 1940–41 the Germans in Athens were in the most unusual position: They lived among English troops and behind an enemy front, so to speak.

During this time a war diary was kept. The *Deutsches Wollen* reproduces in the following pages, as an extract therefrom, the high point: the description of those 21 days which were passed in one of the internment camps.

WREDE, *Landesgruppenleiter.*

April 6, Sunday. "Don't Miss the Bus."

The *Landesgruppe* in Greece had provided in the event of threatening developments for the concentration of the German colony in

German buildings, particularly in view of the very poor accommodations provided for the Italian residents in Athens, who had been confined to a primitive camp. Three buildings were accordingly arranged as general quarters, namely, the former Reich Legation in Academy Street, which enjoyed extraterritorial status, the "Philadelphia", the German clubhouse in Homer Street, and the Archeological Institute in Phidias Street. In each of these buildings good mattresses were provided, and a number of beds were also made available. Food supplies for 150 people were provided in each of the buildings.

Provisions were likewise made for tables, chairs, cooking and eating utensils, laundry supplies, tobacco, oil lamps, medical supplies, and some books. Even air-raid shelters were built. Since the German colony believed that at a given time it would be permitted to withdraw voluntarily to these buildings, an exact plan for the time of transfer was worked out by the local group of the AO. The Athens foreign police had knowledge of these preparations and intimated their agreement.

In the following pages the *Landesgruppenleiter* of the AO in Greece, Party Member Wrede, describes his experiences from the day of the German invasion of Greece to the time when Athens was surrendered to the German mountain troops:

"At 1:30 a.m. I am awakened by an employee of the Legation who requests me to go with him immediately to the German Minister. The Minister has been instructed, he tells me on the way, to inform the Greek Government at 5:20 that the German troops are entering Greece. . . .

"We now discuss briefly what should take place at 5:20 a.m. in order to assure the safety of the German colony as far as possible . . . In a few minutes I awaken the four block leaders who can be reached by telephone and give them the agreed code message, 'Don't Miss the Bus' . . .

"It is 5:25 a.m. when I leave the Legation laden with trunks and bedcovers . . . The two Greek policemen on guard watch for a while as we unload our baggage. Then one of them turns to telephone . . . A party member who tries to enter the building after me is followed into the extraterritorial building by the police and arrested there . . . For several hours I am alone with my family in the Legation. We occupy ourselves in fixing up the rooms and setting up the beds. Will we remain here as the only voluntary internees? That was not exactly the purpose of our coming here.

". . . In the evening the first bombs fall in Piraeus. Finally the first group of German nationals is brought to us.

"The police, following a well-worked-out plan, had within a few hours arrested all Germans in their homes or on the streets. No one was permitted to take with him anything except what he wore. Over a thousand people were finally assembled at the police station, including Germans, stateless persons, Jews, Czechs, and pro-German Greeks. The police had to request the assistance of

Local Group Leader and Party Member Leyh in order to separate this confusion of languages and peoples. Party Member Leyh then energetically sorted the sheep from the goats and there followed a series of heated scenes with emigrants of German and non-German nationality. The transport which followed was not as planned to the three German buildings but to the aforementioned internment camp for Italians . . . Party Member Leyh, however, was able to persuade the police to observe their previous agreement and to distribute the arrested Germans among the three buildings which had been prepared. . . ."

April 7 to 14. Barbed Wire Psychosis? Where Are Our Troops?

". . . On April 11 the Swedish Chargé d'Affaires visits us for the first time with his wife. He reports on pending negotiations concerning the removal of the Legation to Turkey. I request him with great emphasis to see to it that I am not counted as a member of the Legation so that I may be permitted to remain here to take care of the colony."

April 15. New Travel Plans.

". . . The foreign police inform us that tomorrow afternoon the Legation will leave by ship from Lavrion for Smyrna or Istanbul. The official states that the Minister desires me to accompany him. The typists and the employees of the Legation who are living in our building are to proceed immediately to their homes and pack. . . . Five minutes later the Swedish Chargé arrives. He states that we need make no arrangements for our departure and that we should negotiate only with him in these matters. Besides, the question of departure is not so pressing since the German Minister has declared that he will not leave without part of the German colony. In reply to my question as to whether the departure idea is not already as good as overtaken by events, the Swede smiles and says that naturally the arrangements which he is making between the representative of the Reich and the Greek Government have to be worked out correctly and that the German Minister naturally will agree to these negotiations only if the Greek Government fulfils the safety conditions which are proposed. . . . I express to the Chargé my concern for the German nationals who have been left in their homes and discuss with him other questions concerning the transmission of information through the Red Cross to Germany, searching of German homes in absence of the occupants, as well as complaints concerning the conduct of the police.

"No one wants to leave. It is obviously stupid to permit ourselves to be deported shortly before the arrival of the German troops. No one wants to miss that experience and everyone wishes to be at the disposal of our troops."

April 20. We Celebrate the Führer's Birthday.

". . . I speak a few words on the occasion of the Führer's birthday. We sit together at a coffee table decorated with flowers."

April 21. A "Heroic" Appeal.

". . . The Swedish Chargé d'Affaires confirms to us that German troops are south of Larissa. Once again we are to leave but we do not take that seriously any longer. I request the Swedish Chargé that in case of disturbances he demand increased police protection for us. Furthermore, I make it clear to him that the threatening of the population with secret police agents and courts-martial is a source of serious danger for the Germans who remain in their homes. Unfriendly denunciation by an excited neighbor might have the most serious results. The Swede promises to make urgent representations to the Greek Government that every arrest of a German be reported to him. Two racial comrades who since the beginning of the war have been held in police custody and who were thought to have disappeared are brought to our building."

April 27, Sunday. The Swastika on the Acropolis.

"On the flagpole of the belvedere of the castle shines the red of the Reich's flag! The cry 'the swastika flag on the Acropolis' resounds through the building. In a few minutes we all gather in a greeting to the Führer. The national hymns resound through the now open windows to the street below . . . I leave immediately and quickly visit the other quarters, the 'Philadelphia' and the Institute. I instruct the inmates of the building in Academy Street to refrain from returning to their homes today and to hold themselves at my disposal. We want to help the German troops immediately since we are familiar with the local language and customs. Now the moment has come. Work must begin immediately . . . A cavalry officer climbs out . . . who is the first to reach Athens. I report him as the first German officer to the inmates of our building. Then I go with him to the Minister and then to the city hall . . . I find the officer again, who is already at a table with Mayor Plytas . . . The main demand on the German side is the immediate opening of stores, although it is Sunday, and the resumption of normal street traffic. I return to our quarters in Academy Street. Here during the afternoon great activity develops. Soldiers and officers are constantly coming and going. Interpreters and guides are demanded . . . In the meantime I organize the activity of all party members for auxiliary service with the Army. Soon one sees our boys and girls in their Hitler Youth uniforms, proud and radiant beside the field gray, riding on the motorcycles and cars . . . Furthermore, our household must be continued. We still accept guests since our 'well-run establishment' offers guests shelter and first-class food."

DOCUMENT 42

(Translation)

NATIONALSOZIALISTISCHE MONATSCHEFTE, DECEMBER 1940, PAGE 803

THE NEW LEGAL STATUS OF THE FOLK-GROUP IN RUMANIA

By Dr. Otto Liess

Nowadays there are no longer any isolated groups of Germans (Es gibt heute kein Inseldeutschtum mehr). This is especially shown by the agreement between the Rumanian Legionary State and the German folk-group. The new rights of the folk-group in Rumania are not to be evaluated as a single fact but as the expression of a necessary historic development. The leaders of Legionary Rumania, as a result of their own *free* decision, have secured the unrestrained collaboration of the citizens of German blood; they know that in this way German creative power can best offer its contribution to the reconstruction of the new Rumania. The separate articles of the agreement, the conclusion of which Andreas Schmidt, the leader of the German folk-group, announced on October 23 [1940] over the Rumanian radio, are as follows:

"1. The German folk-group in Rumania is declared to be a *legal person* according to public law. It bears the name 'German Folk-Group in Rumania'.

"2. All Rumanian citizens belonging to the German people, who acknowledge their allegiance to the German people and are recognized by the leaders of the folk-group and enrolled in the national register of the German folk-group in Rumania, belong to the German folk-group in Rumania.

"3. The *'National Socialist Workers Party (NSDAP) of the German folk-group in Rumania'* expresses the will and constitutes the executive organ of the German folk-group.

"4. The German folk-group in Rumania, in agreement with the Government of the National Legionary State, decrees the laws concerning its own particular life, and aiming at the preservation and strengthening of the German folk-group.

".5. The symbol of the allegiance of the German folk-group in Rumania to the German people is the flag of the German people. The symbol of the allegiance to the Rumanian state is the flag of the National Legionary State.

"6. The separate personality, here proclaimed, of the German folk-group in Rumania is anchored in the Constitution of the National Rumanian Legionary State.

"7. The leader of the German folk-group in Rumania and the Minister of Justice are entrusted with the execution of this decree."

Folk speaks here to folk.   Questions which for a century seemed insoluble on account of the pretext of preserving an "equilibrium" in the state are banished forever in a few clear sentences.   In the future, one will no longer take away the rights of separate individuals indiscriminately in accordance with a so subtly thought-out democratic system.   The Legionary Rumania will respect as a new community the *separate personality of a folk-group*, which was a guaranty of mutual understanding between two peoples even *before* the beginning of the liberal epoch.

The German folk-group can likewise in its *inner* problems look to a tradition of many centuries, and in its realm of action can aim at the ordering of the entire group.   Consequently, it is no longer necessary to let the denominations administer the schools and education of the youth.   The churches within the German folk-group of Rumania will have the opportunity to lay the emphasis of their work on their own particular realm, namely, care of souls.   As a legal community, the folk-group *itself* will be able to look after political, economic, and social matters, without endangering the existence of the group as was the case in the Versailles interval.   The meaninglessness of a strife within the common state is definitively set aside through the attainment of the new legal status of the folk-group.

On the foundation of mutual respect and friendly collaboration in the common *Lebensraum*, the German folk-group will best play its role as mediator between Greater Germany and Legionary Rumania.   Beyond that, however, the agreement on account of its bold lines will be able to be "typical for the problem of nationalities in the southeast", as Andreas Schmidt emphasized.   What is being initiated in the new relation between the Rumanian people and the Germans of Rumania will sooner or later also be the presupposition for a common life in other states of the southeast.   A Danube realm, with the diverse peoples pacified, will demonstrate the creative power of National Socialist demands.   The coming community of peoples in the southeast will be a workaday unity under the sign of peaceful work and growing accomplishment.

DOCUMENT 43

(Extracts)

WELTWACHT DER DEUTSCHEN (PAN-GERMANIST BI-WEEKLY), DRESDEN-HELLERAU, MARCH 1941

"THE TRANSFORMATION OF THE RUMANIAN-GERMAN

"THE FOLK-GROUP IN POSSESSION OF THE GERMAN SCHOOL

"Important events have taken place in these weeks in the Rumanian-German folk-group, which, united in the NSDAP and working through its organizations, is in a process of development under its young leader, Andreas Schmidt. The Evangelical Church is no longer to supervise the German schools, and these are being placed under the direction of the German folk-group. A newly established province, Gau Bergland, has undertaken the task of doing energetically the educational work among the local Germans. The results of the German census, likewise ordered by Schmidt, are at hand and are being worked over by the folk-group management. The Evangelical Church of the Old Confession held its thirty-seventh and thirty-eighth meetings and named the former pastor, Wilhelm Staedel, as successor of Bishop Victor Glondys.

"Rumania's Germandom is being transformed in these weeks and the task begun of permeating the Germans of this country with the spirit of the new movement.

"THE REPORT OF THE LEADER OF THE FOLK-GROUP"

In a speech February 9 at Hermannstadt, Andreas Schmidt, the leader of the folk-group, reporting on his previous activity, stated in part that the European continent would be a chaos if it were not for Germany and its accomplishments, and that—

"the *Volksdeutscher* has done his share in this accomplishment, for if a new world has arisen today, it has also arisen through the secret sacrifices of this supporter of the idea of the Reich. We, outside, beyond the border of the Reich, have believed eternally in the Great Reich; in whose breast has the ardent yearning for this Reich welled up more strongly than in the breast of the *Volksdeutscher!*

"And the yearning appears to be fulfilled. We are fortunate that the new order is taking place in this region in a peaceful way. Think of the great loss in German blood in other regions, when the German Army has entered the country! Is it not great good luck that the

473

various nations here all stand together! . . . How should we feel then? We should be thankful, thankful to the Reich and thankful to this state."

Concerning the situation of the individual German, no matter where he might be, Schmidt said, "there is *no personal freedom* in a struggle in which the Great German Reich is being established! *In this struggle there is only the freedom of our own people.* Any personal freedom must be subordinated. Every thought and every action, which does not spring from the consciousness that the person is participating in the present work, is alien to us. And I believe that every breast is animated by the desire to participate in some way or other and to be able to say after the victory has been attained: 'I have also given something for this cause, even if it was only my personal freedom!'

"Schmidt gave a résumé of the changes in the German folk-group: 'When I took over the folk-group, 20,000 young people marched in the Youth Organization. Today there are 60,000. There were no party formations at all, and today 35,000 comrades are marching in our formations. There were 7,000 women organized. Today there are 77,000. The workers were not at all organized in the folk-group; today there are 10,000 workers in our organization.'

"Schmidt closed his inspiring talk with the urgent admonition to keep discipline: 'My comrades, strengthen the relations between Germany and Rumania, not just by your convictions but by your deeds! Everyone must stand the test, when it is a matter of duty. Lay everything aside, my folk-comrades, which separates you from one another. *What unites us is greater, and that is the struggle of the German people for Great Germany!*'

"THE ESTABLISHMENT OF THE PROVINCE BERGLAND

"Only a few days after this great demonstration of Germanism in Rumania, on February 16 in Diemrich, the foundation of the new Gau Bergland took place. This Gau extends from Mühlbach to Reschitz and from Diemrich to Schiltal. The German folk-group leader, Andreas Schmidt, gave the German folk-comrades here general instructions concerning their future work: 'Once again for the Germans is beginning a time where the *colonial spirit* is animating their ranks, where the individual no longer goes his own way in order to seek happiness but where the pulse beat of German blood forms the community.'

"Schmidt pointed to the castle Diemrich, the proudest of the old castles which the Rumanian Germans know, and said, 'There were Germans around this castle earlier even than in the environs of Hermannstadt or Kronstadt or Temesburg. It was only our fault and a tragedy that we have forgotten that precisely this Diemrich has been the focal point of all German migrations. This is the highway where thousands of years ago Germanic tribes sought the way to the southeast, where centuries ago there was a Reich of the Goths and Vandals, which was strong, stronger than one can imagine. You are not the first here, to be using this soil for German work. This castle is a token of these centuries and their finest accomplishment.

"The way from the past leads into the future. 'The time must come when the cities Broos, Mühlbach, Diemrich, Kaanschebesch, Lugosch, Reschitz, again exhibit a proud German life. The time is past, thank the Lord, when the German was hated because he accomplished things. We are living in a time when the German is validated and respected for his accomplishments. If we want to proceed in this Province to do creative work again in accordance with the old colonial spirit, this does not mean that we wish to push aside others but rather the opposite.'

"Schmidt described how there are people in this Province, who only speak a few words of German but whose belief in Germanism is unbounded. 'Seek out these people in order to receive them again in your midst. The question, whether they can speak German now as you, is not decisive, rather that they bear the same blood in their veins, have the same physiognomy, and the same clear eyes. When I appeal today for the comradeship of all folk-members, I do this because it is the duty of every German in this region to help bring back in this new Province the conditions that formerly prevailed here.'

"Continuing his address, Schmidt discussed the safeguarding of the folk-group's future through a sufficient number of children, and spoke words in this connection also which merit being recorded. 'If other peoples are able to support ten children, the German, who in accomplishments marches at the head of this world, must also be able to do this. The present struggle is concerned with the display of the *will to live*. Every individual must be a proof for the fact that the German people wants to live and must live. However, one can live only if one creates life. Only if the joy in bearing children is again raised, if it becomes a faith, is this life secure. A family ought not to be a pleasant circumstance for a married couple but the holy cell of the people in which life begins. The goal of the National Socialist idea is to create a *new man*, who is animated by the belief that he must take that path for his people which secures the eternity of his people.'

"The Election of the New Bishop, Wilhelm Staedel"

At the thirty-seventh and thirty-eighth meetings of the Evangelical Church of the Old Confession in Hermannstadt on February 16, at which the pastor, Wilhelm Staedel, was elected the new bishop, the curator of the church, Dr. Hans Otto Roth, praised the fine work of the Evangelical Church in its administration of the German schools.

"Out of the evangelical connection of our church with the German nationality follows the duty to accept this change in the structure of our people, namely the transfer of the schools to the German folk-group. From now on the task of the church will be to think of itself and to seek out the innermost and most intimate spheres of its mission."

"Concerning *the significance of his election,* Bishop Staedel stated, 'Through my election and through the forthcoming important decisions of the thirty-eighth meeting of our church, the church strife which has lasted for years is now finally ended in a way visible from afar. Ultimately it does not matter, especially today and especially in the church, whether the individual or a group wins, but that our Lord and Master and the holy cause of our people win.' "

DOCUMENT 44

(Translation)

EUROPÄISCHE REVUE, JANUARY 1941

POLITICS AND RIGHT

BY BARON VON FREYTAGH-LORINGHOVEN
MEMBER OF THE REICHSTAG, COUNCILOR OF THE PRUSSIAN STATE

In connection with the decisions of the Vienna Court of Arbitration, August 30, 1940, Germany has negotiated with Rumania and Hungary treaties for the protection of the folk-group (*Volksgruppenschutzverträge*). They are inevitably reminiscent, in many details, of the treaties concerning minorities made in 1919. A fundamental difference, however, exists in one essential respect. Whereas the latter were concerned with the protection of the separate individuals, now the folk-group as a whole is given the central position.

Only a short protocol has been negotiated with Rumania, by which it is obliged "to treat the members of the German folk-group as equal in every way to those of Rumanian nationality and to build up further the position of the German folk-group in accordance with the Karlsburg resolutions concerning the preservation of their nationality". These Karlsburg resolutions were made November 18, 1918 by a national convention of Rumanians from Transylvania, Banat, and Hungary. The full political equality of the minorities was set down in these, and beyond that their national autonomy in the realms of education, administration, and legal practice, as well as in that of the church. General Antonescu, in fulfilment of the undertaken obligations, has announced a decree, through which the German folk-group is recognized as a corporate body in public law and is granted the authority, under the reservation of consent from the state, to make obligatory legal prescriptions for its members concerning the preservation and strengthening of their national life.

The German-Hungarian protocol is very much more extensive. The German folk-group is in it guaranteed the right to organize itself and form associations for special purposes, such as sport, care of the youth, etc. Likewise its authority is acknowledged in matters of economic self-help and the development of cooperatives. Its members may practice their vocations under the same presuppositions as the other Hungarian citizens. They have a claim on as many positions in the magistracy and the administrative bodies, as corresponds to

477

their share in the total population. German officials are to be used preferably in the official posts in regions settled by Germans, and in the central offices superior to these. The children shall be assured the possibility of attending German schools, and care will be taken to train a sufficient number of good teachers. The free use of the German language will also be guaranteed. The German language will also be accepted in official matters in those administrative districts in which the members of the folk-group constitute one third of the entire population. The German press will not be subject to any restrictions which do not have general application. No measures will be taken which aim at Magyarization, and the members of the folk-group are to have the right to a free cultural intercourse with the motherland. On the other hand, the Government of the Reich recognizes that the members of the folk-group are obligated to be loyal to the Hungarian state.

With regard to all this, it is of special interest to note the solution reached in the German-Hungarian protocol of the question concerning the determination of membership in the folk-groups, a question which has been much disputed both from the practical and the theoretical side. There are various possibilities here. Originally people were inclined to confer decisive meaning on the so-called "objective signs", such as origin, dialect, family name. Then, however, it was recognized that these are insufficient precisely in regions where nationalities are mixed together.   Everyone, who is acquainted with the east, knows that men named Müller, or Schulze, or some similar name, are not infrequently active as fanatical champions of the Polish or Czech nationality, while, conversely, bearers of Polish or Czech names stand with complete conviction in the German camp. It was still more serious that the authorities of the foreign country usually claimed the right to examine the presence of these objective signs and on this basis to decide for themselves the membership in this or that folk-group. So people began to oppose the subjective principle to the objective one and to accept as authoritative the declaration of the individual. But against this also serious objections were raised, since by the application of this method unreliable elements could creep into the folk-group, who sought personal advantages or else were serving some foreign country or the organizations of some foreign nationality. The proposal was then made, to accept the principle of individual declaration but to demand as well the consent of the folk-group. Without doubt, this is the happiest solution, and it is very much to be welcomed that the German-Hungarian protocol has adopted it.

As important as the two Vienna protocols are in themselves, their full meaning is to be recognized, only when one considers them as an effect of the protective right (*Schutzrecht*) of the mother-state over its folk-groups. This protective right, that became formally a necessity after the breakdown of the inadequate Geneva protection of minorities caused by Poland, was proclaimed by the Führer in his speech before the Reichstag on February 20, 1938. It received the practical acknowledgment of the other great powers in the course of the Czech crisis and was the basis of the Munich Agreement of September 20, 1938. It was validated again in the Polish crisis and, along with the disputability of the Treaty of Versailles, formed the legal basis for the reannexation of West Prussia, Posen, and East Upper Silesia. Likewise it is to be considered as the legal basis for the treaties concerning resettlement, which Germany first concluded, and now, following its example, Bulgaria and Rumania have also concluded. Alongside of reannexation and resettlement, the treaty for the protection of the folk-group appears then as a third form for the realization of the protective right.

In the cases, however, in which the presuppositions for one of these three forms are lacking, still a fourth possibility arises for the exercise of the protective right. This is diplomatic intervention, which if necessary can be supported by the means of pressure which are recognized in international law, especially by retorsion and reprisals. Of course, this possibility also existed formerly, before the recognition of the protective right. But the essential difference lies therein that now such an intervention can be viewed not as inadmissible intrusion in the internal affairs of a foreign state but as representing the consequence of a right acknowledged by international law.

Thus there are an abundance of practical ways in which the protective right of the mother-state has already been realized and can be realized in the future. From the standpoint of the German people that in the course of centuries has sent millions of its sons out in the world and unfortunately has lost a great part of them, whose suppression it has had to endure in silence, it may already be welcomed as one of the most valuable results of this war, that the Reich has now not only attained the possibility, but also the right, to stretch out its protective hand over its sons.

DOCUMENT 45

(Translation)

WESTERMANNS MONATSHEFTE, FEBRUARY 1941, PAGE 368

THE GERMANS IN SLOVAKIA

By Dr. ERNST KEIT

This new order found in the new Slovakian state its visible expression in the unified tight national organization, permeated with the National Socialist spirit, namely, in the "German Party" with its "Voluntary SS" and other organs, such as the "German Youth" and "German Trade Union". There is no German political organization aside from the "German Party". And if on flags and arms the swastika bears witness to the association with all Germans, we recognize therein at the same time a sign that loyalty to the German nationality is compatible with loyalty to a foreign nation's state.

The leader of the "German Party" and the German folk-group is Franz Karmasin, who at the same time directs the German Department of State (*Staatssekretariat*), created in October 1938. He is an old champion of the principle of nationality among the Slovakian Germans and co-founder of the Carpathian German Party, and he became in 1935 Konrad Henlein's representative for the Carpathian district and since then consequently has stood at the head of the German political movement in Slovakia.

In allowing the collection of the German folk-group in an organization, created in accordance with the spirit of the National Socialist revolution, the Slovakian Government has made possible a life-form which can be considered exemplary. For, as President Tiso wrote in the *Kölnische Zeitung* of April 27, 1939, "the acknowledgment of the rights of nationalities was the point of departure for the new ordering of the sovereignty ʳelations in the former territory of Czechoslovakia; it must also be the foundation of the new legal order in the Danube region". The German-Slovakian concord, which was born in the common struggle of the past 20 years and proved so true in the exciting days of March 1939, received its baptism of fire when the young Slovakian state employed its armed forces on the side of the great German Reich against the former Poland, and the Germans in the independent unit of the "German Battalion" could now in turn be pathmakers for the National Socialist will to freedom and order, to which they owed their own liberation.

DOCUMENT 46

(Translation)

WELTWACHT DER DEUTSCHEN, FEBRUARY 1941

GERMANS IN FOREIGN COUNTRIES: IN DENMARK
MEETING OF THE PARTY OFFICIALS IN TINGLEFF

On January 19, the leader of the German Party, Dr. Möller, spoke at this year's first meeting of the party officials in Tingleff. He gave the officials the slogans for the new year, in particular the rallying cry that no German peasant dare leave his farm today, that no agricultural enterprise dare be abandoned, and said about the past year in part as follows:

"By and large we may say at the end of the year 1940 that we have made a *big step forward*. We have completely reorganized the folk-group; . . . we have carried the National Socialist movement right into the whole folk-group.

"We stand *on outposts*. Every single individual is important. We are going forward today, and we shall push on ahead in the coming year also. In the organizations associated with the party, it was the same as with the party. I am referring here to the great accomplishments of the German Relief (*Deutsche Selbsthilfe*), the German Youth, the NS Women's Organization, and Winter Relief.

"Our task must be to take care that the national lines in North Schleswig are not effaced. We serve singly and alone the Führer and the German swastika flag. Above all we ought to work for our German schools. We have just received the announcement that, after long endeavors on our part, our German kindergartens have been allowed the state subsidy which every Danish kindergarten also receives. We can also count on the fact that in a short time only German-thinking teachers will be giving instruction in our communal schools. With regard to the future of our homeland and of our movement, we may be the greatest optimists. Adolf Hitler will shape the future of the new Europe, and in this future we also have our place, not as Europeans, but as Germans."

DOCUMENT 47

(Extracts)

DEUTSCHE ARBEIT, SEPTEMBER 1941

THE SETTLEMENTS OF GERMANS FROM THE PALATINATE IN ZAMOSC COUNTY

By LOTHAR VON SELTMANN

Winning Back Polonized Germans

In the partition of Poland in 1772, Zamosc was given to Austria with Galicia. From 1781 on, Joseph II adopted an official policy whereby German settlements in this region were furthered. In part the colonists were settled in Polish or Ukranian villages already at hand. "For the most part, however, Germans were settled in their own communities, adjunct to the villages of these alien peoples."

In 1815 Zamosc became a part of Russian Poland:

"Thus the German colonists of Zamosc were torn out of their German cultural context and given over to Polonization, which could take place all the more strongly, since the settlers were Catholic and were handed over thus to the Polish clergy, whose activity, in contrast to that of the Catholic clergy in Germany, was always first of all chauvinistic and only thereafter pastoral. The Germans of Hauland-on-the-Bug, who lived much longer amid a foreign environment, could keep themselves German in spirit, even if they succumbed to Polonization with regard to language, because their Protestant faith separated them from the Polish environment and thus impeded racial intermixture. This was not the case with the Germans from the Palatinate; on the contrary, on account of the equating, again and again emphasized, of Catholic with Polish, and Protestant with German, an alienation from their own nationality perforce took place in a very short time. No connections arose with the colonization in Cholm, which began after 1860, because, aside from the purely spatial gap between the Germans in Cholm County and in Zamosc County, both the denominational as well as the ethnic differences—the colonists of Cholm originated for the most part from Pomerania—prevented a closer contact.

"If we visit today the settlements in which the descendants of those colonists lived, i. e. Sitaniec, Ploskie, Horyszow-Colony, Bialobrzegi, Rogozno, Brody, *et al.*, then the construction of the farms and the names of the settlers reveal to us that it is a question here of men of German extraction, but the Polonization with respect to language and spirit is so far advanced that an almost complete slipping away into the foreign nationality has taken place. For a long time the colonists defended themselves against

482

a racial submergence. It is significant that mixed marriages began only rather late, i.e. in the next to the last or the last generation. The instinct of blood still functioned, when already a great part of the settlements had been covered over, with regard to language and spirit, by the alien environment. Up until the World War, and often nowadays also, the Zamosc Germans married only people from their own colonies, although these lie, in part, up to a hundred kilometers distant from one another . . . In view of the fact that the settlers have instinctively avoided mixed marriages up until the latest generations, despite the external Polonization they have kept themselves racially quite pure, so that the idea of introducing a racial and spiritual retrieval of these men of German origin suggested itself, all the more since the Reich today has to permeate an enormous territory with Germans and can resign its claim to no drop of valuable German blood.

"One can view this beginning rather optimistically, when one considers the development of so many German folk-groups in the last years. Just as they have in many cases taken, and are further taking, an unexpected growth through the fact that under the influences of the great German *Volksreich* a spiritual re-orientation is taking place among men who have already been sunk for two or more generations in an alien nationality, likewise it will be all the more possible to win back the German racial elements lost in Zamosc County since we as the sovereign power here in this realm have all the possibilities at our hand for practical ethnic work (*Volkstumsarbeit*). In accordance with this point of view, the leader of the SS and police in the Lublin District, SS Brigade-Leader Globocnik, in his capacity as deputy of the Reich's Commissioner for the Strengthening of the German Nationality, has introduced in these settlements a campaign for the regaining and re-Germanization of the Polonized Germans.

"Let us mention here only briefly the preparation, plan, and execution of this campaign. Before a practical plan of work could be undertaken, the region had to be in some measure defined, and an exact survey of the numerical disposition of the descendants of those Josephinian settlers had to be obtained by a questionnaire. Ten Vienna Hitler Youth leaders in November of last year prepared the basic material after several weeks' work. When one realizes that at that time around 650 families—the number has meanwhile through new inquiries been raised to over 800—were included and exactly described and that for this purpose 80 villages had to be visited despite the most abominable travel conditions, one can judge the difficulties which had to be overcome through the willingness to work and the sympathetic understanding of the Vienna Hitler Youth leaders.

"These questionnaires form the basis for all further plans. Now today there are German school assistants active in eleven villages, so that the young people already enjoy again instruction in German. Beyond that, since January BDM groups have been intensely active in the villages and have achieved great success with regard to instruction in Germanism and social matters. The girls were able in a short time to overcome the initial mistrust and to acquire in the end the unreserved confidence of the village inhabitants. Thus they brought it about that not only the children of the families which they regularly visited gladly attend the German instruction in the school but also that the old people enjoy coming to the evening course and to communal evening meetings. The basic principle for this work of retrieving the Germans is: Those of German origin are to be given pride in their origin, and a consciousness of their origin which is still often present is to be nourished. They must feel that they are a community amidst a foreign environment. In order to deepen this feeling of community, the leader of the SS and the police is publishing a small magazine, 'Letters of Colonists', for these villages. Through the juxtaposition of German and Polish texts, and through the easily comprehensible articles, designed for self-instruction, this magazine moreover facilitates the relearning of German. The first two numbers of the 'Letters of Colonists' have elicited an unexpectedly happy response in the villages.

"Summing up, it may be stated that already today tangible results are to be noted in the German villages of Zamosc County. Certain settlements today are not inferior in their attitude to the German-conscious, now resettled colonies of the Cholm and Lublin countryside. With regard to language, naturally the descendants of the Zamosc Germans still have much to learn, but their village communal life already exhibits today again the old German colonial spirit, which had been buried.

"Thus a valuable 'fragment of our people', which through no fault of its own had slid off into a foreign nationality is being re-won in the Lublin District for the German folk. Thus an essential contribution is being made to the new order of ethnographic relations in the European east which the Führer has proclaimed."

DOCUMENT 48

(Extracts)

Krakauer Zeitung, Cracow, June 15, 1941

GERM CELLS OF A MODERN COLONIZATION EASTWARD

The Results of the Discovery of German Blood in the Zamosc District—
A Report of SS Brigade-Leader Globocnik

Zamosc, June 15.

At a meeting held in the German movie-house, Party Comrade and SS Brigade-Leader Globocnik, deputy of the Reich's Commissioner for the Strengthening of the German Nationality, gave a survey of the presuppositions and the conduct of all ethno-political work, especially how it must proceed in the future in the Lublin District. Globocnik described first—

"the permanent Germanic blood-form which from the beginning of time had wandered in all parts of Europe and of the rest of the world throughout the centuries. Although, on account of the absence of systematic guidance, its human bearers have long been lost, great and impressive traces of its pathmaking efficacy have been right up to the present day left behind everywhere by its cultural and creative energy, superior to all other peoples. Especially in the east of Europe, this Germanic migration gave the Slavs, in almost all aspects of life, the rise from a low backwardness to a higher spiritual and cultural level. It was the superiority of Germans in house-building, cattle-breeding, and agriculture which motivated the landlords in the east again and again to entice German settlers on their farms with favorable offers. . . . In the east one can still find today the descendants of these cultural pioneers in large numbers and in different stages of development. Their fate shows how without planning and without a political consciousness these Germans who came to work in the east have in part always been absorbed and lost because without any protection they were delivered up arbitrarily to the alien peoples who had risen high through them. Moreover, on the basis of the concept of precious German blood, as set down by National Socialism, there results from this the knowledge that only the solid and correct employment of German blood guarantees its steadfastness and the security necessary for development.

"Party Comrade Globocnik declared then that the German element despite centuries of oppression has preserved an astonishingly fresh racial energy, which has suffered only externally up to a certain degree. Without a knowledge of the doctrines of inheritance these Germans have appeared superior to the alien race

485

so that, in an overwhelming percentage, they have only married Germans. This subconscious racial pride of a more valuable race and the negligence of the past give us the important obligation to consider the security of the German race as one of our major tasks and accordingly to shape these regions as a future vital sphere of the German people."

With regard to the resettled Germans of Volhynia, Bessarabia, Bukovina, etc., Globocnik stated that—

"in view of their racial struggles these Germans are the strongest colonists on the new eastern frontier of the Reich and are able to maintain the proper distance from the Slavs. Party Comrade Globocnik discussed then the surprising discovery of still other people who were, racially speaking, Germans, which was made first in the Zamosc District of Lublin during the work of resettlement. Here these men had, while preserving completely the German type, racial characteristics, and religious confession, lost only the German language, or else they exhibited in name and type traces of German origin but no longer possessed a conscious relation to Germanism.

"These discoveries led then to the measures of education previously mentioned by us, aiming to regain spiritually these racial Germans through the courageous activity of the party youth. On the other hand, it introduced a further search for German blood whereby the manner of momentary appearance of the colonist was not decisive for the essential knowledge with regard to racial consideration but rather the essential German characteristics clearly recognizable. On the basis of such considerations Party Comrade Globocnik directed a systematic search for clues in the form of investigations in archives, church registers, gravestones, and ethnic characteristics and forms of the settlements and houses, etc. . . . . Already around six thousand people belonging to the German race have been discovered in this fashion, and the daily arrival of further discoveries and new clues makes one able to infer that a far greater number are present.

"The speaker showed them the systematic work of education in all aspects of life, which has been already applied with full success to those of German race from the Palatinate, who have been up until now discovered in the Zamosc District. He announced thereby that at the end the colonists as also their villages shall again receive old German names. Finally Globocnik outlined a plan according to which all the villages in which those of German race are discovered shall encompass a larger territory which will be determined as a purely German region of settlement. In this new German region of the Lublin District, all those still recognizable as belonging to the German race together with the Germans already settled here shall re-attain the German form of life and attitude of mind, whereby in the course of time also all the institutions of the National Socialistic form of life shall be introduced. Here shall then arise within the *Generalgouvernement* the first German cell of the modern eastern colonization, reawakened by this search to a pulsating German colonial life."

LIST OF CHARTS

(Reproduced Photographically)

CHART 1

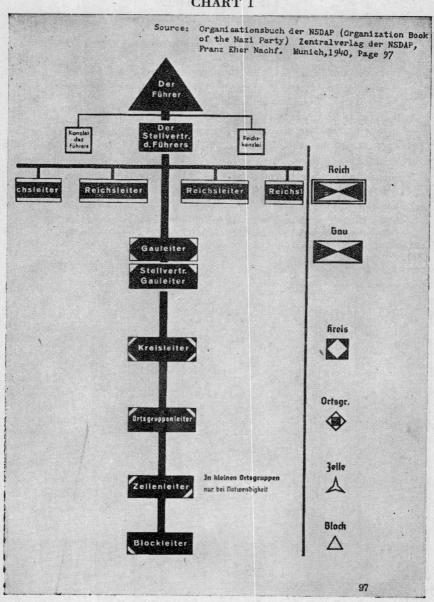

Source: Organisationsbuch der NSDAP (Organization Book of the Nazi Party) Zentralverlag der NSDAP, Franz Eher Nachf. Munich, 1940, Page 97

97

CHART 1-A

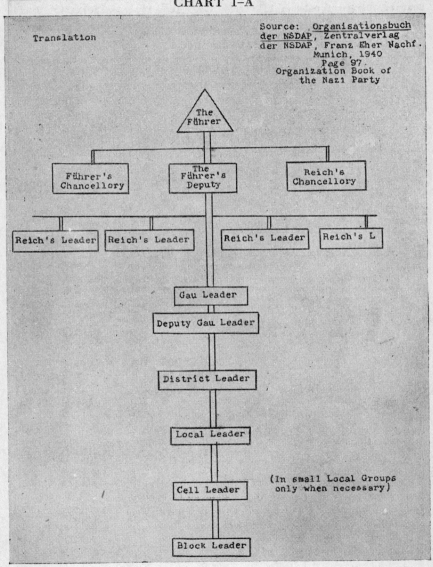

Translation

Source: Organisationsbuch
der NSDAP, Zentralverlag
der NSDAP, Franz Eher Nachf.
Munich, 1940
Page 97.
Organization Book of
the Nazi Party

The Führer

Führer's Chancellory

The Führer's Deputy

Reich's Chancellory

Reich's Leader

Reich's Leader

Reich's Leader

Reich's L

Gau Leader

Deputy Gau Leader

District Leader

Local Leader

Cell Leader

(In small Local Groups only when necessary)

Block Leader

CHART 2

Source: <u>Der nationalsozialistische Staat</u> (The National Socialist State) edited by Dr. Walther Gehl, 1935. Published by Ferdinand Hirt, Breslau. Passed by Official Party Control Commission, November 29, 1935. Page 57.

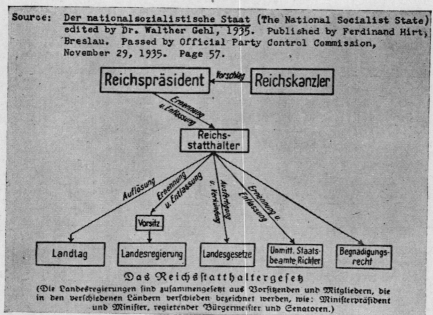

Das Reichsstatthaltergeſetz

(Die Landesregierungen ſind zuſammengeſetzt aus Vorſitzenden und Mitgliedern, die in den verſchiedenen Ländern verſchieden bezeichnet werden, wie: Miniſterpräſident und Miniſter, regierender Bürgermeiſter und Senatoren.)

490

CHART 2-A

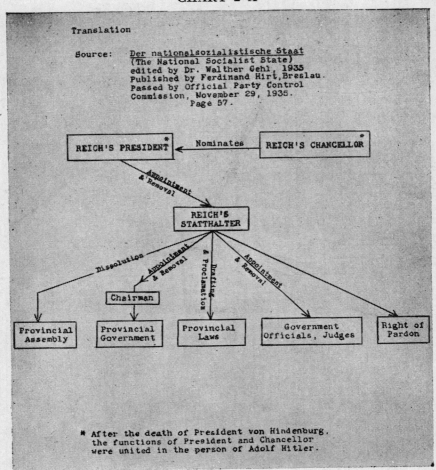

Translation

Source: Der nationalsozialistische Staat
          (The National Socialist State)
          edited by Dr. Walther Gehl, 1935
          Published by Ferdinand Hirt, Breslau.
          Passed by Official Party Control
          Commission, November 29, 1935.
               Page 57.

| REICH'S PRESIDENT* | ← Nominates | REICH'S CHANCELLOR* |

Appointment & Removal

REICH'S STATTHALTER

Dissolution — Appointment & Removal — Drafting & Proclamation — Appointment & Removal

| Provincial Assembly | Chairman / Provincial Government | Provincial Laws | Government Officials, Judges | Right of Pardon |

* After the death of President von Hindenburg,
the functions of President and Chancellor
were united in the person of Adolf Hitler.

491

CHART 3

Reichsleitung der Nationalsozialistischen
Partei- und Oberster
Stellvertreter des Führers in allen

Deutschen Arbeiterpartei
S.A. Führer: Adolf Hitler
Fragen der Parteiführung: Rudolf Heß

Leiter der Politischen Zentralkommission	Stabschef der SA	Reichsführer der SS	Reichsgeschäftsführer
Vorsitz. des Reichs-USchlA (Unterfuchungs- u. Schlichtungsausschuß)	Vorsitz. d. II. Kammer	Stabsleiter der PO (Politische Organisation)	
Reichs-Preßchef	Reichspropaganda	des Reichs-USchlA	Leiter der Reichsleitung	Untsleiter für die Preffe
Leiter des Außenpolitischen Amtes	Reichsjugendführer	Leiter des Wehrpolit. Amtes	Schaftsführer des Nat.-Soz. D. Arbeiter-Vereins

Gliederung der

Reichsleitung

Politische Zentralkommission: a) Kommission für Beratung und Überwachung der national
sozialistischen Arbeit in den Ländern, b) Kommission zur Überwachung der nationalsozialistischen Presse, c) Kommission für Wirtschaftsfragen

Politische Organisation (PO): 1. NSBO (Nationalsozialistische Betriebszellenorganisation),
Abteilung: 5. NS Kriegsopferversorgung, 2. NS Hago (Handwerks-, Handels- und Gewerbeorganisation), 3. NS Frauenschaft, 4. NS Beamten-
6. NS Volkswohlfahrt

Reichsschatzmeister				Agrarpolitisches Amt
Reichsgeschäftsführer	Reichspropagandaleiter	USchlA RL	(Untersuchungs- und Schlichtungsausschuß Reichsleitung)	
Rechtsabteilung RL	Untsleiter der Preffe	Außenpolitisches Amt	Wehrpolitisches Amt	

Landesleiter für Österreich

Landesinspekteure (9)
für je 4-5 Gaue; vom Führer ernannt und abberufen

Gauleiter (36)
vom Führer ernannt und abberufen

Kreisleiter
vom Gauleiter ernannt und abberufen
Unterstellt: Kreis-USchlA-Vorsitzender, Kreisstabsamt, Kreiskassenwart, Kreiskassenwart

Ortsgruppenleiter (Stützpunktleiter)
auf Vorschlag des Kreisleiters vom Gauleiter ernannt und abberufen
Unterstellt: Kulturwart, Preffewart, Wehrwart, Kassenwart

Zellenleiter
auf Vorschlag des Ortsgruppenleiters vom Kreisleiter ernannt und abberufen

Blockwarte
auf Vorschlag des Zellenleiters vom Ortsgruppenleiter ernannt und abberufen

P a r t e i g e n o s s e n

Source: Der Nationalsozialistische Staat (The National Socialist
State) edited by Dr. Walther Gehl, 1935. Published by
Ferdinand Hirt, Breslau. Passed by Official Party Control
Commission, November 29, 1935. Pages 38-39.

Vom Führer infolge ihres besonderen Aufgabenkreises genehmigte Fachbünde:
Volksgesundheit: Nationalsozialistischer Ärztebund,
Volkserziehung: Nationalsozialistischer Lehrerbund (NSLB),
Volksrecht: Bund nationalsozialistischer deutscher Juristen (BNSDJ).
Die vorstehenden Bünde sind in sich ähnlich der Politischen Organisation (Reichs-
leitung, Gauleitung und teilweise noch weiter) gegliedert.

CHART 3-A

Source: Der nationalsozialistische Staat. (The National Socialist State) edited by Dr. Walther Gehl, 1935. Published by Ferdinand Hirt, Breslau. Passed by Official Party Control Commission, November 29, 1935. Pages 38-39

Reich's Leadership of the Nazi Party

Party Leader and Supreme Chief of the SA: Adolf Hitler

Deputy of the Führer in all Questions of Party Leadership: Rudolf Hess

Head of the Central Political Commission	SA Chief of Staff	Reich's Leader of the SS	Reich's Treasurer	Reich's Business Manager
Chairman of the Reich's Uschla (Investigating & Arbitration Committee)	Chairmen, 2d Chamber of Reich's Uschla	PO Chief of Staff (Political Org.)
Reich's Press Chief	Leader of Agrarian Policy Office	Reich's Propaganda Leader	Leader of the Jurist Section	Head of the Press Office
Head of the Foreign Office	Reich's Youth Leader	Head of the Office for Defense Policy	Editor of the Nazi Labor Organizations

Division of the Reich's Leadership

Central Political Commission: a) Commission for the Study and Supervision of Nazi Parliamentary Activity in the Provinces, b) Commission for Supervision of the Nazi Press, c) Commission for Economic Questions

Political Organization (PO): 1. NSBO (Nazi Organization of Active Cells), 2. NS Hago (Crafts, Commercial and Industrial Organization), 3. The Nazi Women's League, 4. Nazi Section for Government Officials, 5. Nazi Organization for the Care of War Veterans.
b. Nazi Public Welfare.

Reich's Treasurer	Reich's Business Manager	Reich's Propaganda Leader Uschla RL (Reich's Leader of Investigation & Arbitration Committee)

| | Office for Agrarian Policy | |
| Reich's Leader of the Justice Section | Head of the Press Office | Foreign Office | Office for Defense Policy |

Provincial Leaders for Austria

Provincial Inspectors (9)
for every 4 or 5 Gaus; appointed & removed by the Führer

Gau Leaders (36)
appointed and removed by the Führer

District Leaders
appointed and removed by the Gau Leaders
Subordinates: the District Uschla Chairman, the District
Cultural Officer, District Press Officer, District Treasurer.

Local Leaders
appointed and removed by the Gau Leaders on
the recommendation of the District Leaders Subordinates:
Cultural Officer, Press Officer, Recruiting Officer, Treasurer.

Cell Leaders
appointed & removed by the District Leaders
on the recommendation of the Local Leaders.

Block Leaders
appointed & removed by the Local Leaders on
the recommendation of the Cell Leaders.

Party Members

The following professional associations have been recognized by the Führer on the grounds of their special fields of knowledge:

Public Health: The Nazi Doctor's League.
Public Education: The Nazi Teacher's League (NSLB).
Public Law: The League of Nazi German Jurists (BNDJ).

These Leagues are organized on a hierarchical basis like the Political Organization (Reich's Leadership, Gau Leadership and so on through the lower subdivisions).

493

CHART 4

Source: Organization Book of the Nazi Party (Organisationsbuch der NSDAP)
Zentralverlag der NSDAP, Franz Eher Nachf., Munich, 1940. Page 145

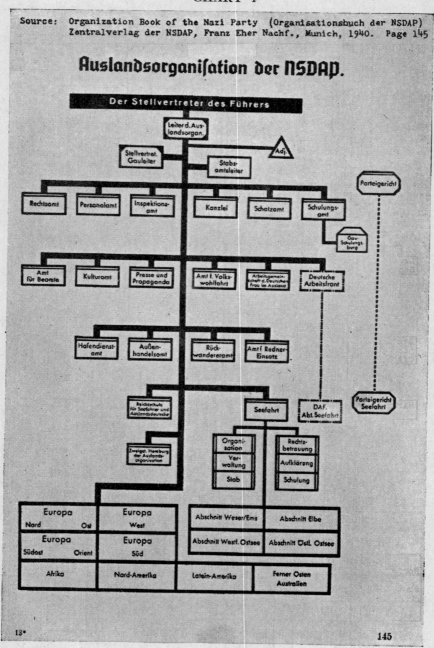

Auslandsorganisation der NSDAP.

CHART 4-A

SOURCE: Organisations-
buch der NSDAP. Zentral-
verlag der NSDAP, Franz
Eher Nachf. Munich,1940
(Organization Book of the
Nazi Party)

FOREIGN ORGANIZATION OF THE NSDAP

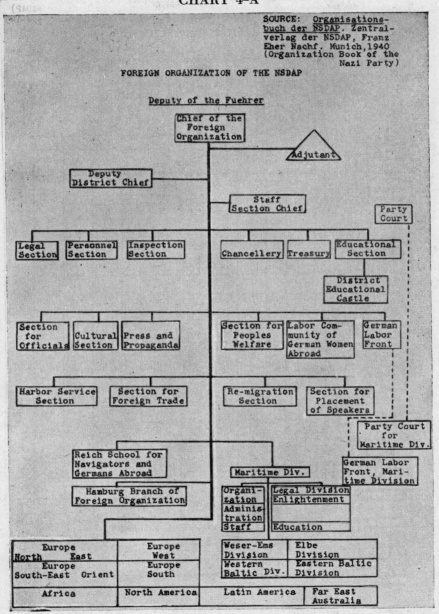

CHART 5

Source: Organization Book of the Nazi Party (Organisationsbuch der NSDAP)
Zentralverlag der NSDAP, Franz Eher Nachf., Munich, 1940. Page 95

Überwachung der Hauptstellen bzw. Abteilungen der Fachämter und angeschlossenen Verbände innerhalb eines jeden Hoheitsgebietes durch die parteiinternen Dienststellen

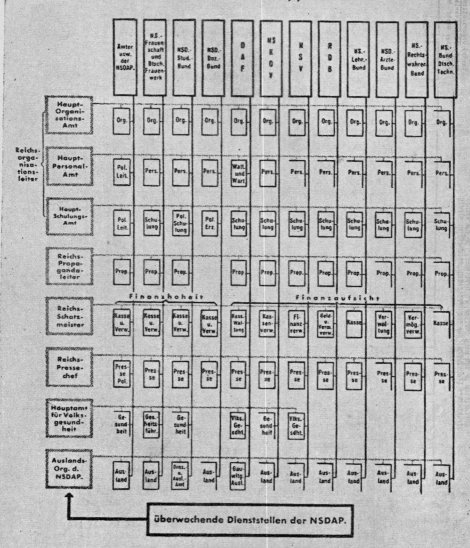

Sinngemäß, wie vorstehend, erfolgt die Überwachung in den Hoheitsgebieten: Gau, Kreis, Ortsgruppe.

CHART 5–A

Source: (Organization Book of the Nazi Party) Organisationsbuch der NSDAP. Zentralverlag der NSDAP, Franz Eher Nachf. Munich,1940 P.95

Translation

SUPERVISION OF THE MAIN OFFICES, (OR DIVISIONS), OF THE SPECIAL DEPARTMENTS (FACHÄMTER) AND THE AFFILIATED ASSOCIATIONS WITHIN EACH SOVEREIGN REGION BY INTERNAL PARTY OFFICES

CONTROL OF FINANCES

SUPERVISION OF FINANCES

SUPERVISORY OFFICES OF THE NSDAP

The Supervision in the spheres of jurisdiction of a Gau, County, Local Group takes place in accordance with the above.

REICH'S DIRECTOR OF THE PARTY ORGANIZATION

- Main Organization Office
- Main Personnel Office
- Main Indoctrination Office
- Reich's Propaganda Director
- Reich's Treasurer
- Reich's Press Chief
- Main Office for Public Health
- Foreign Organization of the NSDAP

Offices, etc., of the NSDAP — Org. — Political Guidance — Political Guidance — Propaganda — Cashier & Mang't. — Press Policy — Health — In Foreign Countries

NS Women's Org. & German Women's Society — Org. — Pers. — In- doctri- nation — Propa- ganda — Cashier & Mang't. — Press — Health Guidance — In Foreign Countries

NS German Students' Assoc. — Org. — Pers. — Political Indoctri- nation — Propa- ganda — Cashier & Mang't. — Press — Health — Border & Foreign Bureau

NS German Pro- fessors' Assoc. — Org. — Pers. — Political Education — Cashier & Mang't. — Press — Health — In Foreign Countries

German Labor Front — Org. — Offi- cials — In- doctri- nation — Propa- ganda — Cashier's Office — Press — Public Health — Gau Mang't. Abroad

NS War Victims' Relief Society — Org. — Pers. — In- doctri- nation — Propa- ganda — Cashier's Office — Press — Health — In Foreign Countries

NS Public Welfare — Org. — Pers. — In- doctri- nation — Propa- ganda — Finance Adm. — Press — Public Health — In Foreign Countries

Reichs' Assoc. of German Govt. Employ- ees — Org. — Pers. — In- doctri- nation — Propa- ganda — Money& Property Mana- g't. — Press — In Foreign Countries

NS Teachers' Assoc. — Org. — Pers. — In- doctri- nation — Propa- ganda — Cashiers' Office — Press — In Foreign Countries

NS German Phy- sicians' Assoc. — Org. — Pers. — In- doctri- nation — Propa- ganda — Mang't. — Press — In Foreign Countries

NS Legal Assoc. — Org. — Pers. — In- doctri- nation — Propa- ganda — Property Mang't. — Press — In Foreign Countries

NS Assoc. for German Tech- nology — Org. — Pers. — In- doctri- nation — Propa- ganda — Cashiers' Office — Press — In Foreign Countries

497

GLOSSARY OF GERMAN TERMS

GLOSSARY OF GERMAN TERMS

AO—See *Auslandsorganisation.*

Ausland—The world outside of the borders of the German Reich.

Ausland-Institut—See *Deutsches Ausland-Institut.*

Auslandsdeutsche—Persons of German blood living outside of Germany, regardless of citizenship.

Auslandsorganisation—The Foreign Organization of the Nazi Party, comprising all party members abroad and exercising jurisdiction over all German citizens abroad.

Auslandsreichsdeutsche—German citizens (*Reichsdeutsche*) residing outside of Germany.

BDM—See *Bund Deutscher Mädel.*

Bewegung—The movement; that is, the Nazi Party and its ideology.

Bund Deutscher Mädel—German Girls' Association.

DAI—See *Deutsches Ausland-Institut.*

Deutsches Ausland-Institut—The German Foreign Institute in Stuttgart, a research and propaganda institute working among *Auslandsdeutsche* under the direction of the Nazi Party's Foreign Organization.

Ersatz—Substitute.

Führer—The Leader, Adolf Hitler, or any subordinate leader with complete authority over his area of jurisdiction.

Führer-Prinzip—The leadership principle, as exemplified in the Nazi Party, whereby the leader exercises absolute authority and his subordinates owe him unquestioning obedience.

Führung—Leadership as exemplified by the *Führer-Prinzip.*

Gau—A major party administrative district; in 1940 Germany was divided into 41 *Gaus*, and a separate *Gau* comprised all party members residing abroad.

Gauleiter—The supreme party leader in the *Gau.*

Gauleitung—The party headquarters in the *Gau.*

Gestapo—Contraction of *Geheime Staatspolizei;* the German secret police under Himmler.

Gleichschaltung—The process of coordination or forcing German organizations of all types to conform to the Nazi pattern and accept party control.

501

Heil Hitler—The standard Nazi greeting implying allegiance to Hitler.

Herrenvolk—Master race.

HJ—See *Hitler Jugend*.

Hitler Jugend—Hitler Youth Organization.

Hoheitsträger—A party leader exercising complete political authority in his respective sphere of jurisdiction and supervising the activities of all specialized party branches therein.

Kameradschaft USA—An organization in Germany of Germans returned from America who had been active in the Nazi movement in the United States; it is sponsored by the *Deutsches Ausland-Institut* of Stuttgart.

Kreis—An administrative subdivision of a *Gau*.

Kreisleiter—The supreme party leader in the *Kreis*.

Länderämter—Offices of the Foreign Organization of the Nazi Party which have jurisdiction in matters of policy relating to specific countries or groups of countries.

Landesgruppe—The Nazi Party organization in any country outside of Germany, under the control of the Foreign Organization.

Landesgruppenleiter—The supreme leader of the Nazi Party organization in any country outside of Germany.

Lebensraum—Literally, living-space; the undefined sphere of influence over which Nazi domination is to be established.

mit deutschem Gruss—Literally, with the German greeting; equivalent to *Heil Hitler*.

Nationalsozialist—A member or supporter of the Nazi Party.

Nationalsozialistische Deutsche Arbeiterpartei—National Socialist German Workers' Party; the Nazi Party.

Nationalsozialistische Kraftfahr-Korps—National Socialist Motor Corps.

Nationalsozialistische Rechtswahrerbund—National Socialist Law Guardians Association.

Nationalsozialistische Volkswohlfahrt—National Socialist Public Welfare Organization.

Nazi—Abbreviated form of *Nationalsozialist*.

NS—Abbreviation for *Nationalsozialist*.

NSDAP—Abbreviation for *Nationalsozialistische Deutsche Arbeiterpartei*.

NSKK—See *Nationalsozialistische Kraftfahr-Korps*.

NSRB—See *Nationalsozialistische Rechtswahrerbund*.

NSV—See *Nationalsozialistische Volkswohlfahrt*.

Ogruleiter—Contracted form of *Ortsgruppenleiter*.

Ortsgruppe—A local group of the Nazi Party, comprising all party members in a certain town or city.

Ortsgruppenleiter—The leader of a local group of the Nazi Party.

Partei—The Nazi Party.

Parteigenosse—Party member.

Pg.—Abbreviation for *Parteigenosse*.

Rasse—Race.

Reich—Germany.

Reichsdeutsche—Persons of German blood and German citizenship.

Reichsgesetzblatt—The official German bulletin of laws, in which important laws and decrees of the German Government are published.

Reichsleiter—A high Nazi Party official having jurisdiction over some line of party activity (e. g. press, propaganda, party courts, storm troops, labor service, etc.) In 1940 there were 21 *Reichsleiter*.

Reichsminister—A Minister in Hitler's Cabinet.

Reichswehr—The German Army.

SA or *Sturmabteilung*—Storm troops; the political shock troops of the party in Germany.

Schulungslager—A party training camp for political indoctrination.

Schutzstaffel—See *SS*.

Sieg Heil—Literally, *Hail Victory;* the rallying cry of the Nazi movement.

SS or *Schutzstaffel*—Elite Guard; the personal bodyguard of the *Führer* and the armed force of the party under Himmler.

Sturmabteilung—See *SA*.

VDA—See *Volksbund für das Deutschtum im Ausland*.

VDVA—See *Verband Deutscher Vereine im Ausland*.

Verband Deutscher Vereine im Ausland—League of German Societies Abroad, an organization aiming at the unification of the countless German clubs and societies in foreign countries into a solid and coordinated Nazi front.

Verlag—Press, publishing house.

Volk—Folk, people, race; more particularly, all persons of German blood. The word *Volk* goes further than the word *people* in its connotation of racial homogeneity and tends rather to mean the tribal community of people of the same blood.

Volksbund für das Deutschtum im Ausland—League for Germandom in Foreign Countries, an old pan-German organization now allied with the Nazis and active in the promotion of pan-German, Nazi ideas among Germans abroad and in the organization of compact German minorities loyal to Hitler.

Volksdeutscher—A person of German blood but of non-German citizenship residing abroad; a member of the German people.

Volksgemeinschaft—People's or racial community; the world-wide community comprising all people of German blood.

Volksgenosse—Racial comrade; a person of German blood regardless of citizenship.

Volksgruppe—A colony or settlement of persons of German extraction outside of the borders of Germany, especially, the organized German minority, "folk-group", in non-German states.

Volkstum—Folkdom; a concept including the racial character and the entire heritage and tradition of the *Volk*.

Weltanschauung—Literally, world-view; philosophy; commonly used in reference to the ideology of the Nazi Party.

Zeitung—Newspaper.

INDEX OF PERSONS AND ORGANIZATIONS

INDEX OF PERSONS AND ORGANIZATIONS

507